by John Collier

NOVELS

Full Circle
Defy the Foul Fiend
His Monkey Wife

COLLECTIONS

Fancies and Goodnights
Presenting Moonshine
The Devil and All
The Touch of Nutmeg

THE JOHN COLLIER READER

THE
JOHN COLLIER
READER

Alfred A. Knopf New York

1972

THIS IS A BORZOI BOOK
PUBLISHED BY ALFRED A. KNOPF, INC.

Library of Congress Cataloging in Publication Data
Collier, John   The John Collier reader.
I. Title.
PZ3.C6903Jo   [PR6005.O36]   823'.9'12   71-154906
ISBN 0-394-46186-x

Some of the stories originally appeared in *Atlantic Monthly,
Ellery Queen's Mystery Magazine, Esquire, Fantasy and
Science Fiction, Harper's Bazaar, Harper's Magazine, International
Magazine,* and *Nugget Magazine.*

The following stories originally appeared in *The New Yorker*:
"Wet Saturday"; "Romance Lingers, Adventure Lives";
"Without Benefit of Galsworthy"; "Incident on a Lake"; "Ah, the
University!"; "Are You Too Late or Was I Too Early?";
"Interpretation of a Dream"; "The Lady on the Gray"; "A Matter of
Taste"; and "The Tender Age."

Manufactured in the United States of America
FIRST EDITION

to my wife, H.H.C.

CONTENTS

INTRODUCTION

Ask the average Englishman about Milton, and he will say it is the name of a patent antiseptic. This is true, though not exclusively. Ask him about John Collier, and he will say that it is the name of a chain men's outfitters, probably adding the television jingle "John Collier, John Collier, the window to watch." There is a nice irony about the fact that the real or immortal John Collier—writer, not tailor—is the last man in the world whose window is to be watched. He eschews fame and has a horror of publicity. He is probably happy enough to know that people regard *The African Queen* as a film with a great script, without being particularly interested in who wrote it, and that the novel *His Monkey Wife* keeps finding a new batch of delighted readers every decade or so, readers too intrigued by the theme and the style to be curious about the author. The situation in America as regards Collier is much the same as in Britain, except that here he cannot be confused with a tailoring firm. Some of his stories must worry Americans who chance upon them. They show a large familiarity with America and even use with ease various kinds of American spoken idiom; yet they seem to be written by a very English Englishman, quaint, precise, bookish, fantastic—the sort of man who might keep to his country estate or college rooms and shudder at the prospect of engaging the New World. And yet John Collier has spent a long time working for that newest sector of the New World, Hollywood, and is a master of the script-writer's craft. Read his short stories and you will see all the script-writer's virtues—intense economy, characterization through speech, the sharp camera-eye of observation. You will also find literature, grace, allusiveness, erudition, the artist as well as the craftsman.

People who read Irving Wallace and Irving Stone and the other Irvings may not be expected to read Collier, but scholars who write about Edith Wharton and E. M. Forster may also be expected to neglect him. Take it further: histories of Anglo-American fiction rarely, even at their most comprehensive, find room for him, but the same may be said of other imaginative writers who share some of his qualities—Saki, for instance, and Mervyn Peake, and the royal physician who wrote the anonymous comic masterpiece *Augustus Carp Esq.* (what a treat is coming to Americans when some publisher decides to reprint it). To write tales about hell under the floorboards, the devil as a film producer, men kept in bottles, a man who marries a chimpanzee is a sure way to miss the attentions of the "serious" chronicler of fiction. The puritanism of the scholarly tradition leads Oxford dons to produce detective stories pseudonymously but to refuse to write "seriously" about the form (T. S. Eliot always promised to produce a considered thesis on the *genre,* but—because of shame or decorum or lack of time or something—the promise was not fulfilled). It also exhibits *pudeur* in the presence of fantasy, especially when it has no evident didactic purpose. *Gulliver's Travels* is all right, but the works of Carroll and Lear are for the depth psychologist rather than the literary historian.

John Collier is essentially a fantasist, but not of the romantic order that purveys Gothick, both paleo- and neo-, and science fiction. He makes literature out of the intrusion of fantasy, or quiet horror, into a real world closely observed, not out of the creation of a parallel world (windy, bosky, and machicolated; steely and computerized; hobbitish). In *His Monkey Wife* it is the world of the 1920's, whose properties shine through a classical and allusive prose that belongs to a more elegant age:

> *The snow's a lady* . . . and, like the rest of her sex, though delightful in her fall (to those who enjoy her), once she has fallen her effect is depressing, particularly in Piccadilly. A heavy blizzard had begun at noon, and continued for a couple of hours, during which time it was whisked and beaten by wheels and feet and sweepers into a kind of stale and ghastly sundae, edging, like Stygian spume, the banks of the stream of black and glassy traffic, which creaked along as slowly and uncouthly as a river of broken ice.

Though we may be said to have sundaes still with us (though not, since the passing of a highly moral Act of Parliament, fallen ladies in Piccadilly), we no longer have the referent of the following "metaphysical" image:

> For the heart is, in a sense, like the Prince of Wales; we would not have it cut in stone, yet how pathetic it is, when, as at Wembley, we see it modeled in butter.

This refers to the British Empire Exhibition of 1924, at which the then Prince of Wales, late the Duke of Windsor, was indeed sculpted fullsize in butter by New Zealand dairy exhibitors. Reading *His Monkey Wife* in the 1970's, we experience the agreeable literary piquancy of seeming to be in three historical periods at the same time—that of the prose, that of the imagery, that of a story which is as potent now as when it was first written, for it is pure myth.

Why write a full-length novel about a chimpanzee that falls in love with, and eventually marries, an undistinguished colonial schoolmaster? Osbert Sitwell enthused many years ago—on the occasion of a reprint—about the deep symbolism: man needs to face his atavistic self, to be refreshed (the hero's name is Fatigay) through contact with the animal world, and so on. This will do well enough; indeed, anything will do, from cartoon charm to Swiftian satire, but we always end up with a chimp falling in love with a man. And we literally end up with this:

> Under her long and scanty hair, he caught glimpses of a plum-blue skin. Into the depths of those all-dark lustrous eyes, his spirit slid with no sound of splash. She uttered a few low words, rapidly, in her native tongue. The candle, guttering beside the bed, was strangled in the grasp of a prehensile foot, and darkness received, like a ripple in velvet, the final happy sigh.

Though Sir Osbert saw here (and who will not say legitimately?) man's soul returning to the anarchic night whence it came, there is something else, forbidden by the eyeshades of decorum—a man copulating with a monkey. There is what is sometimes called *wickedness* in Collier—a quality different from salacity. There is also the logic of the metaphysical conceit (there are enough references to Donne in the book, beginning with the very first sentence, to prepare us for this), which does not balk, as the cartoon fantasy does, at the inescapable conclusion, though it leaves everything to the imagination. The Collierian melodic line deliberately seduces us into accepting reality through the agency of a "double take." It happens, for instance, at the end of the story called "Bottle Party," where the hero is glassed and corked and put on sale:

> In the end, some sailors happened to drift into the shop, and, hearing this bottle contained the most beautiful girl in the world, they bought it up by general subscription of the fo'c'sle. When they unstoppered him at sea, and found it was only poor Frank, their disappointment knew no bounds, and they used him with the utmost barbarity.

That final word covers a great deal, but Collier the scriptman, the visual conceptor, undoubtedly has a number of specific images in mind. Or just one.

An appreciation of many of Collier's effects depends on one's own erudition. In *His Monkey Wife,* Emily the chimp visits the London Zoo, where she encounters an old acquaintance of the jungle, another chimp called Henry:

> "Well, Emily!" he muttered. "Have you too come to haunt me? I know I was wrong to throw that banana skin, and, it's true enough, I meant to do worse still. I determined that, if I could get you on the rebound, so to speak, that day you ran away from the schoolmaster, I'd take it out of you for daring to love anyone but me. But I was punished, Emily, and I'm being punished still. When I was in the very act of making up to you, a leopard sprang on me—no doubt you saw it—and I felt his red-hot teeth and claws, and then all was dark, and I awoke to find myself in the hands of friends, who bore me here—to Hell! Sweet Em, what shall become of Henry, being in Hell forever?"

It is probable that, apart from being able to recognize the *Doctor Faustus* quotation at the end, one needs to be equipped with a knowledge of the history of English fictional dialogue to enjoy this fully. Collier seems to echo, in rhythm as well as idiom, a tradition of speech that could be courtly, melodramatic, colloquial, biblical. His animals know it best. But when his human characters in the short stories seem to speak a respectable enough American, there is always somehow a touch of the bookish, as though Collier is deliberately echoing a *Punch* joke about Americans from the 1850's:

> "I'd have given her the world," said he. "And I would yet. But she's gotta see reason. I'll make her listen to me somehow. Let me get her within reach of my arms, that's all! Landlord, I'll have a bottle of this hooch up in my room, I reckon. I gotta do a bit of thinking. Good night, pal. I'm no company. She's roused up the old caveman in me, that's how it is. I'm not claiming to be any sort of sheik, but this little

Irish wonder lady's gotta learn she can't make a monkey of a straight-forward American businessman. Good night!"

The inversion ("said he") reinforces the slight but flavorsome archaism.

Collier ransacks traditions, but he does not himself seem to belong to any tradition (any more than does Mervyn Peake). *His Monkey Wife* and *Defy the Foul Fiend* do not exemplify any direction in the course of the novel form, and the short stories suggest fable, or grand guignol, more than the naturalistic irony of the *conte*. All this means that he does not play a part in the development of a literature, although he is himself very "literary." It has been regarded by some critics as a sure sign of slightness, the badge of the inconsiderable, for a writer to make some of his effects out of his reading (like the school of essayists that followed Lamb). Add to this an almost exclusive concern with horror and fantasy, and you seem to have a double cause for overlooking Collier. But the interests of the literary critic-historian and of the cultivated fancier of good writing so often fail to meet. One could pursue somewhere, not here, the theory that the books that mean most in the average literate lifetime are not the collected works of Scott, George Eliot, Balzac, Trollope, Zola, Hardy, and other "makers" of the novel, but the unclassifiable "sports"—*Gargantua, Vathek, The Marriage of Heaven and Hell, Les Illuminations, Alice, Mrs. Caudle's Curtain Lectures, Diary of a Nobody, Cardinal Pirelli, The Unquiet Grave, Titus Groan, His Monkey Wife*. If Collier had produced many more full-length works of fiction, then critic-historians would be able to look for patterns and find him a legitimate scholarly niche. As it is, he is chiefly a creator of very wayward miniatures, and all that can be done with these is to enjoy them. In this volume you have most of his stories, as also a part of *Defy the Foul Fiend,* which stands easily on its own, and of course *His Monkey Wife.* Whatever this volume has cost or is going to cost you, it is, believe me, a great bargain.

ANTHONY BURGESS.

Rome
April 1972

HIS
MONKEY
WIFE

Or, Married to a Chimp

Till at the last she set herself to man,

Like perfect music unto noble words.

TENNYSON

MOONSHINE: *All that I have to say, is, to tell you that the lanthorn is the moon; I, the man in the moon; this thorn-bush, my thorn-bush; and this dog, my dog.*

A MIDSUMMER-NIGHT'S DREAM

CHAPTER 1

If thou be'st born to strange sights

and if you don't
mind picking your way through the untidy tropics of this, the globe,
and this, the heart, in order to behold them, come with me into the
highly colored Bargain Basement Toy Bazaar of the Upper Congo.
You shall return to England very shortly.

The tall trees on the edge of the clearing have here and there, it
seems, lifted their skirts of scrub, giving us the same sickening drop
from our expectations as shopwindow ladies do, when their dresses
are opened at back or placket, and we shall see only wire and emptiness. So dead are these vistas into the dark jungle, that if there
emerged from them, into the sun's spotlight at their entrance, one
of those sights we still absurdly expect; an elephant, say, with a
leopard hanging as banderillo from his slaty shoulder, but sliding
down, leaving red tracks grooved in that slatiness, sliding down to
be crushed of course, we should feel that it was just a turn, *Great
Xmas Treat*, materialized from some dressing-room-like pocket in
space, and not native to those scaffoldings and canvas backs with
hanging ropes and sterile floor and darkness. There are birds, naturally, of all sizes and qualities. Their penetrating whistles and clockwork screech and chatter add to the illusion, whichever it is.

This path leads straight to the bungalow of Mr. Fatigay. You see,
he has introduced some English plants into his garden. His is the
only white man's house in Boboma, and this is just as well. The
large man, with his round schoolboy jacket and his honest puzzled
eye, appears to greater advantage alone here among the infant

3

blacks, to whom it is his vocation to bring literacy and light, than he would if there were other white men about, whose coarser codes he might too readily take on. But that is the way with most of us. Sitting on the wide veranda, however, almost alone, his personality expands naïvely, and something quite poetic appears in the twilight of that hour and of his nature, like the sweet but inconsiderable bloom on a ragged nocturnal weed.

I have said *almost alone* in order to prepare you, lest, hearing his voice rise and fall with more point and direction than a man employs who idly mutters to himself, and noticing, as we draw near enough to see into the shadows of the veranda, that no other white-clad figure is stretched out there, you should conclude that he is mad. This is not quite so. Like Vaughan, he is *least alone when most alone*. He has not noticed it, but he, whose shyness limits his conversation to a string of Empire-builder's clichés when he is in the company of his compatriots, he becomes positively fluent and individual only when in the presence of that which moves in the corner behind his chair. He becomes quite a chatterbox. What is it that moves? Look! It's Emily! Here she comes!

Do you wonder, when you see her emerge into the shaft of lamplight, smiling her Irish smile, brushing the floor with the knuckles of her strong capable hands, do you wonder that the branches of the great tree, that which shades the bedrooms from the aching moon, are sometimes torn asunder, when a dark face juts out over a straining hairy torso [Henry's face, who has shared her arboreal infancy, a face all convulsed in the puzzled clown-grief the Prologue speaker plays on us in *Pagliacci*: "A word! A moment. . . ."] But no word comes, naturally, and the moment is lost, and the heavy boughs press inward and close, drowning that woeful face in a flurry of white blossoms and shining leaves, as if in moon-breaking water. Can you wonder that on the silvered grass-patch her mother and sisters sometimes stand, tangled in each other's comforting arms till they look like a Laocoön group cut from a briar root, wondering if she sleeps well, that winsome baffling creature who has left them for a life set farther beyond the scope of their simple minds than is that of Hollywood from the filmstar's folks, Mamma and Poppa in some little hometown on the prairie.

Can you wonder that, *petite*, dark and vivacious, she is the life and soul of the lonely bungalow, so that the passing trader or Colonial Office man has no sooner thrust out his legs into the cool comfort of his evening's rest, than he says, "Now then, old man, where's that chimp of yours? Let's see Emily. Ho! Ho! Ho!"

But as she ambles forward on such occasions, turning a somer-
sault, perhaps, as slowly and gravely as day and night, see! her smile
dawning at the end of it has something of trouble and strain splintering under its sensitive flexibility. Loyal in her support of Mr. Fatigay,
quixotically hospitable in her determination to give such guests
what they are most fitted to enjoy, she is nonetheless ill at ease.
Yet she masks it. This generous hypocrisy is the first sweet ferment
of the noble savage heart. It is civilization. This chimp is civilized.

She had not been so before she had come into the possession of
the good schoolmaster. That was a year ago, before her captor, an
anthropologist, whom she had revered rather than loved, had
exchanged her to Mr. Fatigay for the more conveniently portable
possession of a five-pound note. Then, though eminently deserving
of that second-rate sort of praise implicit in such adjectives as "well-
grown," "sagacious," and the like, she gave no sign, and was herself
unconscious, of any claim to esteem in terms less niggardly and low.
What seeds lay latent in her of qualities with such a claim, sprouted
only under the sunshine of Mr. Fatigay's smiles, and the gentle
warm monotonous rain of the evening monologues, in which, when
work was done, he expressed his hopes, dreams, ambitions to the
friendly dumbness by his side.

"Ah, Emily!" he would say, with something of the gesture as
well as of the onomatopoeia with which he habitually strove to make
English clearer to the infant natives, "How nice to be at ease again!"
lolling his head, and then, in mild explosion, "What a day! What
a day!" And he would continue with a monosyllabic expressiveness
which I, who have never taught the young, am quite unable to
imitate. From simple allusions to physical fatigues and pleasures,
he would proceed to higher matters, and would sometimes have
daubed in a very fair self-portrait, rather larger than life, before an
awareness of his reflection, gesticulating in the dark mirror-bright
eye of the chimp, would bring him back to self-consciousness.

"Why, Emily!" he would say fondly, but with an uneasy titter.
"One would think you understood every word I said."

And, indeed, Emily had soon come to understand the more concrete terms he used, her comprehension falling back only when he
soared into abstractions beyond her experience and his expressiveness. Yet it was in the course just of these, she noted, that his rare
fits of enthusiasm would come upon him, and having seen him thus
transformed and shining, she longed restlessly to know what it was

he said then. She had seen the same light play, but rather more coldly, like an aurora borealis, over his prism and silent face when he sat sometimes with a dry and unattractive object in his hands, evidently voyaging through strange seas of thought, alone. Emily could not read.

She was, however, a schoolmaster's pet, and on the frequent occasions on which she had accompanied him to the schoolroom, she saw pictures enough of cats with the letters C A T printed beside them. Is it so hard to understand how she came by a curiosity as to the nature of letters, and even, perhaps, of the abstracter function of literature? Our scientists may think so, who have chosen to measure the intelligence of the chimpanzee solely by its reactions to a banana. They suspend the delicacy from the ceiling of a cage, and assess the subject's mentality in terms of the number of boxes he or she will pile one upon another in order to secure it. They fail to see that nothing is revealed except the value which that particular chimp chooses to set upon the fruit. And, beyond a certain low limit, this surely is in inverse ratio to intelligence. What boy of ten would not pile up a dozen boxes in an attempt to climb within reach of it? How many would Einstein clamber upon? And how many would Shakespeare? Emily, though a fruitarian by nature, would have disdained an eagerness capable of more than two and a jump.

If you would arrive at a juster estimate of the potentialities of her race, study Emily's conduct following upon her first uncertain inklings as to the nature of the printed word. She now never missed an opportunity of following her master into the schoolroom, where her attention became most concentrated, though unostentatiously, during the elementary reading lessons. With her, the first steps were more difficult by far than they were for her sooty classmates, but the later ones were less so. She was stimulated, moreover, in the powerful effort demanded of her in the early stages, by a new sensation, a feeling of being slightly inflated by a gas lighter than air whenever certain thoughts or memories crossed her mind. These were always connected with Mr. Fatigay. This chimp was awakening to love.

Full consciousness of it, like motor headlights suddenly leaping up behind a nightwalker in a private and violent dawn, came on her one sultry afternoon.

> "What makes the lamb love Mary so?"
> The children all did cry.

chirruped the infant blacks in voices which still echoed so strongly the hollow clicks of their tribal lingo that they sounded as if sticks were being drawn along a wooden paling. And,

"Oh! Mary loves the lamb, you know,"
The teacher made reply.

came Mr. Fatigay's virile tones in response.

A choking gurgle, sadly out of tune, arose from Emily's corner. The sound of his voice, rough and sweet to her as wild honey, took possession of the wilderness of her heart like a John the Baptist. The words, freely translated as to sexes and species, seemed to fill that desert with the suggestion that the Kingdom of Heaven was at hand. Her spirit, a caged lark which hears another in the sky, beat madly against her bars and roof of dumbness. It seemed that only one more effort was needed for her heart to spurt forth a clear, low, wood-sweet voice to harmonize with that resonant bass. A blank agony of concentration resulted. The striving creature dared not abate it, even to inhale. At what seemed the opening of realization, darkness crashed down upon her, like a cloth flung over a birdcage, and she fell forward in a momentary swoon.

As she came up out of it, into the light of consciousness and memory, she paused a little before opening her eyes, in order that she might reassemble the potent impressions which had immediately preceded her collapse. A different, and a sweeter, dizziness was superimposed upon the physical one. Still she kept her eyes fast shut, waiting, like the Sleeping Beauty, and it seemed for a hundred years, for her Prince Charming tenderly to awaken her. Then, far away, falling as from a height infinitely above the near-unnoted stridulations of the little blacks, she heard the awaited voice:

"Drag her out by the legs, and throw a bucket of water over her."

Emily swooned again, and this time more deeply, her spirit, like Ibsen's wounded wild duck, clinging to the cold dark mud in the depths below her consciousness.

The impact of the cold drench revived her, and having now nothing to wait for, nor finding any pleasure in arranging her returning thoughts, she rose to her feet in uncertain haste, and staggered blindly from the arid playground, heedless of the hoots and guffaws of her leaping classmates, who had all too eagerly administered the restorative. For what was such infantile derision to one on whose bowed and nakedly twitching head the laughter of the whole universe was being poured?

The chimpanzee cosmology is highly animistic, and it seemed now to Emily as if the slumbering personality of things had awakened and stood up a moment, to jeer and laugh. The bungalow grinned and looked out of its windows at her; the grass huts were doubled up and shaking. The very airs joined hands and danced in their mean mirth, and the trees threw up their top branches and rained down on her the silvery tinkle of a myriad sun-echoing leaves. For the sun's brazen laughter was the worst of all, and to escape it the poor chimp shuffled in under the cascade from the quivering trees. Like the water of certain high falls, however, this had broken up in its long descent and had become rain, then mist, then nothing, before it reached the ground.

Here, in the dark dry-rottenness of the lower jungle, Emily found escape from the externalized form of her reverse. Here, with the powdering log, and scaly life, woodlouse and small serpent, the bright hot blood fountains from her wounded heart congealed. Soon their brittle larvae flaked away, each sob loosening a little, leaving the subject anemic but sane. It was a suddenly mature chimp that came home from those antifebrile shades, but, tight-lipped and steady-eyed, neither a shattered nor an embittered one.

There is a satisfaction in the bankruptcy of hope and self-esteem, if only it is complete enough. With only the unassailable core of the ego left, one is eased of the intolerable unconscious burden of the debt one's faultiness owes to fortune for preserving its absurdly disproportionate, and nervous, superstructure of greed and pretension. The chimp was aware of this, having heard the schoolchildren sing, "He that is low need fear no fall," and, indeed, having seen some of the elder ones demonstrate it very heartily, in one narrow interpretation at least.

Who would have thought, seeing the trim little brown figure trip so self-containedly through the village, or describe such a suave arc on the end of the swinging bough that landed her pat, here, back again at Mr. Fatigay's feet, as he sat at dinner on the veranda; who would have thought, seeing all this, that beneath that rather Charlotte Brontë exterior, there was actually a Charlotte Brontë interior, full of meek pride, hopeless hope, and timid determination. At one moment, in fact, it became positively Emily B., and that was when Mr. Fatigay, swallowing the last mouthful of his yam, said, with unwonted coarseness:

"Well, Emily, here you are again! I thought you'd got skittish.

Thought there must be a tom about, you know, and you'd gone off for the night."

And, in his blindness, the foolish fellow actually hummed a bar or two from the suggestive chorus of his latest syncopated record, "Those BABoon Blues."

Emily turned her face to the wall. She little thought, as neither did Mr. Fatigay, that this unusual gaucherie of his was expressive of his pleasure at seeing her safely back again. She tried to concentrate on the idea that he, like lesser men, was at heart just a great big boy, with a boy's capacity for the sudden careless blow. This, while it assisted, but perhaps unnecessarily, in repressing any impulse towards anger, did little to salve the new hurt in the barely stanched wound of that afternoon.

As she sat motionless in the gathering darkness, and watched her childhood's home, the jungle, she pondered once more the advisability of withdrawal. The cloudy, smoke-blue billows of that forest washed up almost to where they were sitting, as the sea did to the palace steps in *The Little Mermaid*, and with the same tremendous appeal of depth on depth on depth to dissolve in. It appeared to go on so far that the actual horizon was lost in it, and the moon, which then began to lift directly opposite them, rose like a silver bird from a twiggy blue nest. As the moon rose it got smaller, and time, which it took up with it, got smaller also, and the forest swept on infinite and eternal beneath. Large enough to be a grave for sorrow. A timeless cloudy sea to melt memory away.

"Switch on the light," said Mr. Fatigay, and it was gone.

Before the chimp was a white-painted handrail, a bamboo table with pipes, a whiskey and soda, and the *Overseas Daily Mail.* Beyond these was a wall of darkness in which the moon hung like a word of reminiscence which must pass unnoticed. The white rail and the table stood at the threshold of a new life, stretching beyond her vision, but full, as far as she could see, of strangeness and of pain.

CHAPTER 2

Dust hath closed Helen's eye

Six months slipped swiftly by in the little clearing of Boboma. The seasons, as we know them, are of course tangled up in that locality, caught as they are in the sun's heel, which passes over twice in the course of the year. Spring flew overhead without settling, like a wild bird, tardy migrant! on its way to Hampshire. But Boboma, all unconscious of its distinction, had a little private spring going on in its very center. The new world, which Emily had visualized as opening so aridly before her, had in fact contained one element more than she had bargained for, and that of such aureate quality as to shed a glow even upon the stark and forbidding outlines of her relationship to Mr. Fatigay. Culture this was, in its wider aspects, that made the future seem incredibly rich, not in color and sensation merely, but in possibilities. And at the thought of these possibilities the living principle awoke, like sap, in Emily's heart, so cramped and contracted by an iron resolution she had made to feel and hope no more. This, as when the spring grass cracks stone slabs of pavement, was a signal instance of the futility of the strongest antivital contrivances, when pitted against the forces latent in even the very softest of living tissue. Mr. Bernard Shaw would have been delighted.

So was the chimp. The dawn, spiritually speaking, had come for her when she had passed from reading the flavorless simplified passages in the children's lesson books to groping at the tough and prickly sweetness at the core of her master's little stock of well-chosen classics. The dawn, we must remember, is remarkable for its high and transitory colors, and its deceiving mists. Emily's mind was in many important respects too unsophisticated, too unsuspicious, too generous and eager, for her to estimate at their true worth the various pictures of life which she found in Mr. Fatigay's favorite authors. She believed them all. The world that lay before her was irradiated by Tennyson and Bernard Shaw, by Georgian poetry and Michael Arlen, and, worse than all combined, by love.

But how, you will ask, had she gained so quickly this command of letters, and what did Mr. Fatigay think of it? She had gained it by sheer concentration, and Mr. Fatigay thought nothing of it at all, for, despite his monologues, he was completely unaware that his pet, or plaything, had understanding of any words beyond a few simply spoken commands.

Something better than his dog, a little dearer than his horse! thought Emily, with a momentary bitterness. But it was, she at once admitted to herself with all the warmth of generous self-reproof, largely by her own choice that he continued unmindful of her prowess. For on a day very shortly after her rebuff, and in the first impetuosity of her resolution to become worthy of his regard, she had tried to reveal her intelligence to her master in the classroom.

She had taken a place at an empty desk, instead of her usual one beside the master's stool, and when the children saw her clutch pencil and paper in imitation of themselves, and glance eagerly upward to where Mr. Fatigay stood ready to inscribe model letters on the blackboard, they had cried out with delight. At which Mr. Fatigay had turned round, and, seeing what was afoot, he had said smiling:

"Come, come, Emily! If you are as clever as all that, you must be sold to perform on the halls."

At once the frightened chimp had relinquished the implements of clerkiness, and crept trembling to her old place of subjection. How it all recurred to her when later on she read that Mrs. Virginia Woolf had been denied admittance to a university library! From that moment she gave no sign of possessing an intelligence higher than that with which she was naturally credited. To be debarred from doing so was very grievous to her, less on account of being denied the pleasures of innocent display, which interested her only so far as the impression she made on Mr. Fatigay was concerned, than because she was thus prevented from any opportunity of learning to write, for she could not partake unnoticed in the writing lessons as she could in those on reading. Afterwards she thought that perhaps all had been for the best, for, in her overwrought emotional state at this time, she might have been tempted to fritter away precious hours in the production of a sonnet sequence, to the detriment of her more instructive studies.

So she learned nothing but to read, but, since she was well able to concentrate, which the schoolchildren were not, she learned it at least a hundred times as fast as they. Before the six months had passed she was tolerably conversant with most of the books that a mild idealist takes to the jungle with him in these days, and on these, which help most of us to forget that we are human, she founded her innocent theory of what human life should be. Perhaps, in view of her sex, this was just as well.

There were, in this world she visualized, which must have somewhat resembled a stiff and formal Rousseau wedding group, over which some European tree alarms us by the painter's memory of equatorial frondage, and in whose midst a small hairy nonhuman figure is set, smoldering destructively in its juxtaposition to these starchy nuptials; in this world there were certain elements which seemed alien and antagonistic to its central principle of domestic bliss. These were, to put it bluntly, women. The chief of them was that woman of thirty, on whom G. Moore delivers himself with all the gusto of an egoist and a bachelor. Reading his rhapsody, the chimp was impressed in spite of herself. She recognized the enemy of her faith and her hope, and she hated, yet admired. She toyed with the thought of making this creature her model, and shrank in innocent alarm from even the playful girlish whim. She was repelled, fascinated, and, on Mr. Fatigay's account more than her own, she was filled with vague fears.

"Woman!" she thought, thinking of herself and the negresses, who were the only human kind she had seen, "Woman! The meek hairy shadow, or the glossy black caricature of man! Surely they must be of this second strutting kind who can be imagined as thinking and acting thus!" And, shaking her head, the perhaps old-fashioned chimp had replaced the disturbing volume on the shelf. But for some time this odalisque lay across her path, smiling.

Such forebodings, however, occupied only the more speculative of Emily's reveries. Most of her time was filled, more happily, with the enlarging and remodeling of her conception of her beloved, for, as new ideas expanded the maiden demesne of her heart and mind, so the image of him who was destined lastingly to fill both grew within them, and was ever to be newly explored and additionally loved. That deeper and more workaday grain, which is to be won only by the recognition and cheerful acceptance of blemishes, now marked her feeling for him.

At first, as an apparition from another world, and unrelated to any background, he had possessed for her something of the flat and arbitrary luminosity of a saint in a stained-glass window. Now, seeing him more in the round, she was conscious of certain little weaknesses and blindnesses in him, such as are knit in the fiber of most of us, and while these made him less of the god to her, that earthiness made him more the man—one might say, the anthropoid —to be reached, to be loved possessively. She, who had longed to burn out her heart before him as one renders up the complimentary uselessness of incense to a deity placed high above needs and desires, was now possessed by a more practical tenderness, not less lofty for being practical, as it was not less becoming for being out of date: that is, to strengthen him against the world, to amuse him against himself, and to protect him against treacherous mischance. An opportunity soon came.

Emily was one day with her master in the little arbor which he had made at the end of the garden. He sat at the table, busy writing at some report or other, while his faithful pet was seated high above him on the strong crossbeam which held the structure together. She looked down lovingly upon his rather palm-treed head. Its very untidiness seemed to her expressive of all that was boyish, ingenuous, and enthusiastic in his nature. Its color, debased Nordic, was the aesthetic affinity of her own rich chestnut. How she longed for the right to stroke it caressingly, and to supervise, in her motherly way, its entire well-being!

Suddenly a shadow pitched into the doorway, and in such an inexpressibly businesslike fashion that one could imagine that the black figure, which had clicked into being there, had flung down this outermost skin like a gauntlet. The air at once became tense. Yet it was only Loblulya, wife of the headman of the village, carrying fruit.

Who . . . what is she? Ten years ago she was still the reigning toast of Boboma, though she had already had three husbands, each of whom had been ruler of the little village in his time. No sooner did one of them dwindle and die than she married his successor. Mr. Fatigay, when he had arrived there, had heard of this, and had felt it incumbent upon his unofficially magisterial position, to call her before him and put certain questions to her. But on his asking her if, by any chance, juju or potent vegetable decoctions had played part in the premature demise of her successive spouses, she had replied, with a sniff, that while she would have scorned to deny having taken such measures if brutality or neglect had rendered them necessary, the fact was that the deceased had all of them been very good sorts of men, on whom she had never laid hand save in the way of kindness, and therefore she could only attribute the decline of each of them to some insidious weakness of his own. This was received rather dubiously by Mr. Fatigay, as he was aware that tribal custom decreed the position of headman only to the strongest champion in each particular community, but he felt himself unable to press the inquiry any further.

Loblulya had now been for some years a grass widow, the reigning chief, her fourth, having been accosted by a spirit while he was walking in the wood some two months after their marriage, and this spirit warned him that the tribe would perish to a man if he did not confine himself to a solitary hermitage in a mountain range some miles distant from the village, and if his wife did not, at the same time, take upon her the vows and restraints of a vestal. The village elders, feeling that the fates recently attendant on the succession lent much weight to his pronouncement, decreed that he should want for nothing in his retirement, and that a penalty of painful death should await whoever imperiled the village by disregarding the second of the supernatural edicts.

This obedience had brought a double prosperity upon the settlement. Blessed by the unique possession of an absentee and cheaply maintained headman, it grew peaceful and rich, and its tranquillity was singularly undisturbed by malicious manifestations on the part of those spirits which usually play the very devil with the peace of mind of the blacks. Indeed, save for one, which occasionally pursued young men on their way home from feasts or drinking bouts, the wood demons seemed entirely to have withdrawn. And, among themselves, the villagers lived in a state of goodwill, corroded only by the strong vein of shrewishness which had gradually developed in Loblulya.

That beauty, as she grew older, reflected the steatopygous ideal as if in the convex surface of a spoon. Less and less grew the danger of any hot-blooded young warrior incurring the death penalty by violating the taboo placed upon her charms. And less and less, by the way, grew the danger of the sole remaining wood demon's pursuit. It seemed slower of foot with every passing year, though those young men who were occasionally so fuddled as to be caught by it, testified that the horseplay to which it subjected its victims grew more irresistible, more violent, and more protracted. No man it had once seized in its clutches was ever quite the same again. But for some time, now, it had caught no one.

Loblulya stood in the doorway of Mr. Fatigay's arbor, with her basket of oranges and plums. This, clutched against her mighty bosom, was dwarfed there to the likeness of a large and tasteless brooch.

When Loblulya laughed, it was like war in the village. When she was somber, it was like witchcraft. But when she smiled a powerful odor of musk filled the room.

Mr. Fatigay had stretched out his hand courteously to examine the fruits she set down on his table. Loblulya advanced a pace, and took his hand in hers, and smiled. Emily, silent upon her perch, felt the hairs bristle upon her neck. Mr. Fatigay breathed deeply, then dizzily retreated a pace. Loblulya, with that gracefulness often noted in stout dancers, circumvented the table, and, still smiling, approached still nearer.

"What does this mean?" said Mr. Fatigay, whose wits now rallied to his sense of outrage.

"Om tsang bu t'long umbawa!" thickly replied the charmer, smiling still.

"Begone this moment," said Mr. Fatigay, "or I'll call for help."

"Insensible monster!" returned Loblulya (whose remarks are here translatable into English). "Ingrate, lost equally to the chivalry of a gentleman and to the sensations of a man! Beware! For no sooner shall you raise an outcry impious to my honor and menacing to my life, than, I assure you, I will do likewise, and visit that punishment upon your treachery, which, but for your vicious insensibility, you might by this time have deserved, but not received."

On hearing these words the chimp, paralyzed, remained suspended, but Mr. Fatigay, with a meaning glance at his cigar, on which an inch of ash had developed undisturbed, opened his mouth to summon assistance.

But at that moment, the terrible Loblulya, who had followed his eye, struck the Havana evidence from his hand, and, tearing the kerchief on her bosom, she soon tousled herself into an invidious disarray, while her shouts for assistance rang perjurously through the grove.

Within a minute or two, the sound of running feet was heard, and into the arbor burst three of four of the gigantic elders of the village.

Pale and trembling, Mr. Fatigay gasped for breath, looking the hard-breathed simulacrum of red-handed guilt, whose first stammering denials were drowned in the outcry of his twenty-stone accuser.

"Oh! the beast! the filthy beast!" she cried. "Scarcely had I set foot in this arbor when he offered me bribe, marriage, and violence simultaneously in word and deed."

Not Judge Jefferies himself ever looked so blackly on the shrinking wretch in the dock as did then the fanatical elders upon poor Mr. Fatigay, helpless, alone, remote from any possibility of aid.

Alone? No, not alone, for at that moment something stole up noiselessly behind him, and into his nerveless shaking hand was pressed, by a hairy one, his cigar.

It was hot in his hand. Looking down, he could scarcely believe his eyes. There, upon the end of it, was the full inch of ash which he himself had seen shattered, two minutes before, into a thousand pieces.

Enheartened, he drew himself up, and faced his accusers, collecting all his dignity into a frowning brow.

Imposing silence, demanding attention, with the forefinger of his left hand, he slowly raised his right, and displayed to the astonished elders the fine old testimony of the unbroken ash.

In the breathless moment during which the significance of this simple final proof dawned upon the blacks, the smoke of the Corona rose straight up towards the roof of the arbor.

Many apologies followed, smiles and invitations were exchanged, and within a few minutes the elders had closed upon the gasping Loblulya and had borne her off, instantly to begin her execution. Mr. Fatigay was alone.

Alone? Yes, alone, for, at that moment, Emily, who had crept out unnoticed after placing the cigar in his hand, was being violently sick in the obscurest corner of the garden. It was she, who, seeing the invaluable evidence destroyed, had with a present and inspired mind swooped down upon the cigar, and, taking it into a corner, had so vigorously inhaled its unaccustomed fumes that by the time Loblulya had completed her tirade, the ash was reborn, blushing as ought the snows on Hekla.

"Oh, Emily! Emily!" murmured Mr. Fatigay, hastening to find his pet. "For this, you shall have a new collar with a gold medal, and your name on it."

CHAPTER 3

Thou shalt hear the "Never, never."

Nothing is more sudden than nightfall in the tropics. It resembles the swift transition, in a pantomime, between the fade-out of the principal boy, effulgent in his golden spotlight, on a last dying fall or expiring parrot scream, and the sudden appearance on the other side of the stage, in a silver ray, of the principal girl, with her chorus of fairies star-foreheaded.

On the edges of glades, under bushes white with nocturnal flowers, the long, tousled grass is torn and drenched with blood, black as a hole in appearances. The acetylene moonlight, like a local anesthetic, freezes pain, and the gorilla, standing, staring at the reeking pieces of leopard still clutched in his iron hands, feels the white-hot scratches on his chest and thighs, and his vegetarian disapproval of the carnivorous onslaught, and a certain sneaking sympathy for the tattered fur piece which is all that is left of it, to be part of a problem as remote and cold as some jigsaw mathematic.

Emily crouched, petrified, staring at certain phrases scrawled on a sheet of letter paper, gobbets of a mental organism, oozing and steaming with personality, the mind's blood, felt much the same.

This is what had happened.

Days of peace followed upon the nerve-shattering Loblulya episode, days steeped in that golden classic quality in which our summer arrests itself towards its end, and with the same doomed illusion of eternity. Emily, in her brief periods of introspection, could not help feeling that her action had set a modest hallmark on her development into something far removed from the naïve sylvan creature, dazzled by a first glimpse of civilization, which she had been a few months before. And since, to her, knowledge and experience seemed the greatest addition by which a personality can be enriched, she would not have exchanged even the more melancholy strata of her deepened nature, not even the rich deposit of suffering which caused her suffering still, for all the blind confiding delight of her treetop childhood. For, rating its effects so highly, as she did all that conduced to enlargement, how could she but believe that its fruition in every glance and gesture must gain for her her protector's deeper regard? She had yet to learn that it is not through suffering herself, a condition as common and infectious as the ordinary cold, but through being the cause of it in others, that a woman becomes fatal and fascinating to man. But who would grudge Emily this innocent, if ill-founded, optimism, in the light of the bitter experiences through which, like a tot of brandy, it was to be her only support.

Moreover, Mr. Fatigay himself exhibited certain marked changes of demeanor towards his humble admirer, and if these were slight in comparison to the construction she placed on them, yet let him who would laugh at this poor heart's simplicity beware, for tomorrow may find him running his errand in high fettle, and building up heaven knows what fantastic castles in the air, all because his fine wife, with melting in her voice, and a rose in her cheek, and a note in her bosom, good-humoredly speaks to him as Mr. Fatigay did to Emily, as if he were not a beast, that is, but a human being. Yet our hero was as honest and good-hearted a fellow as any, and a very modest one, too, so that he had no suspicion of the true state of Emily's feelings, and much less any intent to inflame them by the occasional terms of endearment which his affectionate nature proffered, in this solitude, to the nearest deserving object.

"Come, my dear! Come, my pretty!" he'd say, scooping her up on to his knee. "You and I are going to set off to England together very shortly."

And once he added, staring at the desolate wide forest that stretched away on every side: "Yes, by God, I've been a bachelor long enough!" And, biting his lips in a nervous frenzy, he crushed her thin arm in a painful grip. Overcome, she sank her head upon his shoulder.

Her new hopes gave her the happy feeling of a completeness she never before had known. Under their influence, her appearance improved vastly. Her eyes seemed larger and more lustrous than of yore, her smiling face dimpled provocatively, the curves of her slight figure became a shade more rich and ripe.

Her crescent radiance was reflected in her surroundings. When, with her airy tread, she entered the squalid hut of some sick native, and, setting down her little basket of nourishing soup or cooling jelly, she proceeded to shake up the pillow and to lave the fevered brow, the stricken black (the motion of whose rolling eyes, relative to that of his rolling head, it would take four pages of mathematical symbols, or one line of poetry, to describe) would address her now as B'hlongba instead of, as hitherto, B'tongba. At the sound of that dear epithet she would lay her finger on her lips and shake her head at the speaker in smiling reproof, but she could not resist treasuring in her breast the thought that her new status was mirrored, as in a japanned coal scuttle, thus exaggeratedly in the simple sincerity of the blacks.

Mr. Fatigay provided, also, further iridescent materials for the dream palace which thus rose about his gentle pet, in that, now his return to England was decided upon, he began, for certain purposes of his own, to school her in graces of deportment and in the manners and customs of civilized society. An easy carriage and an upright bearing were now imparted to the chimp, and instruction also in the proper method of entering a room, proffering cakes and tea cups, and making a curtsey. So meticulous was the schoolmaster in his training of her in this last respect, that poor Emily began to wonder if she was to be presented at Court, an idea which she would have laughingly dismissed as presumptuous to the point of absurdity, but for a sentence which she read at about that time, which said: "In England the Primate takes precedence of all but Royal Dukes."

The society paper in which these words appeared contained several photographs of personages prominent at Court, and these, combined with its axiom, frequently repeated in one form or another, that nothing was more to be envied than direct descent from an ancient stock, however barbarous, strongly supported the misinterpretation which the innocent creature, unacquainted with the hierarchy of the Church, placed upon the words. She saw herself as one of "this year's brides," and in order that she might be fitted to maintain her husband's dignity in such a position, she attended with her utmost concentration on his instruction.

Why did she not now reveal her talents to Mr. Fatigay? From this delicate motive: so that when he met her, barefooted as it were, at the altar, and there bestowed upon her apparent nothingness and poverty the right to clothe herself henceforth in his material and mental grandeur, she might then surprise and gratify him by revealing that she was not altogether so dowerless as he had supposed, since, though she came to him bare of gold and jewels and securities, she brought with her the treasure of a well-stocked mind, a possession which, all the books said, was infinitely to be preferred.

And as she sat rapt in the contemplation of that moment, she heard him say:

"Come, Emily, shoulders back, please. You mustn't sit all hunched up like that, you know. That would never do in the position you are going to hold in England."

And shortly after, he set the gramophone to work ("What'll I Do?" the song was) and, advancing towards her, he raised her by the hand, and motioned her to follow his movements in sinuous response to the music.

> *"What'll I do*
> *When you*
> *Are far*
> *A-way,*
> *And I*
> *Feel bloo?*
> *What'll I do?"*

One, two, three. One, two, three.

The dolorous words floated off, winged with the poignant notes of the saxophone, blue into the blue darkness about the veranda. From the trees on the slope below, the strain was echoed, more poignantly yet, in a succession of deep, not unmelodious howls.

"That," thought the chimp, pursing her lips, "must be Henry."

It was the most persistent of her admirers in her sylvan days to whom she had given this name, he who haunted the foamy tree beneath her bedroom window.

The kindest of hearts, when happy in devotion to one being, may be inclined to rate a hopeless passion, bestowed on itself, as over-shallow and too easily compensated. Modesty, forbidding too clear a realization of one's power to arouse such a feeling, plays a great part in this, and a still greater perhaps is played by the desire to imagine the whole world as happy as oneself. Emily, prompted thus, took advantage of their next circuit of the dinner table, and, taking a banana from the dessert dish, she flung it in a graceful arc over the rails, with much the careless movement of a dancing film actress disposing of her cigarette ash. For a moment the embittered harmony was stilled. Then, humming like an angry insect, the skin of the banana shot across the veranda, and crashed upon a pane in the window just behind their heads.

"Good God!" said Mr. Fatigay. "What was that? A bat?"

And the gramophone needle scratched and scraped fretfully as the melodious sorrow came to its end.

Emily stepped aside as he hurried to lift it from the record, and, picking up the banana skin, she dropped it flatly over the balcony.

All in a moment a cloud had veiled the moon. Something lay chill at Emily's heart. Had she sinned against love, she wondered wistfully, in the slighting attempt to silence even its intrusive vehicle by the carelessly flung fruit? Though this had not altogether been rejected, something ugly had crept into the Eden of her inner life, and ugliness, where all else was tranquil beauty, was in itself foreboding.

Next day dawned hot and blue, and the passing mood was forgotten. After lunch Mr. Fatigay cried out for his horse, and, smiling at Emily, he said:

"I'm going to ride down to meet the mail boat. There may be a letter for me. You, Emily, must stay at home, as it is such a long way for the horse. I shall be back in time for dinner."

When he was out of sight, Emily turned from the window, and began to wonder how best she might employ her time till evening. Suddenly she smiled: An idea had come into her head. She would devote the long hours of waiting to the practice of a branch of her reading which hitherto had been sadly neglected: the deciphering of manuscript. This, she felt, would be of essential importance in the social life that lay before her.

Sauntering across to her protector's bureau, she opened the blotter which lay upon it, and took up some sheets of letter paper at which Mr. Fatigay had been busy all the morning. Frowning slightly, she peered hard at the crabbed writing. Frowning still more, she peered still harder.

At last the fatal words conveyed their message to her.

"My beloved darling Amy."

It was the draft of a love letter.

Aghast, the stricken chimp reeled back, one hand pressed to her brow. Her dream world lay in ruins about her feet, and, with the deathly faintness which now spread over her, it slowly began to revolve around, evoking a sensation not unlike (yet how unlike!) that procurable on the joy wheel at the fun fairs and luna parks of the carnal capitals of Europe.

"Good Heavens!" she tried to say. "What deceit! What treachery! God! What a fool! What a blind, trusting fool I've been!"

And she crushed the letter and dashed it to the ground (as if that could prevent it clinging to her heart like a flypaper!), and in one leap from where she stood she had sprung out and over the veranda, straight into the branches of a palm below, the near end of one of which she caught, which bore her on an inverse arc to the next tree, and so, like a small boat swinging out on the billows of an hurricane, dizzily on into the jungle.

Lovers' Lane is said by some to be a winding lane, but the path of despised love is as straight as a Roman road. At the moment of disillusion, a red-hot coal smolders where the heart has been, and the victim is impelled forward, heedless of obstacles, bearing with him, like a cow with a thorn under its tail, the very gall he runs so madly to escape. When poetry has fully civilized us, and brought us accidentally into that heaven where the true and the chosen vision are one, and pain and pleasure are no longer divided arbitrarily by superstition, as good and evil once were, we shall find, in this long urgent avidity for relief, a pleasure higher than that now associated with successful love, in that of all appetites, this lasts longest, and endows us with an intenser life, or more reality, the while we attempt to satisfy it.

But Emily's torment was not shot, as it were, by this weft of superior consciousness; it was pure agony, white-hot, that she experienced as she described a beeline of many miles, which ended not because the hellspark in her heart was quenched, but because it had burnt out, temporarily, all the fuel which her cindered nerves had contained. These, like the filaments in a worn-out electric light bulb, could glow no more, so that the spark ceased to act as a motor, though it burned hot as ever, numbly isolated in her bosom, as she sank fordone beneath a mighty tree. From whose branches, some hours later in the night, peered down the dark and eager face of Henry, who had witnessed her rout, and followed, with lesser speed, in hope of advantaging his unrequited desires.

From an ashy sleep, the chimp awoke to see him drop like a vulture, hitting his mark, yet staggering where he landed.

How repellent they seem to us, when the bright Eden where dwells our loved one casts us forth, and we must return to them, those other ordinary people, acquaintance and kin, whose sottish good humor and tasteless tragedy seem drawn by some Dutch realist, after the crisp exaltation of the Hellenic illusion we have lost! Shall we bow our spirits into profane forgetfulness, and turn in with them, pouring their tallowy kindness into our wounds, bemusing sorrow in the treacly vintage of their mirth and their passions?

I, in short, to herd with narrow foreheads, vacant
  of our glorious gains,
Like a beast with lower pleasures, like a beast
  with lower pains!

This was what Emily thought, as her persistent admirer shambled towards her, holding out both his hands, in clownish imitation of the truly biped life of which she had tasted. Yet—he loved her. To love, and to be loved; these, the hemispheres of happiness, how rarely they coincide! Would it not be better, she thought, better for all concerned, to let them follow one upon the other, as some take whiskey and then water, and to complete her experience lopsidedly thus, since it was fated never to be a perfect whole?

He loved her. And let happiness curl its cruel lip as it may, those who have loved in vain will know, only too well, that when love has consumed mind, tastes, standards, character itself, till the victim has become only a void in which that desire functions abstractly, then the elements of choice are gone also, and whose hunger has been raised by one particular dish in all the world, will, if he starves long enough, be satisfied with any. "And that," thought the poor chimp, "without forgetting the least aspect of the truly beloved object, but rather trying, in the final despair of constancy, to inform the husks to which one turns with something of its image, as the families of wild Irish do, who cram their bellies with earthy spuds and fix their eyes on a herring slung out of reach above the table.

I have been faithful to thee, Cynara! in my fashion."

But, as the serpentine quotation writhed in the blasted Eden of her mind, she remembered that the poem had a Latin title, and, whether it was a womanly suspicion of words she could not understand, or whether it was wisdom of that deep kind which circumambulates the guileless, she had a profound distrust of all poems with Latin titles, and this straw, wedging across the gutter, stayed, not her drowning, but the torrent in which she was submerged. She raised her eyes, and gazed indecisively, inquiringly, not untenderly, on the supplicating visage of Henry, who had halted, as halts a tomcat, some feet from where she was crouching. Something in his tortured eyes, something that might have been a spark of her own misery, gave her further pause.

Was it fair to him?

This is a question which takes so long in answering, generally, that the majority of her sex take their conscience's sullen dumbness for assent, but Emily was of different fiber.

Of his misery, wanting her, she could not doubt, for, save for her pestered impulsiveness in the manner of the banana, she was incapable of dismissing lightly any sincere feeling on the part of another, however disproportionate it seemed to its cause. Poor Henry! At that moment it seemed that the only thing left for her to do was to make him happy. Yet how?

For not all the craving of her torn and aching heart for something to hold close and snuggle up to could betray her into the sophistry that she would bestow happiness in bestowing an affection which, like a caged lion, must ceaselessly pace up and down, or sit staring into nothingness, heedless and unresponsive in its obvious longing for its ever-distant ever-present home. That would be worse than sending him away. Was there no solution?

There was. Behind the suppliant swain the tall grasses waved, were parting. Looking over his head she caught a glimpse of a sinewy spotted back, cautiously drawing nearer.

Perhaps it was all for the best. Holding her breath, she held also Henry's attention with her eyes. Time slowed up, as when a clock gaspingly gathers up its powers to strike.

Then, all simultaneously, in one flash, in one scream, in one leap, the leopard was upon poor Henry, and Emily, as if she had been sitting on the other end of a seesaw, was shooting towards and clinging to the bough above her, and ere the long scream had, like a withering fountain, sunk to a gurgle, she was swinging madly on, as if to leave love and death and warm life forever behind her.

Let her go as far, though, and as fast as she may, her blind and mind-shut rush is foredoomed to a limit, as that of a rocket is, which, urged by a similar fire, must, unless it flies clear of the earth's field of gravitation, fall back in exhausted fragments, with a plump exactly proportionate to the momentum of its breakaway.

Mr. Fatigay, we know, was all the world to Emily, and a world of which the gravitational attraction was so far-reaching that there was no practical possibility of her ever flying clear of it. It was hopeless for her to try to escape from jealousy by "going native," for the moment inevitably arrived when, like the dog in Tennyson, she *rose, twofooted at the limit of her chain, roaring to make a third.*

This occurred some days later, when she had traveled exactly a thousand miles, by the way, and, running out along a broad bough, she stopped as suddenly as if she had been pierced by an arrow.

She stood, staring into vacancy, seeing, as if it was flashed upon a cinematograph screen before her, a vision of herself and Mr. Fatigay walking slowly home from the schoolhouse, through the long and treacly beams of the evening sun. It's very strange, how at the moment that one's blind flight stops, it is generally no really important aspect of the dear one that abruptly arrests us, opening up like a firework in the blank behind the fixed neuralgic businesslike mask we have put on, but some detail of the background, seeming to have slipped past the censor by virtue of its obvious unimportance, that brings home to us, and us home, to the dearness we have lost.

Emily visualized Mr. Fatigay's mildly sloping shoulders just before her, and her closed heart opened in such a quick ecstasy that it seemed that if she could only see just that much just once in reality, it would be enough. We do not ask at such moments, "Enough for what?"

But, turning with the shaking eagerness of the long-starved, we run helter-skelter back again, and, as we stumble blubbering into the presence we have hungered for, we scarcely notice at first if it is warm or cold, any more than a famished man does when his porridge is put before him.

So Emily stood motionless, for a moment or an hour, staring before her, with one hand on her heart, which ached now like a cramped limb to which the blood returns, and then she made one slow step back, and then another, and a few doubtful paces, till suddenly she broke into a run and soon was swinging back along the airy forest road as quickly as she had come. And, in effect, as blindly, for the thawed stream in eager spate is as far from clear as it was when set blackly in the cruelest frost.

What thoughts she had, as she toiled in sobbing haste up the long tangled slopes; or stared from their crests as if, ere she had gone a tenth of the way, she hoped to see her goal; or plunged madly down from treetop to treetop on their farther sides, were hardly thoughts, but rather the beams and timbers of the dam she had built up against emotion, and these, now that the torrent had broken through, reversed their purpose, and, if anything, hurried her faster down the swirling race. She longed to feel again, to *know,* the very wound against which she had clenched her mind; it was, even in the very killing of her, life, and, compared with it, all that she could fly to was desert and dead beyond bearing. Besides (and here she took wider leaps) there might be some unimaginable misunderstanding. Perhaps he was writing a novel.

At last the last mile was traversed, and, looking out from the hateful forest, she saw before her the clearing of Boboma, yellow in the afternoon. She paused. It was so much the same, and so unconscious of her, that it seemed as if she was in another world. She almost expected to see her own shape emerge from the schoolhouse. Her lips trembled, and a great booby tear rolled down her face.

As she watched, feeling empty and impotent as a ghost, the singing ceased in the schoolhouse nearby, and the children began to come out, racing and screaming as if no chimp had ever existed. Emily stared at the door, her blood standing still in her veins. Ten minutes crept by like a glacier. Suddenly the well-known figure appeared, and, see! he looks anxiously up and down as if in hope to see the absent one. Emily's eyes, which had yearned so for the sight of him, were blinded with happy tears. Springing to the ground, she totteringly hurried towards him.

"Emily! Emily! Where *have* you been?"

CHAPTER 4

Thus vent thy thoughts;
Abroad I'll studie thee.

A poison cup, if one is sufficiently thirsty, will yield a momentarily invigorating draft, and, at the first renewal of the life-giving contact, Emily was deliriously, thoughtlessly, happy. It was not long, though, before thoughts of the future began to gnaw at her.

At first she tried to postpone dealing with them, but, as they became more insistent, she realized that the situation must be carefully weighed up, and a course of action chosen which would be neither a cowardly abandonment of her struggle, nor, on the other hand, an idealistic attempt at a self-sacrifice high-pitched beyond the ability of her flesh and blood to maintain.

For if there was one thing which even this scarcely tutored chimp had a contempt for, more than any other, it was the type of woman who, having made up her mind to sink differences and accept disadvantages in living in the presence of her beloved, sets out at the first check to infect him with her own discontent, as if she was one of those burnt envenomed lechers Donne refers to, who hope to become sound by giving others their sores.

"Never," said she to herself, "shall his tender heart be tortured by the consciousness of a passion which it is not in his power to return, nor his blithe spirit be oppressed by sullen mood or hysterical outburst of mine. But can I achieve the necessary restraint if I remain beside him? Can I bear to go away?

"I can see no light whatever on the first question," she continued, "but that is the greater reason, not the less, for preventing the unhesitating 'no' with which all my being responds to the second, from influencing my decision. What, now, would be my chief trials in the Tantalus life to which my instinct, but not yet my reason, inclines me?"

The first and greatest would be, she decided, the future Mrs. Fatigay. At the thought of her, the chimp raised her hands to her cold damp forehead, and feeling there the garland of scarlet blossoms with which her rejoicing master had laughingly crowned her, she bitterly tore it away and rent its gaudy beauty to nothingness, as an image of her rival flashed upon that inner eye which is said to be the bliss of solitude. Calming herself at length, she began to realize how important it was that she should at once obtain some definite idea of this woman's personality. But how?

From the letter of Mr. Fatigay's which she had read, it had been apparent that he regarded his inamorata not as a woman, but as an angel. Emily felt that she could not accept this figure, much as she would like to, as literally correct, and for all she knew it might be the very wildest hyperbole. And then: "What a fool I am!" she thought. "That letter must have been part of a long correspondence, and, beyond any question, he has treasured up all that he has received from her."

Brushing aside conventional inhibitions with a weary smile, Emily descended to Mr. Fatigay's bureau, and, finding at the back of one of the drawers a packet of letters carefully secured by an elastic band, she withdrew with these into a private nook, intent on learning all she could from their contents before her master returned from school.

Compressing her lips, the dreary-hearted chimp drew the first missive from its envelope. The letters were neither many nor long, but she read with such concentration that Mr. Fatigay was already approaching his home before she had replaced the last.

She descended to greet him, and both then and while she sat opposite him at tea, there was a something, not of contempt, but of that which we express by "Well! Well! Well!" in her curious regard. For it was now very clear to Emily that the woman whom he had addressed with such passionate adoration had very little sincere feeling to offer in return, and not even enough respect for him or his love to prevent her from parading her indifference with all the needless cruelty common to people of a certain type when they find themselves in possession of the whip hand. So that Emily could not understand, and stared at him as if to read the riddle in his face, now practically eclipsed by a teacup, how this man, kind, wise, and just as she knew him fundamentally to be, could have poured out his heart in slavish devotion to one who wrote, without affection, without respect, without a decent hypocrisy even:

My darling Alfred,

It's lovely to take out your letters, and read them over before answering them, as I do now. It's like going into a quiet dell, away from all the wild glitter and stress that one's restless mind urges one into. I wish, for your sake, I could be simple and wholehearted like you, instead of suffering this tearing hunger to do and do and do—oh, a million things! This month, and last, have been full of people and things—new ideas that seem to remake the world for me, and, side by side with them—the craziest fun you can possibly imagine. It's been so crazy that I daren't describe it to you, as I should feel even in writing it down that you would never understand, and I should see your "schoolmaster" look come between me and the paper.

That's why I missed writing rather longer than I ought, but you mustn't say reproachful things about it, for it makes me feel all hard inside when you do, and then I feel that I *can't* write. It makes me feel as if I wanted to do something you didn't like—flirt or something equally meaningless and mad—out of sheer cussedness.

I feel the same sometimes when you are extra possessive in your letters—stressing the "my own" element—you remember our talk about it before you went away. Don't do it, sweetheart. I can't help being a wincing jade whom the first hint of a fetter makes keen on nothing but bolting. It makes me feel, too, that you've forgotten all you promised then about my personal development—or didn't mean it, perhaps ? ? ? I just can't be anybody's in the way you mean. So that's that.

Don't misunderstand this, dear, or think, as you hint not very kindly in your last two letters, that I am reluctant to keep my promise. I only suggested that you should sign up for the extra two years because it's so clear it would give us a firmer foundation to begin on, and give me time to accustom myself to the idea of being tied up. But having given my word, I should certainly keep it, if you insisted. I haven't time to go into all the pros and cons now, as it's a ballet night, but I'll write you a long letter about it by the next mail.

I think also, dear, that you are being a little selfish about not getting married in a church. It's not fair to say I don't respect your ideas—I do—but I have to think of mother's feelings as well. But, after all, such details are still very far off.

Well, good-bye now, dearest. Don't frown. I think of you always. I enjoy your letters so much, more than I can possibly say. I love them. This is a short poor letter, but I'll write again soon. Forgive your mad bad sad girl.

> All my love, darling
> Amy

Now she knew why he had so often stopped short while they were walking together, particularly, she recollected, in days following the mail boat's arrival, and had fetched a great sigh, looking distractedly about him, or had ground his teeth like a bound man who had been struck a blow in the face. Probably it was the bitter sense of humiliation engendered by the coarsely flaunted indifference in such phrases that had prevented him from including some account of his love in the long discourses on his work and ambition which he had so often drifted into as they sat on the veranda. Knowing him as she did, she could guess how cruelly such treatment must have eaten into his warm heart and his proud spirit.

For, save for the glibly extravagant endearments at the beginning and the end, each of the letters had for its core the insistence that the writer was accepting Mr. Fatigay partly to satisfy most economically an impulse she despised and distrusted and partly because his devotion rendered him the most tractable partner she was likely to get.

"In these letters," thought Emily, "the mean is hardly the product of the two extremes, as it is, when, in love as in arithmetic, so-and-so is to so-and-so as so-and-so is to so-and-so."

This revelation, while it made her painful choice the heavier, left it still undecided, for how, more than ever, could she bear life with Mr. Fatigay when he was married to this woman, and see him, not merely loving another, but being tortured and debased? And how, more than ever, could she leave him now, and know him, not only lost to her, but lost to happiness and to himself?

"How can he? How *can* he?" groaned the unhappy creature, feeling her heart grow hot within her, while she dashed the scalding tears from her eyes with the knuckles of her clenched hand: "How *can* he crawl thus on his knees to his own destruction, crushing in his blind eagerness the heart that loves him so unutterably. So unutterably: that's the curse of it, for, if I could but speak, would I not set maidenly modesty aside, and, taking him frankly by the hand, represent to him the waste, the folly, and the pity of it all? Then, perhaps, though it would be but an outside chance (Fifty to one? Twenty to one? Thirty-three to one?), he might awake suddenly, and, dashing the poisoned sweetmeat to the ground, turn breathless towards me, with 'Emily, my good angel! My twice preserver! My consolation! My love!' "

And, intoxicated by the picture she had conjured up, she fell to wondering if only she might effect this by a combination of eloquent signs, and of thrusting the paltry letters before him, and of putting out books open at telling and relevant passages.

> *Is it well to wish thee happy?—having known*
> *me—to decline*
> *On a range of lower feelings and a narrower*
> *heart than mine!*

This might do as a revelatory conclusion, bringing about the crescendo of exclamations which now pealed like wedding bells on her inner ear.

But then, shaking her head at herself in sad admonition, she dismissed the wild plan from her mind. This was not, it is to be understood, from any tardy revival of old-fashioned conventionalism. Emily considered herself to be as modern, in the worthier sense, as any of her sex, and though she deprecated the way in which many of her contemporaries appeared to fling away all regard for graciousness and responsibility, and even for the true development of their lives, in order to loot and ravage a few masculine privileges, she was capable, as in the case of Loblulya and of her sane benevolence towards Henry, of acting with complete decisiveness and freedom whenever she felt it to be genuinely necessary. It was the harder achievement of applying cold reason to her daydream that now restrained her.

"How could any clumsy interposition of mine turn aside such a love as his?" she thought. "Is love less strong in its defense, or more so, when it is bestowed on the unworthy? And even if I could convince him that chivalry does not bind him there whence reason calls him insistently away, and could bring him to obey that call, what hope have I that he would forthwith turn to me? Did the black on whom he once so unflinchingly operated, without anesthetics, endeavor to kiss the steel which sawed at his gangrened limb?

"No! He would certainly spurn me as a self-seeking, malicious intriguer, none the less cruel in act because I protested that it was for the best. If he turned at all to another love, it would almost certainly be some coalblack mamma, or mammas, he would take to his bosom." Here she shuddered.

"It is more likely, of course," she proceeded, "that he would become a recluse, a hermit, and bury himself here in Boboma with his shattered ideal forever beside him, and that . . . yes! yes! that would be even worse. I would a hundred, nay, a thousand times rather that he found solace in some association which, however degraded, was at least healthy and natural, than that he should thus gratify the vilest and most selfish motive that has ever stirred in my breast." And she curled her lip as she crushed forever the scarce-born wish to spoil for others what she could not have herself, unaware in her innocence that just there, perhaps, lay her closest point of similitude to the human female.

Who treads down an ill motive is generally elevated in the very act to a tall strong generosity, which may bring him too recklessly to engage himself in the opposite direction. Emily had spurned the selfish thought almost before she had properly conceived it, but the bare reminder of such mental processes summoned up all the noble forces of her nature, and she now faced the prospect of a lifelong battle with herself with something of the bellicose confidence of a nation during a period of military maneuvers. And, as if her own weaknesses were an insufficient foe, she bristled more and more eagerly to defend her beloved against those of his future wife.

"Let the future bring what it may," she thought, standing very erect and earnest in the middle of her little white room, "my place is beside Mr. Fatigay, and who knows but that even he may come to be grateful to the humble chimp, when the dawning sense of her love and constancy shines as the only light on the dark path he seems fated to tread."

And, going down to his study, she took from the shelf a pocket encyclopedia, and soon was deeply immersed in an account of the divorce laws of England, which she read, not from vain hopes of its future practical utility, but for its prose, which struck her, in its stark and puritanical terseness, as being far superior to the more exotic phrasing of the marriage service.

CHAPTER 5

Behold! behold, the palace of his pride!
God Neptune's palaces!

Not long after this there was a great bustle in the schoolmaster's pleasant house. Bags were dragged out and packed, livestock and garden appurtenances disposed of, crates filled with curios and souvenirs. Blacks thronged the garden path and sat all day upon the steps. Every time Mr. Fatigay appeared at a window he was cheered to the echo; every time he appeared at the door he was swamped by clustering natives, thick as flies on a roadside fragment, who first loudly, and I believe sincerely, implored him not to go, and then, on his smiling persistence, pressed upon him yams and whatnot.

"Here," they cried, piling these up into his arms, "let us exchange mementos."

And off they went, calling out his praises—one carrying a pair of old shoes, another a collection of used razor blades, yet another a rain-spoiled pith helmet, and a fourth that fine piece of earthenware which had stood beneath his washstand. They gave him all their old rubbish and he gave them his, and everyone was content.

The schoolchildren marched up with flags and music, and performed a masque in his honor on the lawn. In this, the Seven Deadly Sins were mimed with such energy that the pair who enacted Anger were carried gasping to the infirmary, Gluttony was sick on the spot, and when it came to the seventh Mr. Fatigay was obliged to step down and marry the actors before they had completely finished with their parts.

This interposition, however, in no way marred the effect of the whole, in which it had been arranged for an impersonation of himself to appear and to redress the assembled Vices, transmuting them by his mere presence into the corresponding Virtues. And, as they thought he was honoring them by taking up his part in their play, nor did it bear ill fruit afterwards in tying together two adolescents who were yet too young for the cares of domesticity.

"Good-bye!" they cried at the end. "Bless our dear teacher. Hurrah! No more school! Hurrah! Character rather than Intelligence! Hurrah!"

"Good-bye, dear friend," said the headman of Boboma, who, shortly after the execution of Loblulya, had been told by the spirit that he must return to the village.

"Good-bye," replied Mr. Fatigay. "I suppose you don't want to get married again before I go?" For he would have liked to see the whole world married.

"No, thank you," said the headman. "After my last dear wife . . . I shall never marry again. *Mais,*" he continued, unconsciously quoting George II, for he had worked in his youth in the French Congo, *"j'aurai des maîtresses."*

"Good-bye," cried all the servants, their faces so wet and smiling that one instinctively looked for coal-tar rainbows there. Not only the good and faithful ones, but the idlers, thieves, and wastrels among them, even Topsy, the fat cook, found now that they loved Mr. Fatigay and wished he would not go.

"Good-bye," said an old tin can, from which, Emily remembered, as she caught sight of it lying forlorn upon a dunghill, she and Mr. Fatigay had had some delicious pineapple for her name-day tea.

"Good-bye," murmured Emily's heart to it. "And good-bye, village. Good-bye, Arcady. Good-bye, summer. Good-bye. Good-bye."

And the jungle opened up its track, parting like the waters of the Red Sea as they rode away. Mr. Fatigay's ardent heart went on before them, in alternate cloud and fire, on this journey through what wilderness he knew not, to a Canaan other than that of which he dreamed.

Half a day's journey away lay the rotten little pier head, blistering in the mud, where once a month a tiny hiccuping river launch put in an appearance. Sitting on the shaky planks, surrounded by either twenty-five or twenty-seven packages, they stared into the gray heat-haze where the river curved, and the leaden trunks and stream-ers of the trees, prolonged by reflection in the shining slime, mud-dled the distance, as if by a frowzy bead-curtain. Space and time hung about the place like gray, shoddy garments, infinitely too large for man and his shrunken activities here.

After a long wait, a mean and weakly chug chug was heard, and the dirty launch had suddenly appeared to mark where the trees were, after all, divided. Emily stood up in her skimpy cotton frock and watched its approach with fluttering heart. This then was the steamship, a major factor in Tennyson's dictum, *Better fifty years of Europe than a cycle of Cathay.* She was glad she was not going to Cathay.

Its poor appearance, however, did not damp her excitement, for the splendors of the civilization she was now going to visit had been too strongly impressed upon her in her reading to be nega-tived by the shortcomings of a little African mailboat. Nor were they entirely canceled by the prospect of a life of unsatisfied emotion, which was all she had to look forward to.

"For," said the sensible little creature, "mind is still mind, what-ever may befall the heart; perhaps the more so. I will visit Madame Tussaud's and the Tower of London, and become as well-informed as any of my sex, if not as happy. I will drain each new experience to its dregs, as far as is consistent with proportioned and virtuous conduct, and, since my life is to be a tragedy, I will see to it that it does not descend into mawkishness through a deficiency of intel-lectual content."

And, reminding herself that this was her first journey by water, and the beginning of a new life, she looked keenly about her as she tripped up the gangway.

"I hope," she thought fervently, "that I shall not be sick."

Soon the packages were all stowed away on board, and the cap-tain, in accents which boredom rendered as flat and colorless as the mudbanks among which he sailed, declared that all was serene. Ropes were unhitched, the engine strove and stank once more, and they were off. If Mr. Fatigay had been less absorbed in his own thoughts at the moment, he might have noticed that the tall fringes of the jungle were festooned with the innumerable dark faces, like gigantic plums, of a host of chimpanzees, mostly toms, who had come to look their last on this Helen of the jungle. Darkest Africa would be the darker for her going; this she could not doubt, who saw it written so unmistakably in those crowded mournful faces, so simple and sincere.

Day after day the little boat ticked its way through the uneasy stupor of the Congo, under high bluffs where vultures sat, soaked in metallic light, on the gallowsy branches of dead trees; over shallow places where reeds, swarming with filthy larvae, poked up from the mud like mangy hair; past sandbanks hideously alive with the scuttling panic of crocodiles; past squalid settlements where nothing stirred but a scream, or, worse still, a laugh; and on down to where the great estuary began, and the port sweltered behind the roll of hot flashing breakers at the ocean bar.

The boat on to which they were to exchange for the sea voyage was due to sail on the day of their tardy arrival, so that Emily, who had been looking forward to her first sight of a town of size, had to content herself with an inspection of the quays, and with but a distant glimpse of white buildings and tin-roofed shacks dancing in the quivering air. Her disappointment, though, was soon forgotten at the sight of the crowded ship, and at the thought that now she might come into contact, more or less as an equal, with the sort of people among whom she was to live.

It was, as she afterwards discovered, through the generous consideration of her master, that she was not disappointed of this pleasure also, and forced to spend the three weeks of the voyage penned in a narrow cage between decks, in disgusting proximity to crates of serpents and the reeking young of the greater cats.

Mr. Fatigay could not endure the thought of his sensitive pet languishing in such hateful confinement, and his desire for her presence beside him, no less than his fears for her health, had prompted him to apply to the Company for a special ticket, that she might share his stateroom on the voyage. To this they had agreed, providing that she was to be suitably attired, and that he would take all responsibility for her behavior, and that the full passenger's fare was to be paid. As to her good conduct, he had no doubts at all, for she had proved so apt a pupil in even the subtlest points of the etiquette in which he had instructed her; besides, he knew that a sweeter-natured creature had never drawn breath than Emily. The fare had been a serious consideration, for his savings amounted to no great figure, and he had an instinct that Miss Amy Flint, his bride to be, would be ill-content at any rash expenditure on his part. But here, he felt, Amy would agree that he was justified. As for dress, it had been a simple matter to purchase a plain cotton frock and a shady, if unmodish, sunbonnet from the village store.

Emily was pleasedly conscious of her outfit as, holding tightly to his strong hand, she accompanied him through the bustle and life of the promenade deck in search of their cabin. She wondered what all these tall, bronzed men and elegantly costumed women would say to one another about her, and she thought it possible that the simplicity of her dress, and the modest way in which she bent her head as she passed among them, might commend her to their good graces as one who was not inclined to presume nor to give herself airs because her talents had raised her to a *milieu* so widely different from the condition into which she had been born.

"Who can that dumpy little brown creature be?" was what they actually were saying. "The one going along with that shabby fellow there. One of those women anthropologists, I suppose."

And as such they accepted her, taking the silent nods and smiles with which she acknowledged their formal good mornings as resulting from the shyness and reserve of the dowdy student, until, a day or two later, when Mr. Fatigay, on being asked if his wife was not a great traveler, since she stood the sea so well, replied in surprise:

"My wife? Excuse me, but I have no wife. At least, not yet . . ."

"Then who, pray," demanded his interrogator, for, being the wife of a Cape magistrate, she considered herself responsible for the morals of all who met her, and not responsible for those of the lost legion who did not, "who, pray, is that lady in the sunbonnet over there, who, I am told, shares your stateroom, sir, where, for some reason, she always takes her meals?"

"Oh!" said Mr. Fatigay. "That! That's not a lady: That's Emily."

Then, suddenly aware of his interlocutor's puffed and purpled visage, he made haste to add, "That is to say, she's not what you might call a woman at all. She's my pet chimpanzee."

"Oh, really!" cried the lady, the storm which had been gathering on her brow now melting into an expression of astonishment and interest. "Really! In that sunbonnet, and the way she walks, everyone has taken it for granted she was your wife. How extraordinary! Please call her over here. I must have a good look at her. Steward! Some nuts."

And Emily was summoned to make her curtsey before this proud wife, and to listen to the bland and patronizing comments made upon her appearance and manners.

At once the news spread like wildfire round the promenade deck. Cries of "Good heavens!" and "Oh, Mamma, ain't she cute! Won't you buy her for me, Mamma?" were heard on every side, and soon the embarrassed chimp stood nervously in the middle of a ring of grinning faces.

It says much for her native good humor, and for the training she had received from her protector, that she lost neither her temper nor her outward self-possession, but, making a stately inclination or two in acknowledgment of the attention bestowed on her, she gently pressed her way through the crowd and sought the quiet sanctuary of the stateroom.

"You must not mind her shyness," explained Mr. Fatigay courteously. "She is very unused to the society of a large circle of white people."

"Bring her out. Go on, man! Bring her out," shouted the young subalterns and planters, going home on leave. "Will she smoke a cigarette?"

For the two or three days following this Emily's life was little better than a torment, for no sooner did she venture on deck to take a breath of fresh air than she was surrounded by an inquisitive crowd, to whom the least and most ordinary of her actions was a source of loud amazement. When, in the hope of turning aside the derision, and even of enlisting the friendship of two or three of them, who appeared more intelligent than the rest, she ventured to nod approval of some remark they made, or handed them, for example, the Conrad she had secured for herself, with one finger marking a fine descriptive passage, while, with the other hand, she indicated the appropriate sea around them, they would merely burst out into crueler laughter than before.

"Ah!" thought the chimp, "though it is bad enough to be mocked on account of unfashionable clothes and perhaps superfluous hair, these are, after all, admittedly defects. But why should they laugh at me for my understanding? Perhaps they think it ridiculous for one of my sex to aspire to culture. It would be different if I were a tom."

With this, she drew into her shell a little, and, as there was little entertainment in the sight of even a chimp sitting hour after hour staring at a book, the fickle interest of the voyagers soon slackened

and was diverted. A seaman was discovered to be a woman mas-
querading in man's clothes. An actress's pearls were declared missing. A fancy-dress ball was organized, and in the general excitement the chimp soon ceased to be an object of remark.

"We must go to the ball," said Mr. Fatigay, and Emily's heart
bounded with joy. After all, she was young and spirited; nor could
she, any more than the rest of her sex, resist the peculiar thrill of
the prospect of appearing in the most bewitchingly suitable costume,
and among an admiring crowd.

"Perhaps I might go as Carmen," she thought. "If only I could
beg a Spanish shawl from someone, and a red rose to hold in my
lips." And she looked anxiously to where Mr. Fatigay was eating a
dish of Irish stew, to see if there were any bones in it which might
serve as castanets.

"To-re-a-dor!" The quickening strains stirred in her mind, making
her blood tingle as if they had been struck up to hail her entrance
into the ballroom.

"The question is," said Mr. Fatigay, "what shall one go as?"

"Or perhaps Elaine, the lily maid of Astolat." True, it was,
strictly speaking, a part for a blonde, but, after all, there were tiger
lilies. And a white sheet, pinned here and there, would do for the
basic part of the costume. "And I might carry his rowing shield,"
she thought, "and be polishing it! In a way, it wouldn't suit me as
well as Carmen, but supposing he realized that he is my Sir Lancelot,
and *she* his hard exacting Guinevere!"

"Of course, I make a very good pirate," murmured her protector.

"Or supposing I went as Ruth," she thought, "dipping my
morsel in the vinegar. A smile or two, bestowed generally, would
reassure the company that no slight was intended . . ."

"By Jove! I've got it," suddenly cried Mr. Fatigay, slapping his
thigh with a crack like a pistol shot. "Where's that green velvet
smoking jacket mother sent me? It'll be just the thing. I'll go as an
organ-grinder, and I'll get the stewardess to run up a little suit for
Emily, out of some red stuff, and she can be the monkey. Perhaps
we'll get the prize."

Emily gazed at him in consternation. Her first fancy-dress ball!
Why should he demean himself by appearing as a paltry mountebank, and how *could* he force her to appear in the most humiliating
of all possible roles? A hot tide of anger and rebellion surged up
in her heart, and she, even Emily, raised her foot to stamp in
ungovernable rage.

Yet even in the very act she hesitated, and, struck by a new thought, she remained in that stork-like posture, while she considered the matter more seriously.

"After all," she said to herself, "Mr. Fatigay is a man, and no doubt he knows best. To me, this evening's gaiety seems highly charged with glamor and romance, but it is clear that to him, since he elects to behave farcically, it must be a matter of very little importance. His serious attention is, of course, reserved for higher things than this, and though his good breeding forbids him to remain insolently aloof from the company, he saves his dignity by joining them only in a jesting way.

"Or, perhaps," she continued, bringing her right foot gently to the ground, "it is possible that he considers the Comic Muse to be as worthy of reverence as any other, and all the worthier, perhaps, in this degenerate age, when romance is bedecked in the tinsel of Wardour Street, and sentiment is become the pander to every weakly sensual instinct. Then, when all caricature is good, self-caricature is best and most salutary, for our vanities may survive being mocked as ours, but to see another mocking them in himself must leave us in no doubt as to either his sincerity or his knowledge of the subject. Well, if I am to be a jest, I'll see to it that I am a hearty one. I'll dance the cancan. *Ridi, Pagliaccio!*" and she promptly obeyed Mr. Fatigay's eager beckoning, as he set off to gain audience with the stewardess.

That night the lights of the *Stella Mundi* shone bright on its first-class Nordic chivalry, on brave women and fair men. They all looked very vulgar.

In the silence which followed the second dance, a trivial and wispy tune tinkled outside, and the door flew open, revealing the broad shallow steps of the companionway, and standing in them was Mr. Fatigay, cold-colored in the outside starlight, which was very blue, and he was wearing the velvet smoking jacket, and a pair of tight trousers, and a little hat. Before him hung a child's hurdy-gurdy, and, as it dropped reluctantly each strained unearthly note, the tune being the "Barcarolle," Emily, from where she crouched at his feet, arose in her scarlet jacket and trousers, and, shrinkingly brazen, kissed her hands to the company, and began to execute the postures of her dance.

"Oh! How beautiful it is," she thought, as she skipped with exaggerated skimpy care from one extravagant attitude to another, "that this jot of quintessential humor, expressed in an almost meaningless abstraction, should be capable of entering differently every different mental structure that beholds it, and, like a radium needle, can disintegrate each cancerous collection of experiences into pure laughter and virgin chaos.

"One will think of his career," thought she, revolving, with an appearance of painful conscientiousness, upon one leg, "and another perhaps of his love or of his god. Laughter and new beauty must fuse together in the only *aqua regis* which may dissolve these golden illusions." And, bending down, she turned a couple of somersaults very gravely and precisely.

And as she solemnly high-kicked there between the rottenly phosphorescent seas without and the rottenly shining faces of her audience within, she exulted in her conception of a renascent humor, remote from the funny as Picasso is from Louis Wain.

"Bless my dear Mr. Fatigay," she murmured, painfully attempting the splits, "for thus weaning me from my cheap and inartistic romanticism. Garbed according to my original ideas, I could have at best been reflected, albeit glowingly, in the shoddy consciousness of my beholders, but now I am breaking up that consciousness, and shedding a clear and bitter light on the dark deeps below. How they will love me!"

But at that moment a couple of sharp raps were heard, and a volcano of treacle buried all subtleties under the strains of "Maggie! Yes, Ma! Come Right Upstairs."

"Look here, old man," said a subaltern, approaching the suddenly arrested work of art in the doorway, "are you coming in or staying out?"

Like broken instruments of music, the disconcerted pair stumbled in. Not a hand! The dancers shot forward, marked time, and shot back again as hydrometer insects do on the surface film of water. Each pair of eyes was fastened, as if by some quickly grown fleshly tentacle, to the pair opposite, and not so much as even a casual glance was bestowed on the discomfited performers.

An interval followed, and then another dance, then another and another, and still no response was accorded by the feminine element to any of Mr. Fatigay's shy smiles, nor did Emily hear, as still she half hoped to, any manly bass voice at her elbow, murmuring excuses to her partner, and entreating of her the favor of a dance.

Indignation now began to mount the chimp's bosom, less on her own account than because of the effect, becoming increasingly marked in her master's dejected bearing, that their cold reception and this almost pointed neglect was having upon him. It seemed as if he was beginning to feel himself a failure.

All at once an idea came into her head. Unostentatiously, she slipped from his side, and quietly left the great saloon. In a few minutes she had gained the upper deck, whence she clambered perilously down a stanchion till she could gain footing in the porthole which lit the stateroom of an American heiress. She leapt noiselessly to the floor, and, peeping behind the curtain of a hanging cupboard, she drew forth the object of her search, a magnificent scarlet shawl which she had once noticed that lady to be wearing.

In this she hurriedly draped herself, and, taking from the dressing table a pair of large jade earrings, she screwed these on, and hastened from the room in search of a rose and a low-crowned black hat.

In the saloon the heat had grown intense, and the dancers halted more and more frequently for refreshments. Stewards glided easily among the flashing throng, bearing claret cup, Cydrax, and iced lemonade. Champagne was to be purchased at a sufficient price. Bright eyes now shone with an extra brightness; the hot blood bloomed in every cheek. Masculine murmurs, tapping at the heart as a neurologist taps on the patella reflex, or Moses on the rock, elicited silvery laughter in sudden fountains all about the saloon. The bandsmen paused a moment, leaning back to mop their foreheads, yet even without the music the mounting spirit of the evening went on, up to the moment of full tide.

"Now," said the emcee to himself. "Now's the time for the balloons."

But before he could leave the room to call for these, the doors sprang apart, and there stood Carmen, glowing dark and deadly as a poppy, drawing all eyes by her fatal southern attraction, her lips, behind the crimson flower, curving in a smile wherein passion and scorn slumbered lightly side by side.

"Carmen!" The word burst forth simultaneously from every male throat in the saloon. The conductor, an artist to the fingertips, instantly gave the word to the band, and, as Emily advanced towards the spellbound assembly, the opening chords of "Toreador" blazed out into the vibrant air.

"Carmen!" Subalterns, civil servants, diamond smugglers, judges, motor salesmen, confidence men, all that well-tubbed clean-limbed throng advanced to do her homage.

"Carmen!" And as the band rises once more in the more modern and almost equally appropriate notes of "Valencia," the crowd, in one eager husky murmur, entreats her to dance.

But now, with a superb and tigerish gesture of contempt, she passes through their dividing midst to where a single solitary figure droops disconsolate against the wall. Plucking the hot-hued blossom from her lips, she laughingly flings it at his feet, and, extending a graceful hand, she has drawn the suddenly awakened Mr. Fatigay into the whirling mazes of the dance.

CHAPTER 6

We drifted o'er the harbor-bar,
And I with sobs did pray—
O let me be awake, my God!
Or let me sleep alway.

The steamer now drove out of the Gulf of Guinea, and turned her bows to the northeast and home. Mr. Fatigay, who had till then been yearning to starboard, for his love lay there, now felt his heart swing with the swinging needle, and he yearned proportionately to port. Ah, god! The moment when, in its changing course, the swift ship pointed, stern to stem, straight to "The Woodlands," Stotfield nr. Haslemere, where sate Miss Amy Flint, all this particular microcosm's desire!

When, said his pocket compass, that moment had arrived, Mr. Fatigay, for just so long, was accorded the ineffable bliss of being able to yearn, as it were, full-steam ahead. How his poor heart then rose up in his breast, and began to throb and strain to burst free, that it might fly with the velocity of a cannonball (but it was as soft and spicy as a plum pudding) straight to the bosom of his beloved!

But they were to call at Gib, and the course soon fell away some degrees to starboard, so that our hero's heart lost the added impetus of the steamer's straight direction, and it settled into an uneasy stillness again, as a dog's does when his master turns away from the warren.

Now the waves took on a brisker blue, and smokes were seen everywhere on the seaward horizon, and the sails of fishing fleets towards the shore. Electric light cables, dwarfed to the likeness of one-strand wire fences, switchbacked along the undulating coast; corks and orange peel met them on the oil-streaked tide: They were entering the English Channel. Everyone ran suddenly to the side. "There! That's it! There! England! Home!"

"Never forget this day," said a white-haired old commissioner to his son, a bright-faced lad coming home from South Africa for the first time to begin his education at one of our great schools. "That," said he, pointing to the coast of Devon, "is England."

"But, Daddy," replied the youngster in amazement, for he had read his Phillpotts, "it looks like those huts on the goldfields."

A group of South Africans, full of patriotic nostalgia for their colony, stared frowningly at the tactless lad.

"Our Motherland," replied his father, with a dignified glance at these, "may possess neither gold nor fields, but always remember, my boy, that it leads the whole world in building sites.

"If it reminds you of a mining camp," he added, "you must bear in mind that a camp is the most fitting home for heroes, and that it is from surroundings like these that men have risen to go forth to battle, scornful of the horrors of the trenches and careless of the imminence of death."

"Good-bye, dear," whispered a number of straight-limbed, clear-eyed young matrons, glancing tenderly at their well-tubbed squires from under their level brows. "We had better say good-bye now. I expect my husband will be waiting on the quay."

Now the port lay immediately before them, and the hum of life in its narrow streets drifted out on the April breeze. The intermittent nature of this vehicle made the medley of wheels, taxi horns, and voices appear to rise and fall, like the breathing of some vast organism. Emily, feeling incredibly small and brown, peered forth timidly from her niche in the great wall of the floating palace. The crowd on the quay surged forward like a gathering wave, a thin surf of handkerchiefs breaking out upon its crest. A broken spray of self-conscious shouts leapt weakly at the steep side of the liner and drizzled back on the upturned faces whence it had sprung.

A tiny shudder ran through the vast bulk of the ship, and it died happily, and, as the strongest appear weak and small in death, when we are put in mind of the lives they have come through, so it suddenly became a cockleshell that had come five thousand miles, across waters in many places over a mile in depth. And its blissful end, and the pathos of its delivery, and the slackening within each passenger of some strain, which had, it now seemed, all the while been nervously seconding the efforts of the engines—all this moved their hearts so deeply that, if a hymn of thanksgiving had then been struck up, there is little doubt but that many would have joined in under their breaths.

Sirens, which seemed severely meant for everyone, now began to sound, quiet words of command were issued, a rattle of gangways was heard, cries of "There he is! Jim, *Jim!*" arose, and the crowd on the boat and the crowd on the quay rushed together like mouths in a ravenous kiss.

Now up and down among the cleaving throngs ran Mr. Fatigay, dragging Emily tripping and stumbling behind him, and he was looking into every face like a dog that seeks its master.

"Amy! Amy! Where can she be? I say! I wonder where she can be."

As he runs back and forth, growing white and breathless, banging into people, trying to look cool and collected, then not caring how he looks, risking a faint "coo-ee," covering the same ground three or four times over, rushing up to distant figures of the most impossible shapes and sizes, getting something in his eye, whispering intently to the grim custodian of "Ladies," and performing a hundred heartbreaking, mad tricks—that he will blush for to his dying day—let us despise not him alone, but all of us, both those who are capable of such besottedness and those who are not. For the heart is, in a sense, like the Prince of Wales; we would not have it cut in stone, yet how pathetic it is, when, as at Wembley, we see it modeled in butter.

When he had sought her until he was ready to drop, he acknowledged despairingly that she could not have come aboard, and he made haste down the gangway onto the quay, where he commenced his search anew. Soon he saw a Cook's man standing magnificently apart, and, hurrying up to him, he said:

"Excuse me, but have you seen a lady anywhere—a small dark lady—young—looking for anyone?"

"Well, sir, there's a good many," replied the humane official. "Can that be her, perhaps?"

But Mr. Fatigay, turning to follow his glance, saw only Emily, hastening to overtake him with all the speed she might.

Shaking his head sadly, he reached out, and, grasping the poor chimp by the hand, he scurried her off with him. At last, having given up all hope, he drifted out under the entrance arch, to where cars and taxis were ranked in the dock road. And there, in a taxi drawn up by the curb, sat Miss Amy Flint, waiting her love's appearance.

"Amy!"

"Alfred! How brown you're looking! And yet . . . just the same. Have you had a wonderful voyage?"

"Amy!"

"Well? Have I changed so much? Do you think you'll still like me? Have you got lots to tell me?"

"Amy!"

"Well, if I haven't changed outwardly, I've altered a good deal within. You'll have to be very nice and kind and understanding with your wayward girl. But what a time you've been! Most of the people seem to have come out half an hour ago. I was getting quite anxious."

"Why, I've been looking for you everywhere inside," stammered Mr. Fatigay. "That's where everyone was being met. I thought you must have met with an accident or something."

"Ah!" said she with a smile. "Just the same old Alfred! Didn't you guess how I'd feel about the public scene? Never mind, you're forgiven. Hop inside!

"But who . . . ?" she added with a stare. "But what on earth is this?"

Emily, unable to breathe even, looked up supplicatingly at her protector.

"Well," said he, "ha! ha! Well, the fact is . . . I wondered, er . . . I thought perhaps you might like a chimp."

During the pregnant silence that followed, the taxi clock rose thrice.

"Good heavens!" said Amy at last. "Is *that* the wonderful present you've been hinting at in all your letters? A monkey! Darling! My poor old boy! What in the world could you have been thinking of? What should *I* want with a monkey? Covered with fleas, no doubt, and sure to make a filthy mess about the house! You'd better shoot it, or give it to the zoo or something. *I* don't want it."

"Her name's Emily," said Mr. Fatigay, very cast down.

"Anyway," he said, seeing that this communication elicited no response, "we'd better be getting along to your hotel. Get in, Emily."

"I don't want the filthy creature in along with me," cried Amy. "Let it sit beside the driver, or ride on the roof. Oh! I don't know though. Anything is better than being made a public spectacle. Perhaps we'd better have it inside."

Emily had heard little of all this. She stood amazed. To be given away! She felt like something out of *Uncle Tom's Cabin.* And to be given by him, for whom she had renounced all, for whom she had come so far, asking nothing but to watch over him—to be given by him to *her!* She had expected a disillusion to result upon the first sight of Amy, but it seemed to be happening in the wrong quarter.

"Get in, Emily." The words percolated at last, and she automatically obeyed. Taxis were new to her, and, seeing only the back seat within, for the others were sprung back against the partition, she naturally took her place on this, not as one wishing to presume, but because she saw no alternative.

This aspect of the matter did not perhaps occur to Amy, for, seeing the chimp occupying one of the better seats, she took offense, and demanded that it be turned off at once, and be made to sit upon the floor.

"Emily shall sit upon a front seat," said Mr. Fatigay, and he smiled at her reassuringly as he pressed one down.

"You see, my dear," he resumed, as the taxi jolted forward, "Emily is no ordinary chimp. She understands almost everything that is said to her, and, as for having fleas and being ill-trained for the house, why she is as clean and neat and well-behaved as any human being. I have trained her, thinking of you, to bear herself with the utmost decorum. She has her own knife and fork, and her own little bed, and she is not only completely tidy, but also very helpful about the house."

"Then she had better be sold to perform on the halls," said Amy Flint.

At this the poor chimp started violently, and turned her eyes imploringly on Mr. Fatigay. She had a violent prejudice against the stage.

"But, darling," said he, "that wouldn't do at all. I really couldn't bear the thought of parting with Emily to anyone except you. Why, once she saved my life. I thought that might make you look favorably on her, and take her as a novel sort of maid, and if you could only bring yourself to do so, I'm sure you would soon grow to love her for her own sake. My dearest hope," he added, "apart from yourself, has been that you two might come to understand one another, and be friends."

Now, as he said these words, a look of grateful adoration shone from the eyes of the chimp, and Amy, in a flash of feminine intuition, had realized that the humble creature had lost her heart to Mr. Fatigay. And, while well-founded jealousy bears no proportion at all to the love on which it feeds, but only to the possessive element in it, there is a certain fanciful and ill-founded variety which thrives inversely in relation to the strength of what affection may lie beneath it, just as some mountain weeds bloom most flaringly where the soil is thinnest. Of this kind is that sort which is often to be noted in cold and sterile natures, that sort which is most inflamed not by their partner's loving elsewhere, but by their being loved, regardless of whether they return it or not. And if this unrequited gift of affection should glow so warmly as to put their own emotional impotence to shame, as it does the more unmistakably the colder and more sterile they are, then their vindictiveness is sharpened to a surer point than has ever been known among our hot-blooded *señoritas* or ukulele ladies.

A feeling of this description now arose in the bosom of Amy, and, born with all its teeth, it soon fastened on the best method of chastising the impertinence which ventured to love with a strength of which she was incapable.

"Very well," said Amy, "I'll keep the creature, and if it has any intelligence at all I'll train it to wait on me. Otherwise it must be sent away. I suppose it's my only chance of having a maid of my own."

CHAPTER 7

. . . when, sick for home,
She stood in tears amid the alien corn,

the chimp's sad heart was charmed by no nightingale, for the bird had not yet returned to Stotfield, and what corn was showing was but a scanty acid green, ragged among the flints of those chilly fields. It was the blackthorn winter, and Emily, who had been sent out to gather primroses, found the thin stuff dress she now wore, designed by Amy to resemble the drabbest of charity child's garments, to be but a miserable covering against the cruel east wind. A thin and lonely song trembled among the telegraph wires, where the road ran up between the tilted plowlands. It was a disillusioned scene, embittered by the default of spring; yet the primroses seemed loath to leave it. Their crowded sickly faces peered up anxiously at Emily as she knelt shivering beside them and tried to loosen their stems from the tough grasses to which they seemed desperately to cling. A variety of small brown birds, blowing about like dead leaves, uttered cold and colorless notes, much like the whetting together of flint stones.

"Cum, Somer, cum, the suete sesoun and sonne!"

thought Emily, wondering how long it must be before the warm and scented weather came to save her. Perhaps her wistful plea was taken as an impertinent complaint, for the sky darkened forbiddingly, an icy gust made the blackthorn branches rattle against one another, and a sudden rain lashed through her fluttering, shoddy dress. Her fingers were too numb to pick any more, and, as it was, many of the stems were broken off too short, so she crept through the hedge and took the field path towards home, for she felt incapable, in her present dispirited condition, of bearing up under the curious glances of the village people.

48

The path ran out desperately to the shoulder of the hill, then bent and scurried down to where two or three red-brick houses formed a modern and genteel suburb to the village. Nearest of these was "The Woodlands," where Miss Amy Flint, when she was not in town, lived with her mother. This handsome villa of prewar construction formed a delightful residence with gabled elevations, detached, on two floors, affording seven bed and dressing, two servants', two bath, three reception rooms, sun loggia, cloakroom, bright domestic offices, detached garage, surrounded by choice well laid-out grounds of just over one acre, including shrubbery and tennis courts.

Poor Emily stumbled down the path and slipped into the cold house through the back door, as she had been bidden, and, hurrying past the kitchen, whence emanated the rude titters of the cook and parlor maid, she knocked timidly on the door of the drawing room, and, entering, found Amy and Mr. Fatigay at tea.

"Hullo, Emily," said Mr. Fatigay pleasantly.

"Here it is at last," said Amy, and, addressing the sensitive creature briskly rather than unkindly, she said:

"Well, where are the primroses? Show me."

Emily shrinkingly proffered the meager bunch.

"What? Is that all?" said Amy. "And see what miserable little stems you've got to them." And privately she gave the chimp an angry look.

Further than this, however, she did not choose to go, for, though her relationship to the poor chimp was founded, almost entirely, on the feeling that she deserved a good sharp slap, Amy was never brutal to animals, nor was she inclined to appear severe before Mr. Fatigay, who might have been provoked to a defense of Emily, which would have puffed up the chimp undesirably, as well as wasting a quarrel. Amy did not believe in being too prodigal in this direction. "Quarrels with a fiancé," as she put it in one of her witty sallies to her intimate friends, of whom she had many, for she was considered by a large circle to be the Queen of Haverstock Hill, "quarrels with a fiancé, though frequently tonic and diverting, should never be indulged in for wanton pleasure. They are too useful for that, and will be found just as thrilling if saved up till a time when, in the warmth of reconciliation, some important concession is to be obtained."

Amy therefore contented herself with being firm, and with sometimes laughing at Emily, and even this she confined to two main occasions, of which the first was when she laughed at her for being a chimp, and the second was when she laughed at her for behaving like a human.

So this time she said no more, and raised no objection when Mr. Fatigay poured out a milky cup of tea for the half-frozen creature, and bade her bring her little stool to the hearthrug, that she might toast herself before the fire. It had been in Amy's mind to dismiss poor Emily to the solitude of her fireless little garret, but now watching her settle humbly into her place, her ingenious jealousy suggested a more satisfactory way of chastising her impudence, which was by allowing her to remain in the room while she continued her conversation with Mr. Fatigay.

"Come, love," she said softly, stretching herself upon the sofa with a voluptuous grace, modeled on that of Goya's *Maja* (clothed). "Come and sit here on the pouf, and go on telling me what you did, and thought, and felt in Africa."

"Africa?" said Mr. Fatigay, with a touch of that conversational elephantiasis which would surely be listed among the commoner tropical diseases. "Africa? Why, I may have *done* things there, but as for thinking and feeling—how could I think or feel in Africa when my mind and heart were here with you in England?"

And with a tender leer he possessed himself of his lady's hand.

"No. Tell me," she said, in a velvety purr.

"What I thought!" burst out Mr. Fatigay. "What I felt on those long hot nights! Ah, someday I'll tell you. Someday I'll make you understand."

"Tell me now," murmured Amy, who had an infinite capacity for conversation of this kind.

But, alas, Mr. Fatigay, whose feelings had hurried him beyond the limits of his verbal expressiveness, had passed his arm about her waist, and seemed eager to carry out the second of his projects.

"Now! Now! Remember your promise," said she, feeling well pleased that the chimp should witness this display of ardor, but in no way inclined to round it off by any considerable response. "Sit up properly and talk."

"Oh, Amy!" cried the poor fellow, who had been set back in this manner over a score of times since he had come to Stotfield. "Can't you see I'm dying for you? Don't think I am being too physical, dear. I wouldn't, for I know you hate it. But the fact is—after all, we are grown up, aren't we? I've lived so long out there with only your image that when I see you in the . . . in reality, I don't know what to do. Can't we be married at once, darling—do say 'yes'—instead of waiting so long?"

As the tormented water sinks into a momentary quiescence when the cold egg is cast in, so Emily's seething heart subsided into a hot stillness at these words, that she might better catch the answer. "Yet how," thought she, "can anything but assent be given to such a plea, and from such a man?"

"Oh, Alfred!" said Amy, in tones more of sorrow than of anger. "You promised not to pester me till I myself felt ready. I thought you understood how necessary it is to me to be just myself for a little longer. Besides," she went on, to punish him for having forced her to show a reluctance which she could neither overcome nor bring herself to acknowledge, "besides, it's so long since I've seen you, that you can hardly expect me to be quite sure of my feelings till we've been properly engaged for a few months. It wouldn't be fair to you to let you tie yourself up with someone who wasn't quite sure of herself.

"And you ought to have time," she added, "to think over your own feelings. These are your first weeks in England, and you've not seen a white woman for years. Can you be sure that this, joining up with our old feeling for one another, is not making you think that you feel what, perhaps, after all, you don't?"

All this was perfectly reasonable, and even benevolent, in its thoughtfulness for Mr. Fatigay's welfare, nor could any objection be raised to it except, perhaps, by those churlish fellows who are beginning to cry out that women, who have long ago broken in such emotional spontaneities as tears and frowns and smiles to their own use, are now attempting the same with sweet reason, which, if it makes a good master, is a confoundedly bad servant, though an obedient one. "Women," such boors remark, "are unreasonable enough when one wants to reason with them, but when it comes to other matters (as needs it must, if health and good spirits are to retain their seat), then up springs this same forgotten reason, like a garden rake one treads on when picking flowers, and hits you on the nose."

Beside such scurrilities, Amy's words stand arrayed in sweetness and light, except for the trifling fault, since nothing can be absolutely perfect, of being a little insincere. It is extremely difficult for a tenderly nurtured young woman of our race and generation, especially one who is diligent in keeping abreast of contemporary science, to say in so many words, "I like nothing more than being wooed, and nothing less than the prospect of being won," and this must be the reason that so few say it, while so many evince that attitude very clearly in their behavior. Not, indeed, that this is true of every woman, or that there is really a lack of healthy physical instinct among the cultivated shes of today. On the contrary, there is an ample sufficiency, the only trifling criticism to be advanced being connected with the distribution of it, for half, like Amy, have none at all, and the other half have perhaps twice too much.

But, be that as it may, the fact remains that Amy expressed herself thus, and Mr. Fatigay, when he had well pondered her words, began to shake and tremble at the prospect of delay, as if he had been sentenced to a second turn on the rack, and, getting up from the pouf, he took a fling or two about the room.

"Amy!" he cried at last, "Heaven knows I am unwilling to pester you, as you call it, and still more so to obtrude on your notice that side of my nature which your purer one finds so repellent. Do understand! I am not incapable of the higher sort of love which you rightly require of me, but, in spite of that, I am, in short, a man. And if, so to speak, I am repressed much longer, I fear I shall become totally unhinged, and perform, in some awful aberration, a desperate act, which, when you hear of it, will make you hate and shun me. Have pity, therefore, on what is, after all, only the agonizing nature of my sex."

"It may well be the nature of your sex," said she, "in animals and in those men who are nothing more. Doubtless the monkey that sits there could bear you out in that. But I cannot think that any *true* man, least of all you, Alfred, to whom I have given so much, could be so utterly lacking in self-control. Why, George Weeke," she said, "was engaged five years to Adeline Chili, and . . ." But at the sound of these names, which were not unfamiliar to him, Mr. Fatigay uttered a strange sound.

"I see," went on Amy, with some asperity, for she could not bear to hear her friends disparaged, "I see that I am right in resolving to know you more certainly before I entrust my life into your keeping. And if you are that sort of man, who puts *that* before everything else, it surely cannot matter whom you marry. You had better think very seriously before you tie yourself to one who has a life of her own to lead, and can't put *that* thing first in importance."

Hearing these words, Mr. Fatigay was very cast down, for to him Miss Amy Flint was the way and the life, and what disagreed with her least opinion, though it might be the very foundation stone of his being, was not long in appearing to him as both inferior and offensive.

But Emily, on hearing this admonition to him to take thought, could have sprung from her seat, and, going up to Amy, have shaken her warmly by the hand, for she had no idea of the process which fishermen describe in the phrase, "giving him line."

Mr. Fatigay went to the window and watched the dark and rainy wind shake angrily at the numb bewildered boughs, which might have expected by this time to be flecked with translucent green. "The buds," he thought, "seem actually to be retreating."

As she saw him standing there so dismally, drooping in the sudden vacuity of a complete *non plus*, staring at the windowpanes, which, piteous with the cold trickle of raindrops, seemed a fitting mirror for his suddenly colorless and weeping soul, Emily thought to herself, "This pain of his, though it throbs at my heart's root, is perhaps all for the best. Amy spoke the truth, and for better reason than she knew. This deluded ardor of his, the monstrous product of five years' incubation in loneliness under the African sun, must soon dwindle and disappear now it is brought face to face with so manifestly disproportionate an object. While it continues, my master must value this woman's qualities as the highest, which means that his standards must be in utter chaos. But when the bubble is pricked by some word too sharp or prospect too thorny, they will reassert themselves, and he will realize that it is best to give his heart where the warmest return is to be expected. And then . . . Who knows?

"Perhaps he is on the point of revolt now," she continued. "He has reason enough, I am sure. Or perhaps he must have time to see something of normal women before he regains his mental balance."

For poor Emily, in her innocence, believed Amy to be a very chimera of wrath and treachery and greed, and all because she knew how to stand up for herself and was not disposed to be treated as a mere chattel. She thought of her as a cold-blooded variety of that terrible "woman of thirty," whom she regarded as an apocalyptic monster, absolutely transgressing all that Tennyson and the loving heart laid down as beautiful and good. It would be unfair to Amy, however, not to correct this by saying downright that she was, as far as these things can be coexistent, a flower of England's womanhood, beautiful, intelligent, high-principled, a charming companion, a devoted daughter, and the best imaginable comrade.

"He will be a lucky man, on whom Amy bestows her love." So said the dozen or so, each of whom regarded her as their closest friend. But it must be admitted that the male section of these, though they valued her friendship more than anything else in the world, found it possible to maintain it at the pitch of high intimacy she set only by making the most of certain other acquaintances they had among the ladies of Bohemia and the Café Royal.

And now Amy stretched out her hand, and said with a frank and tender smile:

"Come now, old boy! Don't be furious with me for a little plain speaking. After all, we've both said more than we meant, no doubt, but it's a sad case if being honest with one another should estrange us." And she gave him a melting smile, the glutinous sweetness of which he devoured with the avidity of a diabetic who swallows a fatal spoonful of jam. And, not pausing to analyze her words—nay, only too eager, in his trembling desire for reconciliation, to make every surrender he could—he sprang toward her and caught her yielding but elastic frame in his arms. As he was kissing the silky curls at the back of her neck, a process which in itself made the corresponding hairs on Emily even more stiff and straight than usual, Amy peeped out underneath and gave her a glance, and this glance said as plainly as any words might:

"You see?"

CHAPTER 8

And at night along the dusky highway near
and nearer drawn,
Sees in heaven the light of London flaring
like a dreary dawn.

To the outer, if not to the inner, eye, this was rather reversed when Emily first approached the metropolis, for they all went up together on the morning of the first of May, a day so bright in the country, and so conspicuously clouded by London's smoke pall, that it seemed as if they were traveling in time rather than in space, and approaching the outskirts, not of the town, but of yesterday's bad weather. It follows that the highway along which they were being drawn became dusky only as the gray streets engulfed them, for, on the washed hills outside, unpunctual spring had arrived with a rush, all hot and shining, and the railway lines glinted above the hot shingle of the track, as, with a blue glance, she made them her mirror, while she powdered her face with chalk dust and dandelion pollen.

The downs through which the line ran were torn everywhere by new roads, long angry scratches, along which buildings in every stage of erection stood like clots of the earth's red-brick blood. Clustered under the railway embankment, a few white, roughcast villas were being built, the completed ones being already occupied, and, when the fair-haired, bun-faced, bare-armed young matrons came out to pin napkins on their clotheslines, they seemed from one angle like Piero della Francesca angels, against their background of roughcut chalk roadway and roofless walls, and, from another, like advertisements for a labor-saving soap.

Inside the carriage, the heat was bewildering rather than intense. The dust, which had lain congealed all the damp winter, awoke in the cushions behind their heads, issuing out at the least movement to tickle the inflamed membrane at the back of Emily's throat and nose. She had a slight cold, which at once heightened and confused her impressions: she seemed lost among many speeds, many times, many states of existence. Her companions' faces, which had a waxy and artificial look, lolling weakly as dolls' heads, seemed to survive only by a miracle the sudden leap and snap of signal boxes, which flattened themselves on the windows with loud smacks; unsmilingly they still wagged after the temporary annihilation of tunnels, and bobbed like corks on the terrific entrance of concertina-ing hilly streets, volleying into the carriage with the whirr of a watchman's rattle.

But through it all Emily was conscious of a feeling of renewed life and anticipation. London certainly proffered a dawn, though it might be a dreary one. After the icy midnight of "The Woodlands," the prospect of seeing the world's largest capital, rich in public buildings, monuments, stately thoroughfares, and, above all, in associations of the many distinguished figures whose lives and opinions she had read, was one which she could not but find exhilarating.

"Besides," thought she, "my dear master will now have an opportunity of meeting other women, both good and bad, and in the first he will see what his beloved should be, and in the second he will see, with eyes unclouded by love, what she is. He will recognize faults which are the true cause of his present discomfort, and which, in his present blindness, he imagines to be resident more in himself than in her."

"Suitcase," said Amy peremptorily, and the chimp reached up a slim but strong right arm to take it from the rack. Mr. Fatigay began to gather up handbags and papers.

Victoria Station! Emily completely forgot her cold and her problems as she pattered along after the engaged couple, nor did she allow the heavy suitcase with which she was burdened to prevent her from peeping eagerly in all directions. Most of all, of course, when she was once embarked on her first taxi-drive through London, she was impressed by the appearance of our marvelous police. She thought them simply remarkable. For the rest, though the reflections of the untutored chimp are scarcely worth the setting down, she was mostly struck by the appearance of abject misery which was apparent in all the passersby, especially in their sickly complexions, their peevish or anxious looks, their slave's gait, and, most of all, in their rare and rickety smiles.

Do not think, however, that she jumped at once to the conclusion, as some more superficially observant stranger might have done, that the great city is on the whole a nasty mistake, and that it would be better, all things considered, if Highgate Hill were to turn Vesuvius, so to speak, and obliterate, to put it bluntly, all the ugly antheap at its feet. No: she had had experience of her own enough to know that happiness is like some of the lower forms of life, of which, if one of them is cut into pieces, some inconsiderable fragment or other is sure to survive. Thus she had little doubt that, among these hurrying millions, most of whom looked to her (though she knew little of homes and offices) as if they had been both crossed in love and condemned to penal servitude for life, many had compensations, which, however small they might seem to the indifferent spectator, must in logic be so great to each individual concerned that they compensated for the toil, the illness, the worry, and the emotional starvation marked clearly in his face, for they demonstrably withheld him from cutting his throat. "What a wonderful thing a stamp collection must be," thought Emily, "or the construction with one's own hands of a home radio set!"

By now their taxi had reached Haverstock Hill, where Amy had a little upper maisonette in which she spent the greater part of every year. The rooms, unlike the larger, but more stereotyped, apartments of her mother's house, were furnished to express her own personality. The furniture was modern and artistic, but not lacking in occasional evidences of a charming feminine touch. Under a large colored reproduction of Van Gogh's sunflowers, an expensive doll, dressed to represent Polly Peachum, flopped topsily against the telephone. There were bulb-flowers, faded during the owner's absence; a drawing by Augustus John and a huge witch ball.

While her escort set down their burdens, Amy went forward, and flung the windows open, letting in the warm and living air from outside, where a man was selling brown wallflowers.

"Have you everything you want, my dear," said Mr. Fatigay, "before I rush off to the bank?"

"Yes, indeed," said Amy. "Except for a little peace and seclusion. I always want a spell of solitude after staying at home. And now, with you as well as mother and everyone else—well, I'm sure you'll understand, dear, if I want a quiet evening with one or two old friends."

"Why, of course," replied her lover, his face falling a little, for he had hoped that she would go that evening to the theater with him. "Will you come out somewhere with me tomorrow?"

"Well, let's see," said Amy. "Today's Friday, isn't it? Why not come round on Monday evening. I'm having a few friends in then, people you must meet. Till then I really feel that I must be alone. I've such a head, dear." And she passed her hand wearily over her brow.

"All right," said Mr. Fatigay after a moment's pause. "Perhaps I may look in in the morning for Emily, to take her for a walk, and perhaps see you for a moment at the same time."

"Of course, she'll have a good deal to do in helping the char," answered Amy, who noticed with disapproval the sudden beaming of the chimp's ingenuous countenance. But she felt it would look rather bad to refuse without good reason, so she added, "Still, she might be able to go with you in the afternoons. Only I don't want her spoiled. One must begin as one means to go on. Well, good-bye, dear. I'm really terribly tired."

And with that Mr. Fatigay took his leave.

Emily had not done looking after him, nor had Amy done peeping here and there in the uneasy aimlessness which overcomes one when, returning after a long absence, one reestablishes one's rapport with a confusing sunny room, when that black daffodil, the telephone, pealed goldenly through the dusty shafts of sunlight, and Amy (no mother hearing her only child squall could have moved on a quicker instinct) swooped down upon it and took it to her bosom. The rapid but quite natural transition from nerviness and fatigue to a pleasurable excitement was perhaps a shade too frankly realized; a hint of lingering lethargy would have been a seemly compliment to Mr. Fatigay, and to not so much the sincerity of her plea of weariness, for it was sincere enough, but to its depth and stability. What had been important enough to occasion the rather curt dismissal of her lover should hardly have evaporated so quickly at the prospect of speaking to a friend. But Emily—who, not coming of a gregarious stock, had no conception of the thrilling beauty of the telephone, through whose ebon and Plutonic lips our friends address us in voices revived from nonexistence, Lazarus-voices cold and earthy as those of the temporarily awakened dead—Emily felt that Amy had been shamming her headache, and eyed her frowningly. It was hardly the first time, nor was it destined to be the last by many, when the puritanical chimp, seeing Amy at her most ordinary, set her down as being positively criminal instead of simply womanly.

"Now, Emily," said Amy, replacing the receiver, "two or three friends of mine are coming round to tea, and they will probably stay to dinner, and there may be some other people coming afterwards. This means that every single piece of glass and china in the place must be thoroughly washed before teatime, for the dust settles on it. So you'd better start at once."

Emily nodded obediently, for she had no desire to accept Amy's hospitality without giving her ample value in labor in return, and, taking off her sunbonnet, she held it out, and looked about her in a manner expressive of a desire to know where to put her things, that she might prepare herself immediately for work.

"You'd better come up here," said Amy, who had found out some time ago that the chimp understood all that was said to her, though she continued to address her in a few monosyllables except when they were alone. "This is where you'll sleep. You can use the straw in that packing case in the corner." And, as she said this, she pushed Emily into a pokey little garret where lumber and boxes were stored.

"Come down now, and I'll show you the scullery," she went on. "You can boil some water, and begin, while I go out and get you some black dresses and white caps and aprons to wear in the afternoons. Then you'll look more or less respectable when you open the door to visitors. I think, by the way, I'll call you Smithers in future. Emily sounds hardly suitable for one of your species and position."

Emily followed with a sigh. She remembered those distant days when she had studied so absorbedly under Mr. Fatigay's tutelage for the position he had said she was to hold in London. So this was what he had meant her for! The poor chimp sighed once more, then, shrugging her shoulders, she took up the kettle and turned to the ugly sink, accepting, as a now chronic condition of her heart, that painful bursting feeling from which no amount of sighing could afford any real relief.

The next day, though, when her spirits were just at their lowest ebb, Mr. Fatigay appeared shortly after lunch, and said he had come to take Emily for a walk, at which the world seemed suddenly transformed for her, and the enraptured creature, having hurriedly pulled on her shady bonnet, trustingly put her hand in his, and they set forth in the summery afternoon to see the sights of London.

It was that day, of all the year, when the barrowmen who sell sickly roots of daisies do their briskest barter with the sentimental wives of Camden Town; when husbands lean out upon windowsills, and the bugs crawl out upon walls; that day when children swarm in noisy dirtiness on the first hot paving stones of the season, and when the grimiest scrap of newspaper, trundling in warm idleness before the smelly wind, seems to move in a sensuous ritual dance.

The bus they mounted, being either late or sensitive to the spirit of the day, swung wildly down into Camden Town, and before long Mr. Fatigay, who had not Amy's keen perception and had not guessed in over a year what she had seen in less than a month, the extent of Emily's understanding, but who, nevertheless, partly from his natural openness of heart, and partly in unconscious response to her intelligent glances, always spoke to her as if he was aware of it, was pointing out scenes familiar to him in his youth.

"Look, Emily!" he said. "There is the 'Horseshoe.' What a place! When I was at London University, that's where we used to foregather. What a time that was! Well! Well! Well!"

Emily fixed her eyes on the sacred spot. A vision of our hero in the first flush of his youth, ingenuous, idealistic, rose before her:

A young Apollo, golden haired,
Stands dreaming on the verge of strife,
Magnificently unprepared
For the long littleness of life.

As the appropriate lines recurred to her, she saw him, blushing a little in the attempt to overcome his boyish self-consciousness, kindling the divine fire in the ardent, though lesser, breasts of his admiring companions, as he told them in ringing tones of his determination to leave the world better than he'd found it. To that inspiring picture succeeded a softer one, and she saw the band of young students sitting pensive and enthralled, as one of their number, probably that same one, sang the old sweet song, with which, as she had read in *Trilby*, the Paris art students were wont to melt each other's tender hearts—"My Sister Dear."

"What would I not have given," thought Emily, "to have been one of that golden company: to have shared their studies, their vicissitudes, their evenings of grave discussion or innocent mirth! To have been, perhaps, as far as modesty permits, the dear platonic friend of each of them, and, as time went on, something more to one! For the day might have come, when, suddenly breaking off in describing the generous Utopia of his latest dream, he would have hesitated, and, all his swift rhetoric gone, would have said, bluntly and clumsily, 'I need you.' And I, meeting his eyes. . . ." But here the bus jolted on, and Emily awoke from her reverie to hear him say:

"And here's the Charing Cross Road. This is where all the second-hand book shops are. Many's the hour I've spent poking about in some of these places, standing, sometimes, for the whole of lunch-time, reading some book I couldn't afford to buy. Yes, you can stand there as long as you like, reading, and no one says a word."

Emily heard his words with something of a thrill. She determined to avail herself at the first opportunity of the facilities of this enlightened, courteous street.

"How appearances deceive!" she thought, looking at the tall fronts of the dwellinghouses, grayly lustrous in the sun, which rose like cliffs of mud above the sluggish ditch through which they were crawling. It revived memories of her trip down the Congo. A few old booklovers, looking like those dull and crippled water insects which resemble bits of old dry stick, which, again, are exactly like booklovers, hung precariously at the shop fronts, as if in fear of being swept away by the slowly drifting scum, for this is a great street for actors. Here a policeman, dark, shining and clumsy as a huge dytiscus beetle, hung stationary in the middle of the hot colorless stream. Billy and Bertie and Kitty and Gertie coming from rehearsal in their cream and vermilion Mercedes, open and shallow, looked like four pale electric grubs in a water lily. High above the mud banks an airplane, or loud dragonfly, split in relatively wide freedom the limited ashy blue.

"And the palpitations of this slime," thought Emily, "are the effects of mind! The rich silt of all the mental progress of mankind is collected here, radioactive with the living truth. Decidedly I must come. Perhaps," she thought, "I may find a priceless first edition among the musty contents of one of those boxes marked fourpence. I should like to do that."

And so they came to Trafalgar Square, where Emily smiled, for she was no prude, at the statue of Lord Nelson, and where she gazed with regret, though, of course, she had never stayed there herself, at what was once the site of Morley's Hotel.

And so they went down Whitehall on the open-topped bus, and on into the sun's eye, their different figures black and ragged in silhouette as they advanced, on their high and jolty car, solemnly and slowly into that radiance, till at length they drew up in Pimlico, from which they were to start out for a walk along the Chelsea Embankment.

Looking forward, it is possible to catch other glimpses of them, on various of the afternoons when Amy was engaged with her friends. They are either strolling under the sugary flowering chestnuts of Bushey, their slightly unfashionable attire lending a stiff verisimilitude to the beauty of the avenue, or skipping, hand in hand, hurriedly across Fleet Street on their way to Saint Paul's, or emerging, blinking and feeling pale, from the hot maggoty darkness of an Oxford Street movie show, or, what they did more often than was really worthwhile, passing from showcase to showcase in some museum or other, happy in virtuous headaches and the silent friendliness between them.

CHAPTER 9

Stone walls do not a prison make,
Nor iron bars a cage,

thought Emily on certain
thundery afternoons of hot July, when, after lunch, Amy now regularly hurried her upstairs, and locked her in the narrow lumber-room
where her poor straw bed was, before going out herself to concerts,
matinées, or picture exhibitions, or perhaps to tea with a party of
friends. For Mr. Fatigay's brief holiday was over, and he had leisure
no longer to take the chimp for walks in the afternoons, and Amy,
when he had hinted that she might occasionally do this, had replied
woundingly that she did not usually take menials about with her,
even when they happened to be human, and that since the apes at
the zoo managed to exist very comfortably without exercise, she saw
no reason why Emily should not do the same.

"And what's more," she had added, with a stern glance at the
poor dumb creature, who was powerless to contradict, "Emily does
not show, in the sweeping and scrubbing she sometimes has to do,
such an excess of pent-up energy as might indicate any pressing need
for additional exercise. No, Alfred! The chimp is mine now, and
though, as you know, I am incapable of cruelty, even to the hum-
blest and least prepossessing of God's creatures, I don't see why I
should make an exhibition of myself by dragging her about with
me, especially into the company of my friends. And I won't. And
that's that!"

To which Mr. Fatigay had nothing to reply, and Emily, though
she had much, was, of course, unable to put it into words.

It was, therefore, without the satisfaction of having been able to
point out that she would far rather spend her afternoons quietly in
her room than in the company of Amy, even at the most famous of
London's places of interest, that she was now guided, under the
humiliating appearance of compulsion, to the very seclusion of her
choice. And such is the suggestive power of a conventional stand-
point, which can make a terror out of a long period of free board

and lodging, that, on the first afternoon that Amy locked her up, Emily felt quite dejected at her confinement, and was actually hurt at not being held fit company for a person for whom she could feel neither respect nor liking.

As the key turned in the lock she could not prevent herself from standing close to the door, facing it, on the inside, as if appealing that it should be opened—an attitude which exposed her fully to all implied in its forbidding blankness and in the grinding turn of the key. She had to bite her lip very hard to repress a flood of irrational tears.

"After all, though," she said to herself, "I am not a child, though I may not be as old as some people are, and I ought think shame on myself for behaving as such. What wish could I conceive, of all that are handy and practicable, more to my taste than that a locked door should be interposed between me and my oppressor, and though if I had the locking of it, and stood upon the other side, it might be somewhat longer before it was opened, the present arrangement is a very tolerable second-best, and if the gusto with which she thus suits my convenience springs from her belief that she is making me miserable, why, what a fool I should be to make it a reality merely because she imagines it to be one!"

And with a cheerfulness considerably restored, the agile creature bounded lightly about the room, indulging in a series of handsprings, pirouettes, and somersaults, which would have proclaimed clearly, to anyone with an eye to the inner significance of dancing, that she felt herself empress of at least this nutshell and had no intention of becoming prey to heavy dreams.

When her girlish high spirits had abated a little, and something of her usual pensiveness had reasserted its sway, she sat down soberly in the middle of the floor and surveyed her bedroom in its new light as a hermit's or a prisoner's cell.

"And what though some would consider it to be the latter?" she reflected, for her race-consciousness made her unusually sensitive to the suggestion of being caged, so that the idea stuck like a burr to her thoughts. "Even if it was, I should be no worse off than the divine Pankhurst, a martyr to the rights of women."

And gazing around her, she examined, with a pleased interest, the miscellaneous contents of her room. All that Amy thought least of was jettisoned here, she noticed, as if waiting her arrival to head the corner. She could not but feel sympathy and affection for the rest of this Salon des Refusés. They were mostly objects of still life.

All schools seemed fairly represented, as she remembered was the case at the Tate. In one corner a dismembered bedstead and a chalky plaster cast suggested an excellent De Chirico; in another the blurred pale raspberry-pink and silver of an old suspended belt, and the tenuous mistiness of a few discarded stockings seemed newly soft from the palette of Marie Laurencin. Van Gogh, in an early period, was represented by a pair of crumpled boots, sad upon a broken cane chair; Picasso, by a shattered mandolin and a dusty soda-water syphon disposed upon a sheet of newspaper in the fireplace. A strong Camden Town influence emanated from the faded flower-patterned wallpaper and the pale indecent marble of the mantelpiece, for this room had never been redecorated by Amy. A Japanese parasol with a broken rib stood in the corner, and Emily, who had a weakness for these particular trifles, took it up, and, opening it, unconsciously stepped into the place of honor as a very charming Whistler.

After a turn or two, however, the caged bird folded this bright wing, and, betaking herself to the window, she threw up the sash and craned forth her head to stare down between the house backs, where the rank sycamores greened the yellow afternoon into the likeness of water deeps, down to the weedy gardens at the bottom, which were cheaply gay with straggled marigolds and precarious Virginia stock. An enervated subaqueous life persisted on this sub-merged floor. Protruding from the lush and wetly shining foliage of a thicket of Michaelmas daisies, the dark head of a cat, pressed to the ground, stared up like an angler fish at the small shoals of mud-colored birds that skimmed to and fro. Beside it, and near a summer house, battered and faded as a fragment of some sunken ship, a ghastly plaster figure hung on tiptoe, in the erect and weight-less posture of a woman drowned. No anchor was to be seen, but two enormous shells lay half buried in the weeds. The stray notes of a piano, converted into something rich and strange, floated upward toward the light, bursting, as the luminous deep-sea fish do, when they reached the lesser density of the roof level.

Down the sides of the houses ran the encrusted drainpipes, soft puce or dead blue, relics, it seemed, of some abandoned dockyard undertaking. Down the side of the house, riveted firmly to the wall, circular and of six-inch, graspable diameter, ran an iron drainpipe, straight down into the deserted garden, divided on one side, by a low wall only, from the side street, and from Liberty, London, Life, Adventure, Romance. This exhilarating cup, which now flooded up like some divinely effervescent Bethesda pool, and from an ineffably low ebb, up to the very windowsill where Emily rested her chin, caused a delicious chill of excitement to run through her veins. To revisit, lonely as a cloud, in pensive but by no means vacant mood, those scenes with which she had first become acquainted in the company of Mr. Fatigay, perhaps to explore others, to get to know the great city, its highways and its fascinating byways, to scan its changing countenance, to lay fingers on its mighty pulse, to auscultate, however dimly, the eccentric beatings of its mysteriously located heart; this prospect intoxicated the chimp, and, always impulsive, she lightly flung a leg over the sill, in order to descend at once into the magic world whose troubadour voice invited her sweetly from below.

Here, however, she paused a moment. She had learned pretty thoroughly by now the one positively useful lesson which suffering and Geo. Moore have to bestow. This is, that the few pleasures of life are not to be gulped down in bumpkin haste, but savored as a rare claret should be; anticipation, like the voluptuously inhaled bouquet, being the best part, and to be long lingered over, providing only that one has the cup very surely in one's hand. The chimp accordingly flung herself down upon her wretched pallet, and passed the long hours until Amy's return in a most agreeable reverie, stewing gently in the languorous garret heat and happily staring at a low and tawny ceiling, now cinematographically frescoed with images of the adventures which lay before her.

It was therefore not until the next afternoon that she uttered the inspiriting lines which have been mentioned, and she did so as she thrust over the sill a foot, resplendent in one of those very crumpled boots which Amy had discarded, and forthwith she embarked upon the descent with a confidence born of her arboreal youth and of the fact that she had prudently borrowed an old pair of Amy's gym bloomers. A moment later, she was over the wall, and stood upon the gritty sidewalk, beneath the caterpillar-eaten limes. Putting up the parasol, which she had brought down gripped in her teeth, she strolled through the gold siesta of stucco and wisteria, moving with almost the bodiless freedom of a dream, except for the occasional pinches by which Amy's shoes obligingly reminded her that she was awake.

Emerging upon Adelaide Road, she took on a brisker step, and, passing swiftly through the loud and broken streets, she arrived at the spot which, she had decided, must certainly be the object of her first pilgrimage in the great city. To most of her sex this would have been Bond Street or the most super of all cinemas, but Emily, though feminine, was not a woman, and even at the risk of being thought a bluestocking, she gave the British Museum precedence over modes and movies. She had observed, while dusting Amy's writing desk one day, a ticket for the Reading Room lying neglected in a pigeon-hole, and since Amy had sternly forbidden what she chose to call "monkey-tricks" with her own books, the chimp felt justified in borrowing this ticket in the interests of that intellectual urge which it is everyone's duty to forward by all the means in their power.

Emily was not entirely a stranger to the Museum. Mr. Fatigay had taken her there one afternoon, and had even penetrated with her as far as the inner door of the Reading Room, to indulge her with a glimpse of that vast hive, and the swarm of busy creatures engaged in manufacturing a further and diluted yield out of the very honey that gorged its cellular lining. Into this hive, tingling with the apprehensions of an alien wasp, come to contribute nothing, but to carry away all she could, Emily now entered, and, timidly taking a seat, she glanced about under her dark lashes to study the procedure of the habitués.

It was not long before her keen and analytical intelligence had grasped the connection between the consultation of a catalogue, the filling up of an application form, and the subsequent arrival of books. Marking her place with the bright parasol, which, she now realized with unerring judgment, seemed a little too smart and Ascotish for her austere surroundings, where, it appeared, all such sumptuary blossoms had been rigidly nipped in the bud, in order to produce a richer crop of beards and horn-rimmed spectacles, Emily trotted up to where the catalogues were shelved, and, having hoisted DA-DEB onto the shelf, she stood upon tiptoe to peep at it, in search of Darwin's *Origin of Species*, for she was a great believer in beginning at the beginning. But when she came to fill in the form, a most humiliating hitch occurred, humiliating more because she had so stupidly overlooked it than because of the shortcoming from which it derived, for the chimp was by no means an intellectual snob. She was, of course, unable to write. For a moment she was quite overcome.

"It serves me right," she murmured. "What business have I, a mere chimp, to insinuate myself into this Elysium, and by using someone else's ticket, too?"

Then, something of the sterner fiber asserted itself, and, remembering that the writing of many others, which was but little better than her own, not only had its birth here, but its end and its immortality also, she plucked up heart, and, "After all," she thought, "perhaps, in my humble line, I can do as well as these, and by the same means, by careful copying."

And this she proceeded to do, but, alas, her efforts were attended by even less success than that which usually crowns such methods, for what appeared a passable copy of the English characters to her private eye seemed to the official behind the grating to be an inscription in some Eastern alphabet, so that, conscientiously approaching the self-conscious chimp, he asked her, "How d'ye do?" first in Arabic and then in Chinese. On receiving no reply beyond that melancholy and fatalistic smirk with which one naturally disclaims understanding of an unknown tongue, he regarded Emily with great purpose, and, observing her parasol, her prognathous jaw, and a nuance of superfluous hair, he addressed her in the dialect of the hairy Ainus of Japan. At this Emily spread apart her hands, as if to cast to the idle winds a soul ignoble enough to lack understanding of so thorough a courtesy.

Perceiving the pinkness of her palms, the official then spoke to her in Persian, and, as this elicited only a further gesture of self-reproach from the embarrassed chimp, he tried her next, having noted also her dark complexion and diminutive stature, with the four cardinal dialects of the Deccan. All was in vain. For some moments the two gazed at one another, with much genuine liking and respect, across the linguistic gulf which lay between them.

Suddenly Emily conceived a plan. Taking the kind official by the sleeve, she led him to the catalogue, and, putting her finger upon the title of the book she desired, she implored him with her most bewitching smile to fill up for her the form which she proffered. Touched by the sincerity in her eye, the good man, a true friend to all attempts at learning, brushed aside the stifling bonds of red tape, and benevolently made the desired exception to the rule.

How happy was Emily at that moment! She could scarcely contain herself until the book was fetched, and when it arrived she buried herself so earnestly in its pages as to win smiles of sympathy and approval from the blasé veterans of the Reading Room, to whom, for more years than they cared to count, the first glance at the book they had ordered begot nothing but a dyspeptic desire for yet another. So smiles the jaded gourmet upon the hearty youngster whose naïve appreciation plays disproportionate havoc among the dishes of hors d'oeuvres. The officials, too, were appreciative of this single-hearted application of Emily's. One reader at least, they felt, seemed unlikely to add, by a capricious craving for change, to the burden of their hot and swollen feet, and they too smiled upon the eager young student. So smiles the waiter on observing that same youngster settle down to a substantial steak and chips, innocent of the need for titillation which calls for all the porterage of a seven-course meal.

Emily had won the good opinion of the Reading Room, and she had not revisited that spot many times before her demure and sober graces evoked a still warmer feeling from certain of the respectable gentlemen who regularly sat in her section. She was, they unanimously decided, the Belle of the British Museum, and under that title she became the reigning toast of the tearoom, where more than one of her hirsute admirers contracted a mild tannin poisoning from drinking, with no heel taps either, to those dusky charms which had set so many hearts ablaze.

It must not be assumed from these casualties, however, that her influence was mainly of a disintegrating kind. Though one or two of the frailer spirits lost many precious moments in gazing surreptitiously at her unconscious form when they should have been deep in their work, there were others who found in her compelling charm a new stimulus to energy, and scribbled more fiercely than ever in order that they might finish the gigantic works they were compiling, and emerge before her eyes from the dull husk of the reader into the dragonfly iridescence of the famous read. And one and all were conscious of a new spirit born within them, a renascent brightness which blossomed here in a new attaché case, there in a bow tie or a little amateur topiary for a straggling beard, and, in some, in a sparkling vivacity, surprising alike to each speaker and his friends, in their teatime conversation.

"Here's to those bright eyes!" cried one, sluicing a steep wave of tea through the curved baleen of his moustache.

"Here's to her bewitching smile!" "To her orange ear!" "To her wee nose!" clamored others. "And here's to the day she first came among us!" struck in a fifth.

"I remember it well," said a converted editor of Schopenhauer. "I think it was I who saw her first. I thought, 'Another woman!' Yes, that's what I thought. When I came in and saw a parasol lying on the desk beside mine: 'Another woman!' I thought. I always think that. There are too many . . ."

"Then I saw her before you did," burst in a biographer. "I saw her at the doorway. *She stood—a sight to make an old man young!* Well, I don't know, but the effect on a middle-aged one was startling. Perhaps you wouldn't believe it, but my indigestion—well, you know, it was a sort of bowel indigestion before—starchy. From that day to this, believe me or not, just as you like, it changed. . . ."

"Who is she, I wonder? Where does she come from?" said someone else, not for the first time.

"Irish, if you ask me," said a Teague who was present. "She's Irish; Irish with a touch of dusky Southern blood—the passion and magnetism of old Spain."

"Not a bit of it," said a Fabian. "Those eyes are Oriental eyes, bright with the pain of young life born amid fated glories, like a palm tree springing up through the floor of a crumbling palace. They have the meekness too, of Oriental eyes, the eyes of a slave set free from the tyranny of an old exhausting beauty, meekly awaiting the commands of that inexplicable liberator, Western Civilization."

"She walks, it is true, like one accustomed to the courts of India, rather than to those of Wimbledon," said a belated essayist on the Woman Question.

"My ideal!" exclaimed an earnest-looking man, who had never uttered a word before, and he nodded with emphatic approval at the last speaker, before he sank, blushing like the setting sun, behind the wide horizon of his teacup.

"Well, I like her," said a simple fellow, "because she's a little woman. A bouncing little woman. I like them like that. My first wife was a bouncing little woman. My second wife was not. I was deliriously happy with my first wife. With my second—not altogether so. I like a bouncing little woman."

"Well, gentlemen," said the senior member of the company, who ignored the last remark as being the probably carnal utterance of one whose work was merely the compiling of a cyclists' encyclopedia, "well, gentlemen, we had better make a move if we're to catch a last glimpse of her, for like all that's best in life, she comes late and departs early, heaven knows where."

And, rising fragrant-breathed from their tables, the lowing herd wound slowly from the tearoom, and lumbered in clumsy haste, goaded by a small and naked child, to their places in the Augean barton within. But, of the nine, only eight were thus urged home, for one, prodded too painfully perhaps, had jibbed at the gate, and now lurked, restless with uneasy purpose, in the entrance hall.

This was the earnest man who had spoken but two fervent words in the course of this, and all foregoing conversations, and from whom even those two could only have been elicited by the extreme force of his approval of the hint that Emily was an old-fashioned woman, much like his mother, of whom his memories were scented as with lavender, and like a dearly beloved aunt, on whom he had had a boyish fixation of the libido. Like most of the silent kind, he was a man of action. Careless of consequences, he had left his attaché case and his MS derelict upon his desk.

"What," he thought, "is mere property, and the fruits of dry pedantic labor, compared with newborn romance?" "Nothing," he decided, "but the material for a fantastic sacrifice, like that of the beggar who, having come by a ticket in the Calcutta Sweep, flings his last penny into the river or upon the bar, in order to wait, in shiveringly expectant nakedness, for the advent of the capricious goddess."

"*She is coming, my own, my sweet,*" he murmured, as the door swung glassily at the end of the corridor. "And now to follow her home, and find out where she lives!"

Fate, whose initial gifts to lovers are supplied as generously as those free meals an angler offers to the fish, decreed that he should not be disappointed, for in a few seconds the outer door opened, and, surely enough, it was Emily came through, her rapt eye and parted lips proclaiming the student not yet wholly emerged from the magic spell of literature. Peeping out from behind a rack of postcards, he saw her cross the entrance hall. He followed.

"To think," he reflected, as his unconscious quarry turned out of Great Russell Street, "that I should be following an unknown woman up the Tottenham Court Road!" He was relieved when they had ascended into the less compromising air of Chalk Farm.

"Tonight," he decided, "I will rest content with finding out the house in which she lives, and tomorrow I will shift my lodgings into apartments as near to it as possible. Then it will be hard if I cannot find some means of making her acquaintance. I might perhaps venture to address her as she leaves the house, saying, possibly, something like, 'Excuse me, madam,' lifting my hat and bowing with a grave formality which should appeal to one of Eastern origin, 'but have you seen my cat?' I must get a cat. It would be terrible if she found out that I had no cat. But if I had a cat, and she is a cat lover, she must become quite interested. She will very probably express a fondness for the animals. At once I will reply, 'But I have another cat, a little one. Some consider it beautiful. May I, dare I

. . . beg your acceptance . . .' " And, lost in the sweet reverie, he smirked and bowed upon the empty air.

At that moment, Emily chanced to look behind her, and received all the impact of the quivering blandness which her pursuer was bestowing upon her image.

"Good heavens!" she thought. "Is it possible? Am I loved by D.17?"

The idea was distasteful to her. While she saw no reason to doubt his moral integrity, and felt, indeed, a deep gratitude for the honor he bestowed upon her, she knew only too well that she could offer nothing in return but a sincere friendship and a lasting esteem, and there was that in the way he had held one hand to his heart when she glanced at him which suggested he would find such a response worse than nothing. Besides, her present situation was altogether too ambiguous, too unconventional. So the chimp bowed her head and hurried on.

"Did she see me?" he thought. "Provocatively thus to fly? Ah! The witch!" And, quickening his pace, he followed her up Haverstock Hill.

Emily, already late, had no time to make a detour in the hope of giving him the slip. When they reached the quiet turning beside Amy's house, she took a hurried glance about her, and, seeing no one but her impassioned follower, she made a sudden leap at the wall and was over in the twinkling of an eye.

"Oh!" cried the astonished man, and he stood rooted to the spot.

"Oh!" he cried again, for the dainty figure had come once more into view, nimbly ascending the drainpipe which led to her high attic window.

The poor fellow could scarcely believe his eyes. His dream was shattered before it had well begun. To think that one so modest, so prim, almost, to the outward eye, should be such an arrant little tomboy in reality! Biting his lip in deep vexation, he hurried down the hill, cursing himself under his breath for having been an infatuated fool. On the bustop, in his hasty retreat to recover his work, there spasmodically burst from him at every few hundred yards: ". . . modern women! These modern women!"

Now this incident, which was not without its whimsical side (and, indeed, in later life Emily would frequently shake her head smilingly at the recollection of it), this incident was something of a calamity at the time it occurred, and for a good reason: that Emily now felt that it would be too embarrassing and perhaps too dangerous to return to the British Museum. Even if she could have borne the proximity of one puzzled and outraged consciousness, and the possibility of gossip and curious glances from all sides, she dared not incur even a remote risk of some further pursuit or other complication which might result in her exposure to Amy. Reproach, humiliation, mockery, corporal punishment perhaps, and certainly a very strict confinement in future, would follow. And, although a glimpse she had caught of her pursuer's face during her ascent of the drainpipe gave her grounds to hope that his passion was already much abated, she knew from her own cruel experience that, even supposing love to have been wiped out completely by some incident or revelation, it was more than probable that, at the next concurrence of the elements which had produced it, it would be produced again.

She felt, therefore, that it would be better for all concerned if she went no more to the Reading Room, and since the decision, like all thus qualified, was a painful one, she could not entirely banish a rather gloomy expression that evening.

"Emily seems to be frowning rather," said Mr. Fatigay, who was dining there that night. "I wonder if London strains her eyes at all. Perhaps she should wear glasses."

"What nonsense, Alfred!" said Amy.

CHAPTER 10

I am become a name;
For always roaming with a hungry heart
Much have I seen and known.

"Tennyson, *Ulysses,*" Emily thought; and though as a matter of fact she had not yet seen as much as she wished of the city, she felt now that she had too embarrassing a knowledge of the hearts of men to permit of her mingling easily with the general crowd. Besides her experience of yesterday, she had frequently heard Amy recite to Mr. Fatigay detailed accounts of languishing glances or even ardent approaches inflicted on her by complete strangers, sometimes of military or artistic appearance, in the thoroughfares of the town. She had concluded, moreover, from his reception of these accounts, that he resented extremely those happenings to one whom he loved, whereupon she thought to herself, "It is a duty to avoid them, also, on the part of one who loves him."

It happened, therefore, that after a busy morning of sweeping and scrubbing, during which she had had no time to take thought, she effected her escape from confinement, and stood upon the sidewalk with no definite notion of where she should go. The hot walls, the hard stones, and the sharp-edged dust roused by their unfriendliness a keen nostalgia in her, and as a parrot screeched from a foody basement nearby, the poor exile closed her eyes and shudderingly inhaled a sharp whiff of her longing for her native land. For a moment she felt herself dispread in shafted twilight in the still heart of some great tree, sprawling on her back along a monstrous bough, with one sunspot, perhaps, making a jewel of the green plush lichen an inch from her pensive cheek. From a drooping hand half an overripe fruit might fall away, splashing in luscious purple another branch forty feet below, along which a tiny pink and silver monkey would scuttle to seize upon it.

What if, her body thus peacefully reclined, her heart within, straining like some overworked engine, pumped out sorrow equally with blood? There, at least, that sorrow, sprouting from her bosom like a rank and cancerous orchid, would unfurl its deadly beauty unhindered and in quiet. Here, her grief, even, was debased and stunted under a petty oppression, frayed by the sharp meaningless detail of an alien world, brought down from tragedy into shapeless misery by her own thwarted attempts at intellectual development.

"And how," she thought, "am I helping my dear Mr. Fatigay by holding myself an anguished spectator of his decay? Would I have not done better to have remained cloistered in some vaulted grove, weeding all thoughts not of him from his green grave in my breast? Creeping out sometimes, perhaps, to follow, softly as the great moth, ghostly as the white bloom, the leafmold track to the clearing's edge, whence, looking to the lighted veranda, where his strange successor sat with bottle and magazine and bright lamp whereunder the shattered beetles died, I should see, as it were, the opening of the path along which he had gone, leaving no trace on that gateway hardness, but only, in the deep jungle outside, his divine footprint eternal on the desert earth of my heart."

It was not natural to the poor chimp to long for a life of sterile sorrow; the usual trend of her thoughts when her position seemed more than usually hopeless lay rather towards a career of nursing, or some similar selfless benevolence, but this afternoon she was more than ordinarily dispirited.

"She's no use to me," Amy had said, later in the overnight conversation which had followed on Mr. Fatigay expressing anxiety about her eyes.

"I *must* declare," she had continued petulantly, "that, little as I like the two hobbledehoys you introduced as friends of yours, whose idea of mannerly behavior seemed to be to brush aside every conversational opening I gave them, in order to chew to death their revolting reminiscences of what you were before I knew you, little as I liked them. . . ."

"But hang it all, Amy," Mr. Fatigay had replied uneasily, "Grant and Thompson are excellent fellows. We were inseparable in the old days, and I hope we shall be again."

"Then you'll have to be separable from me," she had retorted. "No man can serve two masters, and if you choose to trample on everything I hope I stand for by introducing those clownish philistines into our life together—well, I'm afraid I can't bear with it. I blushed for your connection with them, and for mine with you, at every word they said."

"Oh come!" he had replied, "Amy, you must admit they're not as bad as all that. They're not exactly highbrows, I'll agree, but two better-hearted fellows never breathed. They do their own jobs well enough, I can tell you, and that's more than can be said for the crowd of chatterers you're so fond of, and, as for your disliking them, you can't hate them half so much as I hate that wretched little Dennis Tickler who's always hanging round this place."

At this Amy had become very angry.

"Look here, Alfred," she had said. "My friends are cultured and intelligent people, and Dennis is one of the best friends I have. If you want to say anything against him, or any of them, whom goodness knows I'm always trying to get to like you, you can clear out."

"Well, why should you speak against *my* friends?" he had muttered.

"If I become your wife at all, Alfred," she had said, piercing his

heart with the words, "we must have our friends in common. I'm
not going to be dragged into association with people of that sort,
nor sit by on the shelf like a chattel and see you degraded by them.
Friends, indeed! People you've not seen or heard from for years,
and who came, anyway, only to make a butt of you. Perhaps you
didn't see the glances they gave one another behind your back
while we were talking, but *I* did. I'd like to know any *real* friends
of yours, but these—! Alfred, you surely wouldn't put your relationship to them before your love for me, would you? *Yes or no?*"

Here Mr. Fatigay had looked sadly bewildered, for in such arguments the real tussle lay between his heart and his reason, rather
than between Amy and himself; they were conflicts in which she
played, from outside the region of stress and wounds, the decisive
part of an Homeric goddess.

"And to return to what I was saying," she had said, when she had
extracted a halting negative from him, and had lovingly transformed
it into a gracious and chivalrous promise before storing it safely
away in her memory, "I was saying that Emily's no use to me. She's
either more stupid even than the rest of her species, or else mali-
ciously sulky. To hear you talk of buying spectacles for her, as if
she was human, makes me feel that the jungle must have turned
your brain. The zoo's the proper place for an ape, after all, where
she could have the company of her own kind, and I really think we
ought to send her there. I don't feel that I can stand her stupid
dirty ways much longer."

Emily had here stared openmouthed at her protector. She had
already heard enough to furnish a sleepless night with new meditation on her folly in ever hoping that he would be disillusioned by
hard treatment. And now he was being tried even nearer home.
What would be the result? she wondered.

Fortunately Mr. Fatigay had here a middle course to resort to,
and one which baffled for the time Amy's petulance at his over-
scrupulous regard for the chimp.

"Why, of course, Amy," he had replied, "if you find Emily unsatisfactory, there's no need for you to keep her. I'd hoped she'd please
you, but if she doesn't I can easily take her back now I've got a
place of my own."

"Oh, don't bother," Amy had said crossly. "You'd only spoil her
worse than ever. If she doesn't go to the zoo, she may as well remain
with me. I'll try to put up with her a little longer." For she could
think of no excuse for insisting that Emily was to be sent into cap-

tivity, and, indeed, found her so cheaply useful, and so satisfying to torment, that she would not have suggested it, but for her annoyance at Mr. Fatigay's concern for the humble creature.

Thus the matter had been left, but Emily felt that she had escaped by chance rather than by Mr. Fatigay's power to resist his love on behalf of his lover. This, as much because it augured so ill for his future welfare, as because it implied the nothingness of her claims beside Amy's demands, was the cause of her present depression, which, occurring as it did just when her access to the anodyne of study had been cut off, through no fault of her own, weighed so heavily upon her that her dream of a jungle hermitage now gave place to the more practical consideration of whether she would not, after all, be wise to seek as a cloister the very prison to which Amy had proposed sending her.

"After all," she said to herself, "the jungle would only be so much scenery. The greatest tragedies are played best in the severest of settings. Given peace and loneliness, what matter whether it is the innumerable trunks of trees or the nearer austerer verticals of bars which hem me in?

"But," she added, "I had better go first and see what it's like, lest it should turn out in this case as it has with love and England, from both of which—despite their importance culturally—I would have fled as from the plague, had I but had a true glimpse of them beforehand." And wasting no more time on reflection, Emily set forth, putting up her parasol, which she had again brought down with her, not for vain display, but from a sincere desire to shelter herself from the casual glances of the masculine crowd.

A heavy thundershower, shortly after noon, had discouraged the sightseers, and Emily, descending on the inner side of the fence, found almost unpeopled the wide and stiff-flowered spaces, into which, with their surround of skeleton domes, ringed craters, and Giotto crags; with their watercress teas like memories of childhood; with not knowing which way to turn amid staccato cries of unknown emotion; into all of which one enters as into the excitement of a half-familiar dream. The white sun, which five minutes ago had burnt up the last glittering drop from the paper-faced asters, had heated to their widest and thinnest expansion the humid bubbles of scent risen from the flower beds and the various dung, and now these met and interfusingly burst upon the eye-aching paths, and the chimp, as she inhaled each new cocktail of brittle essences, was switchbacked dizzily over the peaks of jungle fears and raptures, and into the wide dips of its rich and scented ennui. A flamingo spread its rosy wings, the sun stared, a lion sprang in his hollow cage, thunder muttered in the bankéd west, bears, tigers, ounces, pards gamboled before her; the unwieldy elephant, to make her mirth, used all his might, and wreathed his lithe proboscis.

"Back in Eden!" thought Emily, as she watched a child in a dyed frock reward the last-mentioned comedy turn with a bun.

She had not gone very far when she saw, in a quiet corner behind the small cats' house, an empty cage, the door of which was unlocked, and, recalling the purpose of her visit, she congratulated herself on this opportunity of viewing the bars from their hinder side, and accordingly, with a wary glance about her, she nipped into it. But no sooner had she closed the door, she saw two people advancing upon her from different directions, and a sudden panic seized her. "For," thought she, "they will surely be amazed at my costume, and will speedily attract a crowd here, and I shall either be advertised as a runaway, and ultimately haled back to whatever punishment Amy chooses to devise, or I shall be locked in before I have made up my mind whether I want to stay or not. I begin to feel that I don't."

The intruders, however, were still pretty far off when an idea occurred to the sagacious creature, which was that the best she could do was to slip off her dress and pretend to be a true captive, dully asleep, so that she should attract no particular attention, and, when the coast was clear again, she could reassume her clothes and quietly emerge. This course she at once embarked upon, though not without a blush or two, and before the approaching pair had met outside the cage, her dress and parasol were hidden beneath the straw, and nothing more unusual was to be seen than a simian and reclining edition of "September Morn."

"Darling!"

"Beloved!"

These words have an irresistible appeal to every womanly heart, and Emily, hearing them, could not restrain herself from raising an eyelid and taking a sly peep at the enthusiastic speakers.

She almost sat up in her amazement. The woman, though disguised in a tenderer smile than Emily had hitherto noted on her face, was well-known to her as Mrs. Dunedin, a young matron of some few months' standing, and an intimate friend of Amy's. The young man, her interlocutor, was certainly not her husband, who was, the chimp remembered well, a tall and soldierly-looking man, whereas this was as weedy and ill-looking a scrub as ever she had set eyes upon. But Mrs. Dunedin was clearly not of this opinion, for, having sealed her greeting with a hearty kiss, she held his hand in hers and eyed him with obvious gusto.

"Good heavens!" thought the chimp. "Can this indeed be Amy's twin soul, the most high-minded of all her friends? Can it be she who complained so bitterly to Amy, not a fortnight ago, of the carnal side of passion, and the indecency of the male form? If neither the frigidity of his wife nor the inferiority of his rival can protect a husband's honor, why, no man, not even Mr. Fatigay, is safe!"

At that moment, their first raptures having subsided, they glanced perfunctorily into the cage, and:

"Why!" said Mrs. Dunedin. "What an enormous chimp! It's almost as big as that one that Amy Flint now has, and has trained, by sheer force of personality, she told me, to serve her as a maid."

"Well," said the young man, with a sneer, "it might very well be the other way round, for, if you dressed this one up in Amy's clothes, I'm sure I should find it hard to distinguish between them, except that the ape has the sweeter expression of the two."

"What? Do you say so?" said Amy's friend, with a titter. "To tell you the truth, there *is* a likeness, Amy being so small and dark. But I'm greatly surprised to hear *you* mention it, for I always thought you were deeply in love with her. In fact, she told me so."

"Not I," cried the young man. "It's true I visited her a good deal a few months ago, but then I got bored with her superior airs, and . . ."

"Oh, come!" interrupted the lady, with a slightly acid smile. "I know more about it than that. You can't deceive me."

"After all, why should I?" said he. "Well, if you want to know, I *was* rather keen at one time, and hung about her longer than any man in his senses would. But she's one of those who'll allow nothing but a soul passion before marriage, whatever might be the case after. So I withdrew, and left her to this African fiancé of hers. And, if he's the sort of person she hinted he was. . . ."

"Oh, he *is*," interpolated the lady.

"Well, he'll have a pretty thin time, if you ask me," rejoined the young man. "But enough of such a dull subject. Is there anything here that might amuse you?"

"Oh, do let's go and see Monkey Hill," cried his companion, and they passed on.

It was a grave-faced chimp that crept out of the cage and resumed her inspection of the gardens.

"A thin time!" she said to herself. "A thin time . . . !"

Conscious that it was almost madness to hope that she could be of any assistance, unless the extreme thinness of his allotted time should cause the scales to drop at last from his eyes, she nevertheless felt, in some stirring of that instinct which prompts sea captains to sink with their sinking ships, that she must stay by her beloved, though it might mean no good to him and nothing but prolonged torture for herself.

She had made her decision in utter hopelessness, but such was her temper that soon afterwards hope began to flood in, and she felt more and more confident that Mr. Fatigay's pride and manliness would recoil, with a force greater than that which flexed them, after a little experience of what was hinted at in the tinny phrase, "a thin time."

Strengthened by these thoughts, she straightened her bonnet, and, first brushing a little straw off her dress, she reopened her parasol, and resolved to spend the remainder of her afternoon in innocent pleasure among the album of scents and sights about her.

From a quizzical inspection of the lions and leopards, she passed to the softer pleasures of the hornbills and the cranes, which roused in her such a tide of soft remembrance (for all the anthropoids are fond of birds) that it was with suffused eyes and quivering lips that she turned away at last, eager to seek any others of her kind who might be in residence here. A few yards farther on stood a large double cage, in a sort of island on the wide path, and, as she approached this, she saw within it the form of a large female chimpanzee, busily engaged in certain little refinements of her toilette. Emily leaned against the railing. The captive, who apparently went by the name of Sally, cocked a supercilious eye at this new visitor, and was about to return to her occupation, when she gave a second glance, and then, hastening across the cage, she caught hold of two of the bars, and, thrusting her face between them, she stared in silent amazement at the shy figure outside.

"Good afternoon," said Emily, in the tongue of her kind, which, if it contains but few syllables, is rich in nuances of expression.

"Good heavens!" cried Sally. "What are you doing out there, walking about like the rest of the people? Have you escaped or something?"

"Oh, no," said Emily. "I'm living nearby in a little maisonette, as a sort of companion to an Englishwoman, and, hearing that you were here, I thought I'd come in and look you up."

"Living with an Englishwoman, indeed!" exclaimed Sally, in tones in which surprise, envy, and scorn were pretty evenly mingled. "Well, there's no accounting for tastes. Some of the younger set have gone native to a certain extent and take *thé anglais* with one of the stewards every afternoon. I don't myself. Perhaps I'm old-fashioned. When in Rome, they say. . . . Of course, I've *heard* of chimpanzees taking up life among the inhabitants, but I must say I've never seen one before. Still—if you like it. . . . But that dress—is it silk? And the bonnet, really—very attractive. I feel it's the sort of thing that might suit me. Would you care to pass it through the bars for me to try on?"

"Please excuse me," said Emily, "but if anyone happened to come along, I'd have a crowd about me in no time. You know what people are."

"Well, as you like," replied Sally, good-naturedly. "Living in the public eye myself, I can't say crowds bother me much. If it wasn't for this threatening weather, I expect they'd be two or three deep about the place now. They generally come to see me first. I must admit I didn't intend to give the bonnet back to you, as probably you guessed."

Emily shrugged her shoulders with a friendly twinkle.

"I wouldn't take anyone's banana," resumed Sally. "But one doesn't often get a new hat. If there's a drawback to this place, that's what it is. The clothes they offer one are very second-rate. I happened to be taking a sunbath just as you came along, and I'm not sorry either, my dear, for my wardrobe," said she, jerking a thumb to the inner apartment, where in truth nothing but the back sheet of a newspaper and a child's glove were stored, "my wardrobe being what it is, I should have looked a positive frump beside you."

"Well, clothes aren't everything," said Emily spontaneously. "Life's not all honey outside, I can tell you. I expect you have chosen the better part."

"I don't know about that," replied Sally. "It's pretty dreary, being cramped in this drafty hole with a pack of fools pointing and laughing all day long. And as for choosing—I was caught by bird lime myself, and that's that."

"But at least you've got company, haven't you?" asked Emily. "Isn't there someone living in the apartment behind?"

"Oh, there's a poor mad fellow come to live there now," said Sally. "One who got mauled by a leopard and now thinks he's dead and in hell for his misdeeds. And as it seems that the chief of these was, well—being too amorous, he's got a highly inconvenient complex on such matters now, in addition to his insanity. I don't know if there's any chance of him being cured. He's a well-set-up young fellow enough and it goes to my heart to see him in such a state. It seems such a waste, somehow. Go and have a look at him, my dear, and give me your advice."

Emily, a premonition stirring within her, hurried round to the other cage, and there, sitting crouched in a corner, horribly scarred, and adorned with a copious millinery of straw, was Henry, whom she had left in the clutches of the leopard.

"Henry!" she cried in amazement. "Henry! Don't you know me? It's Emily."

Henry looked up dreadfully from where he cowered.

"Well, Emily!" he muttered. "Have you too come to haunt me? I know I was wrong to throw that banana skin, and, it's true enough, I meant to do worse still. I determined that, if I could get you on the rebound, so to speak, that day you ran away from the schoolmaster, I'd take it out of you for daring to love anyone but me. But I was punished, Emily, and I'm being punished still. When I was in the very act of making up to you, a leopard sprang on me— no doubt you saw it—and I felt his red-hot teeth and claws, and then all was dark, and I awoke to find myself in the hands of fiends, who bore me here—to Hell! Sweet Em, what shall become of Henry, being in Hell forever?"

"But why," she asked in amazement, "should you think that you're dead and in Hell?"

"Look!" said he. "Look over there!" pointing across the wide space to where an end of the great cats' cages was in view. "Look! D'you see him? That's the leopard. Perpetually he crouches to spring. Perpetually I crouch in terror. If I hide inside, a fiend comes and turns me out and bolts the door.

"Ah! He's looking at me now. Oh! Oh! Oh!"

"Come, Henry! Be calm," said Emily sympathetically. "He's not looking at you really. Use your reason. Aren't you safe behind those nice strong bars? And, as for this being Hell—it may be for the leopard, but it should be Heaven for you. If it *is* your leopard at all, which I very much doubt, he's certainly being punished for having hurt you. These bars, and those, are arranged to make you safe, so that you can laugh at him, while he longs perpetually to get you. No one gives *him* nuts: they only rattle on the bars with a stick, on purpose, to make him roar. To you, they give apples, bananas, copies of the daily paper, cigarettes, and small pieces of mirror. Is this the behavior of fiends?"

"But . . . ," said Henry.

"Don't keep on saying 'but,' " she said. "Pull yourself together, man, and realize that you're in Heaven, and that you're being compensated for your ill-treatment by the leopard in being able to tantalize him for all eternity, and," she added with a sigh, "for your ill-treatment by me in seeing me as unhappy as when you saw me last, while for you, in the cage behind, lies the opportunity of eternal bliss."

Here Henry began to scratch himself vigorously, as was his habit during strenuous attempts to assimilate new ideas, and, as soon as he had grasped what she said about the leopard, the honest fellow's demeanor changed entirely, and he began to dance about the cage like one possessed, pausing now and then to shout insults at his distant foe.

Leaving him still rapt in this ecstasy, and trusting that her second hint would come home to him when his first transports were calmed a little, Emily slipped away behind the cage to where Sally was awaiting her.

"I think he'll be better now," she said. "Listen He's making all sorts of fun of the leopard to his face. I've persuaded him that he's in Paradise, and I must leave it to you, my dear," she added archly, "charitably to preserve him in the illusion."

"Well, he's certainly a well-set-up young fellow," said Sally, "and I'm one of those who like the matrimonial state, I must say. The only trouble is that, if I've a contempt for one sort of person more than for another, it's for the sort who must always be either in Heaven or in Hell, and will let a few breathy words make all the difference."

"Oh, pray don't mention it," cried Emily generously. "The transition's nothing. It'll require more than words to keep it up, or to make the illusion a fact, rather. That nobler task is yours."

"Oh, I don't feel jealous, really," replied Sally with a smile. "It was just a twinge. Naturally one likes to do everything for the man one's set one's heart on. Look here, my dear: aren't there some people coming? I think he's knocking at the door. So long."

"Good-bye, dear, and lots of orange blossom!" said Emily, rather vulgarly for her, and, noticing that the sun was far declined, she hurried off in the direction of Haverstock Hill, feeling on the whole much stimulated by her eventful afternoon.

CHAPTER 11

I told my love, I told my love,
  I told her all my heart,
Trembling, cold, in ghastly fears.
  Ah! she did depart!

Soon after she was gone from me,
  A traveler came by,
Silently, invisibly:
  He took her with a sigh.

"Darling! What marvelous flowers! Are they really for me?"

"How wonderful you look!" returned Mr. Fatigay, with equal enthusiasm, for on this, the night of the party, Amy had abandoned the rather demurely period sort of frock she usually affected, with its tight bodice and full skirt, and had put on a far simpler garment of black and vermilion, which was, however, so up to date, so deadly Parisian, that its simplicity only lent it the final touch, the hint of the prematurely vicious little girl. Lipstick a shade hotter and drier than usual, startling as a gout of arterial blood coughed up into the midst of Amy's smiling features, added to the effect of sweet innocence playing the cocotte. The speculation aroused, of course, was on how far the game might proceed.

Taking her lover by the hand, Amy ran with him lightly, laughingly, madly up the stairs, drawing ahead a little before they had reached the top, in order to wait for him in an attitude of provocative welcome on her own landing.

"You won't mind just a scratch meal in the kitchen tonight, will you, dear? Nothing's nicer than party clothes in the kitchen. Because the room is all ready for the people who're coming. Put your hat and coat in here." And she flung open the door of her bed-room, and, still prattling, followed Mr. Fatigay inside.

Now, whether it was the novel aspect of Amy in the new dress; or whether it was the touch of abandon she had put on in keeping with it; or whether it was that her chamber, which was to take on for this evening the cold and formal aspect of a cloakroom, was not thus petrified in our hero's eyes by his own entrance, but awaited some more alien garrison of hats and wraps before suffering the change, and was still the rosy, scented sheath of Amy's intimate life; or whether it was that tawny August, cruel oppressor of the long-engaged, had fermented Mr. Fatigay's blood, like Dante's, to a liquor pale and ardent as the most potent of dry sherries; or what-ever it was, the fact remains, that after a minute or two the door slammed violently, and Emily, washing radishes in the kitchen, found that, though she strained very hard to hear the urgent voices within, she could distinguish nothing but a throaty rumble from her master and a few sharp and angry ejaculations from Amy.

Shortly the door was plucked open again, and Amy emerged with the expression of one who has been mortally hurt by a trusted hand, and her lover followed with chagrin and regret mixed on his face in the most hangdog look that any lover can wear. Emily glanced from one to the other and nervously dropped her eyes to the floor.

The meal was eaten nearly in silence, in one of those suspensions of emotional life in which a complex mixture of feelings resolves itself into its elements, each of which ebbs back to the breast to which it is most native, so that before they had finished picking at their food all the humiliation was centered in Mr. Fatigay and all the resentment in Amy.

"I suppose we may as well go into the drawing room," she said, when Mr. Fatigay had heaved a despairing sigh or two across the narrow table. And she got up, leaving him to follow as soon as he could pluck up heart enough to do so. For some time he sat at the table, moodily pushing a match through and through a banana skin, but at last Emily tactfully removed his plate, for it was high time for her to get on with the washing-up. At that he sprang to his feet, and, with some appearance of resolve mingling with the self-reproach on his countenance, he marched across to the drawing room.

Tonight that apartment had something cold and strained in its atmosphere. White wine and claret cup, and a bottle of whiskey for the Chelsea contingent, and nothing less than Pernod for the Bloomsburies, prosciutto and wedges of melon, tempting sandwiches, seductive coffee cakes, the silver box full of Gaulois and Virginian, the Cona and its cups: This chilly and powerful still life exuded an air unpropitious to the heated demands and defenses of an outraged intimacy. Mr. Fatigay, however, thought he was not to be quelled by a cucumber sandwich.

"Amy," he cried. "Amy."

Amy, stiffly reclined in a window seat, where she held a page of *Vogue* to catch the last pale light of the fading sky, looked up after a moment, and said:

"Well?"

"Look here, Amy," he said. "I know I behaved very badly, but after all it's quite understandable—I'm only flesh and blood, after all—and there's no need for you to be so furious about it."

"Indeed?" said she. "I'm glad you think so. I happen to think otherwise, but then my ideas are not the same as yours. But if you think that being engaged to me entitles you to behave like a brute beast—good heavens! I shall never forget the side of your nature you've shown me tonight—if you think that—then the sooner our engagement's at an end, the better."

"I heartily agree," he replied (and Emily, who, though she could not bear these continual quarrels, had found it impossible not to creep out upon the landing to hear what transpired—Emily here pricked up her ears in surprise and pleasure), "I heartily agree, but not perhaps in the way that you mean. Here you've kept me hanging about for years—I only went and buried myself in Africa because you insisted on having time for self-development, as you call it, before you settled down—and now when I come back you keep putting me off till I go nearly mad, and then, when my feelings get the better of me for once, you look at me as if I was something unspeakable. Why? You can't love me a bit, really, or you'd be eager to end this miserable engagement by marrying me as you promised. That's what I mean." Emily here drooped a little.

"I'm sorry you feel it to be a miserable engagement, Alfred," said Amy. "If that's the case now, I don't know that marriage would make things much better. And, as for not caring for you, why, how *can* you say such a thing? I'm always thinking about you and your work, and I give up all my time to you. I scarcely ever see any of my friends nowadays, and it's ages since I've been to see Mother, even; all because of the demands you make upon me."

"Of course, marriage would make things better," he replied. "Do you think that I can be myself, or happy, living as I am, on the rack, so to speak? Do you think it's a satisfying life for a man to come round and spend a few hours with you in the evening, and to have to go off at eleven with nothing but a few kisses, to make him more wretched than ever? As for giving up your friends: You were out seeing them three evenings last week, to say nothing of the fact that they're always dropping in when I'm hoping we shall be alone together. No. If you love me at all, you'll make up your mind to get married, and at once, too."

"As for seeing my friends," she replied, "naturally I still see them now and then. You don't want an absolute *egoïsme à deux,* do you? I don't ask you to give up seeing *your* friends, when they're worth seeing. I always encourage you to. Why should you ask me to give up mine? Why, Alfred, being married to you would be like marrying a Turk or Arab. I wanted us to be comrades and take an interest in each other's interests. But I know now."

"Oh, come!" cried Mr. Fatigay.

"Don't try to deny it," said she. "You've shown me your true nature too clearly for that. You want me for only *one thing.*" And, at this terrible thought, her voice began to quaver, which threw Mr. Fatigay further into confusion, for it added yet another element to the argument, and in discussions of this sort he had the magpie limitation of being unable to count more than three.

"No, Amy," he said, catching at the nearest thread, "I don't want you for only one thing."

"Yes, you do," she cried.

"No, I don't," he said. "But, after all, you're not a Victorian miss, and you know perfectly well that if *that* is unsatisfied everything else gets warped, and one's nerves get upset, and everything's spoilt."

"Only if you choose to let it," said she. "Other men, men I respect, use *some* self-control. And they sublimate. Look at Dennis. I've known him for years; he's always been a sort of brother to me. Well—I could never have anything but a sisterly feeling for him, of course—but I happen to know—I tell you this in utter confidence—he told George, Susan's husband, and she told me—that he's cared for me for years. And he's never even hinted at it."

But here Mr. Fatigay began to curse and swear so very heartily against Dennis Tickler and all his ways, not without including some bitter insinuations against Amy herself, that she, feeling herself to have got on to rather uncertain ground, dissolved into tears in good earnest, hearing which Emily shrugged her shoulders in disgust and retired from her post on the landing, for she knew well what the issue would be, and could not endure to listen to it.

Had she stayed, she would have heard Mr. Fatigay suddenly turn about, and, forgetful of all his case, begin to blame himself bitterly for his lack of self-control, and promise to amend for the future, if only Amy would now dry her tears. This, when he had cursed himself very bitterly for having caused them, she at length consented to do, saying: "Now you've made me cry, I suppose you're happy." And when this suggestion had been suitably denied, she withdrew to her room, in order to remove the traces of her emotion before her friends arrived.

Soon they came, descending from taxis into the rustling lamp-lit cave of the great chestnut tree which overhung the front gate, or walking through the bloomy electric dusk from their dwellings nearby. The men were the sort who have given up art for marriage, but, as if nature was scheming to restore the balance, many of their women appeared likely to give up marriage for art. Dennis Tickler, that shadowy and sinister figure, arrived, and was received very warmly by all. It may have been that what Amy had been told about him was true, or it may have been that he recognized his genius as flowering best in the fields of sentimental friendship—but he had not given up art for marriage, but only for a post in an advertising agency, which bitter sacrifice marked him from the out-set as being a man of sorrows, and therefore well-fitted to hear the sorrows of others. Beyond this, as Emily's discerning eye told her at a single glance, there could be nothing in it whatever, and she wished she could speak, that she might whisper as much to Mr. Fatigay, to clear his spirit of the pain and suspicion which was evident in the glances he occasionally stole at this young man.

It was a good party. Everyone took a glass and joined lustily in "Billy Boy," and, by the time another song or two had been sung, all the characters—and at least half of the people present were characters—had opened exhalingly as evening primroses, and were being thoroughly characteristic. Inseparable friends got their heads together: Mayhew, who painted, demanded guts in a picture; Angela was brilliant and delightfully mad; Peter was clearly in one of his wild moods (it was probably the sight of Susan and Jack, whom he had not seen since their honeymoon, that upset him); Amy was prepared to live partway up to her frock; Simpson tried to teach Elizabeth his Russian dance; and Herbert Houghton's impersonations of everybody were better than ever. Mr. Fatigay had no character at all, beyond being set down as rather possessive by certain of Amy's confidantes. Emily, in her black dress and starched cap and apron, was almost constantly in the room, handing round the drinks and working the gramophone.

When the evening was fairly far advanced, a friend of Amy's arrived, bringing a stranger. Nothing could be more supercilious than the bearing of this young man, though he was as ugly as a toad, for he now found himself among people who did not recognize his name at a first hearing, though it had been on the backs of two or three very advanced booklets, and by the time he had overheard scraps of some of the conversations that were going on, he began to think himself among savages, and behaved accordingly: that is, he stared at the women.

It was not long before his wicked eye lighted on Emily, and, conceiving her to have more blood in her than the rest of them, and, in view of her position, to be less likely to talk, he began to wonder how he could come at her, for he had no more breeding, manners, or scruples than any of his set. This was about the time when the central light of the room had been extinguished, for Millicent to perform at the piano, and for one or two others to sing.

"You'd better wash up all that you can collect," whispered Amy, "and set all the clean things on a large tray. Then you can go to bed." And she sat down in a corner to listen to the music that was beginning, while the young man, who had heard what she said, took a chair very near the door.

"Do you know who that is, that Bella has brought?" whispered Angela, who had been asked by Bella to do so. "It's Wagstaffe, who wrote *Pandarus, or the Future of Bloomsbury.*"

"Ssh!" whispered Amy. "Yes, I know." And she eyed the young man with great interest, and would have gone over and sat by him, but Millicent was just beginning to play, and it would have meant scuffling out from among too many people.

Before very long the young man, having decided the music was less amusing than the little dark-eyed maid might prove to be, quietly opened the door and slipped out, as if he was going to fetch a pocket handkerchief from his overcoat.

As soon as he stepped out upon the landing, he could see the light behind the patterned glass panels of the little scullery, where Emily was drying the glasses, and he had advanced so far as to have his hand already upon the door handle, when he realized that his presence in the scullery must be observed by anyone who might come out of the drawing room. So, feeling that he need stand on little ceremony with the humble maidservant, he thrust his head inside, and with a smile he indicated in dumb show that she was to make haste and finish her task, and join him on the attic stairs which mounted darkly from the landing. Emily, whose innocence prevented her from guessing at all his motive, and who, indeed, disliked this young man far less than any of the others there, nevertheless hesitated before joining him in the nook to which he had already withdrawn himself. "For," thought she, "whatever it is he wants of me at the moment, I am unlikely to be able to satisfy him, being a mere dumb and inexperienced chimp, and if I join him in that secluded spot he may end up by wanting the one thing I can, but will not, give. So it is safer not to go." And with a good-humored smile the prudent chimp turned again to the sink.

Now it happened, a few minutes later, that Amy, released by a momentary pause in the musical program, came out to fetch a pocket handkerchief, and the young man, seeing her pass the foot of the stairs, mistook her for Emily in the dim light, and began to renew his inviting gestures.

"What can he mean?" almost thought Amy. "Perhaps someone has told him I write also, and he wants a more sparkling *tête-à-tête*, more *risqué*, than can be held inside. Walter Wagstaffe! Bella will simply tear her hair." And she gaily ascended to where he was sitting.

"What?" he began, noticing the differences in costume, but deciding to treat the encounter as if it had been fatally ordained since the beginning of things. "Have you come at last?"

"Has it seemed so long?" said Amy, inspired by her wicked new frock, and by her knowledge of his reputation, to adopt that bright tone of sexual gallantry which she understood to prevail in the glittering circles in which he moved.

"Eternity!" he replied, with mechanical efficiency.

"Ah! But," said she, archly, seating herself beside him, "Einstein has shown us that time is only a dimension of space, and space being no longer regarded as infinite, time surely can't be eternal. Only those who have quite the *worst* sort of back to the womb complex. . . ." And here she rattled off into a most informed discourse, now brilliantly playful, now very serious and grave, to which, though he replied only in very hackneyed sentences, the young man listened with great complacency. For though he held the Einstein gambit to be rather a colorless one, he had found it to yield such excellent results that he had come by a generalization from it, which was: that while he had sometimes failed to understand a woman who spoke simply and on the A-B-C of some everyday subject, the more abstruse her matter and the more involved her terms, the more easy he found it to take her.

"Besides," said he to those of similar kidney, "the nearer we approach those altitudes where words must fail us, the sooner comes the time to proceed to action, and for this reason, and no other, I hold that the achievements of science are the greatest blessing which has yet been bestowed upon mankind, for where should we poor bachelors be without Freud and Einstein, poetry having declined as far since Swinburne's glorious day?"

"Why," he had been heard to exclaim on one occasion, to a young man who had come to him for advice, "I began as a poet myself, and had so little success that I developed a painful inferiority complex, which (heaven bless the day!) prompted me at last to glance at a magazine article on psychoanalysis, and it is no exaggeration to say that I owe my present comfortable condition solely to that article, and to a few of the terms I found in it. *So that sport,* as Tennyson finely says, *went hand in hand with science.*

"Why," he went on, "your scientist, or his simulacrum, is to the poor, lean, busy shark of a poet as is the great whale which Donne describes: he has but to open his mouth and his prey flock in:

> *He hunts not fish, but, as an officer*
> *Stays at his court, at his own net, and there*
> *All suitors of all sorts themselves enthrall,*
> *So on his back lies this whale wantoning.*

"Ah! what a poem!" he added, for he was a good fellow at heart. "To forsake such methods for the ugly jargon of science is like laying aside the whole art of angling, and dynamiting a stream for fish. Still, we must move with the times, but I don't mind telling you life is the poorer for it, and if I had my choice I'd live in the days when one cast a fine line of Baudelaire or Dowson, for, if the fish were shyer then, the least of them was a thousand times sweeter than all the shoals which, at the mere reverberation of one exploded hypothesis, turn on their backs and . . ." But here he pressed the metaphor to a grossness beyond the limits of good taste.

This, then, was the young man before whom Amy was innocently displaying her intellectual plumage, and you may be sure that, though he did not much pursue the subjects she touched upon, he had no scruple in exhibiting a great admiration for her understanding of them, a measure which, in a country where the administration of a mere cigar ash in a glass of port wine is, I believe, heavily penalized by law, should surely be punishable by a long term of penal servitude. And so it is, in the sense that many who adopt the pose end by hypnotizing themselves as well as their victims, and are ultimately distorted into a reverence sottishly real. But this, like other of the penalties of license, falls chiefly on the ingenuous amateur, while the practiced libertine escapes unscathed.

"But, surely," he said, "you must write? What is it—poems? Brilliant essays? Or perhaps on some technical, scientific subject? How is it I've lived so long without coming across anything you've published?"

"Oh," said she, "I have, tentatively, tried to catch an impression here and there. What I should like to do would be to experiment with form. But publication . . . well, hardly, in these days! But you —you write a great deal, of course."

"Well, I have," he replied, "up till tonight. But now I'm going to *live*." And with that he took hold of her, and in a manner which showed he had no illusions as to the main purpose of vertebrate existence. But Amy, though shaken, and though terrified of being thought a suburban prude, found the transition a little too precipitate for her sense of balance. More words were required.

"Stop," she said. "Why, you hardly know anything about me. Supposing I happened to be fond of someone else?"

"Why," said he, "you may well be. For I'm not so blind as to think your loveliness can have failed to attract a hundred hearts, or that your gallant generosity can have failed to reward the best of them. But you don't think me such a Victorian fool as to mind that? After all, how contemptible it would be to study science and not to live according to its discoveries! And if there's one thing which modern advances have shown us, it is that it is the best and not the worst person who can love many, and the truly moral rather than the immoral who has the courage to attain full self-realization in this respect. Besides, matter flickering, as it does, in and out of existence, insures that we are born again every second, so that I no more feel that you are part of your past at this perfect moment, than you, when you have gone on from it into some radiant tomorrow, need feel, unless you wish, that what happens now is part of you then."

"But," murmured Amy, blushing with very shame, "I'm afraid I have no past; not in that sense, I mean."

"What," cried he, "then all the more reason that you should have a present, and *here it is!*"

"Stop," said she. "But, you see, *he* may not think as you do, and I should hate to hurt him."

"What?" exclaimed the young man, glad to fall back on poetry again. "But you think as I do. *Let me not to the marriage of true minds admit impediments . . . to thine own self be true, and it must follow, as the night the day, thou can'st not . . .* But how I run on! The thing is that he can't be moved by you as I am, who could not bear to sit inside there and see you surrounded by a crowd of fools. Do you think he understands you as I do?"

"I think he loves me well enough," said Amy. "Indeed, I should be a rotter if I let you doubt it. But," she added with equal, though widely separated, sincerity and truth, "I don't think he understands me as you do."

"Why, then . . . !" cried the young man, and clipped her closer.

At that moment Mr. Fatigay came out upon the landing to fetch a handkerchief from his overcoat and switched on a new light. Emily, who had by now ventured to creep out from her retreat, followed his glance to where the unheeding couple were just visible above, and her heart opened with pity and contracted with apprehension as she saw him grow white to the lips, and then clench his hands in a sudden gust of fury. The poor man had, by this time, however, well learned that whenever he was moved very violently he was pretty sure to be culpably in the wrong, and knowing, too, that Amy would never forgive any demonstration of possessiveness in front of her friends, he made a tremendous effort at self-control, and he turned on his heel and rejoined the company, where, as very few of them ever addressed a word to him, he thought he might sit quietly and try to see Amy's point of view in this unconventional behavior.

For some time he sat in a corner with his glass in his hand, and this he very frequently replenished in hope to still the restlessness of his mind, which hovered constantly outside upon the staircase.

And, as a certain boredom which had overcome him during the earlier part of the evening had then prompted him to drink rather more than was his custom, he was very soon tipped off his balance into a moody and reckless confusion, in which things began to seem rather unreal, and not to matter very much anyway.

It was at this stage that he was joined by a very close friend of Amy's, Bella, the young woman who had brought Walter Wagstaffe, in fact. She had noticed the strained look upon his face when he reentered the room, and, going out shortly afterwards to fetch a handkerchief from her handbag, had quickly perceived the cause, and not without some feeling of injury. It occurred to this young woman that what was sauce for the goose was not only sauce for the gander, but also for any other goose who happened to be about, so that as her husband, who was a foolishly jealous person, happened not to be present, she thought it no harm to approach Mr. Fatigay and to embark upon a little flirtation with him.

"Why is it," said she, seating herself beside him, "why is it that you never say a word to me?"

"Well," replied Mr. Fatigay, after a little conscientious consideration, "I didn't think you wanted me to."

"How too deliciously modest of you!" cried she, with great enthusiasm. "Whatever can have made you think that? Perhaps it's that I've always felt so shy of you, since you're so much the lion of the party, with your too thrilling Conrad sort of background. I should love to live alone in the jungle."

"The lion, indeed!" said Mr. Fatigay with a titter. "I thought people generally regarded me as a bear, rather."

"Well, only because you look as if you could hug so terribly," replied the lady, and then, as if realizing that she had said something very foolish and indiscreet, she blushed and lowered her eyes in confusion, though not before those orbs had, in the merest fraction of a second, held a brief correspondence with Mr. Fatigay's, in which time they had come to a very perfect agreement, which only needed the ratification of their more cumbrous principals.

"When I was a child," she resumed, with the agility of a dancer, who, having just shown you that she can do the splits, returns in bewildering *da capo* to a remotely earlier and more formal movement. "When I was a child I used to dream of the jungle. My schoolgirl heroes were always Conrad's and what's-his-name's, men carrying on their work among savages and wild beasts and fever and loneliness. Tell me about *your* work."

Mr. Fatigay had already learned that there are only two sorts of women in the world: those who are interested in one's work and those who are not, but, like the rest of his fickle sex, as soon as he found himself in conversation with one of either sort, he wished she was of the other, so he tactfully changed the conversation.

"That's a wonderful dress you're wearing," said he.

"Do you think so. I'm afraid you wouldn't if you cared much about the fashion. The fact is I have to wear them rather longer than most people, because I've got a terrible scar halfway up my shin, where I fell on some rocks when I was young. It positively sticks out through my stocking."

"Oh no!" said Mr. Fatigay, utterly incredulous of this.

"Yes, indeed!" said she. "It's most extraordinary. Give me your hand. There—you see." And at this moment their eyes met to endorse the treaty which had been made before.

"Well, I know something about scars," said Mr. Fatigay rather hoarsely, and after a short silence. "The blacks practice cicatrization a great deal, of course. I wish I could have a look at this. I believe it could be removed."

"Do you really?" cried the charmer. "How interesting. I wish I could show you it. But I can't here, in front of all these people."

"I wish I could examine it," said Mr. Fatigay, with something of the annoyance of the thwarted specialist. "Look here, if you like, I'll wait for you in the room at the back, and give you my opinion."

"Well . . . I don't see why not," murmured the lady. "Very well, then."

And Mr. Fatigay, first taking a further deep pull at his glass, got up and walked very carefully across to the door.

Waiting among the hats and coats, the poor fellow found himself assailed by a host of painful reflections, among which, however, those concerned with Amy and her violent flirtation so strongly insisted on precedence over those connected with his own procedure that he was still far from giving attention to the latter when the door opened and the young woman entered.

"Here I am," she unnecessarily whispered. "How absurd! Do you really understand these things?"

"I know a bit about them," muttered Mr. Fatigay, whose hands had begun to tremble a little.

"Well," said she, turning aside to pull down her stocking, "here it is."

Mr. Fatigay approached and examined it very closely.

"It's very small," he said. "How white your skin is! Is it as smooth as it looks?" And with a stern and scientific expression he put out his hand to make sure.

But at this the charmer let fall her skirt, and edged away half a pace, on which Mr. Fatigay, leaning toward her, caught both her hands in his, at the same time experiencing an electric shock throughout his flurried nervous system.

"You bewitch me!" he cried, and, slipping an arm behind her, he pressed her to him for a hungry kiss.

"Stop," said she, as soon as she was able. "Are you sure we ought to do this? Wouldn't Amy dislike it? I'd hate to do anything that would hurt her."

"Oh, *she* won't mind," said Mr. Fatigay, with a touch of bitterness in his voice. Here, however, he was mistaken, for at that moment the door opened, for Amy, who had found her gallant adventure advancing a little too quickly for her, and who had, also, seen from her point of vantage the entrance of first her fiancé and then her friend into the bedroom, had decided to follow them, and now entered just as Mr. Fatigay was embarking upon his second kiss.

Neither the advanced nature of the lady's ideas nor the clouded condition of the gentleman's were proof against such a conventionally dramatic situation, and they stood awkwardly, with faces as red as fire, while Amy, after a freezing glance, said in a small thin voice:

"Oh, pray don't let me disturb you. I only came to look for something." And she withdrew, closing the door with ostentatious firmness.

Mr. Fatigay and his charmer stared at one another.

"I think we'd better go into the other room," said she, making for the door. "I do hope Amy hasn't misunderstood."

"I hope she has," said Mr. Fatigay, "but I'm afraid she hasn't."

"What a fool I've been!" he thought to himself. "Still, it's Amy's fault, for if she hadn't behaved so wantonly herself—and especially after our quarrel before dinner—I'd never have dreamt of flirting with anyone else. Oh, dear!" And he, who had entered the room with the expression of a doctor, left it with that of an undertaker's mute.

CHAPTER 12

While, like a ghastly rapid river,
Through the pale door
A hideous throng rush out forever
And laugh—but smile no more.

Beauty, which some of us experience (as opposed to noting it merely) only when we are distraught by love, awakens, as far as the all-night Corner Houses and soda fountains are concerned, at about one in the morning, and there she waits the pale and burning few who come to seek her consolations. I refer to beauty of the supersensual kind, though the other sort is, I believe, to be found at the same time and place, but that is a matter of taste, and not mine, though if it is yours I shall not quarrel with you, but I mean abstract beauty, and of the sort that De Quincey digested out of his opium, beauty made out of the mysterious presence of monsters in scenes of frigid and marmoreal splendor; the apparition, for one is not the only lover in the world, of white and twitching faces and the wringing of despairing hands.

As it is not on a diet of moonlight and night-dew only that the nicotiana expands its cadaverous sweet bloom, but, like the blushing, bouncing rose, it is nourished fundamentally on a homelier product, so this insomniac atmosphere, whether you penetrate like a jetty beetle into the ruby air of some sinister saloon, creeping silently over red carpets, sitting on red plush, staring at the rich satin panels whence the spongy air absorbs the color of pigeon's blood; or whether you advance into an arena walled by cliffy marble, which seems to have sweated immense nodules of pale ice in which the waxy lights gleam like reflections, and take your seat somewhere on the wide mosaic pavement, on a gilt cane chair incredibly small and hard and frail, and perhaps at the foot of a tall squat-looking pillar, cut nevertheless with such dash and smooth precision out of the once difficult stone, and so wantonly placed and crudely and effectively capitaled, that it has all the violent facility of a rough sketch, or of the décor of an opium dream; or whether you sit in some gilded mirror-hall, down whose illusory aisles your somnambulist image steps from space to space, lit, like the mind exploring Coleridge's caves of ice, by lights increasingly tangled, flickering and faint—whichever it is of these you may happen to choose, and a true lover is likely to be stung on from one to another till he has seen them all in the course of a night; whichever atmosphere it is, its beauty and its mysteriousness are derived largely from the fact that it was smaller twelve hours ago, when it was filled from wall to wall and from Eden to Apocalypse with the rosy or milky or golden faces, all shot with satin iridescence, of innumerable sweet girls, now poutingly asleep under their sheeny eiderdowns at Wimbledon, or Enfield, but then bright in the bright light, flashing it back in sudden bird refractions, while under the many-jetted, iris-jetted fountains of the band they preserved their roses with the bitumen-dark interiors of steak and kidney puddings. Inheriting from these, fed on them as they were on the dark hearts of the puddings, your pallor and grief, and the Dantean frigidity or poisonous soft redness of your surroundings, are not desolate and evil only, which would be pretty, but are damned, which is a sufficient foundation for the beautiful.

He who tastes this peculiar beauty, however, or any that is seen when love's strong claws have, in getting at him, rent asunder the silken caul of trance in which most of us pass through the world, had better beware, lest he gets a craving for it, so that he, who found this one crazy flower staring out of the upas tree which is killing him, may in the end find little satisfaction in laughter and inn fires, and actually seek again those poisonous shades for the sake of their strange glamor, as De Quincey did with his drug. Sooner or later such a one will find the dreadful stimulant beginning to lose its effect, and then he will be marooned far from all that Rupert Brooke greatly loved, and on an island speedily growing desert of all that attracted him. His fate then, such is the cruel power of passion, will be little better than that of a chronic dyspeptic, who can find pleasure in nothing.

Mr. Fatigay was approaching this condition, as he would have found out during his nocturnal wanderings after the party, but for the unfortunate chance that he belonged to the large majority of the amorous, who, though their contortions are as lovely as any, are conscious of nothing but their pain. These, like unhappy mules blinkered, and bleeding from the goad, serve to carry the imagination through the rocky and romantic scenery to which they are native, where otherwise its frail foot might fail to tread.

Poor Mr. Fatigay had slunk out from Amy's flat without making his adieux, all his longing for an intimate half-hour after the others had gone having been slain by two wounds, anger and fear, either of which alone might have polished him off. At his own lodging, he found that sleep had been murdered by the same fell agents, and, after spending an hour or so partly in staring at the dingy appointments of his bedroom, which, from previous associations of something of the kind, had grown extremely distasteful to him, and partly in reviewing the events of the evening and the prospect of the morrow, which were infinitely so, he sprang from the bed, where he had thrown himself still half-dressed, and, pulling on the rest of his clothes, he fled from the torture chamber into the empty chalky street, which ached under the sleepless lamplight like a row of rotten teeth.

Before long, the ennui of suffering in the void avenues and crescents of Hampstead had turned his steps, as unconsciously as, through his weariness, the downhill streets had drawn them, toward the center of the town, and soon he had passed one by one the long chain of lamps that swoops down to Charing Cross, much as a damned soul passes star after star on its way to perdition.

On such excursions there is a fine balance to be noted between the aching of the heart and that of the feet, and, while the second pain is the baser, its cause, after all, is a present and a cumulative one, while the cause of our heartache lies in the past or the future, so that it is not liable to immediate material increase. This being so, it is inevitable that, sooner or later, the feet must weigh down the balance, and that attention, sliding down the beam, must come to rest upon them. Then it is that the wise man cries out in joy, for the physical anguish is infinitely to be preferred to the mental, from whose dominion it filches the light of consciousness. This wise man at once sets out on a wider circle, which, to another, would seem to be a circle of red-hot iron, but which to him represents comparative oblivion.

The foolish lover, however, has no sooner had attention distracted a little from the worst of his pain, than he conceives a hankering to examine it further, and he hastens to find a seat, where, it must follow, his feet soon become easier and his heart becomes hot and swollen again, and the balance is once more tipped the other way, and he springs up from his seat and stumbles out upon the next lap of his mad career.

Mr. Fatigay was not the wisest of lovers, his experience having been a schoolmaster of the tyrannous kind, who cow and bewilder rather than instruct. So, when the inevitable pain in his feet began to intrude upon his thoughts, he entered the next all-night café that he passed. It was a blood-red one. Disposed droopingly at the tables about its walls were the forms of other disconsolate lovers, their faces incredibly white and Beardsleyesque against their background of Edwardian satin, some reading and rereading letters of dismissal, some gazing at photographs, and some staring at mental images in the vacancy before them. In the center were one or two groups of night birds, whose appearance seemed, at this hour, finally to establish the fact that life was ugly and obscene, and that whatever dreams may once have possessed these lovers were but futile bubbles, foredoomed, by the mere pressure of normality, to fade and die.

Mr. Fatigay began to stare at a succession of images of Amy, each in a different attitude, like a strip of snapshots from an automatic machine. He saw her simply as herself, the star which had burned on his inner eye in the velvety darkness of every African night. Then, and appareled in a frostier light, he saw her as she had stood a few hours ago, icily and bitterly thrusting back his feverish approaches. "You brute!" she had said. To *him*, after all these years: "You brute!"

"This next image, then," he thought, "cannot be true. I must be mad. After that, how *can* she have lightly embraced that ugly, sneering stranger? Yet she did. I saw it. And yet she said, 'You brute!' "

All this drew up his mind into an erect figure of accusation, which crumpled up suddenly, though, as if hit behind the knees by a beam, when the last image inexorably asserted itself.

There she stood, the witness of his folly and his shame. "Don't mind me," she had said. Mr. Fatigay broke into a heavy sweat. How could he explain? How could he express resentment? He began, for the fiftieth time, to compose a long speech, in which he made it clear that he had most to forgive, and at the end of which, his bursting heart relieved a little, he forgave freely and lovingly.

"It's only natural. We've been living an impossible life. Now it's all over. We'll marry and be all in all to each other." He fancied he caught a tremulous assent.

"Good god!" he thought, "perhaps she's suffering now, just as I am." And, bemused by the last stage of his reverie, he hurried out to the telephone booth in the entrance hall to ring her up and reassure her.

But there was no reply. Mr. Fatigay returned to his table in a state of stupefaction.

"She must have heard," he thought. "Why doesn't she answer? She must know it's me. Is it because she hates me? She's got no right to hate me. She began it, after all. It can't be anything but that . . . surely? I wish I'd not gone before that ugly fellow went. Good god!"

And, unable to sit still any longer, he made his way out to the street, along which he drifted from call box to call box, at each of which he was injected, by the agency of mere silence, with a jealousy more insidious, more fertile, and more irresistible than could have been conveyed by the most venomous of positive slanders.

It was not until, not his feet merely, but his whole body was aching with an insupportable fatigue, that he staggered at last into a vast and polar hall and sank fordone beneath a marble pillar, from whose cold shelter he at length looked out across the wide spaces under the heavy ceiling, oppressively low as an arctic snowcloud, to where at intervals a few exhausted lovers leant over the glass-topped tables, like corpses waiting to be hoisted completely on to those mortuarial slabs. On the farther side of the hall a little group of people radiated an edgy gaiety, like that of the moonlight picnickers under the gibbet of Montfaucon. They were by no means rollicking, but, in this petrified waste, the fact merely that they ate up their eggs and bacon, broke their rolls, raised coffee cups, and spoke, and looked at one another when they did so, lit them up with a stagy Dionysian light, and drew all eyes wearily and resentfully towards them.

Mr. Fatigay gazed awhile in the same vacant annoyance. Then, as if his eyes, their glaze broken, had acted as fire alarms, summoning his wits from nightmare to come tumbling down to deal with a fiery reality, he grasped at the edge of his table and half rose to his feet. For there was Amy (that was why she had not answered the telephone), taking an after-party breakfast with the abominable Tickler and her smart friends, Mr. and Mrs. Dunedin, and certain others.

To collect himself, he leaned back behind the pillar. His worst surmise, then, had been a false and a ridiculous one. The sun rose, just over the horizon, on his arctic winter. Assuming, a little too readily, that it must ascend uninterruptedly to a summer zenith, melting all the black ice, he rose to his feet, and, baring his bosom to its warm shafts, and to her shafts, he hurried towards the group, knocking over a chair on his arrival.

"Amy!" he said, with a look of naked, indecent rapture. "Well . . . Amy!" And the poor clown, tired and glad beyond all restraint, bent over to give her a kiss.

Amy, bright and dry as a calico rose, had come out to establish these qualities of hers in the minds of her friends, as an inoculation against the story they were bound to hear, of how Bella had raided her private possession. With deft touches, she had, she hoped, modified the tone values in their idea of her relationship to Mr. Fatigay, so that he and she should be felt to be a hard and frivolous couple, to whom such incidents were part of life's wit merely.

As she did so, a small tight resentment had hardened in the core of her heart, not so much at the necessity of doing this, as at its probable inefficacy. No remote hints, much less any downright statement, if that were possible, would persuade Mrs. Dunedin that Alfred felt like that, although she might easily believe that Amy herself did. He had too often behaved, when they had been drinking cocktails, with a clumsy and provincial fondness more appropriate to high tea. And while her friends knew that Alfred was at heart crudely romantic and sentimental, her own reputation for modernity and cynicism was insufficient, for still it held that these qualities of his, valuable in a subject, had been, for a time at least, entirely subverted.

Upon her now, at the moment of greatest strain, advanced the palpitating Mr. Fatigay, positively with tears in his eyes, stretching out two shaking hands, uttering her name in the rich moo of Italian opera, bending over, while the others looked on observantly, to engulf the last vestiges of the character she had given him in a heavy tremulous kiss.

Amy darted into the advancing mass a kiss of her own, as swift, hard, and destructive as the knife Hugo's hero darted into the center of the octopus. Mr. Fatigay sank, punctured, upon a chair, his tentacles all awry.

Amy saw, somewhere deep within herself, that there was nothing for it but to leave him to the part he insisted on. Her only protection against the smiles the Bella episode would provoke must, then, lie in the stressing of her own fairy-like capriciousness. People must say, "Amy doesn't care."

"Hullo, Alfred!" she said, giving him an appropriate smile. "Have you been with Bella? I hope she was nice to you. Isn't she too attractive for words?"

"Good heavens no, Amy!" said Mr. Fatigay heavily. "You don't think I'd do that, do you?"

"Well, why on earth not?" said Amy with an amused glance at her friends. "Why, you blundering old African jumbo, you! You don't think I'd mind, do you, surely? Why, you'd find it the most delightful thing in the world, a little affair with Bella. I'm sure I could never resist her if I was a man. I don't know that I could even now, as it is, if she tried to flirt with me. Sometimes she looks so sweet one simply has to jump up and kiss her." And she gave a little laugh so frank and friendly in its confidential audacity that it completely deceived one of its hearers, if not the other three.

Mr. Fatigay sat silent, trying to sum up the conflicting jumble of false and true impressions that heaved his tired brain, a task in which, as he did not allow for the plus and minus signs which should have qualified them, he found it difficult to arrive at a result which looked even possible.

"In the ideal world, of course," went on Amy, making the point a general one, "it will be with everyone as it is with us. In every set there'll be a number of these divinely desirable little animals like Bella who'll carry their perfect irresponsibility like a flag of neutrality under which heavy engaged couples may shelter for a space. I'm sure it will make us ever so much nicer afterwards."

"But why be engaged at all?" said Susan Dunedin, and the conversation proceeded along the usual lines.

Mr. Fatigay did not join in. His brain had almost stopped working. With his chin sinking onto his breast, and his mouth gaping like that of a dead codfish, he sat mechanically registering each blow that Amy gave to his old African dream. Every sally of hers, which was expressive merely of ideas, and very usual ideas, to the others, was to him related to the two great poles of his present agitation, her bitter repulse before the party and her behavior with the ugly stranger. His dream world lay in ruins about his feet, and, when he heard her make a light reference to the fascinations of this particular man, and to an arrangement she had made to have tea with him, it began slowly to revolve around him, evoking a sensation not unlike (yet how unlike) that obtainable on the joy wheel at Wembley. He felt he must summon up fury, or die.

Suddenly he got up, lifting his forgotten body with a gigantic dreary effort.

"Excuse me," he said, and walked out across the enormous hall to the lavatory on the staircase.

"When I get there," he thought, as one makes plans for the end of a three weeks' journey, "I will hang myself, and write a note saying why. Then she'll be sorry."

When he had arrived at the chosen place, however, he found that he had no paper in his pocket, which made the second part of his project difficult, and no pencil, which made it impossible. His exhausted mind was halted on its single track. To die without uttering a few well-chosen words—there is the sting!

"I have only my braces to do it with," he thought idiotically, "and then my trousers, being loose at the waist (for he had fallen very thin of late) might fall down. I'd be bound to kick a little. And then I should look absurd. It would be in the papers. She might only laugh. Would she laugh? Laugh? Surely I'm going mad."

And he rushed out of the place, and, calling a taxi, fled to his lodgings, where he fell upon the bed utterly prostrated, and was soon deep in the sleep of exhaustion, for these Africans are not used to late nights.

CHAPTER 13

Her warbling voice, a lyre of widest range
Struck by all passion, did fall down and glance
From tone to tone, and glided thro' all change
Of liveliest utterance.

When he awoke, it was already afternoon. He arose stiffly, and while dressing he moved aimlessly about the room, absorbing the blessed normality of his surroundings. Outside the window a bank of tangled Michaelmas daisies bloomed starrily in the shade of a sooty tree. His walking shoes, well-worn brogues, experienced, rich, and glossy, stood in a shaft of mellow light. A snapshot of himself on his horse, taken in Boboma, stood on the mantelpiece: through it he looked into a vista of the life that he had lost. Amy's photograph, set framed beside it, compelled his reluctant mind back to the nightmare it was instinctively avoiding. He saw, in a compound vision of all that had passed since his return to England, a series of inevitable corridors along which he had been lured and hustled to the crazy amphitheater where he had finally collapsed. To be tantalized, bewildered, and betrayed, this might be his fate. "But not," said his brown brogues, "not in an all-night soda fountain."

As his thoughts became more collected, they resumed the aspect of his last conclusions of the previous night, but with this difference, that he was no longer half dead physically. The choice between fury and death, therefore, was decided automatically in favor of the former, and, calling for his tea, and for two eggs to be brought up with it, he paced up and down rehearsing expressions of resentment.

Swallowing the penultimate mouthful, and cramming the last into his mouth, he seized his hat and hurried forth to deal summarily with Amy.

The chimp opened the door at Haverstock Hill. She gave him a sympathetic look.

"Amy?" he demanded. And, seeing that she shook her head, he asked:

"Amy soon?"

Emily, who would have preferred not to be addressed in this pidgin English, nodded with a friendly smile.

Mr. Fatigay ascended to the drawing room. This, since Emily had spent the day in tidying up, had resumed its normal appearance. Mr. Fatigay threw down his hat and began to stride about. He was so full of words that he could not restrain himself to wait for Amy's return before speaking, but began to unburden his mind to the chimp, little suspecting that she understood such complex utterances.

"If Amy was shocked at the way I behaved to her," he said, "and called me 'You brute' when she's supposed to love me, how could she go on like that with that horrible little literary beast? And if she went on like that, how could she give me that dreadful look just because I kissed that wretched little vamp when I'd had a drop too much because she made me so miserable by flirting with that dirty libertine? And if she gave me that look, how could she say before all her friends in that cursed all-night café that she didn't mind, and wouldn't mind if I'd gone home with her? And if she doesn't mind, how can she love me?"

The chimp, who would have been unable to answer any of these questions, even if she had been as voluble as humans of her sex, expressed her growing concern on behalf of her beloved in a heavy sigh.

"Alas!" she thought, "I wish I had stayed in the zoo. How can I bear to see him suffer so? And when she does marry him, it'll be even worse, if her behavior last night is anything to go by. If only I could console him somehow. Perhaps someday I may."

And, crossing the room, she laid a gentle hand upon his knee, and gazed mournfully at him with her dark and eloquent eyes.

"What, Emily?" he said. "Are you there? Ah! Emily, I begin to wish we were back in the old days at Boboma."

"Shall I—" thought Emily, "dare I—press my lips upon his hand?"

At that moment the door opened, and Amy came in.

"Hullo, Alfred?" she remarked. "I hardly expected to see you, you behaved so strangely last night." And mentally she took up Mr. Fatigay's misconduct in her right hand, and her own new light attitude in her left, as if she were taking up sword and buckler. "Where did you get to, in the end?"

"Did you mean all that you said in that place last night?" said Mr. Fatigay, in tones of considerable momentum.

"What exactly do you refer to?" asked Amy, with a glance of surprise flung like a dart at his ill-mannered emphasis.

"You know what I mean," he said brutally.

"If you mean the various ideas I expressed about people enjoying a certain amount of freedom," said Amy, "what of it? Those are very usual ideas nowadays."

"Did you mean them for us—for you and me?" he demanded. "That's what I want to know."

"I may have, and I may not," she replied loftily. "But supposing I didn't; supposing I think as you want to make me think: how are you going to defend your conduct last night?"

"And what about you and that dirty scribbler?" asked Mr. Fatigay. "How do you explain that, if you didn't mean what you said?"

"I haven't said I didn't mean it," said Amy. "As a matter of fact, you won't get anywhere by being abusive. It wasn't at all the same as your behavior with Bella. You showed me earlier in the evening what part of your beastly nature was dominant, and what you did later on was obviously the outcome of it, and in mean spiteful revenge because I refused to be treated like a common prostitute.

"No, don't dare interrupt me," she continued. "I mean to say what I think. You showed clearly enough that you haven't an inkling of what finer feelings are, so I can't expect you to understand that a girl can be momentarily dazzled by contact with a great mind, and perhaps be thrown off her balance for a moment without having the same hateful motives as yours."

"Well," said Mr. Fatigay, even more rudely than before, and with the additional offensiveness of an apparent resolution. "Well, you could have had me, as you know, but, since you choose to react like that to what you consider a great mind, you'd better stick to it. I'm off. You've got too many bright friends for me ever to feel safe." And he walked towards the door.

Amy, though shaken by his insolent parade of firmness, might have let him go, had he not turned, and said:

"I know you don't want Emily, so I'll take her. Come, Emily!"

Emily sprang out of the scullery, to which Amy had banished her on entering.

"Wait a minute," said Amy. "You can't go like that. We must thrash this matter out first. Perhaps I said I was dazzled only in order to punish you. You began it, Alfred, by your brutal assault on me before dinner. I was never so overcome in my life. It made me feel that everything I'd trusted, every clean and decent thing, everything that made me prefer you to the average intellectual, was done for. I felt that what you stood for was, after all, a sham, and there was no chivalry and self-control anywhere. So I just didn't care what I did. I just felt that you ought to be punished for destroying everything good."

"Oh!" said Mr. Fatigay with a sneer. "That's what you call 'mean spiteful revenge' in me, isn't it? To say nothing of the fact that I've got the excuse of having drunk too much because what I saw made me so miserable, and of having normal desires which you don't seem to have, as far as I'm concerned anyway. And having them all pent-up, because of your tantalizing tricks, which God knows you've never had to complain of in me. If you'd loved me, as you pretended to, we'd have been married by this time. And now we'll never be. I'm off!" And again he started for the door.

Amy, who had contemplated very seriously saying the words, "Be off!" at her next meeting with Alfred, found that she could not bear the initiative to be taken by her worshipper. There seemed to be all the difference in the world.

"I suppose you're going to that hateful Bella of yours," she said bitterly, using the first thought that came into her head to arrest him. But as soon as it was said, she almost believed it, and at the idea of such a calamity she burst into tears.

Mr. Fatigay did not run to her at once to console her.

"What does it matter to you?" he said, with cruel duplicity. "If you drive me away by your conduct, as you'd have driven me away a long time ago, if I'd had the sense of a flea, just by your refusal to keep your word about fixing our marriage—since you've now driven me away, what does it matter to you where I go?"

"Don't go to her," bellowed Amy. "Please, Alfred! Even if you hate me now, and can't forgive me, don't go to her just to hurt me."

"I don't hate you," he said. "And I forgive you, if that's what you want. But I'm not going to be played with any longer, and I'm not going to make any stipulations as to what I do next."

"Wait, Alfred," said Amy, and for a few moments she did battle with herself.

"Alfred," she said, "I *will* fix it, if only you won't go. Only give me six months more."

Mr. Fatigay made a vulgar grimace of contempt. "You ought not to be married at all," said he, "and I wish I'd seen that from the first." And he made as if to turn away.

"Stop!" said she. "I *must* wait till Mother comes back from Scotland. Would early in November do? Please, Alfred! You *know* I love you."

Mr. Fatigay could withhold himself no longer. He saw only the piteous surrender, and pitied, and loved, not caring to think that such a surrender implied a siege, a war in which, as in all wars, there can be no victor, but only two losers.

"Truly, darling?" he cried.

"Truly, truly."

"Amy! My own!"

Outside, in the scullery, some crockery fell with a shattering sound.

CHAPTER 14

The Violet invited my kiss—
I kiss'd it and call'd it my bride:
"Was ever one slighted like this?"
Sigh'd the Rose as it stood by my side.

November arrived, and in its chilly heart, like the core of all its darkness, Emily thought, came the day of the wedding, appropriately dulled and muffled in an icy fog. At eight o'clock, Emily rose from a hot and sleepless pillow and shuffled miserably into the dark little kitchen to boil the water for Amy's early tea. Standing in the chilly dirt, among the soiled plates and glasses, staring at the evil gas ring, she tried to review the situation for the last time. At first her benumbed mind, which had been locked in a rigid cramp all night, seemed like a galvanized corpse, capable of but one spasmodic movement—"This must not be!"—but a sudden hateful stirring in the kettle, signaling the moment when the dreadful day's procedure must begin, painfully goaded it beyond its pain-wracked impotence, and she began wildly to catch at even remotely possible means of saving her dear protector at this eleventh hour.

In such mental disorder, the extremest conclusions usually present themselves first, so it came about that the desperate chimp, from the trough of dejection, whence she could see nothing to be done, was next flung up into a contemplation of the stormiest future, which seemed to justify the most violent measures.

"Murder!" she thought, aghast, and she turned the ill word loathingly in her mind, until, as if it were some wicked bright blade she was handling, she seemed to see in it her own anguished reflection. "Murder!"

Those whose virtue is but the negative outcome of the triumph of a little good over less evil may here conceive an aversion to our heroine because she entertained such a thought, but to do so would be as unjust as to condemn a neighbor because his house has been entered by burglars, forgetful of the fact that such violent visitors come uninvited, and usually only to the richest establishments. And, moreover, while the general statement that the more we know of our fellows the more ready we are to forgive and understand may not be quite true in all cases, it may be confidently invoked in this connection, for he is singularly fortunate who has much acquaintance in the world and has not been seized by the same impulse as now possessed Emily, and that not once but many times, and on but a hundredth part of her grievous provocation.

For here she was, face to face with her final ruin, not merely of her own, but of her adored one's happiness. One by one she had seen her hopes crumble away at the acid touch of reality.

She saw herself, infinitely far off and long ago, standing in some moment, one of many, in Africa, standing as simple in her equipment and her intention as any figure in an old morality play, standing in a lion-colored patch of sunlight at the doorway of some hut, and thinking, "When he sees the author of those letters, the enslaver of his boyish fancy, he will surely recognize the gulf between her as she really is and the vision of her that he has treasured all these years." At the thought of such simplicity, the poor chimp writhed in humiliation.

She saw herself again, as from outside the house here; she saw herself looking out over the flowerpots on the windowsill, a wistful smile in chocolate and beige behind the dusky scarlet of the geraniums, looking to see who was coming up the front-door steps, hoping against hope that it might at last be that not impossible she, who (wise, kind, and gentle) should set up in Mr. Fatigay's misguided passion the disintegrating process of a damaging comparison.

But all the shes who came were impossible, and at length Emily had come to understand that the awaited one who never came must be impossible also, and though in her eyes nine-tenths of Amy's circle were preferable to Amy, she realized that this impression was probably the result only of her ignorance of them—a display of common sense which, if it were only emulated by the many discontented husbands who exist among us, and who imagine that they can achieve happiness by a change of partner, would save us a large proportion of the expensive divorce suits which are rapidly robbing us as a nation of our reputation for fortitude and farsightedness.

Turning in from the window one evening, she had thought despairingly, "But perhaps he will fly from her." Glancing out again at the bevy by the gate, she had murmured, "But to whom?

"Besides," she had gone on, miserably, "from what I have seen of the married couples who frequent this house, it seems that those men who are treated hardest find it hardest to tear themselves away, as wretched flies find that poisonous flypapers are less easy to break free from than is nourishing jam or treacle. Part chained, part drugged, it depends on the fiber of the man whether he becomes a doting sot or a sulky slave."

Moreover, a certain *tête-à-tête* between Amy and her friend Susan Dunedin, only the previous evening, had made it more apparent than ever, to the chimp's way of thinking, that poor Mr. Fatigay, if the drunken and enervating pleasures of besottedness were to be his portion, must qualify for them by a blindness so absolute that he must fail to see that there would be no attempt at hiding, and, if he was to become a conscious but helpless slave, he would be one whose torments were even more exquisite than the ordinary.

"The trouble, of course, with men," Susan had said, staring pensively into the gas fire, "is that they are so possessive.

"And the trouble with women," she added, when Amy had hinted acquiescence in a sigh, "the trouble with women is that they let themselves be possessed."

"Not every woman," Amy had murmured.

"Practically every one," said Susan severely. "And I'll tell you why. When they first get married, they let their emotions run away with them, and give themselves entirely, and promise to do so forever. And once that's done, with all the tradition of servitude to back it up, a woman's made a chattel of herself, and the man keeps her so."

"Well," said Amy, "tomorrow I marry. What would you have me do?"

"Not what *I* did, anyway. Not if you value your individuality, that is. Last April, on our honeymoon, I was so keen on *giving* everything that Jack began to regard me as a mere piece of property at once. He objected to certain of my friends. I gave them up. He objected to my trying to get a part in a film. I gave it up. And each demand and each concession only paved the way for more and more."

"Who *were* the friends he asked you to give up?" asked Amy.

"Oh! there were enough of them. Dennis was one, and George was another. And there are one or two you don't know. Anyway, by going on like that, Jack has taken all the bloom off our relationship, for he makes it impossible for me to be frank with him, and it even spoils my relationship with the men concerned, besides making himself look ridiculous. Yet, if he *will* insist on my giving a lot of promises, which are utterly impossible to keep without hurting people I like very much and who are part of my life, what can I do?"

"Yes," said Amy.

"Don't mention that to anyone else, though," said Susan. "I don't want it to get about—yet, at any rate. I should hate to hurt Jack.

"If ever I *do* marry again," she resumed, "and it's not unlikely, owing to one or two things . . . if ever I marry again, I shall begin as I mean to go on. After all, all this ridiculous jealousy is just a habit, and the only way to break it is to be firm at the start. That's what I advise you to do, though I suppose advice is no good."

"I don't know," said Amy. "Alfred certainly is terribly possessive, and he seems to be getting more so. He can't seem to realize that there are moments when one must be oneself. Still, I should hate to hurt him."

"I think Alfred's fond enough of you to be got to understand," said Susan. "Men don't like it at first, of course, because they're so bitterly opposed to progress. But I don't think Alfred would make trouble. Sooner or later he'd understand."

"Well, certainly I think things ought to be on an open footing between people," said Amy.

"Yes, it's a hateful life for a woman, otherwise," said Susan. "I know. You'll be careful not to say anything to anyone, won't you, because otherwise. . . ."

"Of course," said Amy.

Emily, who had been clearing away the coffee cups, had lost control of herself for a moment, and tossed her head.

"One thing I've already put my foot down over," said Amy, giving her a severe glance. "And that is, that that monkey is to go straight to the zoo, immediately after the ceremony tomorrow. Clumsy thing!"

How far the conclusions Emily had drawn from all this were the illusory outcome of her limited experience of civilization, who can tell? But the fact remains that her view of the position, and of the menace to which her beloved appeared to be helplessly exposed, was nonetheless terrible to her because, in estimating it, some knowledge of the Dunmow Flitch and of the domestic life of the Brownings did not form part of her data.

Now she stood in the kitchen. In her hand was the teapot, there the cup from which Amy would shortly drink. Powerful disinfectants stood officiously beneath the sink.

The cutlery was in the basket on the dresserette.

The bedroom window was thirty-odd feet from the ground, to say nothing of the area.

But no! Not from fears of the consequences to herself, for on these she never bestowed a thought, but because of the danger of breaking Mr. Fatigay's heart, and because (she was, after all, but young and ingenuous) of her conviction that it is fundamentally wrong to obtrude steel, spirits of salts, or other such material arguments upon problems of the inner life, she cast the crude solution from her mind. She strangled the luxurious desire in her heart.

A partition as thin and as doubtfully located as that which divides genius from madness is all that lies between the tragic and the ridiculous. Emily next thought of appealing to Amy by the only means in her power, pantomime and passages from the printed works of great minds.

"For," said she to herself, "the fact that she so despises me might here be not an objection, but an advantage. Who, impervious to familiar voices, would dare to disregard the dust if it should rise up in accusation? Why, even those haughty emperors who retaliated dire displeasure on receiving good counsel from those about them have been known to tremble and turn back from their evil courses at the admonitions of filthy fakirs and the miserable mad."

But her native good sense admonished her at this point that there was, however, no case on record of an empress being thus affected, and the bubble collapsed into nothingness before heavier arguments had need be brought to bear on it.

"There is no hope," thought Emily, taking up the teapot, "and no resource for me but to suffer up to the limit of my capacity, and then, renouncing a guardianship which it was presumptuous folly ever to have thought I could fulfill, to seek tardy oblivion in a self-inflicted death."

Then, finding in the depths of despair a firmness to which she had long been a stranger, she took up the flimsy tray, and, spilling no drop from the brimming cup upon it, she crossed the narrow landing, knocked resolutely on Amy's bedroom door, and, entering, found that lady awake upon her pillow, with her hands clasped behind her head and her dark eyes fixed thoughtfully upon the ceiling.

Amy, who had awakened early, and to emotions compounded pretty equally of triumph and misgiving, was not displeased when the chimp came in to her, for the sight of one who had become somehow connected with the politics behind her marriage served to direct her thoughts to that successful quarter, and away from certain doubts which had been troubling her as to some of the deeper but *démodé* aspects of the affair. With Emily, though, she had some business in hand, and Amy owed much of her briskness and brightness to the fact that whenever she was attacked by what she called "mental dyspepsia," she took the first opportunity of thrusting the qualmy thoughts behind her and embarking upon some sort of action.

Leaning on one elbow, her teacup raised to her lips, she eyed Emily with what had been called, in her last year at school, her Mona Lisa smile.

Emily felt profoundly uneasy. Had she been a hundred times less intelligent, she would by now have recognized that smile with much the same discomfiture as does a performing animal the dainty loaded cane.

There is, perhaps, no fairer maxim among all the many which our national genius has brought forth, than that which advises us not to hit a man when he is down. For, apart from its implicit generosity, to which every true Briton must wholeheartedly respond, it is, like most of our more exalted precepts, full of the soundest practical sense, since, in mental as well as in physical combats, he who flings himself upon his fallen adversary must needs stoop to a something similar position himself and thereby run great risk either of exposing himself to some unconventional blow, or of being dragged down in the same grapple by which his enemy manages to rise. It is, as a matter of technical interest, far better to wait till the fallen man has half, but not more than half, scrambled to his feet, before rushing in to finish him off.

Amy, however, would have thought very meanly of herself if she had accepted schooling from a mere copybook, and to the lessons of experience, of which she had not had a full course, she had brought rather too much prejudice to profit greatly by them, so that, in what she instinctively felt to be her hour of victory, as far as the chimp was concerned, she saw no reason to deny herself the contrivance of an artistic little *coup de grâce* to the poor creature's presumptuous though unspoken criticism.

"Emily," she said, speaking very slowly and distinctly, "I have a little surprise for you. It struck me that it might be amusing—and

Mr. Fatigay, needless to say, has raised no objection—if you were to perform the part of bridesmaid this morning. Freak weddings are quite the thing in these days, and 'The Monkey Bridesmaid' will be very attractive to the gossip writers, if to no one else.

"Open that box," she continued, pointing an imperious finger. "There are two white dresses in it. Bring them here.

"This," she said, "is yours, and you may get into it, and lay the other out for me, while I take my bath. Unpack the hats also, which are in that box above the wardrobe. It's a pity Mother's ill, and can't come, but she'll love the photographs."

And, drawing a batik silk dressing gown about her shoulders, she went to the bathroom, leaving the poor chimp to savor the full bitterness of the cup now placed before her.

Emily drew a deep breath.

To say that fury at the manner in which Mr. Fatigay's kindly motives were broken in and exploited to further his bride's vindictiveness was the single element in her anger would be to exaggerate her selflessness into something not of this world, but it bore an extraordinarily high proportion to the hot personal resentment with which it was fused. There was room enough, in Emily's feeling at the moment, for an almost infinite quantity of each of these factors. And, as a stunned man may be revived by the sting of a new blow, her mental forces threw off the numbness into which despair had cast them, and began feverishly to act.

When Amy returned from her bath, she found the chimp arrayed in her white dress, waiting submissively to perform her office of tiring maid.

"It's getting late," said Amy, "so please try not to be clumsy, and attend to what I say. Here, help me on with this."

With trembling fingers the downtrodden chimp pulled on Amy's robe of triumph, so similar to that victim's garment which oppressed her own frail form.

"Come, dress my hair," said Amy. "And be sure you do it well. Alfred adores my hair, and, apart from that, I always like to be well groomed."

The chimp obeyed. One by one the stages of the toilette drew on towards completion. The clock crept remorselessly on. Then—it brought a reverse so sudden that no words can express it—willfully misinterpreting a humiliating but very natural request from Amy, the chimp handed her a certain volume of tales, and it was open at a page describing the simian *Murders in the Rue Morgue*.

Amy took in the familiar passage at a glance. She felt the chimp's hand upon her shoulder, and her freezing gaze became riveted upon the carving knife, of which Emily had possessed herself a few minutes before, and which she now brandished at about the level of Amy's fallen chin.

"Oh! Good god!" cried Amy. "What are you going to do?"

The chimp drew back a pace, and, smiling in bitter scorn, took up the bridal wreath and veil and clapped their flimsy finery upon her own brown head. Then she handed the bridesmaid's lowlier headwear to the trembling Amy, and, with a terrific gesture, commanded her to don it.

Amy, scared out of her wits, obeyed in faltering haste.

When she had done so, her wrist was taken in an iron grasp, and Emily, first showing her that she had the knife in her right hand, concealed under a fold of her garment, then drew her out from the disheveled bedroom, down to where the hired car waited below.

"What can I do?" thought Amy. "What can I do?"

She dared not scream, for she was too well aware that the resolute being beside her would plunge the gleaming blade into her shrinking flesh long before any rescue could be effected.

"It will be all right," she thought, as the car crawled through the foggy streets. "When Alfred sees us, he will be prompt to act. The stupid beast has not considered that."

The car stopped with a jolt outside the little Bloomsbury church where the ceremony was to be performed, and, still holding Amy by the wrist, leading her as if she were a heathen chimp who had never set foot in a place of worship before, Emily escorted her into the church.

A flashlight flared unhealthily into the fog as they ascended the steps.

"So *that's* the Monkey Bridesmaid!" said the photographer in audible tones. "Why, the bride's just the same height as she is. Myself, I like a good upstanding woman. . . ."

"Good heavens!" thought Amy. "Is it possible he didn't realize I was human?"

How often her lover had had reason to conceive, on different grounds, a similar misapprehension!

A sudden cold fear seized on her heart as they passed up the aisle to where Mr. Fatigay stood awaiting them.

No one else save he, and now the clergyman, was in the dark little church. Amy's mother, who had insisted on a church, was confined to her bed with flu, and, as a result of their agreement to a religious ceremony, neither of them had invited friends to be present, preferring to enlist the verger, who now appeared, to their support in the procedure.

They were some minutes late, for Amy, who had a strong objection to waiting herself, had ordered the car to call for her at the time appointed for the service to begin, in order to avoid any possibility of this.

As Mr. Fatigay advanced to meet them, Amy parted her lips to call for his help, but a sudden pressure on her wrist, and a sudden steely glance flashed at her from beneath the bridal veil, gave her pause.

"After all," she thought, "Alfred will recognize me, and she will then have no excuse from act of mine to murder me, nor opportunity neither, for he will overpower her in a moment."

But they were late, and the church was darker than a registry office would have been, and Mr. Fatigay slipped his hand under Emily's arm, and meeting an appealing look from the bridesmaid with that kindly smile with which he had responded to many such glances from (he thought) that quarter, he turned to face the waiting clergyman, and the service began.

The bridegroom's responses were clear and emphatic; the bride's, as is often the case, were the merest inaudible murmur.

His eyes misty with happy tears, Mr. Fatigay slipped the ring upon Emily's extended finger, and they were man and wife.

Emily's heart beat hot and fast.

They entered the vestry, and Mr. Fatigay had just signed his name in the register, and the chimp had tremblingly taken the pen in her hand, when a heavy fall was heard in the body of the church. Amy, who had been standing rooted to the spot, had fallen in a swoon, knocking over a rush-bottomed chair in her sudden collapse.

Mr. Fatigay rushed to the door of the vestry, to which the chimp followed him, when she had scrawled her illegible but characteristic signature below his.

"Oh!" said he. "It is only Emily, fallen over a chair." For Amy was already beginning to stir a little in the throes of a painful returning consciousness.

The ardent bridegroom, instead of rushing up to set his fallen pet, as he imagined, upon her feet, turned again towards his bride, and, lifting her veil with a gentle hand, he bent down to imprint a passionate kiss upon her lips. The chimp, in the tumult of whose consciousness all but her invulnerable love was lost, protruded these responsively.

A pause, an abyss in time, followed.

Then the astounded man, turning to where the clergyman was departing the church, cried out in the voice of agony:

"Hi, sir! Hi, sir! You've married me to a chimp!"

The clergyman, suave, debonair, equal to any emergency his ragtag and bobtail parish could thrust upon him, conscious too, that standing in the carven doorway, haloed in his blondness against the murky air without, he must look rather like the St. George in his stained-glass window, especially with the bowed and writhing form of the verger cringing at his knee, replied in befitting tones:

"Well, sir, what of that? The Church, you should be aware, is inspired from on High, and is therefore always abreast with the latest discoveries of science. Marriage between cousins, though I never encourage it myself, is perfectly legal. You must excuse me, sir, but I am a busy man. Good day!"

Mr. Fatigay pressed both his hands to his brow, and sank upon a chair.

Emily stood irresolute. She felt a strong and very natural impulse to go to the stricken man, and, taking his hand in hers, to endeavor, by loving glances and a consoling caress or two, to persuade him that things were probably not quite as black as they seemed. On the other hand, a subtle and penetrating feminine instinct warned her that this was almost certainly one of those moments in which, as young wives are warned in the articles on husband management in the daily press, "Hubby is best left quite alone."

Thus, like figures in a problem picture, they remained for many minutes, during which time the coughing verger, waiting at the door to lock up the church, wondered impatiently how long the queer party meant to be.

Then Amy, who, having regained consciousness enough to hear the clergyman's departing admonition, had on hearing it sunk into a deeper swoon, began at last to stir and sigh again, which brought Mr. Fatigay to his feet in an electric bound, and, forgetting his own anguish in his solicitude for her, he hurried anxiously to her side.

"Amy! Amy!" he cried. "Good heavens! What nightmare is this?

"Amy! Amy! Speak! Move! You cannot be dead! Oh, Amy!"

Soon Amy's eyelids fluttered once more and her limbs made some feeble spasmodic movements. At these Mr. Fatigay evinced an uncontrollable joy, so small a fraction of what we usually take for granted is sufficient to raise us to transports of pleasure, if only we are first brought low enough to appreciate it.

"She lives! She lives!" he breathed ecstatically, turning a working countenance upon the verger, who by now had come up the aisle to see what it was that induced these people to keep him waiting so long.

"What? The bridesmaid having a fit?" said the verger. "Why, I've seen worse than that happen in this church, and to the bride, too, and before the ceremony was over, sometimes." And, considering this often remunerative business to be his own particular monopoly, he demanded that the patient should be given air, and he pushed aside the bewildered Mr. Fatigay, who was reduced to utter docility by the conflict of his emotions, and proceeded with great confidence to apply his own methods of reviving the prostrate lady.

All this time Emily had hung doubtfully upon the outskirts of the action, anxious, in her kind heart, for Amy's recovery, and still more so for Mr. Fatigay's emergence from his unrecognizably distraught condition, that he might become once again the man she had known so long. Now, when the hypnotized fixity of his gaze began to slacken a little, its object having begun to sip water from a glass which the verger held to her lips, Emily could restrain herself no longer, and, creeping up, she laid her hand upon his arm, in hope of consoling him a little, and of winning some response, which, however heated, might contain some faint evidence that she was not utterly anathema to her adored one.

But Mr. Fatigay, as soon as he felt her touch, started away as if he had been stung by a serpent, and, fixing upon her a gaze full of a cold resentment, heavy beyond all thoughts of revenge, he took thought as best he might as to how he could efface her forever from the lives of himself and the sweet being whom her action had stricken to the ground.

"Here," he said at last, in a strained, hoarse tone, and, lugging out his pocketbook, he drew from it the bundle of notes which he had obtained to see them through their honeymoon in Paris. "Here: take this hundred pounds. It's no good to me anymore. And, since you've shown yourself to be so intelligent, go, get yourself your passage back to Africa, and never let me see your face again.

"No! Never!" he exclaimed in a voice of thunder, as the chimp, who from a habit of obedience had taken the money he thrust upon her, extended towards him her pleading hands. "Go!"

And, stretching forth his right arm, he pointed inflexibly to the door, through which the poor chimp, her own arm bent upwards across her brow, staggered in unutterable despair.

CHAPTER 15

> "O my cousin, shallow-hearted! O my Amy,
>   mine no more!
> O the dreary, dreary moorland! O the barren,
>   barren shore!"

Ere Emily's stricken figure had disappeared into the fog, Mr. Fatigay had turned, and, without a second glance, he had rushed back to where Amy was sitting up and beginning to moan.

"Come!" he cried to the verger, and, linking hands, they bore Amy between them, but a little lopsidedly, for the verger's form was meager and bowed with age, out to where the hired car was waiting. Himself almost fainting, he took the seat beside her, and, rewarding the man with what loose silver he had, he bade him instruct the driver to proceed, not to the hotel where they had arranged to lunch, but back to Haverstock Hill. As the door closed and the car started, he turned to her with a countenance brimming with woebegone tenderness, and made as if to take her drooping head onto his bosom.

"Amy!" he murmured. "What a catastrophe has befallen us! How on earth could it have happened? Dearest, don't look so pale! We are still ourselves, and we must face this together. Love me as I do you, and nothing can harm us. It will, it *must* all come right in the end."

But, as he said these words, Amy's form stiffened antagonistically, and, jerking her head away, she replied with a vindictiveness which equally surprised and wounded him.

"Don't touch me! Let me alone, I say! I hate you. I believe you did it on purpose."

"Amy! My poor darling! You are still overwrought, and no wonder. There! Close your eyes, and try to quiet yourself till we get back home."

"No!" cried she. "Let me alone! I'm well enough, at any rate, to see through the trick you've played on me, with your mean, vengeful nature. I suppose you did it to get your own back because I wouldn't give in to you in everything. Oh! Oh! Oh! If only Dennis were here, to give you the thrashing you deserve!"

"What—*him*?" retorted Mr. Fatigay warmly, but he checked himself, and after a moment he said very earnestly:

"Dear, if you think for just a moment you'll see how impossible it is that I should do such a thing. I swear to you I did not. I was never more astounded or horrified in my life than when I found out."

"Do you mean to say that you didn't recognize me from the moment we entered the church?" cried Amy, as furiously as ever. "It says a lot for the 'love' you talked so much about that you should think I was that ugly, murderous monkey you burdened me with. No, Alfred, I can't believe that even you could be as blind as that."

"But I never looked properly at the bridesmaid," said Mr. Fatigay miserably. "I was looking all the time at what I thought was you."

"And do you mean to tell me you didn't see that that creature, with *that* figure, wasn't me?" retorted Amy. "It comes to exactly the same thing."

"I didn't," said Mr. Fatigay. "I was so agitated, I suppose. And you being the same height and everything. . . ."

"Well, if you *are* innocent," said Amy, "you must be the biggest and blindest fool on earth. What do you think my friends will say when they hear of it? I shall be the laughingstock of all London! Oh! Oh! Oh!"

And, at this thought, her grief arose in her more agonizingly than before, and she collapsed in a flood of scalding tears.

Mr. Fatigay, to whom the sight of his beloved's anguish and the revelation of the chief cause of it were like a blow on the mouth, rendering him dumb, looked on in silent misery till the car stopped outside Amy's house.

"Come," said he then, "let us go inside and talk over this dreadful business more quietly." And Amy, who had still much to say to him, suffered him to escort her up the stairs to where the disordered rooms were awaiting the arrival of the charwoman who was to have cleared up and taken away the key.

"Amy," said Mr. Fatigay, when he had lit the gas fire. "Tell me what happened, please. My head is in a whirl."

"And what about mine?" said she. "All you wanted was to get married, and I don't believe you cared twopence who it was. Well, perhaps you've got a wife who'll be more a wife to you, in your beastly sense of the word, than I could ever be. I don't see what you've got to worry about. But I'm disgraced forever. I shall never dare to look any of my friends in the face again. What does it matter to me whether you're a scoundrel or only an idiot. I never want to see you again."

"Amy," said Mr. Fatigay, "for God's sake tell me what happened. How could you have let Emily play such a trick? I can't believe that you did it willingly, just to get out of marrying me at the last moment."

Amy, who could not stomach the least implication reflecting on her conduct, opened her mouth to deny this with an emphasis which lent something slightly canine to her expression, and was about to rebuke Mr. Fatigay for entertaining the idea even negatively. But suddenly she closed it again, for an idea had crossed her mind. There seemed an avenue of escape from the worst result of the catastrophe, the mockery of her friends. "Supposing," she thought, "I were in a position to imply at least that this came about through my own desire. Supposing I *had* made Emily play the part. It would be taken as a very dazzling, though unscrupulous, action. I could always find some way of justifying it. And I might even hint that some makeup was employed. I must think it over. I must admit nothing. I've already been too open in the car."

"Alfred," she said, with an expression of severe reserve, "I won't even trouble to deny such an infamous suggestion. I will make no statement at all. I'm sorry to have to say it, but I don't trust you enough."

Mr. Fatigay's chilled mind fumbled numbly at these sentences, as one's fingers do at one of those abominable Chinese puzzles, consisting of two interlocked nails which are supposed to be capable of disentanglement.

Amy quite pitied him as she watched him knit his brows and pace up and down the room, and stammer out the beginnings of half a dozen sentences. "But," she thought to herself, "I must be strong. He has brought it on himself by his ridiculous blindness."

"Well, Amy," said he at last, trying a new tack, "I won't question you any more at present, if that's how you feel about it. But what shall we do now? Surely, in spite of what the clergyman said, this marriage can't be legal. There's a law against chimps."

"There's no law against marrying them that *I* know of," replied Amy. "And if there was," she added, for she was determined to avoid at all costs any appearance of pledging herself to a course of action which might end in exposing her to the ridicule she dreaded —"And if there was, I couldn't go behind the marriage service on a legal quibble. It would hurt Mother's feelings too terribly. She would regard it as no better than living in sin."

"What? Even if I could get a proper divorce?" cried Mr. Fatigay. "I'm sure she wouldn't. I'll ask her."

"Well, how can you get a divorce?" said Amy. "Where *is* the animal, anyway?" For she had overheard him dismissing the poor chimp to Africa.

"I've sent her away," said Mr. Fatigay. "I told her to go back to where she came from. But I could bring the suit, citing some chimp or chimps unknown, and she'd never appear to defend it."

"No, Alfred," said Amy very nobly. "I can't agree to anything dishonest."

"Everyone will say," she thought to herself, "isn't it just too uncanny of Amy to have got out of it at the last moment like that? She's like a changeling, or a piece of quicksilver, or something."

"Well, Amy," continued Mr. Fatigay, with a hopelessly supplicating glance at her. "I know it's no good asking you to face it out honestly with me, and live with me openly. After all, our love should be stronger than any outside opinion."

"I'm sorry, Alfred," she replied, understandingly.

"And you won't consent to a divorce, or any sort of annulment," continued the unhappy man, no longer inquiringly, even, but in flat recapitulation. "Well, then, what *can* I believe but that you did it on purpose. How could you? Amy! How *could* you? And what's worse than all," he added in a keening wail, "what's worse than all is the way you put the blame on me in the car just now. *You* did it, and you put the blame on me! That's cold-blooded. . . ."

"Cold-blooded!" said Amy. "Look here, Alfred! That sort of thing from you just shows me what all this vaunted affection of yours amounts to in reality. I tell you, I'm not going to descend to reply to your insults. Since you've shown me what your opinion of me really is, you'd better keep to it. And keep to your monkey wife into the bargain. She'll put up with anything—I expect. She'll have to. You'd better go after her before it's too late."

"But, Amy . . . ," cried Mr. Fatigay beseechingly.

"No, don't touch me," she cried in disgust. "I'm finished. The best thing you can do is to go away. You've done me enough harm. I mean what I say. Can't you *see* that I mean it? Leave me alone. Cold-blooded! You can think whatever you like, and, whatever you think, I'll consent to nothing. That's final. Go!"

And, stretching forth her right arm, she pointed inflexibly to the door, through which poor Mr. Fatigay, his own arm bent upwards across his brow, staggered in unutterable despair.

A little later, Amy took down the telephone, and dialed the number of an intimate friend.

"Is Mrs. Dunedin there?" she might have been heard to say. "It's Miss Flint speaking. Oh, it *is* you, is it, darling? I didn't recognize your voice. . . . Yes, I said Miss Flint. . . . Yes, the ceremony *is* over. . . . No, I *meant* to say Miss Flint. . . . Well, it's *too* ridiculous, but the fact is, your Amy got a little nervous at the last moment. . . . Yes, I said the ceremony was over. . . . Well, Alfred's very short-sighted, you know . . . Yes, he nearly went blind in Africa. But don't interrupt. Well, there was that chimp hanging around, looking the very image of a perfect wife and mother, so with the help of the bridal veil—it covers a multitude of . . . wait a minute . . . and with the aid of a little makeup for the bridesmaid. . . . No, no, *I* was the bridesmaid. You should have seen me shuffle! . . . What? . . . Yes! Yes! that's it. Darling, it went off perfectly. . . . Well, perhaps *un peu de chagrin* just at first, but, really, I think he was rather relieved. . . . Oh, no, he can get out of it if he wants to, I should think, but I expect he'll absolutely love it before long. She'll suit him far better than I would. . . . Yes, if you like. Anytime this evening. Tell Deirdre to come too, if you see her. Good-bye. Good-bye."

CHAPTER 16

"Who calls that wretched thing that was Alphonso?"

The snow's a lady . . . and, like the rest of her sex, though delightful in her fall (to those who enjoy her), once she has fallen her effect is depressing, particularly in Piccadilly. A heavy blizzard had begun at noon, and continued for a couple of hours, during which time it was whisked and beaten by wheels and feet and sweepers into a kind of stale and ghastly sundae, edging, like Stygian spume, the banks of the stream of black and glassy traffic, which creaked along as slowly and uncouthly as a river of broken ice.

Mr. Fatigay, whose trousers and jaw, both terribly thin, had alike sprouted a short and ragged fringe, felt it enter over the tops of his shallow shoes, which gaped the more loosely about his piteous ankles because he no longer wore socks. For having in agony averted his face whenever the future rose before him, for he had found it too horrible to contemplate, he had prevented himself from observing one detail in which it resembled all other of the states of man, that it demanded money. So that he had not gone very far into it, when, his small supply running out, he found this one most ordinary detail to have developed into the most hideous part of all its aspect.

With Amy's last scornful word of dismissal ringing in his ears, he had gone out into the streaky opening clearing air, into whose sudden rifts of clarity, hard and colorless as a photograph, or as the inside of a crevasse, he had stared madly, as if he was seeing everything for the first time. His brain was numbed. Tensely and automatically he called for his bags, left his apartments, canceled the address he had given, offered no other, and went out into his new and empty world, the brittle walls of which, cupping its devastating hollowness, began to split before sharp jags of pain, like those of a hollow tooth at which the dentist has failed, and to which sensation returns as the anesthetic begins to wear thin. This pain was more than Mr. Fatigay could bear.

When a young man, almost alone in London, and, possessed of a modicum of intelligence and a small deposit account, is afflicted with pain greater than he can bear, he is likely to find himself, in obedience to an inexplicable law, in the company of artists. This was the fate of our unfortunate hero, who, only a fortnight later, might have been seen in a bar near the Tottenham Court Road, exchanging short nods with certain young men who wore black hats and long glances with certain youngish women who wore none.

He had already been there three nights in succession, and might have been described as an habitué. The women, to whom he politely offered drinks, found his politeness refreshing, and excused his lack of artistic outfit by saying that he was *real* and unhappy.

Mr. Fatigay's reality, however, was fated to be but brief, for the fact is that he was living upon his capital, having cut adrift from his employment in cutting adrift from the rest of the unbearable associations of his previous life. Whenever he thought of this, which he did the more often as his capital grew less, he ordered another whiskey, and whenever he thought of the cause of it, which he always did when waiting for his whiskey, he exchanged glances with one of the Bobbies, Billies, or Trilbies, who either painted, or were painted, over and over again as the old song says, during the hours that this public house was closed.

But this was but a passing phase, for, as he grew poorer, his reality suffered in the eyes of these charmers: he was discovered to be ordinary, which is quite another thing, and at last they found him to be dry, empty, a mere nobody, and were unable to see him at all. When he was finally exiled from this noisy limbo, and forced to keep the squalid garret he had descended to because he was completely penniless, he found that the devil which had possessed him during the period we have been examining had partaken of the general decay and become a little unreal also—it appeared to have been a mere *poseur*, its place being taken by what seemed a larger and more genuinely menacing relative.

In short, while to love and not to be rich has been set down as a great misfortune, our hero, in loving hopelessly and now being hopelessly destitute, had discovered a far greater. He proceeded to explore it thoroughly.

It may well be wondered that he did not entirely sink under his distresses, and take his leave of a life which had become so inexpressibly bitter, either by precipitating himself from one of the many suitable bridges, or by the even less difficult process of merely waiting for a day or two longer, until grief, weakness, and his cough should release him. But the fact is that at the very depth and bottom of all his misery, at a moment when, having stood long beneath a railway arch because he could walk no more, and then having begun to walk to save himself from falling forward, he had suddenly felt, through a sort of rift in his waking trance, a keen nostalgia for the racy flavor of a cabbage stump, portions of which, he remembered, are occasionally to be picked up in the purlieus of Covent Garden Market, and, being then no farther away than Charing Cross, he had begun to totter briskly in that direction.

Before the end of an hour, he was already in sight of his goal, but had begun to doubt if his legs would carry him the few additional yards that intervened, when suddenly his eyes had fallen upon the very article of which he was in search, and, resting for a space against the doorposts of a set of offices there, he began eagerly to gnaw at it, when there emerged a tall and stylishly-dressed gentleman, who, observing with good humor the gusto which our hero brought to his simple meal, had said to him, "Come, come, my good fellow, take this shilling, and get yourself something a little more tasty and nourishing."

The grateful tears which welled up in the poor wretch's eyes magnified the coin to the size of a half-a-crown. Nor did this entail any danger of an anticlimax, for to one in his condition of bitter necessity a shilling fences in the whole horizon with its milled edge, for his longest view extends only to the next meal, unless he is a person of exceptional foresight and intelligence, in which case he may be gratified by a vision of a second repast, as the wanderer discerns, it seems beyond the earth's rim, what is perhaps a further Himalaya, or perhaps only a cloud.

Mr. Fatigay had given evidence of these qualities, when after a moment's reflection he put the cabbage stump into his pocket, saying to himself, "I will keep this in order to make a light breakfast on it one of these fine days, so that I need not gorge myself now as if I were taking my last meal on earth, and, being satisfied at a lesser expense, I shall have some money left over, on which, if I decide to do so, I may start life anew."

He had lost no time in seeking out an unconventional little restaurant behind St. Martin's Lane, where, after some moments' deliberation, he had ordered an egg and rasher, with extra fat, three slices of bread, and a cup of strong tea, milky and with plenty of sugar. Leaning back luxuriously after this repast, he had decided to take up, temporarily at any rate, the extended lease of life which had been offered him.

"For," he had thought, "I cannot recollect, and, what is more to the point, nor can I imagine, any bliss arising from the love of woman at all comparable to the ecstasy with which I have just devoured this meal, from which, moreover, when I have paid my just sixpence, I shall depart feeling completely satisfied, and with my sixpence change clutched firmly in my hand. Is it possible that my values have hitherto been wrongly pitched? To consider this thoroughly will take a considerable time, and, in order that I may eat and drink while I do so, I had better invest that remaining sixpence in the stock-in-trade of some modest business, for I am thoroughly tired of the ups and downs of Bohemianism.

"I remember," he had continued, "it was my custom in the old days, when buying matches from men who sold them in the street, to put down threepence upon the tray when taking up a box worth only a penny or three ha'pence. Now, I will buy six penny boxes with my sixpence, and offer them for sale in some crowded thoroughfare, where hundreds of people pass by every few minutes. It cannot be long before I have sold them all for, say, eighteenpence. I shall then buy eighteen more boxes and repeat the operation, plowing back my profits into the business, until at evening I have a respectable sum in hand, part of which I'll spend on creature comforts, and part on a studs and laces department.

"Later on, when profits increase, I might consider taking on an assistant, or renting a suitable shop. But that is a decision best left until I know the ropes a little. It is mere foolhardiness to settle such things in advance. One way or another, at any rate, I should be proprietor of a very pretty little business in the course of a year or so, and, indeed, I might enter into competition with Harrods, from which all the Flints derive their incomes, and then, when Amy is reduced to utter poverty, I might drive up to her mean lodging in my car, and say, with a look of tender understanding which would melt away all thoughts of old scores, apologies, humiliation, and such rubbish, 'Amy! I would say . . .' "

But at this moment the voice of the waitress, demanding his sixpence, had aroused him from his reverie, and, stepping manfully forth from the shop, he had entered a tobacconist's, where he had made his investment, and then advanced upon the street, no longer a pauper, but a respectable tradesman.

Probably owing to the prevailing depression in trade, business had been hardly as brisk as he had anticipated. Indeed, two or three days later, when he carried out a postponed audit of his accounts, he found that he had sold only three boxes of matches, two of them at cost price, and one at a profit of a penny, so that he was in possession of fourpence in cash and three-penny-worth of unsold stock. With inflexible determination he had purchased three more boxes of matches, and had spent only the penny of profit on a piece of bread, to the proteins in which he had been enabled, by his display of foresight, to add the vitamins in his cabbage stump.

Two more days had passed, and our hero, whether it was owing to international complications, or, as he had begun to fear, to his having chosen a line to which he was naturally unfitted, had sold no boxes at all. With a careworn look he had determined to go into liquidation.

"I will write," he said to himself, "a little card, with the words: 'Great Bargain Sale. Business in Liquidation. Stock MUST be cleared at 25 percent below cost,' and thus I will be in possession of fourpence ha'penny before very long. I will spend three ha'pence on food, and the rest on apples, or bars of chocolate, or some other merchandise which can, if the worst comes to the worst, provide me with a meal if it remains unsold."

But, going out that morning with his little notice, he had been appalled to find that it attracted no attention whatever, and two o'clock found him trudging dejectedly along the gutter of Piccadilly, with so cold and heavy a heart that he began to feel that it must indeed be descended into his shoes, into which, as has been noted, the vile and icy slush slopped at his every step.

"Can it be," he thought, "that it is today that my burdensome life is to be demanded of me? God knows, I have no great fondness for it. On the day I received the shilling I was ready enough to let it pass from me. But somehow the gleam of hope which that coin shed into my abyss, or the high living to which I treated myself on getting it, has made me rather critical and high-stomached in this matter. If I am to perish, so be it; but let it be on a golden afternoon of late May, or June, or even July, rather than in this black repellent air, and, above all, not from cold and retchy hunger, but from a surfeit of lampreys, of green ducks of eight weeks old, with the first peas of the season."

For the poor fellow's mind was almost unhinged by his distresses, so that he wandered, and in a moment he was thinking himself a boy again, playing puff-puff through the gulleys of crisp leaves in frosty autumn, and, lost in the hallucination, he spattered up the slush to the left and right of him as he toiled along.

A few threatening words having burst this happy bubble about his ears, he mooned on vacantly for two or three hundred yards, when, as he was creeping by a famous taxidermist's window, he happened to raise his eyes, and, seeing before him various lifelike specimens of tropical fauna, he found himself, like poor Susan, momentarily gaping in a world precariously built out of the wreckage of the real one about him. Taxi horns were transmuted into the cries of that creature, whatever it is, which barks loudest in zoos and in equatorial film effects; two popular writers, threading through the crowd on their way to confession, joined as back and front legs of an elephant, parting the slim and dingy grasses on either side. There was a monkey-chatter of teeth in his head. Piccadilly. Pickaninny. The air was full of blacks.

"Ah!" said he, rapturously inhaling a rank and orchidaceous fume of patchouli from an antelope-eyed undergraduate who passed at that moment. "Ah!" said he. "Boboma! Boboma!"

"What's that?" cried the undergraduate with an angry look, and he gave the enfeebled Fatigay a hard and spiteful prod with his clouded cane, and retired petulantly down a side street.

The flesh, in retreating from the unhappy creature's ribs, had left the nerves, it appeared, stranded behind it, perhaps like helpless and self-conscious starfish upon the furrowed shore, and while to the ear of an outsider the blow would have seemed merely to be one upon an empty cardboard box, to the more intimate senses of the recipient its effect was agonizing. A groan, attenuated to the keenness of wind whistling in a keyhole, escaped through his chattering teeth. No longer under any illusion as to his whereabouts, he shuffled westwards, in more senses than one, he thought, along the squelching gutter.

When he had got as far as the Ritz, still without disposing of any of his stock, his tottering steps were arrested by the glossy backside of a gigantic Hispano-Suiza which had swept up to the imposing entrance to receive one of the favored few who had been lunching therein. Mr. Fatigay peeped humbly out from behind the sumptuous car to feast his eyes with a glimpse of this happy being. The door swung, a commissionaire bowed respectfully, and our hero's eyes protruded from their hollow sockets. For there, smartly groomed and fastidiously fastening a glove, stood Emily, his monkey wife.

Mr. Fatigay blinked as if to clear from his gaze what must surely be a filmy vestige of his recent vision of Boboma. But, no: there was the Ritz, and there surely enough was Emily. Her expression, though sweet as ever, was pensive, even melancholy, but perhaps on that account more spiritual even than before. She was a little thinner, but, such being the fashion, it suited her.

As she put forward a daintily shod foot to cross the pavement to her car, she hesitated, and, with a startled eye, she held one hand to her heart, as if perhaps that organ had halted within her, super-sensually aware of its mate, fluttering in the crazy cage on the curb-stone. Her eyes met those of Mr. Fatigay, and, with all her soul and sorrow melting in her look, she hurried towards him with eager outstretched hands.

Before she reached him, the strained axle of the whirling scene had snapped in his brain, and, pitching forward, he fell in a swoon at her feet. In spite of her tumultuous feelings, the chimp remained mistress of herself and the situation. Before a crowd could collect, she made a sign to the chauffeur, and, assisting his efforts with all the energy of her well-knit frame, she had the pitiful unconscious form gently lifted into the luxuriously cushioned limousine, where, following, she took his ragged, verminous head upon her bosom, and they started for her little home in South Audley Street.

CHAPTER 17

And she turn'd—her bosom shaken with
 a sudden storm of sighs—
And the spirit deeply dawning in the dark
 of hazel eyes—

Saying, "I have hid my feelings, fearing they
 should do me wrong";
Saying, "Dost thou love me, cousin?" weeping,
 "I have loved thee long."

As, with the whitening dawn, the lotus holds itself less tightly shut
and heavy to the bitter lifeless mud, and, rising through clear inky
depths, breaks open into the sunlit languor of its life, which, though,
is less energetic by far than was the strained blank intensity of its
shutting into nothingness, so the spirit of Mr. Fatigay, having
remained a long while tensely furled, in a sort of rigid antilife,
antinightmare constriction, detached itself from the frozen black
depths of his being, to which it had sunk, and rose into the pearly
shallows of semiconsciousness, where the light was the light under
the white ceiling of a Venetian-blinded room, into which this spirit
diffused itself a little when finally it broke surface in the imper-
ceptibly popping twin blossoms of his vacant eyes.

The street outside the green slats must have had its grayness
enriched a little by the hazy sun of a February afternoon, for the
light that percolated was not utterly cold, and joining with, diluting,
the coppery radiance from an electric fire, it warmed, without much
coloring, the milky dimness of the bedroom air. What color there
was in these two lights precipitated itself on the surfaces of various
objects in the room, causing these to glow with a somber richness,
which, to one detached from the present, with the body forgotten in
that tepid bed, and the eye forgotten in the ease of that tepid air,
was evocative of the Orient and immortal aspect with which simple
objects are endowed by all of us in childhood.

Through this tender colorless translucency, which was no more
emptiness than is the sweet light of the horizon at bedtime in June,
into which one longs, and is nearly able, to bathe one's outstretched
hand; through this, and with the intimate nearness of the youngest
moon, the palely shining crescent of a spoon described a gracious
arc, rising from somewhere behind Mr. Fatigay's head and setting
in a voluptuous kiss on that Endymion's lips.

Bouillon! Slipping away beneath the horizon of his languid gaze,
it rose again, and again the silver argosy, piled high, full moon, full
spoon, bore its delightful freight to the invalid. Chicken jelly! Then,
in its third quarter, lined with darkness, it rose and set again. Stewed
mushrooms! With that savory, the tempting little luncheon came to
an end, and the sufferer, as if the last of his liquid courses had been
spooned up from a superior Lethe, dropped his heavy lids in a
slumber inexpressibly sweet.

When he opened them again, he was more himself. Objects no
longer leaned against his eyes, staring in, but were regarded through
them as, when an empty house is tenanted again, the prevailing gaze

shifts round to a course from within outwards, instead of fitfully from outside through the vacant windows to the dim and empty rooms within. And from the newly inhabited interior, curtained to a dark rich secrecy by personality, interest, suddenly awakened, advanced a pale and staring face to the pane. Mr. Fatigay looked out in bewilderment.

Something in the disposal of the furniture, though he was sure he had seen no individual piece of it before, reminded him strongly of his airy white room in Boboma. Every detail was slightly different, but no detail of furniture can, by being changed, alter the identity of a room. It was as if his salary had been raised in Africa, and he had gradually changed each chair for a better one of the same sort, and the table also, and added a bureau, and got a very much more comfortable bed. Some orchids scented the room. Something moved in the corner behind the bed.

"What is it that moves?" he wondered suddenly, for to him this room seemed to be his fancy, but he recognized the movement, which yet was in it, as real. "Look!" cried his awakening heart. "Look! It's Emily! Here she comes!"

Smiling, the chimp advanced, and, with a nurse-like air, she laid a kind finger on her kinder lips. "Calm yourself," this gesture said. "Don't try to think. Excitement will only make you worse." But Mr. Fatigay, staring out of his preconceptions, goggle-eyed and mouthing, as a goldfish seems to stare out of its glass globe, gazing at a familiar room which he was seeing for the first time, gazing at Emily, whom, a few months ago, he had seen for the last time, rapidly retracing his experience till the long Elijah trail of footsteps in the slush of Piccadilly ended in nothing outside the Ritz, he felt all this, or even much of it, could not be, and falteringly he asked, in a sudden weak sweat of anxiety:

"Am I mad?"

At once the trim figure turned, and hurried to the bureau by the fireplace. Two or three quick clicks were heard. Mr. Fatigay rolled his eyes in further doubt and more dismal apprehension.

But then, returning with all the speed she might, the ministering chimp held up before him a sheet of paper, on which were typed the brief consoling characters:

"NO."

The poor man's bursting heart deflated in a long sigh of relief. "Emily!" he said quaveringly, too weak and lost even to remember the part she had played in the events that had brought him so low. "Emily! But where am I? What does it all mean?"

Placing a cool hand on his brow, and with a pressure inexpressibly gentle, yet strong enough to restrain him from raising himself in the bed, as he was attempting to do, she enjoined patience with a tender gesture, and hurriedly slipped to the typewriter, whence soon she brought a sheet which said:

"All is well. Soon you shall know everything. But first regain a little of your strength. Eat and sleep."

And when he had read these words, she gave him what to the broken in spirit and body are the two best things in the world: a smile of infinite kindness and as much food as he could eat. And by repeating these benefits as often as he wakened during the next day or two, she cherished him at last to a condition of sufficient strength and calm for him to hear what she had to tell.

It seemed strange to her that his first questions were not concerned with the trick she had played upon him, for she was unaware, of course, of how Amy had taken over the chief responsibility for this, and of how Mr. Fatigay, who still greatly underrated her intelligence and initiative, had settled with himself that she had been Amy's uncomprehending tool in this matter, so that he felt little resentment and no curiosity as far as she was concerned. Had he known, at this juncture, that she had organized the whole coup, there is little doubt but that he would have raised himself from the bed and rushed from the flat, if only to collapse and perish on the doorstep. But he did not know as yet. If this, the turning point in Emily's fortunes, owes much to luck, let it be remembered that this is the case with even the best of us, for the most able and well-lived life is merely that which is prepared to meet and to receive the good chance, and to shoulder off the bad.

Mr. Fatigay, then, began to feel much restored, and, "Now, Emily," said he, in a tone in which, though it was still weak, there rang something of the old Fatigay, to smite upon the taut chords of her heart. "Now, Emily, since you seem to have become literate: what I want to know is, what place is this, and whose, and whence came the fine clothes you were wearing when I met you, and the expensive car? You know you can be quite frank with me."

At once the docile chimp hurried to the typewriter, whence a few minutes later she drew a sheet on which was written:

"This place, my dear master, is a desirable first-floor flat in South

Audley Street, W.1, and until you entered it I have considered it mine, but upon that auspicious day it automatically became yours, with all else that belongs to me, including, needless to say, such trifles as my body and soul."

"Thank you, Emily, very much indeed," said Mr. Fatigay in the deceptively matter-of-fact accents of one who is dazed to a degree far beyond the shock of any further surprise.

"But," he went on, clinging to his own train of thought as if it were the only possible thread that might lead him out of this maze, and back to reality. "But tell me how you came by all these fine things. That's what I want to know."

The chimp nodded smilingly, as if to say, "Only wait and you shall be satisfied," and with that she began typing again and soon brought him a closely covered sheet of paper, which ran as follows:

"When you bade me begone, I was so miserable as to be unable to think connectedly for many hours, during which time I wandered about until I had at last overcome by physical weariness those paroxysms of emotion which tumultuously prevented the voice of reason from making itself heard. When, at last, thought became possible to me, I applied it first to test a certain strong feeling which remained like a rock in the center of my being after the raging tide of other emotions had shrunken back to its lowest ebb. This feeling was that, in spite of my reluctance to disobey you, I could not leave this country, either by a liner or by suicide, until I had ascertained that you were at least in a fair way to recover from the shock and disappointment for which I had been responsible. This feeling was endorsed by every rational consideration which I could bring to bear upon it.

"My first duty, it followed, was to return to you the hundred pounds you had given me for my fare to Africa, and I accordingly hastened to your lodgings that I might thrust them through the letter box, but, as I crept towards the house, I saw your figure emerge and enter a waiting taxicab, and, remembering that you had spoken of giving up the apartments on the day of your marriage, I assumed it to be likely that you were now leaving them for the last time. I watched for some days, but you did not return."

(Here the paper was blotched a little, as if a reminiscent tear had fallen upon it.)

"I soon began," it continued, "to suffer acutely from cold and hunger, and resolved I must earn some money (for that which I had of yours I regarded as a sacred trust, which I have kept for you to this day. It is in the drawer of the little table by your bed). Compelled by this cruel necessity, and unfitted, by physical and educational shortcomings, to earn my bread in any of the fields normally open to lonely spinsters in this city, I very reluctantly, and with many private tears and sighs, determined to sacrifice my self-respect and . . ."

Here the sheet came to an end, and Mr. Fatigay looked anxiously at Emily's stylishly draped back, where she sat industriously typing the next page.

"Good heavens!" he thought. "What is she going to tell me?" And he began to twitch and stir in the bed, and to look uneasily about the room with an expression of quick distaste for its natty and expensive appointments.

"Emily fallen!" he thought, and he looked back across the dirty, corpsey floodwaters that had drowned the last few months, back to what he suddenly realized had been the happiest days of all his life, dream days in Boboma.

And he stared aghast at two almost coincidental visions, one spoiling the other, as happens with snapshots superimposed upon the same film, first of the Emily of those idyllic hours

> *Wading in bells and grass*
> *Up to her knees,*
> *Picking a dish of sweet*
> *Berries and plums to eat,*
> *Down in the bells and grass*
> *Under the trees*

and second, of a new Emily, fated, like Eve, to be considered a true woman only after her fall.

"Emily!" he cried, wondering a little at the tremor and huskiness of his voice. "Say—what *was* it you did? It wasn't—*that*? Say it wasn't *that*!"

The chimp, unable to comply with his request, dearly as she would have liked to, bethought herself quickly how she might allay his anxiety, and, pulling the next sheet, still uncompleted, from the typewriter, she tripped across and placed it in his hands.

"and go," it continued, "as an organ-grinder's monkey.

"Having been forced to this humiliating resolution, I wasted no time in putting it into practice. Making my way to an obscure corner of the town, I patrolled its streets until I came upon an organ playing outside a public house, and, entering the saloon bar, I removed my bonnet, and distorting my face into a smiling caricature of the monkey kind, I executed the little *pas seul* which you taught me, my dear master, for the fancy dress ball on the ship.

"The proletarians present seemed quicker than the first-class revelers had been to perceive the tragic humor in the little turn, for they accorded me attention and applause, and were by no means ungenerous when I passed among them with my bonnet extended in the style of an offertory bag.

"The pennies I thus received I unhesitatingly appropriated to my own use, they were so evidently given entirely as a reward for the dance, and, as I gave my unconscious accompanist a small *douceur* on leaving, I had no misgivings as to the honesty of this way of life, whatever were my regrets as to its lack of dignity. I must confess, though, to some qualms of conscience when, on looking back one day after leaving a public house near Hammersmith Broadway, I saw the unfortunate grinder, who had evidently looked in at the door to collect on his own behalf, being very roughly handled by two or three men who had already behaved most generously to me. After that I doubled the fee I had been giving.

"With the pence I thus earned I was able to purchase bananas from the street stalls, and to receive a bed every night in a respectable women's lodging house, where I was treated with much consideration on account of being supposed to be dumb, and this life (which would have been more tolerable if only I could have discovered some trace of your whereabouts) continued until a day arrived, when, dancing in the wide lounge of a public house in St. Martin's Lane, I noticed that I had attracted something more than usual regard from an opulently dressed, but coarse and rather flashy man, who, however, had in his eye enough of a certain rough kindliness to compel a second glance from a creature as lonely as myself.

"Catching this glance, he beckoned me towards him, and what hesitancy I felt being counteracted by a sudden strong feeling, or hunch, that this meeting might mark a turning point in my career, I joined him at his table.

" 'Baby!' surprisingly began this stranger. 'You're too slick a piece of goods to be going round with a wop and a lot of canned numbers. I'm going to take you right away from all that worry and strain. And now, Baby, I want you. . . .' "

Here, again, the page came to an end, and, when he read the last words upon it, Mr. Fatigay fell into the same feverish anxiety as before. It was, if anything, the intenser for a certain subconscious process of disentanglement which had been set up by his previous alarm and relief. His emotions were not dissimilar to those that a poverty-stricken peasant of South Africa might experience, who, having spurned peevishly a dull pebble in the road, sees a sophisticated-looking stranger pounce eagerly upon it, and disappear, all singing, all talking, all dancing, into the distance.

"Emily!" he cried. "How could you? Ah, the libertine! Did you? You couldn't! You didn't? Yes or no?"

At once, the kind creature, to disembarrass him of his fears, drew the next sheet from the machine and hurried to give it him.

" 'to take a big part in my new revue,' " he read, and experienced the relief of a peasant, similarly situated to the one previously described, who notices that the joyously bounding stranger has jolted the rough diamond from his pocket in his excited retreat.

"At this," continued the typescript, "I looked very doubtfully at the stranger, for I have a very strong antipathy to the theater, and I had heard of strange developments following upon proposals of this kind. But I reminded myself that an increase in my earning capacity meant increased facilities in my quest for some knowledge of your condition, and an ability, also, to be of material assistance to you if you had been overtaken by misfortune, so I prepared myself to come to terms with the stranger.

" 'Come,' said he, looking shrewdly into my face, in which perhaps traces of my dubiety still lingered. 'What do you say to a level twenty a week?'

"It took some moments for the exact significance of this phrase to dawn upon me, and when I realized that I, a mere chimp, was being offered this sum, I was too overcome immediately to nod my acceptance. Before I could do so, the manager, for such was his rank, gave me a further shrewd look, and, addressing me as 'Chicken,' said he saw that I was not a stranger to the theater world and, swearing that he hated equally meanness and taking advantage, proposed that we should be on the level straight away, and, as if to establish us there, advanced his offer in one bound to £50.

"At this, I gazed at him with a certain degree of amazement, partly at the idea of being worth £50, and partly that so bluff and downright a man should speak so far out of character as to have offered a novice what now appeared to be less than half her market value. You may imagine my surprise, when, again misreading my expression, the manager brought his hand down upon the table with a crash, and, laughing heartily, observed that I had him taped. He then expressed a determination that we should not fall out over the contract, and offered me the same as he had given the principal dame in his last production, that is, £100 a week. On that, he offered me his hand, which I shook with considerable enthusiasm, and then, with an appearance of the utmost satisfaction, he led me to his office, where a contract was immediately made out and presented to me for signature. I signed with a scrawl as nearly like human handwriting as I could manage.

" 'Ah!' said he, after a glance at it. 'Juanita Spaniola? Is that it? Spanish, I presume?'

"Thinking no harm of the white lie, I nodded, suppressing a smile.

" 'So I thought,' said he. 'Now that's what I call a very fair hand for a ballerina. Say, don't you know English, señorita? You seem to understand it all right.'

"I shook my head.

"It was not until after my first appearance upon the boards, where my success, for what it is worth, was prodigious, that my patron arrived at an inkling of my true species, which I had used every means to conceal, lest my exposure in a position entirely devoid of civil rights should render me a prey to the unscrupulous and perhaps a slave to the immoral. This dreaded consummation did not follow, for my patron, flushed by the success of his under-taking, and genuinely grateful for my part in it, shook me warmly by the hand and swore that he would see to it that I had fair play, damning, incidentally, the eyes of all stars, leading ladies, and chorus girls of human origin.

" 'For,' said he, 'with their everlasting chatter chatter chatter and grab grab grab they make my life a hell upon earth between them, while you, señorita,' (for so he gallantly persisted in addressing me) 'say never a word, either jealous, quarrelsome, or cajoling. You per-form your steps without a lot of —— temperament, and you take your paycheck at the end of the week without making a lot of fuss about the size of it.'

"I need not describe, my dear master, the various steps by which I made myself at home in the peculiar world I had entered. Suffice it to say that I early acquired a proficiency on the typewriter, by means of which I gained all the advantages of communication with others. At the end of my contract with my good patron, I found myself able to bargain for the highest salary in my profession, and to set myself up on the scale of luxury in which you have found me, and I have, moreover, accumulated a comfortable private fortune against the longed-for day when I should cross your path again, for knowing that your mind is concerned with more important matters than the mere acquisition of wealth, it appeared to me that it would be well for you if any property you owned (for such I hope I may still consider myself to be) should perform that menial function on your behalf. What luxurious display I have entered upon has been only in the interests of my professional status: the address, the clothes, the car, and the Ritz, for example, to which last, may I assure you, I should have preferred the most humble of vegetarian restaurants, though now I shall ever hold it dear on account of it having been the point to which our paths converged.

"Now, my dear master, I have answered to the best of my ability the questions you put to me. Allow me, in return, to ask one of you. Is there any little dainty you could especially fancy for your tea?"

"No, Emily," replied Mr. Fatigay, on reading this last sentence. "Nothing but a lightly boiled egg, and some slices of thin bread and butter."

When she had left the room to arrange for the preparation of these, he reread the document she had handed him. Whether it was that his momentary apprehensions during the first reading had stimulated his general awareness of her personality, and of hitherto unsuspected depths in his feeling for her, or whether his long period on a restricted diet had had that effect of clearing the vision and sharpening the wits which those who indulge in voluntary fasts claim for the practice, it is impossible to decide, but the fact remains that he was not so satisfied with this mere record of events, from which, with rare selflessness, Emily had omitted so much personal feeling and motive, as he would have been had he still considered her as an ordinary chimp, however talented.

After his last experience of the sex, this absence of egotism affected him with the new restlessness that a city dweller finds, when he retires into the complete quiet of the country in order to cure the insomnia caused by the cacophony of London nights. He wanted just a little of it in order to feel at peace.

"Emily," he said, when she came in bearing a dainty tray, "is it true that you remained in England, which you hate, in order to be near me, who cast you out? And that you took up a profession which you abhorred in order to gain money for my assistance, when I had sent you away with nothing but your fare back to Boboma, and without even knowing that you were able to make use of the money? Why, you might have been robbed!"

Emily nodded, with a meek and tender smile.

"But why?" asked Mr. Fatigay. "And how, if your devotion is such, could you have brought yourself to wreck my life by upsetting my marriage to Amy?"

At this, the chimp began to tremble a little, for she imagined that he knew all, and thought the moment had now come when he would spurn her; but she bravely made her way to the typewriter, whence shortly she produced a sheet for his inspection, which said:

"The answer to both your questions, my dear master, is that which truth would have compelled me to make had you asked me the motive of even the least of my actions in Africa, almost from the day when I came into your possession. It is—because I love you.

"What I did, I did from cruel necessity. Was it wholly bad? Consider. Do you remember one happiness received from that affair for which you have not paid many times its value in pain? Which of your friends have you seen married to a human female without well-founded misgivings as to his future? Ponder these questions gravely, and, if you still wish it, I will, at whatever cost to my own feelings, give you grounds for divorce. You can then rejoin your fiancée, who, if she loves you as I do, will no doubt gladly receive you. I perceive that I have typed the last line with a certain degree of malice (which please forgive and discount), so I will say no more."

When Mr. Fatigay had read these words, he said nothing, but lay for a long time staring sadly into space, and every now and then he fetched a heavy sigh.

As with a drowning man whom mermaid hands draw down to what is probably, after all, far better than the life he has hitherto led, yet who kicks and struggles regardless of this consideration, until he sees his whole past unfold before him in a series of vivid pictures, when he folds his hands and fills his lungs and sinks without further protest, so did Mr. Fatigay rebel bitterly against Emily's invitation into reason, an element as unfamiliar and as fatal to lovers as the sea is to any land creature, and it was not until he had begun to review his past life in hard detail that he ceased his first instinctive resistance.

Oddly, perhaps significantly, it was not those pictures which might have been given such titles, if they had been shown at the Academy, as *The Rebuke, Waiting, The Green-Eyed Monster,* or

So Near and Yet so Far, that moved him most in this direction, but rather those in which a shadowy third appeared, a small melancholy figure, bowed by tyranny on one side and neglect on the other. When he thought of Emily at her most painful corner of that most scalene and painful triangle, a position in which she was thrust the farther from him, and to a more acutely pointed humiliation, by his own obtuseness; when he thought of what she must have suffered, and when he contrasted her constant good humor and control with Amy's pampered peevishness, he began to feel for her not as a chimp, but as a woman, or, at the very least, as an angel.

"After all," he thought, "Emily had to do what Amy told her in that matter of the wedding, and her lesser part was actuated by love for me, though I neglected her, while Amy, whom I loved (and here he gave a groan), Amy invented that unspeakably cruel way of dismissing me."

Sheltered by this illusion from the cold facts which might at the present stage have easily destroyed it, a new feeling for Emily began to spring up in his heart, nourished equally by certain old memories, by his convalescent gratitude, and by some faint but ineffably thrilling hopes for the future: it sprang up much as a hedge does, sheltered for the first season or so by hurdles, which, when they rot, it will more than replace as a bulwark against the storm.

Everyday this feeling made new growth, and yet without a word about it passing between them. It was too subtle and frail a thing, both of them felt, to be born save in a secure and holy silence, for, like the soul in Wordsworth, this love had had elsewhere its setting, and, since it trailed no clouds of glory, it needed repose and forgetfulness for its unencumbered delivery.

Not until Mr. Fatigay was almost completely recovered from the effects of his privations, and might sit, on the sunny March days, wrapped in warm rugs on the little balcony, did he make the remotest allusion to the past, and even this he did so vaguely that it was some time before the chimp realized the misapprehension which Amy had engendered in his mind.

When at last she understood, her heart stood still in her breast.

"Oh dear!" she thought, her whole life suddenly arrested, as if that of the cancer cure who one day feels, it seems, a twinge of the old familiar pain. "Oh dear! Supposing everything goes wrong now? What will he say when he finds out?"

"Emily," called Mr. Fatigay from the balcony. "That, over there, must be the top of the Ritz, surely. To think that it was down there that I was trudging in the snow only last month! Now all that, and all that led to it, seems part of another life. It seems I died then, and am here with you in heaven. Let it always be so, Emily. We will live like the blessed angels."

Emily bowed her head.

As soon as she might, she withdrew into a back room to wrestle with the temptation that shook her.

"Can I bear it?" she thought.

"Should I destroy his newborn happiness? Dare I take the dreadful responsibility? Is it fair to him?"

She sat for a long time, staring at the wall. Once, already, she had wrung the truth out of this last treacherous question, a pitfall which cowardly instinct digs for one sex, but which ultimately engulfs the other. Emily stared at the wall.

"No," she said, at last. "What grows between us must be based on truth, or, though it kills me, it must not grow at all."

And she sat down at the typewriter, to make a complete statement; but this, either because of the trembling of her hands, or because of a not unnatural impulse to express it in a rather finer prose than usual, she was a long time in completing, and she had not yet finished when the doorbell rang peremptorily, interrupting her painful task.

CHAPTER 18

Fly a shadow, it still pursues you,

and so, adds the poet, does a woman. But he might have elaborated his conceit with a reservation that during the darkest hours both have a tendency to disappear, the pursuit being renewed only when the sun rises again, in the opposite quarter.

A woman who has sent a man about his business will hear very complacently that he is shunning all company and diversion and moping unprofitably alone, and if it is said that he has morosely flouted all his material interests, has flung up his job, or has been thrown out of it for a display of sullen temper: "Why," says she, "a very little will suffice to keep a single man in comfort, and perhaps, for one so emotionally unstable as he is, it is better that he has no money, considering the temptations of the metropolis."

And if she is told that he is drinking like a madman, so that his best friends can no more have truck with him, she will show how the charity of love is superior to that of friendship, for she will say, "Poor fellow! It is as well we did not marry, clearly, but I can easily forgive him, for I know what he has suffered. He wrote telling me. . . . After all, why should I grudge him an anodyne which may be a blessing in disguise, preventing him from turning to worse things?"

But should it come to her knowledge that he has dared actually to go about his business, his business as a man, I mean, and is warming his starved heart in the new-risen sun of another affection, she will say nothing to anybody, but will at once go and pay him a visit; when in her first sentence she will propose, "Let us forget all that, and be just the perfect friends we were really meant to be." And in her next she will try to arouse his jealousy, and, in the third, and the many that follow it, she will bitterly reproach him for desecrating all that has passed between them.

Amy, when she had recovered from her first chagrin at the sensation of defeat, found it possible to admit to herself that she had been prevented, after all, only from something which she could easily do without. Indeed, her relationship to her lover, for she still regarded him as hers, as kings and queens consider banished men as still their subjects, her relationship to him had never been more satisfactory. Registered letters, and some borne by district messengers, arrived continuously, and in reading these she was conscious of a receptiveness luxuriously free to devote itself to the writer's manner, and the pure feeling which this conveyed, instead of being bothered at every other sentence by the necessity for dealing with some point of fact, as might have been the case had she contemplated making an answer.

It was not long before these letters were written on a poorer paper than formerly, and the addresses from which they were dated became more and more doubtful, till the last of them, as she learned from a discreet inquiry of Dennis Tickler, who knew his London, was nothing but a slum dosshouse, where a journalist friend of his had once spent a night in search of copy.

"Poor Alfred!" thought Amy that evening. "Yet perhaps such an experience as this is just what he wanted to make him pull himself together. He never had enough backbone." And she gave her thoughts a turn to: "How fortunate men are, to be able to go and live roughing it in the queerest, most thrilling places, whence women are debarred by a set of silly conventions. No wonder that men write all the best books."

"I quite agree," said her friend, for Amy had been thinking aloud, so to speak. "I quite agree. It's a part of a great conspiracy, which shows them to be conscious of weakness. Purdah! Absolute purdah!

"But tell me," she went on, after a moment's bitter rumination on the guarded privileges of men, "tell me, dearest, unless you'd rather not—you've never told me, and I've never liked to ask—just what *was* it made you decide not to marry Alfred at the last moment?"

Amy stared into the gas fire as if in hesitation, or perhaps as if to collect her mind into a stark and unflinching sincerity. But, in fact, she knew what she was going to say, for she had said it before, and unflinchingly, to one or two other confidential inquirers.

"I don't know," she said at last. "I hate to seem to criticize Alfred: he was such a dear, and there was such a bond between us in one way—not mental, perhaps, at least, not exactly, our tastes weren't much the same, but that didn't seem to matter—I suppose it was spiritual. I think it was some instinct stopped me. Perhaps it was an awareness of certain deeps in me that Alfred never succeeded in arousing. I feel I ought to marry someone who could make me feel—*mad*. That's what it was, dear, in absolute confidence, of course; Alfred didn't attract me sufficiently in that way. So it seemed only fair to him. Supposing—afterwards—someone else—one might have been carried away, and he'd have hated it *too* terribly. He got terribly upset once, over something absolutely trivial. And yet—I don't know. I sometimes think I'm strange in that way. Have some more of this coffee, darling. Do you like it? It's supposed to be very special."

Amy's contentment survived another month or so, until a very extraordinary piece of news came to her ears. Mr. Fatigay, clad in a singularly sumptuous dressing gown, had been seen sitting in the spring sunshine on the balcony of a certain house in South Audley

Street. Beside him, and dressed up to the nines, Dennis Tickler said, the chimp had been sitting, and they had been actually holding hands.

Amy listened, aghast.

All this time, her sexual life had been balanced and satisfied by the vision of Mr. Fatigay suffering for her in an exile in which there were the fewest possible counterattractions to her image. She had felt inexpressively tender towards him. On many nights, she had lain down to sleep in a warm surrender to the idea of a recall, and in a vision of their rapturous reunion. Though with each new morning's severer light there reappeared substantial reasons against it, the dream had become very dear to her, for it supplied all that she needed from marriage, and demanded nothing she was unwilling to give. And now this happy dream world lay in ruins about her feet.

"Really?" she said. "Did you say that house with all that lovely ironwork? How awfully lucky for Alfred! I've always thought that to live with that balcony must be perfect. Well! Well!" and with a light laugh she turned the conversation.

The next few days were perhaps the most emotional Amy had ever known. A burning resentment against her lover filled her heart. She felt stifled at the thought of the deceitful way in which he had been trampling on all the almost holy feelings that had grown up in her heart. This rebellion must be quelled at all costs, she felt, though it might necessitate the lending of her own person, temporarily at least, to effect a complete subjugation, a loan which Machiavelli advises to princes in their treatment of the unruly conquered.

At last she could restrain herself no longer; her heart, the chemistry of which had so long been giving off the mild vapors of an Heloïse part, seethed violently under the new acid and emitted a stinging intoxicating gas which inflated her to the proportions of a Cleopatra cognizant of Antony's marriage. Outwardly calm, she set forth one afternoon to reclaim the wanton Alfred, and it was her ring which interrupted the last sentences of Emily's confession, and it was her form that the disconcerted chimp beheld when she opened the door of the flat.

"Alfred!" cried Amy from the doormat, ignoring the lifted eyebrows of the chimp.

A faint sound emanated from the drawing room. Amy, assuming a light and friendly air, made her way towards it.

"Hullo, Alfred!" she said, as he arose in confusion at her entrance. "I hope you won't mind my coming to look you up. You don't mind, do you? I thought, 'Even if our love affair did come to a horrible sticky end, yet there's so much between us. We may have been a misfit sexually, but nothing can destroy the fact that we are, underneath, the best friends in the world.' Isn't that so? Best friends, Alfred?"

And she extended, frankly and freely, a hand.

"Well, Amy," said Mr. Fatigay, giving it a clumsy shake, "I don't know. I don't know that I bear any grudge. I must say, I've had a pretty bad time."

"A bad time? Poor old chap!" said Amy, giving him a look. "Well, I've not been too happy, myself, wondering what's been happening to you. I've missed your companionship and your . . . terribly."

A multitude of dead emotions rose from their graves in Mr. Fatigay's heart, like souls on the last day. In his tremulous surprise at seeing all these old friends again, he failed to perceive at once, that, battered by their violent end, they had become still more the worse for wear during their entombment.

"Amy . . ." he said, and halted.

At that moment, the chimp, in a simple afternoon frock of maizey green and yellow silk, entered with the tea tray. She placed it steadily on a low table, and, seating herself beside it, she glanced inquiringly at Amy, as if to ask, would she take tea?

"What, tea?" said Amy. "What a charming pot! Shall I pour out for you, Alfred, as in the old days?" And she began at once to do so, still utterly ignoring poor Emily, who exercised self-control.

Yet this was more natural than wise of Amy, for Mr. Fatigay, who had come to see Emily's early hardships with the same new eye which had lent perspective to his own, was inevitably reminded of both by seeing his sweet-natured benefactress thus slighted in her own house.

"Well. . . . Oh! Thank you," he murmured, taking the cup. "Of course, Emily usually pours out tea, you know."

"Yes, I see you've got Emily," replied Amy brightly. "And what a nice place you've got, Alfred. You *must* have prospered. But why do you dress the monkey up in that gaudy thing? Surely it's unsuitable for a servant? It would be for anyone, for that matter." For she meant to show how utterly impossible it was for any normal civilized person to conceive that the chimp could exist on any other footing.

"Emily isn't a servant," said Mr. Fatigay firmly. "If either was the servant here, it would be me. This place is hers, for she's now a well-known dancer, and she simply saved my life by taking me in when I was starving."

"Good heavens!" said Amy. "Well! Of course, I know that *legally* she's your wife. But. . . . Well, I suppose it's not for me to ask questions. Dennis told me that he'd seen you sitting together very intimately on the balcony. It was from him I found out where you were. I've been looking everywhere for you, though perhaps with a quite ridiculous thought in my mind. . . . I wish I'd questioned Dennis more closely now. I didn't like to, for I didn't want to hurt him. He's been *too* marvelous."

"I wrote to you often enough," said Mr. Fatigay, "till I got too poor and hopeless. You can't have been looking for me very long."

"It takes a woman some time to get over a shock like that," replied Amy. "That's the sort of thing you could never understand, Alfred. We might have been happy together now if you could ever have understood that."

"And apparently you needed the assistance of Dennis Tickler," rejoined Mr. Fatigay. "Good Lord! What a choice of a consoler! And goodness knows what shock you've had to get over. I should think I was the one who had the shock."

"Don't run down Dennis, please," said Amy. "I haven't *said* that he was my 'consoler,' as you call it. He's been perfect, absolutely. If anyone's consoler is to be criticized, it's yours, if you only knew," she went on, getting her trump card played as best she might. "And not because she's a filthy monkey, either, but something far, far worse even than that. You don't know what she did about our wedding. I came round meaning to tell you, and put matters right between us, but, finding you living, God knows how, with this admirable wife of yours, dragging everything that was good and lovely between us—or so I was fool enough to think—in the mire, I won't. I expect she was your—your *creature*—all the time, and you put her up to doing what she did. Good God! To think what I've given my love to! To think that I should have come round this afternoon, feeling and hoping what I did—to this!"

"You know perfectly well," said Mr. Fatigay, "that none of your insinuations about Emily and myself are true—put that teapot down, Emily—either in the past or now. Whatever it was you felt when you came here, you've not gone the right way to bring it off. And vague accusations will carry us no farther. Why don't you say it downright?"

"Oh, I don't know, Alfred," she replied. "I'd better not spoil whatever happiness you seem to have contented yourself with. It wouldn't do any good. You've made it pretty clear that you hate me now."

"I don't know what I feel," said Mr. Fatigay. "But you owe it to Emily, and to me, and to yourself, unless you wish me to think you a mere slanderer, to say everything now you've said so much. Otherwise, we'd better say good-bye."

"Well, if you force me to, I will," said Amy. "You don't know just one thing that may alter your opinion of your beloved wife. You don't know that it was she who threatened me with a carving knife, and made me put on the bridesmaid's hat, and would have killed me if I'd said a word—it was she who spoiled everything I'd been longing for—and on my bridal day, too."

"Good god!" cried Mr. Fatigay. "Emily! Emily, is this true?"

The chimp nodded piteously.

Mr. Fatigay sank back in his chair. His whole mind seemed shattered by this revelation. His thoughts raced wildly round from point to point of his riven firmament like the needle of an overturned compass. It was significant, though, that, when their wild oscillations settled at last into a trembling stillness, they should concentrate on Emily. Was she, after all, their true pole?

"Emily," he said hoarsely. "But how *could* you do such a thing?"

Emily laid an eloquent hand upon her heart.

"Of course," said Amy with a short laugh, "the ridiculous creature's been hankering after you from the first. Anyone could see that in her shameless looks."

Mr. Fatigay looked at the chimp more in sorrow than in anger, for even in his shaken state he found the motive thus indicated to be at least a possibly forgivable one.

"Poor chimp!" he said. "Even if in your ignorance you hoped to advantage yourself by such an act, how could you have deceived me now? I said only today that . . ."

"Why," cried Amy vindictively, "she's as deceitful as anything. She reeks of deceit."

Emily held up her hand arrestingly. Both stared at her. Quickly she bounded from the room, and, in a moment, had returned with the typewriter, in which fluttered the nearly completed page on which she had been making her confession.

Mr. Fatigay took it out and glanced at it.

"My dear master," it began. "One or two recent remarks of yours have made me doubt, and something you said today has made me certain, that you are under some misapprehension as to the part I played in preventing your marriage to Amy, and in marrying you myself. I had not thought it possible that she should not have told you, or I would have enlightened you earlier, though I know that it may make you hate me, and drive me from you into a still more hopeless darkness than before. I alone am guilty. I could not bear to see you engaging yourself for a lifetime into that cruel subjection under which I had myself suffered so often and so bitterly. That is what I meant when I said I had acted from cruel necessity. I had reason to believe that still worse lay in store for you, and, determined to save you from this fate, rather than from the least hope of gaining you for myself, I forced Amy to play the part of bridesmaid, while I, trembling, assumed that of the bride. I justified myself by the thought that I was only intruding upon a legal formality, and that if by some remote chance I had underestimated Amy's affection for you, this would have an opportunity to demonstrate itself in an acceptance of you in spite of what had happened, and in spite of the gossip and scandal which might ensue."

Mr. Fatigay looked up from this sheet, with a countenance which, after some seconds of utter blankness, began to work as a man's does when devils are being cast out of him, and, after he had amazed Amy and alarmed Emily by the protracted violence of this symptom of internal conflict, he leaned back in his chair, with a countenance pale and bedewed with sweat, and spoke, in a pale cold voice, these words:

"It seems that Emily had no intention of deceiving me, Amy! Why did you deceive me, though? What excuse have you for poisoning my whole existence with a belief, compared with which the real event, and even your straightforward rejection of me after it, would have been nothing—nothing at all?"

"I never actually *said* that I'd made Emily do it," said Amy, and then, terrified by the expression on Mr. Fatigay's face, she added: "Oh, Alfred! I couldn't bear to be laughed at. *Do* understand."

"I understand one thing," said Mr. Fatigay, with cold vehemence, "and that is that a man would be better off with any chimp in the world, much less Emily, than with a woman of your sort.

"No, Emily," he went on, "remain where you are. *I* will show Amy to the door."

"Well," said Amy with a dry sob of humiliation, "if you treat me like this, don't be surprised at anything you hear about me and

Dennis, that's all. Or anyone else for that matter. You'll have driven me to it by your hardness." And she began to weep.

"Don't cry, Amy," said Alfred. "The people in the street will see you."

And he closed the door.

"Emily!" he cried, as he turned back to where the chimp stood, waiting with downcast doubtful gaze. "Emily! My twice preserver! My good angel! My consolation! My wife."

The chimp, drowned in happiness, heard his words falling like the sound of bells from an infinite height.

"Had he but said 'my love,' " she thought, "my wildest, fondest dream would have all come true. But what a happy task, to spend the future years in winning that last dear epithet from his truthful lips!"

It was perhaps a train of thought following on this last idea, and confirmed by her careful consideration of what would be best for his future happiness, that led her, two or three days later, to suggest that they should leave the country in which they had both suffered so much, and return to the warmer climate and happier associations of Boboma.

"Yes, Emily," said Alfred, when he had read the neat typescript in which she conveyed this proposal. "I'll see if I can get the school-master's position again, and we'll start as soon as ever we can."

CHAPTER 19

And I lie so composedly,
  Now, in my bed
(Knowing her love),
  That you fancy me dead—
And I rest so contentedly,
  Now in my bed
(With her love at my breast),
  That you fancy me dead—
That you shudder to look at me,
  Thinking me dead.

The dirty white boat train, its windows bedewed as if with tears, ran out from under the vast indigo cloud, which lowered and billowed saddeningly over a hundred miles of silvery khaki and darkly silvered green, and it drew up in a burst of pale sunshine at the harbor platform. The baggy cloud rolled off eastward over the glimpse of sea, leaving bright waters pitching in the southwest prospect, and on the horizon a glimpse of ultimate blue. Through gaps in raw planks, gangways and derricks were to be seen, and, high above them, and above a flash of white paint, the surprising funnels stood up to proclaim that all that is best and sincerest in poster art is true.

Mr. and Mrs. Fatigay were among the first to descend from the train, and a glad haste winged their heels as they tripped, arm in arm, up the ridgy gangway. Several cameras clicked; it had been impossible to conceal the monkey dancer's romance from the press.

"My message to your readers," said Mr. Fatigay, when he had escorted his shy bride to her stateroom, and was able to give his attention to the group of slick young interviewers who surrounded him, "is simply this. It is true my wife is not a woman. She is, in fact, an angel in more or less human form. But though I believe that there is no chimp like my Emily, I can heartily recommend my fellow men to seek their life's pal, so to speak, among the females of her modest race. My experience has taught me that they are unequaled as soul mates, if that is the correct term, when skies are either gray or blue. Behind every great man there may indeed be a woman, and beneath every performing flea a hot plate, but beside the only happy man I know of—there is a chimp."

At these words, those among the reporters who were young and single looked a little dubious, but those who were older, or married, nodded their heads as if more than half convinced, and eyed Mr. Fatigay with something of friendly envy in their gaze.

The ship's sirens then began to sound, and lover from lover, husband from wife, parent from child, the one was taken and the other was left. The gangways were withdrawn.

"Write soon."

"Yes, I'll write from Gib."

A strip of emerald water was there, widening, dividing them from England; the land slipped by them; it sank to the appearance of a sandbank, and next day was gone; a sultrier coast smoldered to port; they drew in under the shadow of the Rock, some officers disembarked; three palm trees sprang up from a cluster of rickety white where the flat warm water lapped the sand. It was Africa. Some smallish whales were seen. Guinea lay beside them, hot as brass; then they ticked in the colored circle of sea, passing, save for their frothy white or boiling phosphorescent wake, through time only, to a dull and steamy coast lagooned with islands of mud. On the shining shores of these, crippled dugouts, the craft of splayfooted fishermen, were beached. Behind them, sunlit beyond mudflat after mudflat, more and more water was seen, paler than the sea. Emily's heart swelled: there was the Congo.

Mr. Fatigay's heart swelled also. He came softly up behind the almost childish figure that stood gazing over the rails of the foremost boat deck and laid his hand very tenderly on hers.

"Well, Emily!" he said. "Here we are, so to speak, and I must say I'm happy to have arrived. I've quite a longing to taste a yam again."

Emily smiled up at him contentedly.

"By Jove!" he cried. "I vote we have a marvelous spread in Cazembe. We ought to be there in time for dinner. New-picked fruit for you, Emily, and for me, well, it's hard to decide. Something with plenty of flavor to it, anyway. I hate the pallid food that most of the English keep to out here." And he proceeded to express some very decided views on this subject, every particular of which Emily noted, although in fact she had heard the greater part already.

Now a dead branch drifted past them, and they stood in towards the port. A broad boat advanced to receive the Fatigays, who were the only passengers landing here, and, with a quiet farewell or two (for they had elected to live in a happy seclusion on the ship, and so had made little acquaintance among their fellow voyagers), they descended the side, and settled themselves in the stern of the tender, impatient to set foot again on African soil.

When their excellent evening meal was done, Mr. Fatigay lit a cigar and suggested to Emily that they should stroll abroad a little and see the sights of the town. But she, with one or two of those quiet signs by which she managed to express to his now subtler understanding almost all that she desired to communicate to him (*my gracious silence*, he sometimes laughingly called her), with one or two such signs she indicated that she had seen enough of cities, and that they made her sick to her stomach, so that she would be well content to await him in the hotel while he took a walk, and perhaps a little refreshment in any congenial company he might find.

Mr. Fatigay, having been smilingly reassured that the chimp would suffer no sort of loneliness during his absence, consented to wander about for an hour or so, and, as he sat outside the principal café, comparing their present brand of lager beer with that which they had provided on his previous visit, four years or so ago, he mused contentedly on the singular difference between his circumstances now, and then.

"Was it indeed I?" he murmured, as his cigar smoke oozed from his nostrils into the blue and gold of the lamplit evening air. "Was it I who sat here at this same table with my very bones aching with misery at the thought of three years' separation from the she who was all I held dear, and with my heart already broken, so it seemed, by the thought that it was herself who had decreed my exile?

"Was it I whose life in Boboma was spaced and divided, and with a punctuation which grew more and more modernist in its increasing infrequency, by those letters, which, when they came, sucked all my heart's blood to fill their emptiness of affection, as if they were cupping glasses applied to that swollen and exhausted member?

"Was it I who spent that agonizing night in the Corner House, descending to the very verge of suicide because Amy kissed that fellow at her party; a reaction so extreme in this age, when men are what they are, and when so few women are what they were, that it must have been in itself an obvious symptom, to any rational mind, of a lunatic abandonment of all sense of balance and proportion?

"Was it I," he thought, with his twentieth spicy sigh of repletion, "who was brought down to mixing with artists, and eating cabbage stumps, and wearing no socks, like a damned highbrow, by my despair at the trick Amy played on me? And here's that poor fellow writing from Boboma full of gratitude for being bought out of his job and asking if I'll mind if he leaves a week before my arrival, as he is anxious to get quickly home to be married! I wonder if he's got a chimp."

"A chimp," the very word was like a bell; one of those bells which, struck only once by the skilled hand of the trap drummer, arrests the melancholy heartsearchings of the verse, and turns the treacly current into the richer rhythms of the chorus.

Mr. Fatigay arose, and, his feet moving as if to music of this luxuriously slothful kind, he made his way back to where, at the end of the now darkening palm-rustling street, the lights of the hotel glittered like a collection of fireflies in a broken cardboard box.

"Good night, Emily," he said, thrusting his head through the door which joined their rooms. But Emily, though she was still awake, pretended to be sleeping. "For," thought she, "if he thinks I go to sleep quite normally when he stays out late, he will never feel constrained to leave his enjoyment earlier on my account. It is best to begin as one means to go on."

As last he blew out his candle, and, with the extinction of that, the last resistant spark of humanity in Cazembe, the night flooded in, dark as water under the mighty trees, hard as sapphire where it wedged in the white alleys, and, high above, as dry and light and thin as spangled gauze. Reptiles moved in the river and lions on the land, desires in the heart and dreams in the mind. Then, tearing through the light upper night, blowing it away, the sun came, and, in a moment, all values were reversed.

Nothing is more sudden than daybreak in the tropics. It is as when, in a village cinema, the screen vibrates again, after a pitchy break, with that compelling white light in which move images shallowly common to all. Stars, or cigarette ends, fade; screams and embraces cease. The close-up of the beloved's enormous eye fades out before the still more illusory close-up of the world's sweetheart —Apollo or Rudolph Valentino, it's all one. The business we are here for is suspended, as the great cats run home, and the business we all pretend we are here for now begins. All of us, that is, except our hero and heroine, whose only end is to get home to Boboma.

As the sun sprang up, the respective shutters of Mr. Fatigay and his Emily popped open simultaneously, and, as they thrust their heads out into the singing morning, they at once caught sight of one another, and were glad.

"Look! Look, Emily!" cried Mr. Fatigay, and pointed to where the scabby little boat was moored, which was to take them up the river.

The streets opened up into life, mats were shaken, breakfasts eaten at doorways, greetings shouted, merchandise spread out on the pavements. The cripples, crawling as if tangled in their own black shadows, like wet flies, made for the shady nooks in which they passed the day.

"Come, Emily," said Mr. Fatigay, "and I'll buy you a new parasol before we go on board."

The journey was delightful. The captain and his mate were enchanted by Emily's quiet charm, so different from the loud mixture of arrogance and querulousness with which the wives of other officials had so often frayed their nerves. Shyly, and with the manly delicacy characteristic of their profession, they hinted to Mr. Fatigay, during a pleasant game of Nap, that, if she had any sisters at home at all resembling herself, they would be more than honored by an opportunity of making their acquaintance next time they put in at Boboma. The crew plucked water lilies.

The river narrowed. They were nearing their own parts. Looking up, they saw a dark figure suspended from the overhanging branch of a gigantic tree, watching their approach with idle curiosity. But, as they passed beneath, this figure showed signs of amazement, and ran out along the bending branch to get a closer view.

"That looks like a cousin of mine," thought Emily, and, standing up in the boat, she impulsively waved a handkerchief in greeting. The effect was electrical. The simplehearted fellow performed a hundred superb feats in joyous trapeze. Finally, after nods promising his speedy return, he disappeared, swinging, with rustle and crash and low sweet birdcall, from treetop to treetop through the haunts of his acquaintance and kin.

From that hour, their progress was processional. Dark faces and flying limbs switchbacked along the sheer green wall of the jungle, scattering flocks of gaudy parrots like fluttering confetti. Rustic bouquets sailed through the air. It seemed as if all the chimps in the world were present at the carnival. Mr. Fatigay bowed right and left. Emily kissed her hand.

At last they rounded a bend and saw the landing stage before them. It was crowded with the young men of the village, come out to escort them home. A mighty cheer arose as they came alongside. Mr. Fatigay was now dearer to these honest hearts than was Livingstone, who had discovered Boboma, or any of the white men who had visited it since, for he was the only one who had ever come back after once having left it.

"*Au revoir!*" cried the captain and the mate, and the crew's faces were split with smiles expressive of all the good humor to which their humbler station forbade them to give voice.

The blacks gaily hustled the happy pair into a state litter, which was raised upon the shoulders of the chief's bearers, music was struck up, Chinese lanterns, contemptuous of the day, were hoisted before them, and they set off back along the forest road.

"Welcome home!" said the headman graciously. "The residents of Boboma are unanimous in hearty welcome and goodwill and best wishes for connubial bliss. Accept the freedom of Boboma. Be pleased to attend a fête organized in your honor by the Corporation of Boboma and by her hearty healthy happy townsfolk."

As he concluded, the music struck up again, and the whole population began to dance and sing, even those who brought in the victuals to the high festal table at which the Fatigays were seated with the chief between them.

When at last the evening's merriment was done, and Mr. Fatigay and his bride had been escorted to the dear house in which they had first met, which had been swept and garnished to receive them, they sat a long while on the veranda, watching the lights in the village fade out one by one, and the moon rise like a clear and simple idea in a happily tired mind. Not a word was spoken. They almost ceased to think.

"Well, we must to bed," said Mr. Fatigay at last, and, rising only half-reluctantly, he switched on the light. Home, with chairs and tables, sprang up about them, like a comfortable wooden cage for the nocturnal feelings, shy as birds, which the blue moon-silences had lured from out their timid hearts.

Soon afterwards, Mr. Fatigay came from his room and sat on Emily's little white couch, wherein she sat upright, dark and dainty as a Spanish princess.

"Emily!" he said, and was silent for a long time.

"Emily!" he said. "My Angel! My Own! My Love!"

At this last word, for which she had been waiting, Emily raised her eyes, and extended to him her hand.

Under her long and scanty hair, he caught glimpses of a plum-blue skin. Into the depths of those all-dark lustrous eyes, his spirit slid with no sound of splash. She uttered a few low words, rapidly, in her native tongue. The candle, guttering beside the bed, was strangled in the grasp of a prehensile foot, and darkness received, like a ripple in velvet, the final happy sigh.

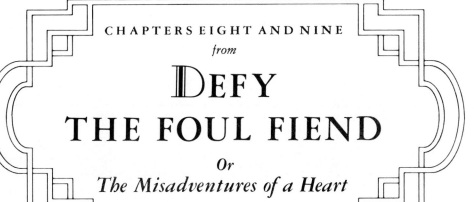

CHAPTERS EIGHT AND NINE

from

Defy

THE FOUL FIEND

Or

The Misadventures of a Heart

8 WILLOUGHBY IN THE COUNTRY

Willoughby was as gay as a lark when he left Paddington for Gloucestershire. The train he went by was the ten o'clocker; it was the first of October, and a day fit to advertise any ale in the world. His happiness fell one degree short of perfection, as everything must; the cause of this was that he was wearing a suit of his father's clothes, which he suspected did not become him to the best advantage.

The good old man, whose benevolence was all practical, as benevolence should be, had not forgotten to ask some pertinent questions as to his kit. When he learned it comprised two town suits and some evening clothes only: "That will never do," said he. "Your uncle hates a townee worse than the devil. Go to him in such an outfit, he'll think you just such another as your Uncle Ralph, and show you the door before you have time to broach our notion. Look, my boy," said the old chap eagerly, "at home in my trunk I've a suit or two of tweeds, which many a time I've meant to sell, for what's the good of 'em to me, these days? No time to have them taken in, they'll hang a bit loose; that does very well in the country."

When their evening was done, they had gone back to Pimlico and lugged out the suits. It was impossible to deny that the material was excellent: one was holly-green, t'other something the mustard color of a horsecloth. All the same, they were rather museum pieces and cut in the Norfolk style.

"You can fold the breeches under your belt," said the old man. "The coat is ample enough to conceal any little protuberance."

"Yes, that is true," said Willoughby.

Never mind, he was in the train. Believe it or not, he knew no other country than that which surrounds Reigate, or lies along its railway line to London. When the train left Oxford his excitement reached its highest: the carriage was empty, and he went from window to window, to see the ridges rolling away and the clouds rolling over them. The woods were yellowing, boisterous in a brave wind. "I don't care a damn whether I have the money or no," cried he, and murmured some phrases, which we will forbear to repeat, concerning tramping the road, darkening shires, inn fires.

He got out at Kingham. "I want to get to a place called Olle-beare," he said. "Five miles the other side of Stow, I believe."

"Hi, Alfred!" called the ticket collector, to a lean pale fellow who was cooling his heels outside. "Gennelman wants to go to a place called Ollebeare, t'other side o' Stow."

"Near the Slaughters, I'm told," said Willoughby.

"Oh, aye!" spoke up the lean fellow. "I've heerd tell on un. Honorable Corbo?"

"That's it," cried our hero in delight.

"Aw! Aw! Honorable Corbo!" said the ticket collector. The lean man, without saying any more, began to crank up a dusty taxi.

"I'll sit beside you," said Willoughby.

"Pleasure, sir," said the lean man. They were soon out of King-ham, an inconsiderable place; the taxi went fifteen miles an hour. Willoughby had time for a refreshing conversation with the driver.

After running along a high ridge, they went downhill between stone walls. On the left, the walls were lined with chestnuts, fine timber trees, evenly spaced; the stubble was already under plough, two teams of fine horses worked on it; there were some trim build-ings, good gates, a cart track well patched up with flints. Our hero got only a very general impression from this; nevertheless he per-mitted himself the use of the word "jannock," which was well received. On the right, the land appeared to be a waste.

"This is Ollebeare," remarked the driver.

"Which? Where?" cried Willoughby in great excitement.

"That on the right," replied the driver.

They turned in by a lodge, of which all the windows were gone, and the roof was singularly well ivied. A heap of sorry coops was stacked in the garden of it, the gates were hospitably open, and would never again be shut. An avenue ran up from this deserted lodge; some of the trees were down, sprouting from the stumps. Brakes of elder and bramble swallowed up the trunks of the remaining trees. The land on either side was a sort of tuffety pasture, ungrazed, halfway back to warren. "This is very picturesque," said Willoughby to the driver, who made no reply.

In a minute or two they made a turn, and our hero was confronted with the home of his forefathers. It was a fine house of the Cotswold stone, gabled, long, and low, but, to say much in little, it stood in need of repair. The turf on either hand came to an end, the avenue opened into a wide terrain of gravel which ran right up to the façade, the nettles hissed under the runningboards of the car. They drew up at the handsome porch, the steps of which were cushioned to the feet by stone crops and mosses.

On an obscure impulse, Willoughby had his bag put down and dismissed the driver. He turned and surveyed the door, which was of studded oak, magnificent, but it bore the look of not having been opened for a very considerable time. A rod and ring appeared to be some sort of bellpull. Willoughby pulled and let go; the iron obeyed inertly, unresponsively; it was like lifting and dropping a dead man's hand. Nevertheless, the sun was shining as brightly as ever. He rapped with his knuckles upon the oak. "That won't do," he said, perceiving its solidity. "Perhaps there's a back door somewhere."

He walked along the front of the house, looking in at the uncurtained windows. There was a huge room, with busts on pillars, leather furniture, bookshelves, and the floor was covered with apples laid out on newspapers. The next was completely empty, except for a pail standing in the middle of the floor. Half the ceiling was down. The next he could not see into—the blinds had fallen. Nothing could be more silent. There were the dead windows, the dead rooms, the nettles, the façade, the sun. A human being would have been quite terrible.

Luckily the end room was reassuring: It contained a trundle bed, a chamber pot, a chair covered with candle grease. Willoughby went around the corner, and came to the back of the house; a little flagged terrace, well bethistled, gave down into a walled couple of acres. He went along the whole length of this terrace, pushed his way through a shrubbery, came out on another walled garden, with cabbage plots, bristling espaliers falling down from the walls, a line stretched between two old standard trees; on the line, shirts, like blue flags on a desert reef. On this kitchen side a door was open. He looked in; there was an old woman with her elbows in a tub of lather. He tapped for her attention.

"I've come to see my uncle," said he. "Mr. Corbo."

"Why, sir, he's not here."

"Not here?" cried our hero in some dismay.

"Being the first, sir. Not but what he's out every day now. But—on the first, sir—*the Honorable George Corbo is never at home.*" The old woman made this announcement with a smile of innocent pride.

Willoughby found it mysterious. However, at last he discovered that his uncle was shooting pheasants, it being the first of October, in company with William Bucknell, keeper, who lived in the house with him, and that the old woman came once a fortnight to do the washing, and every afternoon in the season to put a bit of dinner on against his uncle's return. He got his bag round, and put it in the washhouse: the old woman told him he might find his uncle below Pinnigers. He rejoiced at this, and learned that Pinnigers was a hangar which he might discern unmistakably once he was beyond the garden wall.

He retraced his steps along the garden front, took a good look at it: "This is fine," said he. "What's even finer is the thought it may come to me someday, if I play my cards well, which I certainly must. I should have to live simply, to live in it at all; all the same, I think I could trim it up a bit, and very contentedly eat bread and cheese. My uncle seems to live strangely: still, strange people are easiest to approach. Besides, he is a Corbo, and may do as he likes, and so am I, and so may I. Fine!"

He plowed through the tangle in the garden; came out by a little wicket gate, saw the park land sweeping down, a few scraps of plow further on, coppices scattered about everywhere, the stone walls mostly lost in bramble and briar; a valley, and a long wood on the slope opposite: that must be Pinnigers Hangar. "What a lot of land!" he cried in delight.

He saw two men sitting under a tree in the bottom, eating. A black retriever, a liver-colored spaniel with a very small head, and a barrel-bodied white spaniel, set up a harmless bark. "This looks very easy and pleasant," said Willoughby to himself. "I wonder who those two men can be."

Both were dressed the same: big coats, huge pockets, breeches close about the knee, all of an old, smooth, hard-looking material, very much the color of cow dung, homemade stockings. One wore boots, the other anklets, that was all the difference. They both had long, pointed noses, haggard cheeks with a streaky red spot high up on the bone, tufts of hair on these spots, long thin moustaches, little keen eyes, overhanging brows.

"Good afternoon," said Willoughby. They looked at him with no interest whatsoever.

"What does he want?" said the man in anklets to his fellow.

"What do you want?" said that fellow to Willoughby.

"I want Mr. Corbo," replied our hero, frowning at the first speaker. "I was told he would be somewhere about here."

"Oh, aye he's about here," said the booted man.

"What d'ye want with him?" said he of the anklets.

"My dear sir," said Willoughby politely, "no doubt I shall be delighted to tell you when you have told me what the devil it has to do with you."

"Maybe my name is Corbo," replied the man with the anklets, whose coat Willoughby now perceived to be unquestionably the oldest in the world.

"You can't be my uncle," said he.

"No, by God I can't," said the other. "No tricks! I've not a nephew in the world, nor want one."

"Are you the Honorable George Corbo?" demanded our hero with some impatience. "If not, kindly take me to him at once."

"Maybe I am," replied the old fellow, with a convincing complacency.

"Then you have got a nephew," said Willoughby. "I'm him."

"No tricks!" cried his uncle with a frown.

"You're trespassing," said the other man suddenly.

"My name's Willoughby Corbo," cried our hero, thrusting out his hand. "And if you're my uncle: how d'ye do? My father's Lord Ollebeare."

"That's a lie," said the other very doggedly. "I met Ollebeare, February four or five years back—when we went to Crufts, Bucknell, and it wasn't on—he said no woman had got her hooks in him."

"True as that onion's on that bit o' paper, sir," replied his companion. "You're trespassing," he said to Willoughby.

"I know all about you, Bucknell," said Willoughby. "Heard about you from Walter Burfoot."

"Walter Burfoot?" cried the keeper, utterly undone.

"Walter Burfoot?" said his master. "What Walter Burfoot's that?"

"Why, that'll be Jim's older brother, sir," replied the keeper. "Jim Burfoot at plough t'other side of the road this very moment. I knew him well. Walter Burfoot went for groom to Mr. Ralph. Why, sir, that seemingly proves it."

"Proves it, my—!" cried his master in a rage. "A scoundrel!"

"No, sir. Walt warn't never that."

"Must have been, to go off with my ugly brother Ralph," cried the Honorable George Corbo.

"No indeed," said Willoughby determinedly. "One of the very best."

"That he was," chimed in Bucknell.

"He brought me up," said Willoughby.

"Told me a dozen things about you," he added to Bucknell.

"I warrant he did," cried that worthy with enthusiasm. "It's so, sir; he's your nephew, he's your nephew, he's a Corbo. Look at his great big nose. You must shake him by the hand, sir, that you must."

"Some by-blow of that dirty devil Ollebeare's," said the old man, not acting on his keeper's suggestion.

"Good god!" replied Willoughby, very haughty. "If you'll think more of me for that, it can be put straight. My father's offered to marry: I can be legitimate son *and* heir, all in a week. Then perhaps you'll receive me properly. 'Twas that very thing I came down to see you about, fearing it might upset your convenience. Never mind."

"It's blackmail," cried the old man. "That's what it is. Take it down. Note every word he says, Bucknell. Wait a minute, I must think about this."

"While you think," said Willoughby very coldly, "I'd be glad if you'd let me have a crust and an onion. I don't travel empty a hundred miles to see an uncle every day. I believe your brother Ralph would greet me better."

"Bread and cheese and an onion," said his uncle in derision. "For a smarty like you? No. You want champagne and chicken. You won't get that here."

"Smarty!" cried Willoughby. "What? Don't you know your own brother's clothes? Look," said he, plucking at his baggy breech. "Look," plucking at his belt. "Don't you know the shape of your own brother?"

"Say he may eat, sir," begged the keeper. "The young gentleman's fair flagging for want of a bite and a sup."

"No, I'm not," said Willoughby, but giving the basket a very particular look.

"Let him eat," said the old man, "and be damned to him: coming here to disturb me on the first day of all the year."

"Eat hearty, sir," said the keeper, offering Willoughby an open clasp knife.

"Eat quickly," said his uncle. "We're waiting to get on. I'll not move till I've settled you one way or another. Ollebeare's not married, you say?"

"Not yet," said Willoughby, with his mouth full. "Nor need not be if you don't wish it."

"What's the trick?" said the old man.

"No trick at all," said Willoughby. "He sent me down to make an arrangement with you. It's all very simple, but why let it spoil your day? It can wait till this evening. That's a fine gun. That's a more beautiful gun than they seem to make nowadays."

"Give the rascal some beer," said the old man. "That gun," said he to Willoughby, "is one of a pair, made forty-four years ago this very summer. For my twenty-first birthday I had that pair of guns. Your grandfather was a funny sort of man; all the same, he didn't believe in giving a young chap a second-rate pair of guns. Because it spoils his style. I was out with that pair of guns at a certain place not a hundred miles from here . . ." and he told a story which convinced his nephew he had to deal with one who dearly loved shooting, for otherwise he'd not have brought so much imagination to it.

Willoughby, while he listened, ate at speed. An unaccountable exhilaration possessed him, whether it was hearing old Burfoot's speech again and no longer needing to check his tongue from following it—anyway, that member felt as one who puts on old loose clothes and gave a frisk or two. He was relieved, too, to find his uncle so rustic. Most would have thought him a very unpromising card, but an uncle he could not tell from a keeper was comfortable to one who had dreaded some unapproachable Stumber or icy Ralph.

When his uncle had done praising the gun, he looked at Willoughby very hard, then, a certain itch getting the better of him: "You're here," said he. "You may be a scoundrel; in fact, I know you're one. All the same, the first day of the year, eh? Ha! Ha! I don't know we can have a fellow about, Bucknell, and never give him a shot."

"No, indeed," said the keeper, "not a nephew."

"Besides," pursued the old man, "he can try my other gun. I think it will interest you," says he to Willoughby, in the politest tone. "You'll find it such a gentle, *gentle* gun. Not like these banging short-barreled things."

"It would interest me very much to know how to load it," thought Willoughby.

A boy was hallooed up, and, after a good many cautions, sent to get this matchless weapon. "Meanwhile," said the old man, "we're done lunch—you eat well, I'll say that for you. Bucknell, the boys might work through the little spur, just to keep us busy till the gun comes. Lend him yours, Bucknell, till then."

"With pleasure," said the keeper, offering Willoughby a positive fowling piece.

"No, no," said he, "I can very well wait." The fact is, he suffered a little from the foolish vanity of his years, and was afraid to say he knew nothing of the business, lest these stern votaries should despise him. He wanted to see how it was done. That was foolish, for an indifferent performer is the object of toleration at best, and often of a hatred singularly keen, while the eager novice is a creature to be begotten into venery, stamped with one's own image, molded like the child in the womb, encouraged, his errors forgiven, his achievements exaggerated, his first right and left rejoiced over—it amounts to being loved.

So he was fool enough to hold his tongue. They moved off to a point in the bottom under an arm of the hangar: three or four hobbledehoys, carrying long sticks, got up from the other side of a clump of brambles, and took an upper path to the top of the wood. Old Corbo explained to his nephew the disadvantages of all those oversized shoots where more land was shot over, more guns lined up, more beaters employed, more birds killed. Willoughby agreed heartily. His uncle was not without a sense of proportion; he next exclaimed against that piddling form of the sport which some mean spirits had the impudence to conduct upon a smaller scale. Willoughby agreed, with all the sincerity in the world, that shooting should take place over 752 acres of hilly ground, the woods being parceled out into small copses and hangers, lying mostly south; the beaters should be few, the guns two or three, the bag a hundred birds in a proper day, a dozen to a walk around, and three dogs should be employed for the picking-up—a Clumber spaniel, a liver spaniel of what is called "the old-fashioned sort," and a curly-coated retriever, old and rather blind.

He deplored the vulgar grandiose; he mocked the nasty little piddling rough-shooter, who was pretty sure to feed for another man's birds. What a change of heart this was, for one who had shot only five acres hitherto, his gun a Daisy air rifle, his bag one cat in a lifetime, and that a runner, his only beater the butler at Kent Court, who had beaten the game out of the sportsman's backside.

What's more, our hero had for some time past indulged in humanitarian impulses of the highest spiritual level. His good Uncle Ralph had begotten in him a strong aversion to the rich in themselves; his experience of lackeys had prejudiced him against the effect of riches on other men. His ideas were still without form, and void, but over their chaos brooded the dove-like spirit of nineteenth-century liberalism. He believed the human race to be perfectible, and, by long consequence, disapproved of blood sports. He was the friend of the bottom dog, as all young men should be. Regard him, then, under the necessity of directing a load of 1⅛ oz. of No. 6 shot against the bottom dog, if a feathered biped clattering at forty yards above one's head can be so termed, and about to impel this load not only with the force of one ounce of black powder of the smokeless diamond variety, but also with the deadly hope of prowess. Alas, poor Willoughby! You shall soon point your gun, and hope. In every load there is one more pellet than can be counted: it is a long shot, but yet that pellet may prick the dove-like spirit of nineteenth-century liberalism. A pricked bird may flutter on seemingly unharmed, but after a time it dwindles and pines away.

His uncle was not one of those who insist on the greatest possible silence in their beaters, lest sudden cries should disturb the concentration of the guns. "I like to *know* I'm out shooting," said he. The beaters assisted him toward this realization by shouts of *Mark over* and *Cock forrard, hare coming down to you, sir, coming forrard, coming down to you;* the dogs lifted their noses and whined in eagerness; old Corbo, with exactly the same expression, also lifted his nose. Willoughby felt a tingling in all his nerves, which he was kind enough to ascribe to the beauty of the yellowing sweep of trees, the tuffety grass, the dogs like dogs in an old print—liver, white, and black.

The hare must have turned off; the woodcock, like a god in a legend, metamorphosed into mistle thrush ere it burst out from the promontory of trees; for a moment, the voices were hushed, the sticks tapped in the wood, there was a gathering silence, a pregnancy in the high, cliffy yellow. Well away to their left, a single cock flew out low and steady, the sun on his copper, his tail rippling behind like the tail of a dragon. But that was in another country.

"Come *on,*" said the keeper under his breath. "Damn my eyes!" The next moment a crackling cry sprang up like a ladder in the wood. From the top of it, a fine cock launched himself magnificently upon the blue. Bucknell, standing below, lifts up his gun, stops, looks at his master, it's the first day of all the year. The old fellow, as greedy as a schoolboy, gives a grunt, takes the long shot. The bird, so struck, and seen from the side, seems hardly to fall, but to swerve, stoop, nay, *dash* itself down: it strikes the turf like a thunderbolt.

"Thank'ee, Bill Bucknell," calls out the old boy, not loud, trying to pass off as a smile of thanks the smile of exultation that irradiates his weather-beaten chops. He cannot resist stealing a glance at Willoughby. Our hero receiving it: "Upon my word!" says he in equal delight. "I've not come a hundred miles for nothing."

Now the beaters are very near, the first real rise is flushed, a proper little bouquet, right between the guns. These, just less than cool, pick their first birds, but fire a little chancy with the left. Three are down, one of them so far from clean-killed he bounces up six feet into the air again, falls, flutters up again, and continues to do so for the space of a minute or more. The dogs eye him, so does Willoughby, but the guns take no notice whatever. Willoughby feels a considerable qualm; he'd like to go and wring the bird's neck. Two things prevent him; one is that he doesn't know how, the other that he fears to make a fool of himself, for which I do not blame him at all. Nineteenth-century liberalism labors his bosom, and it is only by way of anodyne, so far, that he applies his mind to this consideration: *"These things have been done for many hundred years, and by better men than I am: I had better know more before I say aught."*

It's only a little branch of the wood, there are two more rises, one of which goes astray; then that drive is over. The beaters stumble out through the brambles, the dogs get up. Bucknell sets them to quarter the ground after a couple of runners.

"This is a lovely sight!" cries Willoughby.

"You will not see three better dogs," says his uncle, "not for forty miles round, though they're old, too old—like their master, some would say—and poor old Carlo's as blind as a bat. See how he works them! 'Lo, 'lo, 'lo, 'lo, Prince! 'Lo, 'lo, 'lo, Floss! I los'! I los'! Go in, you devil, go in!"

"Now, master, you made me a promise not to go shouting on, when I'm a-trying to get these three damn dogs to work," calls out old Bucknell from the other side of the scrub.

"Damn you, Bucknell! Damn the fellow! Damn his eyes . . . impudence . . . my own dogs . . . talk like that in front of my nephew . . . ," mutters the old chap, to keep his face. At this moment the boy comes up, carrying the gun.

"Here we are. Just try that. Just try the handling on't. Try how it comes up. Like a living thing, eh?"

"Like a living thing," says Willoughby, making a poke with it, and wishing to god it had life enough to shoot of itself.

"That's a well-balanced gun," the old chap rattles on. "You don't feel the weight of it. Now, just you take a guess at the weight of that gun."

Willoughby gives himself up for lost, can't decide whether it weighs twenty pounds or forty, lifts it up again with a critical look in his eye, purses his lips; fortunately the old enthusiast can wait no longer. "What is it?" says he. "Six and a half pound, seven pound—what?"

"Feels no more than six and a half to *me*," says Willoughby, with the air of one abdicating reason in the presence of the supernatural.

"Seven pounds, seven ounces," says his uncle.

"Good God Almighty!" cries Willoughby.

"You may well say, Good God Almighty!" says his uncle, with a very affable nod.

They are now walking round to stand under the main part of the hangar. "If only my luck holds!" says Willoughby to himself.

What follows happened under Pinnigers Hanger, on Ollebeare, estate of the Honorable Corbo, near the Slaughters, at three o'clock on a fine afternoon, the first of October, 1922. They were lined up again, a cock came out just as before, straight over Bucknell's head, a bit higher if anything. That worthy fires, the bird's on the swerve, he misses both barrels. "Round to you, sir," he calls to Willoughby.

Poor Willoughby feels his heart going fit to burst, lifts his gun, and tries to *sight* the bird along it, using the wrong eye. He sees the bird at the end of his gun, makes up his mind to pull the trigger, an admirable resolution which he fairly soon puts into effect. By this time the bird is round on its swerve, coming t'other way. As he's pointing six feet to the left of where 'twas, and pulling late, he's just in time to catch it on the way back: the taut crossbow breaks, a dark star twinkles. Down it comes.

"*Got him!*" cries Willoughby, convulsed with joy, and runs up to where it lies, picks it up, to have a good look at it.

"What's up?" cries his uncle. "What's the fellow doing? Think he'd never brought down a bird in his life before!"

"No more I have," cries Willoughby in his delight. "No more I have. But, by God! I'll shoot many another, I hope."

His uncle looks at him this way and that; can't make him out at all.

"Young gennelman shows a good deal of promise, then," says the keeper. "Well done, young sir, I say! There's instinck there, sir, if ever I did see it in all my life—save once, sir, *save once.*"

"What are *you* talking about?" says old Corbo, still in two minds about it all.

"Sir, that shot . . . ," says Bucknell, very impressive. "That shot is like the first shot as ever you took, out along o' me and my dad, as like as that 'ere gun is like that 'ere gun—pair to't. Year of grace 1874," he adds.

"I remember it," says the old chap, "but that was a higher bird."

"Mebbe a leetle bit higher, sir," says the keeper, "but you'd a-bin a-rabbit-shooting many a time."

"I had that," says his master. "But he's been rabbit-shooting too."

"No I haven't," cuts in Willoughby.

"But I wasn't more than seventeen," says his uncle.

"That evens it then," says the keeper. "Bred in the bone! Nothing like it. Brings me back my younger days again. Just such another, as never I expected to see."

"You think he'll make a first-class shot, then?" says the old man.

"Bred in the bone," says Bucknell, avoiding the implication.

"I'll make some sort of a shot, anyway," says Willoughby. "For if ever I enjoyed myself in all my life, it was when I saw that blasted bird come down."

"Got the instinck!" cries Bucknell. "I *know* the instinck; told you Carlo had it, eight year come second week in February, when you was taken about drownden on un."

"Better get on," says George Corbo, with a long look at Willoughby. "Take his cartridges, Bucknell. Let him point an empty gun. Don't want to be shot by my own nephew, not on the first day of all the season."

Bucknell touches his hat, blows his whistle, the beaters come down through the wood.

"Is this right?" says Willoughby, stabbing the air. "Is this the way?"

"Don't you say too much, young sir," says the keeper, speaking low. "You come out with me an hour or two, sometime, and try at the rabbits."

9 WILLOUGHBY VISITS OLLEBEARE

Well, they went back to the house at the end of the day, and sat, keeper and all, in an enormous kitchenish room, not impressive, only rather like a taproom, eating a steak-and-kidney pudding the old woman had put by for them. The Honorable George, who bent down pretty close to his plate, found time to direct several piercing glances at Willoughby from under his shaggy eyebrows. Willoughby needed pull no special sort of face; he was happy, and his nature was, when he was happy, to show it. What's more—poor, untaught lad!—he was liable to sudden affections and had come by a singular liking for this old uncle of his.

"Why the devil," said he to himself, "was I ever taken in by those pompous fools I met at old Stumber's, whose shirtfront starch any grocer might put on? This chap, and my dad, are the only two positive gentlemen I've ever met: the others are less than men, their distinction lies in what they *fear* to do. These show their silly natures in every word and look, and their silly natures are noble. Damn it, they're fine!"

He was greatly struck by the relationship between his uncle and the keeper: what little they said was so easy and pleasant, it was clear there were never two better friends, and just as clear that one was master and t'other man. "And if I couldn't be one, I'd next soon be the other," thought Willoughby, *"that's the point of it.* However, I hope I shall be that one some day."

The impression it made on him was tremendous; it confirmed his unthought thoughts, as poetry does. "How *true* it all is!" he said, noting that in his uncle's face there was a good deal more than he had observed at first. He thought he saw traces of knowledge and disillusion there, their equation worked out to much the same simplicity as was native to Bucknell's honest jowl.

While they ate, the talk was all of the day's sport, mapped out by crusts and cruet-pots. Immediately afterwards Bucknell got on his stiff legs: "I'm stepping down to the Five Alls," said he tactfully.

"That's right, Bucknell," said the Hon. George.

"Well, now," said he to his nephew, when they were left alone, "I don't doubt it, you're Ollebeare's son all right. I'm glad to see you, though we live pretty simple here. How long were you thinking of staying?"

"I'd like to stay a bit," said Willoughby. "If I'd not be in your way."

"Have no fear of that," said the old man in a peculiar tone. "However, we'll talk about that later. Tell your story, boy."

Willoughby told about Kent Court, didn't say much, but said it pretty well: his uncle was much taken by it. "That's my sneaking brother Ralph all over," said he. "Now he was begotten wrong side of the blanket, that I'll swear: not our sort at all. Now, your grandfather, he was true sire to Ollebeare and me. You're the same breed: come and have a look at his likeness."

He took up the oil lamp, and led Willoughby into the better part of the house. Our hero glanced around: "How heavy the stone looks out at the back there," he said, "and how light it arches here!"

"That room we were in," said his uncle, "that was the dining hall of the old house, before they put all this front on, reign of George the First. Then it became the servants' hall. I use it now—one can live alone, and rough, under the rougher stone. Living as I do, in this part, that 'ud put me in mind of those old prints of Bedlam: you know, the light pillar, the fine arch, and underneath—altogether too faded a company."

"I know what you mean, sir," said Willoughby, very pleased to find his uncle had this side to him. "Out there, you and Bucknell eating a steak-and-kidney pudding together—it's somehow natural, right, the best possible thing: here it would be damned odd, and here oddness is madness. Yet, it's a pity the library should have apples all over the floor. Why don't you open the place and entertain people of your own standing?"

"My boy," answered his uncle, "better these civilized walls should look down on a couple of madmen than on a score of idiots.

Besides, I have no money, not for that sort of thing. Come in here," said he, opening a door. "I used to use this room to write letters in years ago, when still I wrote 'em. There's your grandpa."

Willoughby saw, over a fireplace, a gentleman who looked very much like a tame bear, tricked out in a high collar. He looked at it for awhile, felt his nose: "Yes," he said. His uncle made no move, only looked several times from the portrait to Willoughby and back. Our hero felt it was unnecessary for him to go on looking at the bear-like gentleman; he stole glances right and left. Over a bureau in the shallow bay beside the fireplace was another picture. This one, vilely painted, was of a girl of the uttermost beauty: I mean of that vivid flesh and that vivid spirit that gives one a new idea of the gods. The lamplight fell on it clearly enough. Willoughby was struck to the heart by this astonishing face. "Good god!" he cried.

"Come on," said his uncle.

"No," said Willoughby, who had not had the restraining influence of education. "May I look at this? I must. I've never seen anything like it in my life. Yet it's the sort of face one thinks one *has* seen."

"Oh, ah!" remarked his uncle.

"Who was she?" babbled our hero. "Did you know her well? I suppose she's an old woman now. Is she still beautiful? I thought that was all rot, in Browning, 'a face to lose youth for,' but it's so. I'll never fall in love again."

"Will 'ee come on," cried his uncle in the roughest tones. "You talk too much. Too much by half."

Willoughby heartily pitied the dried-up old codger, unkindled before such burning loveliness. However, he bethought him of his manners as they went through the door: "I'm sorry I kept you waiting, Uncle," said he. "I didn't mean to offend you, but I was so much struck."

"You don't offend me, boy," replied his uncle, "but come back to the dogs and the fire."

When they were seated again, Willoughby took up his tale, mentioned his job, described in more detail his meeting with his father. "Go on," said his uncle.

"Well, do you see," said Willoughby, "he wants to provide for me. We rather took to one another, you see? Let me get it clear. When he dies, this place and the title go to you; when you die, they go to Uncle Ralph."

"Ah, damn him! So they do," replied the Honorable George.

"Well, the obvious thing," said our hero, "would be for my father to marry my mother; then they'd come to me, and I suppose, I should at once have your handle. He'd have a sort of nurse for his old age, too."

"Well, if that's all right by law, why don't he marry her?" said the old chap.

"He's only known me a few days," said Willoughby. "He's known you all his life, do you see? He says it wouldn't be fair to put you out."

"Oh, ah!" said his uncle, with a peculiar glance. This glance recalled to Willoughby's notice the fact that he was lying, or, rather, since he had no objection to lying in the abstract, the fact that he was swindling this very concrete old man to whom he had taken a liking. However, one must live.

"Perhaps he isn't specially keen on marrying her," said he. "Anyway, he proposed an alternative."

"Go on," said his uncle.

"Oh, hell!" thought Willoughby. "Why do you leave it all to me?"

"He suggests," he continued, "that you, as heir to the estate, could consent to the breaking of the entail, so that he could leave me the land when he dies, with you to have a life's lease of it at the same figure, and have the title into the bargain. Thus you go on as you are for the rest of your life, and, when you die, Ralph gets only the title and I get the land."

His uncle pondered over this, looking into the fire. "That looks plain and straightforward, like all Ollebeare's schemes," said he. "If it's as square as it looks, it'll be the only one that ever was. Look 'ee, boy, what do you know about it?"

"What I've told you," said Willoughby, rather flat.

"I can understand you coming down to someone you've never seen," said his uncle, "with one of Ollebeare's notions to broach. All right. There's a lot of lawyer's details to be ferreted out, that's certain. I can put the ferret to 'em if need be. Myself, being no ferret, I stay above ground—why live simple, else? Likewise, it's no odds to me, the matter of the rent: if I didn't pay it, it would lay by. I've my own income, which I hardly spend, though it's small. Supposing your father dies before me, I should not care that" (with a snap of his fingers) "about the matter of a year or two's rent. On the other hand, supposing he marries, and all's square in law, you could put me out on his death: that would be the end of me. I could not live elsewhere but here."

"I should not do that," cried Willoughby, forgetful of his father's advice. "Don't think that, Uncle, for that I'd never do."

"Why not?" said his uncle, very suddenly.

Willoughby could not, without resorting to emotional terms, describe the impression made on him that afternoon and evening. He said, therefore: "I will not say why, but I'd not do it, nor will I have the possibility taken into reckoning."

"I believe you are a very decent sort of young chap," said his uncle. "I see no reason, boy, why I should not consent. You certainly brought that bird down very well. What's more, I believe you've something of our nature in you. God help you! Your father lives a wretched life, and people call me mad. Never mind, one can do well enough on this place. I'd rather you had it than that Ralph. It seems aboveboard: I'd not trust your father, but you've a straight eye, spoken me very fair. I'll trust you. Give me your word there's no trick, and the thing shall be done. Your word?" With this, the old chap looked very frankly at Willoughby. Willoughby thought of two hundred pounds a year, and of inheriting this stone house, the tangled garden, the wild fields, the yellowing woods. He thought of becoming such another, with certain modifications (such as the girl in the picture), as his uncle was.

"I see nothing wrong in it," he said. "I see much that is wrong, foolish, criminal, in throwing away a settled income, freedom, and the hope of coming into this place, and ending up like you. Oh, dear! I wish you had received me less kindly: I would then have given you my word. Curse it!" he cried in much stress. "I would not mind being a rogue, not a bit—I am not such a fool, Uncle— yet I am fool enough to jib at this, because you have said I am of your kind, and so I am. I'd do it to anyone else in the world. I wish you were my Uncle Ralph. But there it is—I'll not give you my word."

"Don't tell me you're not my nephew after all," cried the old man.

"Too much so," said Willoughby. "No, the fact is, my mother has long been dead. I shall never forgive myself for this. It was my poor old father's idea. He is to die, so he says, in six months or so, and he wanted to see me settled."

"Never forgive yourself?" said his uncle. "Why, there's no harm done."

"No, indeed?" remarked Willoughby. "No harm in throwing away this place? I shall never forgive myself, never."

"Oh, I thought you meant for joining in the trick," said his uncle.

Willoughby permitted himself the use of an impatient expression.

"You could not have forced my hand," said his uncle. "I believe your father's law is poppycock. We are governed by grocers, witness my fallows for one thing. All the same, I believe in no bill that could put me out by legitimizing a bastard twenty-one years after his birth. But, bill or no bill, I'd not have stood for Ollebeare's blackmail. However, you seemed to believe in it. Yet you gave up the poaching trick when it came to the pinch. Very well, my boy. You're my nephew when all's said and done. Your Aunt Clara was fond of you, you say?"

"So I was told," said Willoughby.

"And you were the death of her?"

"That's why Uncle Ralph so hated me," replied Willoughby.

"I'll get to know you, boy," said his uncle. "To me, you seem a rum un. If my thoughts should chance to turn that way—which I don't say they will—there's one thing your father overlooked— your Uncle Ralph must consent to break the entail."

"Well then, I'm done," cried Willoughby. "For he hates me like poison."

"He cares nothing for the place," said his uncle. "And I'd rather the devil had it than him. That could be managed. Look, boy, stay on. I'll get to know you. I make no promise, mind, but I'll get to know you."

"I should like to stay on," said Willoughby. "I've never been in a place I liked yet."

"So Ollebeare's to die, if he tells the truth," said the old chap. "I'm sorry to hear it, if it's true. If he's not lying, then, I shall be Lord Ollebeare, and that fat bitch, who looks down her nose at me, and her stockbroking husband, they'll—well, if it's not all lies, that is."

They sat on beside the great fireplace, glad to have done with discussion. Willoughby had his beer in a mug with Lord Nelson on it; his uncle had one with sportsmen and pointer on. The beer in those parts is the cleanest, the bitterest, the best in England. Willoughby was not at all unhappy; he believed life to be a fountain of such fine things as this—lose one, another will come along. His uncle smiled at him. William Bucknell returned, said there was a frost. His face had the dahlia glow of it: frost, wood-smoke, taste of bitter beer. It was soon time to make up a bed for the visitor. Nothing could be more pleasant than the way they all three said good night.

Or, if anything could be, it was Willoughby's waking next morning. He woke between blankets, on a hard bed, in a little hard whitewashed room, with a deep window. This window was full of blue, ambrosial blue, it was so rich and so strong. A pear branch, by being bathed in it, had become a mighty gold and breathed easy in the lower part of the window. Willoughby, washed in sleep, sprang up and looked out. Below him was the kitchen garden; beyond it, meadows and stubbles, and woods and copses standing very still. There was a sting of frost in the air, the shadows were amethyst with it, and in all the holy, jolly blue there was no speck of cloud.

From this height, Willoughby could see over the right-hand wall of the kitchen garden into a strip of old orchard, where, under a giant apple tree, there were a broken wooden table and a bench overturned into the frosty grass. Our hero indulged in the fancy that Slender and Shallow had sat there overnight, a little while ago. "I can take my mug of beer and join them," he said, for he was used to shadowy company.

He found plenty to please his fancy during the days that followed, for life in this large rough country had necessities and pleasures quite other than those of the parky lands around Reigate, where there seems to be no dung. A little indifferent farming continued on the estate; Willoughby rejoiced in finding a whole race of Burfoots, who allowed him to hinder them with the greatest good humor.

The Hon. George bore very well with our hero's prattle for a week; at the end of that time, Bucknell passed a hint that the governor had no great stomach for young company. "He don't like being drawed," said that worthy, "into book talk, though it properly tempts him. Dunno why, I'm sure; he likes enough the reading on 'em."

Willoughby expected nothing more of an uncle, and very philosophically withdrew, but no further than his little room, for it had a fireplace, and he understood that little rooms upstairs were the prerogative of nephews.

The old man had expected a completer retreat. However, this did well enough, except when Willoughby talked too much at mealtimes. As for our hero, he thought it, save in one respect, the best life in the world.

Its single small deficiency engrossed a good deal of his thoughts. Soon after Christmas he had reason to go into the front part of the house, and, his eye falling on the door of the little study, he was moved to go inside and have another look at the picture that had taken his fancy. It was as perfect as before. Willoughby was induced to revert to an odd habit of solitary childhood and address certain words to it. He was rewarded by the agreeable illusion of a response in the pictured face. He remained there half an hour, and returned next day. In a word, he fell half in love with this beauty of thirty years ago, and at last could no longer refrain from bursting forth with all manner of questions and speculations at the dinner table.

The Hon. George was a little morose that evening. Next morning, Willoughby was surprised to see him appear in a town rig of some seniority.

"I shall be away a day or two," said he. "Keep the boy in order, Bucknell. And Bucknell. . . ."

"Yes, sir?" said the keeper.

"Hold your tongue."

Two or three days later, the old man returned, and looked and sniffed about him as if he had been away a year.

"I've done your business," said he to Willoughby.

"What business, Uncle?" asked our hero.

"That," replied his uncle, who was a little addicted to the rustic riddling habit, "that which to think of it makes you a rogue, and not to think of it makes you a fool. Now do you know what I mean?"

"I *half* think," replied Willoughby, "that you must mean something to do with my father's little arrangement."

"True enough," returned the other. "I've seen your poor old father—God! who'd think we'd been boys together here, no longer ago, it seems to me, than yesterday? He's struck hard, and won't last much longer. You must go to see him, boy; he's in a bad way. They've got him in a doctor's home: I don't know who pays the piper. Three months they give him, cooped up there on slops and soda water. He begged and prayed of me to get him out: 'One good meal,' said he, 'would cure me of all my trouble.' True enough, so 'twould. And he frets so, I nearly gave way to him. Ah, well!

"Well, I saw the other fellow. We'll say nothing about that. He's agreed; your father's made a will; 'tis all done. When he's gone, my bank will go on every week as before; you arrange it with his. Till then, I'm giving you something to go on with, so you may go at once, and see if you can keep him from fretting over being cooped up so and fed on slops."

"Why," said Willoughby, "perhaps I should have gone before. The truth is, I hardly knew how, for I've only a few shillings, and hardly liked to ask you for any. I hope I've not been a nuisance to you. I've never liked being anywhere so much before, but sometimes I've been afraid I've offended you."

"No, no, my boy," said his uncle. "You're young for me, that's all. Let me hear from you. I'll send word when I'd like you to come for a couple of days."

Willoughby felt that so small an invitation was almost invisible. Still, he knew uncles were strange beings, and, though he was sorry to leave Ollebeare, he was extremely glad to be going to London, which he thought might prove a very pleasant place to a gentleman of two hundred a year.

STORIES

Bottle party

Franklin Fletcher dreamed of luxury in the form of tiger skins and beautiful women. He was prepared, at a pinch, to forgo the tiger skins. Unfortunately, the beautiful women seemed equally rare and inaccessible. At his office and at his boardinghouse, the girls were mere mice, or cattish, or kittenish, or had insufficiently read the advertisements. He met no others. At thirty-five he gave up, and decided he must console himself with a hobby, which is a very miserable second best.

He prowled about in odd corners of the town, looking in at the windows of antique dealers and junk shops, wondering what on earth he might collect. He came upon a poor shop, in a poor alley, in whose dusty window stood a single object; it was a full-rigged ship in a bottle. Feeling rather like that himself, he decided to go in and ask the price.

The shop was small and bare. Some shabby racks were ranged about the walls and these racks bore a large number of bottles, of every shape and size, containing a variety of objects which were interesting only because they were in bottles. While Franklin still looked about, a little door opened, and out shuffled the proprietor, a wizened old man in a smoking cap, who seemed mildly surprised and mildly pleased to have a customer.

He showed Franklin bouquets, and birds of paradise, and the Battle of Gettysburg, and miniature Japanese gardens, and even a shrunken human head, all stoppered up in bottles. "And what," said Frank, "are those, down there on the bottom shelf?"

"They are not much to look at," said the old man. "A lot of people think they are all nonsense. Personally, I like them."

He lugged out a few specimens from their dusty obscurity. One seemed to have nothing but a little dried-up fly in it; others contained what might have been horsehairs or straws, or mere wisps of heaven knows what; some appeared to be filled with gray or opalescent smoke. "They are," said the old man, "various sorts of genii, jinns, sibyls, demons, and such things. Some of them, I believe, are much harder, even than a full-rigged ship, to get into a bottle."

"Oh, but come! This is New York," said Frank.

"All the more reason," said the old man, "to expect the most extraordinary jinns in bottles. I'll show you. Wait a moment. The stopper is a little stiff."

"You mean there's one in there?" said Frank. "And you're going to let it out?"

"Why not?" replied the old man, desisting in his efforts, and holding the bottle up to the light. "This one. . . . Good heavens! *Why not,* indeed? My eyes are getting weak. I very nearly undid the wrong bottle. A very ugly customer, that one! Dear me! It's just as well I didn't get that stopper undone. I'd better put him right back in the rack. I must remember he's in the lower right-hand corner. I'll stick a label on him one of these days. Here's something more harmless."

"What's in that?" said Frank.

"Supposed to be the most beautiful girl in the world," said the old man. "All right, if you like that sort of thing. Myself, I've never troubled to undo her. I'll find something more interesting."

"Well, from a scientific point of view," said Frank, "I . . . ."

"Science isn't everything," said the old man. "Look at this." He held up one which contained a tiny, mummified, insect-looking object, just visible through the grime. "Put your ear to it," he said.

Frank did so. He heard, in a sort of whistling nothing of a voice, the words, "Louisiana Lad, Saratoga, four-fifteen. Louisiana Lad, Saratoga, four-fifteen," repeated over and over again.

"What on earth is that?" said he.

"That," said the old man, "is the original Cumaean Sibyl. Very interesting. She's taken up racing."

"Very interesting," said Frank. "All the same, I'd just like to see that other. I adore beauty."

"A bit of an artist, eh?" said the old man. "Believe me, what you really want is a good, all-round, serviceable type. Here's one, for example. I recommend this fellow from personal experience. He's practical. He can fix you anything."

"Well, if that's so," said Frank, "why haven't you got a palace, tiger skins, and all that?"

"I had all that," said the old man. "And he fixed it. Yes, this was my first bottle. All the rest came from him. First of all, I had a palace, pictures, marbles, slaves. And, as you say, tiger skins. I had him put Cleopatra on one of them."

"What was she like?" cried Frank.

"All right," said the old man, "if you like that sort of thing. I got bored with it. I thought to myself, 'What I'd like, really, is a little shop, with all sorts of things in bottles.' So I had him fix it. He got me the sibyl. He got me the ferocious fellow there. In fact, he got me all of them."

"And now he's in there?" said Frank.

"Yes. He's in there," said the old man. "Listen to him."

Frank put his ear to the bottle. He heard, uttered in the most plaintive tones, "Let me out. Do let me out. Please let me out. I'll do anything. Let me out. I'm harmless. Please let me out. Just for a little while. Do let me out. I'll do anything. Please. . . ."

Frank looked at the old man. "He's there, all right," he said "He's there."

"Of course, he's there," said the old man. "I wouldn't sell you an empty bottle. What do you take me for? In fact, I wouldn't sell this one at all, for sentimental reasons, only I've had the shop a good many years now, and you're my first customer."

Frank put his ear to the bottle again. "Let me out. Let me out. Oh, please let me out. I'll. . . ."

"My god!" said Frank uneasily. "Does he go on like that *all* the time?"

"Very probably," said the old man. "I can't say I listen. I prefer the radio."

"It seems rather tough on him," said Frank sympathetically.

"Maybe," said the old man. "They don't seem to like bottles. Personally, I do. They fascinate me. For example, I. . . ."

"Tell me," said Frank. "Is he really harmless?"

"Oh, yes," said the old man. "Bless you, yes. Some say they're tricky—Eastern blood and all that—I never found him so. I used to let him out; he'd do his stuff, then back he'd go again. I must say, he's very efficient."

"He could get me anything?"

"Absolutely anything."

"And how much do you want for him?" said Frank.

"Oh, I don't know," said the old man. "Ten million dollars, perhaps."

"I say! I haven't got that. Still, if he's as good as you say, maybe I could work it off on the hire-purchase system."

"Don't worry. We'll say five dollars, instead. I've got all I want, really. Shall I wrap him up for you?"

Frank paid over his five dollars and hurried home with the precious bottle, terrified of breaking it. As soon as he was in his room, he pulled out the stopper. Out flowed a prodigious quantity of greasy smoke, which immediately solidified into the figure of a gross and fleshy Oriental, six feet six in height, with rolls of fat, a hook nose, a wicked white to his eye, vast double chins, altogether like a film producer, only larger. Frank, striving desperately for something to say, ordered shashlik, kebabs, and Turkish delight. These were immediately forthcoming.

Frank, having recovered his balance, noted that these modest offerings were of surpassing quality and set upon dishes of solid gold, superbly engraved, and polished to a dazzling brightness. It is by little details of this description that one may recognize a really first-rate servant. Frank was delighted, but restrained his enthusiasm. "Gold plates," said he, "are all very well. Let us, however, get down to brass tacks. I should like a palace."

"To hear," said his dusky henchman, "is to obey."

"It should," said Frank, "be of suitable size, suitably situated, suitably furnished, suitable pictures, suitable marbles, hangings, and all that. I should like there to be a large number of tiger skins. I am very fond of tiger skins."

"They shall be there," said his slave.

"I am," said Frank, "a bit of an artist, as your late owner remarked. My art, so to speak, demands the presence, upon these tiger skins, of a number of young women, some blonde, some brunette, some *petites*, some Junoesque, some languorous, some vivacious, all beautiful, and they need not be overdressed. I hate overdressing. It is vulgar. Have you got that?"

"I have," said the jinn.

"Then," said Frank, "let *me* have it."

"Condescend only," said his servant, "to close your eyes for the space of a single minute, and opening them you shall find yourself surrounded by the agreeable objects you have described."

"O.K.," said Frank. "But no tricks, mind!"

He closed his eyes as requested. A low, musical, humming, whooshing sound rose and fell about him. At the end of the minute, he looked around. There were the arches, pillars, marbles, hangings, etc., of the most exquisite palace imaginable, and wherever he looked he saw a tiger skin, and on every tiger skin there reclined a young woman of surpassing beauty, who was certainly not vulgarly overdressed.

Our good Frank was, to put it mildly, in ecstasy. He darted to and fro like a honeybee in a florist's shop. He was received everywhere with smiles sweet beyond description, and with glances of an open or a veiled responsiveness. Here were blushes and lowered lids. Here was the flaming face of ardor. Here was a shoulder turned, but by no means a cold shoulder. Here were open arms, and such arms! Here was love dissembled, but vainly dissembled. Here was love triumphant. "I must say," said Frank at a later hour, "I have spent a really delightful afternoon. I have enjoyed it thoroughly."

"Then may I crave," said the jinn, who was at that moment serving him his supper, "may I crave the boon of being allowed to act as your butler, and as general minister to your pleasures, instead of being returned to that abominable bottle?"

"I don't see why not," said Frank. "It certainly seems rather tough that, after having fixed all this up, you should be crammed back into the bottle again. Very well, act as my butler, but understand, whatever the convention may be, I wish you never to enter a room without knocking. And above all—no tricks."

The jinn, with a soapy smile of gratitude, withdrew, and Frank shortly retired to his harem, where he passed the evening as pleasantly as he had passed the afternoon.

Some weeks went by, entirely filled with these agreeable pastimes, till Frank, in obedience to a law which not even the most efficient of jinns can set aside, found himself growing a little overparticular, a little blasé, a little inclined to criticize and find fault.

"These," said he to his jinn, "are very pretty young creatures, if you like that sort of thing, but I imagine they can hardly be first-rate, or I should feel more interest in them. I am, after all, a connoisseur; nothing can please me but the very best. Take them away. Roll up all the tiger skins but one."

"It shall be done," said the jinn. "Behold, it is accomplished."

"And on that remaining tiger skin," said Frank, "put me Cleopatra herself."

The next moment, Cleopatra was there, looking, it must be admitted, absolutely superb. "Hullo!" she said. "Here I am, on a tiger skin again!"

"*Again?*" cried Frank, suddenly reminded of the old man in the shop. "Here! Take her back. Bring me Helen of Troy."

Next moment, Helen of Troy was there. "Hullo!" she said. "Here I am, on a tiger skin again!"

"*Again?*" cried Frank. "Damn that old man! Take her away. Bring me Queen Guinevere."

Guinevere said exactly the same thing; so did Madame de Pompadour, Lady Hamilton, and every other famous beauty that Frank could think of. "No wonder," said he, "that old man was such an extremely wizened old man! The old fiend! The old devil! He has properly taken the gilt off all the gingerbread. Call me jealous if you like; I will not play second fiddle to that ugly old rascal. Where shall I find a perfect creature, worthy of the embraces of such a connoisseur as I am?"

"If you are deigning to address that question to me," said the jinn, "let me remind you that there was, in that shop, a little bottle which my late master had never unstoppered, because I supplied him with it after he had lost interest in matters of this sort. Nevertheless, it has the reputation of containing the most beautiful girl in the whole world."

"You are right," cried Frank. "Get me that bottle without delay."

In a few seconds, the bottle lay before him. "You may have the afternoon off," said Frank to the jinn.

"Thank you," said the jinn. "I will go and see my family in Arabia. I have not seen them for a long time." With that, he bowed and withdrew. Frank turned his attention to the bottle, which he was not long in unstoppering.

Out came the most beautiful girl you can possibly imagine. Cleopatra and all that lot were hags and frumps compared with her. "Where am I?" said she. "What is this beautiful place? What am I doing on a tiger skin? Who is this handsome young prince?"

"It's me!" cried Frank, in a rapture. "It's me!"

The afternoon passed like a moment in paradise. Before Frank knew it, the jinn was back, ready to serve up supper. Frank must sup with his charmer, for this time it was love, the real thing. The jinn, entering with the viands, rolled up his wicked eyes at the sight of so much beauty.

It happened that Frank, all love and restlessness, darted out into the garden between two mouthfuls, to pluck his beloved a rose. The jinn, on the pretense of serving her wine, edged up very closely. "I don't know if you remember me," said he in a whisper. "I used to be in the next bottle to you. I have often admired you through the glass."

"Oh, yes," said she. "I remember you quite well."

At that moment Frank returned. The jinn could say no more, but he stood about the room, inflating his monstrous chest and showing off his plump and dusky muscles. "You need not be afraid of him," said Frank. "He is only a jinn. Pay no attention to him. Tell me if you really love me."

"Of course I do," said she.

"Well, say so," said he. "Why don't you say so?"

"I have said so," said she. "Of course I do. Isn't that saying so?"

This vague, evasive reply dimmed all Frank's happiness, as if a cloud had come over the sun. Doubt sprang up in his mind and entirely ruined moments of exquisite bliss.

"What are you thinking of?" he would say.

"I don't know," she would reply.

"Well, you ought to know," he would say, and then a quarrel would begin.

Once or twice he even ordered her back into her bottle. She obeyed with a malicious and secretive smile.

"Why should she give that sort of smile?" said Frank to the jinn, to whom he confided his distress.

"I cannot tell," replied the jinn. "Unless she has a lover concealed in there."

"Is it possible?" cried Frank in consternation.

"It is surprising," said the jinn, "how much room there is in one of these bottles."

"Come out!" cried Frank. "Come out at once!"

His charmer obediently emerged. "Is there anyone else in that bottle?" cried Frank.

"How could there be?" she asked, with a look of rather overdone innocence.

"Give me a straight answer," said he. "Answer me yes or no."

"Yes or no," she replied maddeningly.

"You double-talking, two-timing little bitch!" cried Frank. "I'll go in and find out for myself. If I find anybody, god help him and you!"

With that, and with an intense effort of the will, he flowed himself into the bottle. He looked all around: There was no one. Suddenly, he heard a sound above him. He looked up, and there was the stopper being thrust in.

"What are you doing?" cried he.

"We are putting in the stopper," said the jinn.

Frank cursed, begged, prayed, and implored. "Let me out!" he cried. "Let me out. Please let me out. I'll do anything. Let me out, do."

The jinn, however, had other matters to attend to. Frank had the infinite mortification of beholding these other matters through the glassy walls of his prison. Next day, he was picked up, whisked through the air, and deposited in the dirty little shop, among the other bottles, from which this one had never been missed.

There he remained for an interminable period, covered all over with dust and frantic with rage at the thought of what was going on in his exquisite palace, between his jinn and his faithless charmer. In the end, some sailors happened to drift into the shop, and, hearing that this bottle contained the most beautiful girl in the world, they bought it up by general subscription of the fo'c'sle. When they unstoppered him at sea and found it was only poor Frank, their disappointment knew no bounds, and they used him with the utmost barbarity.

Evening Primrose

In a pad of Highlife Bond, bought by
Miss Sadie Brodribb at Bracey's for 25¢

MARCH 21   Today I made my decision. I would turn my back for good and all upon the *bourgeois* world that hates a poet. I would leave, get out, break away—

And I have done it. I am free! Free as the mote that dances in the sunbeam! Free as a housefly crossing first-class in the largest of luxury liners! Free as my verse! Free as the food I shall eat, the paper I write upon, the lamb's-wool-lined softly slithering slippers I shall wear.

This morning I had not so much as carfare. Now I am here, on velvet. You are itching to learn of this haven; you would like to organize trips here, spoil it, send your relations-in-law, perhaps even come yourself. After all, this journal will hardly fall into your hands till I am dead. I'll tell you.

I am at Bracey's Giant Emporium, as happy as a mouse in the middle of an immense cheese, and the world shall know me no more.

Merrily, merrily shall I live now, secure behind a towering pile of carpets, in a corner nook which I propose to line with eider-downs, angora vestments, and the Cleopatraean tops in pillows. I shall be cozy.

I nipped into this sanctuary late this afternoon and soon heard the dying footfalls of closing time. From now on, my only effort will be to dodge the night watchman. Poets can dodge.

I have already made the first mouse-like exploration. I tiptoed as far as the stationery department, and, timid, darted back with only these writing materials, the poet's first need. Now I shall lay them aside, and seek other necessities: food, wine, the soft furniture of my couch, and a natty smoking jacket. This place stimulates me. I shall write here.

DAWN, NEXT DAY   I suppose no one in the world was ever more astonished and overwhelmed than I have been tonight. It is unbe-lievable. Yet I believe it. How interesting life is when things get like that!

I crept out, as I said I would, and found the great shop in min-gled light and gloom. The central well was half illuminated; the circling galleries towered in a pansy Piranesi of toppling light and shade. The spidery stairways and flying bridges had passed from purpose into fantasy. Silks and velvets glimmered like ghosts, a hundred panty-clad models offered simpers and embraces to the desert air. Rings, clips, and bracelets glittered frostily in a desolate absence of Honey and Daddy.

Creeping along the transverse aisles, which were in deeper dark-ness, I felt like a wandering thought in the dreaming brain of a chorus girl down on her luck. Only, of course, their brains are not so big as Bracey's Giant Emporium. And there was no man there.

None, that is, except the night watchman. I had forgotten him. As I crossed an open space on the mezzanine floor, hugging the lee of a display of sultry shawls, I became aware of a regular thudding, which might almost have been that of my own heart. Suddenly it burst upon me that it came from outside. It was footsteps, and they were only a few paces away. Quick as a flash I seized a flamboyant mantilla, whirled it about me and stood with one arm outflung, like a Carmen petrified in a gesture of disdain.

I was successful. He passed me, jingling his little machine on its chain, humming his little tune, his eyes sealed with refractions of the blaring day. "Go, worldling!" I whispered, and permitted myself a soundless laugh.

It froze on my lips. My heart faltered. A new fear seized me.

I was afraid to move. I was afraid to look around. I felt I was being watched, by something that could see right through me. This was a very different feeling from the ordinary emergency caused by the very ordinary night watchman. My conscious impulse was the obvious one: to glance behind me. But my eyes knew better. I remained absolutely petrified, staring straight ahead.

My eyes were trying to tell me something that my brain refused to believe. They made their point. I was looking straight into another pair of eyes, human eyes, but large, flat, luminous. I have seen such eyes among the nocturnal creatures which creep out under the artificial blue moonlight in the zoo.

Their owner was only a dozen feet away from me. The watchman had passed between us, nearer him than me. Yet he had not seen him. I must have been looking straight at him for several minutes at a stretch. I had not seen him, either.

He was half reclining against a low dais where, on the floor of russet leaves, and flanked by billows of glowing homespun, the fresh-faced waxen girls modeled spectator sports suits in herring-bones, checks, and plaids. He leaned against the skirt of one of these Dianas; its folds concealed perhaps his ear, his shoulder, and a little of his right side. He, himself, was clad in dim but large-patterned Shetland tweeds of the latest cut, suede shoes, a shirt of a rather broad *motif* in olive, pink, and gray. He was as pale as a creature found under a stone. His long thin arms ended in hands that hung floatingly, more like trailing, transparent fins, or wisps of chiffon, than ordinary hands.

He spoke. His voice was not a voice; it was a mere whistling under the tongue. "Not bad, for a beginner!"

I grasped that he was complimenting me, rather satirically, on my own, more amateurish, feat of camouflage. I stuttered. I said, "I'm sorry. I didn't know anyone else lived here." I noticed, even as I spoke, that I was imitating his own whistling sibilant utterance.

"Oh, yes," he said. "*We* live here. It's delightful."

"We?"

"All of us. Look!"

We were near the edge of the first gallery. He swept his long hand around, indicating the whole well of the shop. I looked. I saw nothing. I could hear nothing, except the watchman's thudding step receding infinitely far along some basement aisle.

"Don't you see?"

You know the sensation one has, peering into the half-light of a vivarium? One sees bark, pebbles, a few leaves, nothing more. And then, suddenly, a stone breathes—it is a toad; there is a chameleon, another, a coiled adder, a mantis among the leaves. The whole case seems crepitant with life. Perhaps the whole world is. One glances at one's sleeve, one's feet.

So it was with the shop. I looked, and it was empty. I looked, and there was an old lady, clambering out from behind the monstrous clock. There were three girls, elderly *ingénues*, incredibly emaciated, simpering at the entrance of the perfumery. Their hair was a fine floss, pale as gossamer. Equally brittle and colorless was a man with the appearance of a colonel of southern extraction, who stood regarding me while he caressed mustachios that would have done credit to a crystal shrimp. A chintzy woman, possibly of literary tastes, swam forward from the curtains and drapes.

They came thick about me, fluttering, whistling, like a waving of gauze in the wind. Their eyes were wide and flatly bright. I saw there was no color to the iris.

"How raw he looks!"

"A detective! Send for the Dark Men!"

"I'm not a detective. I am a poet. I have renounced the world."

"He is a poet. He has come over to us. Mr. Roscoe found him."

"He admires us."

"He must meet Mrs. Vanderpant."

I was taken to meet Mrs. Vanderpant. She proved to be the Grand Old Lady of the store, almost entirely transparent.

"So you are a poet, Mr. Snell? You will find inspiration here. I am quite the oldest inhabitant. Three mergers and a complete rebuilding, but they didn't get rid of me!"

"Tell how you went out by daylight, dear Mrs. Vanderpant, and nearly got bought for 'Whistler's Mother.' "

"That was in prewar days. I was more robust then. But at the cash desk they suddenly remembered there was no frame. And when they came back to look at me—"

"—She was gone."

Their laughter was like the stridulation of the ghosts of grasshoppers.

"Where is Ella? Where is my broth?"

"She is bringing it, Mrs. Vanderpant. It will come."

"Tiresome little creature! She is our foundling, Mr. Snell. She is not quite our sort."

"Is that so, Mrs. Vanderpant? Dear, dear!"

"I lived alone here, Mr. Snell, for many years. I took refuge here in the terrible times in the 'eighties. I was a young girl then, a beauty, people were kind enough to say, but poor Papa lost his money. Bracey's meant a lot to a young girl, in the New York of those days, Mr. Snell. It seemed to me terrible that I should not be able to come here in the ordinary way. So I came here for good. I was quite alarmed when others began to come in, after the crash of 1907. But it was the dear Judge, the Colonel, Mrs. Bilbee. . . ."

I bowed. I was being introduced.

"Mrs. Bilbee writes plays. *And* of a very old Philadelphia family. You will find us quite *nice* here, Mr. Snell."

"I feel it a great privilege, Mrs. Vanderpant."

"And, of course, all our dear *young* people came in '29. *Their* poor papas jumped from skyscrapers."

I did a great deal of bowing and whistling. The introductions took a long time. Who would have thought so many people lived in Bracey's?

"And here at last is Ella with my broth."

It was then I noticed that the young people were not so young, after all, in spite of their smiles, their little ways, their *ingénue* dress. Ella was in her teens. Clad only in something from the shop-soiled counter, she nevertheless had the appearance of a living flower in a French cemetery, or a mermaid among polyps.

"Come, you stupid thing!"

"Mrs. Vanderpant is waiting."

Her pallor was not like theirs; nor like the pallor of something that glistens or scuttles when you turn over a stone. Hers was that of a pearl.

Ella! Pearl of this remotest, most fantastic cave! Little mermaid, brushed over, pressed down by objects of a deadlier white—tentacles—! I can write no more.

MARCH 28   Well, I am rapidly becoming used to my new and

half-lit world, to my strange company. I am learning the intricate laws of silence and camouflage which dominate the apparently casual strollings and gatherings of the midnight clan. How they detest the night watchman, whose existence imposes these laws on their idle festivals!

"Odious, vulgar creature! He reeks of the coarse sun!"

Actually, he is quite a personable young man, very young for a night watchman, so young that I think he must have been wounded in the war. But they would like to tear him to pieces.

They are very pleasant to me, though. They are pleased that a poet should have come among them. Yet I cannot like them entirely. My blood is a little chilled by the uncanny ease with which even the old ladies can clamber spider-like from balcony to balcony. Or is it because they are unkind to Ella?

Yesterday we had a bridge party. Tonight, Mrs. Bilbee's little play, *Love in Shadowland*, is going to be presented. Would you believe it?—another colony, from Wanamaker's, is coming over *en masse* to attend. Apparently people live in all the great stores. This visit is considered a great honor, for there is an intense snobbery in these creatures. They speak with horror of a social outcast who left a high-class Madison Avenue establishment, and now leads a wallowing, beachcomberish life in a delicatessen. And they relate with tragic emotion the story of the man in Altman's who conceived such a passion for a model plaid dressing jacket that he emerged and wrested it from the hands of a purchaser. It seems that all the Altman colony, dreading an investigation, were forced to remove beyond the social pale, into a five-and-dime. Well, I must get ready to attend the play.

APRIL 14   I have found an opportunity to speak to Ella. I dared not before; here one has a sense always of pale eyes secretly watching. But last night, at the play, I developed a fit of hiccups. I was somewhat sternly told to go and secrete myself in the basement, among the garbage cans, where the watchman never comes.

There, in the rat-haunted darkness, I heard a stifled sob. "What's that? Is it you? Is it Ella? What ails you, child? Why do you cry?"

"They wouldn't even let me see the play."

"Is that all? Let me console you."

"I am so unhappy."

She told her tragic little story. What do you think? When she was a child, a little tiny child of only six, she strayed away and fell asleep behind a counter, while her mother tried on a new hat. When she woke, the store was in darkness.

"And I cried, and they all came around, and took hold of me. 'She will tell, if we let her go,' they said. Some said, 'Call in the Dark Men.' 'Let her stay here,' said Mrs. Vanderpant. 'She will make me a nice little maid.' "

"Who are these Dark Men, Ella? They spoke of them when I came here."

"Don't you know? Oh, it's horrible! It's horrible!"

"Tell me, Ella. Let us share it."

She trembled. "You know the morticians, 'Journey's End,' who go to houses when people die?"

"Yes, Ella."

"Well, in that shop, just like here, and at Gimbels, and at Bloomingdale's, there are people living, people like these."

"How disgusting! But what can they live upon, Ella, in a funeral home?"

"Don't ask me! Dead people are sent there, to be embalmed. Oh, they are terrible creatures! Even the people here are terrified of them. But if anyone dies, or if some poor burglar breaks in, and sees these people, and might tell—"

"Yes? Go on."

"Then they send for the others, the Dark Men."

"Good heavens!"

"Yes, and they put the body in Surgical Supplies—or the burglar, all tied up, if it's a burglar—and they send for these others, and then they all hide, and in they come, the others—Oh! They're like pieces of blackness. I saw them once. It was terrible."

"And then?"

"They go in, to where the dead person is, or the poor burglar. And they have wax there—and all sorts of things. And when they're gone there's just one of these wax models left, on the table. And then our people put a dress on it, or a bathing suit, and they mix it up with all the others, and nobody ever knows."

"But aren't they heavier than the others, these wax models? You would think they'd be heavier."

"No. They're not heavier. I think there's a lot of them—gone."

"Oh, dear! So they were going to do that to you, when you were a little child?"

"Yes, only Mrs. Vanderpant said I was to be her maid."

"I don't like these people, Ella."

"Nor do I. I wish I could see a bird."

"Why don't you go into the pet shop?"

"It wouldn't be the same. I want to see it on a twig, with leaves."

"Ella, let us meet often. Let us creep away down here and meet. I will tell you about birds, and twigs and leaves."

MAY 1 For the last few nights the store has been feverish with the shivering whisper of a huge crush at Bloomingdale's. Tonight was the night.

"Not changed yet? We leave on the stroke of two." Roscoe has appointed himself, or been appointed, my guide or my guard.

"Roscoe, I am still a greenhorn. I dread the streets."

"Nonsense! There's nothing to it. We slip out by two's and three's, stand on the sidewalk, pick up a taxi. Were you never out late in the old days? If so, you must have seen us many a time."

"Good heavens, I believe I have! And often wondered where you came from. And it was from here! But, Roscoe, my brow is burning. I find it hard to breathe. I fear a cold."

"In that case you must certainly remain behind. Our whole party would be disgraced in the unfortunate event of a sneeze."

I had relied on their rigid etiquette, so largely based on fear of discovery, and I was right. Soon they were gone, drifting out like leaves aslant on the wind. At once I dressed in flannel slacks, canvas shoes, and a tasteful sport shirt, all new in stock today. I found a quiet spot, safely off the track beaten by the night watchman. There, in a model's lifted hand, I set a wide fern frond culled from the florist's shop, and at once had a young, spring tree. The carpet was sandy, sandy as a lakeside beach. A snowy napkin; two cakes, each with a cherry on it; I had only to imagine the lake and to find Ella.

"Why, Charles, what's this?"

"I'm a poet, Ella, and when a poet meets a girl like you he thinks of a day in the country. Do you see this tree? Let's call it *our* tree. There's the lake—the prettiest lake imaginable. Here is grass, and there are flowers. There are birds, too, Ella. You told me you like birds."

"Oh, Charles, you're so sweet. I feel I hear them singing."

"And here's our lunch. But before we eat, go behind the rock there, and see what you find."

I heard her cry out in delight when she saw the summer dress I had put there for her. When she came back the spring day smiled to see her, and the lake shone brighter than before. "Ella, let us have lunch. Let us have fun. Let us have a swim. I can just imagine you in one of those new bathing suits."

"Let's just sit here, Charles, and talk."

So we sat and talked, and the time was gone like a dream. We might have stayed there, forgetful of everything, had it not been for the spider.

"Charles, what are you doing?"

"Nothing, my dear. Just a naughty little spider, crawling over your knee. Purely imaginary, of course, but that sort are sometimes the worst. I had to try to catch him."

"Don't, Charles! It's late. It's terribly late. They'll be back any minute. I'd better go home."

I took her home to the kitchenware on the subground floor, and kissed her good-day. She offered me her cheek. This troubles me.

MAY 10   "Ella, I love you."

I said it to her just like that. We have met many times. I have dreamt of her by day. I have not even kept up my journal. Verse has been out of the question.

"Ella, I love you. Let us move into the Trousseau Department. Don't look so dismayed, darling. If you like, we will go right away from here. We will live in that little restaurant in Central Park. There are thousands of birds there."

"Please—please don't talk like that!"

"But I love you with all my heart."

"You mustn't."

"But I find I must. I can't help it. Ella, you don't love another?"

She wept a little. "Oh, Charles, I do."

"Love another, Ella? One of these? I thought you dreaded them all. It must be Roscoe. He is the only one that's any way human. We talk of art, life, and such things. And he has stolen your heart!"

"No, Charles, no. He's just like the rest, really. I hate them all. They make me shudder."

"Who is it, then?"

"It's him."

"Who?"

"The night watchman."

"Impossible!"

"No. He smells of the sun."

"Oh, Ella, you have broken my heart."

"Be my friend, though."

"I will. I'll be your brother. How did you fall in love with him?"

"Oh, Charles, it was so wonderful. I was thinking of birds, and I was careless. Don't tell on me, Charles. They'll punish me."

"No. No. Go on."

"I was careless, and there he was, coming round the corner. And there was no place for me; I had this blue dress on. There were only some wax models in their underthings."

"Please go on."

"I couldn't help it. I slipped off my dress and stood still."

"I see."

"And he stopped just by me, Charles. And he looked at me. And he touched my cheek."

"Did he notice nothing?"

"No. It was cold. But Charles, he said—he said—'Say, honey, I wish they made 'em like you on Eighth Avenue.' Charles, wasn't that a lovely thing to say?"

"Personally, I should have said Park Avenue."

"Oh, Charles, don't get like these people here. Sometimes I think you're getting like them. It doesn't matter what street, Charles; it was a lovely thing to say."

"Yes, but my heart's broken. And what can you do about him? Ella, he belongs to another world."

"Yes, Charles, Eighth Avenue. I want to go there. Charles, are you truly my friend?"

"I'm your brother, only my heart's broken."

"I'll tell you. I will. I'm going to stand there again. So he'll see me."

"And then?"

"Perhaps he'll speak to me again."

"My dearest Ella, you are torturing yourself. You are making it worse."

"No, Charles. Because I shall answer him. He will take me away."

"Ella, I can't bear it."

"Ssh! There is someone coming. I shall see birds—real birds, Charles—and flowers growing. They're coming. You must go."

MAY 13   The last three days have been torture. This evening I broke. Roscoe had joined me. He sat eying me for a long time. He put his hand on my shoulder.

He said, "You're looking seedy, old fellow. Why don't you go over to Wanamaker's for some skiing?"

His kindness compelled a frank response. "It's deeper than that, Roscoe. I'm done for. I can't eat, I can't sleep. I can't write, man, I can't even write."

"What is it? Day starvation?"

"Roscoe—it's love."

"Not one of the staff, Charles, or the customers? That's absolutely forbidden."

"No, it's not that, Roscoe. But just as hopeless."

"My dear old fellow, I can't bear to see you like this. Let me help you. Let me share your trouble."

Then it all came out. It burst out. I trusted him. I think I trusted him. I really think I had no intention of betraying Ella, of spoiling her escape, of keeping her here till her heart turned towards me. If I had, it was subconscious. I swear it.

But I told him all. All! He was sympathetic, but I detected a sly reserve in his sympathy. "You will respect my confidence, Roscoe? This is to be a secret between us."

"As secret as the grave, old chap."

And he must have gone straight to Mrs. Vanderpant. This evening the atmosphere has changed. People flicker to and fro, smiling nervously, horribly, with a sort of frightened sadistic exaltation. When I speak to them they answer evasively, fidget, and disappear. An informal dance has been called off. I cannot find Ella. I will creep out. I will look for her again.

LATER Heaven! It has happened. I went in desperation to the manager's office, whose glass front overlooks the whole shop. I watched till midnight. Then I saw a little group of them, like ants bearing a victim. They were carrying Ella. They took her to the Surgical Department. They took other things.

And, coming back here, I was passed by a flittering, whispering horde of them, glancing over their shoulders in a thrilled ecstasy of panic, making for their hiding places. I, too, hid myself. How can I describe the dark inhuman creatures that passed me, silent as shadows? They went there—where Ella is.

What can I do? There is only one thing. I will find the watchman. I will tell him. He and I will save her. And if we are overpowered . . . Well, I will leave this on a counter. Tomorrow, if we live, I can recover it.

If not, look in the windows. Look for three new figures: two men, one rather sensitive-looking, and a girl. She has blue eyes, like periwinkle flowers, and her upper lip is lifted a little.

Look for us.

Smoke them out! Obliterate them! Avenge us!

WITCH'S MONEY

Foiral had taken a load of cork up to the high road, where he met the motor truck from Perpignan. He was on his way back to the village, walking harmlessly beside his mule, and thinking of nothing at all, when he was passed by a striding madman, half naked, and of a type never seen before in this district of the Pyrénées-Orientales.

He was not of the idiot sort, with the big head, like two or three of them down in the village. Nor was he a lean, raving creature, like Barilles's old father after the house burned down. Nor had he a little, tiny, shrunken-up, chattering head, like the younger Lloubes. He was a new sort altogether.

Foiral decided he was a kind of *bursting* madman, all blare and racket, as bad as the sun. His red flesh burst out of his little bits of colored clothes—red arms, red knees, red neck, and a great round red face bursting with smiles, words, laughter.

Foiral overtook him at the top of the ridge. He was staring down into the valley like a man thunderstruck.

"My God!" he said to Foiral. "Just look at it!" Foiral looked at it. There was nothing wrong.

"Here have I," said the mad Jack, "been walking up and down these goddam Pyrénées for weeks—meadows, birch trees, pine trees, waterfalls—green as a dish of *haricots verts!* And here's what I've been looking for all the time. Why did no one tell me?"

There's a damned question to answer! However, madmen answer themselves. Foiral thumped his mule and started off down the track, but the mad fellow fell in step beside him.

"What is it, for God's sake?" said he. "A bit of Spain strayed over the frontier, or what? Might be a crater in the moon. No water, I suppose? God, look at that ring of red hills! Look at that pink and yellow land! Are those villages down there? Or the bones of some creatures that have died?

"I like it," he said. "I like the way the fig trees burst out of the rock. I like the way the seeds are bursting out of the figs. Ever heard of surrealism? This is surrealism come to life. What are those? Cork forests? They look like petrified ogres. Excellent ogres, who bleed when these impudent mortals flay you, with my little brush, on my little piece of canvas, I shall restore to you an important part of your life!"

Foiral, by no means devout, took the sensible precaution of crossing himself. The fellow went on and on, all the way down, two or three kilometers. Foiral answering with a "Yes," a "No," and a grunt. "This is *my* country!" cried the lunatic. "It's *made* for me. Glad I didn't go to Morocco! Is this your village? Wonderful! Look at those houses—three, four stories. Why do they look as if they'd been piled up by cave dwellers, cave dwellers who couldn't find a cliff? Or are they caves from which the cliff has crumbled away, leaving them uneasy in the sunlight, huddling together? Why don't you have any windows? I like that yellow belfry. Sort of Spanish. I like the way the bell hangs in that iron cage. Black as your hat. Dead. Maybe that's why it's so quiet here. Dead noise, gibbeted against the blue! Ha! Ha! You're not amused, eh? You don't care for surrealism? So much the worse, my friend, because you're the stuff that sort of dream is made of. I like the black clothes all you people wear. Spanish touch again, I suppose? It makes you look like holes in the light."

"Good-bye," said Foiral.

"Wait a minute," said the stranger. "Where can I put up in this village? Is there an inn?"

"No," said Foiral, turning into his yard.

"Hell!" said the stranger. "I suppose someone has a room I can sleep in?"

"No," said Foiral.

That set the fellow back a bit. "Well," said he at last, "I'll have a look around, anyway."

So he went up the street. Foiral saw him talking to Madame Arago, and she was shaking her head. Then he saw him trying it on at the baker's, and the baker shook his head as well. However, he bought a loaf there, and some cheese and wine from Barilles. He sat down on the bench outside and ate it; then he went pottering off up the slope.

Foiral thought he'd keep an eye on him, so he followed to the top of the village, where he could see all over the hillside. The fellow was just mooning about; he picked up nothing, he did nothing. Then he began to drift over to the little farmhouse, where the well is, a few hundred yards above the rest of the houses.

This happened to be Foiral's property, through his wife: a good place, if they'd had a son to live in it. Seeing the stranger edging that way, Foiral followed, not too fast, you understand, and not too slow, either. Sure enough, when he got there, there was the fellow peering through the chinks in the shutters, even trying the door. He might have been up to anything.

He looked round as Foiral came up. "Nobody lives here?" he said.

"No," said Foiral.

"Who does it belong to?" said the stranger.

Foiral hardly knew what to say. In the end he had to admit it was his.

"Will you rent it to me?" said the stranger.

"What for?" said Foiral.

"Damn it!" said the stranger. "To live in."

"Why?" said Foiral.

The stranger holds up his hand. He picks hold of the thumb. He says, very slowly, "I am an artist, a painter."

"Yes," says Foiral.

Then the stranger lays hold of his forefinger. "I can work here. I like it. I like the view. I like those two ilex trees."

"Very good," says Foiral.

Then the stranger takes hold of his middle finger. "I want to stay here six months."

"Yes," says Foiral.

Then the stranger takes hold of his third finger. "In this house. Which, I may say, on this yellow ground, looks interestingly like a dice on a desert. Or does it look like a skull?"

"Ah!" says Foiral.

Then the stranger takes hold of his little finger, and he says, "How much—do you want—to let me—live and work—in this house—for six months?"

"Why?" says Foiral.

At this the stranger began to stamp up and down. They had

quite an argument. Foiral clinched the matter by saying that people didn't rent houses in that part of the world; everyone had his own.

"It is necessary," said the stranger, grinding his teeth, "for me to paint pictures here."

"So much the worse," said Foiral.

The stranger uttered a number of cries in some foreign gibberish, possibly that of Hell itself. "I see your soul," said he, "as a small and exceedingly sterile black marble, on a waste of burning white alkali."

Foiral, holding his two middle fingers under his thumb, extended the first and fourth in the direction of the stranger, careless of whether he gave offense.

"What will you take for the shack?" said the stranger. "Maybe I'll buy it."

It was quite a relief to Foiral to find that after all he was just a plain, simple, ordinary lunatic. Without a proper pair of pants to his backside, he was offering to buy this excellent, sound house, for which Foiral would have asked twenty thousand francs, had there been anyone of whom to ask it.

"Come on," said the stranger. "How much?"

Foiral, thinking he had wasted enough time, and not objecting to an agreeable sensation, said, "Forty thousand."

Said the stranger, "I'll give you thirty-five."

Foiral laughed heartily.

"That's a good laugh," said the stranger. "I should like to paint a laugh like that. I should express it by a sort of cascade of the roots of recently extracted teeth. Well, what about it? Thirty-five? I can pay you a deposit right now." And, pulling out a wallet, this Croesus among madmen rustled one, two, three, four, five thousand-franc notes under Foiral's nose.

"It'll leave me dead broke," he said. "Still, I expect I can sell it again?"

"If God wills," said Foiral.

"Anyway, I could come here now and then," said the other. "My god! I can paint a showful of pictures here in six months. New York'll go crazy. Then I'll come back here and paint another show."

Foiral, ravished with joy, ceased attempting to understand. He began to praise his house furiously: he dragged the man inside, showed him the oven, banged the walls, made him look up the chimney, into the shed, down the well . . . "All right. All right," said the stranger. "That's grand. Everything's grand. Whitewash

the walls. Find me some woman to come and clean and cook. I'll go
back to Paris and turn up in a week with my things. Listen: I want
that table chucked in, two or three of the chairs, and the bedstead.
I'll get the rest. Here's your deposit."

"No, no," said Foiral. "Everything must be done properly, before
witnesses. Then, when the lawyer comes, he can make out the papers.
Come back with me. I'll call Arago, he's a very honest man. Guis,
very honest. Vigné, honest as the good earth. And a bottle of old
wine. I have it. It shall cost nothing."

"Fine!" said the blessed madman, sent by God.

Back they went. In came Arago, Guis, Vigné, all as honest as the
day. The deposit was paid, the wine was opened, the stranger called
for more, others crowded in. Those who were not allowed in stood
outside to listen to the laughter. You'd have thought there was a
wedding going on, or some wickedness in the house. In fact, Foiral's
old woman went and stood in the doorway every now and then, just
to let people see her.

There was no doubt about it, there was something very magnificent about this madman. That evening, after he had gone, they
talked him over thoroughly. "To listen," said little Guis, "is to be
drunk without spending a penny. You think you understand; you
seem to fly through the air; you have to burst out laughing."

"I somehow had the delectable impression that I was rich," said
Arago. "Not, I mean, with something in the chimney, but as if I—
well, as if I were to spend it. And more."

"I like him," said little Guis. "He is my friend."

"Now you speak like a fool," said Foiral. "He is mad. And it is I
who deal with him."

"I thought maybe he was not so mad when he said the house was
like an old skull looking out of the ground," said Guis, looking side-
ways, as well he might.

"Nor a liar, perhaps?" said Foiral. "Let me tell you, he said also
it was like a dice on a desert. Can it be both?"

"He said in one breath," said Arago, "that he came from Paris.
In the next, that he was an American."

"Oh, yes. Unquestionably a great liar," said Quès. "Perhaps one
of the biggest rogues in the whole world, going up and down. But,
fortunately, mad as well."

"So he buys a house," said Lafago. "If he had his wits about him,
a liar of that size, he'd take it—like that. As it is, he buys it. Thirty-
five thousand francs!"

"Madness turns a great man inside out, like a sack," said Arago. "And if he is rich as well—"

"—money flies in all directions," said Guis.

Nothing could be more satisfactory. They waited impatiently for the stranger's return. Foiral whitewashed the house, cleaned the chimneys, put everything to rights. You may be sure he had a good search for anything that his wife's old man might have left hidden three years ago, and which this fellow might have heard of. They say they're up to anything in Paris.

The stranger came back, and they were all day with the mules getting his stuff from where the motor truck had left it. By the evening, they were in the house, witnesses, helpers, and all. There was just the little matter of paying up the money.

Foiral indicated this with the greatest delicacy in the world. The stranger, all smiles and readiness, went into the room where his bags were piled-up, and soon emerged with a sort of book in his hand, full of little *billets*, like those they try to sell for the lottery in Perpignan. He tore off the top one. "Here you are," he said to Foiral, holding it out. "Thirty thousand francs."

"No," said Foiral.

"What the Hell now?" asked the stranger.

"I've seen that sort of thing," said Foiral. "And not for thirty thousand francs, my friend, but for three hundred thousand. And afterwards—they tell you it hasn't won. I should prefer the money."

"This is the money," said the stranger. "It's as good as money anyway. Present this, and you'll get thirty thousand-franc notes, just like those I gave you."

Foiral was rather at a loss. It's quite usual in these parts to settle a sale at the end of a month. Certainly he wanted to run no risk of crabbing the deal. So he pocketed the piece of paper, gave the fellow good-day, and went off with the rest of them to the village.

The stranger settled in. Soon he got to know everybody. Foiral, a little uneasy, cross-examined him whenever they talked. It appeared, after all, that he *did* come from Paris, having lived there, and he *was* an American, having been born there. "Then you have no relations in this part of the world?" said Foiral.

"No relations at all."

Well! Well! Well! Foiral hoped the money was all right. Yet there was more in it than that. No relations! It was quite a thought. Foiral put it away at the back of his mind; he meant to extract the juice from it some night when he couldn't sleep.

At the end of the month, he took out his piece of paper, and marched up to the house again. There was the fellow, three-quarters naked, sitting under one of the ilex trees, painting away on a bit of canvas. And what do you think he had chosen to paint? Roustand's mangy olives, that haven't borne a crop in living memory!

"What is it?" said the mad fellow. "I'm busy."

"This," said Foiral, holding out the bit of paper. "I need the money."

"Then why, in the name of the devil," said the other, "don't you go and get the money, instead of coming here bothering me?"

Foiral had never seen him in this sort of mood before. But a lot of these laughers stop laughing when it comes to hard cash. "Look here," said Foiral, "this is a very serious matter."

"Look here," said the stranger, "that's what's called a check. I give it to you. You take it to a bank. The bank gives you the money."

"Which bank?" said Foiral.

"Your bank. Any bank. The bank in Perpignan," said the stranger. "You go there. They'll do it for you."

Foiral, still hankering after the cash, pointed out that he was a very poor man, and it took a whole day to get to Perpignan, a considerable thing to such an extremely poor man as he was.

"Listen," said the stranger. "You know goddam well you've made a good thing out of this sale. Let me get on with my work. Take the check to Perpignan. It's worth the trouble. I've paid you plenty."

Foiral knew then that Guis had been talking about the price of the house. "All right, my little Guis, I'll think that over some long evening when the rains begin." However, there was nothing for it. He had to put on his best black, take the mule to Estagel, and there get the bus, and the bus took him to Perpignan.

In Perpignan they are like so many monkeys. They push you, look you up and down, snigger in your face. If a man has business—with a bank, let us say—and he stands on the pavement opposite to have a good look at it, he gets elbowed into the roadway half a dozen times in five minutes, and he's lucky if he escapes with his life.

Nevertheless, Foiral got into the bank at last. As a spectacle, it was tremendous. Brass rails, polished wood, a clock big enough for a church, little cotton-backs sitting among heaps of money like mice in a cheese.

He stood at the back for about half an hour, waiting, and no one took any notice of him at all. In the end one of the little cotton-backs beckoned him up to the brass railing. Foiral delved in his pocket, and produced the check. The cotton-back looked at it as if it were a mere nothing. "Holy Virgin!" thought Foiral.

"I want the money for it," said he.

"Are you a client of the bank?"

"No."

"Do you wish to be?"

"Shall I get the money?"

"But naturally. Sign this. Sign this. Sign on the back of the check. Take this. Sign this. Thank you. Good-day."

"But the thirty thousand francs?" cried Foiral.

"For that, my dear sir, we must wait till the check is cleared. Come back in about a week."

Foiral, half dazed, went home. It was a bad week. By day he felt reasonably sure of the cash, but at night, as soon as he closed his eyes, he could see himself going into that bank, and all the cotton-backs swearing they'd never seen him before. Still, he got through it, and, as soon as the time was up, he presented himself at the bank again.

"Do you want a checkbook?"

"No. Just the money. The money."

"All of it? You want to close the account? Well! Well! Sign here. Sign here."

Foiral signed.

"There you are. Twenty-nine thousand eight hundred and ninety."

"But, sir, it was thirty thousand."

"But, my dear sir, the charges."

Foiral found it was no good arguing. He went off with his money. That was good. But the other hundred and ten! That sticks in a man's throat.

As soon as he got home, Foiral interviewed the stranger. "I am a poor man," said he.

"So am I," said the stranger. "A damned sight too poor to pay you extra because you can't get a check cashed in a civilized way."

This was a peculiarly villainous lie. Foiral had, with his own eyes, seen a whole block of these extraordinary thirty-thousand-franc *billets* in the little book from which the stranger had torn this one. But once more there was nothing to be done about it; a plain honest man is always being baffled and defeated. Foiral went home, and put his crippled twenty-nine thousand-odd into the little box behind the stone in the chimney. How different, if it had been a round thirty thousand! What barbarous injustice!

Here was something to think about in the evenings. Foiral thought about it a lot. In the end he decided it was impossible to act alone, and called in Arago, Quès, Lafago, Vigné, Barilles. Not Guis. It was Guis who had told the follow he had paid too much for the house, and put his back up. Let Guis stay out of it.

To the rest he explained everything very forcefully. "Not a relation in the whole countryside. And in that book, my dear friends— you have seen it yourselves—ten, twelve, fifteen, maybe twenty of these extraordinary little *billets*."

"And if somebody comes after him? Somebody from America?"

"He has gone off, walking, mad, just as he came here. Anything can happen to a madman, walking about, scattering money."

"It's true. Anything can happen."

"But it should happen before the lawyer comes."

"That's true. So far even the curé hasn't seen him."

"There must be justice, my good friends. Society cannot exist without it. A man, an honest man, is not to be robbed of a hundred and ten francs."

"No, that is intolerable."

The next night, these very honest men left their houses, those houses whose tall uprights of white plaster and black shadow appear, in moonlight even more than in sunlight, like a heap of bleached ribs lying in the desert. Without much conversation, they made their way up the hill and knocked upon the stranger's door.

After a brief interval they returned, still without much conversation, and slipped one by one into their extremely dark doorways, and that was all.

For a whole week there was no perceptible change in the village. If anything, its darks and silences, those holes in the fierce light, were deeper. In every black interior sat a man who had two of these excellent *billets,* each of which commanded thirty thousand francs. Such a possession brightens the eyes, and enhances the savor of solitude, enabling a man, as the artist would have said, to partake of the nature of Fabre's tarantula, motionless at the angle of her tunnel, remembering the gaudy fly. But they found it no longer easy to remember the artist. His jabbering, his laughter, even his final yelp, left no echo at all. It was all gone, like the rattle and flash of yesterday's thunderstorm.

So, apart from the tasks of the morning and the evening, performing which they were camouflaged by habit, they sat in their houses alone. Their wives scarcely dared to speak to them, and they were too rich to speak to each other. Guis found it out, for it was no secret except to the world outside, and Guis was furious. But his wife berated him from morning till night, and left him no energy for reproaching his neighbors.

At the end of the week, Barilles sprang into existence in the doorway of his house. His thumbs were stuck in his belt, his face was flushed from lead color to plum color, his bearing expressed an irritable resolution.

He crossed to Arago's, knocked, leaned against a doorpost. Arago, emerging, leaned against the other. They talked for some little time of nothing at all. Then Barilles, throwing away the stump of his cigarette, made an oblique and sympathetic reference to a certain small enclosure belonging to Arago, on which there were a shed, a few vines, a considerable grove of olives. "It is the very devil," said Barilles, "how the worm gets into the olive in these days. Such a grove as that, at one time, might have been worth something."

"It is worse than the devil," said Arago. "Believe me or not, my dear friend, in some years I get no more than three thousand francs from that grove."

Barilles burst into what passes for laughter in this part of the world. "Forgive me!" he said. "I thought you said three thousand. Three hundred—yes. I suppose in a good year you might make that very easily."

This conversation continued through phases of civility, sarcasm, rage, fury, and desperation until it ended with a cordial handshake and a sale of the enclosure to Barilles for twenty-five thousand francs. The witnesses were called in; Barilles handed over one of his *billets*, and received five thousand in cash from the box Arago kept in his chimney. Everyone was delighted by the sale: it was felt that things were beginning to move in the village.

They were. Before the company separated, *pourparlers* were already started for the sale of Vigné's mules to Quès for eight thousand, the transfer of Lloube's cork concession to Foiral for fifteen thousand, the marriage of Roustand's daughter to Vigné's brother with a dowry of twenty thousand, and the sale of a miscellaneous collection of brass objects belonging to Madame Arago for sixty-five francs, after some very keen bargaining.

Only Guis was left out in the cold, but, on the way home, Lloubes, with his skin full of wine, ventured to step inside the outcast's doorway, and looked his wife Filomena up and down, from top to toe, three times. A mild interest, imperfectly concealed, softened the bitter and sullen expression upon the face of Guis.

This was a mere beginning. Soon properties began to change hands at a bewildering rate and at increasing prices. It was a positive boom. Change was constantly being dug out from under flagstones, from the strawy interiors of mattresses, from hollows in beams, and from holes in walls. With the release of these frozen credits, the village blossomed like an orchid sprung from a dry stick. Wine flowed with every bargain. Old enemies shook hands. Elderly spinsters embraced young suitors. Wealthy widowers married young brides. Several of the weaker sort wore their best black every day. One of these was Lloubes, who spent his evenings in the house of Guis. Guis in the evenings would wander round the village, no longer sullen, and was seen cheapening a set of harness at Lafago's, a first-rate gun at Roustand's. There was talk of something very special by way of a fiesta after the grape harvest, but this was only whispered, lest the curé should hear of it on one of his visits.

Foiral, keeping up his reputation as leader, made a staggering proposal. It was nothing less than to improve the mule track all the way from the metaled road on the rim of the hills, so that motor trucks could visit the village. It was objected that the wage bill would be enormous. "Yes," said Foiral, "but we shall draw the wages ourselves. We shall get half as much grain for our produce."

The proposal was adopted. The mere boys of the village now shared the prosperity. Barilles now called his little shop "Grand Café Glacier de l'Univers et des Pyrénées." The widow Loyau offered room, board, and clothing to certain unattached young women, and gave select parties in the evenings.

Barilles went to Perpignan and returned with a sprayer that would double the yield of his new olive grove. Lloubes went and returned with a positive bale of ladies' underclothing, designed, you would say, by the very devil himself. Two or three keen cardplayers went and returned with new packs of cards, so lustrous that your hand seemed to be all aces and kings. Vigné went and returned with a long face.

The bargaining, increasing all the time, called for more and more ready money. Foiral made a new proposal. "We will all go to Perpignan, the whole damned lot of us, march to the bank, thump down our *billets*, and show the little cotton-backs whom the money belongs to. Boys, we'll leave them without a franc."

"They will have the hundred and ten," said Quès.

"To hell with the hundred and ten!" said Foiral. "And, friends, after that—well—ha! ha!—all men sin once. They say the smell alone of one of those creatures is worth fifty francs. Intoxicating! Stair carpets, red hair, every sort of wickedness! Tomorrow!"

"Tomorrow!" they all cried, and on the morrow they went off, in their stiffest clothes, their faces shining. Every man was smoking like a chimney, and every man had washed his feet.

The journey was tremendous. They stopped the bus at every café on the road, and saw nothing they didn't ask the price of. In Perpignan, they kept together in a close phalanx; if the townspeople stared, our friends stared back twice as hard. As they crossed over to the bank, "Where is Guis?" said Foiral, affecting to look for him among their number. "Has he nothing due to him?" That set them all laughing. Try as they might, they couldn't hold their faces straight. They were still choking with laughter when the swing doors closed behind them.

ARE YOU TOO LATE
OR WAS I TOO EARLY?

In the country I accept the normal and traditional routine, doing what every man does: rising early, eating when I should, turning up my coat collar when it rains. I see the reason for it, and shave at the same hour every morning.

Not so in town. When I live in town I feel no impulse in the starling migrations of the rush hours. There is no tide, in any submarine cave, anywhere, that is not more to me than the inflow and outflow at the cold mouths of offices or the hot mouths of restaurants. I find no growth in time, no need for rain, no sense in sobriety, no joy in drinking, no point in paying, no plan in living. I exist, in this alien labyrinth, like an insect among men, or a man in a city of ants.

I despise the inconsiderable superiority of the glum day over the starless night. My curtains are always drawn; I sleep when my eyes close, eat when I remember to, and read and smoke without ceasing, allowing my soul to leave my wastrel and untended carcass, and seldom do I question it when it returns.

My chambers are in the stoniest of the Inns of Court. I keep no servant here, for I mean always to go back to the country within the week, though sometimes I stay for months, or . . . I don't know how long. I supply myself with immense stocks of cigarettes, and such food as I happen to remember, so that I shall have no reason to return from the landscapes of Saturn or the undescribed gardens of Turgenev in order to go out into the streets.

My fingers are horribly blistered by the cigarettes that burn down between them while still I walk in the company of women with the heads of cats. Nothing seems strange to me when I wake from such reveries unless I part the curtains and look out into the Square. Sometimes I have to press my hands under my heart to resume the breathing that I have entirely forgotten.

I was constantly ambushed and defeated in I forget what journeys, or what loves, or where, by the fullness of a saucer in which a hand of mine failed to find room to crush out its cigarettes. Habit, which arranges these things, demanded some other receptacle. I rose, holding my thoughts as one holds a brimming glass, and was moved into the bathroom, drawn by the vague memory of a soap dish, which lay stranded like an empty shell on the empty beaches of a blank mind. But, swallowed by God knows what high-reaching wave, that shell was gone, and my reviving eyes, straying at first aimlessly, soon called me all back again, poor Crusoe, to regard on the cork mat the new, wet, glistening imprint of a naked foot.

It was not long before I assured myself that I was dry, dressed in my pajamas and slippers, and that I was not clean. Moreover, this foot, the prints of whose toes were as round as graded pearls, was neither long, like that of a man, nor hideous, like that of a bear; it was not my own. It was that of a woman, a nymph, a new-risen Venus. I conceived that my wandering spirit had brought me back a companion from some diviner sea's edge, and some more fortunate shell.

I drank up this moist footprint with my hot eyes; it dried as I looked upon it. It was not the air took it, but I; I had it for my own. I examined it for days and nights, building, upon its graceful rotundities, arched insteps, ankles equally graceful, and calves proportionately round. I deduced knees, haunches, breasts, shoulders, arms, plump hands and pointed fingers, full neck, small head, and the long curl, like the curve when the wave breaks, of the green-gold hair.

Where there falls one footprint there must fall the next; I had no doubt I should soon be vouchsafed the dull gleam of her hair. For this, I at once became ravenous, and slunk restlessly from room to room.

I noticed, with half-unconscious approval, that even the neglected furnishings seemed responsive to the goddess, and stood clean and tidy as onlookers at a holiday. The carpet, as if she were Persephone instead of Venus, bloomed with new flowers beneath her invisible feet. The sun shone through the open window, and warm airs entered. At what moment had I swept back the curtains and extended this invitation to sun and air? Perhaps she had done so herself. It was, however, impossible to attend to such lovely trifles. I desired the gleam of her hair.

"Forgive me for having rejoiced in the pallor of the dead! Forgive me for having conversed with women who smelled like lions! Show me your hair!"

I was devoured by a cruel nostalgia for this being who was always with me. "Supposing," I thought, waking in my strangely fresh bed, "supposing she appeared terrifyingly in the darkness, white as marble, and as cold!" At that moment I felt an intermittent warmth on my cheek, and knew that she breathed beside me.

There was nothing to clasp but the empty air. For days I moved to and fro, my blood howling in me like a dog that bays at the moon. "There is nothing but the empty air."

I persuaded myself that this was nonsense. I had seen the trace of beauty, and felt the warmth of life. Gradually one sense after another would be refracted on this divine invisibility, till she stood outlined like a creature of crystal, and then as one of flesh and blood. As soon as I was well-persuaded, I saw her breath dimming upon a mirror.

I saw some flowers, which had appeared, part their petals as she bent her face to them. Hurrying there, I smelled, not the flowers, but her hair.

I threw myself down, and lay like a dog across the threshold, where, once or twice in the day, I might feel the light breeze of her passing. I was aware of the movement of her body, or an eddy in the light where she moved; I was aware of the beating of her heart.

Sometimes, as if out of the corner of my eye, I saw, or thought

I saw, not her bright flesh, but the light of her flesh, which vanished as I widened my eyes upon it.

I knew where she moved, and how she moved, but I was destroyed by a doubt, for she did not move towards me. Could there be some other existence, to which she was more responsive, some existence less tangible than her own? Or was she my unwilling prisoner here? Were those movements, of which I was not the object, the movements of one who longed only to escape?

It was impossible to tell. I thought I might know everything if only I could hear her voice. Perhaps she could hear mine.

I said to her, day and night, "Speak to me. Let me hear you. Tell me you have forgiven me. Tell me you are here forever. Tell me you are mine." Day and night I listened for her answer.

I waited in that unutterable silence, as one who, in a darkness equally profound, might await the arrival of a gleam of light from a star in whose existence he had good reason to believe. In the end, when I had ceased to hope or believe, I became aware of a sound— or something as near to a sound as the light on her cheek was near to the flesh of her cheek.

Now, living only in my eardrum, not moving, not breathing, I waited. This ghost of a sound increased; it passed through infinite gradations of rarity. It was like the sound in the second before the rain; it was like the fluttering of wings, the confused words of water; it was like words blown away in the wind; like words in a foreign tongue; it grew more distinct, closer.

Sometimes my hearing failed me, exactly as one's sight fails, dimmed suddenly by tears, when one is about to see the face one has always loved, after an ineffable absence. Or she would fall silent, and then I was like one who follows the sound of a brook, and loses it under the muffling trees, or under the ground. But I found it again, and each time it was clearer and stronger. I was able to distinguish words; I heard the word "love," I heard the word "happy."

I heard, in a full opening of the sense, the delicate intake of her breath, the very sound of the parting of her lips. She was about to speak again.

Each syllable was as clear as a bell. She said, "Oh, it's perfect. It's so quiet for Harry's work. Guess how we were lucky enough to get it! The previous tenant was found dead in his chair, and they actually say it's haunted."

Fallen Star

In Hell, as in other places we know of, conditions are damnably disagreeable. Well-adjusted, energetic, and ambitious devils take this very much in their stride. They expect to improve their lot and ultimately to become fiends of distinction.

In the great mass of ordinary, plodding, run-of-the-mill devils, any escapist tendencies are sufficiently ventilated by entertainments akin to radio and television, which offer them glimpses of what they take to be Paradise, interrupted by screaming commercials.

There are, however, certain idle, worthless, and altogether undevilish devils who dream incessantly of getting away from it all, and a few of them have actually managed to do so. The authorities are at no great pains to recapture them, for they are invariably chronic unemployables and nothing but a burden on the community.

Some of the fugitives have established themselves on sundry minute planetoids which are scattered here and there along the outer fringes of the Pleiades. These tiny worlds rise like green atolls in the everlasting blue. Here the deserters build their sorry shacks and subsist on a little desultory soul-fishing. They live like beachcombers, growing fatter and lazier every year, and they compare themselves to the mutineers of the *Bounty*.

When they want a bit of change, they take a swim in the azure ether, and sometimes go as far as the cliffs of Heaven, just to take a look at the girls, who, naturally enough, are as beautiful as angels.

The cliffs of Heaven, you may be sure, are studded with summer resorts and well-supervised bathing beaches. There are also some quiet creeks and unfrequented bays where the ether washes in sapphire waves upon golden rocks, and over sands of a quality to make any honest digger call for spade and pail. Here, where no lifeguard stands with unfolded pinions, bathing is strictly prohibited. This is because of the occasional presence of one of those lurking, sharkish, runaway devils, and whoever goes in defiance of the regulations must be prepared to face the consequences. But, in spite of the risk, or because of it, some of the younger set of Heaven take a huge delight in breaking the rules, as the younger set do everywhere.

Thus a certain delightful young she-angel came down one morning into one of these forbidden coves. The weather was heavenly and her heart was as vibrant as one of her own harpstrings. She felt that her blissful existence might blossom into something even more blissful at any moment. She sat a long while on an overhanging rock, and sang as gaily as the lark of the morning. Then she stood up, made a pose or two, she hardly knew why, and finally she took off with a swan dive into the exhilarating ether.

An elderly, fat, and most unprepossessing devil had been hanging offshore in the shallows for no other purpose than to play the Peeping Tom. The sight of this lovely creature aroused a ticklish and insistent longing in the old reprobate; it rose up in his black heart like a belch in a tar caldron. He swung in and seized her as a shark might seize on a bathing beauty, and he swept her swooning off to his little verdant planet, and on to the rickety porch of his cabin, which jutted out from the rocks for all the world like one of those fishing shacks which are to be found on any island in the tropics.

She came to herself with a gasp, and looked with horror at her repulsive captor, whose paunch sagged over his greasy belt, and whose tattered jeans scarcely sufficed to conceal his devilishness. He, with a rusty pair of shears, was already at work clipping her wings, and, gathering up the feathers: "These," said he, "will clean my pipe out to perfection. I like to smoke while I fish. Here is my favorite line: It is stronger and longer than it looks. With this I can dabble deep into the dormitories of the YMCA. For bait I use some pleasant little dreams I've had at one time or another. I keep 'em in this bucket over here, and you can take one right now and put it on the hook."

"The nasty, wriggly, slimy things!" cried she, shrinking away from the sight. "I wouldn't touch them for anything."

"You'd better," said he, "if ever you want to taste the heart and sweetbreads of a tender young divinity student."

"I'll feed myself," said she, with a curl of her lip. "I eat nothing but honey and flowers, and sometimes the egg of a hummingbird, when I'm extra hungry."

"Very uppish!" said he. "Very snooty! If you think you're here to play the fine lady, you'd better think again. Soft, silly, and good-hearted—that's old Tom Truncheontail if you stroke his fur the right way! But cross me up, and I can be rough, I can be tough, and I can be quarrelsome. You'll bait my hooks when I tell you, and you'll scrub and you'll scour and you'll sweep, and you'll cook the dinner and tend the still and make the bed . . ."

"The bed?" said she. "I'll make my own bed. As to yours . . . !"

"Do one without doing the other," said he, "and you shall ride me back to Heaven with a bridle of daisies. I said *bed*. It's singular, that is, and it'd be a lot more singular if it were plural." With that, he laughed fit to split his sides.

The angel thought it a very poor joke. "I know I broke the rules," said she. "And I know you can make me work and slave for you. But what I did wasn't a real sin, so you can't make me suffer a fate worse than death."

"Worse than death, eh?" said the devil, his vanity wounded. "That shows how much *you* know about it."

"If I wished to know more," she replied, "I wouldn't choose you for my teacher."

"Not if I made you a sparkling necklace," said he, "out of the tears of innocent chorus girls?"

"Thank you!" said she. "Keep your trumpery jewelry, and I'll keep my virtue."

"Trumpery!" said he indignantly. "It's clear you don't know what's what in the jewelry line, or in the virtue line either. All right, my dear, there are more ways than one of taming an absolute little spitfire!"

The old sensualist, however, reckoned without his host. In the days that followed, he tried this and he tried that, but neither tyranny nor cajolery availed him in the very least against her snowy virtue and his own sooty complexion. When he frowned she feared him, but when he smiled she hated him worse than ever devil has been hated before.

"I can," said he, "put you into a whiskey bottle, from which you will have to emerge when a cloak-and-suit buyer takes out the stopper."

"Do so," said she. "He can be no uglier than you, and no more of a nuisance."

"You think not?" said he. "It's clear you have very little experience of cloak-and-suit buyers. I can feed you to an oyster, from which you'll come out imprisoned in a pearl, and find yourself traded, in the most embarrassing circumstances, for a whole wagonload of the chastity you hold so dear."

"I shall scream 'culture,' " said she, very coolly. "And the victim will reach for her .22, and thus we shall both be saved."

"Very neat," said he. "But I can send you to earth as a young girl of nineteen or twenty. That's the age when temptations are strongest, and resistance is very low. And the first time you sin, your body, soul, virtue, and all are mine at seven years' purchase. And that," said he, with an oath, "is what I'll do. I was a fool not to have hit on it before."

No sooner said than done. He took her by the ankles and heaved her far out into the seas of space. He saw her body descending, turning, glimmering, and he dived after it like a schoolboy after a silver coin flung into a swimming bath.

Some ordinary people, going home very late over the Brooklyn Bridge, pointed out to each other what they took to be a falling star, and a little later a drunken poet, returning from an all-night party, was inspired by what he thought was the rosy dawn, glimmering through the skimpy shrubbery of Central Park. This, however, was not the dawn, but our beautiful young she-angel, who had arrived on earth as a young girl who had lost both her clothes and her memory, as sometimes young girls do, and who was wandering about under the trees in a state of perfect innocence.

It is impossible to say how long this would have continued, had she not been found by three kindly old ladies, who always were the first to enter the Park in the morning, for the purpose of taking crumbs to their friends the birds. Had our young angel remained there till lunchtime, anything might have happened, for she retained all her original beauty, and was pinker and more pearly than any dawn. She was round, she was supple, she was more luscious than peaches; there was a something about her that was irresistibly appealing.

The old ladies, with a twittering and fluttering like that of their feathered favorites, charitably surrounded this pink perfection of innocence and desirability. "Poor creature!" said Miss Belfrage. "Undoubtedly some man has brought her to this condition."

"Some devil!" said Miss Morrison. This remark afforded infinite amusement to the lubber fiend, who stood invisibly by. He could not resist giving Miss Morrison a little pinch, of a sort entirely new to her experience. "Dear me! Did you do that, Miss Shank?" cried Miss Morrison. "Surely you did not do *that*?"

"I? I did nothing," said Miss Shank. "What is it?"

"I felt," said Miss Morrison, "a sort of pinch."

"So did I," cried Miss Belfrage. "I felt one that very moment."

"So do I," cried Miss Shank. "Oh, dear! Perhaps we shall all lose our memories."

"Let us hurry with her to the hospital," said Miss Morrison. "The Park seems all wrong this morning, and the birdies won't come near. *They* know! What experiences she must have gone through!"

These kind old ladies, now escorted by an increasing crowd, took our beautiful but unfortunate she-angel to a hospital for nervous diseases, where she was received charitably and to some extent enthusiastically. She was soon hurried into a little room, the walls of which were of duck's-egg green, this color having been found very soothing to girls discovered wandering in Central Park with neither their clothes nor their memories. A certain brilliant young psychoanalyst was put in charge of her case. Such cases were his specialty, and he seldom failed to jog their memories to some purpose.

The fiend had naturally tagged along to the hospital, and now stood there picking his teeth and watching all that transpired. He was delighted to see that the young psychoanalyst was as handsome as could be. His features were manly and regular, and his eyes dark and lustrous, and they became more lustrous still when he beheld his new patient. As for hers, they took on a forget-me-not glimmer which caused the devil to rub his hands again. Everyone was pleased.

The psychoanalyst was an ornament to his much maligned profession. His principles were of the highest and yet no higher than his enthusiasm for his science. Now, dismissing the nurses who had brought her in, he took his seat by the couch on which she lay.

"I am here to make you well," said he. "It seems you have had a distressing experience. I want you to tell me what you can remember of it."

"I can't," said she faintly. "I can remember nothing."

"Perhaps you are in a state of shock," said this excellent young analyst. "Give me your hand, my dear, so I may see if it is abnormally warm, or cold, and if there is a wedding ring on it."

"What is a hand?" murmured the unfortunate young she-angel. "What is warm? What is cold? What is a wedding ring?"

"Oh, my poor girl!" said he. "Quite evidently you have had a very severe shock. Those who forget what wedding rings are often get the worst of all. However, this is your hand."

"And is that yours?" said she.

"Yes, that is mine," he replied.

The young angel said no more, but looked at her hand in his, and then she lowered her delightful eyelashes, and sighed a little. This delighted the heart of the ardent young scientist, for he recognized the beginning of the transference, a condition which indescribably lightens the labors of psychoanalysts.

"Well! Well!" said he at last. "We must find out what caused you to lose your memory. Here is the medical report. It seems you have not had a blow on the head."

"What is a head?" she asked.

"This is your head," he told her. "And these are your eyes, and this is your mouth."

"And what is this?" said she.

"That," said he, "is your neck."

This adorable young angel was the best of patients. She desired nothing more than to please her analyst, for, such is the nature of the transference, he seemed to her like some glorious figure out of her forgotten childhood. Her natural innocence was reinforced by the innocence of amnesia, so she pulled down the sheet that covered her, and asked him, "And what are these?"

"Those?" said he. "How you could have possibly forgotten them. I shall not forget them as long as I live. I have never seen a lovelier pair of shoulders."

Delighted by his approbation, the angel asked one or two more questions, such as at last caused this worthy young analyst to rise from his chair and pace the room in a state of considerable agitation. "Unquestionably," he murmured, "I am experiencing the counter-transference in its purest form, or at least in its most intense one. Such a pronounced example of this phenomenon should surely be the subject of experiment. A little free association seems to be indicated, but with a bold innovation of technique. In my paper I will call it 'The Demonstrative Somatic Method as Applied to Cases of Complete Amnesia.' It will be frowned upon by the orthodox, but, after all, Freud himself was frowned upon in his time."

We will draw a veil over the scene that followed, for the secrets of the psychoanalytic couch are as those of the confessional, only more interesting. There was nothing sacred, however, to Tom Truncheon-tail, who by this time was laughing his ugly head off. "Because," thought he, "what sin in the world could be greater than to make such an exemplary young psychoanalyst forget himself, his career, and all the ethics of his profession?"

At a certain moment the wily old devil allowed himself to become visible, leaning over the end of the couch with a cynical smile on his weather-beaten face.

"Oh, what is that, darling?" cried the young she-angel, in accents of frustration and dismay.

"What is what?" asked the analyst, who was at this moment somewhat preoccupied by his researches.

The young she-angel became very silent and melancholy. She knew what she had seen, and now remembered things she wished she had thought of before. It is well-known that this makes sins of this sort no smaller. "Alas," said she, "I think I have recovered my memory."

"Then you are cured," cried the analyst in delight, "and my method has been proved correct, and will be unanimously adopted in the profession. What an inestimable benefit I have conferred upon my colleagues, or at least on those whose patients are half or a quarter as beautiful as you are! But tell me what you remember. I ask you, not as your doctor, but as your future husband."

How easily one sin follows upon another, particularly the sin of lying upon that which had just been committed! The poor angel could not find it in her heart to destroy his happiness by telling him that after seven years he would have to relinquish her to the gross and bristly fiend. She murmured something about having fallen asleep in her bath, and having a tendency to somnambulism. Her story was eagerly accepted, and the happy young analyst hastened out to procure a marriage license.

The fiend immediately made himself visible again and smiled upon his victim with abominable good nature. "Quick work!" said he. "You've saved me a lot of trouble. There are girls in this town who'd have shilly-shallied for the best part of a week. In return, I'll get you a box or two with some clothes in 'em, so your story will hold together, and you can marry the guy and be happy. You have to hand it to old Tom T.—he hasn't a jealous hair in his tail!" The truth is, the old rascal knew she'd sooner or later get hooked up with some-one or other, and, as actually he was as jealous as a demon, he thought it better to be jealous of one rather than a whole series. Also, he felt she might just as well choose a good provider, with a well-stocked icebox and liquor cabinet, and a basement furnace in which he could sleep warm of nights. Psychoanalysts are always well furnished in these respects. And what had finally decided him was the reflection that a marriage which is founded on a lie is usually fertile in other transgressions, as pleasant to the nostrils of a fiend as are roses and lilies to the rest of us.

In this last respect, we may say at once that the old villain was bitterly disappointed. No wife could possibly be more angelic than our angel. In fact, the sweet odors of domestic virtue became so oppressive to the devil that he took himself off to Atlantic City for a breath of fresh air. He found the atmosphere of that resort so exhilarating that he remained there most of the seven years. Thus the angel was almost able to forget the future in the extreme happiness of the present. At the end of the first year she became the mother of a sturdy boy, and at the end of the third she had a beautiful little girl. The apartment they lived in was arranged in the best of taste; her husband rose higher and higher in his profession, and was cheered to the echo at all the principal meetings of psychoanalysts. But as the seventh year drew to a close, the fiend came around to see how things were getting along. He told her much of what he had seen in Atlantic City, and embroidered on the life they would live together when her time was up. From that day on he appeared very frequently, and not only when she was alone. He was utterly without delicacy, and would permit himself to be seen by her at moments when even an elephant-hided devil should have realized his presence was embarrassing. She would close her eyes, but fiends are seen more easily with the eyes closed. She would sigh bitterly.

"How can you sigh so bitterly at such a moment as this?" her husband asked her. The angel could hardly explain, and it almost made a rift between them.

"I wonder," said the analyst on another such occasion, "if this can be connected with your experiences before you lost your memory. Is it possible your cure is not complete? It almost shakes my faith in my method."

This thought preyed upon his mind until he was on the point of a breakdown. "My work is ruined," said he one day. "I have lost faith in my great discovery. I am a failure. I shall go downhill. I shall take to drink. Here is a gray hair! What is worse than an old, gray, drunken psychoanalyst, who has lost faith in himself and his science, both of which he believed equal to anything? My poor children, what a father you will have to grow up with! You will have no pleasant home, no education, and probably no shoes. You will have to wait outside saloons. You will get inferiority complexes, and

when you are married you will take it out on your unfortunate part-
ners, and they too will have to be psychoanalyzed. Of course, it is
all good for the business."

At this the poor young angel gave way altogether. After all, there
were only a few weeks left. She thought it better to destroy the
remnant of her happiness than to ruin the lives of her husband and
children. That night she told him all.

"I would never have credited such things," said her husband, "but
you, my dear, have made me believe in angels, and from that it is
a short step to believing in fiends as well. You have restored my
faith in my science, which has frequently been likened to the casting-
out of devils. Where is he? Can I get sight of him?"

"All too easily," replied the angel. "Go upstairs a little earlier than
usual, and hide yourself in my wardrobe. When I come up and begin
to undress, he'll be quite certain to show himself."

"Very well," said her husband. "Perhaps tonight, as it is rather
chilly, you need not . . ."

"Oh, my dear," said she, "it is far too late to bother about trifles
of that sort."

"You are right," said he, "for, after all, I am a psychoanalyst, and
therefore broad-minded, and he is only a devil."

He at once went upstairs and concealed himself, and his angelic
wife followed him soon after. Just as she had expected, the devil
appeared at a certain moment, lying stretched out on the chaise
longue and leering insolently at the angel. He went so far as to give
this innocent creature one of his humorous little pinches as she went
by. "You're getting thin," said he. "However, you'll soon be back
in your old form, once we've started our honeymoon. What fun we
shall have together! You've no idea how much I've learned in
Atlantic City!"

He went on like this for some time. In the end the husband
stepped out of the wardrobe and took him by the wrist.

"Let go of my wrist!" said the devil, trying to pull himself free,
for these old, gross, and sensual devils are like scared and sullen
children when a psychoanalyst gets hold of them.

"It is not your wrist that interests me," said the analyst in a tone
of lofty detachment. "It's that tail of yours."

"My tail?" muttered old Tom, taken altogether aback. "What
about my tail? What's wrong with it?"

"I'm sure it's a very good tail," replied the analyst. "But I
imagine you'd like to get rid of it."

"Get rid of my tail?" cried the startled devil. "Why in the name of all that's unholy should I want to do that!"

"Everyone to his taste," said the analyst with a contemptuous shrug. "Did you see any little appendages of that description in Atlantic City?"

"Well, no, as a matter of fact, I didn't," replied the crestfallen fiend. The truth is, devils, who suggest so very much to the rest of us, are themselves extremely suggestible. That is how they got that way.

"In my opinion that tail is purely psychic in origin," said the analyst. "And I believe it could be cured without much difficulty."

"Who said I want it cured?" retorted the devil angrily.

"No one said so," replied the man of science in a tranquil tone. "But you have *thought* so, and tried to suppress the thought. By your own admission you are very pronouncedly a *voyeur*—I'll touch on the disadvantages of that later. At least you have seen what is considered normal and pleasing in a well-formed male, and no doubt you would like to be in the mode."

"I have a good time," said the devil, now very much on the defensive.

The analyst allowed a pitying and incredulous smile to overspread his features. He turned to his wife. "My dear," said he, "I must ask you to leave us alone. The confidences of these twisted and unhappy creatures are sacred."

The angel at once withdrew, closing the door very quietly behind her. The analyst took a seat near the head of the chaise longue on which the unfortunate devil was lying. "So you think you have a good time?" said he in the gentlest tone imaginable.

"I do," responded the fiend defiantly. "And what's more, very soon I expect to have a better one."

"It is a mere hypothesis, of course," said the analyst. "It can be nothing more at this early stage of analysis. But I suggest that what you claim as a good time is just a mask for a very profound maladjustment. The physical symptoms are noticeable. You are appallingly overweight, and I suspect that this in turn has produced a heart condition."

"It's true I breathe a little hard now and then," said the devil uneasily.

"Do you mind telling me how old you are?" said the analyst.

"Three thousand four hundred and forty," replied the devil.

"I should have thought you at least a thousand years older than that," said the analyst. "However, I don't claim to be infallible. But, one thing is quite certain: you were very much a misfit in your original surroundings, otherwise you would not have run away. And now you are trying to run away from analysis. It is a threat to that tail of yours. Consciously, you know it's a terrible disfigurement, but you are unwilling to give it up."

"Oh, I don't know about that," said the fiend uncertainly.

"Oh, yes, you cling to it as a mark of your devilishness," said the analyst sternly. "And what does this devilishness amount to? I think we shall find it is a protest, arising out of a sense of rejection which may very well date to the actual moment of your becoming a devil. Even human birth is a traumatic experience. How much worse must it be to be born a poor, rejected devil!"

The wretched fiend shifted his shoulders, pulled at his dewlaps, and showed other signs of distress. Thereupon the analyst drove home the attack, referring to fits of depression, vague fears, a sense of guilt, an inferiority complex, spells of insomnia, a compulsion to eat and drink too much, and psychosomatic aches and pains. In the end the poor devil positively begged to be analyzed; all he asked was that he might be given extra sessions so that the cure could be accomplished more quickly.

The analyst was willing to oblige. He sent his wife and children away for a long summer holiday, and worked day and night upon his difficult patient. Before the angel returned, this transformed devil had left the house clad in a pearly gray suit, tailless, comparatively slim, and mentally alert. He shortly afterwards became engaged to a Mrs. Schlager, a widow who had also been a troublesome patient in her time.

He visited his benefactor's home, bounced the children on his knee, and apologized to his hostess for all the inconvenience he had caused her. She eagerly forgave him, for, after all, his misbehavior had been the effect of unconscious impulses, and had resulted in her marriage, so that she felt he was a friend of the family. He was a little wearisome in recounting the history of his case, but this is very usual in those who have benefited from analysis. In the end, he went on to Wall Street, where he did so extremely well that he was soon able to endow a superb clinic for the young psychoanalyst.

THREE BEARS COTTAGE

"Our hen has laid two eggs," said Mrs. Scrivener, "and I have boiled them for breakfast." As she spoke, she unfolded a snowy napkin and displayed the barnyard treasures, and she placed the white one in her husband's eggcup and the brown one in her own.

The Scriveners lived in a house with a steep roof and a white gable, set in a woodland tract among juvenile birch trees. It was extremely small, but so was the rent, and they called it "Three Bears Cottage." Their ménage was frugal, for Henry had retired at forty, in order to study Nature. Nevertheless, everything was as neat as a pin, and everything was carefully regarded. Each week, in their tiny garden, a new lettuce approached perfection. Its progress was minutely inspected from day to day, and, at that hour when it reached the crest and pinnacle of its development, they cut it, and ate it.

Another day, they had the cauliflower.

People who live thus, from one cherished detail to the next, invariably have complexions clear to the point of transparency, and bright and bird-like eyes. They are also keenly sensitive to the difference between one new-laid egg and another, which, like many other fine points, is often overlooked by the hurrying multitudes in cities. The Scriveners were both well aware that, contrary to a commercially fostered superstition, it is the brown egg that is superior in nourishment, in appearance, and in flavor. Mr. Scrivener noted that his wife had retained the brown egg for herself, and his eyes grew rounder and more bird-like than before. "Ella," said he, "I notice that you have given me the white egg, and retained the brown one for yourself."

"Well," said she, "why not? Why should I not have the brown egg? It is I who keep everything neat and trim in the house, and polish the canary's cage, which you, if you were a man, would do for me. You do nothing but scratch about in the garden, and then go lounging around the woods, studying Nature."

"Do not call Dickie 'the canary' in that fashion," responded her husband. "I sometimes think you have no affection for any living creature about you, least of all for myself. After all, it is I who feed our dear hen every day, and, when she lays a brown egg, I think I should at least be *asked* if I would like it."

"I think I know what the answer would be," said his wife with a short laugh. "No, Henry. I have not forgotten your conduct when the tomato ripened. I think the less said about who has what in this house, the better."

Henry was unable to think of a fitting reply. He gazed moodily at the white egg, which seemed more than ever contemptible to him. His wife sawed off the top of her own egg with a grating and offensive sound. Henry took another look at his. "By God," thought he, "it is not only white! It is smaller!"

This was altogether too much. "Ella," said Henry, "you probably are uninterested in Ripley's *Believe It or Not*, for you despise the marvels of Nature. I am not sure he did not have a picture of a boiled egg with an undigested worm coiled up inside it. I believe the egg was a brown one."

"There is no worm in this egg," replied Ella, munching away imperturbably. "Look in your own. Very likely you will find one there."

Henry, like an unskillful operator of a boomerang, was forcibly struck by the idea he had launched at Ella in the hope of making her abandon her egg to him. He looked closely at his own egg, essayed a spoonful, and found he had no taste for it. "Hell and damn it!" he muttered, for, like many a mild man, he was subject to fits of fury, in which he was by no means guarded as to his language.

His wife looked at him quietly, so that he was ashamed without being mollified. "Selfishness and greed," said he, "have made the world what it is today." Ella, with unconcealed relish, devoured a heaping spoonful. With tight lips and burning eyes, Henry rose from the table, reached for his cap, and stamped out of the house. Ella, with a lift of her eyebrows, took over his neglected egg, which she found not noticeably inferior in flavor to the first. This put her in an excellent humor, and it was with a whimsical rather than a gloating smile that she set about her household tasks.

Henry, on the other hand, slashed savagely at the tall weeds and grasses as he strode along the path to the woods. "What a fool I was," muttered he to himself, "to retire so early, believing that happiness is to be found in a cottage! I conceived a simplicity as pleasurable as a tale for children. Two cups, one adorned with roses, and the other with cornflowers. Two plates, one with a blue ring, and the other with a red ring. Two apples on the tree, both rosy, but one slightly larger than the other. *And that should be for me!* I am a man, and it is right that I should have the larger one. Yes, it could be a divine life, if Ella only had a sense of the fitness of things. How happy I might be, if only she was less greedy, better tempered, not addicted to raking up old grudges, more affectionate, with slightly yellower hair, slimmer, and about twenty years younger! But what is the good of expecting such a woman to reform?"

He had just reached this point in his meditation when his eye fell upon a singularly handsome mushroom, of the genus *Clavaria,* and he uttered an exclamation of delight. It was part of their frugal economy at "Three Bears Cottage" to enliven their menus with all kinds of gleanings from the woods and fields, with wild berries and hedge salads, and, above all, with various sorts of edible fungi, which they found singularly palatable and nutritious.

Henry therefore gathered this one and wrapped it in his handkerchief. His natural impulse was to make tracks for the cottage, and burst in radiant upon his mate (or perhaps enter lugubriously, holding his treasure trove behind his back for a surprise), but, in any case, sooner or later to come out with it exultingly, with, "Here it is, my love, an admirable specimen of the genus *Clavaria*! Rake together your fire, my dear, and serve it up piping hot for lunch. You shall nibble a little, and I will nibble a little, and thus we shall have half each." This generous urge was dashed by the thought that Ella was neither as good-tempered, nor as yellow-haired, nor as slim, nor as young as she ought to be. "Besides," thought he, "she will certainly contrive to keep the better half for herself, and, in any case, it is a mistake to cut a mushroom, for its allows the nutritious juices to escape."

He looked about on all sides in the hope of finding another, but this was the only one. "How eagerly I would take it home," thought he, "if I might be greeted by such a creature as I have often imagined! I would willingly sacrifice the juices. As it is, I had better toast it on a stick. It is a pity, for they tend to dry up that way."

He began to hunt about for some twigs with which to make a little fire, and almost at once his eye fell upon another fungus, of singularly interesting shape, and of a pearly pallor that spoke volumes to the student of Nature. He recognized it at once as the Death Angel, that liberal scientists give a grosser name, calling it *Amanita phalloides*, if the ladies will pardon the Latin. It combines the liveliest of forms with the deadliest of material, and the smallest morsel will fell a man like a thunderbolt. Henry gazed respectfully at this formidable fungus and was unable to repress a shudder. "Nevertheless," said he, "it is certainly very appropriately named. It is around such a toadstool that one might expect to see a fairy tripping, a delicious little creature with golden hair . . .

"And, by all that's wonderful," cried he, "figuratively speaking, I believe that is just what I *do* see!"

With trembling hands he garnered the lethal titbit, and wrapped it in his handkerchief beside the other, carefully interposing a fold of the linen to avoid any contact between them. "Ella has always made nasty cracks at Nature," said he. "Now Nature shall have a crack at her."

He at once hurried back to the cottage, where Ella greeted him with a smile. "It is easy to smile when you have had two eggs for breakfast," thought our hero. "Let us see how you'll manage after having *Amanita phalloides* for lunch." This reflection struck him as being highly diverting, and he accorded his wife a very creditable smirk in return, from which she concluded their little tiff was all forgotten. This she found especially gratifying, for she was a simple, primitive creature, and her double breakfast ration had caused the blood to flow warm and sluggish in her veins.

"See what I have found," said Henry. "Two mushrooms, and of different varieties. This one is a *Clavaria*, a wholesome fungus, with a decent, satisfying flavor."

"And what," said she, "is this other, which looks so white and pearly?"

"Oh, that," said he deceitfully, "that is *Eheu fugaces.*"

"What a pretty name!" said she. "But what a very odd shape! I mean, of course, for a mushroom."

"Pay no attention to that," said he. "It is more nutritious than you can possibly imagine: it is rich in vitamins D, E, A, T, and H. What's more, it has a flavor fit for a king, so I shall eat it myself, for you can hardly be called kingly, not being built that way."

"Ah, that is true," said she, with a giggle. "That is perfectly true, darling. Ha! Ha! I am not built that way."

This reply set Henry back a hundred leagues, for he had expected her to assert a strong claim to the deadly mushroom, as soon as she heard him credit it with a superior vitamin content and flavor. However, he was quick-witted, and at once changed his tack. "Nevertheless," said he, "you shall have this excellent mushroom, for I think you thoroughly deserve it."

"Why, Henry," she said, "that is very sweet of you. How can I reward you for your kindness? What can a mere woman do, to show how she appreciates a good husband?"

"Mince them up," said he, "and cook them separately, so as not to confuse the flavors. Serve them each on a toast, and cover them liberally with grated cheese."

"I will do that," she said, "though it goes to my heart to chop it." She gave him a nudge and went into the kitchen, and began to dress and prepare the mushrooms. Henry waited in the sitting room, thinking of a delicious creature not a day more than twenty years old. Ella, peeking lovingly round the door, recognized the glimmer in his bird-like eye, and continued her cookery with a song in her heart. "He deserves nothing but the best," thought she, "and he shall have it. He shall have the better mushroom, for he is a king among men, and he said it is highly nutritious. After all, I had two eggs for breakfast, and those, tra-la-la, were sufficient for me.

"Come, my dear," said she, when all was done. "Here is our lunch ready, and here are our two plates, mine with a blue ring and yours with a red one. Eat heartily, my angel, and soon you shall be rewarded for your kindness and consideration."

Henry, who was peckish by reason of his diminished breakfast, wished moreover to fortify his tissues against the day when the true Goldilocks should arrive at "Three Bears Cottage." He therefore sawed himself off a sizable morsel and crammed it into his maw. He at once shot out of his chair, and began to leap, writhe, stagger, spin, curvet, gyrate, loop, and flounder all over the room. Simultaneously, he was seized with giddiness, nausea, spots before the eyes, palpitations, convulsions, flatulence, and other symptoms too hideous to mention.

"What on earth is the matter, darling?" said his wife. "Are you feeling unwell?"

"The devil!" he gasped. "I have eaten the Death Angel! I have eaten *Amanita phalloides!*"

"Really, my dear!" said she in amazement. "What an expression! Whatever can you be thinking of?"

"You b—!" cried he. "Will you stand there bandying words? I am dying! I am poisoned! Run for a doctor. Do you hear?"

"Poisoned?" said she. "By that mushroom? Why, Henry, that is the one you tried to palm off on me!"

"I confess it," said he. "I was feeling aggrieved and resentful. Forgive me. And, for heaven's sake, fetch me a doctor, or in five minutes I shall be dead."

"I forgive you for trying to poison me," said Ella. "But I cannot forget that awful name you called me just now. No, Henry, a lady dog cannot run for a doctor. I shall go no further than to that powerfully built young woodcutter who is chopping away at an elm tree down in the hollow. He has often whistled when I passed him, like an oriole in full song. I shall ask him what *he* thinks of a man who calls his wife such a name, and what he thinks of a man who brings home a thing like that to his wife. And I have no doubt at all he will tell me."

Pictures in the Fire

Dreaming of money, I lay half asleep on the Malibu sand. A desolate cry reached me from out of the middle air. It was nothing but a gull, visible only as a burning, floating flake of white in the hot, colorless sky, but wings and whiteness and a certain deep pessimism in the croak it uttered made me think it might be my guardian angel.

The next moment, from the dank interior of the beach house, the black telephone raised its beguiling voice, and I obeyed. It was, of course, my agent.

"Charles, I've made a date for you. For dinner tonight. Have you ever heard of a man called Mahound?"

"A Turk?"

"He *could* be a Turk."

"Never."

"I'll be honest with you, Charles, neither had I. But, believe me, he's solid. Money, new ideas, wonderful organizing power—everything."

"What does he want from me?"

"Everything."

"It seems almost superfluous."

"Look, Charles, this guy wants to make pictures. Pictures have to be written, Charles, and they have to be produced. Now this guy . . ."

"Does he know my wages?"

"I'm trying to tell you, Charles, it'll be more than salary. A lot more."

"Where, and at what hour?"

On the first stroke of eight I entered the foyer of the Beverly-Ritz. Precisely on the last stroke, an elevator boy, with an air of triumph, flung back his softly clanging lattice, and disclosed, like a Kohinoor in a casket, a personage of such distinguished bearing that I thought for a moment he must be a dummy, put there to lend tone to the hotel. I was wrong. He inhaled the smoke of a cigar of surpassing diameter; he swept a dark and flashing glance over the squalid congregation in the foyer; this glance came to rest on my hair, which I arrange in an unaffected style. He knew me; I knew him. "Mr. Rythym, this is very, very good of you. You have come all the way up from Malibu."

"Yes. Why do things by halves?"

"An excellent principle, Mr. Rythym. I have impressed it on my chef, who travels with me. If you'll come up to my little suite here, you shall tell me if I've been successful."

He fell silent as we entered his suite, awaiting my cry of surprise and admiration. It was with some difficulty that I repressed it. I was enchanted to hear him say, with the faintest discernible chagrin in his voice, "I hope this sort of decoration is not distasteful to you?"

"Not in the least. I like the baroque; I admire Titian."

"I confess I like my comfort. I like to travel with my own things. I had some little architectural changes made also."

"Excellent taste, if I may say so, and excellent judgment!"

He knew that I was impressed, but I knew that he wished to impress me. This made us even, except of course that *he* still had the money.

"I shall put that compliment to the test," said he. "Will you trust my taste so far as to let me give you a completely new cocktail?"

"I look forward to an important experience. How pleasant to talk like this! Which of us started it? I feel that at any moment we may exchange bows."

The new cocktail was a sizable affair, with something of the cloudy opalescence of absinthe, and one of those vague but fiery flavors—memories, regrets, contempt for regrets. I swallowed the first glass; the second swallowed me; I emerged, rather larger and greedier than life, in the midst of a banquet and a conversation. "Have a little more wine, Mr. Rythym. As I was saying, I should like to be the recognized leader of a revived and superior film industry."

"All you need is money, and, of course, talent."

"You are with me, then?"

"My agent permitting. A sordid soul, I must warn you!"

"He is to join us later this evening. I think I can talk to him in a language he will understand. Have a little brandy, Mr. Rythym. We'll drink to a long and happy association."

Next day, I visited Joe's offices at an early hour. Our eyebrows waved like the antennae of encountering ants. "Well, Joe? Did I sign something last night?"

"Think of a number," said he.

"Come on! I've been thinking of it all night."

"Multiply it by five," said he, smiling.

"Impossible! I'm not Einstein."

"Here's the contract, Charles. See for yourself."

"What a lot of pages! Hey! Here's rather a long string of options!"

"Well, like you said last night—'For all eternity, at that figure!' "

"Joe, I'd like to read this contract over with you, word by word."

"Sorry," said Joe. "I've got another client waiting. Did you notice her?"

"I saw, I must admit, what seemed like a patch of sunlight in your anteroom."

"That was Miss Belinda Windhover from England. Take another look as you go out."

"Before I do that, Joe, tell me some more about that fellow Mahound."

"Well," said my agent, hedging a little. "What did you think of him yourself?"

"Seems to have been everywhere."

"He certainly does."

"Knows everybody."

"He seems to, indeed."

"Amazing eyes, Joe."

"Yes, Charles, quite extraordinary."

"Anyway," said I, "he seems to have pots of money."

"Rich as the . . . Rich as Croesus," cried Joe, at once becoming his sunny self again.

"He must be older than he seems, Joe. He described an incident in the Boer War."

"Did he, indeed? Ha! Ha! I thought you were going to say the Crusades."

"What's that? He *didn't* describe an incident in the Crusades?"

"He did, though, to me. Of course, people say anything to an agent."

"Joe, does this Mahound remind you of anybody? Is his name in any way familiar?"

"I never could fit a name to a face, Charles. But I'll swear I've never seen him before."

"No, but frankly, Joe," said I uneasily, "who do you think he is?"

"It's not my business, old chap, to think who people are. That would never do. My job is to sell a client."

"You've sold me, Joe. Damned if you haven't! Damned anyway! Hell!"

"Look here, old boy. You don't want to get temperamental. After all, it's pictures. Think of the people I've sold you to in the past."

"Yes, Joe. But these damned options. You didn't really give him options on me for all eternity?"

"Well, it's just a phrase."

"A phrase! Oh, boy!"

"After all, he's a wonderful organizer. I bet he'll get some amazing effects, too. You work well with him, Rythym, and you've got a blazing future. You'll be the hottest writer in town."

"Joe, this contract's got to be bust. I'm out."

"Sorry, old chap, it's cast-iron. Besides, think of the money. Think of me. An agent needs his percentage, Charles. Anyway, he may not be what you suppose. You're a writer, a dreamer; you've got to remember this is the twentieth century. Maybe he's just some old guy who found out monkey glands in the Crusades or somewhere."

"With those ears?"

"Maybe he was a money lender in those days. Maybe he got 'em clipped a bit."

"Those nails?"

"Look, Rythym, you don't want to start being satirical. I know what producers are. I'm a man of taste, same as yourself. All the same, this is the industry, you know. I do a lot of business with these fellows. I can't go picking 'em to pieces just for a laugh."

"Joe, I think I'm going to walk about the streets a bit."

"That's the stuff. I knew you'd shape up to it. God! I'd give the world to undo it, Charles. I just made a fool mistake."

I went out, passing Miss Belinda Windhover on the way. She looked like an angel. What was that to me? That evening I called again at the Beverly-Ritz, and this time I was shown up to Mr. Mahound's suite. His dressing jacket was stupendous.

"Mr. Mahound, were you by any chance in the Crusades?"

"Mr. Rythym, that was a very interesting assignment."

"It makes you rather old, doesn't it?"

"Well, one's as old as one feels. I feel devilish young today, my dear Rythym. To be in the Beverly-Ritz Hotel, signing up talent, about to re-create the American Film Industry!"

"Avaunt!"

"My dear fellow! This is the twentieth century."

"Well then, clear off! Scram!"

"Have a cigar."

"Listen. I'm a tough customer."

"So am I. Which reminds me: I thought we might do a new version of Jekyll and Hyde. I could play the lead. Watch!"

"Phew!"

"Queer! Everyone hates seeing me like that. There was a saint I once looked in on. She said she'd rather spend the rest of her life on red-hot needles than see me like that for one second. Flattering, in a way. But, don't you worry, Rythym, you and I are going to get along like a house afire."

"Yes! Yes, indeed! Stay as you are now, that's all. I see that I'm in for it. I'll do anything you like."

"That's what I like about writers. Well, now, what are we going to do about making films?"

"Take a friendly word of advice. You don't want to make pictures. It's nothing but worry. Besides, you'll get mixed up with a lot of actors."

"I have always found the players very congenial."

"I guess you've been rather out of things recently. You haven't seen some of our stars."

"My dear Rythym, forgive me, but I'm supposed to have rather a good way with people. As for the worry—pooh! I've been a top executive in one of the biggest organizations in existence. Nothing but grumbling and complaints! Now I've retired, and I mean to enjoy myself."

"Well, why not sit back?" said I. "Sit back and take it easy?"

"You should see my throne! No, my dear fellow, I'm crazy to start in making pictures. You concentrate on finding a story. I'll stay here to interview the press. And, by the way, there's someone coming here to see me soon. Your excellent agent found her for me. A clean English girl. Fresh! Unspoiled!"

"I know that sort."

"I think not, Rythym. She's a mere child! I'm going to groom her for stardom. In fact, she may be here already." He rang a bell. "Has a Miss Windhover arrived?"

"Yes, sir. She's waiting."

"Show her in."

In a moment Miss Windhover had entered, again like a patch of sunshine, outdoing the costly electric glare.

"Oh, Mr. Mahound. I . . . I . . . I . . ."

He patted her hand reassuringly. "Now, now, my dear! Not nervous, surely? Always remember that you have talent, the thing that money can't buy. Remember that. It will give you poise. Miss Marlene Dietrich has poise. I want you to have poise, too."

"If you knew what it's been like, Mr. Mahound. The struggle for small parts. The cheap boardinghouses. And Daddy's been so cross. And Mummy cries. Why are one's people always such snobs? They're dears, of course, old-fashioned dears. Why are one's people always so old-fashioned?"

"There, there, my dear! It's all over now. Think of the big lights. Wealth! Fame! Parties in Beverly Hills!"

"And my art!"

"Yes. Yes. Your art."

"It comes first. And, of course, doggies."

"Yes, indeed. My dear Rythym, Miss Windhover loves dogs. Could you, possibly . . . ?"

Not too pleased, I took the telephone and called room service. "Some dogs. For Miss Belinda Windhover."

"Sorry, sir. Pet shops all shut by now."

"Do you call this service? Are there none in the hotel?"

"Only Myra de Falla's."

"She's slipping. Send 'em up."

The page soon arrived with two Borzois, four Scotties, and a pug. Belinda Windhover was delighted. "Oh, doggies!"

"See how she kisses them, my dear Rythym. You think she will make a star?"

"Listen, Mahound, I can see you're going to spoil that girl."

"Nonsense. I flatter myself I have a way with people. I want you to take her out, study her psychology, write her a big part."

"Let her study the part. To hell with her psychology!"

"Oh, come, my dear Rythym!"

"I won't," said I. "That's flat."

"Well! Well! I say, just look at this parquet floor. One of the blocks is loose."

As I looked, he dislodged a block with his toe. The effect was extraordinary. I seemed to be looking down to an infinite depth, at a vast number of highly animated figures in a flame-colored setting. Mr. Mahound edged the block into place again, and the vision was gone.

"Phew!"

"What did you say, my dear Rythym?"

"I said, 'Yes.'"

"You will spend the evening with Miss Windhover?"

"Yes."

"And explore her psychology?"

"Yes."

"Ah, here are the reporters! Come in, gentlemen! Come in. I want you all to meet Miss Belinda Windhover. She gave up a refined home for her art. Write it down."

"O.K. We know it. Old-fashioned parents."

"Well, take a photograph. Here she is, being groomed for stardom in Mahound Pictures Incorporated. Here are her beloved dogs."

"O.K. We know them. Hallo, Mirza! Hallo, Bobbles! Remember when Nancy North had 'em, boys?"

"She's slipped."

"And Lucille Lacey. She was always took with the pug."

"She's slipped, too."

"Maybe they ain't housebroken. O.K. Frame up. What about this gent?"

"I'm a writer."

"Fine! You can hold the leg of my tripod. O.K. Shoot. Miss Belinda Windhover. And you're Mr. Mahound?"

"I will tell you my intentions with regard to the renascence of the American film industry."

"Sure. Let's get Belinda with the big white dogs. They're class. Where's your sables, Miss Windhover?"

"Sables for Miss Windhover, my dear Rythym."

"Yes." Annoyed, I took up the telephone again.

"Sables."

"Sorry, sir. Can't buy sables at this hour."

"What sort of joint is this? Are there none in the hotel?"

"Plenty, sir. There's Miss Pauline Powell's."

"She's slipping. Bring 'em up."

Soon the photographs were all taken. The pressmen withdrew.

"Now, young people, I'm going to send you off to make friends with one another."

"Oh, Mr. Mahound, aren't you coming along?" cried Belinda with an arch pout and wiggle.

"Call me Nicholas, my dear. Tonight, alas, I can't be with you. I've a great deal to attend to."

"But," said she, "do you think I ought to be seen about with a writer?"

"Mr. Rythym is a very distinguished writer, my dear. What's more, he's my right-hand man."

"Yes, and I'm going to explore your psychology."

This cheered the future star a little. "I want to know all about my psychology," said she as we went down in the elevator. "I'm not going to be an ordinary actress, Mr. Rythym. I'm going to be intellectual. And at the same time I like nothing better than cooking, just simple things, in a simple playsuit. I'm going to ask Clark Gable, and Katherine Hepburn, when I get properly known, and Gary Cooper, and give them little cookies I bake myself."

"Fine! Stick to that idea. I like it."

"And you'll tell me all about my psychology?"

"Sure," said I. "We'll go into it together. Come on."

Next day, I spent a lot of time with Mr. Mahound. His suite was full of orchids and cablegrams.

"People are getting excited," said he, rubbing his hands.

"Yes."

"We're going to do great things."

"Yes."

"Now, what about our Belinda? Can you fit a part to her psychology?"

"Yes. I'm sure of it."

"Did she . . . talk about me at all last night?"

"She did. She thinks you're the cat's pajamas."

"The cat's pajamas, eh? Rythym, we're going to do great things. Great things! Run along."

I ran along to the restaurant where I was to meet Belinda. She seemed to have acquired poise overnight.

"Mr. Rythym. How do you do?"

"Listen. A film studio is the greatest democracy in the world. You can call me Charlie."

"Yes. I'm just simple. I like to cook. How's Mr. Mahound?"

"Belinda, he's wild about you."

"Tell me. Is he one of the *really* great producers?"

"The biggest of all. He's got all the money in the world."

"Yes, Charlie. But there's one thing money can't always buy, not in England, anyway. Or is that just a thought of my own?"

"You mean talent. I can guess your thoughts, Belinda."

"Don't do that. You see, my people are old-fashioned. I think I'd like to play Juliet."

"It's been done."

"Not as I shall do it. You shall write a new script, specially for me."

"O.K. We'll modernize it. The Capulet apartment is in a New York skyscraper. Romeo's a young G-man, from Harvard, but disguised as a Yale man in order to outwit the gangsters. Capulet's Harvard, you see. It builds for a reconciliation, a happy ending. Romeo's keen on mountain climbing; that builds up for the balcony scene. On a skyscraper, you see. Only his name's not Romeo. It's Don."

"Isn't that making him different?"

"Well, you know what Shakespeare said, 'Wherefore art thou Romeo?' "

"Juliet said that."

"Well, anyway, it showed there were doubts."

"You're right. I've only just thought of it. Charlie, you write my thoughts in a book on Shakespeare, and I'll sign it. I don't want to be an ordinary actress."

"You won't. But let's go and join Mahound. He's wild about you."

"And he's really one of the very big producers?"

"He is. But, a word in your ear. (God! It's like a shell! A lovely, rosy shell!) I was going to say, remember you've got the talent. Last night you were just a discovery. Today—you are what you are today. You're developing fast. Think in a big way. Don't let anybody cramp your style. Not even Mahound."

"No. Because of my art. That's sacred."

"Grand!"

Mr. Mahound, when we entered his suite, took both her hands in his. "What a very, very lovely thing to do, on the part of a very, very lovely lady, to come and see a poor old film man, in his little hideout in the Beverly-Ritz!"

"Nicky, Charlie's thought me up a part. Juliet, only better."

"Splendid. Have you anyone in mind for Romeo, my dear Rythym?"

"Oh, some guy."

"He's got to climb up the face of a skyscraper, Nicky. For me to do the balcony scene, holding a rose."

"Will your Hollywood leading men manage that, Rythym? They are not all as young as they used to be."

"Sure. They'll climb anywhere. And, look, we've got to work in a Joan of Arc touch to build up the part. She's got to save New York."

"From what?"

"Gangsters. And listen to the payoff."

"What's that?"

"Real bullets."

"Oh, Rythym! Come, come! After all, there are rules to the game, you know. Even I . . ."

"Hear me out," I cried. "The part demands it. Doesn't it, Belinda? How's she going to act up, give all she's got, if you let her down on the bullets?"

"I think I ought to have real bullets, Nicky."

"Of course," I insisted. "Do you think Theda Bara would have played Cleopatra without a real pearl?"

"Not a real asp, though," said Mahound, clutching at a straw.

I twitched it away. "Yeah, a real asp, only an old one. With its teeth out. You can use old bullets. Say, you can use old gangsters and let on they died of heart failure."

"You sound rather tough all of a sudden, my dear Rythym."

"Tough? You wait till I get on the set!"

"Perhaps the set will have parquet flooring."

"Yes, perhaps it will," said I, despondently. "Perhaps we'll have blank cartridges. Perhaps I'll go out and buy some real pearls, instead. Because I'm going to write in a Cleopatra touch, where she comes in rolled up in a carpet."

"Do so, my dear fellow. We've got a writer of talent, Belinda."

"Charlie's all right, but he gives way so. Please, Nicky, I want real bullets."

"Listen, folks," said I. "I'm off to buy those pearls. You talk it over."

On the way back, I was overcome by misgivings. Had I gone too far? Maybe the pearls were a little vulgar. I thought I'd go to my room and see how they looked with two or three of the largest taken from the middle. As I walked along the corridor, the elevator came humming down. Mr. Mahound was in it. He saw me. His lips shaped the words, "She's wonderful!" Then he was gone.

Later on, I went up to his suite. Belinda was there alone, tearing up orchids.

"They look like confetti," she said. "I find him a leetle . . . fascinating, your Mr. Mahound."

I noted her middle-European accent. "You have your bullets, then?"

"Charlie, we're going to have me save the city from a red navy. Real shells."

"That's right, Belinda, honey. Nick's a grand guy. He's a white man, Belinda. He's got background. If I were a girl, I'd think a lot of Nick. But don't forget it; you're the one with the talent. Don't let anybody cramp your style. You've got a big future, Belinda. Maybe you think you're in the money. Baby, that's chicken feed to what's coming to you, all so long as you don't get your style cramped."

"You're right, Charlie. It's my art. It's sacred."

In the evening I saw Mahound alone. "She's wonderful, Charles! But . . . I say . . ."

"Yeah?"

"Did she say anything to you about shells?"

"She said *you'd* said something to her about shells."

"Maybe I did. In a moment of emotion. It's tough, Charles. Real shells! There'll be trouble. I don't want to be dragged into court."

"What do you care?"

"I care about my ambitions in pictures. What's more, Charles, I don't like your script. Forgive me, old fellow. It's a grand script, but I don't like it. The fact is, it's too expensive."

His eyes could not meet mine. I saw he was ashamed that his millions were not entirely unlimited. I reflected that where vanity of that sort is to be found on one side of a contract there is always hope on the other. I goaded him. "I thought you had all the money in the world. I thought you were solid. They say, 'Rich as the devil,' you know." He couldn't bear to say frankly he was only *a* devil. He muttered something about a budget being a budget.

"I can do you a western," said I, sarcastically. "Will you run to a real horse?"

"I've run to a real trap already, my dear Rythym."

"Maybe you have. Very well, I'll get something on paper."

Next day I called Belinda early. "Well, lovey, our script's got panned. I'm writing you a little old period piece in a small-town setting. You wear one of those big bonnets that hide the face."

"Charlie, you don't say so! I want to come in in a carpet, with three big pearls."

"The pearls are out, ducky. There's an economy ramp on. Listen, even your shells are gone. It's you and a horse."

"Don't write a word, Charlie. Wait till I've seen Nick."

After lunch, the telephone summoned me to Mr. Mahound. Belinda was there, flushed and radiant.

"Real shells, Charlie!"

"And bells, Charles. Belinda and I are going to be married. Isn't that so, sweetie?"

"Yes, and I'm going to have real shells."

"Real battleships, too," said I. "How about that for an idea? Let me put 'em in the script. Coming up the Hudson, blazing away! My present to the bride."

"Do you hear what he says, Nick? Oh, Charlie, you *can* write! Real battleships!"

"I'm afraid Charles is joking, my dear. He likes jokes about blazing away. But you and I—let's talk about our wedding."

"All right, Nicky. We'll fly to New York. We'll go to the Little Church Around the Corner."

"Did you say the little *judge* around the corner?"

"No, honey, the Little *Church*."

"Not for us, honey. Us for a quiet wedding, in front of a judge."

"What? What do you think I am? Your chattel? Your slave? Am I a filmstar, or not?"

"But a good little wife, too, honey. Remember, you're a simple girl. Doggies . . . cookies . . . Her fans want her to be an ideal little wife, don't they, Charles?"

"Yes, Nicky. But I'm not signed up for the wife part yet awhile. I'm not acting any part before I'm signed up for it. Mummy said a girl shouldn't ever act like a wife till she is one. She's old-fashioned. Why are one's people so old-fashioned?"

"I'm old-fashioned, too, dear," said Nick. "I can't go to the Little

246 — THE JOHN COLLIER READER

Church Around the Corner. I should sink through the floor. Look, darling, make it just a plain judge, and maybe I can stretch a little on the budget. Maybe I'll get you a battleship or two."

"Well, don't forget you've promised."

"What a relief! What happiness!" cried he. "Real happiness! Let's start at once."

"Linda," I whispered, while he was telephoning for a plane. "Don't forget your prestige. Make it a good long honeymoon. Two months at least, honey, or the world'll think there's something wrong with your glamor."

"You're right, Charlie. I will."

So they went to Yuma. After some weeks I got a telegram. "*Home on Friday. Love. Nick and Linda.*" Soon afterwards came another. "*Confidential. Can you possibly outline alternative script? Western, South Sea, or other simple natural background. Repeat confidential. Nick.*"

After some thought, I drafted a rather humorous farm story, of the sort that made Mabel Normand in the good old days. I thought it would hardly appeal to Belinda, but I was under contract. Orders were orders.

I was at the airport to meet them. Linda alighted first, and was at once seized on by the press. I heard the words "husband," "doggies," "cookies."

"Charles," whispered Mahound. "A word in your ear. Have you got that outline? That rough script?"

"Yes. I've got it. What's the matter? Are you stalling on the real battleships?"

"Charles, she wants the real New York."

"Well! Well! Well! Never mind. I've got a farm story. She can have real striped stockings."

"She thinks big, Charles. She may feel it rather a letdown after the real New York."

"Don't worry. You go off to the hotel. Everything's fixed up for you. I'll look in after supper."

Late that evening I went round to see them. Something told me that all was not harmony in the romantic ménage. Mahound was frowning over a heap of bills.

"You've bought a lot of rather impressive orchids, Charles," said he, in a worried tone.

"Nothing's too good for you and Linda," said I, smiling. "You're my best friends in pictures."

"Yes, but it all goes down on the expense account."

"There you go again, dear!" cried Linda. "He's got all mean, Charlie. He says he can't afford to buy me New York. For the bombardment scene. Where I save it. *I* can't act in front of a lot of pasteboard, Charlie. You tell him."

"There's something in that, Nick," said I. "Still, listen, Linda, I've got a new script for you. The part's sort of lovable. Farm. Birds singing. Real birds. Hens, too. You come in scattering the corn. With comedy stockings on. Real stockings. Real comedy."

"Nick, is this just a bad joke, to welcome me home?"

"Now, listen, honey," said Nick. "Give the writer a chance. He's put his life's blood into this story. Go on, Charlie."

"That's true, Linda. There's smiles and tears in this script."

"Smiles?"

"Where you get a sock in the puss with a custard pie. A real . . ."

"Say. What have you got lined up for me next? A burlesque act? I'm out. I'm through."

"Joan of Arc started on a farm, honey."

"Joan of Arc never got no custard pie."

"She got worse than that, milking the cows, sweetie," said Nick. "I was there. I fixed it."

"What do you mean, you were there?" cried Belinda. "Are you starting in lying to me already? I'll fly to Reno. No, I won't, though. Don't forget what you put in my contract, out in Yuma. I've got to O.K. every script."

"Well, sweetie, Charles'll write you one you'll really like. Maybe where you're a young girl, mad to get on the stage. Then you can do your Juliet speech at a party. Where there's a big producer."

"No, he won't."

"Yes, he will."

"No, he won't. That's flat."

"Yes, he will," said Mahound. "A lovely script. A part that'll make you drive the whole world crazy. The real world. Won't you, Charles?"

"Well, as a matter of fact," said I. "I won't."

"What?"

"Look at the clock. Didn't you hear it strike twelve?"

"What of it?"

"Well, Nick," said I, "it's two months. Today—but now it's yesterday—my first option came up for renewal. I'm afraid you've let it slip by. I'm free!"

"Hell! I could sink through the floor!"

"Nicky, you got to sign a writer who'll put me in New York. And parts for my doggies."

"Your doggies are dead," I told her. "They ate your cookies."

"Ow! Charlie! My doggies!"

"I could sink through the floor!" muttered Nick. "To slip up on an option!"

"Yeah," said I. "You've slipped. Sink away!"

"I will, too," cried he, stamping his foot.

And with that he seized Belinda, and, WHOOSH, they were gone through the floor.

I chose one of the smaller orchids for a buttonhole, and went off to a nightclub. Next day, I returned to Malibu.

WET SATURDAY

It was July. In the large, dull house they were imprisoned by the swish and the gurgle and all the hundred sounds of rain. They were in the drawing room, behind four tall and weeping windows, in a lake of damp and faded chintz.

This house, ill-kept and unprepossessing, was necessary to Mr. Princey, who detested his wife, his daughter, and his hulking son. His life was to walk through the village, touching his hat, not smiling. His cold pleasure was to recapture snapshot memories of the infinitely remote summers of his childhood—coming into the orangery and finding his lost wooden horse, the tunnel in the box hedge, and the little square of light at the end of it. But now all this was threatened—his austere pride of position in the village, his passionate attachment to the house—and all because Millicent, his cloddish daughter Millicent, had done this shocking and incredibly stupid thing. Mr. Princey turned from her in revulsion and spoke to his wife.

"They'd send her to a lunatic asylum," he said. "A criminal-lunatic asylum. We should have to move away. It would be impossible."

His daughter began to shake again. "I'll kill myself," she said.

"Be quiet," said Mr. Princey. "We have very little time. No time for nonsense. I intend to deal with this." He called to his son, who stood looking out of the window. "George, come here. Listen. How far did you get with your medicine before they threw you out as hopeless?"

"You know as well as I do," said George.

"Do you know enough—did they drive enough into your head for you to be able to guess what a competent doctor could tell about such a wound?"

"Well, it's a—it's a knock or blow."

"If a tile fell from the roof? Or a piece of the coping?"

"Well, guv'nor, you see, it's like this—"

"Is it possible?"

"No."

"Why not?"

"Oh, because she hit him several times."

"I can't stand it," said Mrs. Princey.

"You have got to stand it, my dear," said her husband. "And keep that hysterical note out of your voice. It might be overheard. We are talking about the weather. If he fell down the well, George, striking his head several times?"

"I really don't know, guv'nor."

"He'd have had to hit the sides several times in thirty or forty feet, and at the correct angles. No, I'm afraid not. We must go over it all again. Millicent."

"No! No!"

"Millicent, we must go over it all again. Perhaps you have forgotten something. One tiny irrelevant detail may save or ruin us. Particularly you, Millicent. You don't *want* to be put in an asylum, do you? Or be hanged? They might hang you, Millicent. You must stop that shaking. You must keep your voice quiet. We are talking of the weather. Now."

"I can't. I . . . I . . ."

"Be quiet, child. Be quiet." He put his long, cold face very near to his daughter's. He found himself horribly revolted by her. Her features were thick, her jaw heavy, her whole figure repellingly powerful. "Answer me," he said. "You were in the stable?"

"Yes."

"One moment, though. Who knew you were in love with this wretched curate?"

"No one. I've said a—"

"Don't worry," said George. "The whole goddamned village knows. They've been sniggering about it in the Plow for three years past."

"Likely enough," said Mr. Princey. "Likely enough. What filth!" He made as if to wipe something off the backs of his hands. "Well, now, we continue. You were in the stable?"

"Yes."

"You were putting the croquet set into its box?"

"Yes."

"You heard someone crossing the yard?"

"Yes."

"It was Withers?"

"Yes."

"So you called him?"

"Yes."

"Loudly? Did you call him loudly? Could anyone have heard?"

"No, Father. I'm sure not. I didn't call him. He saw me as I went to the door. He just waved his hand and came over."

"How *can* I find out from you whether there was anyone about? Whether he *could* have been seen?"

"I'm sure not, Father. I'm quite sure."

"So you both went into the stable?"

"Yes. It was raining hard."

"What did he say?"

"He said 'Hullo, Milly.' And to excuse him coming in the back way, but he'd set out to walk over to Bass Hill."

"Yes."

"And he said, passing the park, he'd seen the house and suddenly thought of me, and he thought he'd just look in for a minute, just to tell me something. He said he was so happy, he wanted me to share it. He'd heard from the Bishop he was to have the vicarage. And it wasn't only that. It meant he could marry. And he began to stutter. And I thought he meant me."

"Don't tell me what you thought. Exactly what he said. Nothing else."

"Well . . . Oh dear!"

"Don't cry! It is a luxury you cannot afford. Tell me."

"He said no. He said it wasn't me. It's Ella Brangwyn-Davies. And he was sorry. And all that. Then he went to go."

"And then?"

"I went mad. He turned his back. I had the winning post of the croquet set in my hand—"

"Did you shout or scream? I mean, as you hit him?"

"No. I'm sure I didn't."

"Did he? Come on! Tell me."

"No, Father."

"And then?"

"I threw it down. I came straight into the house. That's all. I wish I were dead!"

"And you met none of the servants. No one will go into the stable. You see, George, he probably told people he was going to Bass Hill. Certainly no one knows he came here. He might have been attacked in the woods. We must consider every detail . . . A curate, with his head battered in—"

"Don't, Father!" cried Millicent.

"Do you want to be hanged? A curate, with his head battered in, found in the woods. Who'd want to kill Withers?"

There was a tap on the door, which opened immediately. It was little Captain Smollett, who never stood on ceremony. "Who'd kill Withers?" said he. "I would, with pleasure. How d'you do, Mrs. Princey. I walked right in."

"He heard you, Father," moaned Millicent.

"My dear, we can all have our little joke," said her father. "Don't pretend to be shocked. A little theoretical curate-killing, Smollett. In these days we talk nothing but thrillers."

"Parsonicide," said Captain Smollett. "Justifiable parsonicide. Have you heard about Ella Brangwyn-Davies? I shall be laughed at."

"Why?" said Mr. Princey. "Why should you be laughed at?"

"Had a shot in that direction myself," said Smollett, with careful sang-froid. "She half said yes, too. Hadn't you heard? She told most people. Now it'll look as if I got turned down for a white rat in a dog collar."

"Too bad!" said Mr. Princey.

"Fortune of war," said the little captain.

"Sit down," said Mr. Princey. "Mother, Millicent, console Captain Smollett with your best light conversation. George and I have something to look to. We shall be back in a minute or two, Smollett. Come, George."

It was actually five minutes before Mr. Princey and his son returned.

"Excuse me, my dear," said Mr. Princey to his wife. "Smollett, would you care to see something rather interesting? Come out to the stables for a moment."

They went into the stable yard. The buildings were now unused except as old sheds. No one ever went there. Captain Smollett entered, George followed him, Mr. Princey came last. As he closed the door he took up a gun which stood behind it. "Smollett," said he, "we have come out to shoot a rat which George heard squeaking under that tub. Now, you must listen to me very carefully or you will be shot by accident. I mean that."

Smollett looked at him. "Very well," said he. "Go on."

"A very tragic happening has taken place this afternoon," said Mr. Princey. "It will be even more tragic unless it is smoothed over."

"Oh?" said Smollett.

"You heard me ask," said Mr. Princey, "who would kill Withers. You heard Millicent make a comment, an unguarded comment."

"Well?" said Smollett. "What of it?"

"Very little," said Mr. Princey. "Unless you heard that Withers had met a violent end this very afternoon. And that, my dear Smollett, is what you are going to hear."

"Have you killed him?" cried Smollett.

"Millicent has," said Mr. Princey.

"Hell!" said Smollett.

"It *is* Hell," said Mr. Princey. "You would have remembered—and guessed."

"Maybe," said Smollett. "Yes, I suppose I should."

"Therefore," said Mr. Princey, "you constitute a problem."

"Why did she kill him?" said Smollett.

"It is one of these disgusting things," said Mr. Princey. "Pitiable, too. She deluded herself that he was in love with her."

"Oh, of course," said Smollett.

"And he told her about the Brangwyn-Davies girl."

"I see," said Smollett.

"I have no wish," said Mr. Princey, "that she should be proved either a lunatic or a murderess. I could hardly live here after that."

"I suppose not," said Smollett.

"On the other hand," said Mr. Princey, "*you* know about it."

"Yes," said Smollett. "I am wondering if I could keep my mouth shut. If I promised you—"

"I am wondering if I could believe you," said Mr. Princey.

"If I promised," said Smollett.

"If things went smoothly," said Mr. Princey. "But not if there was any sort of suspicion, any questioning. You would be afraid of being an accessory."

"I don't know," said Smollett.

"I do," said Mr. Princey. "What are we going to do?"

"I can't see anything else," said Smollett. "You'd never be fool enough to do me in. You can't get rid of two corpses."

"I regard it," said Mr. Princey, "as a better risk than the other. It could be an accident. Or you and Withers could both disappear. There are possibilities in that."

"Listen," said Smollett. "You can't—"

"Listen," said Mr. Princey. "There may be a way out. There *is* a way out, Smollett. You gave me the idea yourself."

"Did I?" said Smollett. "What?"

"You said you would kill Withers," said Mr. Princey. "You have a motive."

"I was joking," said Smollett.

"You are always joking," said Mr. Princey. "People think there must be something behind it. Listen, Smollett, I can't trust you. Therefore you must trust me. Or I will kill you now, in the next minute. I mean that. You can choose between dying and living."

"Go on," said Smollett.

"There is a sewer here," said Mr. Princey, speaking fast and forcefully. "That is where I am going to put Withers. No outsider knows he has come up here this afternoon. No one will ever look for him unless you tell them. You must give me evidence that you have murdered Withers."

"Why?" said Smollett.

"So that I shall be dead sure that you will never open your lips on the matter," said Mr. Princey.

"What evidence?" said Smollett.

"George," said Mr. Princey, "hit him in the face, hard."

"Good god!" said Smollett.

"Again," said Mr. Princey. "Don't bruise your knuckles."

"Oh!" said Smollett.

"I'm sorry," said Mr. Princey. "There must be traces of a struggle between you and Withers. Then it will not be altogether safe for you to go to the police."

"Why don't you take my word?" said Smollett.

"I will when we've finished," said Mr. Princey. "George, get that croquet post. Take your handkerchief to it. As I told you. Smollett, you'll grasp the end of this croquet post. I shall shoot you if you don't."

"Oh, hell," said Smollett. "All right."

"Pull two hairs out of his head, George," said Mr. Princey, "and remember what I told you to do with them. Now, Smollett, you take that bar and raise the big flagstone with the ring in it. Withers is in the next stall. You've got to drag him through and dump him in."

"I won't touch him," said Smollett.

"Stand back, George," said Mr. Princey, raising his gun.

"Wait a minute," cried Smollett. "Wait a minute." He did as he was told.

Mr. Princey wiped his brow. "Look here," said he. "Everything is perfectly safe. Remember, no one knows that Withers came here. Everyone thinks he walked over to Bass Hill. That's five miles of country to search. They'll never look in our sewer. Do you see how safe it is?"

"I suppose it is," said Smollett.

"Now come into the house," said Mr. Princey. "We shall never get that rat."

They went into the house. The maid was bringing tea into the drawing room. "See, my dear," said Mr. Princey to his wife, "we went to the stable to shoot a rat and we found Captain Smollett. Don't be offended, my dear fellow."

"You must have walked up the back drive," said Mrs. Princey.

"Yes. Yes. That was it," said Smollett in some confusion.

"You've cut your lip," said George, handing him a cup of tea.

"I . . . I just knocked it."

"Shall I tell Bridget to bring some iodine?" said Mrs. Princey. The maid looked up, waiting.

"Don't trouble, please," said Smollett. "It's nothing."

"Very well, Bridget," said Mrs. Princey. "That's all."

"Smollett is very kind," said Mr. Princey. "He knows all our trouble. We can rely on him. We have his word."

"Oh, have we, Captain Smollett?" cried Mrs. Princey. "You *are* good."

"Don't worry, old fellow," Mr. Princey said. "They'll never find anything."

Pretty soon Smollett took his leave. Mrs. Princey pressed his hand very hard. Tears came into her eyes. All three of them watched him go down the drive. Then Mr. Princey spoke very earnestly to his wife for a few minutes and the two of them went upstairs and spoke still more earnestly to Millicent. Soon after, the rain having ceased, Mr. Princey took a stroll round the stable yard.

He came back and went to the telephone. "Put me through to the Bass Hill police station," said he. "Quickly. . . . Hullo, is that the police station? This is Mr. Princey, of Abbott's Laxton. I'm afraid something terrible has happened up here. Can you send someone at once?"

SQUIRRELS HAVE BRIGHT EYES

I had what appeared to be the misfortune to fall in love with a superb creature, an Amazon, a positive Diana. Her penthouse *pied-à-terre* was a single enormous room, liberally decorated with the heads and skins of the victims of her Lee-Enfield, her Ballard, her light Winchester repeater. Bang—a hearthrug! Crack—a fur coat! Pop, pop—a pair of cozy mittens!

But, as a matter of fact, clothes suffocated her. Supremely Nordic, she ranged her vast apartment clad only in a sort of kirtle. This displayed four magnificent limbs, sunburned several tones darker than her blonde and huntress hair. So I fell in love. What limbs! What hair! What love!

She only laughed. "Squirrel," she said—she called me "Squirrel" —"it's no good. You're a real pet, though; you remind me a little of Bopotiti. He lived in a tree on the Congo.

"Bogey," she said to her hateful little female adorer, who was always curled up on some skin or other, "Bogey," she said, "show him that snap of Bopotiti."

"Really," I said, "this is not like me at all. I am more graceful, more bird-like."

"Yes, but he used to bring me *mjna-mjnas*. Every morning."

"I will bring you love, at all hours. Marry me."

"No."

"Live with me."

"No, no. I live with my guns. The world cannot utter its gross libidinous sneers at a girl who lives chastely with her Lee-Enfield, her Ballard, her light Winchester."

"Love is better."

"Ha! Ha! Forgive me. I must laugh now." And she flung herself upon a polar bear skin in a paroxysm of giant mirth.

Utterly crushed, I went out to do myself in. Racking my brain for the most expressive method, I suddenly remembered a man called Harringay, a taxidermist who was often at her cocktail parties, where he had eyed me with a friendly interest.

I went to his shop. He was there alone. "Harringay! Stuff me!"

"Sure. What shall it be? Steak? Chop suey? Something fancy?"

"No, Harringay, bitumen. Harringay, I want you to employ your art upon me. Send me to Miss Bjornstjorm with my compliments. For her collection. I love her." Here I broke down.

Harringay, that owl-like man, acted magnificently. He gave me his philosophy, put new heart into me. "Go just as you are," said he. "Perhaps love will come. Fortunately your eyes are somewhat glassy by nature. You have only to hold the pose."

"You think love will come?"

"She must at any rate recognize you as an admirably motionless companion for a—it's on the tip of my tongue—one of those things up in a tree to shoot from."

"It's on the tip of mine, too. I'll gamble on it. Harringay, you are a friend."

"No, no. It will be an advertisement for me."

"No, no. You are a friend. In one moment I shall be ready."

I was. He carried me to her apartment. "Brynhild, here is something more for your natural history museum."

"Why, it's Squirrel! Is he stuffed?"

"For love of you, Brynhild."

"How lifelike! Harringay, you are the king of taxidermists."

"Yes, and I service him every day. It's a new method. It's all arranged for. Shall I put him in that alcove?"

"Yes, and we'll have a cocktail party. Right away. Everybody must come. Bogey, call everybody."

"Even Captain Fenshawe-Fanshawe?"

"Yes, by all means the Captain."

She collapsed, roaring with laughter, upon a flamboyant tiger skin. She was still laughing when the guests poured in. The gigantic Captain Fenshawe-Fanshawe, my rival with the monocle and the Hapsburg chin, taller than Brynhild herself, towered among them.

Everybody laughed, chattered, and admired. "Marvelous work, Mr. Harringay! When our dear Pongo dies, I shall send him to you."

"I hope you will do our Fifi, Mr. Harringay."

Harringay bowed and smiled.

"He did it for love, they say."

"Love!" boomed the Captain, filliping me under the nose. I trembled with rage and mortification.

"Be careful! He's very delicately wired," said Harringay.

"Love!" boomed the Captain. "A squirrel! Ha! Ha! It takes a full-sized man to hold a worthwhile amount of love. What sort of heart did you find in him, Harringay?"

"Quite a good sort," said Harringay. "Broken, of course."

Brynhild's laughter, which had been continuous, stopped.

"A squirrel!" sneered the Captain. "Didn't know you went in for small deer, Brynhild. Send you a stuffed mouse for Christmas."

He had not observed Brynhild's expression. I had. It looked like one of those bird's-eye views of the world you see before a newsreel, with everything going round and round: clouds, continents, seas, one thing after another. Suddenly, in a single convulsive movement, she was off her flamboyant tiger skin, and stretched superbly prone on the funereal pelt of a black panther. "Leave me!" she cried chokingly. "Go away, everybody! Go away! Go away!"

The guests felt something was wrong. They edged out.

"Does that mean me?" said the Captain.

"Go away!" she cried.

"Me, too?" said Bogey.

"Everybody," sobbed Brynhild. Nevertheless, a woman must have a friend; she clutched her by the hand.

"Brynhild! What is it? You are crying. I have never seen you cry. Tell me. We are alone."

"Bogey, he did it for love."

"Yes."

"I've just realized what that means, Bogey. I didn't know. I've been all my life hunting things—killing them—having them stuffed. Bogey, that's all done now. He's everything to me. I'll marry him."

"I don't think you can, if he's stuffed, Brynhild, darling."

"Live with him, then."

"The world—?"

"The world's gross libidinous sneers can't touch a girl who lives with a man who's stuffed, Bogey. But I shall seat him at table and talk to him, just as if he were alive."

"Brynhild, you're wonderful!"

I agreed. At the same time my position was a difficult one. It is no joke to have to seem stuffed when your beloved adores you, passionately, remorsefully, seats you up at table, talks to you in the firelight, tells you all, weeps even. And yet, if I unbent, if I owned up, I felt her newborn love might wither in the bud.

Sometimes she would stroke my brow, press a burning kiss upon it, dash off, fling herself down on a leopard skin, and do her exercises, frantically, hopelessly. I needed all my control.

Harringay called every morning, "to service me" as he said. He insisted that Brynhild should go out for an hour, pretending that a professional secret was involved. He gave me my sandwich, my glass of milk, dusted me thoroughly, massaged my joints where they were stiff.

"You can't massage the stiffness out of this absurd situation," said I.

"Trust me," he said.

"All right," I said. "I will."

Brynhild returned, as usual, five minutes or so too early. She couldn't stay away the full hour. "I miss him so," she said, "when I'm out. And yet, when I come back, he's stuffed. It's too terrible."

"Perhaps I can help you," said Harringay.

"I dare not believe it," she said, clutching her heart.

"What?" cried he. "And you the little girl who shoots tigers? Pluck up your courage. Would you be too scared to believe in an artificial leg?"

"No," said she. "I could face that."

"One of those modern ones," said he, "that walk, kick, dance even, all by machinery?"

"Yes," she said. "I believe in it."

"Now," said he, "for his sake, believe in two of them."

"I will. I do."

"Be brave! Two arms as well."

"Yes! Yes!"

"And so forth. I can make his jaw work. He'll eat. He'll open and shut his eyes. Everything."

"Will he speak to me?"

"Well, maybe he'll say, 'Mamma.' "

"Science! It's wonderful! But—what will the world say?"

"I don't know. 'Bravo!' Something of that sort."

"No. Gross libidinous sneers. If I live with him, and he says 'Mamma.' And I can't marry him because he's stuffed. Oh, I knew it would be no good."

"Don't worry," said Harringay. "These are just technicalities. I'll straighten it all out. More tomorrow."

She saw him out, and came back shaking her head. She was in despair. So was I. I knew the Diana element in her. So did she. She spent the afternoon on the skin of an immense grizzly. I longed to be with her. I felt myself as if I were on the skin of a porcupine.

Suddenly, just as the shadows were falling thick in the vast apartment, there was a knock at the door. She opened it. It was the abominable Fenshawe-Fanshawe.

"What do you want?" said she.

"Guess," said he.

"I wouldn't dream of it," said she.

"No need to," said he, removing his jacket.

"What are you doing?" said she.

"I have waited long enough," said he. "Listen, I don't like that kirtle. It doesn't suit you."

She made a bound, however, and reached the wall. Her guns were there. She pointed the Lee-Enfield. "Stand back!" she cried.

The Captain, sneering, continued to advance.

She pulled the trigger. A hollow click sounded. The Captain smiled and came nearer.

She caught up the Ballard. Click! The Winchester light repeater. Click! Click! Click!

"I removed the cartridges," said the Captain, "when you were laughing so heartily at the cocktail party."

"Oh, Squirrel! If you could help me!"

"He can't. He's stuffed."

"Oh, Squirrel! Help me! Squirrel! Squirrel—" At that moment, he seized her. She broke free. "Help me!"

"You're darn tootin' I will," said I, rising stiffly from my seat. The effect, in the shadowy alcove, was probably uncanny. The Captain gave a throbbing cry. He turned and fled for the door. My blood was up, however, and, regardless of the pins and needles, I pursued him, snatching a prize elephant's tusk as I ran. While yet he scrabbled at the latch I let him have it. He fell.

I felt Brynhild beside me, a true comrade. "Forgive me," I said. "I have deceived you."

"You have saved me. My hero!"

"But I'm not stuffed," I murmured.

"At least," said she, "you have more stuffing in you than that great beast."

"He will need it now, Brynhild. Or the mountainous carcass will become offensive."

"Yes. We'll call in Harringay."

"Good old Harringay!"

"A clean kill, Squirrel mine! Great hunting!"

"Thank you."

I put one foot on the mighty torso, then the other. Our lips were on a level.

"Brynhild! May I?"

"Yes."

"Really?"

"Yes."

It was a divine moment. We sank upon the skin of a giant panda. Bogey knocked in vain.

Next day, of course, we were married.

Halfway to Hell

Louis Thurlow, having decided to take his own life, felt that at least he might take his own time also. He consulted his bankbook; there was a little over a hundred pounds left. "Very well," said he. "I'll get out of this flat, which stinks, and spend a really delightful week at Mutton's. I'll taste all the little pleasures just once more, to say good-bye to them."

He engaged his suite at Mutton's, where he kept the page boys on the run. At one moment they had to rush round into Piccadilly to buy him chrysanthemums, in which to smell the oncoming autumn, which he would never see. Next they were sent to Soho to get him some French cigarettes, to put him in mind of a certain charming hotel which overlooked the Seine. He had also a little Manet sent round by the Neuilly Galleries—"To try living with," he said, with the most whimsical smile. You may be sure he ate and drank the very best—just a bite of this and a glass of that, he had so many farewells to take.

On the last night of all, he telephoned Celia, whose voice he felt inclined to hear once more. He did not speak, of course, though he thought of saying, "You should really not keep on repeating 'Hallo,' but say 'Good-bye.'" However, she had said that already, and he had been taught never to sacrifice good taste to a bad *mot*.

He hung up the receiver and opened the drawer in which he had stored his various purchases of veronal tablets.

"It seems a great deal to get down," he thought. "Everything is relative. I prided myself on not being one of those panic-stricken, crackbrained suicides who rush to burn out their guts with gulps of disinfectant; now it seems scarcely less civilized to end this pleasant week with twenty hard swallows and twenty sips of water. Still, life is like that. I'll take it easy."

Accordingly, he arranged his pillows very comfortably, congratulated himself on his pajamas, and propped up a photograph against his bedside clock. "I have no appetite," he said. "I force myself to eat as a duty to my friends. There is no bore like a despairing lover." And with that he began to toy with this last, light, plain little meal.

The tablets were not long in taking effect. Our hero closed his eyes. He put on a smile such as a man of taste would wish to wear when found in the morning. He shut off that engine which drives us from one moment to the next and prepared to glide into the valley of the shadow.

The glide was a long one. He anticipated no landing, and was the more surprised to learn that there is no such thing as nothing, while there is quite definitely such a thing as being dead in the most comfortable bedroom in all Mutton's Hotel.

"Here I am," he said. "Dead! In Mutton's Hotel!"

The idea was novel enough to make him get out of bed at once. He noticed that his corpse remained there, and he was glad to observe that the smile was still in place and looked extremely well.

He strolled across to the mirror to see if his present face was capable of an equally subtle expression, but when he came to look in he saw nothing at all. Nevertheless, he obviously had arms and legs, and he felt that he could still do his old trick with his eyebrows.

From this he assumed that he was much the same, only different.

"I am just invisible," he said, "and in that there are certain advantages."

He decided to go out at once, in order to have a bit of fun. He went down the stairs, followed a departing guest through the revolving door, and in two minutes he was walking down Cork Street. It appeared to be just after midnight; there were a bobby, a taxi or two, and a few ladies, none of whom took any notice of him at all.

He had not gone twenty yards, however, and was, as a matter of fact, just passing his tailor's, when a lean dark figure detached itself from the shadows which hung about the railings in front of the shop, and, coming up close behind his elbow, said, "Damn and blast it, man, you *have* been a time!"

Louis was a little put out at finding himself not so invisible as he had thought. Still, he glanced at the stranger and saw that his eyes were as luminous as a cat's eyes, from which it was plain that he could see better than most.

"Do you mean," said Louis, "that I've been keeping you waiting?"

"I've been hanging about here, freezing, for a week," said the stranger peevishly.

Now, it was only September, and the nights, though nippy, were not as cold as all that. Louis put two and two together. "Is it possible," said he, "that you have been waiting to—to take me in charge, so to speak, on account of my recent suicide?"

"I have," said the fiend. "You'll come quietly, I suppose."

"My dear fellow," said Louis, "I know you have your duty to do, and in any case I'm not the sort of person to make a scene in the street. I'm sorry if I've kept you hanging about in the cold, but the truth is I had no idea of your existence, so I hope there'll be no ill feeling."

"I've got an ill feeling all right," replied the other, grumpily. "I swear I've got the flu, curse it!" And with that he sneezed miserably. "The worst of it is," he added, "we've got such a *human* of a way to go. I shall be fit for nothing for weeks."

"Really, I can't bear to hear you sneeze like that," cried our hero. "Have you ever tried the Quetch at the Rattrap Club?"

"What's Quetch?" asked the other, between sneezes.

"It tastes like liquid fire," replied Louis. "I believe it's made from plum stones, though why I can't tell you. Possibly to cure your cold."

"Liquid fire, eh?" observed the stranger, his eyes glowing like cigarette ends.

"Come and try it," said Louis.

"I don't know," said the other. "We're a week late through your fault. I don't see why we shouldn't be half an hour later through mine. I suppose there'll be trouble if they hear of it."

Louis assured him that this last half-hour must be put down to his account also. "You caught the cold through my delay," said he. "Therefore, I am responsible for the time you take to cure it." The fiend obviously believed this, which caused our hero to reflect that he must be a very simple fiend.

They set out for the Rattrap Club. Passing through Piccadilly Circus, the fiend indicated the Underground, saying, "That's where I'm going to take you when we've had this drop of what-d'ye-call-it."

"That does not take you to Hell," said Louis, "but only to Baron's Court. The mistake is pardonable."

"No mistake," replied the fiend. "Let's cross the road this way, and I'll show you what I mean."

They went in, and traveled down the escalator, chatting very affably. It was fairly crowded with more ordinary passengers, but our friends attracted no attention whatever. There are a great many fiendish-looking individuals traveling on this subway, and others of a corpsy appearance. Besides, now I come to think of it, they were invisible.

When they had reached the ordinary lowest level, where the trains run, "Come," said the fiend, and drew Louis into a passage he had never before noticed, up which there came a huger clanking and a sultrier blast. He saw a notice saying, KEEP TO THE WRONG. A few paces brought them to the top of an escalator such as our hero had never dreamed of: it swooped down from under their feet with a roar and a groan, down into the close innards of the earth. Its passage was lit by the usual lamps. Louis, whose sight seemed to have become extremely keen, saw that at some far point on its vast curve the black shades changed to blue, and the lamps gave place to stars. However, it seemed to go on the devil of a long way past that.

For the rest, it was made just like all other escalators, except in matters of detail. Its sides were adorned with pictorial advertisements of temptations, some of which Louis thought might be very interesting. He could have stepped on, for there was no barrier or ticket collector, but, as we have seen, he liked to take his time.

Now and then, he and his companion were jostled by other fiends and their charges. I am afraid some of the latter were behaving in rather an undignified manner, and had to be marched along in a sort of policeman's grip. The effect was degrading. Louis was interested to see, however, how tremendously the escalator accelerated once it felt the weight of these infernal policemen and their victims. It was a tremendous spectacle to see this narrow moving chain, dimly lit, roaring, rushing down, looping the distance between Earth and Hell, which is greater than one would imagine.

"What did you do before this sort of thing was invented?" asked Louis.

"We had to leap down, like chamois, from star to star," replied the fiend.

"Splendid!" said Louis. "Now, let's go and have that drink."

The fiend consenting, they went off to the Rattrap, and, slipping into a cubbyhole behind the bar, they helped themselves to a full bottle of the famous Quetch. The fiend disdained a glass, and put the bottle to his lips, whereupon Louis saw, to his great amazement, this powerful form of brandy was actually brought to the boil. The fiend appeared to like it. When the liquid was gone, he sucked away at the bottle, the melting sides of which collapsed like the skin of a gooseberry sucked at by a child. When he had drawn it all into his mouth, he smiled, pursed his lips, and blew out the glass again, this time more like a cigarette-smoker exhaling his first puff. What's more, he didn't blow the glass into bottle shape as formerly, but into the most delightful statuary piece, most realistic, most amusing. "Adam and Eve," said he laconically, placing it on the table to cool.

"Oh, very, very good!" cried Louis. "Can you do Mars and Venus?"

"Oh, yes," said the fiend. Louis immediately commandeered several more bottles of Quetch.

He called for one or two other subjects, of a nature that would hardly interest the reader. The fiend, however, thought each more amusing than the last, and nearly split his sides over the effect of a hiccup on Lady Godiva. The fact is, he was getting rather tight. Louis encouraged him, not so much for the love of art as because he had no great desire to ride on that escalator.

At last the fiend could drink no more. He got up, jingled his money (fiends have money—that's where it's all gone to), and puffed out his cheeks. "Whoop!" said he, with a hiccup. "My cold's better, I believe. If it isn't, well, then—to Hell with it! That's what I say. Ha! Ha!"

Louis, you may be sure, told him he was a fine fellow. "Well," said he, as they stood on the steps of the Club, "I suppose you're going that way; I'm going this." He made a bit of a face, pleasantly, raised his hat, and set off along the street, scarcely daring to breathe till he had rounded the corner.

When he thought himself in safety, "By Jove," said he. "I'm well rid of that fellow. Here I am, dead, invisible, and the night is yet young. Shall I go and see what Celia's doing?"

Before he could embark on this rash project, he felt a very hard hand on his arm, looked round, and saw his custodian.

"Oh, there you are," said Louis. "I wondered where you'd got to."

"Drunk as a lord," said the fiend, with a smile. "Got to see each other home, eh?"

There was nothing for it. They set out for Piccadilly Circus. The fiend kept his hand on Louis's wrist, quite inoffensively, of course, only Louis would rather it had not been there.

So they went chatting into the subway again. Just as they got to the level of the Piccadilly line, which is where the infernal aperture gapes for those who are privileged to see it, whom should Louis see, in top hat, white silk scarf, and all the rest, but his damned nasty rival, catching a late train home.

"I bet," said Louis at once, addressing the fiend, "that you are not strong enough to carry me on your back from here to the escalator."

The fiend, with a sneer of contempt, immediately bent down. Louis, with a desperate effort, picked hold of his rival round the waist and dumped him on the back of the fiend, who gripped his legs, and started off like a racehorse.

"Carry you all the way to Hell for tuppence!" cried he, in drunken pride.

"Done!" cried Louis, who was skipping along beside them to enjoy the spectacle.

He had the delicious pleasure of seeing them jump on the escalator, whose terrific acceleration seemed even more marked and more admirable than before.

Louis returned to the street as happy as a king. He walked about for a bit, and suddenly decided to look in at Mutton's Hotel to see how his corpse was getting on.

He was rather annoyed to see, even as he stood looking at it, that the effective smile, over which he had taken so much trouble, was slipping. In fact, it was beginning to look altogether idiotic. Without giving the matter a thought, he instinctively nipped inside to hook it back into place. In doing so he twitched his nose, found it necessary to sneeze, opened his eyes, and, in a word, discovered that he was quite alive and no longer kicking, in that excellent bedroom of Mutton's Hotel.

"Well, upon my word!" said he, glancing at the bedside table. "Is it possible I dropped off to sleep after taking only two of those tablets? There is really something to be said for taking one's time. It must have been just a vivid dream."

In short, he was glad to be alive, and still gladder a day or two afterwards, when some news came through that made it seem that it was not a dream after all. Louis's rival was announced as missing, having last been seen by two friends at the entrance of Piccadilly Circus Station shortly after midnight on Tuesday.

"Who'd have thought it?" said Louis. "Anyway, I suppose I had better go and see Celia."

However, he had learned the advantage of taking his time, and before he went he thought better of it, and, in fact, did not go at all, but went to Paris for the autumn, which shows that girls should not play fast and loose with the affections of small men with blue eyes, or they may find themselves left in the lurch.

THE LADY ON THE GRAY

Ringwood was the last of an Anglo-Irish family which had played the devil in County Clare for a matter of three centuries. At last all their big houses were sold up, or burned down by the long-suffering Irish, and of all their thousands of acres not a single foot remained. Ringwood, however, had a few hundred a year of his own, and if the family estates had vanished he at least inherited a family instinct which prompted him to regard all Ireland as his domain and to rejoice in its abundance of horses, foxes, salmon, game, and girls.

In pursuit of these delights, Ringwood ranged and roved from Donegal to Wexford through all the seasons of the year. There were not many hunts he had not led at some time or other on a borrowed mount, nor many bridges he had not leaned over through half a May morning, nor many inn parlors where he had not snored away a wet winter afternoon in front of the fire.

He had an intimate by the name of Bates, who was another of the same breed and the same kidney. Bates was equally long and lean, and equally hard-up, and he had the same wind-flushed bony face, the same shabby arrogance, and the same seignorial approach to the little girls in the cottages and cowsheds.

Neither of these blades ever wrote a letter, but each generally knew where the other was to be found. The ticket collector, respectfully blind as he snipped Ringwood's third-class ticket in a first-class compartment, would mention that Mr. Bates had traveled that way only last Tuesday, stopping off at Killorglin for a week or two after the snipe. The chambermaid, coy in the clammy bedroom of a fishing inn, would find time to tell Bates that Ringwood had gone on up to Lough Corrib for a go at the pike. Policemen, priests, bagmen, gamekeepers, even the tinkers on the roads, would pass on this verbal *pateran*. Then, if it seemed his friend was on to a good thing, the other would pack up his battered kitbag, put rods and guns into their cases, and drift off to join in the sport.

So it happened that one winter afternoon, when Ringwood was strolling back from a singularly blank day on the bog of Ballyneary, he was hailed by a one-eyed horse dealer of his acquaintance, who came trotting by in a gig, as people still do in Ireland. This worthy told our friend that he had just come down from Galway, where he had seen Mr. Bates, who was on his way to a village called Knockderry, and who had told him very particularly to mention it to Mr. Ringwood if he came across him.

Ringwood turned this message over in his mind, and noted that it was a very particular one, and that no mention was made as to whether it was fishing or shooting his friend was engaged in, or whether he had met with some Croesus who had a string of hunters that he was prepared to lend. "He certainly would have put a name to it if it was anything of that sort! I'll bet my life it's a pair of sisters he's got on the track of. It must be!"

At this thought, he grinned from the tip of his long nose like a fox, and he lost no time in packing his bag and setting off for this place Knockderry, which he had never visited before in all his roving up and down the country in pursuit of fur, feather, and girls.

He found it was a long way off the beaten track, and a very quiet place when he got to it. There were the usual low, bleak hills all around, and a river running along the valley, and the usual ruined tower up on a slight rise, girdled with a straggly wood and approached by the remains of an avenue.

The village itself was like many another: a few groups of shabby cottages, a decaying mill, half-a-dozen beer shops, and one inn at which a gentleman, hardened to rural cookery, might conceivably put up.

Ringwood's hired car deposited him there, and he strode in and found the landlady in the kitchen, and asked for his friend Mr. Bates.

"Why, sure, your honor," said the landlady, "the gentleman's staying here. At least, he is, so to speak, and then, now, he isn't."

"How's that?" said Ringwood.

"His bag's here," said the landlady, "and his things are here, and my grandest room taken up with them (though I've another every bit as good), and himself staying in the house best part of a week. But the day before yesterday he went out for a bit of a constitutional, and—would you believe it, sir?—we've seen neither hide nor hair of him since."

"He'll be back," said Ringwood. "Show me a room, and I'll stay here and wait for him."

Accordingly, he settled in, and waited all the evening, but Bates failed to appear. However, that sort of thing bothers no one in Ireland, and Ringwood's only impatience was in connection with the pair of sisters, whose acquaintance he was extremely anxious to make.

During the next day or two he employed his time in strolling up and down all the lanes and bypaths in the neighborhood, in the hope of discovering these beauties, or else some other. He was not particular as to which it should be, but on the whole he would have preferred a cottage girl, because he had no wish to waste time on elaborate approaches.

It was on the second afternoon, just as the early dusk was falling, he was about a mile outside the village and he met a straggle of muddy cows coming along the road, and a girl driving them. Our friend took a look at this girl, and stopped dead in his tracks, grinning more like a fox than ever.

This girl was still a child in her teens, and her bare legs were spattered with mud and scratched by brambles, but she was so pretty that the seignorial blood of all the Ringwoods boiled in the veins of their last descendant, and he felt an overmastering desire for a cup of milk. He therefore waited a minute or two, and then followed leisurely along the lane, meaning to turn in as soon as he saw the byre, and beg the favor of this innocent refreshment, and perhaps a little conversation into the bargain.

They say, though, that blessings never come singly, any more than misfortunes. As Ringwood followed his charmer, swearing to himself that there couldn't be such another in the whole county, he heard the fall of a horse's hoofs, and looked up, and there, approaching him at a walking pace, was a gray horse, which must have turned in from some bypath or other, because there certainly had been no horse in sight a moment before.

A gray horse is no great matter, especially when one is so urgently in need of a cup of milk, but this gray horse differed from all others of its species and color in two respects. First, it was no sort of a horse at all, neither hack nor hunter, and it picked up its feet in a queer way, and yet it had an arch to its neck and a small head and a wide nostril that were not entirely without distinction. And, second—and this distracted Ringwood from all curiosity as to breed and bloodline—this gray horse carried on its back a girl who was obviously and certainly the most beautiful girl he had ever seen in his life.

Ringwood looked at her, and as she came slowly through the dusk she raised her eyes and looked at Ringwood. He at once forgot the little girl with the cows. In fact, he forgot everything else in the world.

The horse came nearer, and still the girl looked, and Ringwood looked, and it was not a mere exchange of glances, it was wooing and a marriage, all complete and perfect in a mingling of the eyes.

Next moment, the horse had carried her past him, and, quickening its pace a little, it left him standing on the road. He could hardly run after it, or shout; in any case, he was too overcome to do anything but stand and stare.

He watched the horse and rider go on through the wintry twilight, and he saw her turn in at a broken gateway just a little way along the road. Just as she passed through, she turned her head and whistled, and Ringwood noticed that her dog had stopped by him, and was sniffing about his legs. For a moment he thought it was a smallish wolfhound, but then he saw it was just a tall, lean, hairy lurcher. He watched it run limping after her, with its tail down, and it struck him that the poor creature had had an appalling thrashing not so long ago; he had noticed the marks where the hair was thin on its ribs.

However, he had little thought to spare for the dog. As soon as he got over his first excitement, he moved on in the direction of the gateway. The girl was already out of sight when he got there, but he recognized the neglected avenue which led up to the battered tower on the shoulder of the hill.

Ringwood thought that was enough for the day, so he made his way back to the inn. Bates was still absent, but that was just as well. Ringwood wanted the evening to himself in order to work out a plan of campaign.

"That horse never cost two ten-pound notes of anybody's money," said he to himself. "So, she's not so rich. So much the better! Besides, she wasn't dressed up much; I don't know what she had on—a sort of cloak or something. Nothing out of Bond Street, anyway. And lives in that old tower! I should have thought it was all tumbled down. Still, I suppose there's a room or two left at the bottom. Poverty Hall! One of the old school, blue blood and no money, pining away in this godforsaken hole, miles away from everybody. Probably she doesn't see a man from one year's end to another. No wonder she gave me a look. God! If I was sure she was there by herself, I wouldn't need much of an introduction. Still, there might be a father or a brother or somebody. Never mind, I'll manage it."

When the landlady brought in the lamp: "Tell me," said he. "Who's the young lady who rides the cobby-looking, old-fashioned-looking gray?"

"A young lady, sir?" said the landlady doubtfully. "On a gray?"

"Yes," said he. "She passed me on the lane up there. She turned in on the old avenue, going up to the tower."

"Oh, Mary bless and keep you!" said the good woman. "That's the beautiful Murrough lady you must have seen."

"Murrough?" said he. "Is that the name? Well! Well! Well! That's a fine old name in the West here."

"It is so, indeed," said the landlady. "For they were kings and queens in Connaught before the Saxon came. And herself, sir, has the face of a queen, they tell me."

"They're right," said Ringwood. "Perhaps you'll bring me in the whiskey and water, Mrs. Doyle, and I shall be comfortable."

He had an impulse to ask if the beautiful Miss Murrough had anything in the shape of a father or a brother at the tower, but his principle was, "Least said, soonest mended," especially in little affairs of this sort. So he sat by the fire, recapturing and savoring the look the girl had given him, and he decided he needed only the barest excuse to present himself at the tower.

Ringwood had never any shortage of excuses, so the next afternoon he spruced himself up and set out in the direction of the old avenue. He turned in at the gate, and went along under the forlorn and dripping trees, which were so ivied and overgrown that the darkness was already thickening under them. He looked ahead for a sight of the tower, but the avenue took a turn at the end, and it was still hidden among the clustering trees.

Just as he got to the end, he saw someone standing there, and he looked again, and it was the girl herself, standing as if she was waiting for him.

"Good afternoon, Miss Murrough," said he, as soon as he got into earshot. "Hope I'm not intruding. The fact is, I think I had the pleasure of meeting a relation of yours, down in Cork, only last month. . . ." By this time he had got close enough to see the look in her eyes again, and all this nonsense died away in his mouth, for this was something beyond any nonsense of that sort.

"I thought you would come," said she.

"My god!" said he. "I had to. Tell me—are you all by yourself here?"

"All by myself," said she, and she put out her hand as if to lead him along with her.

Ringwood, blessing his lucky stars, was about to take it, when her lean dog bounded between them and nearly knocked him over.

"Down!" cried she, lifting her hand. "Get back!" The dog cowered and whimpered, and slunk behind her, creeping almost on its belly. "He's not a dog to be trusted," she said.

"He's all right," said Ringwood. "He looks a knowing old fellow. I like a lurcher. Clever dogs. What? Are you trying to talk to me, old boy?"

Ringwood always paid a compliment to a lady's dog, and in fact the creature really was whining and whimpering in the most extraordinary fashion.

"Be quiet!" said the girl, raising her hand again, and the dog was silent.

"A cur," said she to Ringwood. "Did you come here to sing the praises of a half-bred cur?" With that, she gave him her eyes again, and he forgot the wretched dog, and she gave him her hand, and this time he took it and they walked toward the tower.

Ringwood was in seventh heaven. "What luck!" thought he. "I might at this moment be fondling that little farm wench in some damp and smelly cowshed. And ten to one she'd be sniveling and crying and running home to tell her mammy. This is something different."

At that moment, the girl pushed open a heavy door, and, bidding the dog lie down, she led our friend through a wide, bare, stone-flagged hall and into a small vaulted room which certainly had no resemblance to a cowshed except perhaps it smelt a little damp and moldy, as these old stone places so often do. All the same, there were logs burning on the open hearth, and a broad, low couch before the fireplace. For the rest, the room was furnished with the greatest simplicity, and very much in the antique style. "A touch of the Cathleen Ni Houlihan," thought Ringwood. "Well, well! Sitting in the Celtic twilight, dreaming of love. She certainly doesn't make much bones about it."

The girl sat down on the couch and motioned him down beside her. Neither of them said anything; there was no sound but the wind outside, and the dog scratching and whimpering timidly at the door of the chamber.

At last, the girl spoke. "You are of the Saxon," said she gravely.

"Don't hold it against me," said Ringwood. "My people came here in 1656. Of course, that's yesterday to the Gaelic League, but still I think we can say we have a stake in the country."

"Yes, through its heart," said she.

"Is it politics we're going to talk?" said he, putting an Irish turn to his tongue. "You and I, sitting here in the firelight?"

"It's love you'd rather be talking of," said she with a smile. "But you're the man to make a byword and a mockery of the poor girls of Eire."

"You misjudge me entirely," said Ringwood. "I'm the man to live alone and sorrowful, waiting for the one love, though it seemed something beyond hoping for."

"Yes," said she. "But yesterday you were looking at one of the Connell girls as she drove her kine along the lane."

"Looking at her? I'll go so far as to say I did," said he. "But when I saw you I forgot her entirely."

"That was my wish," said she, giving him both her hands. "Will you stay with me here?"

"Ah, that I will!" cried he in rapture.

"Always?" said she.

"Always," cried Ringwood. "Always and forever!" For he felt it better to be guilty of a slight exaggeration than to be lacking in courtesy to a lady. But as he spoke she fixed her eyes on him, looking so much as if she believed him that he positively believed himself.

"Ah," he cried. "You bewitch me!" And he took her in his arms.

He pressed his lips to hers, and at once he was over the brink. Usually he prided himself on being a pretty cool hand, but this was an intoxication too strong for him; his mind seemed to dissolve in sweetness and fire, and at last the fire was gone, and his senses went with it. As they failed, he heard her saying, "Forever! Forever!" and then everything was gone and he fell asleep.

He must have slept some time. It seemed he was awakened by the heavy opening and closing of a door. For a moment, he was all confused and hardly knew where he was.

The room was now quite dark, and the fire had sunk to a dim glow. He blinked, and shook his ears, trying to shake some sense into his head. Suddenly he heard Bates talking to him, muttering as if he, too, was half asleep, or half drunk more likely. "You *would* come here," said Bates. "I tried hard enough to stop you."

"Hullo!" said Ringwood, thinking he must have dozed off by the fire in the inn parlor. "Bates? God, I must have slept heavy! I feel queer. Damn it—so it was all a dream! Strike a light, old boy. It must be late. I'll yell for supper."

"Don't, for heaven's sake," said Bates, in his altered voice. "Don't yell. She'll thrash us if you do."

"What's that?" said Ringwood. "Thrash us? What the hell are you talking about?"

At that moment a log rolled on the hearth, and a little flame flickered up, and he saw his long and hairy forelegs, and he knew.

INCIDENT ON A LAKE

Mr. Beaseley, while shaving on the day after his fiftieth birthday, eyed his reflection, and admitted his remarkable resemblance to a mouse. "Cheep, cheep!" he said to himself, with a shrug. "What do I care? At least, I wouldn't, except for Maria. I remember I thought her kittenish at the time of our marriage. How she has matured!"

He knotted his thread-like necktie and hurried downstairs, scared out of his life at the thought of being late for breakfast. Immediately afterwards, he had to open his drugstore, which then, in its small-town way, would keep him unprofitably busy till ten o'clock at night. At intervals during the day, Maria would drop in to supervise, pointing out his mistakes and weaknesses, regardless of the customers.

He found a brief solace every morning when, unfolding the newspaper, he turned first of all to the engaging feature originated by Mr. Ripley. On Fridays he had a greater treat; he then received his copy of his favorite magazine, *Nature Science Marvels*. This reading provided, so to speak, a hole in his otherwise hopeless existence, through which he escaped from the intolerable into the incredible.

On this particular morning the incredible was kind enough to come to Mr. Beaseley. It came in a long envelope and on the handsome notepaper of a prominent law firm. "Believe it or not, my dear," Mr. Beaseley said to his wife, "but I have been left four hundred thousand dollars."

"Where? Let me see!" cried Mrs. Beaseley. "Don't hog the letter to yourself in that fashion."

"Go on," said he. "Read it. Stick your nose in it. Much good may it do you!"

"Oh! Oh!" said she. "So you are already uppish!"

"Yes," said he, picking his teeth. "I have been left four hundred thousand dollars."

"We shall be able," said his wife, "to have an apartment in New York or a little house in Miami."

"You may have half the money and do what you like with it," said Mr. Beaseley. "For my part, I intend to travel."

Mrs. Beaseley heard this remark with the consternation she always felt at the prospect of losing anything that belonged to her, however old and valueless. "So you would desert me," she said, "to go chasing about after some native woman? I thought you were past all that."

"The only native women I am interested in," said he, "are those that Ripley had a picture of—those with lips big enough to have dinner plates set in them. In the *Nature Science Marvels Magazine* they had some with necks like giraffes. I should like to see those, and pygmies, and birds of paradise, and the temples of Yucatan. I offered to give you half the money because I know you like city life and high society. I prefer to travel. If you want to, I suppose you can come along."

"I will," said she. "And, don't forget, I'm doing it for your sake, to keep you on the right path. And, when you get tired of gawping and rubbering around, we'll have an apartment in New York *and* a little house in Miami."

So, Mrs. Beaseley went resentfully along, prepared to endure Hell herself if she could deprive her husband of a little of his Heaven. Their journeys took them into profound forests, where, from their bare bedroom—whose walls, floor, and ceiling were austerely fashioned of raw pine—they could see framed in every window a perfect little Cézanne, with the slanting light cubing bluely among the perpendiculars of pine trees or exploding on the new green of a floating spray. In the high Andes, on the other hand, their window was a square of burning azure, with sometimes a small, snow-white cloud like a tight roll of cotton in a lower corner. In the beach huts on tropical islands, they found that the tide, like an original and tasteful *hôtelier,* deposited a little gift at their door every morning: a skeleton fan of violet seaweed, a starfish, or a shell. Mrs. Beaseley, being one of the vulgar, would have preferred a bottle of Grade A and a copy of the *Examiner.* She sighed incessantly for an apartment in New York and a house in Miami, and she sought endlessly to punish her unfortunate spouse for depriving her of them.

If a bird of paradise settled on a limb above her husband's head, she was careful to let out a raucous cry and drive the interesting creature away before Mr. Beaseley had time to examine it. She told him the wrong hour for the start of the trip to the temples of Yucatan, and she diverted his attention from an armadillo by pretending she had something in her eye. At the sight of a bevy of the celebrated bosoms of Bali, clustered almost like grapes upon the quay, she just turned around and went straight up the gangplank again, driving her protesting husband before her.

She insisted they should stay a long time in Buenos Aires so that she could get a permanent wave, a facial, some smart clothes, and go to the races. Mr. Beaseley humored her, for he wanted to be fair, and they took a suite in a comfortable hotel. One afternoon, when his wife was at the races, our friend struck up an acquaintance with a little Portuguese doctor in the lounge, and before long they were talking vivaciously of hoatzins, anacondas, and axolotls. "As to that," said the little Portuguese, "I have recently returned from the headwaters of the Amazon, where the swamps and lakes are terrific. In one of those lakes, according to the Indians, there is a creature entirely unknown to science—a creature of tremendous size, something like an alligator, something like a turtle, armor-plated, with a long neck, and teeth like sabres."

"What an interesting creature that must be!" cried Mr. Beaseley in a rapture.

"Yes, yes," said the Portuguese. "It is certainly interesting."

"If only I could get there!" cried Mr. Beaseley. "If only I could talk to those Indians! If only I could see the creature itself! Are you by any chance at liberty? Could you be persuaded to join a little expedition?"

The Portuguese was willing, and soon everything was arranged. Mrs. Beaseley returned from the races, and had the mortification of hearing that they were to start almost immediately for a trip up the Amazon and a sojourn on the unknown lake in the dysgenic society of Indians. She insulted the Portuguese, who did nothing but bow, for he had an agreeable financial understanding with Mr. Beaseley.

Mrs. Beaseley berated her husband all the way up the river, harping on the idea that there was no such creature as he sought, and that he was the credulous victim of a confidence man. Inured as he was to her usual flow of complaints, this one made him wince and humiliated him before the Portuguese. Her voice, also, was so loud and shrill that, in all the thousands of miles they traveled up the celebrated river, he saw nothing but the rapidly vanishing hinder parts of tapirs, spider monkeys, and giant anteaters, which hurried to secrete themselves in the impenetrable deeps of the jungle.

Finally they arrived at the lake. "How do we know this is the lake he was speaking of?" Mrs. Beaseley said to her husband. "It is probably just *any* lake. What are those Indians saying to him? You can't understand a word. You take everything on trust. You'll never see a monster. Only a fool would believe in it."

Mr. Beaseley said nothing. The Portuguese learned, from his conversation with the Indians, of an abandoned grass hut, which in due time and after considerable effort they located. They moved into it. The days passed by. Mr. Beaseley crouched in the reeds with binoculars and was abominably bitten by mosquitoes. There was nothing to be seen.

Mrs. Beaseley succeeded in taking on a note of satisfaction without in the least abating her tone of injury. "I will stand this no longer," she said to her husband. "I've allowed you to drag me about. I've tried to keep my eye on you. I've traveled hundreds of miles in a canoe with natives. Now I see you wasting our money on a confidence man. We leave for Para in the morning."

"You may, if you wish," said he. "I'll write you a check for two hundred thousand dollars. Perhaps you can persuade some native in a passing canoe to take you down the river. But I will not come with you."

"We will see about that," said she. She hadn't the faintest intention of leaving her husband alone, for she feared he might enjoy himself. Nevertheless, after he had written out the check and given it to her, she continued to threaten to leave him, for if he surrendered, it would be a triumph, and if he didn't, it would be another little black cross against him.

She happened to rise early one morning and went out to make her ungrateful breakfast on some of the delicious fruits that hung in profusion all around the hut. She had not gone far before she happened to glance at the sandy ground, and there she saw a footprint that was nearly a yard wide, splayed, spurred, and clawed, and the mate to it was ten feet away.

Mrs. Beaseley looked at these admirable footprints with neither awe nor interest—only annoyance at the thought of her husband's triumph and the vindication of the Portuguese. She did not cry out in wonder, or call to the sleeping menfolk, but only gave a sort of honking snort. Then, picking up a sizable palm frond, this unscrupulous woman obliterated the highly interesting footprints, never before seen by a white person's eyes. Having done so, she smiled grimly and looked for the next set, and she wiped out that one, too. A little farther on, she saw another, and then still one more, and so on, till she had removed every trace down to the tepid of the lake, where the last was printed at the very edge of the water.

Having obliterated this final trace, Mrs. Beaseley straightened up and looked back toward the hut. "You shall hear of this," she said, addressing her sleeping husband, "when we are settled down at Miami and you are too old to do anything about it."

At that moment there was a swirl in the water behind her and she was seized by a set of teeth which quite exactly resembled sabres. She had no leisure to check up on the other points mentioned by the Portuguese doctor, but no doubt they came up to specification. She uttered one brief scream as she disappeared, but her voice was hoarse by reason of the strain she had put on it during the previous weeks, and her cry, even if it had been heard, could easily have been confused with the mating call of the megatherium, thought to be extinct. As a matter of fact, the last surviving megatherium emerged from the jungle only shortly afterward, looked around in all directions, shrugged his shoulders resignedly, and went back the way he had come.

A little later, Mr. Beaseley awoke, noted the absence of his wife, and finally went and woke the Portuguese. "Have you seen my wife?" said he.

"Really!" said the little Portuguese, and went to sleep again.

Mr. Beaseley went out and looked around, and at last returned to his friend. "I'm afraid my wife has run away," said he. "I have found her footprints leading down to the lake, where she has evidently encountered some native in a canoe and persuaded him to transport her down the river. She was always threatening to do so in order to take a small house at Miami."

"That is not a bad town," said the Portuguese, "but, in the circumstances, perhaps Buenos Aires is better. This monster is a great disappointment, my dear friend. Let us go back to Buenos Aires, where I will show you some extraordinary things—in quite a different line, of course—such as your Ripley has never dreamed of."

"What an agreeable companion you are!" said Mr. Beaseley. "You make even city life sound attractive."

"Well, if you get tired of it, we can always move on," said the little Portuguese. "I know some tropical islands where the girls—

though their lips are not designed to hold dinner plates—are nevertheless marvels of nature, and their dances are wonders of art."

OVER INSURANCE

Alice and Irwin were as simple and as happy as any young couple in a family-style motion picture. In fact, they were even happier, for people were not looking at them all the time and their joys were not restricted by any censorship code. It is therefore impossible to describe the transports with which Alice flew to embrace Irwin on his return from work, or the rapture with which Irwin returned her caresses.

It was at least two hours before they even thought about dinner. Even then, it took a long time to get food on the table, there was so much patting and petting, nibbling at the nape of the neck, mumbling of ears, kissing, fondling, and foolishness to the carrying of every single dish.

When at last the meal was ready, you may be sure they ate with excellent appetite. Nevertheless, whatever was best on his plate, he found time to put it on hers, and she was no slower in picking out some dainty tidbit to pop between his eager and rather rubbery lips.

After dinner, they would sit in one chair, for all the world like two innocent lovebirds in a cage, and he would entertain her with a detailed catalogue of her charms, which gave her the highest possible opinion of his taste and judgment. However, these delights did not endure very long, for they found it necessary to go to bed at an early hour, in order to rise bright and fresh in the morning.

It was a dull and heavy night when he did not wake up once or twice and switch on the light to assure himself she was not merely a delightful dream. She, blinking through the rosy radiance, was not in the least annoyed at being thus awakened, and they would have a very delightful little conversation and soon would fall happily asleep again.

It is not likely that a husband whose evenings are so contentedly spent at home will often linger in saloons and barrooms when the day's work is done. It was only on rare occasions that Irwin suffered himself to be persuaded, and even then he would suddenly think of his darling—how plump, how soft, how deliciously rounded she was—and he would give a sort of frisk or leap into the air.

"Why the hell do you do that?" his friends would demand. "Did you think someone was giving you a hotfoot or something?"

"No, no," he would reply evasively. "I was just feeling peppy. I was just feeling full of beans."

With that, he would grin all over his face like a fool, and take hasty leave of them, and rush home at top speed, eager to reassure himself as to the genuine existence, and his own miraculous possession, of those tender, those rounded, those infinitely sweet details that made up his delectable little wife.

On one of these occasions he was darting home as fast as his legs would carry him, when he forgot to look about him in crossing the street, and a taxi came swiftly around the corner. Fortunately, the driver jammed on his brakes; otherwise Irwin would have been bowled over like a ninepin, and might never have seen his honeybun any more. This idea appalled him, and he was unable to dismiss it from his mind.

That night they were seated as usual in their single chair, she tenderly stroking his somewhat sallow chops, and he protruding his lips, like some eager ape at the approach of a milk bottle, in the attempt to imprint kisses on her passing hand. In this interval, it was his custom to recite all the events of the long day, and especially how he had missed her. "And that reminds me," said he, "I was very narrowly missed myself, by a taxi, as I was crossing the street, and if the driver had not put his brakes on I should have been bowled over like a ninepin. And then maybe I should never have seen my honeybun any more."

At these words her lips trembled, and her eyes brimmed over with tears. "If *you* didn't see me any more," she said, "then I wouldn't see *you* any more."

"I was just thinking of that," said Irwin.

"We always have the same thoughts," said she.

This, however, was no consolation; their thoughts that evening were so unutterably sad. "All day tomorrow," said Alice, weeping,

"I shall be seeing you lying all squashed in the gutter. I'm sure it will be too much for me. I shall just lie down and die."

"Oh, I wish you had not said that," said Irwin. "Now I shall be thinking of you lying all crumpled on the hearthrug. I shall go mad, or die."

"Now it's even worse," lamented Irwin. "Supposing you should die because you think that I've died because . . . It's too much! I can't bear it!"

"Nor can I," said she.

They hugged each other very tightly, and exchanged kisses rendered surpassingly salty by their tears. This is thought by some to add relish, as with peanuts, by bringing out the sweetness. Irwin and Alice were too overcome to appreciate fine points of this nature; they could think of nothing but of how each would feel if the other should suddenly die. Consequently they got never a wink of sleep all night long, and Irwin was deprived of the pleasure of dreaming of his Alice and of switching on the light to find that she was true. She, on her side, was denied the joy of blinking up in a sudden rosy radiance to see him hovering and goggling over her. They made up for this by the passion and fervor of their embraces. Consequently, when the dawn came cool and gray and rational in at their window, the unhappy pair were themselves feeling cooler, grayer, and more rational than at any time since they had first met.

"Alice," said Irwin, "we must look at this bravely. We must face up to what may happen, and do our best to provide ourselves with whatever consolation we can."

"My only consolation will be to cry," said she.

"Yes, and mine, too," said he. "But would you rather cry in a fireless garret, and have to stop and get up and do your own housework, or would you rather cry in a fine apartment, with a mink coat on, and plenty of servants to bring in your meals?"

"I would rather have my meals brought in," said she. "Because then I could go right on crying. And if I had a mink coat on I should not catch cold and sneeze in the middle of it."

"And I would rather cry on a yacht," said he, "where my tears could be ascribed to the salt spray, and I should not be thought unmanly. Let us insure each other, darling, so that, if the worst happens, we can cry without interruption. Let us put nine-tenths of our money into insurance."

"It will leave us very little to live on now," said she. "But that is all the better, beloved, because then it will be all the more of a consolation."

"That was exactly my idea," said he. "We always have the same thoughts. This very day I will take out the policies."

"And let us," cried she, "insure our dear bird also," pointing to the feathered cageling, whom they always left uncovered at night, in order that his impassioned trills might grace their diviner raptures.

"You are right," said he. "I will put ten bucks on the bird. His chirpings would be as a string of pearls to me, if ever I were left alone."

That day Irwin made arrangements for the investment of nine-tenths of his earnings. "We are poor," said he, on his return, "but we have each other. If ever we are robbed of that joy, we shall at least have many thousands of dollars."

"Do not speak of them," said she. "Hateful dollars!"

"By all means," said he. "Let us have dinner. I was very economical at lunchtime, and I am unusually hungry this evening."

"It will not take long," said she. "I was economical at the market, and have bought a new sort of food. It is amazingly cheap, and it contains a whole alphabet of vitamins, enough to keep a whole family in pep and energy for a week. It says so in the description on the packet."

"Splendid!" said he. "Depend upon it; your dear, sweet, tender little metabolism and my great, gruff, bearish metabolism will spell all the honey-dovey-love-words in creation out of that same alphabet of vitamins."

No prospect could be more agreeable, but as the days passed it appeared that their metabolism would have put up a poor show at Scrabble. Or perhaps the manufacturer of the product had been misled by some alien-minded scientist, and had thus erred slightly in the description on the packet. Irwin grew so weak that he could no longer leap into the air at the thought of his darling, his tender, his deliciously-rounded little wife. On the other hand, Alice grew so thin that he no longer had any reason to do so.

Her stockings now wrinkled unappetizingly upon her stick-like legs.

"I think," thought Irwin, "she no longer rushes to greet me with eager rapture as of yore. Perhaps it's as well. How much more delightful to be greeted by a porterhouse steak!"

What with this new, disturbing thought, and his sawdust diet, and the innumerable financial worries that increasingly beset the young lovers, now that nine-tenths of their income went into insurance, Irwin frequently passed wakeful nights, but he no longer felt impelled to switch on the light and feast his eyes on his beloved. The last time he had done so, she had mistaken his face for an omelet. "Oh, it's only you!" she had murmured, turning crossly away.

They fed their new diet to the bird, who soon afterwards flopped on his back, threw up his feet, and died. "At least we get fifty bucks on him," said Irwin. "And he is only a bird!"

"I hope we are not thinking the same thought," said Alice.

"Of course not," said he. "How can you imagine it?"

"*I* certainly am not," said she. "How shall we spend the money? Shall we buy another canary?"

"No," said he. "Let us have something bigger. Let us buy a big, fat roasting chicken."

"So we will," said she, "and potatoes, and mushrooms, and string beans, and chocolate cake, and cream, and coffee."

"Yes," said he. "And coffee. Get some good, strong, bitter coffee; something with a real kick to it, if you know what I mean."

"I will get," said she, "the best, the strongest, and the bitterest I can."

That night they were not long in carrying in the dishes, nor in emptying them when they were on the table.

"This is certainly good, strong coffee," said Irwin. "And bitter."

"Is it not?" said she. "You didn't, by any chance, change the cups round while I was in the kitchen?"

"No, dear," said Irwin. "I was just wondering if you had. It certainly seems to have a kick in it."

"Oh, Irwin!" cried Alice. "Is it possible we had the same thought after all?"

"It feels like it," cried Irwin, legging it for the door faster even than he had done in the old days, when he used to leave saloons and barrooms with such impetuous speed. "I must get to a doctor."

"So must I," said she, fumbling also for the latch.

The poison, however, acted extremely quickly on their weakened constitutions. Even as they scuffled for precedence, they fell prone upon the doormat, and the postman came and covered them with bills.

THE FROG PRINCE

Two young men were discussing life. Said the richer of them to the poorer, "Paul, you had better marry my sister."

"That is a very strange thing to say," said Paul, "considering I have told you all about my debts."

"I am not worldly," replied Henry Vanhomry. "I should prefer my sister to marry a clean, decent, and kindly fellow like yourself, than some rich but blasé roué, cynic, near-man, sub-man, or half-man."

"I am certainly not blasé," said Paul. "On the other hand, I had not the pleasure of meeting your family when I was in Boston."

"I am very fond of my sister," said Henry, "in a way."

"How delightful! No doubt she was a mother to you when you were small. A little mother!"

"No. No. She is ten years younger than I am; only twenty-eight, in fact."

"Aha! She would have come into her fortune just in the rockiest year of our financial history."

"Fortunately it is well invested, and yields her an income of forty thousand dollars."

"An objection occurs to me. We are men of the world, Henry. If we were of the other sex, we might also make mistakes. Fond as I am of children—"

"That would be a matter entirely for you to decide."

"Henry, your sister sounds charming. Tell me more about her. She is not by any chance a *teeny* little woman?" And Paul held his hand some thirty inches from the floor.

"Quite the reverse."

"*Quite* the reverse, eh?"

"My dear Paul, I do not mean that she is six-feet-four."

"Six-feet-three, perhaps?"

"And-a-half. But, perhaps, I should tell you she is rather plump. Disproportionately so, in fact."

"Upon my word! I hope she is good-tempered."

"Angelically. You should hear her petting her dolls."

"Pardon me, Henry, but is she at all—backward?"

"A matter of opinion. She reads and writes admirably."

"How delightful. We could correspond, if I happened to be away."

"I will be frank with you, Paul; her letters to famous boxers are quite amazingly expressive, though by no means perfect in orthography."

"Henry, she is capable of hero-worship; she has an affectionate nature."

"Almost embarrassingly so. It appears from these letters of hers, which we censor, that she would make a devoted wife. However, my family are old-fashioned, and the boxers are cowardly brutes. I should like to see her safely married."

"But, as yet, if I understand you, she is pure as the driven snow? Charming!"

"Hers has been a cloistered girlhood. Yet there is something romantic in her nature which causes me alarm. Supposing one of the boxers responded. He might not treat her politely."

"I, on the other hand, would write her the most devoted letters, and bow, with old-world courtesy, whenever we met. Hm! All I fear, to be perfectly candid, is that a certain confounded coldness, a defect of my nature, might be a cause of pain, dissatisfaction, or longing."

"Well, my dear Paul, that is hardly a matter for me to speculate upon. I can only remind you that faint heart never won fair lady."

"Very well, Henry. I will at least come with you and see your sister."

"I am afraid I cannot accompany you. You forget that I am off to Europe next week. However, I'll give you a letter of introduction to the family."

All this being arranged, our good Paul took leave of his friend, and, after walking about for a little with an air of distraction, he paid a visit to the apartment of another friend of his.

"My dear Olga," he said, after a time, "I'm afraid I have some very ridiculous news for you. I am going to be poor no longer."

"Tell me only one thing, Paul. Is she beautiful?"

"Not very, it seems. I have not seen her, but she is over six feet three, and disproportionately fat."

"My poor Paul! She is simply bound to have hair on her face. What will become of you?"

"Besides all this, she is not very bright, I hear."

"And, now I come to think of it, what will become of me?"

"She has forty thousand a year, my dear Olga."

"Paul, we women are given to incredible follies when we are jealous. I might refuse everything. I find myself capable of jealousy."

"But, on the other hand, are you, or am I, capable of living any longer without a little of that forty thousand a year?"

"Or some other."

"But what other, my dear Olga? Where is another forty thousand?"

"It is true, Paul. Am I right in believing that your gigantic bride-to-be is mentally nine years, or is it twelve years old?"

"Seven, I should think, by all that Henry told me of her. She has an exuberant innocence. She writes to boxers, but caresses dolls."

"Really? That is very interesting. Dolls are so featureless. Now, is there any great hurry, Paul? I still have that bracelet you found at Palm Beach. It would provide us with a few last weeks together."

"I was going to suggest, as a matter of fact, that it should be my present to the bride, for I like to do things in good style. However, something may turn up. I admit that I love you."

"You shall promise me not to go near Boston for at least a month. I shall be busy. I have decided to wear my hair short, but at least we shall meet at weekends. In between, you may say farewell to all your bachelor life."

"Yes, that is true, Olga. I shall have to do that, I suppose."

Everything being agreed, this young couple spent the next month or so as Olga had suggested, and, at the end of it, she saw him off to Boston, with a restraint that he found almost too admirable.

He arrived in Boston, presented his letter of introduction, and was very well received by old Mrs. Vanhomry.

They got on admirably. "You are still a bachelor?" she asked.

"I cannot," he replied, "bring myself to regard the modern girl as a true mate. Those clipped locks, that flat masculine figure, that hardness, that ultrasophistication! Where are the curves, the innocence, the warm-heartedness of yesteryear? But why am I telling you all this—?"

"You would have liked our dear Ethel. Such a big, healthy, affectionate, old-fashioned girl! You must meet her, and her fiancé. Perhaps you will come to the wedding?"

"Nothing could be more delightful. Unfortunately, I have to return to New York almost immediately."

On his return, Paul called at once on Olga, but found that her flat was locked-up. She had left no address; you may depend, he sought her everywhere, but no one could tell him where she had gone.

He saw in the papers an account of the wedding of Miss Vanhomry to a Mr. Colefax. It appeared that the happy pair were on their way to the Ritz-Carlton.

"I really must go and sit in the lobby," said he, "and console myself with a peep at the disadvantages attached to that forty thousand a year."

Very well, he sat in the lobby. Before very long, he saw the enormous form of what was evidently the happy bride crossing from the elevator.

"Upon my word!" he thought. "There is a great deal to be said for the simple life after all. One at least preserves one's individuality."

He peered about for the husband. At last he saw a sensitive face in the neighborhood of the bride's hips. "That must be the husband," he said. "Very charming! Very charming, indeed. But surely I have seen him before."

In order to make sure, he edged closer, and was amazed to find that this husband was none other than his own Olga, in male attire.

He at once applied for a private interview. "My dear Olga, this is a very pretty trick you have played on me. And what can your bride—soi-disant—think of it all?"

"You must regard the matter rationally, my dear Paul."

"I am so afraid there may be a scandal. You have no idea what spiteful tongues might make of it."

"You underestimate the innocence of my wife, whose dolls, as I suspected, were very ordinary dolls. And you must admit, Paul, that if either of us is to be in this position, I at least offer less grounds for jealousy. You had better be my secretary."

Paul submitted with a good grace, and for a long time enjoyed his occupation very tolerably. Fortunately, Henry Vanhomry remained in Europe.

On one occasion there was a dinner party at the Colefax home, and a few of the male guests, with Paul, the friendly secretary, and dapper little Mr. Colefax, remained smoking together long after the gigantic bride had retired to bed. The conversation turned on women, a subject which the so-called Mr. Colefax enjoyed more than his secretary. They talked of attractions.

"My wife," said this charming impostor, "is disarmingly simple. Why try to disguise it? Nevertheless, she has an amazing personality buried, as it were, beneath her naïveté. I am convinced it is there, I sense it, and yet I could hardly find an example to describe. How do you account for that?"

"It is very simple, my dear Colefax," said a very eminent doctor. "Your wife, if I may say so, owes her adorable simplicity, as she does her admirably robust physique, to a little glandular maladjustment, which—always supposing you should desire what professionally we should regard as an improvement—could easily be put right. Who knows what she is like underneath?"

"It would certainly be interesting to find out," said her false husband, intrigued.

"She might be slim, vivacious, a positive butterfly," continued the doctor.

"It would be like carving out ambergris from a whale," observed a well-known adventurer who was present.

"Or opening a Neolithic barrow," added a famous archaeologist.

"Or undressing an Eskimo girl at Christmas," put in a notorious Don Juan.

"You might find more than you bargain for," observed Paul, overcome by an inexplicable foreboding.

He spoke too late. Everyone was desperately keen on the experiment.

"You must bring your dear wife to a little home I have in Paris," said the doctor, "where I have every facility for the treatment."

"We shall come at once. You, Paul, had better remain behind, to deal with everything we shall have to leave unsettled."

Paul, therefore, was left. Ethel and her spouse went on the next boat to Paris, accompanied by the doctor, and, as a matter of fact, by the adventurer, the archaeologist, and the Don Juan as well.

My dear Paul,

You will be amazed at the result of our experiment, and possibly a little disconcerted, though you were always a connoisseur of poetic justice. Under the treatment, Ethel has lost no less than a hundred pounds. The removal of this prodigious quantity of blubber has left her exposed as a lean, agile, witty, and very handsome man. "How absurd that I should have been called Ethel so long!" he observed to me when first he was apprised of this transformation. In order to put him at his ease, I replied at once, "No more absurd than that I should have been called your husband." After all, the cat was, so to speak, out of the bag, and there was nothing else to do.

He took it extremely well, saying with a smile, "We must make the punishment fit the crime." On my part, I was not long in promising never to deceive him again.

We are remaining on this side to avoid gossip, for the situation has a ludicrous side which we might find painful. But not nearly so ludicrous or painful, my dear Paul, as it might have proved, in all the circumstances, had you had your original wish.

Once more,
Olga

SEASON OF MISTS

I was ready for anything when I came to the town of T——. It was already late in the year. Dead leaves crawled like crabs over the asphalt of the deserted esplanade. Winds raced along the corridors of the larger hotels, barging into the wrong rooms.

It is at such a place, and at such a season, that one finds the desperate grass widow, or young things whose natural credulity snaps starvingly at the grossest counterfeit. The illusion of teeming possibilities has gone with the licentious carnival of summer, the masks of coarse sunburn, and he who may be sitting alone among the sand dunes. Ravenous dreams pace the unvisited sitting rooms of villas, or stalk between rising waves and falling leaves.

The concealed smile in my smile, and the concealed meaning in my words, would have made me seem a sort of scheme-riddled Machiavelli in the ephemeral mating-dance of July. I should have been condemned as heavy-going, would-be clever, even unpleasant or dangerous. Now, on the other hand, my slightly involved personality would be as welcome as a jigsaw puzzle in hands already fidgety with boredom. Nevertheless, I had gone so far as to purchase a ready-made sports jacket, and if my black moustache had had an objective existence I should have taken the precaution of shaving it off. I had decided to go as a young man called Christopher, well-bred, sensitive, unsuccessful, capable of nothing but love.

I still had a little money. I was not after profit, but pleasure. I desired to intoxicate myself on a real emotion, and I wondered in which of the still occupied villas, in what sort of absurd drawing room, treading softly in fear of what husband or what aunt, I should perform what drunken antics my chosen potion would inspire in me.

Meticulous in my observance of protective mimicry, I could not of course omit the "snorter" or "quick one" before dinner on my first evening in the hotel. I entered the bar in jaunty style, my mouth already writhing with a classy catchphrase, like the eye socket of a provincial actor (but all actors are provincial) in travail with his waggish monocle.

This witticism was never uttered. I thought I saw a golden fish. It was the honey head of the barmaid, bent over a love story, but, as the place had the appearance of the tourist cocktail lounge of a liner sunk two years previously in a hundred fathoms of gray-green ocean, I thought it was a golden fish. I was sharply corrected when she raised a face so dappled with flush and sun-gleam that I looked instinctively for the orchard boughs above her head.

All this was disconcerting, and effective in shattering my pose. It happens that these fresh and almost eatable faces have a peculiar effect on me. "Farewell before hail," I thought, "to the sailor's languishing wife, and to the ardent anemia at the vicarage! I am off."

I ordered one of the far inferior intoxicants that stood ranked behind her, and retired a pace, changing my name to Bert, a young fellow already doing well, at once cheeky and shy, but probably capable of being serious. One never knew what I could come out with next.

I was wondering about that myself when I saw that she, affecting to take no particular notice of me, had retired into the flowery thicket of her reverie. I realized that this must have grown very wild and tangly in the last month or two, because, before she could turn for a parting glance, it swallowed her up entirely, like a prospective sleeping beauty, and indeed she yawned.

I analyzed this yawn with the aloof precision of one of those scientists who are always helping Scotland Yard. I discovered it to be heavy with a supersaturation of sigh, its origin a plaintive protest against the difference between dreams and reality. Though this was only the middle of November, I diagnosed it as a premature December yawn, *and in December they settle for reality.* This emboldened me to act at once.

Affecting to consult my heart, exactly as if it had been a pocket watch, I gasped, bit my lip, and stared at her in wild surmise. You could never tell when I was joking. "Do you believe," I said fervently, "in love at first sight?"

"No, sir," she said severely. "That sort of thing doesn't appeal, thank you."

It was clear she had not been a barmaid more than seven or eight weeks. From behind her professional hauteur, she peeped out to watch for its effect, as bewitchingly as if she were a child wearing her mother's terrible hat.

"I'm not fooling," I said (taken down a peg or two, you understand). "The fact is, believe it or not, I'm a bit psychic." On this word, the most useful though not the most beautiful in our language, she raised her eyes to mine, which I had baited with pieces of an old sincerity which I carry about for just such purposes. I put a little in my voice, too, as I added, "Do you know what I thought, the minute I saw you?"

"What?" said she.

"I'll tell you," said I. " 'That girl's tragic,' I thought. 'She's being wasted. There's a sort of bar between her and all sorts of delightful surprises. I wish it could be melted away.' "

"Not really!"

"I did," said I. "Give me your hand. I can read it like a book, probably by your favorite author. Oh, I'm psychic all right. I had a sort of premonition when I came here. I knew I was going to fall desperately in love."

"I know you're kidding," said she, but she offered me her open hand, which proved to be quite illegible.

Nevertheless I spoke with confidence. "You've been thinking of love today. You've been dreaming of a stranger. Now, don't deny it, because it's written in your hand. And that's not all."

"What else does it say?" said she.

"Call it Fate," said I solemnly. "Call it Kismet if you like; I can deny you nothing. Or, look here, let's call it Destiny. You can't go back on Destiny, you know. It would absolutely ruin it. It says . . . Guess what?"

"I can't," she said. "Do tell me."

I couldn't guess either. Dumbly I scrutinized her palm. She leaned a little farther over the bar, joining me in the study. Our foreheads touched. I remained conscious, but the shock had dislocated all connection between awareness and volition. With a divine shudder I heard myself reply, "It says we are going to be married."

"Oh," said she. "I don't know about that."

"What?" I cried, hurt to the quick, all caution forgotten. "Is this mutual understanding? Is this two hearts beating as one? Don't let's start off with a rift like this between us."

"I didn't mean it that way," she replied remorsefully.

"Splendid," I said. "Our first little quarrel healed already. And don't we sort of know one another better for it? Aren't we somehow closer? If not, we ought to be. Lean over a little farther."

Fate had evidently triumphed. Her kiss was like cowslips and cream. I was unquestionably in love, and I felt I was no longer responsible for my actions.

At that moment, however, a gong sounded in the echoing depths of the hotel. "Better go," she said, already wifely. "Go and get your dinner. I'll be here later on."

I bowed before the importance of Bert's dinner, and went. When I returned, the bar was still empty of intruders, and she was still there. I rushed forward, I flung my arms about her, and resumed the kiss that had been so coarsely interrupted.

I had just been struck by the nice thought that perhaps after all it tasted of cream and honeysuckle, rather than cowslips, when I was also struck by a tremendous blow in the face.

"What?" I said, staggering back. "Are you tired of me already? You might at least have broken it more gently."

"I'll call the manager," said she.

"Do so," said I. "Call the boots, too. Call the waiters. Call all the principal residents of T—— on Sea. Let them hear how you promised to marry me before dinner, and socked me in the puss for a kiss immediately afterwards."

"Promised to marry you?" she cried. "Before dinner? Oooh! It must have been Bella. Fancy! Bella!"

"What is your name?" said I.

"Nellie," said she.

"That's who it was," said I. "Nellie. You. To the devil with this interfering, designing Bella, who . . ." But, as I spoke, she turned and darted through the door behind her.

I heard some delicious squeals and giggles. "I hope," I thought, "she is giving that abominable Bella a good pinch. Pretending to be her! She had the poor girl all confused." At that moment the door opened again, and out they came, hand in hand.

"I'm Nellie."

"I'm Bella."

"Keep quite still," said I, clowning astonishment. "I must think for a little while about this."

"Look! He's all bowled over."

"Isn't he sweet?"

"Yes, he's a duck. Bella, you *are* lucky."

"Your turn next."

That was the rub. My mind darkened at the thought of a brother-in-law. You know what beasts men are. A thousand intricate jealousies tangled themselves before me. The girls were so exactly alike; they *went together,* as we say. Besides, who can choose between cowslips and honeysuckle?

It was time I said something. "Well!" said I. "By all that's wonderful I wish old Fred were here tonight!"

"Who's Fred?"

"Fred? You'll like Fred. He's a splendid fellow. We're twins."

"No!"

"Yes, identical twins. More alike than you are. Same looks. Same tastes. Same thoughts. I always know what he's thinking. Listen! He's sort of trying to get through to me now. I bet he knows I'm happy. He does. He's sending congratulations. In waves. He's asking something. What is it, Fred, old boy? Is there what? Oh, 'Is there one for me, Bert?' *That's* what he's trying to say. What shall I tell him, Nellie?"

"Don't know, I'm sure."

"Why don't you bring him along one day?" said Bella.

"I can't," said I. "We're on a very special job. It's just half the time off for each of us. But I'll tell you what—I'll *send* him along."

This was agreed upon. I spent the rest of the evening delightfully, and in the morning bought a new sports coat, brushed my hair a little differently, and returned as Fred.

I entered the bar peering through my fingers. "Which are you?" I cried. "I don't want to look at you properly till I know. I might fall in love with the wrong one."

"I'm Nellie."

"Good! To make it absolutely perfect, I'm Fred." With that I dropped my hand. "Good old Bert!" I cried. "Wonderful taste he's got! Wonderful fellow!"

"He's nice. But you're nice, too."

"Do you really think so?"

In short, we were happy. Soon afterwards Bella came in. There was nothing but giggles, comparisons, talk of future joys.

"It really ought to be a double wedding," they said.

"Can't be done," I replied. "Truly. Ask Bert, if you don't believe me. He'll tell you it's out of the question."

The next few days passed like lightning. All went twice as merrily as the ordinary marriage bell. I rented two bungalows, semi-detached, furnished them from the same store, took a week off for my honeymoon as Bert, and the next week for my honeymoon as Fred.

I then settled down to lives of singular contentment and regularity. One evening Nellie and I would have Bella to dinner, and spend the time saying what a grand fellow Bert was, and the next evening Bella and I would entertain Nellie and do the same for Fred.

It was a full month before I asked myself: Which is the happier of the two, Fred or Bert? I was unable to answer. The doubt persisted until it tortured me.

I became a little moody, and sometimes would retire to the next room, under the pretense of a headache, in order to ponder the question over again. On one of these occasions, I went into the hallway to get cigarettes from my overcoat and I heard the girls' voices through the flimsy door of the drawing room. "The darlings!" I thought. "They are discussing their husbands again. This may shed some light on my problem. Bella thinks Bert has the nicer voice. Nellie claims that Fred knows more songs. What is this? Really, Bella! Come, come, Nellie, you flatter me! Bella, what an exaggeration! Nellie, that is a downright lie!"

Soon afterwards I heard Nellie go home. I rejoined Bella, who was obviously much exercised in her mind. "Bert," she said, "who is the best swimmer, you or Fred?"

"We never compete, darling, we are so sure we are equal."

"I wonder if you would be if you tried," said Bella, still looking extremely thoughtful.

When I returned to the other bungalow next evening, I found Nellie equally ill at ease. "Tell me something," said she. "Of course, I know Bella's my sister, my twin. Nobody could love her more than I do. But tell me, Fred, would you say she was absolutely truthful?"

"Absolutely," said I. "I'd stake my life on it. Bert's life, too. She is incapable of a lie."

"Oh!" said Nellie, lapsing into a deeper reverie than before.

It was with a sardonic pleasure that I watched the increasing wistfulness of both my wives. "I have an idea," said I to myself, "that I shall soon learn whether Bert or Fred is the happier."

Sure enough, it was not long before Nellie sent round one evening to ask if Bert would help her move some heavy furniture. I went to her aid, and afterwards we sat talking for a while on twins, likenesses, differences, marriage, conventions, love, and what would have happened if Fred had met Bella before I had, and whether what hurts nobody can really be said to be wrong.

It took a long time to resolve all these problems to our complete satisfaction, and I was deprived of a good deal of Bella's company that evening. But this was made up to me on the following day, for she came round to ask if Fred would help her with a leaky tap, and we had an almost identical discussion which took just as long for its complete resolution.

I was now in a state of extreme and complicated bliss. It was clear that Bert had no reason to envy Fred, and that Fred's happiness was in all respects equal to Bert's. Not only had I two charming wives, but my double domestic happiness was multiplied by a dual and delicious infidelity.

But, I was one day in the character of Bert, sitting before the fire enjoying the more legal of my happinesses with Bella, charmed by her prattle and pleased by the complete restoration of her good spirits, when suddenly I was struck, as if by a thunderbolt, by the thought, "This woman is deceiving me!"

I leapt up with a muttered excuse and rushed out of the now hateful house. I walked on the shore till late that night, prey to the most bitter reflections. I had to admit I was largely responsible, but I at least knew that it made no difference. She had no such excuse; it was she who had blighted our Eden.

I went home long after midnight, slept uneasily, and hurried off in the morning, eager to exchange the pitiful personality of the deceived husband for the roguish character of his betrayer.

As Fred, I returned with a jaunty sneer. Nellie greeted me. "How was Bert," said she, "when you left him?"

"Bert?" said I. "Bert!"

Without another word I went heavily upstairs, and looked at myself in the mirror. The sight maddened me. I itched to get my fingers round my throat. I longed to rush next door and pour out my troubles to my adorable mistress, but I knew in my heart that she was as false as her sister below.

I thought of divorce, working out the actions and counteractions on my fingers, and badly spraining two of them in the process. Besides, there was the unsavory publicity.

At last I made up my mind. I hurried off to catch the last train to the town. Arrived there, I wrote two notes, as follows:

"Dear Nellie, I have found you out. I am asking Bert to come for a swim. He will never return. Fred."

"Dear Bella, I know all. Am persuading Fred to take a midnight bathe. He will not come back. Bert."

Having posted my letters, I took my two sports coats to the beach, where I left them side by side.

There was just time to get the train for B——, and it was there that I met Mrs. Wilkinson.

WITHOUT BENEFIT OF GALSWORTHY

The minute I left the golf links, I gave a sort of sniff. "Damn it! Poetry about!" I said. I can always tell it; I've got that sort of streak in me. "Where does it come from?" I said. "Sunset tints? Going round in eighty? Or what?" Passed a couple of schoolgirls, giggling in a gateway. I could just imagine their conversation: one saying to the other, "Who's the wicked moustache?" and the other replying, "Why, that's our handsome Major."

Life suddenly seemed like a bottle of champagne. Cheltenham looked like a first-class oil painting, only with a lot of decent people living in it. There was *Poona Lodge*. "Good old *Poona Lodge!*" There was *Amritsar*. "Cheerio, *Amritsar!*" There was my little box,

The Laurels. Poetic streak again, you see, calling it that. Better, maybe, if I'd just been an ordinary, damnfool, wooden-headed soldier man. Still, if it wasn't for these sneaking socialists . . .

Well, in I went. Adela looked out of the drawing room. Good old Adela! Sound through and through. Troopships, kids, marvelous head of hair, everything. She gave me a sort of hiss. "She's come," she said.

I knew whom she meant. We had that sort of understanding. It was the new parlormaid. "Grand!" I said. "Tell her to bring my tea into the den."

I went into the den. Snug little cubbyhole. Mixed myself a peg. "Hullo! What's this? Poetry's getting stronger!" Had a good look round; caught sight of my moustache in the looking glass. "Wicked moustache, eh?" That was the word. Gave it a pat. "Well," I said, "damn it!" Very nearly burst out laughing.

In she came with the tea. Ten minutes past five: the moment my life changed completely. Here had I been going about with a streak of poetry all my life; this was the woman it was meant for. Woman, did I say? Little more than a girl. Slip of a girl. Yet, mind you, a touch of the goddess.

I was down. I was out. "Jack," I said, "you're done for." Talk about poetry—I tell you I saw that girl, nude, on a beach, in a sort of dawn. The impression was overwhelming. Do you know what I very nearly said? I very nearly said, "Look here, my dear! Bathing costume, please! Might be trippers about."

Of course, I said nothing of the sort. But I looked it. She seemed to understand. You know what I mean. Goddess—all very well. Moustache—all very well. But if a woman doesn't understand a man, and if a man doesn't understand a woman, there isn't much in it, is there? Still, she seemed to. If it wasn't for these bloody Bolsheviks . . .

Anyway, there I was, sparring for time, fighting like a madman to get on my feet, face up to it, grip the controls, anything. I said, "What's your name?" She said, "Gladys."

After that, neither of us said anything for a while. There we were.

Then she said, "Please, sir, shall I pour out your tea?"

I said, "Yes. Always." Just that, you see? Nothing about the beach. Nothing about anything. Just "Always."

And all she said was, "Very well, sir."

You see the delicacy? I thought, "That girl's got breeding." I'm the true democrat, you see. Or was, rather. I thought, "There was some young dog of a subaltern hovering around the cottage where you were born, my dear." But I didn't say so, naturally. Might have been someone in the diplomatic, anyway. "Very well, sir."

That was all. She went out. Went up to her little room, I expect. I was left alone, staring at the fire, like a fellow in a play.

I heard Adela going upstairs. "Good god," I thought, "there's Adela!" I'd forgotten her. "And the kids!" Clean, decent youngsters. "God," I thought, "there's the Carrington-Joneses, too!" Bitch of a woman. Tongue like a Gurkha's kukri. I thought of the old General, over at Lucknow Grange—dear old boy! Thought of the regiment; young chaps in the mess, keen as mustard, lead 'em to Hell and back. What would they say? Thought of my round in eighty. Thought of a fellow called Uglow. Met him one day in the bar of the Chutna Club. Never saw him again. Don't know why I thought of *him*.

But Adela was in my thoughts all the time, dodging in and out among the others. Then there was a sort of mirage, only not upside down, of this little goddess, on a beach, as it were. Pretty hard to concentrate.

Shall I tell you the words that came into my mind then? "Play the game!" Woman's heart broken, life ruined, old campaigner like Adela. No! Thought of the day we found a snake in the bed up at Chundrapore. That's another story. Still, it's a link, you know, that sort of thing. Only, what's a snake against a goddess? If it wasn't for these blasted agitators . . .

I did my best. I ignored her all Sunday. Monday morning I came out into the hall. There she was, sweeping the stairs. With a dustpan and broom. You know what I mean. I found Adela in the drawing room. I said, "Adela, I've got to go up to town. I've got to see Doggie Weaver."

She saw something was up. When I'm in a tight place, I like to see Doggie Weaver. Been in tight places together. "You go," she said. "Come back on the eight-forty-five." I said, "All right, I will."

So I went up to town. I saw Doggie. I told him everything. I said, "I've got to choose. And I can't face it." He said, "I advise a compromise." I said, "What?" He gave a sort of wink. He said, "Least said, soonest mended." I said, "What?" He said, "What the eye doesn't see, the heart doesn't grieve for." I said, "Doggie, you and I have been in some tight places. Now I think you're a dirty rotten cynic. You don't know what a good woman is, and I wish I'd never been in a single tight place with you."

So I went out. Then I thought of Piggy Hawkins. Can't say he was ever the most popular man in our mess; still, I had an idea Piggy was all right—a sort of intuition. I looked him up. I told him everything. "Jack," he said, "there's nothing for it. There it is —as clear as daylight. You've got to play the game."

You see? The very words I'd said to myself. So I knew he was right. I shook hands with him. I said, "Piggy, we've never been in very many tight places together, but if ever I'm in a tight place again, I hope you'll be there beside me."

I went back. I had another look at her, just to make sure. I called Adela into the den. I said, "Adela, keep a stiff upper lip. You're a soldier's daughter."

She said, "Yes, Jack. A soldier's wife, too."

I said, "Well, yes. Up to the present."

She said, "Don't tell me it's another woman."

I said, "I won't. It's a goddess."

She said, "I see. Now I'm just the mother of a couple of soldier's children."

I said, "Clean, decent kids, Adela. Keen as a couple of well-bred sporting terriers."

She said, "Yes, clean. I must have them, Jack. I'll keep them— clean."

I said, "Take them, Adela."

She said, "Keep a stiff upper lip, Jack. They've got to have the right sort of school."

I said, "Yes, Adela."

She said, "And the right sort of home to come home to. The right sort of mother, too. Do you know what they call me?" she said. And she almost broke down as she said it. "They call me their 'lovely mother.' I can't be a 'lovely mother,' Jack, in a ragged old last-season's frock, can I?"

I said, "All right. I want nothing. I shall be living at Waikiki or somewhere. On a beach."

She said, "You must have your baccy, Jack." The way she said it—I almost broke down myself.

Then, of course, there was her family, and her lawyers, and resigning from everything, and being cut, and the Carrington-Joneses —bitch of a woman—everything. I kept a stiff upper lip, signed everything, never said a word, kept my eyes to myself in the house

—didn't want to drag the little goddess into it. Time enough for that when we got to Waikiki or wherever it was.

In the end they took all the furniture out. There I was with my polo cup and a bag of golf clubs in the old den. Never mind—off to Waikiki or somewhere before you could say knife. Damn these reptiles from Moscow—they're un-English.

I called for Gladys. She came in. I gave her a look. Suddenly the words burst out for me. Did you ever see a light drumfire barrage moving briskly forward in advance of a battalion of the best men God ever made? That's how it sounded to me.

"Here I am," I said. "Take me. Play with my moustache. Cut it off, if you like. It's yours. So's all the rest of me."

She said, "What?"

I said, "I've given it up. Everything. Adela. Children. The old General—dear old boy, but never mind. Carrington-Joneses. Cheltenham. Club. Regiment. Money. Even a fellow called Uglow—met him in the Chutna Club—never mind him, either. I'm yours. I saw you, nude, on a beach—dawn, everything. Get your hat on, Gladys. We're going into that dawn. We're going to find that beach. Not a tripper for miles!"

She looked at me. Of course, I knew she'd be surprised. Hadn't liked to say anything, not while Adela was in the house. Kept it clean, you know. Still, there was that word "Always." And "Very well, sir."

I thought she was going to say it again. Going to say it, not as she'd said it before, like a mouse talking out of a hole with all the cats of wealth, rank, station, convention, and god knows what prowling about the room, if you know what I mean, but loudly, triumphantly, and with a sort of spring at the end of it.

She was loud enough. Did you ever see a buzz bomb go off? With some poor fellow under it? That's how it seemed to me. I thought, "Jack, you're knocked out. You're done for." I looked round. She was gone.

I saw what it was. They'd been at her. The scum! From Moscow. The blasted agitators. The cursed reds. Nobody's too young for 'em, or too pure. Damn it, they're in the Sunday schools—everywhere. Goddess—what's that to them? Eyes, little ears, everything—they don't give a damn. Class against class, that's their motto. Class hatred. Class war.

THE DEVIL GEORGE AND ROSIE

There was a young man who was invariably spurned by the girls, not because he smelt at all bad, but because he happened to be as ugly as a monkey. He had a good heart, but this soured it, and though he would grudgingly admit that the female kind were very agreeable in shape, size, and texture, he thought that in all other respects they were the most stupid, blind, perverse, and ill-natured bitches that had ever infested the earth.

He expressed this view very forcefully, and on all possible occasions. One evening he was holding forth to a circle of his cronies; it was in the Horseshoe Bar, at the bottom of the Tottenham Court Road. He could not help noticing that his remarks attracted the interest of a smart and saturnine individual seated at the next table, who had the rather repulsive look of a detective dressed up in evening clothes for the purpose of spying on a nightclub.

Our friend was in no way abashed by this scrutiny, but continued to say exactly what girls were, and what they did whenever they got the chance. He, who had least evidence for it of any man in the world, seemed to think they were unduly inclined to lasciviousness. "Or else," said he, "in the other extreme, they are mercenary prudes, or sadistical Dianas, whose delight it is to kindle the fires of Hell in a man's bosom and elsewhere, and triumphantly to describe his agonies to their little friends. I speak of the fires of Hell—I wish they existed in reality, so that these harpies and teasers might be sent there, and I myself would go willingly, if only I could watch them frizzle and fry."

With that, he got up and went home. You may imagine his astonishment, when he had climbed the high stairs to his poor student's room, to find the dark and cynical stranger, who had been watching him in the bar, now standing very much at his ease upon the hearthrug. At the very first glance, he realized this was none other than the Devil himself, in whom for many years he had had no belief at all. "I cannot easily describe," said that worthy, with the easy air of a man of the world, "the pleasure it gives me to meet one of such insight and intelligence as Mr. George Postle-thwaite."

George made several sorts of protest, but the Devil smiled and bowed like an ambassador. In the end he had buttered up George to some effect, and carried him off to supper in a little restaurant in Jermyn Street. It must be admitted, he stood a superb bottle of wine.

"I was vastly intrigued," said he, "by the views I heard you expressing earlier this evening. Possibly, of course, they were born of a mere passing petulance, pique, wounded vanity—call it what you will?"

"The devil take me if they were!" cried George.

"Splendid!" said his companion. "I like nothing better than a man who says what he means. Now, my dear chap, my little difficulty is this. The domain over which I have the honor and pleasure to preside was designed originally on the most ample scale, but, nevertheless, certain recent tendencies are fast rendering its confines too narrow, and its supervision too onerous for one who is not as young as he was."

"Sorry to hear that," said George.

"I could cope with the increase of the population of this planet," said the Devil. "I might have coped even with the emancipation of women. But unfortunately the two are connected, and form a vicious circle . . ."

"I see your point," said George.

"I wish I had never invented that particular sin," said the Devil. "I do indeed. There are a thousand million women in the world at this moment, and, with one or two negligible exceptions, every single one of them is damned."

"Fine!" said George.

"Very fine indeed," said the Devil, "from the artistic point of view. But consider the pressure on space, and the ceaseless strain of organization."

"Squeeze 'em in!" cried George with enthusiasm. "Jack 'em tight. That's what I say."

"They would then imagine themselves at a party," replied his new friend, "and that would never do. No, no. Everyone who comes to me must have individual attention. I intend to open a new department. The site is chosen. The builders are at work. All I need is a superintendent of iron personality."

"I should like to know a little about the climate, salary, and prospects," said George, in a businesslike tone.

"The climate, much like that of Oxford Street on a summer afternoon," replied the Devil. "The salary is power, and the prospects are infinite. But if you are interested, my dear fellow, allow me to show you over the place. In any case, I should value your opinion on it."

No sooner said than done. They sank into the bowels of the earth, and came out in a suburb of Sydney, N.S.W.

"Here we are, then!" cried George.

"No, no," said the Devil. "Just a little farther on."

They proceeded with the speed of rockets to the northeast corner of the universe, which George now perceived to be shaped exactly like a pint of beer, in which the nebulae were the ascending bubbles. He observed with alarm a pair of enormous lips approaching the upper rim of our space. "Do not be alarmed," said the Devil. "That is a young medical student called Prior, who has failed his exam three times in succession. However, it will be twenty million billion light-years before his lips reach the glass, for a young woman is fixing him with her eye, and by the time he drinks all the bubbles will be gone, and all will be flat and stale."

"Poor fellow!" cried our hero. "Damn these women!"

"Do not pity him," said the Devil very tolerantly. "This is his fifth pint, and he is already as drunk as a lord, and closing time draws near. What's more, our destination is at hand."

George saw that they were nearing what is sometimes called a "fish" in this considerable pint of beer. As they approached it, he saw it was a dark star of gigantic proportions, about which circled a satellite many hundred times larger than the earth.

"That satellite," said his conductor, "is the spot I am proposing to colonize with my new department. We will go straight there, if you have no objection."

George assenting, they landed in a sterile and saturnine country, close by a palace of black basalt, which covered about a square mile of ground.

"That's a snug-looking box!" observed our hero.

"Merely a pioneer's hut," said his companion. "My future overseer will have to rough it there until something better can be fixed up for him."

George, however, noticed a prodigious number of barrels being run down into a cellar on the hinder side of this palace. What's more, he saw several groups of fiends, who should have been at their work, squatting in one of the unfinished galleries with cards in their hands.

"You actually play poker here?" said he, in tones of the liveliest satisfaction.

"We are connoisseurs of every pleasure," replied the Devil, with a smile. "And when we play cards, everyone has an excellent hand."

He showed George a number of masterly pictures; some of them were a little indecent. There were also very splendid kitchens, already staffed with cooks; kennels, stables, falconries, gun rooms, music rooms, grand halls, little cozy rooms, rooms devoted to every sort of pastime, and gardens laid out rather like those of Versailles, only very much larger. There was a whole cellar full of fireworks of every description. Not only these, but there were a number of other delights, of a nature entirely new to the visitor. There was an observatory, for example, from which the behavior of any young woman in the world could be closely inspected. "This is really a very interesting device," murmured our hero.

"Come!" said the fiend. "We must not stay here all day. Doubtless you will want to see the rest of your domain."

"Yes, indeed," said George. "Show me where the prisoners are to be confined. I suppose that now and then I can have one haled up for special admonishment."

The Devil then flew with him over the whole surface of the planet, which, once they were clear of the palace and its lands, proved to have an aspect not unlike that of the Great West Road, where it approaches London. On every hand, rows of cells were being run up. To add the final refinement of misery, they were designed exactly like houses in a modern building project. Imitation husbands, who could neither speak nor hear, were planted in armchairs with their feet on the mantelpieces. The wardrobes were full of unfashionable garments. Small imps disguised as children were already rehearsing by dozens in all the upper rooms. The peculiar property of the walls was to translate the noise of those next door into the sound of a party going on, while the windows were so designed as to make the dowdiest passerby appear to be arrayed in the very latest mode.

Vast bunion factories belched smoke among the crazy villas; truckloads of superfluous hair clattered along the streets. George was shown the towering gasometers of the halitosis works, and a number of other things I do not dare imagine. He saw a great concourse of fiends being instructed in door-to-door salesmanship; others were being fitted out as relations-in-law, rent-collectors, and bailiffs. He himself made two suggestions that were immediately put into force: one was for a stocking ladderer, and the other for an elastic that would break in the middle of any crowded thorough-fare.

As a final encouragement, the Devil took him over to the main-land of Hell itself, which is girdled by the Styx, as Saturn by his ring. Charon's vast liner had just come to dock, and our hero had the pleasure of seeing a multitude of filmstars, baby blondes, unfaith-ful wives, disobedient daughters, frivolous typists, lazy serving-maids, wantons, careless waitresses, cruel charmers, naggers, sirens, clogs, unpunctual sweethearts, bridge-playing grandmas, extravagant helpmeets, mischief-making gossips, tantalizers, female novelists, crazy debutantes, possessive mothers, neglectful mothers, modern mothers, unmarried mothers, would-be, should-be, in fact, all who could be, mothers: They were all there, as naked as your hand, and they filed down the gangway, some weeping, some brazen, and some in attitudes of affected modesty.

"This is a magnificent sight," remarked our hero.

"Well, my dear sir," said the Devil, "are you the man for the job?"

"I will do my best!" cried George enthusiastically.

They shook hands on it. All the little details were arranged. Before evening George was installed as principal vassal of all the Devil's host and overlord of a planet populated only by women and fiends.

It must be admitted, he enjoyed himself with a vengeance. Every day he would go out, having donned his cap of invisibility, and regale himself upon his subjects' endeavors to cope with the hard-ships he had designed for them. Sometimes he would hold up the ceaseless self-dirtying of plates, put the children to sleep, and amuse them with the prospect of a matinée. He saw to it, though, that they had to queue up for the cheap seats, and arranged for it to rain. In the end, he would announce that the show was post-poned.

He had a thousand other ways of tantalizing them; I shall not enumerate them all. One of the best was to send for any newly arrived young thing who was reported to be vain of her beauty and give her the impression for an hour or two that she had made a conquest of him, and then (as far as was possible) undeceive her.

When the day's work was done, he sat down to cards with his principal officers, and sure enough everyone had a good hand, but his was the best. They drank like champions; the Devil was constantly sending over the choicest delicacies from Hell; the word "fine" was continually upon our hero's lips; and the time passed like lightning.

One day, toward the end of the second year, our potentate had just got through his levee, and was refreshing himself with a stroll on a little private terrace which he much affected, when word was brought to him that the senior port official desired an audience. Our hero was the easiest fellow in the world to approach, never stood upon his dignity. "Send the old chap along here," said he. "And, hi! Bring a bottle and a couple of glasses back with you when you come."

The fact is, George dearly loved a chat with these old petty officers, who occasionally brought him reports of diverting little incidents at the Ellis Island of Hell, or scraps of gossip concerning the irrelevant affairs of the world, such as sometimes strayed in among Charon's cargo, as lizards or butterflies travel to Covent Garden among the bananas.

On this occasion, however, the harbor master's face bore an extremely worried expression. "I'm afraid, sir," he said, "I've got a little irregularity to report."

"Well, we all make mistakes sometimes," said George. "What's the trouble?"

"It's like this here, sir," replied the old salt. "Young gal come along o' the last cargo—seems as if she didn't ought to be here at all."

"Oh, that'll be all right," cried George. "Bound to be. It's understood we take the whole issue in these days. She's a woman, and that's enough. What's on her charge sheet, anyway?"

"Lot o' little things, sir, what don't amount to much," replied the honest fellow. "Fact is, sir, it ain't added up." And he pursed his lips.

"Not added up?" cried George in amazement.

"That's how it is, sir," said his subordinate glumly. "This young gal *ain't properly dead!*"

George was absolutely bowled over. "*Whew!*" said he. "But this is serious, my man."

"It *is* serious, sir," said the old chap. "I don't know what's to be done, I'm sure."

A score of fine legal points were involved. George dispatched an SOS for one of the leading casuists of Hell proper. Unfortunately, they were all engaged in committee, on some fine point concerning an illuminated address which was being prepared for the saviors of Germany. George therefore had nothing but precedent to go upon, and precedent made it clear that a mortal must sin in such and such a way, die in such and such a condition, be checked in, checked out —it was as complicated as a case in Court Leet under a Statute of Ed. Tert. Rex, that statute being based on precedents from the Saxon and Norman codes dually and differently derived from a Roman adaptation of a Greco-Egyptian principle influenced prehistorically by rites and customs from the basin of the Euphrates or the Indus. It was quite like an income-tax form. George scratched his head in despair.

What made it all the worse was, the Devil himself had given him a most serious warning against the least infringement of protocol. "This is," he had said, "little better than mandated territory. We have built up, step by step, and with incredible ingenuity, a system under which we live very tolerably, but we have done it only by sailing devilishly close to the metaphysical wind. One single step beyond the strict legal limits, and I am back on my red-hot throne, in that pit whose bottomlessness I shall heartily envy. As for you—"

George therefore had every incentive to caution. He turned over a large number of volumes, tapped his teeth. In the end, he knew not what to make of it. "Send the young person in to me," said he.

When she arrived, she proved to be no more than seventeen years of age. I should be telling a downright lie if I said she was less beautiful than a peri.

George was not a bad fellow at heart. Like most of us, he was capable of tyranny upon the featureless mass, but when he came to grips with an individual his bark was a good deal worse than his bite. Most of the young women he had had up for admonishment had complained of little except his fickleness.

This young girl was ushered into his presence; the very lackeys who brought her in rolled their eyes till the whites flickered like the Eddystone Lighthouse. She was complete in every particular, and all of the highest quality; she was a picture gallery, an anthology of the poets, a precipitation of all that has ever been dreamed of love:

her goodly eyes like Saphyres shining bright, her forehead yvory white, her cheeks lyke apples which the sun hath rudded, her lips lyke cherryes charming men to byte, her brest lyke to a bowle of creame uncrudded, her paps lyke lyllies budded, her snowie neck lyke to a marble towre; and all her body like a pallace fayre, ascending up, with many a stately stayre, to honours seat and chastities sweet bowre.

Her name was Rosie Dixon. Moreover, she gained enormously in contrast to her surroundings, by the mere fact of being alive. It was as though a cowslip were to bloom miraculously between the dark and sterile metals of the Underground; as if its scent were wafted to one's nostrils on the nasty, sultry, canned sirocco of that region. It is no exaggeration to say that she was as good as she was beautiful. It is true her pretty face was a little blubbered with tears. "My dear," said George, taking her hand, "there is no reason for you to cry in that fashion. Don't you know the good old saying, 'Never holler before you're hurt'?"

"Pray, sir," cried she, having taken a long, dewy peep at his monkey-phiz, and seeing a vast amount of good nature there, "Pray, sir," said she, "tell me only, where am I?"

"Why, in Hell, to be sure," said he, with a hearty laugh.

"Oh, thank goodness!" cried she. "I thought I was in Buenos Aires."

"Most of 'em think that," said our hero, "owing to the liner. But I must say you are the first who has shown any gratification on learning otherwise."

They had a little more conversation of this sort; he questioned her pretty closely as to how she came to be stowed away on Charon's vessel. It appeared that she was a shopgirl who had been much tormented by her workmates; why, she could not say. However, she had to serve a young man who came in to buy some stockings for his sister. This young man had addressed to her a remark that brought her soul fluttering to her lips. At that very moment, the cruelest of her envious colleagues had maneuvered to pass behind her, and had bestowed on her a pinch so spiteful, so sudden, and so intensely and laceratingly agonizing, that her poised soul was jolted from its perch. It had spread its wings and borne off her swooning body as a woodcock bears off its young. When she had regained her senses, she was locked in one of the narrow staterooms of a vast ship, stewarded by what she took to be black men, and resounding with the hysterical laughter and screams of captives of her own sex, all of whom seemed to think they were on the way to Buenos Aires.

George was very thorough. He minutely examined what little evidence she had to offer. "There is no doubt," said he at length, speaking in tones of the greatest sympathy, "that you have received a very cruel pinch. When your tormentor comes into my hands, I myself will repay it a hundredfold."

"No, no," said she. "She did not mean so much harm. I'm sure she is a good girl at heart. It is just her little way."

George was overcome with admiration at this remark, which, however, caused a tremor to pass through the whole of the vast black palace. "Upon my word!" said he. "I can't keep you here. You will bring the whole place crashing about my ears. I dare not put you in one of our punishment cells, for, if I did so against your will, all our system of home rule would be snatched away from us, and we should return to the crude discomforts of primitive times. That would be intolerable. There is a museum over on the mainland that would make your blood run cold."

"Could you not send me back to earth?" said she.

"No woman has ever left this place alone!" cried he in despair. "My position is so delicate I dare not make an innovation."

"Do not take on so," said she. "I cannot bear to think of so kind a gentleman being plunged into fiery torments. I will stay voluntarily, and perhaps then no fuss will be made. I hope it will not be terribly painful."

"You adorable creature!" cried he. "I must give you a kiss for that. I believe you have solved the difficulty."

She gave him back his kiss, as sweetly and purely as you can possibly imagine. "This is terrible," he cried in great anguish of spirit. "I cannot bear to think of you undergoing the miseries of this place. My dear, good girl—"

"I don't mind," she said. "I have worked in a shop in Oxford Street."

He gave her a pat or two, and signed up a form for her: "Remanded in custody at own request."

"It is only temporary, after all," he said. "Otherwise I would not permit it."

Very well, she kept a stiff upper lip, and was carted off to a hateful box as cruelly equipped as any of the others. For a whole week George kept his head, reading love lyrics to distract his mind. At the end, he could put the matter behind him no longer. "I must go," said he, "and see how she is getting on."

In Hell, all the officials travel with incredible speed. In a very few minutes George had passed over a couple of continents, and was tapping at the mean front door of poor Rosie's little habitation. He had not chosen to put on his cap of fern-seed virtue, or perhaps he never thought of it. Anyway, she came to the door with three or four of the imps hanging about her apron strings, and recognized him at once. He observed that she was wearing the drab and unfashionable garments provided by the authorities, in which her appearance was that of a rose in a jam-pot.

What raised an intolerable burden from his heart was the fact that the superfluous hair had obviously failed to take root upon her living flesh. He found on inquiry that she had used it to stuff a pillow with, which she had placed behind the head of the snoring imitation husband who gracelessly sprawled before the fire. She admitted a little tuft flourished on the bruise where she had been pinched.

"No doubt it will fall off," said our hero scientifically, "when the tissues resume their normal condition. These things were designed to flourish upon carrion only, whereas you—" and he smacked his lips.

"I hope it will fall off," said she, "for scissors will not cut it. And since I promised some to the eldest of these toddlers, to make him a false moustache of, no more has arrived."

"Shall I try to cut it off?" said our hero.

"No, no," said she, with a blush. "He has stopped crying now. They were all very querulous when first I came here, but now they are improved out of all knowledge."

While she spoke, she busied her fingers with a succession of little tasks. "You seem to be terribly busy," complained George.

"Forgive me," said she, with a smile, "but there is such a terrible lot to do. Still, it makes the time pass."

"Do you never," said he, "wish to go to the matinée?"

"That would never do," she replied. "Supposing *he* should wake up" (pointing to the imitation husband) "and call for his tea. Besides, I have plenty of entertainment. The people next door seem always to have a party; it does me good to hear them laugh and sing. What's more, when I'm cleaning the windows, as needs doing rather often, I see girls going by, dressed more beautifully than you can possibly imagine. I love to see people in pretty clothes."

"Your own are not very attractive," said George in a melancholy tone.

"They are plain enough," said she, with a laugh. "But I'm far too busy to think about that. All I could wish is that they were of slightly stronger materials. The stockings laddered so often I've had to give up wearing them. And whenever I go out shopping—Still, you don't want to hear all this."

George was so devoured by remorse that he had not the spirit to ask an interesting question. "Good-bye," said he, pressing her hand.

She gave him the sweetest glance; he felt it no more than his duty to offer her an encouraging kiss. At once the doors began to bang, the fire belched smoke, the imps opened their mouths to yell.

"No, no," said she, with just so much of inexpressible regret as to soften the cruelty of it. And she pointed to the dummy husband before the fire.

"Don't worry about him!" cried our hero. "He's only a dummy." With that, he gave the image a kick, capsizing it into the hearth.

"Well, if he's not a real husband," said Rosie, "I suppose there is nothing wrong in it." And with that she gave George a kiss, which he found altogether delightful, except that, as it increased the high esteem in which he held her, so also it increased his misery in having placed her in such a predicament.

When he got home, the poor fellow could neither eat nor sleep. He called up a few of his officers to pass away the night at poker, but, though he held four straight flushes in succession, he could take no pleasure in it. In the morning, the telephone bell rang. George's was the only instrument on the planet which did not go wrong as soon as one began to speak; on this occasion he would willingly have surrendered the advantage. The Devil was at the other end, and he was in a towering rage. He made no bones about accusing our hero of downright morality.

"You curse and swear very well," said the victim in an injured tone. "All the same, it was not my fault she came here. I clearly see she may prove a disintegrating influence if I keep her, but, if I may not send her back, I don't see what else I can do."

"Why, tempt her, you idiot!" replied the Devil. "Have you never tempted woman before?"

"As far as I know, no," said George frankly.

"Well, do so now," said the Devil in quite a silky tone, which, nevertheless, caused blue sparks to crackle from the instrument. "Once we get possession of her soul, there will not be much fuss made about her body. I leave the matter in your hands entirely. If you fail me, there are one or two ancient institutions over here which I shall take pleasure in reviving entirely for your benefit."

George detested the idea of tempting this singularly good and beautiful young girl; however, the prospect was not so unredeemedly repulsive as that of immersion in boiling brimstone. He took a glass or two, to stifle what regrets he had, and sent for Rosie to attend him in a silken pavilion, which he had had rigged up among the groves and fountains which surrounded his citadel. He considered this fabric to be preferable to blocks of black basalt, in the event of some disruptive phrase of hers bringing the roof about their ears.

It was not very long before she arrived, although it seemed so. Heaven knows how she preserved her radiant health in the nasty gray air of Hell's outer suburbs, but she looked as fresh and bright as ever, and seemed to glow through her cheerless wrappings as a peach glows through tissue paper. Nevertheless, George was naturally a slow starter, especially when his conscience was involved. He certainly greeted her very warmly, but, if all the scientists in the world had had these hugs and kisses in a test tube, they could not have separated one atom of sin out of them, for they were as simple as could possibly be desired.

I admit that the simple and natural is as good a beginning as any other. George, however, proceeded only to the offer of a cup of tea, which is not sinful except at the university. They began to chat; he was unable to resist telling her of his joys and sorrows in the neighborhood of the Tottenham Court Road, and the reason for this was that he wished her to know everything about him. She herself was no less frank. It is impossible to describe the emotion with which George heard that she had become an orphan at the age of fourteen, and had since then lived with an old aunt who was inclined to severity. The moments passed like flowers of that precious edelweiss joy which blooms on the brink of the abyss.

The light began to fade; the warbling of blackbirds and thrushes now sank into a stillness from which soon arose the diviner strains of the nightingale. In this far, wild corner of the garden, the effect was a little Chinese, with a profusion of willow trees, which now turned blue in the dimming air. Our young people, seated at the entrance of the tent, found their tongues fall idle, and sat in a divine languor which, like another silence, a silence of the soul, permitted the first faint notes of a new music to become audible in their hearts.

Their fingers interlocked. The moon, which in those parts is of gigantic size, being no other than Hell itself, rose behind the shadowy trees. "They say," said Rosie in a dreamy voice, "that those marks on it are craters."

One person's dream may well be another's awakening. George was at once galvanized into activity. "Come," said he. "It is time we began dinner. It's my birthday, so there's lots of champagne."

He hoped by these words to inveigle the simple girl into making a feast of it. However, he started under a handicap, for he was already as drunk as a lord on the very sound of her voice. A man's true nature appears when he is in that condition: George was prepared to jeopardize his whole future for an amorous whim. His brain reeled under the onslaught of a legion of virtuous thought. He even conceived the notion of suggesting to the Devil that it should be the dummy husband who should be cast into the boiling brimstone, and that he should take that useless effigy's place, but from this act of madness the thought of the imps restrained him.

The remembrance of his master brought him back to Hell for a moment. "My dear," said he, patting her hand, "how would you like to be a filmstar?"

"Not at all," said she.

"What?" said he.

"Not at all," said she.

"Oh!" said he. "Well! Well! Well!"

He had a diamond necklace in his pocket, ready to tempt her with, but could not restrain himself from hanging it unconditionally about her neck, he was so delighted by this answer of hers.

She was pleased even more than by the gift itself by the spirit in which it was given. She thought George the kindest and the best of men, and (whether it was the wine or not, I'll not say) she would have even stuck to it that he was handsome.

Altogether, the meal went off as merry as a marriage bell. The only drawback was that George could see no signs of a fitting sequel. Some would say the brimstone was a sequel sufficiently appropriate, but that was not George's idea at all. In fact, when he had played all his cards in this halfhearted fashion, he was suddenly overcome by a hideous prevision of his fate, and could not repress a most alarming groan.

"What is it, my dear?" cried Rosie, in the tenderest of voices.

"Oh, nothing," said he, "nothing at all. Only that I shall burn forever if I fail to seduce you."

"That is what the young man said at the stocking counter," said she in dismay.

"But I mean in brimstone," said he dolorously, "and that, I assure you, is altogether a different proposition from love, whatever the poets may say."

"You are right," said she, in a happier voice than seemed entirely fitting, "love is altogether different from brimstone," and with that she squeezed his hand.

"I fear it will give me no peace in which to remember you," said he, positively photographing her with his eyes.

"You shall not go there," said she.

"He said I must!" cried George.

"Not," said she, "if—if it will save you to—"

"To what?" cried George.

"To seduce me," faltered Rosie.

George protested very little; he was altogether carried away by the charming manner in which she expressed herself. He flung his arms about her, and endeavored to convey, in one single kiss, all his gratitude for her kindness, his admiration for her beauty, his respect for her character, and his regret that she should have been orphaned at the age of fourteen and left to the care of an aunt who was a little inclined to severity. This is a great deal to be expressed in one single kiss; nevertheless, our hero did his best.

Next morning, he had to telephone his report to the Devil. "I'll hold your hand," said Rosie.

"Very well, my darling," said he. "I shall feel better so."

His call was put through like lightning. The Devil, like thunder, asked him how he had got on.

"The young woman is seduced," said George, in a rather brusque tone.

"Excellent!" returned his master. "Now tell me exactly how it happened."

"I thought," said George, "that you were supposed to be a gentleman."

"I am inquiring," said the Devil, "in a strictly professional capacity. What I wish to get at is her motive in yielding to your almost too subtle charm."

"Why?" cried George. "You don't think that splendid girl would see me frizzling and frying in a lake of boiling brimstone?"

"Do you mean to say," cried the Devil in a terrifying voice, "that she has sacrificed her virtue merely to save you from punishment?"

"What other inducement," asked our hero, "do you imagine would have been likely to prevail?"

"You besotted fool!" cried his master, and proceeded to abuse him ten times more roundly than before.

George listened in fear and rage. When he had done cursing him, the Devil continued in a calmer voice, "There is only one thing to be done," said he, "and you may consider yourself very fortunate that you—you worm!—are needed to play a part in it. Otherwise, you would be frizzling before sunset. As it is, I see I must give the matter my individual attention, and the first step is that you must marry the girl."

"By all means," replied our hero briskly.

"I shall send you a bishop to perform the ceremony," continued the fiend, "and, next week, if I am better of my present fit of gout, I shall require you to present me to your wife, and I myself will undertake her temptation."

"Temptation to what?" asked George, in a tone of great anxiety.

"To that sin to which wives are peculiarly fitted," replied the Devil. "Does she like a waxed moustache?"

"Oh, dear! He says," whispered George to Rosie, "do you like a waxed moustache?"

"No, darling," said Rosie. "I like a bristly, sandy one, like yours."

"She says she likes a bristly, sandy one, like mine," said George, not entirely without complacency.

"Excellent! I will appear in one yet bristlier and sandier," replied the fiend. "Keep her by you. I have never failed yet. And, Postle-thwaite—"

"Oh, yes, yes," said George. "What is it now?"

"Be discreet," said the Devil, in a menacing tone. "If she gets wind of my intentions, you shall be in the brimstone within an hour."

George hung up the receiver. "Excuse me, my dear," he said. "I really must go and think over what I have just heard."

He walked out among his groves of willows, which were then all freshened by the morning dew and resounding with the songs of birds. It was, of all the mornings of his life, that on which he would most have appreciated his first cigarette, had it not been for his conversation with the Devil. As it was, he did not bother to light one. "The thing is," he said to himself, "he must either succeed or fail. In the latter case his fury will be intolerable; in the former case mine will be."

The problem seemed to defy solution, and so it would have done, had it not been that love, whose bemusing effects have been cele-brated often enough in song and story, has another and an ungratefully neglected aspect, in which the mind receives the benefits of clarifying calm. When the first flurry of his perturbation had passed, our hero found himself in possession of a mind as cool and unclouded as the sea-strand sky of earliest dawn. He immediately lit his cigarette.

"After all, we have some days to go," he murmured, "and time is entirely relative. Consider, for example, that fellow Prior, who is at this very moment about to drink up the universe, and who will still be arrested in the act of doing so long after all our little lives have passed away. On the other hand, it is certainly not for me to deny that certain delightful moments can take on the aspect of eternity. Besides, we might always escape."

The thought had entered his mind as unostentatiously as, no doubt, the notion of writing *Paradise Lost* entered Milton's— "H'm, I'll write *Paradise Lost*." "Besides, we might always escape." Just a few words, which, however, made all the difference. All that remained, in one case as in the other, was to work out the little details.

Our hero was ingenious. What's more, he was assisted in his reflections by the hoarse cry, like that of a homing swan, of Charon's siren. It was the hour when that worthy, having cast loose from the quays of Hell, where he dropped his male cargo, turned his great ship towards George's planet. It came into sight, cleaving the morning blue, flashing in the beams of the local sun, leaving behind it a wake like that of a smoke-trailing airplane, only altogether better. It was a glorious sight. Soon George could see the women scampering up and down the decks, and hear their cry: "Is that Buenos Aires?"

He lost no time. Repairing to his palace, and seating himself in the most impressive of its salons, he sent forth a messenger to the docks, saying, "Bid the skipper come up and have a word with me."

Charon soon came stumping along in the wake of the messenger. He might have been inclined to grumble, but his eyes brightened at the sight of a bottle George had on his desk. This contained nothing less than the Old Original Rum of Hell, a liquor of the fiercest description, and now as rare as it is unappreciated.

"Skipper," said George, "you and I have got on well enough hitherto, I believe. I have to ask you a question, which may seem to reflect a little on your capacities. However, I don't ask it on my own behalf, you may be sure, and, in order to show my private estimation of you as a friend, as a man, and, above all, as a sea dog of the old school, I am going to ask you to do me the favor of taking a little tipple with me first."

Charon was a man of few words. "Aye, Aye!" said he.

George then poured out the rum. When Charon had wet his whistle, "The Chief," said George, "is in a secret fury with you over Mrs. Soames of Bayswater."

"Avast," said Charon, with a frown.

"Has it slipped your memory that I mentioned her to you on two previous occasions?" continued our hero. "She is now a hundred and four, and as cross as two sticks. The chief wants to know why you have not brought her along months ago." As he spoke, he refilled Charon's glass.

"Avast," said that worthy again.

"Perhaps," said George, "among your manifold onerous duties, his express commands concerning one individual may have seemed unworthy of your attention. I'm sure I should have forgotten the matter altogether, had I such a job as yours. Still, you know what he is. He has been talking of changes at the Admiralty; however, pay no attention to that. I have to visit the earth myself on important business, and I find that the young woman you brought by such a regrettable mistake has had training as a hospital nurse. Between us, I assure you, we will shanghai the old geezer in a brace of shakes; the Chief will find her here when he recovers from his gout, and foul weather between you will be entirely averted."

With that, he poured the rest of the rum into the old salt's glass.

"Aye! Aye!" said that worthy.

George at once pressed the bell, and had Rosie ushered in, in a bewitching uniform. "To the ship, at once!" he cried.

"Aye, Aye!" cried Charon.

"I can take you back," whispered George to his beloved, "as long as you don't cast a glance behind you. If you do, we are lost."

"Depend upon me," she said. "I have too much to look forward to."

Very well, they got aboard. Charon believed all landlubbers were mad; moreover, he had long suspected machinations against him at headquarters, and was obliged to George for giving him word of them. George ordered a whole case of the admirable rum (the last case in existence) to be placed in his cabin, lest Charon should remember that old Mrs. Soames had never been mentioned to him at all.

Amid hoots and exclamations in technical language, the great ship left her moorings. George, on the pretext that he had to maintain constant communication with his chief, took over the wireless operator's cabin. You may be sure Satan was in a fury when he heard what had happened; but the only effect of that was that his gouty members became a thousand times worse inflamed, and grew still more so when he found it impossible to establish communication with the ship.

The best he could do was to conjure up, in the trackless wastes of space, such dumb images as might tempt Rosie to glance behind her. A Paris hat would bob up like a buoy on the starboard bow, and a moment later (so great was the speed of the ship) be tossing far astern. On other occasions, the images of the most famous film actors would be descried sitting on the silver planets of far constellations, combing their hair. She was exposed to a hundred temptations of this sort, and, what was crueler, she was subjected, by pursuant imps, to ceaseless tweakings of the hair, tuggings of the garments, sensations as of a spider down her back, and to all sorts of odious familiarities, such as would be very offensive to describe! The devoted girl, holding fast to the forward rail of the boat deck, never so much as flickered an eye.

The result of this devotion, coupled with George's vigilance at the earphones and Charon's drunkenness below, was that they soon heaved to in the latitudes of the earth. George and Rosie were set to slide at dizzy speed down an invisible rope, and they found themselves safely in bed beside the old centenarian, Mrs. Soames.

She was in a tearing rage when she found this young couple beside her. "Get out of here at once," she cried.

"All right," they said, "we will."

The very next day I met them in Oxford Street, looking in the windows of the furniture shops, and George acquainted me with the whole story.

"And you say," said I, "that the universe is really a vast pint of beer?"

"Yes," said he. "It is all true. To prove it, I will show you the very place where Rosie was pinched by the envious young woman."

"The very place?" I cried.

"Yes," said he. "It was in that shop over there, at the counter to the right as you go in, just at the end of the stockings, and before the beginning of the lingerie."

Ah, THE UNIVERSITY!

Just outside London there lived an old father who dearly loved his only son. Accordingly, when the boy was a youngster of some eighteen years, the old man sent for him and, with a benevolent glimmer of his horn-rimmed spectacles, said, "Well, Jack, you are now done with school. No doubt you are looking forward to going to the university."

"Yes, Dad, I am," said the son.

"You show good judgment," said the father. "The best years of one's whole life are unquestionably those which are spent at the university. Apart from the vast honeycomb of learning, the mellow voices of the professors, the venerable gray buildings, and the atmosphere of culture and refinement, there is the delight of being in possession of a comfortable allowance."

"Yes, Dad," said the son.

"Rooms of one's own," continued the father, "little dinners to one's friends, endless credit with the tradespeople, pipes, cigars, claret, Burgundy, clothes."

"Yes, Dad," said the son.

"There are exclusive little clubs," said the old man, "all sorts of sports, May Weeks, theatricals, balls, parties, rags, binges, scaling of walls, dodging of proctors, fun of every conceivable description."

"Yes! Yes, Dad!" cried the son.

"Certainly nothing in the world is more delightful than being at the university," said the father. "The springtime of life! Pleasure after pleasure! The world seems a whole dozen of oysters, each with a pearl in it. Ah, the university! However, I'm not going to send you there."

"Then why the Hell do you go on so about it?" said poor Jack.

"I did so in order that you might not think I was carelessly underestimating the pleasures I must call upon you to renounce," said his father. "You see, Jack, my health is not of the best; nothing but champagne agrees with me, and if I smoke a second-rate cigar, I get a vile taste in my mouth. My expenses have mounted abominably and I shall have very little to leave to you, yet my dearest wish is to see you in a comfortable way of life."

"If that is your wish, you might gratify it by sending me to the university," said Jack.

"We must think of the future," said his father. "You will have your living to earn, and in a world where culture is the least marketable of assets. Unless you are to be a schoolmaster or a curate, you will gain no great advantage from the university."

"Then what am I to be?" the young man asked.

"I read only a little while ago," said his father, "the following words, which flashed like sudden lightning upon the gloom in which I was considering your future: 'Most prayers are weak.' These words are in fact the monolithic opening sentence of a little brochure upon the delightful and universally popular game of poker. It is a game which is played for counters, commonly called chips, and each of these chips represents an agreeable sum of money."

"Do you mean that I am to be a cardsharper?" cried the son.

"Nothing of the sort," replied the old man promptly. "I am asking you to be strong, Jack. I am asking you to show initiative, individuality. Why learn what everyone else is learning? You, my dear boy, shall be the first to study poker as systematically as others study languages, science, mathematics, and so forth—the first to tackle it as a student. I have set aside a cozy little room with chair, table, and some completely new packs of cards. A bookshelf contains several standard works on the game, and a portrait of Machiavelli hangs above the mantelpiece."

The young man's protests were vain, so he set himself reluctantly to study. He worked hard, mastered the books, wore the spots off a hundred packs of cards, and at the end of the second year he set out into the world with his father's blessing and enough cash to sit in on a few games of penny ante.

After Jack left, the old man consoled himself with his glass of champagne and his first-rate cigar and those other little pleasures which are the solace of the old and the lonely. He was getting on very well with these when one day the telephone rang. It was an overseas call from Jack, whose existence the old man had all but forgotten.

"Hullo, Dad!" cried the son in tones of great excitement. "I'm in Paris, sitting in on a game of poker with some Americans."

"Good luck to you!" said the old man, preparing to hang up the receiver.

"Listen, Dad!" cried the son. "It's like this. Well—just for once I'm playing without any limit."

"Lord have mercy on you!" said the old man.

"There's two of them still in," said the son. "They've raised me fifty thousand dollars and I've already put up every cent I've got."

"I would rather," groaned the old man, "see a son of mine at the university than in such a situation."

"But I've got four kings!" cried the young man.

"You can be sure the others have aces or straight flushes," said the old man. "Back down, my poor boy. Go out and play for cigarette ends with the habitués of your doss house."

"But listen, Dad!" cried the son. "This is a stud round, and nothing wild. I've seen an ace chucked in. "I've seen all the tens and fives chucked in. There isn't a straight flush possible."

"Is that so?" cried the old man. "Never let it be said I didn't stand behind my boy! Hold everything! I'm coming to your assistance."

The son went back to the card table and begged his opponents to postpone matters until his father could arrive, and they, smiling at their cards, were only too willing to oblige him.

A couple of hours later the old man arrived by plane at Le Bourget, and shortly thereafter he was standing beside the card table, rubbing his hands, smiling, affable, the light glinting merrily upon his horn-rimmed spectacles. He shook hands with the Americans and noted their prosperous appearance. "Now what have we here?" said he, sliding into his son's seat and fishing out his money.

"The bet," said one of the opponents, "stands at fifty thousand dollars. Seen by me. It's for you to see or raise."

"Or run," said the other.

"I trust my son's judgment," said the old man. "I shall raise fifty thousand dollars before I even glance at these cards in my hand." With that he pushed forward a hundred thousand dollars of his own money.

"I'll raise that hundred thousand dollars," said the first of his opponents.

"I'll stay and see," said the other.

The old man looked at his cards. His face turned several colors in rapid succession. A low and quavering groan burst from his lips and he was seen to hesitate for a long time, showing all the signs of an appalling inward struggle. At last he summoned up his courage and, pushing out his last hundred thousand (which represented all the cigars, champagne, and other little pleasures he had to look forward to for the rest of his life), he licked his lips several times and said, "I'll see you."

"Four kings," said the first opponent, laying down his hand.

"Hell!" said the second. "Four queens."

"And I," moaned the old man, "have four knaves." With that, he turned about and seized his son by the lapels of his jacket, shaking him as a terrier does a rat. "Curse the day," said he, "that I ever became the father of a damned fool!"

"I swear I thought they were kings," cried the young man.

"Don't you know that the 'V' is for *valets*?" said his father.

"Good god!" the son said. "I thought the 'V' was something to do with French kings. You know, Charles V, Louis V, V one, V two, V three. Oh, what a pity I was never at the university!"

"Go," said the old man. "Go there, or go to Hell or wherever you wish. Never let me see or hear from you again." And he stamped out of the room before his son or anyone else could say a word, even to tell him it was high-low stud they were playing and that the four knaves had won half the pot.

The young man, pocketing his share, mused that ignorance of every sort is deplorable, and, bidding his companions farewell, left Paris without further delay, and very soon he was entered at the university.

BACK FOR CHRISTMAS

"Doctor," said Major Sinclair, "we certainly must have you with us for Christmas." Tea was being poured, and the Carpenters' living room was filled with friends who had come to say last-minute farewells to the Doctor and his wife.

"He shall be back," said Mrs. Carpenter. "I promise you."

"It's hardly certain," said Dr. Carpenter. "I'd like nothing better, of course."

"After all," said Mr. Hewitt, "you've contracted to lecture only for three months."

"Anything may happen," said Dr. Carpenter.

"Whatever happens," said Mrs. Carpenter, beaming at them, "he shall be back in England for Christmas. You may all believe me."

They all believed her. The Doctor himself almost believed her. For ten years she had been promising him for dinner parties, garden parties, committees, heaven knows what, and the promises had always been kept.

The farewells began. There was a fluting of compliments on dear Hermione's marvelous arrangements. She and her husband would drive to Southampton that evening. They would embark the following day. No trains, no bustle, no last-minute worries. Certain the Doctor was marvelously looked after. He would be a great success in America. Especially with Hermione to see to everything. She would have a wonderful time, too. She must see the skyscrapers. Nothing like that in Little Godwearing. But she must be very sure to bring him back. "Yes, I will bring him back. You may rely upon it." He mustn't be persuaded. No extensions. No wonderful post at some super-American hospital. Our infirmary needs him. And he must be back by Christmas. "Yes," Mrs. Carpenter called to the last departing guest, "I shall see to it. He shall be back by Christmas."

The final arrangements for closing the house were very well managed. The maids soon had the tea things washed up; they came in, said good-bye, and were in time to catch the afternoon bus to Devizes.

Nothing remained but odds and ends, locking doors, seeing that everything was tidy. "Go upstairs," said Hermione, "and change into your brown tweeds. Empty the pockets of that suit before you put it in your bag. I'll see to everything else. All you have to do is not to get in the way."

The Doctor went upstairs and took off the suit he was wearing, but, instead of the brown tweeds, he put on an old, dirty bathrobe, which he took from the back of his wardrobe. Then, after making one or two little arrangements, he leaned over the head of the stairs and called to his wife, "Hermione! Have you a moment to spare?"

"Of course, dear. I'm just finished."

"Just come up here for a moment. There's something rather extraordinary up here."

Hermione immediately came up. "Good heavens, my dear man!"

she said when she saw her husband. "What are you lounging about in that filthy old thing for? I told you to have it burned long ago."

"Who in the world," said the Doctor, "has dropped a gold chain down the bathtub drain?"

"Nobody has, of course," said Hermione. "Nobody wears such a thing."

"Then what is it doing there?" said the Doctor. "Take this flashlight. If you lean right over, you can see it shining, deep down."

"Some Woolworth's bangle off one of the maids," said Hermione. "It can be nothing else." However, she took the flashlight and leaned over, squinting into the drain. The Doctor, raising a short length of lead pipe, struck two or three times with great force and precision, and tilting the body by the knees, tumbled it into the tub.

He then slipped off the bathrobe and, standing completely naked, unwrapped a towel full of implements and put them into the washbasin. He spread several sheets of newspaper on the floor and turned once more to his victim.

She was dead, of course—horribly doubled up, like a somersaulter, at one end of the tub. He stood looking at her for a very long time, thinking of absolutely nothing at all. Then he saw how much blood there was and his mind began to move again.

First he pushed and pulled until she lay straight in the bath, then he removed her clothing. In the narrow bathtub this was an extremely clumsy business, but he managed it at last and then turned on the taps. The water rushed into the tub, then dwindled, then died away, and the last of it gurgled down the drain.

"Good God!" he said. "She turned it off at the main."

There was only one thing to do: the Doctor hastily wiped his hands on a towel, opened the bathroom door with a clean corner of the towel, threw it back onto the bath stool, and ran downstairs, barefoot, light as a cat. The cellar door was in a corner of the entrance hall, under the stairs. He knew just where the cut-off was. He had reason to: he had been pottering about down there for some time past—trying to scrape out a bin for wine, he had told Hermione. He pushed open the cellar door, went down the steep steps, and just before the closing door plunged the cellar into pitch darkness, he put his hand on the tap and turned it on. Then he felt his way back along the grimy wall till he came to the steps. He was about to ascend them when the bell rang.

The Doctor was scarcely aware of the ringing as a sound. It was like a spike of iron pushed slowly up through his stomach. It went on until it reached his brain. Then something broke. He threw himself down in the coal dust on the floor and said, "I'm done for. Done for!"

"They've got no *right* to come," he said. Then he heard himself panting. "None of this," he said to himself. "None of this."

He began to revive. He got to his feet, and when the bell rang again the sound passed through him almost painlessly. "Let them go away," he said. Then he heard the front door open. He said, "I don't care." His shoulder came up, like that of a boxer, to shield his face. "I give up," he said.

He heard people calling. "Herbert!" "Hermione!" It was the Wallingfords. "Damn them! They come butting in. People anxious to get off. All naked! And blood and coal dust! I'm done! I'm through! I can't do it."

"Herbert!"

"Hermione!"

"Where the dickens can they be?"

"The car's there."

"Maybe they've popped round to Mrs. Liddell's."

"We must see them."

"Or to the shops, maybe. Something at the last minute."

"Not Hermione. I say, listen! Isn't that someone having a bath? Shall I shout? What about whanging on the door?"

"Sh-h-h! Don't. It might not be tactful."

"No harm in a shout."

"Look, dear. Let's come in on our way back. Hermione said they wouldn't be leaving before seven. They're dining on the way, in Salisbury."

"Think so? All right. Only I want a last drink with old Herbert. He'd be hurt."

"Let's hurry. We can be back by half past six."

The Doctor heard them walk out and the front door close quietly behind them. He thought, "Half past six. I can do it."

He crossed the hall, sprang the latch of the front door, went upstairs, and, taking his instruments from the washbasin, finished what he had to do. He came down again, clad in his bathrobe, carrying parcel after parcel of toweling or newspaper neatly secured with safety pins. These he packed carefully into the narrow, deep hole he had made in the corner of the cellar, shoveled in the soil, spread coal dust over all, satisfied himself that everything was in order, and went upstairs again. He then thoroughly cleaned the bath, and himself, and the bath again, dressed, and took his wife's clothing and his bathrobe to the incinerator.

One or two more little touches and everything was in order. It was only a quarter past six. The Wallingfords were always late; he had only to get into the car and drive off. It was a pity he couldn't wait till after dusk, but he could make a detour to avoid passing through the main street, and even if he was seen driving alone, people would only think Hermione had gone on ahead for some reason, and they would forget about it.

Still, he was glad when he had finally got away, entirely unobserved, on the open road, driving into the gathering dusk. He had to drive very carefully; he found himself unable to judge distances, his reactions were abnormally delayed, but that was a detail. When it was quite dark he allowed himself to stop the car on the top of the downs, in order to think.

The stars were superb. He could see the lights of one or two little towns far away on the plain below him. He was exultant. Everything that was to follow was perfectly simple. Marion was waiting in Chicago. She already believed him to be a widower. The lecture people could be put off with a word. He had nothing to do but establish himself in some thriving out-of-the-way town in America and he was safe forever. There were Hermione's clothes, of course, in the suitcases; they could be disposed of through the porthole. Thank heaven she wrote her letters on the typewriter—a little thing like handwriting might have prevented everything. "But there you are," he said. "She was up-to-date, efficient all along the line. Managed everything. Managed herself to death, damn her!"

"There's no reason to get excited," he thought. "I'll write a few letters for her, then fewer and fewer. Write myself—always expecting to get back, never quite able to. Keep the house one year, then another, then another; they'll get used to it. Might even come back alone in a year or two and clear it up properly. Nothing easier. But not for Christmas!" He started up the engine and was off.

In New York he felt free at last, really free. He was safe. He could look back with pleasure—at least after a meal, lighting his cigarette, he could look back with a sort of pleasure—to the minute he had passed in the cellar listening to the bell, the door, and the voices. He could look forward to Marion.

As he strolled through the lobby of his hotel, the clerk, smiling, held up letters for him. It was the first batch from England. Well, what did that matter? It would be fun dashing off the typewritten sheets in Hermione's downright style, signing them with her squiggle, telling everyone what a success his first lecture had been, how thrilled he was with America but how certainly she'd bring him back for Christmas. Doubts could creep in later.

He glanced over the letters. Most were for Hermione. From the Sinclairs, the Wallingfords, the vicar, and a business letter from Holt & Sons, Builders and Decorators.

He stood in the lounge, people brushing by him. He opened the letters with his thumb, reading here and there, smiling. They all seemed very confident he would be back for Christmas. They relied on Hermione. "That's where they make their big mistake," said the Doctor, who had taken to American phrases. The builders' letter he kept to the last. Some bill, probably. It was:

Dear Madam,

We are in receipt of your kind acceptance of estimate as below and also of key.

We beg to repeat you may have every confidence in same being ready in ample time for Christmas present as stated. We are setting men to work this week.

We are, Madam,

Yours faithfully,
PAUL HOLT & SONS

To excavating, building up, suitably lining one sunken wine bin in cellar as indicated, using best materials, making good, etc.

. . . .£ 18/0/0

ANOTHER AMERICAN TRAGEDY

A young man entered the office of a prominent dentist, and seated himself in the chair. He scornfully waved aside the little probe and mirror with which the dentist smilingly approached him. "Rip 'em all out," he said.

"But," said the dentist, "your teeth seem perfectly good."

"So," said the young man, "is my money."

The dentist hesitated a little. "It would hardly be ethical," said he, "to take out teeth which are sound—unless there is a very good reason for it."

The young man, who had begun to smile at the word "ethical," here extended his smile into a cavernous gape, which laid bare the hindermost of his ivories. At the same time he twitched out a small roll of bills from his vest pocket, and held them noticeably in his hand.

The dentist utterly ignored these bills. "If you want those excellent teeth out," said he, "you must certainly be mad. Now I have a little theory: *mental* derangement is caused by *dental* derangement. It is a sign of something wrong way up behind the roots of the teeth, especially those of the upper row. Viewed from that angle—"

"Cut it, and pull them out," said the young man, impatient of these professional niceties.

The dentist shrugged and obeyed. As if in fear that the young man might become altogether too sane at the end of the operation, he humorously tweaked away the roll of bills with a thirty-third frisk of his forceps.

The young man made no comment, but only called for a mirror, in which he surveyed his numb and fallen chops with every appearance of satisfaction. He asked when his denture would be ready, made the appointment, and went his way.

"Dear me!" thought the dentist. "Perhaps the trouble was not in his teeth after all. Certainly he is still as crazy as a coot."

Here the dentist made a big mistake. The young man was perfectly sane, and knew very well what he was about. It happened that he had spent all his money in some years of the vilest dissipation, but he had a very far-reaching and watertight plan for getting some more. His views on the subject of teeth were directly opposite to the common attitude towards insurance. He held it is better not to have them, and to need them, than to have them but to find no sort of use for them.

He accordingly returned to the dentist on the appointed day, and was equipped with his artificial grinders, which he sucked at and gnashed in the most ordinary fashion. He paid for them with almost his last dollar, went out, and got into his racy-looking roadster, and drove out of town as if pursued by the finance company, as he certainly would have been had they caught sight of him.

He drove till nightfall, and resumed his journey next day. Late in the afternoon he arrived in that part of the country where old and miserly uncles live in remote, dilapidated farmhouses. Our young man was more or less fortunate in possessing one of the oldest and richest of these uncles, whose house was the remotest and most dilapidated of all.

Arriving at this secluded dwelling, our hero drew up before a porch upon which no money had been squandered for years. "So much the more in the old sock," reflected the nephew, as he knocked upon the door.

He was a little disconcerted to hear the tap of high heels within, instead of the shuffle of a deaf and surly retainer, and his jaw dropped when the door was opened by a plump and squarish blonde, a baby of some thirty-odd years and about a hundred and fifty pounds. Her mouth was as wide and as red as a slice of watermelon; she had well-darkened lashes and brows, and an abundance of phony gold hair flowing girlishly down over her shoulders. Our friend was to some extent reassured when he realized that she was dressed in what might be called a nurse's uniform, but the extreme shortness of the skirt and the fact that her garters were bright scarlet and adorned with enormous bows caused him to wonder if his dear uncle was getting the very best of professional care.

Nevertheless, it is important to get on the right side of the nurse, especially when she stands solidly in the doorway. Our hero removed his hat, and put on so soapy a smile that his false teeth nearly dropped out of his head. "I have driven all the way from the big city," said he, "to see my poor, dear, bedridden old uncle—God bless him! I did not expect to see so charming a nurse."

The nurse, not budging an inch, responded with a surly and suspicious stare.

"I fear he must be sinking," continued the nephew. "In fact, I had an intuition, a sort of telepathic SOS, telling me to hasten out here before it was too late. Let me rush to his bedside."

The nurse still hesitated, but at that moment a peculiar sound, resembling the croaking of giant bullfrogs, arose in the dim depths of the house. This was the good old uncle himself, vociferating toothlessly for an immediate sight of his nephew, whose expressions of affection and concern had been audible in every corner of the dwelling. The old boy knew very well that his young relative was after his money, and he was eager for the pleasure of turning him down.

The nurse somewhat grudgingly stepped aside. Our hero, with a well-rehearsed whinny of delight, scuttled into the bedroom.

Nothing is more affecting than the greetings of near relatives after a long separation, especially when they are as fond of each other as these two. "My dear Uncle!" cried the nephew. "What a pleasure it is to see you again! But why is your voice so hollow? Why are your eyes so sunken? Why are you so thin and pale?"

"If it comes to that," said his uncle, "you are not too stout and rosy yourself. No, you are very worn and emaciated, my boy. Your hair is thin and gray; you have lines, bags, and creases all over your face. If it were not for your handsome white teeth, I believe you would look every bit as old as I do."

"That," said the nephew, "is the effect of ceaseless toil and moil. It is a hard struggle, Uncle, to make good in these days, especially without any capital."

"So you are making good?" said the old man. "Do you not drink anymore?"

"No, Uncle, I never drink now," replied the nephew.

"Well, that's tough," said his uncle, producing a giant flask from under his pillow. "In that case I can't ask you to join me." With that, he took a mighty swig, and, wiping his lips, he continued, "I have, thank heaven, a good doctor. A typical tough, bluff, hard-hitting, straight-shooting country sawbones of the old school. We call him the horse 'n' buggy doc. He recommends me this as medicine."

"Perhaps that is why your hand trembles so," said his nephew.

"Your own is none too steady," rejoined his uncle. "Evidently you work too hard. Tell me, Nephew, do you ever take a little flutter with the cards?"

"Good heavens, no!" cried the nephew. "I cured myself of that folly long ago."

"I am sorry to hear it," replied his uncle. "We might have played a little cutthroat. The old horse 'n' buggy doc says the excitement keeps me lively. We often play together till after midnight."

"That is why your eyes are sunken so deep," said the nephew.

"I think yours are equally hollow," replied the old man. "You should take a little rest now and then. I suppose, my dear Nephew, you still have an occasional frolic with the girls."

"Girls!" cried the nephew, lifting up his hands. "What an odious suggestion! It is years since I have even looked at a girl."

"Well, that's too bad," said his uncle. "The old horse 'n' buggy doc has up-to-date views. It was he who sent me Birdie." And, turning to the nurse, who happened to be arranging his pillows, he gave her a certain sort of caress, such as is mentioned nowhere in the pharmacopoeia.

"No wonder!" cried his nephew, when the nurse had gone bridling and smirking from the room. "No wonder, my poor Uncle, that you are so extremely thin and pale!"

"You are equally so," replied his uncle, "and you are only half my age."

"Well," said the nephew, trying a new tack, "perhaps your doctor is right. Perhaps I had better take your treatment."

"I heartily advise it," said the old man.

"The only thing is," said the nephew, "that I can hardly work at the same time. I suppose you would not care to give me a little money, so that I can enjoy the benefits of the system."

"Well, no," said his uncle. "I would not. Definitely not."

"I thought as much," said his nephew. "I fear I shall have to keep on toiling. How upset your good old horse 'n' buggy doc would be! Tell me one thing, however; indulge my curiosity in one trifling respect. Is there any hope I shall come into your money? Have you arranged it in your will?"

"Oh, come!" said his uncle. "Why bother your head with matters of that sort?"

"Do tell me," pressed the nephew. "You have no idea how interested I am."

"Well, if you really want to know," said his uncle, "I have left it all to the old horse 'n' buggy doc, a true, downright, straight-living, crusty, hard-faced, softhearted country croaker of the old school, and you cannot imagine how agreeable his treatment is to me."

"Is that really so?" said the nephew. "I must say, I expected something of the sort. Fortunately I have made my plans against just such a contingency. Allow me, my dear Uncle."

With that, he twitched a pillow from under the old man's head, and pressed it over his face. The old uncle gave a petulant kick or two, but what with one thing and another there was very little life left in him, and soon that little was gone.

The nephew, with a wry glance at the door, quickly divested himself of his clothing, which he stowed under the bed. Next, possibly feeling a little chilly, he took the liberty of borrowing his uncle's nightshirt. Then, stowing his uncle's shrunken body under the bed also, he climbed into his place between the sheets. Finally, he expectorated his false teeth into a clean pocket handkerchief, which he had brought especially for the purpose, and leaned back upon the pillows, the very spit and image of the old man.

Soon he set up a pipe: "Birdie! Birdie!"

At his call the nurse came hurrying in. "Why, honey-boy," said she, "where's your worthless nephew gone?"

"He has just slipped out for a stroll around the old place," croaked our hero. "Moreover, I don't think you should call him worthless. No, I have misjudged that young man, and I want you to send for the lawyer, so that I can do him justice in my will."

"Why, Daddy?" cried the nurse. "What's made this change in you?"

"Change?" said the nephew hastily. "There's no change in me, my dear, except perhaps I feel my latter end approaching. Otherwise I am just the same." And to reassure her on this point, he gave her a friendly little caress, exactly as his uncle had done. She emitted an hilarious squeal and went giggling on her errand.

The nephew lay at his ease, waiting only for the arrival of the lawyer. "I shall dictate a new will," thought he, "and sign it before the very eyes of the lawyer, in a shaky imitation of the old man's crabbed hand. I shall then express a desire to be left alone for a short nap, replace my poor uncle in the bed, put on my clothes, put back my teeth, and step out of the window, to march in at the front door as if newly returned from my walk. What bucketfuls of tears I shall shed, when we discover that the poor old boy has passed peacefully away!"

Pretty soon there was a heavy footstep on the porch, and a large and roughhewn individual strode into the room, bearing a sizable black bag.

"I am glad you have come," said our hero. "I am eager to make out a new will. I wish to leave everything to my nephew."

"My dear old friend," replied the newcomer, "I fear your malady has reached the brain. Who would have thought my old pal could have mistaken me for the lawyer? You must let me make a brief examination." With that, he pulled down the sheet, and began to probe the nephew with a hard and horny finger. The nephew realized too late that this was no lawyer, but the horse 'n' buggy doc himself, and he uttered a hollow groan.

"I feared as much," said the doctor. "There is something very wrong somewhere in here. I must act at once, if you are to recover your reason." As he spoke, he turned the nephew over in the bed, and whisked out a monster hypodermic from his black bag. "Fortunately," said he, "I am always ready for emergencies."

Our hero tried to protest, but he hardly knew what to say, fearing that his uncle would be discovered under the bed, and the circumstance would tend to his prejudice. The doctor, all in a moment, injected a pint of icy fluid into the small of his back, which numbed his whole middle, and paralyzed all his faculties, except that of rolling the eyes, which he indulged to the point of excess.

"I am only an old, rough, goldarn horse 'n' buggy doc," observed the doctor, "but I keep abreast of the times. Mental derangement is often caused by abdominal derangement. If you will get out my instruments, nurse, I think we shall soon find the source of the trouble."

In a moment, the unfortunate nephew was laid open under his own eyes, which he never ceased to roll. The doctor, unpacking him like a Gladstone bag, kept up a running commentary. "Take this," said he to the nurse, "and put it on the washstand. Put these on the chair. Don't get them mixed up, or I shall have the devil of a job getting them back again. It is a pity that nephew is not back; it is more ethical to have the consent of a relative before operating. I see nothing wrong with this pancreas, considering the age of the patient. Put it on the chest of drawers. Hang these over the bed-rail.

"Hold the light a little closer," he continued. "I still have not found the cause of his madness. Don't let the candle drip; that is hardly hygienic. Anyway, he is certainly mad, or he would not think of leaving his money to that scalawag of a nephew. It is as well you let me know, my dear, instead of bothering the lawyer. When this is all over, we must take a little trip together."

Saying this, he gave the nurse a caress, similar to that which both uncle and nephew had bestowed on her. The sight of this caress not only shocked our hero, but depressed him beyond description, and lowered his powers of resistance. "It is most unprofessional," thought he, "and, what's even worse, it smacks abominably of conspiracy." This thought caused him to roll his eyes for the last time, and the next moment he was a goner.

"Dear me," said the Doctor, "I fear I have lost my patient. Sometimes I quite envy the city doctor, with his well-appointed operating theater. However, their autobiographies usually sell very poorly, and, after all, I did my best for the old boy, and he has remembered me in his will. Had he lived, he might have altered it. What an extraordinary trick of fate! Pass me over the various organs, my dear, and I will put them roughly into position, for I expect the nephew will be back very shortly, and he would hate to see them lying around."

COLLABORATION

There was a certain Ambrose, who was proud of his superior profile and his superior taste. His wife was supposed to be a testimony to both. She was a honey-blonde with a wide mouth, and a bewitching eye, better than a bowl of strawberries and cream, but she was too simple to be fit for any but an adoring role, and this was what he assigned to her. He managed, however, to teach her to demand sherry, and sneer at cocktails, and sometimes she wondered if she was sighing for an old-fashioned.

They had a little house on Long Island, and another in the South of France. On one occasion he was opening his letters: "All is well," said he. "We shall set off for Provence next month. We shall see our dear house, our terrace, our garden, all in perfect taste, all designed by me. I shall take you with our little Moviola, and you," said he, throwing back his wavy hair, "will take me."

"Yes, my dear," said she.

"If only," said he, "we had a couple of ideal children, the image of their father. They could be taken running to meet me. We could take them here on Long Island and show them to our friends in Provence, and we could take them in Provence, and show them to our friends on Long Island. I can't understand why you don't have a couple of ideal children. You know I wish it."

"I gave up cocktails because you wished it," said she. "And now I drink sherry."

He put his fine hand to his brow. "I talk of ideal children," he moaned, "and you reply with an idiotic irrelevancy about cocktails. Leave me. You jar. I will open my letters alone.

She obediently withdrew, but soon a bitter cry brought her scurrying back again. "Oh, my dear, what in the world is it?" cried she. "Whatever is the matter?"

"Read that," said he, handing her a letter. "Don't talk to me about cocktails. Read that."

"What is this?" she cried. "Your money gone!"

"I tried to double it," said he. "I thought it would be nice. This comes of being an artist, a dreamer. Spare me your reproaches."

"We have each other," said she, allowing a large, booby tear to trickle down her cheek, as women often do when they seek comfort in this particular reflection.

"Yes," said he. "And may take films of each other in the bread-line, and show them to our friends. You may be taken so if you wish. I have my pride."

"But I have my jewels," said she. "We can live on them while you write that book you have always been talking of."

"*Always* been talking of?" said he. "I hardly know what you mean. Still, a great many fools write books, and sell a hundred thousand copies. What would be the royalty on five hundred thousand? Put a heap of high-grade paper in my study. Tell everyone I am not to be disturbed. If only we had a couple of ideal children, you could keep them quiet while I was at work. You could tell them what their daddy was doing."

Pretty soon he was in his study, and visitors were impressed. Sometimes he would wander out among them with a fine, vague air. The only trouble was, he was equally vague when he returned to his desk, and not a line appeared on even the first sheet of his high-grade paper; nothing but drawings of profiles. "I am too much of an artist, I suppose," said he to himself. "I have no appetite for the coarse and crude material of which plots are made. I am all style. There will be no book, we shall become beggars, and Daphne will cease to adore me. I must go out and see life. Perhaps I will find a plot."

He went out and hung about the Bohemian cafés in Greenwich Village, where he saw writers in plenty, but not enough life to go round, and not a plot among the whole crowd of them.

In the end he fetched up in the cheapest and shabbiest of dives, such as might be frequented by one who could not finish his book, who had no money, whose wife had ceased to adore him, and who consequently had less chance than ever of a couple of ideal children.

It was extremely crowded. Possibly there are many writers in this disagreeable situation. Ambrose had to share a table with a young man who had the appearance of a tomcat whose ears have been bitten short in a hundred rigorous experiences. He had a bullet head, a broad nose, magnificent teeth, and a ravenous expression. His shirt was ragged, and his chest bore a plentiful growth of absolutely genuine hair.

His hands were somewhat battered. "That thumb," said he to Ambrose, "a dame shot off. Holding up a candle. One-horse circus show. Never missed ordinarywise. Jealous. That finger a croc got. Marlinspike that one. Third mate. Mutiny. This thumb got frostbit. Hitchhiking across Labrador in a blizzard. Some of them bites is horse-bites, some's wolves', some's dames'."

"Certainly," said Ambrose, "you have seen life."

"Life, birth, death, and passion in the raw," returned the other. "I'd rather see a hamburger."

"Look, there is one cooking on the stove over there," said Ambrose. "Are you by any chance a writer?"

"A second Jack London," said the other. "But I got the publishing racket against me. I give 'em blood, sweat, lust, murder, everything. And they talk about style." He pronounced this last word with an air of contempt.

"Style," said Ambrose reprovingly, "is ninety-nine percent of the whole business. I am a stylist myself. Waiter, bring over that hamburger. This is what you wished to see, is it not?"

"Thank you," said the young man.

"Yes," said Ambrose. "You can now look at it closely. I have this ability to gratify my friends—call it power if you will—because I am a fine stylist. I count on my forthcoming book to sell half a million copies. Eat the hamburger. It is nothing to me."

"O.K.," said the young man, falling to.

"You seem to like hamburgers," said Ambrose. "I need a sort of secretary with a good experience of life; a prentice, in short, such as the old masters had, who could rough out plots for me. You seem to have an unlimited supply of material. I have an unlimited supply of hamburgers."

"Sell out?" cried the young man. "For a hamburger? Not me!"

"There would be large steaks—" said Ambrose.

"But—" said the young man.

"—smothered with mushrooms," said Ambrose. "Fried chicken. Pie. New clothes. Comfortable quarters. Maybe a dollar a week pocket money."

"Make it two," said the young man. "You can't take a dame out on a dollar."

"Certainly not," said Ambrose. "No dames. All must go into the plots."

"That's tough," said the young man.

"Take it or leave it," said Ambrose.

The young man, after a struggle, succumbed, and soon was tied up with a long-term contract, and taken home to the little house on Long Island. Ambrose described him as a secretary, in order to conceal the true arrangement from his wife, for he feared it might lessen her adoration.

The young man, whose new clothing became him very well, ate and drank very heartily, and relished all that was set before him, all except the sherry. This he absolutely refused, demanding a cocktail. "Mix him an old-fashioned," said Ambrose to his wife, for he felt it might help to nourish up a plot full of life in the raw.

His lovely wife opened her eyes very wide, first at her husband, then at his secretary, and finally at the old-fashioned, of which she could not resist taking a surreptitious sip. "How extremely delicious!" she thought. "How delightful life is, after all! In comes this young man, and at once I get what I have been sighing for. I wonder if he ever sighs for anything. He seems too vital. He would just ask for it. Or take it. Oh, dear!"

With that, she handed the cocktail to the young man, who received it shyly, gratefully, and yet as if it were his due. He drank it in a straightforward, manly fashion, yet with a keen, primitive, simple enjoyment, holding the glass just so, throwing back his head just so —I cannot describe how handsomely this young man disposed of his cocktail.

All went well in the house. Ambrose ceased to worry. His wife ceased to sigh. Soon the plot was ready. It had everything. "You will remain here," said Ambrose to his secretary, "and we shall go to our little house in Provence, where I shall cast this rough clay into something rather like a Grecian vase. Meanwhile, you can think up another."

So off they went, Ambrose rubbing his hands. His wife perversely showed some disposition to sigh again when they boarded the liner, but of that he took no notice. He soon, however, had reason to sigh himself, for when he began work in his stateroom he found his style was not quite as perfect as he had imagined it to be. In fact, by the end of his voyage his high-grade paper was still as blank as before.

This put Ambrose back into the depths of despair. When they got to Paris, he slunk out of the hotel, and drifted into the dingiest café he could find, where the poorest writers forgathered, who were all destitute of plots, money, adoring wives, ideal children, and everything.

Such cafés abound in every back street of Paris, and enjoy a numerous and cosmopolitan custom. Ambrose found himself sitting beside a young Englishman whose features were sensitive to a degree, and almost transparent by reason of their extreme emaciation. Ambrose observed that this young man's eyes were full of tears. "Why," said he, "are your eyes full of tears?"

"I am a writer," said the young man, "and as the barbarous publishers pay no heed to style, but insist upon plots about beastly men and women, you may understand that I have to live very simply. I was making my frugal dinner on the smell of a superb dish of *tripes à la mode*, which that fat fellow over there is eating, when in came an abominable newspaperman, who sat down in our neighborhood and poured out such a flood of journalese that I was obliged to move away. And I am so hungry!"

"Too bad!" said Ambrose. "I'll tell you what. I'll order a portion for myself, and you shall sniff as heartily as you wish."

"I am eternally grateful," said the other. "I don't know why you should benefit a stranger in this way."

"That's nothing," said Ambrose. "Have you ever tasted a piece of bread dipped in the gravy?"

"Yes, indeed!" cried the other. "I did so last Christmas. It lent a special richness to my style all through the first half of this year."

"How admirably you would write," said Ambrose, "if someone fed you *boeuf en daube!*"

"I could write an *Iliad* on it," cried the other.

"And on *bouillabaisse?*"

"An *Odyssey.*"

"I need someone," said Ambrose, "to put a few little finishing touches to some more modern but equally magnificent conceptions of my own. I have a little house in Provence, with an excellent kitchen—"

In a word, he soon had this unfortunate in his hands, and tied up with options and loans as securely as any white slave in Buenos Aires.

The young man first lived in a rapture of sniffing, then grew quite used to bread dipped in the gravy, and finally ate all that was going, to the utmost benefit to his physique and style. He would not, however, drink any of Ambrose's sherry. "Let me have a cocktail," said he. "It will impart a modern and realistic smack to my prose, which is particularly desirable for the scenes laid in America."

"Not only that," thought Ambrose, "but it will provide a link, a *rapport*, between him and the other." Accordingly, he called in his wife, at whose appearance the young man inhaled deeply. "Mix him an old-fashioned," said Ambrose.

His wife, as before, opened her bewildering eyes wide, on husband, secretary, and cocktail, of which, as before, she took a secret sip. She experienced the same delicious sensation. "Perhaps I was wrong to begin sighing again," she thought. "Perhaps there is very seldom any real reason to sigh. This young man looks as if he sighed a good deal, which is a pity in anyone so graceful and delicate. I wonder if he knows the cure for it."

Life, however, is not all play—the book progressed rapidly, and soon took shape as the four-star classic of all time, thrilling enough for the most hardened lowbrow, and so perfectly written as to compel the homage of the connoisseurs.

It sold like hot cakes, and Ambrose was fêted everywhere. His cellar was full of the most superlative sherries. His wife no longer sighed, not even when they left Long Island for Provence, or Provence for Long Island. "It makes a change," said she to the interviewers.

It was not very long before she crowned his happiness by presenting him with a sturdy son. "Soon," said Ambrose, "he will be able to run to meet me, and you shall take us on the Moviola. He is not quite as like me as he ought to be; it must be your cruder nature coming out in him. But perhaps he will improve, or perhaps you will do better next time."

Sure enough, there was a next time, and Ambrose rejoiced in two ideal children. "This one," said he, "is still a little short of the ideal. He has your rather effeminate look. However, they average out very like their father indeed, and that is as much as could be hoped for."

So time went by, and no man was more pleased with himself than Ambrose. "What a happy man I am," said he to himself, "with my fame, my riches, my beautiful wife who adores me, my forceful plots, my exquisite style, my houses, my two secretaries, and my two ideal children!" He had just called for the Moviola to have them taken running to meet him, when a visitor was announced—a literary pilgrim who had come to do him homage.

Such were always very welcome to the great man. "Yes," said he. "Here I am. This is my study. Those are my books. There, in the hammock, is my wife. And down there, in the garden, are my two ideal little children. I will take you to see them. You shall watch them run to meet their papa."

"Tell me," said the visitor, "do they reflect the genius of their father?"

"Probably," said Ambrose. "In a small way, of course."

"Then," said the visitor, "let us approach them quietly. Let us overhear their prattle. Suppose they are telling stories to each other. I should like to tell the world, sir, that they have inherited their father's genius."

Ambrose was indulgent, and they tiptoed to the edge of the sand-pit, where the two youngsters, squatting in the dirt, were busy gabbling their heads off. Sure enough, they were telling a story.

"An' the ole dragon," said the elder, "sprung out on him like mad, spittin' out flames—"

"And the monster," said the younger, "rushed forth upon him, breathing fire—"

"He hopped out of the way, and stuck his sword in its belly—"

"He leapt nimbly aside, and thrust his gleaming blade into its black heart—"

"And over it went—"

"And it fell—"

"Done in."

"Dead."

GAVIN O'LEARY

There was a young, bold, active, and singularly handsome flea, who lived as blissful as a shepherd in Arcady upon the divine body of Rosie O'Leary. Rosie was an eighteen-year-old nursemaid in the comfortable home of a doctor in Vermont, and no flea had been better pastured than this one since the beginning of the world. He considered himself a landowner in a country overflowing with milk and honey, and he delighted in every undulation of the landscape.

Rosie was the merriest, most ardent, laughing, bounding, innocent, high-spirited creature that ever trod on earth, from which it follows that our flea was equally blessed in temperament and general physical tone. It is widely known that the flea imbibes more than half his weight at a single repast, from which it follows that not only the bodily health, but the nervous condition, the emotions, the inclinations, and even the moral standards of whoever provides the meal are very directly transmitted to his diminutive guest.

Thus it came about that this particular flea bounded higher than most, and ceaselessly extolled his good fortune. All his nourishment came fresh and ruby from her untroubled heart, and there was never such a gay, silly, glossy, high-jumping, well-developed flea as Gavin O'Leary. Gavin was his given name; the other he took from Rosie, as a nobleman takes his title from his domain.

There came a time when Gavin found something a little heady in his drink, and his whole being was filled with delicious dreams. On Thursday evening this sensation rose to a positive delirium. Rosie was being taken to the movies.

Our flea at that time had no great interest in the art of the motion picture. He sat through the first half of the performance in a nook that offered no view of what was going on. At ten o'clock he began to feel ready for his supper, and, as Rosie showed no signs of going home to bed, he resolved to picnic, as it were, on the spot. He inserted his privileged proboscis in the near neighborhood of her heart. His earlier exhilaration should have warned him that great changes were taking place in the nature and quality of the nectar on which he lived, but, as Rosie was guileless and heedless, so therefore was Gavin equally unwary. Thus he was taken by surprise when his light and sparkling sustenance changed to warm and drowsy syrup, with a fire smoldering under its sweetness, which robbed him of all his bounding enterprise. A tremor ran through his body, his eyes half closed, and when his shy retreat was suddenly and inexplicably invaded by an alien hand, he was neither amazed nor hopping mad, but crawled half-reluctantly away, looking over his shoulder with a languid simper, for all the world as if he were a mere bug.

Gavin took refuge in a cranny of the plush seat, and surrendered himself to the throbbing intoxication that filled his veins. He woke from his drunken sleep several hours later, with a slight sense of shame. It was early morning; Rosie and her companion were gone;

the picture house was empty and no food was in sight. Gavin waited eagerly for the place to reopen, for his appetite was of the best. At the proper hour people began to file in. Gavin's seat was taken by a pale youth, who fidgeted impatiently until the performance began, and when the performance began he sighed. Gavin, brushing his forefoot over his proboscis, for all the world like a toper who wipes his lips before taking a swig, entered between a pair of waistcoat buttons, and, without any affectation of saying grace, tapped his new host between the fourth and fifth rib, in order that he might drink as fresh and pure as it came.

I think it is Dante who describes a lover's blood as running pale and fiery like old wine. By this comparison, the draft now sucked up by Gavin was vodka or absinthe at the very least. No sooner had he swallowed this potent philter than he began to pant, moan, and roll his eyes like a madman, and he could not clamber up fast enough out of the young man's shirt to a spot whence he could catch a glimpse of the object of what was now their joint adoration. It was none other than Miss Blynda Blythe, whose infinitely famous, infinitely glamorous face at this moment filled the greater part of the screen.

Gazing upon her, our flea was in the condition of one who has made a whole meal of a love potion. He felt his host's blood positively boiling within him. He was devoured, wrought-up, hysterical; his proboscis burned, throbbed, and tingled at the sight of that satiny skin; he wept, laughed, and finally began to rhyme like a demon. The fact is, his host was a poet, or he could never have been such a lover. In consequence, no flea has ever loved, longed, and hungered as Gavin did, at his very first sight of Miss Blynda Blythe. (Except for that one, dear Madame, which was availing itself of my hospitality, when you passed in your limousine last Thursday.)

All too soon the film came to its end, and Gavin rode home to a hall bedroom, where he spent the night on the young man's coat collar, looking over his shoulder at the fan magazines which this youth incessantly studied. Every now and then he would take a quick shot of that burning brew that was the cause of his furious passion. A number of lesser fleas, and other creatures of a baser sort, refreshed themselves at the same source, and shared the night-long bacchanal. Their besotted host, confused between his itches, was too far gone even to scratch. The crazy drinkers were free to take their perilous fill, and the scene was worse than any opium den. Some wept and moaned their lives away in corners; some, dirty, unkempt, lost to the world, lay abandoned in feverish reverie; others sprang from the window, drowned themselves in the slop pail, or took Keating's. Many, mad with desire, blunted their probosces on one or other of the glossy photographs of Blynda Blythe which adorned the mantelpiece and the screen.

Gavin, though he sipped and sipped till the potent liquor entered into the very tissues of his being, was made of sterner stuff. It was not for nothing that he had spent his youth on the finest flower of the indomitable immigrant stock. With the dawn, his bold plan was made. His host rose from his uneasy slumbers, dashed off a few lines, and went out to seek his breakfast at a drugstore. Gavin rode boldly on the rim of his hat, taking his bearings from the position of the sun.

The poet walked westward for two or three blocks, and Gavin was grateful for the lift. But no sooner did the fellow veer off in a northerly direction in quest of his coffee and doughnut than Gavin was down on the sidewalk, and hopping furiously on the first stage of his three-thousand-mile trek to the Coast. He hitchhiked when he could, but as he left the town behind him these opportunities grew fewer. The dust choked him, the hard surface proved lacerating to those sensitive feet, accustomed to nothing coarser than the silken skin of Rosie O'Leary. Nevertheless, when the red sunset beaconed where the long trail crossed the distant hills, a keen eye might have discerned the speck-like figure of Gavin, jiggling lamely but gamely on.

It was long afterwards, and after heaven knows what adventures by prairie, desert, and mountain, that a travel-worn, older, and gaunter Gavin entered Hollywood. He was gaunt, not merely by reason of his incredible exertions, but because of the knight-errant asceticism he had practiced through all the hungry miles of the way. Fearing lest any full meal should fill him with some baser, alien mood, he had disciplined himself to take the merest semi-sip, except where he was well assured that his entertainer was also an adoring fan of Blynda Blythe.

He now hastened along Hollywood Boulevard in search of the world-famous Chinese Theater. There, sinking on one knee, he reverently pressed his long proboscis to a certain beloved footprint set here in the cement of eternity. A keen-eyed producer noticed the knightly gesture as he drove by, and instantly conceived the idea of doing a new version of Cyrano de Bergerac. Gavin, having accomplished his act of homage, took the innocent equivalent of a glass of milk from the dimpled shoulder of a baby star, and began to ponder on how he might make contact with his idol.

He thought at first of striking up an acquaintance with some of the lounging, idle, dissipated fleas of the town, to find out from them which laundry she patronized, so that he might arrive like a male Cleopatra rolled up in some intimate article of her apparel. His wholesome pride rejected this backstairs approach. He dallied for a shuddering moment with the fierce temptation to perch on the cuff of an autograph hunter, and make a Fairbanks leap upon her as she signed the book. "To spring upon her!" he muttered. "To wreak my will upon her regardless of her cries and struggles! To plunge my cruel proboscis into her delicate epidermis!" But Gavin O'Leary was no brutal, cowardly rapist. There was something upright and manly in his nature that demanded he meet his mate as a friend and as an equal. He was fully conscious of the immense social gulf that lay between a poor, unknown flea and a rich and famous filmstar. Painful as the thought was to him, he did not avert his eyes from the racial barrier. But to Gavin, barriers were made to be overleaped. He felt that he must be recognized as a fellow being, and respected as . . . as what? "Why, that's it!" he cried as the inspiration struck him. "Respected as a fellow artist! Who has not heard of performing fleas? Whenever did a troupe of players travel without a numerous companionship of my dark, brittle, and vivacious kin?"

The decision made, nothing remained but to crash the studios, as the ambitious phrase it. Gavin had certain misgivings at the thought of permitting an agent to handle him. The only alternative was to mingle with the ranks of shabby extras who hung about the gates of Blynda's studio in the hope of being called in on some emergency. Fortune favors the brave; he had not been waiting there many weeks when an assistant director dashed out, crying in an urgent voice: "Say! Any of you guys got a performing flea? Anybody know where I can hire one?"

The word was spread. The extras on the sidewalk began to search themselves hastily. Genuine professional flea masters patrolled the boulevards rounding up and coralling their troupes, which they had, with the inhumanity of their kind, turned out to forage for themselves during the bad times. While all this *brouhaha* was spreading through the town, with "Yipee-i-ay! Yipee-i-ay!" reechoing from Gower Street to Culver City, Gavin boldly entered the studio, and took up a point of vantage on the producer's desk. "At least," thought he, "I am first in line."

Some flea masters soon entered, carrying their recaptured artistes in pillboxes and phials. Gavin surveyed his rivals, and saw that every one of them bore the indefinable stamp of the bit player. He could hardly suppress a sneer.

When all were assembled: "We've got a part here for the right flea," said the producer. "It's not big, but it's snappy. Listen, this flea's going to have the chance to play opposite Blynda Blythe. It's a bedroom scene, and there's a close two-shot. He's going to bite her on the shoulder when she's down and out in a rooming house. Say, where are your fleas from, feller?"

"Dey're Mex, boss," replied the impresario he had addressed. "Mexican flea, him lively, him jumpa, jumpa . . ."

"That's enough," replied the producer coldly. "This scene's laid in the East, and when I shoot a scene it's authentic. You can't fool the public these days. Come on, boys, I want a New England flea."

As he spoke he spread the contract out before him. A babble arose from the flea masters, all of whom swore their fleas had been bred on Plymouth Rock and raised on none but Lowells, Cabots, and Lodges. While they still argued, Gavin dipped his proboscis in the ink bottle and scrawled his minute signature on the dotted line.

The effect was electrifying. "The darned little guy!" said the producer admiringly. "He's got what it takes. While all you fellers are shooting off your mouths, he muscles right in and gets his moniker on the contract. Reminds me of the time when *I* broke into this industry," he added to a sycophant who nodded smiling agreement. Gavin was hurried onto the set, where his coming was eagerly awaited. "You wouldn't like your stand-in to do this scene, Miss Blythe?" said an overobsequious assistant. Gavin's heart sank.

"No," said Miss Blythe. "When it's a champagne scene, I want real champagne, and when I get bitten by a flea I stand for a real flea bite."

"Get that written down and over to the publicity department," said the producer to another hanger-on. "O.K., Jack," to the director. "I'll watch you shoot."

"Better run it over once or twice in rehearsal," said the director. "Somebody stand by with a glass of brandy for Miss Blythe."

"You're not to go on if you feel faint, Blynda," said the producer.

"It's all right, Benny," said Blynda. "It's for my art."

"Look how it is, Blynda," said the director, taking up the script. "This is where you've walked out on Carew, just because you're nuts about him. You want to see if he'll follow you down to the depths. You're yearning for him. And you're lying on the rooming house bed, crying. And you feel a bite, just where he kissed you in the scene we're going to shoot when that goddam art department gets the country club revel set done. Get the point, Blynda? You feel the bite. For a moment you think it's Carew."

"Yes, Jack. I think I see that. I think I understand."

"And, Jesus! you turn your head, hoping against hope it's him . . ."

". . . and it's only the flea!" She nodded gravely. "Yes, I can feel that. I can play it."

"Bet your life you can play it! Okay, get on the bed. Where's makeup? Got Miss Blythe's tears ready?"

Blynda waved the crystal vial aside. She shook her head and smiled bravely at the director. "I shan't need phony tears, Jack. Not if it's Carew."

At these words, a look and a murmur passed through all the numerous company. Actors and technicians alike felt sympathy and admiration for the plucky girl, for her unrequited real-life passion for the handsome, sneering leading man was no secret. In fact, it was the subject of almost hourly bulletins from the publicity department.

It was whispered that "Repressed Carew," as he was nicknamed by the psychology-conscious younger set of Hollywood, was a man contemptuous of love in any form whatever. Only those who had seen him at his mirror knew that he made an exception in favor of his own supercilious profile. This was the man Blynda hopelessly adored, and Blynda was the girl Gavin was about to bite.

Next moment the director had said a quiet word to his assistant, and the assistant, like a human megaphone, blared the command to the farthest corner of the vast sound stage. "QUIET for Miss Blythe and Mr. Gavin O'Leary rehearsing."

Gavin's heart swelled. To become at one stroke a successful film actor and a happy lover is enough to intoxicate a more down-to-earth personality than a flea's. Blynda pressed her face to the pillow and wept. Her delicious shoulder blades heaved with emotion, and Gavin stood ready for the leap. He wished only that he had a delicate scrap of cambric, that he might wipe his proboscis and fling it into the hands of a nearby grip. He felt the gesture would have shown a nice feeling.

His regrets were cut short by a crisp word: "Mr. O'Leary!" He sprang high into the air, landed, and struck deep.

"Boy! did you see that jump?" cried the director to the producer. "Watch him bite! The little guy gives it all he's got."

"Make a note for me to get him under long-term contract," said the producer to his secretary.

"What the Hell am I doing on this floozy's shoulder?" murmured Gavin in a petulant voice. "I wonder when my gorgeous Carew is going to make his entrance." Forgive him, reader! It was the drink speaking.

At that very moment a deep, rich, jocular voice was heard. "Hey, what goes on here? New talent, eh? Stealing my scene!"

All turned to eye the newcomer with respect, Blynda and Gavin with something more. Blynda wallowed as invitingly as she could upon the bed; Gavin, with a leap that approached if not surpassed the world's record, flung himself upon his new idol's breast, sobbing mingled ecstasy and shame.

"The little fellow seems to take to me," said the actor good-humoredly. "Going to be buddies, eh? Good material that, Jack, for the publicity department." These words marked the beginning, and, as far as the speaker was concerned, the motivation, of a friendship between the oddly assorted pair. Soon they became inseparable.

The biographer prefers to draw a veil over the next stage of Gavin's career. To know all is to excuse all, but to know less in a case of this sort is to have less to excuse. Suffice it to say that Carew's love for himself continued what Blynda's love for Carew had begun, and, as it was marked by a fervor and a constancy very rare in Hollywood, fervid and constant was Gavin's unhallowed passion for Carew.

It was not long before ugly rumors were in circulation concerning the flea star. People whispered of his fantastic costumes, his violet evening suits, his epicene underwear, his scent-spray shower-bath, and of strange parties at his bijou house in Bel Air. A trade paper, naming no names, pointed out that if individuals of a certain stripe were considered bad security risks by the State Department, they must be even more of a danger in the most influential of all American industries. It seemed only a matter of time before Gavin would be the center of an open scandal, and his pictures picketed by the guardians of our morals.

But time works in many ways, and the actor's face withered even faster than Gavin's reputation. Soon he was rejected everywhere for the role of the lover, and must either play character parts or go in for production. Character never having been his strong point, he felt himself better fitted to be a producer. Now, producers are known to be god-like creatures, and the chief point of resemblance is that they must either create new stars or have no public.

Carew, of course, had Gavin as an ace up his sleeve. Splendid parts, full of nimble wit and biting satire, were written for the flea actor, but nowhere could a new beauty be found who was worthy to play opposite him. The talent scouts ranged far and wide, but their eulogies carried little conviction. At last, however, a short list was made. Carew read it over, shook his head, and threw it down on his dressing table. "There's not a winner among them," he muttered. "That means I'm not a genius as a producer."

He retired to bed feeling thoroughly dissatisfied with himself for the first time in many years. To Gavin, his supper that night seemed to have a smack of clean and salutary bitterness about it. His nerves steadied themselves, his mind cleared; he saw Carew for what he was, and the hour of his salvation was upon him. At such moments the mind naturally reverts to thoughts of old times, early days, youth, innocence, and the bright faces of the past.

Gavin O'Leary rose and ripped off the flimsy, decadent night attire he had recently affected. He sought, with a leap that was already less mincing and effeminate, the list upon the writing table. The inkwell stood open; to him, its sable depths were a positive Jordan, in which, if he dipped seven times, he might yet cease to be a moral leper. He immersed himself with a shudder, and, clambering painfully out, he stood for a moment upon the dark rim of the inkwell, nude, shivering, gasping, yet tensing his muscles for a leap to a certain spot at the head of the list. He made it, and made it without splash or blot. With the accuracy of a figure skater, but with all the slow difficulty of a treacle-clogged fly, he described the word "Rosie" in a perfect imitation of the sprawling hand of the chief talent scout.

Another painful leap, and he was back, sobbing and choking, in the bitter, glutinous ink. The hot weather had thickened it. This time, he completed the word "O'Leary." Five times more, and her address was written below. Gavin, utterly worn-out, black as your hat, half-poisoned by ink, sank exhausted on the blotting pad. But a great gladness had dawned in his heart.

The ruse was successful. Rosie was brought to the Coast for a screen test. Needless to say, she passed it triumphantly. Gavin, with a thankful sigh, nestled once more upon her heart, and drank deep of its cleansing, life-giving vintage. With that draft, the last of his aberration fell away from him like a shoddy, outworn garment. The past was dead. He was a new flea, and he had earned his right to be the lover of the most beautiful Irish colleen, and the greatest little actress, and the most important human being in the world. And as Miss O'Leary soon began to think of herself in the same terms, you may be sure they lived happily ever after.

If YOUTH KNEW,
IF AGE COULD

The first thing one noticed about Henri Maurras was inevitably his gaunt and quixotic Spanish nose, flanked by a pair of enormous eyes, extremely dark and melancholy, but capable of fire. This romantic equipment was unfortunately betrayed by the childish, petulant mouth of a Parisian, and a ridiculous little moustache.

For the rest, he was a mere thread of a young man, a veritable nailpairing, and wore a paper-thin gray suit, under which his little buttocks presented all the appearance of a hairpin. He worked as assistant bookkeeper in a big general store in Marseilles, and he desired ardently to be married.

Frequently he would lose count of a column of figures and turn up his dark eyes, as he visualized the bride of his dreams, youthful, devoted, passionate, deliciously rounded, and yet of immaculate reputation. Our passionate *petit bourgeois* was especially set upon the immaculate reputation.

His little moustache would twitch as he imagined the promenades they would take on Sundays, envied by all who beheld them. She would hang fondly on his arm, driving all the men to despair; he would wear a smart suit from Marquet's, and carry a fashionable cane.

"Pleasure is all very well," said he to his fellow clerks, when they proposed some little frolic on payday. "But what pleasure can compare to being married? I mean, to a beautiful wife, gay, amiable, sympathetic, and—" His hands sketched certain outlines in the air. "For that," said he, "one must save. One must wait."

"Nonsense," said the others. "Come with us to Madame Garcier's. It may make saving a little harder, but the waiting becomes infinitely more tolerable. After all, a young man is entitled to a little happiness on account."

"No. No," said he. "I have certain ideals. You would hardly understand."

Henri's ideals, as lofty as the bridge of his nose, preserved him from the venal affections so popular among the youth of Marseilles. Yet that phrase, *"a little happiness on account,"* took fatal root. Under its influence he succumbed to the attractions of a superb malacca cane, displayed in the window of the most expensive shop in all the Rue St. Ferréol. "After all," said he to himself, "I shall have to buy one sooner or later. Why not now?"

As soon as he had paid over the money, he was almost ready to kill himself, he was so mortified at his extravagance. Yet he trembled with joy as he twirled his new treasure, leaned upon it, and hung it over his arm. On leaving the shop, he fancied that several well-dressed men eyed it with envious interest. "Wait," thought he, "till they see me in a suit from Marquet's, and with my lovely wife walking by my side."

When he got home he put his new acquisition into his wardrobe. It would never do to get it scratched, or even to have the least gloss taken off it, before the day of his nuptials. On that day, everything was to be immaculate; everything must have its gloss absolutely unimpaired.

Nevertheless, every night, before he undressed, he put on his hat again, and took out his cane for a few minutes, holding it this way and that way in front of the mirror. He swung it as gracefully as the narrowness of his bedchamber allowed, and, seating himself on the side of his bed, he drew a heart on the carpet.

This cane had a horn ferrule of the highest quality. It was as smooth and round as anything you can possibly imagine, and it was girdled with a slim circlet of gold, for all the world like a wedding ring.

Now that he possessed such a cane as this, Henri could no longer resist casting glances at the girls, although his saving was at far too early a stage to justify such boldness. He was a little bothered by a certain look on the more attractive faces he saw, a look which can be described only as suggesting worldly experience. "Where shall I find a bride," thought Henri, "as fresh, immaculate, and shining as my new cane?" He did not reflect that this cane had come to him, not leafy from the swamp in which it had grown, but smooth and sophisticated from the hands of the polisher.

However, Henri still hoped, and every evening he rode home on the bus to his dwelling at the far end of the Prado. At this hour, at the beginning of May, the streets of Marseilles are full of golden light. The new leaves of the innumerable plane trees exude their soft yellow into the radiance of the declining sun.

One evening a girl got on the bus. Henri looked up; his magnificent nose made a true point, his dark eyes flamed, his little moustache quivered, and his childish mouth pouted as if it had been stung by a bee. She was an Italianate Marseillaise, and as lovely as a black grape—her skin had that sort of bloom upon it. This dusky bloom concentrated into a delicate, adorable down along the line of her upper lip, which was bewitchingly lifted. Her eye was like the eye of a gazelle, her cheek was soft, and her figure was at once young and ample, such as any man must admire, but especially he whose buttocks are as lean as a hairpin under his skimpy pants.

To crown it all, she was dressed very simply, in one of those non-descript black dresses affected by the well-to-do peasantry, who are so much better off than the little bookkeepers. She wore black cotton gloves. It must have been a careful family, of the proper old-fashioned type, that had brought her up so completely out of the dubious mode. Such old-fashioned people are usually extremely conscientious about the *dot*. Henri admired, approved, and loved.

"It is true," he thought, "I have yet to win her affections, gain the approval of her family, and save up a whole mountain of francs. All that is possible, but how am I to make her acquaintance? At any moment she may get off the bus. If I speak to her, she will either answer me, in which case she cannot be as virtuous as she looks, or she will not answer me, and I shall never see her again." Here, Henri experienced one of the greatest dilemmas known to mankind, and one which had been sadly neglected by the philosophers.

Fate, however, was altogether on his side. The bus stopped for a whole minute at a corner where a family of Gypsies were giving the traditional exhibition. A goat mounted precariously upon a step-ladder; a mangy bear stood by, shifting his feet in melancholy reminiscence of his training; a nervous monkey presented a miniature tambourine for the sous of the passersby.

The girl, as simple as a child, was ravished by this familiar spectacle. She pressed her face against the glass, smiled in rapture, and turned a bright gaze on the other passengers, to see if they were enjoying it, too. Henri, leaning over, was emboldened to offer the comments of a man of the world.

"Very amusing, the little monkey," said he.

"Yes, monsieur, very amusing."

"The bear, he is droll."

"But yes, monsieur, very droll."

"The goat, also. For a domestic animal, he is droll, too."

"Yes, monsieur, he is truly droll."

"The *gitanos* are very picturesque, but they are a bad type."

At this point the bus jolted on. A brilliant conversation had been interrupted, but acquaintance was established, and in such a simple and innocent fashion that the most fastidious of future husbands could find nothing to object to. Henri ventured to seat himself beside her. The jolting of the bus provided the briefest but most delicious of contacts. A *rapport* was established; their tongues uttered banalities, but their shoulders were supremely eloquent. "Madamoiselle," said Henri at last, "dare I hope that you will take a little promenade with me on Sunday?"

"Oh, but I am afraid that would hardly be possible," replied the young girl, with an adorable appearance of confusion.

Henri urged his plea with all the feeling at his command, and at length his charmer, whose name was Marie, decided that she might overcome the obstacles, which doubtless had their origin in the excessive respectability of her upbringing.

The rendezvous was made. Henri, left alone upon the bus, rode far past his destination, lost in an ecstasy far transcending any description. The excess fare amounted to two francs.

That night he spent a whole hour before his mirror, conducting his cane in the manner in which he hoped to parade it on Sunday. "There is no doubt about it," said he to himself, "such a cane, and such a girl, absolutely demand that new suit from Marquet's. Tomorrow I will pay them a visit." He drew several hearts, all of them transfixed by arrows, and surrounded by initials. "I will take her to the *calanque*," said he to himself, "and there, seated beside her on a rock, I will draw something of this sort on the sand. She will guess what I mean."

On Sunday everything went as well as any lover could wish. Henri was first at the trysting place, and soon saw her tripping along. This time she was wearing a summer frock and white cotton gloves. She had the happy air of a little girl let out from school. "Her parents must be very severe," thought Henri. "So much the better. I wonder by what artless excuses she managed to get away."

Their greeting was all the heart could desire. Every true lover, and some whose aims are less creditable, knows the delicious promise of those first meetings in which both parties act as frankly and simply as children, and take hands even as they make their way to the bus. Days beginning thus should always be spent in the open air, and no place under all the sky is more propitious to them than those deep and cliffy creeks near Marseilles, which are called the *calanques*. Snow-white rocks descend into water as clear as glass, edged by tiny beaches of sand, perfectly suited for the inscription of hearts and arrows. Little pine trees cover all the slopes, and, when the afternoon sun is hot, there is all the more reason to take advantage of their shade.

Henri and his Marie did this. "Take off your gloves," said he, "and I will tell your fortune."

She willingly removed the glove from her right hand, which she extended to him with the utmost grace.

"No," said he, "I beg you to take off both."

Marie blushed, and hesitated, and began with tantalizing slowness to draw off the other glove.

"It does not seem to come off very easily," said Henri.

"You demand too much," said she. "This is only the first time I have been out with you. I did not think you would ask me to remove my gloves."

"At last," thought Henri, "I have found a girl of a simplicity, of a virtue, such as must be absolutely unique in the world of 193–."

"Marie," cried he, pressing his lips to her hands, "I adore you with every fiber of my being, I implore you to be mine. I long, I burn, I die for the happiness of being married to you."

"Oh no," said she. "That is impossible."

"Then you do not love me," said he. "I have spoken too soon."

"No," said she. "Perhaps I do. But how can I answer you? It could not be for a year, perhaps two, possibly even three."

"What of that?" cried he. "I will wait. In fact, I shall have a great deal of money to save." He told her of the prospect of the furniture business, and of the situation of his old mother, who had been treated abominably by certain relatives.

Marie was less explicit in her description of her background. She said, though, that she was treated very strictly, and could hardly introduce into her home a young man she had met so unconventionally on a bus.

"It is inconvenient," said Henri, "but it is as it should be. Sooner or later we will manage something. Till then, we are affianced, are we not? We will come here every Sunday."

"It will be very hard for me to get away," said she.

"Never mind," said he. "It will arrange itself. Meanwhile, we are affianced. Therefore, I may embrace you."

An interlude followed in which Henri experienced that happiness which is revealed only to young men of the meagerest proportions in the company of girls as delightfully rounded as Marie. At the close of the day Henri had drawn almost as deeply on his future marriage as he had upon his costume and his cane. "They are right," thought he, "one is entitled to a little happiness on account."

He went home the happiest young man in Marseilles, or in all France, for that matter, and next day he actually carried his cane to the office with him, for he could not bear to part with it.

That evening, on the bus, he fixed his eyes on the people waiting at every stopping place. He felt that fortune might grant him an unappointed glimpse of his beloved. Sure enough, after a false alarm or two, he caught sight of her shoulder and the line of her neck as she stood in a knot of people two or three hundred yards up the street. He recognized this single curve immediately.

His heart pounded, his hands shook, his cane almost fell from his grasp. The bus came to a stop, and he turned to greet her as she entered. To his horror and dismay, she appeared not to recognize him, and, as he blundered toward her, she gave him a warning frown.

Henri saw that behind her was an old man, a man of nearly eighty, a colossal ruin of a man, with dim and hollow eyes, a straggly white moustache horribly stained, and two or three yellow tusks in a cavernous mouth. He took his seat beside the adorable Marie, and folded his huge and grimy hands, on which the veins stood out like whipcord, over the handle of a cheap and horrible cane, an atrocity fashioned out of bamboo. He wore the expensive and ugly broadcloth of the well-to-do peasant.

Henri fixed his eyes on the pair. "Possibly he is her father," thought he.

A lover, however, has an eye which is not easily deceived. Henri knew perfectly well that this old man was not her father. He tried to repress a feeling of acute uneasiness. "He is very old," thought Henri. "It is more likely he is her grandfather. Possibly she has something to endure from him. He seems to be sitting beside her in a very familiar way. How I wish we could be married at once!"

At this point the conductor approached the old man, and jingled his little ticket machine under his nose. "Demand it of Madame," said the old man in a low and thunderous rumble.

Henri sat as if struck by lightning. "It is impossible," said he to himself over and over again. "After all, what is more natural than for a man to speak of his female companion as 'Madame,' whether she is married or not, when he is addressing a waiter, a bus conductor, or someone of that sort? Besides, the old fool dotes; he doesn't know what the Hell he is saying. He thinks it's his wife, her grandmother; his mind is in the past."

As he said this, he saw before his eyes a picture of her left hand, with the white glove on it, which she had removed so slowly and with so much trouble.

"She is a pure, sincere, serious, straightforward girl," thought he. "Yes, but that is why she had so much trouble with that glove. An artful girl would have removed her wedding ring before meeting me. So much the more terrible!

"No, no. I am going mad. He *is* her grandfather. Possibly her great-grandfather. See how old he is! People should be killed before reaching that age. Look at his mouth, his teeth! If he *should* be her husband, and fondle her! Nonsense! I am mad. The idea is absurd."

Nevertheless he lived in torment till the end of the week, when a note reached him saying that Marie could slip out for an hour or two on Sunday. She would be at the same rendezvous at two o'clock.

Nothing could be more simple and reassuring than this note, which breathed innocence and affection. One or two words were artlessly misspelled, which always gives an effect of sincerity. Henri's suspicions departed as suddenly as they had come. "What a brute I was!" he thought, as he hastened to meet her. "I will beg her forgiveness. I will go down on my knees. But no, not in this suit. On the whole, I had better say nothing about it. What sort of a husband will she think I will make if I am already suspicious of a disgusting old man? Ah, here she comes! How lovely she is! How radiant! I certainly deserve to be thrashed with my own cane."

She came smiling up to him, and put out her hand with the white cotton glove upon it. Henri's eyes fell upon this glove, and his debonair welcome died upon his lips. "Who," said he hoarsely, "who was that old man who was with you?"

Marie dropped her hand and stared at Henri.

"He is not your father," said Henri, in a tone of rage and despair.

"No," said she, obviously terror-stricken.

"He is not your grandfather!" cried Henri. "He is your husband."

"How did you know?" cried she.

"You have deceived me!" cried Henri. "I thought you pure, true, artless, without fault. I—I—I—Never mind. *Adieu*, Madame! Be so good as to look at the newspaper in the morning, and see if any unfortunate has fallen from the ramparts of the Château d'If."

With that he turned on his heel and strode away, in the ominous direction of the port, where the little boats take sightseers out to the Château d'If. Marie, with a cry, ran after him, and clasped his arm in both her hands.

"Do nothing rash," she begged. "Believe me, I adore you."

"And yet," said he, "you marry a disgusting old man."

"But that was before I knew you."

"So be it, Madame. I wish you every felicity."

"But, beloved," said she, "you do me an injustice. He is rich. I was young. My parents urged me. You cannot think I love him."

"Leave me, prostitute!" cried Henri.

"Ah, you are unkind!" said she. "Why should you be jealous? You are young. You are dressed in the mode, even to your cane. You are handsome. You are my dream. How could you threaten to commit a desperate act? The old man will not live forever. You and I would be rich. We could be happy. Henri, were we not happy last Sunday, out at the *calanque?* I am just the same."

"What?" cried Henri. "Do you think I care for his dirty money? Could I be happy with you again, thinking of that old man?"

"Nevertheless," said she, "it is nearly a million francs."

"To the devil with it!" said Henri. "Supposing we stayed at the best hotels, traveled, had an apartment in Paris, even, how could I enjoy anything, thinking of you and him together?"

"But he is so old," said she. "He is nearly blind. He can scarcely speak. He is deaf. He has lost the use of all his senses. Yes, Henri, *all* his senses."

"What do you mean, *all* his senses?" said Henri, halting in his stride.

"*All* his senses," said she, facing round and nodding gravely at Henri. "All. All. All.

"He is eighty years of age," said she. "Who is jealous of a man of eighty? What is there to be jealous of? Nothing. Nothing at all."

"All the same," said Henri, "they are sometimes worse than the rest. A thousand times worse. Leave me. Let me go."

"He is a log of wood," said she earnestly. "Henri, is it possible to be jealous of a log of wood? It is not what you would choose, perhaps, and nor would I, if I could help it. But, after all, it is nothing. The same cannot be said of a million francs."

Henri demanded ten thousand assurances, and was given them all. The Parisian in him urged a common-sense view of the situation. "After all, we must be broad-minded," thought he. "Provided, of course, that it is really nothing. Absolutely and certainly nothing!"

"I shall be able to see you every Sunday afternoon," said Marie. "I have suggested to him that he take a little stroll and a drink at the café between two and six. I made very poor excuses for not accompanying him, but to my surprise he assented eagerly. I had expected a lot of trouble."

"He is jealous, then?" cried Henri. "A log of wood is not jealous."

"But all the more," said Marie. "After all, is it so unreasonable, darling?"

"Nevertheless," said Henri, "I cannot understand why he should be jealous. I am jealous; that is natural. But a log of wood. . . ."

Marie soothed him again with another ten thousand assurances, and when at last he bade her farewell his happiness was completely restored.

Only one fly remained in his ointment. "When I consider," thought he, "how extremely scrupulous I have been, unlike any other young man in Marseilles, it certainly seems very unfair. I have never spent my money on girls. I have never visited an establishment such as Madame Garcier's. And now I am to marry a girl who . . . It is true he is eighty. At eighty, a man is no better than a log of wood. Nevertheless, it is a difference between us. It will give rise to a thousand bitter reflections when we are married. She is so beautiful. And there is the million francs. What a pity there should be any cause for bitterness! How lovely she looked today! I wish we could have been reconciled under that little pine tree out in the *calanque*. I should be able to view matters more calmly."

At this moment, a certain idea came into his head. It is impossible to say where it came from. Probably it was from the Parisian in him. "It would certainly balance accounts between us," said he to himself. "It would go far to prevent bitterness. She would be all the happier for it. After all, it is not my fault we could not go to the *calanque*."

Reflecting thus, he bent his steps toward the famous establishment of Madame Garcier, so highly recommended by his fellow clerks. This discreet haven had all the appearance of a private house; the door was answered by a maidservant, who ushered callers into an anteroom.

"Madame will be with you immediately," said this maidservant to Henri, taking his hat and stick and depositing them in an old-fashioned hall-stand. With that she showed him into the anteroom, and departed, leaving the door open behind her.

"This is an excellent idea," thought Henri. "Now there will be two of us, and I shall be the worse of the two, as a man should be! So I shall not feel bitter. How happy we shall be! And, after all, what is a little extravagance, when we are going to inherit a million francs?"

At that moment he heard footsteps on the stairs, and the voice evidently of the Madame, who was ushering out some favorite patron.

"This has been a delightful surprise," she was saying. "When I heard of your marriage, I declared we had seen the last of you. Delphine and Fifi were inconsolable."

"What would you?" came the reply in a thunderous rumble, which caused Henri's hair to stand erect upon his head. "A man must settle down, Madame, especially when he is no longer as young as he was. It is, so to speak, a duty to the Republic. But, Madame, I am, thank God, still in my prime, and, when he is in his prime, a man demands variety. Besides, Madame, the young women in these days—"

Henri nearly fainted. He heard the front door close, and the footsteps of the proprietress approaching the room in which he sat. He felt he must get out at all costs.

"Pardon me, Madame," he muttered. "I fear I have changed my mind. A sudden indisposition."

"Just as you please, Monsieur," said the old trot. "There is no compulsion in this establishment. But if Monsieur would like at least to *inspect* a young lady—to exchange a few pleasant remarks—"

"No, no, thank you," said Henri, desperately, edging into the hallway. "I must go. Ah, here is my hat. But my cane! Where is my cane?"

He stared, but his cane was gone. In its place, the last visitor had left a cheap, nasty, battered old bamboo.

THUS I REFUTE BEELZY

"There goes the tea bell," said Mrs. Carter. "I hope Simon hears it."

They looked out from the window of the drawing room. The long garden, agreeably neglected, ended in a waste plot. Here a little summerhouse was passing close by beauty on its way to complete decay. This was Simon's retreat. It was almost completely screened by the tangled branches of the apple tree and the pear tree, planted too close together, as they always are in the suburbs. They caught a glimpse of him now and then, as he strutted up and down, mouthing and gesticulating, performing all the solemn mumbo jumbo of small boys who spend long afternoons at the forgotten ends of long gardens.

"There he is, bless him!" said Betty.

"Playing his game," said Mrs. Carter. "He won't play with the other children anymore. And if I go down there—the temper! And comes in tired out!"

"He doesn't have his sleep in the afternoons?" asked Betty.

"You know what Big Simon's ideas are," said Mrs. Carter. " 'Let him choose for himself,' he says. That's what he chooses, and he comes in as white as a sheet."

"Look! He's heard the bell," said Betty. The expression was justified, though the bell had ceased ringing a full minute ago. Small Simon stopped in his parade exactly as if its tinny dingle had at that moment reached his ear. They watched him perform certain ritual sweeps and scratchings with his little stick, and come lagging over the hot and flaggy grass toward the house.

Mrs. Carter led the way down to the playroom, or garden-room, which was also the tearoom for hot days. It had been the huge scullery of this tall Georgian house. Now the walls were cream-washed, there was coarse blue net in the windows, canvas-covered armchairs on the stone floor, and a reproduction of Van Gogh's *Sunflowers* over the mantelpiece.

Small Simon came drifting in, and accorded Betty a perfunctory greeting. His face was an almost perfect triangle, pointed at the

359

chin, and he was paler than he should have been. "The little elf-child!" cried Betty.

Simon looked at her. "No," said he.

At that moment the door opened, and Mr. Carter came in, rubbing his hands. He was a dentist, and washed them before and after everything he did. "You!" said his wife. "Home already!"

"Not unwelcome, I hope," said Mr. Carter, nodding to Betty. "Two people canceled their appointments; I decided to come home. I said, I hope I am not unwelcome."

"Silly!" said his wife. "Of course not."

"Small Simon seems doubtful," continued Mr. Carter. "Small Simon, are you sorry to see me at tea with you?"

"No, Daddy."

"No, what?"

"No, Big Simon."

"That's right. Big Simon and Small Simon. That sounds more like friends, doesn't it? At one time, little boys had to call their father 'sir.' If they forgot—a good spanking. On the bottom, Small Simon! On the bottom!" said Mr. Carter, washing his hands once more with his invisible soap and water.

The little boy turned crimson with shame or rage.

"But now, you see," said Betty, to help, "you can call your father whatever you like."

"And what," asked Mr. Carter, "has Small Simon been doing this afternoon? While Big Simon has been at work."

"Nothing," muttered his son.

"Then you have been bored," said Mr. Carter. "Learn from experience, Small Simon. Tomorrow, do something amusing, and you will not be bored. I want him to learn from experience, Betty. That is my way, the new way."

"I have learned," said the boy, speaking like an old, tired man, as little boys so often do.

"It would hardly seem so," said Mr. Carter, "if you sit on your behind all the afternoon, doing nothing. Had *my* father caught me doing nothing, I should not have sat very comfortably."

"He played," said Mrs. Carter.

"A bit," said the boy, shifting on his chair.

"Too much," said Mrs. Carter. "He comes in all nervy and dazed. He ought to have his rest."

"He is six," said her husband. "He is a reasonable being. He must choose for himself. But what game is this, Small Simon, that is worth getting nervy and dazed over? There are very few games as good as all that."

"It's nothing," said the boy.

"Oh, come," said his father. "We are friends, are we not? You can tell me. I was a Small Simon once, just like you, and played the same games you play. Of course, there were no airplanes in those days. With whom do you play this fine game? Come on, we must all answer civil questions, or the world would never go round. With whom do you play?"

"Mr. Beelzy," said the boy, unable to resist.

"Mr. Beelzy?" said his father, raising his eyebrows inquiringly at his wife.

"It's a game he makes up," said she.

"Not makes up!" cried the boy. "Fool!"

"That is telling stories," said his mother. "And rude as well. We had better talk of something different."

"No wonder he is rude," said Mr. Carter, "if you say he tells lies, and then insist on changing the subject. He tells you his fantasy; you implant a guilt feeling. What can you expect? A defense mechanism. Then you get a real lie."

"Like in *These Three,*" said Betty. "Only different, of course. *She* was an unblushing little liar."

"I would have made her blush," said Mr. Carter, "in the proper part of her anatomy. But Small Simon is in the fantasy stage. Are you not, Small Simon? You just make things up."

"No, I don't," said the boy.

"You do," said his father. "And because you do, it is not too late to reason with you. There is no harm in a fantasy, old chap. There is nothing wrong with a bit of make-believe. Only you must learn the difference between daydreams and real things, or your brain will never grow. It will never be the brain of a Big Simon. So, come on. Let us hear about this Mr. Beelzy of yours. Come on. What is he like?"

"He isn't like anything," said the boy.

"Like nothing on earth?" said his father. "That's a terrible fellow."

"I'm not frightened of him," said the child, smiling. "Not a bit."

"I should hope not," said his father. "If you were, you would be frightening yourself. I am always telling people, older people than you are, that they are just frightening themselves. Is he a funny man? Is he a giant?"

"Sometimes he is," said the little boy.

"Sometimes one thing, sometimes another," said his father. "Sounds pretty vague. Why can't you tell us just what he's like?"

"I love him," said the small boy. "He loves me."

"That's a big word," said Mr. Carter. "That might be better kept for real things, like Big Simon and Small Simon."

"He is real," said the boy, passionately. "He's not a fool. He's real."

"Listen," said his father. "When you go down the garden there's nobody there. Is there?"

"No," said the boy.

"Then you think of him, inside your head, and he comes."

"No," said Small Simon. "I have to make marks. On the ground. With my stick."

"That doesn't matter."

"Yes, it does."

"Small Simon, you are being obstinate," said Mr. Carter. "I am trying to explain something to you. I have been longer in the world than you have, so naturally I am older and wiser. I am explaining that Mr. Beelzy is a fantasy of yours. Do you hear? Do you understand?"

"Yes, Daddy."

"He is a game. He is a let's-pretend."

The little boy looked down at his plate, smiling resignedly.

"I hope you are listening to me," said his father. "All you have to do is to say, 'I have been playing a game of let's-pretend. With someone I make up, called Mr. Beelzy.' Then no one will say you tell lies, and you will know the difference between dreams and reality. Mr. Beelzy is a daydream."

The little boy still stared at his plate.

"He is sometimes there and sometimes not there," pursued Mr. Carter. "Sometimes he's like one thing, sometimes another. You can't really see him. Not as you see me. I am real. You can't touch him. You can touch me. I can touch you." Mr. Carter stretched out his big, white dentist's hand, and took his little son by the nape of the neck. He stopped speaking for a moment and tightened his hand. The little boy sank his head still lower.

"Now you know the difference," said Mr. Carter, "between a pretend and a real thing. You and I are one thing; he is another. Which is the pretend? Come on. Answer me. Which is the pretend?"

"Big Simon and Small Simon," said the little boy.

"Don't!" cried Betty, and at once put her hand over her mouth, for why should a visitor cry, "Don't!" when a father is explaining things in a scientific and modern way? Besides, it annoys the father.

"Well, my boy," said Mr. Carter, "I have said you must be allowed to learn from experience. Go upstairs. Right up to your room. You shall learn whether it is better to reason, or to be perverse and obstinate. Go up. I shall follow you."

"You are not going to beat the child?" cried Mrs. Carter.

"No," said the little boy. "Mr. Beelzy won't let him."

"Go on up with you!" shouted his father.

Small Simon stopped at the door. "He said he wouldn't let anyone hurt me," he whimpered. "He said he'd come like a lion, with wings on, and eat them up."

"You'll learn how real he is!" shouted his father after him. "If you can't learn it at one end, you shall learn it at the other. I'll have your breeches down. I shall finish my cup of tea first, however," said he to the two women.

Neither of them spoke. Mr. Carter finished his tea, and unhurriedly left the room, washing his hands with his invisible soap and water.

Mrs. Carter said nothing. Betty could think of nothing to say. She wanted to be talking for she was afraid of what they might hear.

Suddenly it came. It seemed to tear the air apart. "Good god!" she cried. "What was that? He's hurt him." She sprang out of her chair, her silly eyes flashing behind her glasses. "I'm going up there!" she cried, trembling.

"Yes, let us go up," said Mrs. Carter. "Let us go up. That was not Small Simon."

It was on the second-floor landing that they found the shoe, with the man's foot still in it, much like that last morsel of a mouse which sometimes falls unnoticed from the side of the jaws of the cat.

Special Delivery

It was with his eyes wide open, and with a reluctance amounting to dread, that Albert Baker slowly surrendered to the passion that was to change his whole life. "Am I mad?" he asked.

He addressed this inquiry, at the end of a long letter, to a certain Big Brother Frank, who gave candid advice in the Heart Correspondence Column of the popular *Tails-Up Weekly*. They printed his letter in full.

Dear Sir,

Excuse my writing to you, but you say write your difficulties. I am in a difficulty, and cannot ask anyone else, they will say I am mad. I am in love. Only the young lady is not like others. She is different.

Have you been along Oxford Street at eight in the morning? I have to go every morning, that is where I work. In all the shopwindows you can see the young men carrying in the artificial young ladies they have to dress for the day. All the way along you can see them, like the old master picture of the Romans and the stolen women, only not so fat. Some struggle, some have their arms round the young men's necks but are looking out of the window. She does not struggle or look out of the window. She is one of those young ladies and I am one of the young men.

Surely it is not much difference from falling in love with a filmstar. I have been in London on this job four years, no one to really talk to. She seems to know everything I try to say. She has those very long blue eyes, thinking about the Riveera, but very kind.

After all, what do you really want with a girl, if not higher things? It isn't only the Riveera, either, but I look after her every way, and you would really think she knew. Ordinary girls don't know, take it from me.

I take her in and keep well in front of her till she is full-dressed, no one shall write to the papers about *her*. Anyway, what is it they make all the fuss about—*nothing*.

I am not mad, she is what I want, not everybody wants a lot of chatter or a family. You want someone to understand you, so you can be happy. I would look after her. But they cost £30, you might as well cry for the moon. Besides, if I got £30, they would say to me, you are mad. Or immoral purposes. It is not like that.

In the shop they heard me speak to her and are ribbing me all the time. I shall know what to do if I know what I am. My plans are made. Please tell me Big Brother if you think they are right. Am I mad?

Yours truly,
Albert Baker

Big Brother Frank's reply was printed below. "Take cold baths and plenty of open-air exercise," said this amiable adviser. "Change your occupation. If you find yourself unable to put aside this degraded and perverse attachment, by all means consult a reliable psychiatrist, and if necessary, enter an institution for treatment."

"So I'm crazy," said Albert, when the paper was delivered on Friday morning. "All right, then. My plans are made." There was a touch of braggadocio in this speech. Albert's only plan was to keep quiet and see what he could do.

At half past seven in the morning there is only one thing a shop assistant can do; that is, hurry off to work as fast as he may, especially if he has to walk from Paddington. To be crazy is one thing; to be late at Rudd & Agnew Ltd. is quite another; Albert was not as mad as all that.

So he started out from his lodgings with his mouth open and his eyes wide. "If I'm late," said he, "they're bound to get hold of her. They'll bend her over. They'll do anything. I must hurry."

"I'll be in time," said Albert to Eva, speaking across the desolate glory of the new day's sunlight, the sunlight, that is, of the day on which he was definitely crazy, and anything was possible; the sunlight in which he and she were utterly and terribly alone. "I wouldn't let you down."

Unfortunately, Albert now abandoned himself to a dream, the dream of his every morning rush toward Rudd & Agnew. This was of entering first upon the empty salon, lifting the dust sheet. "Wake up," he would say. "Is it all right? Put your arms round my neck. Helpless, aren't you? Here's your brassiere. Here's your things." (The models at Rudd & Agnew were lifelike to a degree, perfect in almost every particular.) "Come on," Albert would say. "Nobody can see you. Hurry up, and we'll have a minute before they come in. What did you dream about? Did you dream about the house?"

In abandoning himself to this rehearsal, Albert unconsciously fell into his normal pace. Awakening, he found himself in the glazed brick employees' entrance, devoured by the dry smell of big shops, facing a time clock that stood at three minutes past eight. "They'll be here," he said.

He fled through the catacombs below, into the main shop, downstairs, upstairs, over an interior bridge. From the gallery on the other side he could look down into the long aisles behind the principal windows. Like laden ants in a disturbed anthill, the shopmen ran to and fro with their still, pale burdens. Albert could see the daily joke pass, from the lips of one to the eyes of another, wherever their paths crossed, as they carried their waxen Circassians, these proud, long-suffering, far-eyed, enchanted princesses, out of their mad mysterious night to their odious toilettes, to make them ready for the long slavemarket of the day. There was a slap, and a guffaw.

"Here, none of that," said the shopwalker, himself unable to restrain a scurvy grin at what Clarkie was doing.

But, rounding the gallery, Albert could see three or four gathered in the corner where Eva lay, where he put her to sleep properly, after they had all gone at night. They were out of sight of the shopwalker. They were bending over. Miller's hateful voice sounded out of the middle of the group. "Oh, my God!" cried Albert. "They've got her."

He went down the stairs as one flies downstairs in a nightmare, heedless of the steps, round the satins, into the French models. "Living statue, number three," he heard Miller say. "Albert's 'oneymoon, or—" His hands dived out before him, without waiting to be told; his fingers were on the back of Miller's neck. They slipped on the brilliantine. He drove his nails in.

Next moment, Miller was up, facing him. "You think you can do that to me?" said Miller. "You poor loony!" There was a crack, shatteringly loud; Miller had struck him openhanded on the cheek.

"You leave her alone," said Albert, "or by heaven I'll be the death of you."

"What in the world is this?" cried the shopwalker, hurrying up.

"Stuck his nails in the back of my neck, that's what," said Miller, truculent, standing up for his rights, justified. "I reckon I'm bleeding."

Albert's lower lip was jerking, as if something quite independent of himself had got inside it. "He had hold of her," he said at last.

They all looked down at Eva, naked, her eyes staring out far beyond her shame, like a lion's eyes staring past the bars and the crowd. Albert bent down, and pressed her into a more seemly position. She ignored him. Properly let down, angry, she ignored him.

"What if he had got hold of her?" said the shopwalker. "You think Rudd & Agnew waits for *you* to come in any time and fix the windows?"

"I'm sorry sir," said Albert.

"I shall have to make a report on you," said the shopwalker. "Get on with your work."

Albert was left alone with Eva. "If they give me the sack," he murmured, "who'll look after you? Don't be hard, Eva. I couldn't help it. And I had something to tell you. Don't you want to know what it is? You do? Really? Well, listen—"

Eva had given him an unmistakable look of understanding and forgiveness. It raised Albert to a precarious exaltation. Twice he actually risked slipping out into the entrance, where he could catch the sidelong glance from her eyes. It seemed to him impossible he could get the sack.

After the midday break, however, things took a different turn. Albert spent his lunchtime walking up and down in front of the shop, an exercise which was not forbidden because no one had ever thought it possible. Soon after he got in, Miller entered, full-blown, triumphant, carrying a copy of *Tails-Up Weekly*. As he passed Albert he showed it to him, and grinned.

"What a fool!" thought Albert. "What a fool I've been!"

"Look here, boys," cried Miller as loudly as he dared. "Come in behind here. Clarkie! Sid! Come on. Just half a tick. It's worth it."

"Get back to your counters," said the shopwalker, perceiving the excitement. "What is it now, Miller, for heaven's sake?"

"Only something that proves something," said Miller with an air of righteousness, handing the shopwalker the fatal page.

"This is serious!" cried the shopwalker, staring at Albert. "This is a matter for the Secretary. I'm taking this paper, Miller. I'm taking it to Mr. Schilberg himself."

He went, and Albert was left alone standing, stared at, like a man brought out to be hanged. "It's the sack all right," he said to himself. "Who knows? They might have me shut up."

The thought set his legs in motion. "Here, you'd better stand by," cried a good-natured man. "They'll be sending for you in a minute."

"Let 'em," said Albert. "I'm off."

"Well, I ain't seen you go," said the other defensively.

"I'm off!" cried Albert aloud, as he passed others of the department. They all stared at him; then pretended not to notice. He went up the stairs and round the gallery, through the corridors, out past the timekeeper. "I'm off," said he, punching the clock for the last time.

"You look it," said the timekeeper indifferently.

He went into the street, and round into Oxford Street, crossing to the other side in the hope of making some undetected signal to Eva. As soon as he saw her, he knew what his real purpose was. He walked on without a change of pace, and entered the farther doorway, into the hardware department, where as yet the news could hardly be known, and where he himself would be unrecognized.

He went through a staff door, into a maze of corridors, and found his way to a nook in a storeroom, where he could lie hidden till closing time. There he lay, with his eyes closed and his hands folded, like a dead man, but there was a clock ticking in his brain.

At exactly seven o'clock he got up and stepped out quietly. He was cool, collected, utterly different. The whole place was different. A little daylight leaked in through the blinds at the back of the windows; the high glass dome was blueing, the galleries were drowned in darkness; flying staircases leapt out where the light struck them, and stopped short in midair, where darkness bit them off. Vast stacks of shadow, the leaning façades of towering dreams, mounted like the skyscrapers of a new-risen city from floor to unsubstantial floor, up to the dome itself. The watchman, a being of the shadows, drifted unhurriedly across the diminishing territories of the light. Albert, a deeper shade, followed him, blacker and quieter than the watchman, more utterly of the dark.

The watchman entered the main hall, crossed the region of the French models, and disappeared into a deep vista of darkness on the farther side. Albert, absolutely master of the situation, knowing exactly how many minutes were his before the watchman could stumble round again, ran noiselessly forward.

He pulled aside the dust-sheets. The models were huddled there, grouped like victims in the sack of some forgotten city. Some stood upright, unable to relax, tense to meet new outrage; some, on hands and knees, bowed their faces to the floor, straining for the relief of tears. Others, their wits wiped out by horror, sat with their legs straight out, their hands flat and dead beside them, staring idiotically into a darkness deeper than that of the night.

"Eva!" whispered Albert. "Where are you?" She was a little apart from the others, sitting as if waiting to be taken away.

"You knew I'd come," said Albert, lifting her. Her face fell forward on his, her lips touched his cheek. "You're cold," said Albert. "You're used to your bed."

He caught up the dust sheet and tucked it about her neck. Its pale folds fell over her and him.

This cloaked double figure, this walking embrace of life and death, this beautiful nightmare under its carapace of cotton cloud, now ran noiselessly, staggering a little, up the light spirals of fretted iron, over the flying bridges, now to be seen rounding some high gallery, now swallowed by darkness, now seen higher, still mounting like a spider, till at last it reached the uppermost corridors, and the sanctuary of the little storeroom.

Albert closed the door, spread a bed of wrapping papers, laid Eva upon it, took her head upon his lap, and spread the dust sheet over them. Eva gazed up at him. There was still light here, through a little round window like a porthole. He could see her eyes, steady and cool, gazing at him, weighing him up: his weak face with its tremulous, rickety outline; his flossy, inconsiderable hair. All the same, he was her savior. More than that, for that was a job merely, he was for her the only man in the world. If ever she loved, she must love him. Whatever her memories were, there was no one else now. All the rest were monsters, raging in blindness. In all his unworthiness, he was the only living creature she could love. "What can I do?" thought Albert, overwhelmed by the responsibilities laid on him by this tremendous act of chance, which blackmailed her into the necessity of loving him, and left it to him to make herself worthy.

The dawn, with its threat, recalled him from a thousand fine spiritual issues to a very practical one. "I can't leave you here," said he. "What can I do?"

Albert was not a man of action. His mind was weak, broken, bound by the hundred habits of timid servitude. He crouched, with his head in his hand, conscious less of the problem than of Eva's blue gaze, which expected a decision.

Suddenly Albert stood up. "I've got it," said he. "They've driven me to it. Never mind. You do what I tell you. You trust *me*." He actually emphasized the word "me." He lifted Eva, and set her in the corner, as if she were a mere dummy. "Keep quiet," he said. "I'm going to deliver you, like a chap in a book."

He went out into the twilight of the vast shop, a dawn twilight, altogether different from that of the evening. Albert was equally changed. He was no longer a shadow scurrying ratlike from dark to dark, but a young man of nerve and decision. He was perfectly prepared, if he met him in the silks, to stun the night watchman with a roll of art-shade ninon, or to hood him with a girdle if their paths crossed in the lingerie, or gag him with gloves in the gloves, or strangle him with a stocking in the hosiery, or fell him with a cucumber in the fruit. He devoutly hoped the encounter would not take place in the hardware or cutlery, for Albert was the mildest, gentlest creature that ever breathed, and abhorred the sight of blood. As it happened, the night watchman was no believer in burglaries at six o'clock on a June morning, and was now in his cubbyhole far away in the basement, engaged in the nice preparation of a cup of cocoa to keep at bay the ill effects of the night air.

Albert, not knowing this, and resolved to deal with a dozen night watchmen if necessary, was intoxicated by his only experience of courageous action, and rose from height to height. When he had gathered up a complete wardrobe for Eva, of a rather gayer fashion than she had ever enjoyed before, he went boldly up to the main office, to a desk where forms were made out for special deliveries, and, finding a block of such forms, he chose a name from a list of customers on the desk: "Raymond Pinckney, Esq., 14 Mulberry Grove, Hampstead." This he scribbled on the form; filled in the words, "One model, special arrangement: deliver 9 A.M.—" "Now what the Hell day is this?" murmured Albert. His heart sank; he was done for; he had come upon that blind spot which brings the greatest criminals to their downfall. But no! There was a calendar: yesterday was a Friday because his washing had to be made up; this, therefore, was Saturday. "Who says I'm crazy?" said Albert. "Deliver 9 A.M. Saturday, 14 June, without fail." Now for the rubber stamp. He looked in the middle drawer, and there it was. Everything was going swimmingly. It was with a light heart that he drew out the cash for expenses and hurried back to Eva.

She looked at him questioningly. "Don't worry," said he. "I been man enough. Here, I'm going to wrap you up. When I've got you dressed, of course."

Albert dressed Eva. That was no difficult task. He wrapped the gray-white paper about her, leaving a chink for light and air to come through. Then he set himself to wait for the striking of eight o'clock. In the long interval he was as still as Eva was. He dared not move, nor think, nor scarcely breathe, even; he sat holding a tourniquet on his courage, which had already begun to ebb away. He did not hear seven o'clock strike at all, or the clashing of the scrubwomen's pails, or the drone of the vacuum cleaners; he heard only one bronzy reverberation, and knew it for the last stroke of eight.

He picked Eva up and ran down the back stairs, out to where a raw service-lift clanked him down into the goods yard, whence, without stopping, he walked straight out, holding up his form to the indifferent custodian. "Special delivery," he said. "Got to get a cab."

Albert looked around: he was in the street. "Oh, good heavens!" he said. "What have I done?" People were looking at him, only waiting a split second before they knew and would begin to hound him down. He forgot all about the cab; all his thought and will were concentrated on the single effort of keeping himself from breaking into a run.

Automatically, he took the way to his lodgings. Four times he saw a policeman in the distance, and walked step by leaden step under the awful eyes till he drew abreast of him, crossed the razor edge between brazen approach and guilt-proclaiming flight, felt the eyes on his back, and waited for the shout.

He passed a knot of children on their way to school. "Look what he's got!" they cried. "Hi, Crippen!"

He had had no lunch, no supper, no breakfast, no sleep. The morning sun was already sultry. Eva, whom he could carry like a baron or a brigand when he was in the shop, now became an insupportable weight. He ached in every joint, his knees gave, his head swam; every one of the thousands in the streets was a pursuer; never was creature so universally hunted, nor moved so pitiably slow.

He turned at last into the mean street where he lived. He stumbled into the smelly passage. His landlady, who had spied him from the basement window, now called to him up the kitchen stairs. "Is that you, Mr. Baker?" cried she.

Albert stopped dead. His room was two floors above, but he could already see it as if he were in the doorway: its dimness, its frowziness, its promise of a few hours' safety with Eva. He had thought of nothing beyond that. All he wanted was just a few hours in that room. He had gone through the hellish streets for that, and now, from the tone of his landlady's voice, he knew he would never see his room again. He began to cry.

"Yes, it's me, Mrs. Budgen," he said haltingly, using the breaths between his sobs.

"Mr. Baker, there's been inquiries," shouted the landlady. "Looked like the plainclothes to me. I'd like a word, *now*. I—"

"All right, Mrs. Budgen," said Albert. "I'll be down in half a tick. Just got to go to the WC."

He allowed himself a few seconds to breathe, then took up Eva again, and crept out of the front door and into the hideous street. He reached the corner, and saw Praed Street with its taxicabs. "Got to take a cab," he said aloud, as if he were still addressing the man in the goods yard. *"I* dunno where I'm going.

"Hi!" called Albert to a passing taxi. It went on unheeding. "Hi!" he called. "Stop, won't you? Are you mad?" He actually galvanized his bending knees into a pitiable stagger, and overtook the taxi a few yards on, where it had stopped at a crossing. The driver looked at him as he panted alongside.

"Here you are," said Albert, staring at the delivery slip he had held all this time in his hand. "Pinckney, 14 Mulberry Grove, Hampstead."

"O.K.," said the driver. Albert fell into the cab, and they were off.

Albert held Eva propped against him, and closed his eyes. A jerk, such as the dead will feel on the last day, recalled him to his senses. There was sunlight, altogether unlike the menacing glare in the loud streets: it was filtered through the leaves of lime trees. There was a heavenly quiet, a green iron gate, a gravel drive, a smiling housefront, peaceful, prosperous, and not unfriendly.

Albert stood in a wide porch, with his arm round Eva. A soft-faced man, in blue serge trousers and waistcoat, stood in the doorway. "Never 'eard of a tradesman's entrance?" said he mildly.

"This 'ere's special," said Albert, holding out his slip.

"Well, you've come wrong," said the man. "Mr. Pinckney's down at the Hall. Two Rivers Hall, Baddingly, Suffolk. They ought to have known at the shop. You take it back quick."

"Wanted very special," murmured Albert in despair, proffering his slip.

The man weighed up the situation for a moment. "Hand it over," said he. "The chauffeur's going down. He'll take it."

"He'll take me, too," said Albert. "This is special."

"All right," said the man. "You'll have to get back by yourself, though."

"Don't you worry about me," said Albert.

There followed another dream, with Albert sitting in the back of a large touring car, Eva beside him, and the wrapping dislodged a little so that she could get the fresh air and see the fields go by. Not a word was said. Albert ceased trying to fit things together in his brain. He wished the drive would go on forever, but, since it had to end, he was glad that it ended at a quiet house, standing on a gentle Suffolk knoll, surrounded by red walls and green gardens, full of the shade of senior trees.

"The master's in the studio," said an old woman to the chauffeur.

"You come along with me," said the chauffeur to Albert.

Albert followed with his precious burden into a cobbled stable-yard. The chauffeur knocked at a door. "Young man from Rudd & Agnew. Special delivery," said he.

"What's that?" said a voice. "Send him in."

Albert found himself in a giant room. It was a loft and stable knocked into one, with a vast, cool window all down one side. A large canvas stood on an easel; there were hundreds of brushes, several palettes, boxes of colors. On a cane sofa was a young man reclining in great comfort, reading a thriller.

This young man looked up at Albert. He was a true monkey-face, hideously ugly, with a quick brown eye, hair fallen over his forehead; cotton jersey, beach trousers, straw shoes, and a pipe. "Well, what is it?" said he.

"I've brought—" said Albert. "I've brought—I've brought this." He pulled aside a little more of the wrapping.

"I didn't order anything of this sort," said the young man. "You've brought her to the wrong place."

"Here it is," said Albert, offering his slip. "Written down."

"I don't use that sort of model," said the young man. "Might be an idea, though. However, you ask them to give you some beer in the kitchen, and then take her back."

"No," said Albert. He began to shake and tremble. He stared at Mr. Pinckney with a rabbit desperation. Mr. Pinckney stared back at him. "What *is* all this?" said he.

"Mister," said Albert, "have you ever been in love?"

"We won't discuss that," said the ugly young man.

"If you don't know, it's no good me talking," said Albert. "All right, I'll get out. Come on, Eva. I can't help it. We got to get out."

"Wait a little," said Mr. Pinckney. "Take it easy. Tell me all about it. I shall understand."

"It's like this," said Albert, and told, very strangely, his strange story.

"You are quite mad," said Pinckney at the end of it.

"So they say," said Albert. "I'm a human being, ain't I? I could be happy."

"I like your philosophy," said Pinckney. "Mad but happy."

"Have I ever been happy?" said Albert.

"Go on," said Pinckney.

"And what about her?" said Albert. "But you are laughing. You're ribbing me." His voice rose dangerously.

"What would you do with her?" said Pinckney.

"I'd look after her," said Albert. "But not to be ribbed. No. I'll go out."

"Listen, you," said Pinckney. "If you want to look after her, don't leave her propped against the table there. Set her in the armchair comfortably."

"Yes, sir, I will," said Albert. "I didn't like to ask."

"Take off those stuffy wrappings," said Mr. Pinckney harshly. Albert smiled at Mr. Pinckney.

"So, you're in love with her," said Mr. Pinckney, "and you want to be happy. What's your name, by the way?"

"Albert Baker. Hers is Eva."

"Well, Baker," said Pinckney, "I'm not making you any promises; you're just here for the time being. How long depends on a lot of things. Most of all, on how you behave. You're mad. Don't forget it. It doesn't matter a bit, but you've got to be sensible about it. Listen to this. If ever you feel an overpowering impulse—if ever you feel you simply must do something—whatever it is, you're to tell me first. Do you hear?"

"Yes, sir," cried Albert. "If you please, I must—I must go to the lavatory. I'm so happy."

"Excellent!" said Pinckney. "Then go and sit under the tree over there. Eva will be perfectly all right. She's resting."

"She's all right," said Albert. "She trusts you."

When he had gone, Pinckney went to the telephone, and he called his lawyer.

"I'm going to keep him here," said he, in conclusion. "Well, I'm going to, that's all—Yes, but you tell them their damned model's going to be paid for. That's all they care about—Yes, I'm responsible for him—That's it, our respected client—As long as you fix it—Oh, hideous, absolutely hideous—Might do to paint for a lark—Well, you'll let me know? Good man! That's fine."

Pinckney hung up. "He'll fix it," said he to himself. "But I'll keep that bit of news, in case he needs calling to order. If he seems depressed, I'll tell him."

Albert, however, did not seem depressed. The journey through the London streets had left him with some comfortable blanks in his mind. He wore a slightly dazed look; his mouth hung open, and his eyes filled with tears now and then, when a thought came to a happy end, transforming itself into a feeling, like a flower opening inside his mind. To the outward view, there was nothing very odd about him. "He's a bit queer, isn't he?" said Mabel the housemaid.

"Nervous breakdown," said the housekeeper. "That's what Mr. Pinckney says. My sister's boy had one. They put him in a home."

"He's no trouble," said Mabel. "Does his own room, anyway. Funny, he locks that door as if he had the Crown Jewels to look after."

"He's very willing and obliging," said the housekeeper. "And he's got to be let alone."

Albert had an old chauffeur's room, away over the end of the stables. He shined the shoes, he fetched and carried for the housekeeper, who was told never to send him down to the village. Most of the time he helped the gardeners in the green gardens that were almost all lawn and trees. From the dusty window Eva watched him working for her in the yellow shade of the limes, in the black shade of the mulberries, and in the green shade of the mighty beech.

In the evening Albert had his supper in the housekeeper's room. At the end of it, "Thank you, ma'am," said he, and, "Thank you, miss," to Mabel. He was very polite; to him they were lesser angels, instruments of the great power that kept the world at bay. Then, he hurried away to his room, to tell Eva all about it.

"He came up to me today," he would say. "Oh, he's no *nice,* Eva. I can't tell you how nice he is. Always speaks rough, only it's in a joking way. But when he mentions you—it's most respectful. He knows what you are. I ought to have told you, it was his idea about bringing up the roses. Only I thought you'd like it to be me."

This was only the beginning of their evening, which stretched far into the light summer night, for Albert slept very little, and, when he did, Eva came to life in his dreams. "Are you miserable?" he asked her. "Are you still longing for the Riveera?"

"Not me," she replied softly.

"It's better than the shop, isn't it?" said he, anxiously.

"It's nice being with you," said Eva.

"Do you mean it?" cried Albert eagerly. "With me?"

"I can see what you're like," said Eva.

These tender passages passed between them in dreams so mingled with his summer wakefulness that he passed from one to another as easily and unnoticingly as he passed from shade of beech to shade of lime on the lawn. Sometimes Albert and Eva never lay down at all, but passed the night at the window, watching the glow fade from the red roofs of the village at the foot of the slope, and not moving till the dawn brought them into sight again.

One evening, under one of these friendly red roofs, a meeting was in progress. The proceedings were concerned with the organization of the village flower show and fête. Officials were appointed to the charge of the show-tent, the gate, the sideshows, and the collection of subscriptions. "I propose Mr. Bly be asked to go round for subscriptions," said the vicar's gardener. "I beg to second that," said the blacksmith. "If Mr. Bly will be so kind," said the secretary, cocking an inquiring eye at the village constable, whose official position marked him out for this responsible office. Mr. Bly nodded formidable assent, the proposal was unanimously accepted, entered in the minutes, and the meeting was adjourned.

Next morning, Mr. Bly mounted his bicycle, and pedaled slowly in the direction of the Hall.

"Oh, God!" cried Albert, peering from behind a hedge. "They've tracked us down."

Bending double, he ran to his little stableroom. "Come on, Eva," he said. "It's no good. It couldn't last. He can't save us this time. It's the police."

He took Eva in his arms and ran down under the field hedges to a wood in the bottom, and thence across country, along the edges of dusty summer fallows, crawling through standing corn, taking to the woods whenever possible, scuttling across the roads when he came to them, shouted at by one or two men in the fields, flown at by a dog when he blundered on a keeper's hut in a clearing, stared at by an awful eye from above. All around, he could sense a network of cars and men, policemen, shopwalkers, the Secretary himself, searching for him and Eva.

Night came. He could creep only a hundred yards at a time, and then must lie still a long time, feeling the earth turn over and over, and the network of pursuit close in. "Eva," said he, "we've got to go on all night. Can you stand it?"

Eva made no response. "You're weak," said he. "Your head's going round. You can feel your heart giving way. But we've got to go on."

The last part of that night journey was a blank to Albert. They must have come to a common. He found himself sprawled in a deep bay in a clump of furze. Eva lay tumbled beside him, in a horrible attitude, as she had lain that fatal morning in the shop. "Stretch yourself out," he said. "I'll come to in a minute. I'll look after you."

But the sun was already high when he sat up, and Eva was still sprawled as she had been before. A yellow fly crawled on her cheek: before he could move, it had crawled right over her unwinking blue eye. "Eva!" he cried. "What's up? Wake up. Has it been too much for you? Say something, do.

"She's dead!" he cried to the world at large. "Carrying her about like that—I've killed her."

He flung himself upon the sprawling figure. He opened her dress, he listened for her heart. He lay like that for a long time. The sun poured down, glimmering on the worn blue suit, parching the flossy hair, devouring the waxen cheeks, fading the staring blue eyes.

Albert's face was as dead as Eva's, till suddenly it was galvanized by an expression too distracted and too fleeting to be called hope. Thump, thump, thump, he heard: he thought it was her heart beating again. Then he realized it was footsteps coming near.

He raised his head. Someone was on the other side of the bushes. "They shan't disturb you, my darling," he said to Eva, and got up and stumbled round to face the intruders.

It was not policemen: it was two ordinary men, filthy, unshaven, looking at Albert out of wicked eyes.

"Nice goings-on," said one of them.

"We seen you," said the other.

"There's a law against that sort of thing," said the first. He gazed up at the sky. "Might be worth a couple of quid, not to be run in for that sort of thing."

"For a decent girl it would," said the other.

"Not to be dragged along to the copper-station with her thing-ummys hanging round her ankles," said the first.

"You keep off," said Albert. "I haven't got no money. Straight. You can search me if you like."

"Perhaps the young lady 'as," said the first man, having verified this point.

"If she *is* a young lady, she 'as," said the second.

"And if not," said the first. "If not, Alf— What do you say? Looked O.K. to me. Nice bit of goods!"

"I'm game," said Alf, glancing round.

The men made a move. Albert got in front of them, his arms spread wide. "Keep back," he said again, feeling how light and flat and useless the words were.

"Sit on him, Alf," said the first man. "Then I will."

There was a scuffle. Albert, heaven knows how, tore himself away from Alf, and rushed after the first man, seizing him by the collar and raining blows on his hard head. "Strewth!" cried the man. " 'Ere, take him off, Alf, 'e's stinging me."

Albert felt a hand seize him. He turned; there was Alf's grinning face. "Come on, dearie," said Alf. Albert, yielding for a moment, suddenly kicked as hard and viciously as he could. There was a terrifying howl. Alf was rolling on the ground.

"What'll they do to me?" thought Albert. "Eva! I did it for you."

"He's done it to me!" cried Alf. "He's done it to me. Kill the— Kill 'im!"

Something hit Albert on the side of the jaw, and a bombshell burst in his brain. "The knockout," said the first man, turning again to go round to where Eva lay.

"Let me get my boots on him," said Alf, scrambling to his feet.

"Gawd's trewth! Look here, Alf," cried the first man from the other side of the bushes. "It's a bloody dummy."

"You come back here," said Alf. "You 'it 'im. *I* didn't!"

"What's up?" cried the other, hurrying round.

"He's a goner," said Alf. "I'm off."

"Wait a minute, pal," cried the first man. "Have some sense. You're in it as much as me. Look here, you kicked him. Do you think I can't see? Never mind. Let's get him hid; that's the main thing."

"Chuck 'em down in the chalk pit, both of 'em," said the other. "Come on! It'll look as if he fell in of his own accord. We've never seen him, have we?"

A few minutes later the men were gone. The sun poured down on the glinting common, scorching everywhere except in the cool bottom of the chalk pit, where Eva and Albert lay unsought and undisturbed. His head lay limp on her neck; her stiff arm was arched over him. In the autumn, when the overhang crumbled down on them, it pressed him close to her forever.

Rope enough

Henry Fraser, well assured that almost everything is done by mirrors, was given a job in India. No sooner had he set foot on shore than he burst into a horse laugh. Those who were meeting him asked in some alarm the cause of this merriment. He replied he was laughing at the mere idea of the Indian Rope Trick.

He emitted similar startling sounds, and gave the same explanation, at a tiffin where he was officially made welcome; likewise, on the Maidan, over *chota peg,* in rickshaws, in bazaars, in the Club, and on the polo ground. Soon he was known from Bombay to Calcutta as the man who laughed at the Indian Rope Trick, and he gloried in the well-deserved publicity.

There came a day, however, when he was sitting in his bungalow, bored to death. His boy entered, and, with suitable salaams, announced that a mountebank was outside, who craved the honor of entertaining the *sahib* with a performance of the Indian Rope Trick. Laughing heartily, Henry consented, and moved out to his chair upon the veranda.

Below, in the dusty compound, stood a native who was emaciated to a degree, and who had with him a spry youngster, a huge mat basket, and a monstrous great sword. Out of the basket he dragged some thirty feet of stout rope, made a pass or two, and slung it up into the air. It stayed there. Henry chuckled.

The boy then, with a caper, sprang at the rope, clutched it, and went up hand over hand, like a monkey. When he reached the top he vanished into thin air. Henry guffawed.

Soon the man, looking upwards with an anxious expression,

began to hoot and holler after the boy. He called him down, he ordered him down, he begged him down, he began to swear and curse horribly. The boy, it seemed, took no notice at all. Henry roared.

Now the black, clapping his abominable great scimitar between his teeth, took hold of the rope himself, and went up it like a sailor. He, also, disappeared at the top. Henry's mirth increased.

Pretty soon some yelps and squeals were heard coming out of the empty air, and then a bloodcurdling scream. Down came a leg, thump on to the ground, then an arm, a thigh, a head and other joints, and finally (no ladies being present) a bare backside, which struck the earth like a bomb. Henry went into fits.

Then the black came sliding down, holding on with one hand, fairly gibbering with excitement. He presented to Henry, with a salaam, his reeking blade for inspection. Henry rocked in his chair.

The black, seemingly overwhelmed with remorse, gathered up the fragments of his little stooge, lavishing a hundred lamentations and endearments upon each grisly member, and he stowed them all in the giant basket.

At that moment Henry, feeling the time had come for a showdown, and willing to bet a thousand to one they'd planted the whole compound full of mirrors before calling him out there, pulled out his revolver, and blazed away all six chambers in different directions, in the expectation, of splintering at least one of those deceiving glasses.

Nothing of that sort happened, but the black, doing a quick pirouette in alarm, looked down in the dust at his feet, and held up a villainous little snake, no thicker than a lead pencil, which had been killed by one of Henry's stray bullets. He gave a gasp of relief, touched his turban very civilly, turned round again, and made a pass or two over the basket. At once, with a wriggle and a frisk, the boy sprang out, whole, alive, smiling, full of health and wickedness.

The black hastily hauled down the rope, and came cringing up to Henry, overflowing with gratitude for having been saved from that villainous little snake, which was nothing more nor less than a krait—one nip and a man goes round and round like a Catherine wheel for eleven seconds; then he is as dead as mutton.

"But for the Heavenborn," said the black, "I should have been a goner, and my wicked little boy here, who is my pride and delight, must have lain dismembered in the basket till the *sahib's* servants condescended to throw him to the crocodiles. Our worthless lives, our scanty goods, are all at the *sahib's* disposal."

"That's all right," said Henry. "All I ask is, show me how the trick is worked, or the laugh will be on me from now on."

"Would not the *sahib*," said the black diffidently, "prefer the secret of a superb hair restorer?"

"No. No," said Henry. "Nothing but the trick."

"I have," said the black, "the secret of a very peculiar tonic, which the *sahib*—not now, of course, but in later life—might find—"

"The trick," said Henry, "and without further delay."

"Very well," said the black. "Nothing in the world could be more simple. You make a pass, like that—"

"Wait a minute," said Henry. "Like that?"

"Exactly," said the black. "You then throw up the rope—so. You see? It sticks."

"So it does," said Henry.

"Any boy can climb," said the black. "Up, boy! Show the *sahib*."

The boy, smiling, climbed up and disappeared.

"Now," said the black, "if the *sahib* will excuse me, I shall be back immediately." And with that he climbed up himself, threw down the boy in sections, and speedily rejoined Henry on the ground.

"All that," said he, scooping up legs and arms as he spoke, "all that can be done by anyone. There is a little knack, however, to the pass I make at this juncture. If the *sahib* will deign to observe closely—like that."

"Like that?" said Henry.

"You have it to perfection," said the black.

"Very interesting," said Henry. "Tell me, what's up there at the top of the rope?"

"Ah, *sahib*," said the black with a smile, "that is something truly delightful."

With that he salaamed and departed, taking with him his rope, his giant basket, his tremendous great scimitar, and his wicked little boy. Henry was left feeling rather morose; he was known from the Deccan to the Khyber Pass as the man who laughed at the Indian Rope Trick, and now he could laugh no more.

He decided to keep very quiet about it, but this, unfortunately, was not enough. At tiffin, at *chota peg,* at the Club, on the Maidan, in the bazaar, and at polo, he was expected to laugh like a horse, and in India one has to do what is expected of one. Henry became extremely unpopular, cabals were formed again him, and soon he was hoofed out of the Service.

This was the more distressing as, in the meantime, he had married a wife, strong-featured, upstanding, well-groomed, straight-eyed, a little peremptory in manner, and as jealous as a demon, but in all respects a *memsahib* of the highest type, who knew very well what was due her. She told Henry he had better go to America and make a fortune. He agreed, they packed up, and off they went to America.

"I hope," said Henry, as they stood looking at the skyline of New York, "I hope I shall make that fortune."

"Of course," said she. "You must insist upon it."

"Very well, my dear," said he.

On landing, however, he discovered that all the fortunes had already been made, a discovery which very generally awaits those who visit America on this errand, and, after some weeks of drifting about from place to place, he was prepared to cut his demand down to a mere job, then to a lesser job, and, finally, to the price of a meal and a bed for the night.

They reached this extremity in a certain small town in the Middle West. "There is nothing for it, my dear," said Henry. "We shall have to do the Indian Rope Trick."

His wife cried out very bitterly at the idea of a *memsahib* performing this native feat in a middle-western town, before a middle-western audience. She reproached him with the loss of his job, the poor quality of his manhood, with the time he let her little dog get run over on the Bund, and with a glance he had cast at a Parsee maiden in Bombay. Nevertheless, reason and hunger prevailed; they pawned her last trinket, and invested in a rope, a roomy grip, and a monstrous old rusty scimitar they discovered in a junk shop.

When she saw this last, Henry's wife flatly refused to go on unless she was given the star part and Henry took that of the stooge. "But," said Henry, drawing an apprehensive thumb down the notched and jagged edge of the grim and rusty bilbo, "but," said he, "you don't know how to make the passes."

"You shall teach me," she said, "and if anything goes wrong you will have only yourself to blame."

So Henry showed her. You may be sure he was very thorough in his instructions. In the end, she mastered them perfectly, and there was nothing left to do but to stain themselves with coffee.

Henry improvised a turban and loincloth; she wore a *sari* and a pair of ashtrays borrowed from the hotel. They sought out a convenient waste lot, a large crowd collected, and the show began.

Up went the rope. Sure enough, it stuck. The crowd, with a multiple snigger, whispered that everything was done by mirrors. Henry, not without a good deal of puffing, went up hand over hand. When he got to the top, he forgot the crowd, the act, his wife, and even himself, so surprised and delighted was he by the sight that met his eyes.

He found himself crawling out of something like a well, onto what seemed to be solid ground. The landscape about him was not at all like that below; it was like an Indian paradise, full of dells, bowers, scarlet ibises, and heaven knows what all. However, his surprise and delight came less from these features of the background than from the presence of a young female in the nearest of these bowers or arbors, one which happened to be all wreathed, canopied, overgrown, and intertwined with passionflowers. This delightful creature, who was a positive houri, and very lightly attired, seemed to be expecting Henry, and greeted him with rapture.

Henry, who had a sufficiently affectionate nature, flung his arms round her neck and gazed deeply into her eyes. These were surprisingly eloquent. They seemed to say, "Why not make hey-hey while the sun shines?"

He found the notion entirely agreeable, and planted a lingering kiss on her lips, noting only with a dim and careless annoyance that his wife was hooting and hollering from below. "What person of any tact or delicacy," thought he, "could hoot and holler at such a moment?" and he dismissed her from his mind.

You may imagine his mortification when his delicious damsel suddenly repulsed him from her arms. He looked over his shoulder, and there was his wife, clambering over the edge, terribly red in the face, with the fury of a demon in her eye, and the mighty scimitar gripped firmly between her teeth.

Henry tried to rise, but she was beforehand with him, and while yet he had but his left foot on the ground, she caught him one across the boiling parts with the huge and jagged bilbo, which effectually hamstrung him, so that he fell groveling at her feet. "For heaven's sake!" he cried. "It's all a trick. Part of the act. It means nothing. Remember our public. The show must go on."

"It shall," said she, striking at his arms and legs.

"Oh, those notches!" cried he. "To oblige me, my dear, please sharpen it a little upon a stone."

"It is good enough for you, you viper," said she, hacking away all the time. Pretty soon, Henry was a limbless trunk.

"For the love of God," said he, "I hope you remember the passes. I can explain everything."

"To Hell with the passes!" said she, and, with a last swipe, she sent his head rolling like a football.

She was not long in picking up the scattered fragments of poor Henry, and flinging them down to earth, amid the applause and laughter of the crowd, who were more than ever convinced it was all done by mirrors.

Then, gripping her scimitar, she was about to swarm down after him, not from any softhearted intention of reassembling her unfortunate spouse, but rather to have another hack or two at some of the larger joints. At that moment, she became aware of someone behind her, and, looking round, there was a divine young man, with the appearance of a maharaja of the highest caste, an absolute Valentino, in whose eyes she seemed to read the words, "It is better to burn upon the Bed of Passion than in the Chair of Electricity."

This idea presented itself with an overwhelming appeal. She paused only to thrust her head through the aperture, and cry, "That's what happens to a pig of a man who betrays his wife with a beastly native," before hauling up the rope and entering into conversation with her charmer.

The police soon appeared upon the scene. There was nothing but a cooing sound above, as if invisible turtledoves were circling in amorous flight. Below, the various portions of Henry were scattered in the dust, and the bluebottle flies were already settling upon them.

The crowd explained it was nothing but a trick, done with mirrors.

"It looks to me," said the sergeant, "as if the biggest one must have splintered right on top of him."

GREEN THOUGHTS

Annihilating all that's made
To a green thought in a green shade.

—MARVELL

The orchid had been sent among the effects of his friend, who had come by a lonely and mysterious death on the expedition. Or he had bought it among a miscellaneous lot, "Unclassified," at the close of the auction. I forget which it was, but it was certainly one or the other of these. Moreover, even in its dry, brown, dormant root state, this orchid had a certain sinister quality. It looked, with its bunched and ragged projections, like a rigid yet a gripping hand, hideously gnarled, or a grotesquely whiskered, threatening face. Would you not have known what sort of an orchid it was?

Mr. Mannering did not know. He read nothing but catalogues and books on fertilizers. He unpacked the new acquisition with a solicitude absurd enough in any case toward any orchid, or primrose either, in the twentieth century, but idiotic, foolhardy, doom-eager, when extended to an orchid thus come by, in appearance thus. And in his traditional obtuseness he at once planted it in what he called the "Observation Ward," a hothouse built against the south wall of his dumpy red dwelling. Here he set always the most interesting additions to his collection, and especially weak and sickly plants, for there was a glass door in his study wall through which he could see into this hothouse, so that the weak and sickly plants could encounter no crisis without his immediate knowledge and his tender care.

This plant, however, proved hardy enough. At the ends of thick and stringy stalks it opened out bunches of darkly shining leaves, and soon it spread in every direction, usurping so much space that first one, then another, then all its neighbors had to be removed to a hothouse at the end of the garden. It was, Cousin Jane said, a regular hopvine. At the ends of the stalks, just before the leaves began, were set groups of tendrils, which hung idly, serving no apparent purpose. Mr. Mannering thought that very probably these were vestigial organs, a heritage from some period when the plant had been a climber. But when were the vestigial tendrils of an ex-climber half or quarter so thick and strong?

After a long time, sets of tiny buds appeared here and there among the extravagant foliage. Soon they opened into small flowers, miserable little things—they looked like flies' heads. One naturally expects a large, garish, sinister bloom, like a sea anemone, or a Chinese lantern, or a hippopotamus yawning, on any important orchid; and should it be an unclassified one as well, I think one has every right to insist on a sickly and overpowering scent into the bargain.

Mr. Mannering did not mind at all. Indeed, apart from his joy and happiness in being the discoverer and godfather of a new sort of orchid, he felt only a mild and scientific interest in the fact that the paltry blossoms were so very much like flies' heads. Could it be to attract other flies for food or as fertilizers? But, then, why like their heads?

It was a few days later that Cousin Jane's cat disappeared. This was a great blow to Cousin Jane, but Mr. Mannering was not, in his heart of hearts, greatly sorry. He was not fond of the cat, for he could not open the smallest chink in a glass roof for ventilation but the creature would squeeze through somehow to enjoy the warmth, and in this way it had broken many a tender shoot. But, before poor Cousin Jane had lamented two days, something happened which so engrossed Mr. Mannering that he had no mind left at all with which to sympathize with her affliction, or to make at breakfast kind and hypocritical inquiries after the lost cat. A strange new bud appeared on the orchid. It was clearly evident that there would be two quite different sorts of bloom on this one plant, as sometimes happens in such fantastic corners of the vegetable world, and that the new flower would be very different in size and structure from the earlier ones. The bud grew bigger and bigger, till it was as big as one's fist.

And, just then—it could never have been more inopportune—an affair of the most unpleasant, the most distressing nature summoned Mr. Mannering to town. It was his wretched nephew, in trouble again, and this time so deeply and so very disgracefully that it took all Mr. Mannering's generosity, and all his influence, too, to extricate the worthless young man. Indeed, as soon as he saw the state of affairs, he told the prodigal that this was the last time he might expect assistance, that his vices and his ingratitude had long ago canceled all affection between them, and that for this last helping hand he was indebted only to his mother's memory, and to no faith on the part of his uncle either in his repentance or his reformation. He wrote, moreover, to Cousin Jane, to relieve his feelings, telling her of the whole business, and adding that the only thing left to do was to cut the young man off entirely.

When he got back to Torquay, Cousin Jane was nowhere to be found. The situation was extremely annoying. Their only servant was a cook who was very old and very stupid and very deaf. She suffered, besides, from an obsession, owing to the fact that for many years Mr. Mannering had had no conversation with her in which he had not included an impressive reminder that she must always, no matter what might happen, keep the big kitchen stove up to a certain pitch of activity. For this stove, besides supplying the house with hot water, heated the pipes in the "Observation Ward," to which the daily gardener who had charge of the other hothouses had no access. By this time, she had come to regard her duties as stoker as her chief *raison d'être,* and it was difficult to penetrate her deafness with any question which her stupidity and her obsession did not somehow transmute into an inquiry after the stove, and this, of course, was especially the case when Mr. Mannering spoke to her. All he could disentangle was what she had volunteered on first seeing him, that his cousin had not been seen for three days, that she had left without saying a word. Mr. Mannering was perplexed and annoyed, but, being a man of method, he thought it best to postpone further inquiries until he had refreshed himself a little after his long and tiring journey. A full supply of energy was necessary to extract any information from the old cook; besides, there was probably a note somewhere. It was only natural that before he went to his room Mr. Mannering should peep into the hothouse, just to make sure that the wonderful orchid had come to no harm during the inconsiderate absence of Cousin Jane. As soon as he opened the door his eyes fell upon the bud; it had now changed in shape very considerably, and had increased in size to the bigness of a human head. It is no exaggeration to state that Mr. Mannering remained rooted to the spot, with his eyes fixed upon this wonderful bud, for fully five minutes.

But, you will ask, why did he not see her clothes on the floor? Well, as a matter of fact (it is a delicate point), there were no clothes on the floor. Cousin Jane, though of course she was entirely estimable in every respect, though she was well over forty, too, was given to the practice of the very latest ideas on the dual culture of the soul and body—Swedish, German, neo-Greek and all that. And the orchid house was the warmest place available. I must proceed with the order of events.

Mr. Mannering at length withdrew his eyes from this stupendous bud, and decided that he must devote his attention to the gray exigencies of everyday life. But although his body dutifully ascended the stairs, heart, mind, and soul all remained in adoration of the plant. Although he was philosophical to the point of insensibility over the miserable smallness of the earlier flowers, yet he was now as much gratified by the magnitude of the great bud as you or I might be. Hence it was not unnatural that Mr. Mannering while in his bath should be full of the most exalted visions of the blossoming of his heart's darling, his vegetable godchild. It would be by far the largest known, complex as a dream, or dazzlingly simple. It would open like a dancer, or like the sun rising. Why, it might be opening at this very moment! Mr. Mannering could restrain himself no longer; he rose from the steamy water, and, wrapping his bathrobe about him, hurried down to the hothouse, scarcely staying to dry himself, though he was subject to colds.

The bud had not yet opened; it still reared its unbroken head among the glossy, fleshy foliage, and he now saw, what he had had no eyes for previously, how very exuberant that foliage had grown. Suddenly he realized with astonishment that this huge bud was not the one which had appeared before he went away. That one had been lower down on the plant. Where was it now, then? Why, this new thrust and spread of foliage concealed it from him. He walked across, and discovered it. It had opened into a bloom. And as he looked at this bloom his astonishment grew to stupefaction, one might say to petrification, for it is a fact that Mr. Mannering remained rooted to the spot, with his eyes fixed on the flower, for fully fifteen minutes. The flower was an exact replica of the head of Cousin Jane's lost cat. The similitude was so exact, so lifelike, that Mr. Mannering's first movement, after the fifteen minutes, was to seize his bathrobe and draw it about him, for he was a modest man, and the cat, though bought for a tom, had proved to be quite the reverse. I relate this to show how much character, spirit, *presence*—call it what you will—there was upon this floral cat's face. But although he made to seize his bathrobe, it was too late. He could not move. The new lusty foliage had closed in unperceived; the too lightly dismissed tendrils were everywhere upon him; he gave a few weak cries and sank to the ground, and there, as the Mr. Mannering of ordinary life, he passes out of this story.

Mr. Mannering sank into a coma, into an insensibility so deep that a black eternity passed before the first faint elements of his consciousness reassembled themselves in his brain. For of his brain was the center of a new bud being made. Indeed, it was two or three days before this at first almost shapeless and quite primitive lump of organic matter had become sufficiently mature to be called Mr. Mannering at all. These days, which passed quickly enough, in a certain mild, not unpleasant excitement, in the outer world, seemed to the dimly working mind within the bud to resume the whole history of the development of our species, in a great many epochal parts.

A process analogous to the mutations of the embryo was being enacted here. At last, the entity which was thus being rushed down an absurdly foreshortened vista of the ages slowed up and came almost to a stop in the present. It became recognizable. The Seven Ages of Mr. Mannering were presented, as it were, in a series of close-ups, as in an educational film. His consciousness settled and cleared. The bud was mature, ready to open. At this point, I believe, Mr. Mannering's state of mind was exactly that of a patient who, wakening from under an anesthetic, struggling up from vague dreams, asks plaintively, "Where am I?" Then the bud opened, and he knew.

There was the hothouse, but seen from an unfamiliar angle. There, through the glass door, was his study. There, below him, was the cat's head, and there—there, beside him, was Cousin Jane. He could not say a word, but, then, neither could she. Perhaps it was as well. At the very least, he would have been forced to own that she had been in the right in an argument of long standing; she had always maintained that in the end no good would come of his pre-occupation with "those unnatural flowers."

It must be admitted that Mr. Mannering was not at first greatly upset by this extraordinary upheaval in his daily life. This, I think, was because he was interested not only in private and personal matters, but in the wider and more general, one might say the biological, aspects of his metamorphosis. For the rest, simply because he *was* now a vegetable, he responded with a vegetable reaction. The impossibility of locomotion, for example, did not trouble him in the least, or even the absence of body and limbs, any more than the cessation of that stream of rashers and tea, biscuits and glasses of milk, luncheon cutlets, and so forth, that had flowed in at his mouth for over fifty years, but which had now been reversed to a gentle, continuous, scarcely noticeable feeding from below. All the powerful influence of the physical upon the mental, therefore, inclined him to tranquillity. But the physical is not all. Although no longer a man, he was still Mr. Mannering. And from this anomaly, as soon as his scientific interest had subsided, issued a host of woes, mainly subjective in origin.

He was fretted, for instance, by the thought that he would now have no opportunity to name his orchid, or to write a paper upon it, and, still worse, there grew up in his mind the abominable conviction that, as soon as his plight was discovered, it was he who would be named and classified, and that he himself would be the subject of a paper, possibly even of comment and criticism in the lay press. Like all orchid collectors, he was excessively shy and sensitive, and in his present situation these qualities were very naturally exaggerated, so that the bare idea of such attentions brought him to the verge of wilting. Worse yet was the fear of being transplanted, thrust into some unfamiliar, drafty, probably public place. Being dug up! Ugh! A violent shudder pulsated through all the heavy foliage that sprang from Mr. Mannering's division of the plant. He became conscious of ghostly and remote sensations in the stem below, and in certain tufts of leaves that sprouted from it; they were somehow reminiscent of spine and heart and limbs. He felt quite a dryad.

In spite of all, however, the sunshine was very pleasant. The rich odor of hot, spicy earth filled the hothouse. From a special fixture on the hot-water pipes, a little warm steam oozed into the air. Mr. Mannering began to abandon himself to a feeling of *laissez-aller*. Just then, up in a corner of the glass roof, at the ventilator, he heard a persistent buzzing. Soon the note changed from one of irritation to a more complacent sound; a bee had managed, after some difficulty, to find his way through one of the tiny chinks in the metalwork. The visitor came drifting down and down through the still, green air, as if into some subaqueous world, and he came to rest on one of those petals which were Mr. Mannering's eyebrows. Thence he commenced to explore one feature after another, and at last he settled heavily on the lower lip, which drooped under his weight and allowed him to crawl right into Mr. Mannering's mouth. This was quite a considerable shock, of course, but on the whole the sensation was neither as alarming nor as unpleasant as might have been expected. "Indeed," thought the vegetable gentleman, "it seems quite agreeable."

But Mr. Mannering soon ceased the drowsy analysis of his sensations when he saw the departed bee, after one or two lazy circlings, settle directly upon the maiden lip of Cousin Jane. Ominous as lightning, a simple botanical principle flashed across the mind of her wretched relative. Cousin Jane was aware of it also, although, being the product of an earlier age, she might have remained still blessedly ignorant had not her cousin—vain, garrulous, proselytizing fool!—attempted for years past to interest her in the rudiments of botany. How the miserable man upbraided himself now! He saw two bunches of leaves just below the flower tremble and flutter, and rear themselves painfully upwards into the very likeness of two shocked and protesting hands. He saw the soft and orderly petals of his cousin's face ruffle and incarnadine with rage and embarrassment, then turn sickly as a gardenia with horror and dismay. But what was he to do? All the rectitude implanted by his careful training, all the chivalry proper to an orchid-collector, boiled and surged beneath a paralytically calm exterior. He positively travailed in the effort to activate the muscles of his face, to assume an expression of grief, manly contrition, helplessness in the face of fate, willingness to make honorable amends, all suffused with the light of a vague but solacing optimism; but it was in vain. When he had strained until his nerves seemed likely to tear under the tension, the only movement he could achieve was a trivial flutter of the left eyelid—worse than nothing.

This incident completely aroused Mr. Mannering from his vegetable lethargy. He rebelled against the limitations of the form into which he had thus been cast while subjectively he remained all too human. Was he not still at heart a man, with a man's hopes, ideals, aspirations—and capacity for suffering?

When dusk came, and the opulent and sinister shapes of the great plant dimmed to a suggestiveness more powerfully impressive than had been its bright noonday luxuriance, and the atmosphere of a tropical forest filled the orchid-house like an exile's dream or the nostalgia of the saxophone; when the cat's whiskers drooped, and even Cousin Jane's eyes slowly closed, the unhappy man remained wide awake, staring into the gathering darkness. Suddenly the light in the study was switched on. Two men entered the room. One of them was his lawyer, the other was his nephew.

"This is his study, as you know, of course," said the wicked nephew. "There's nothing here. I looked when I came over on Wednesday."

"I've sat in this room many an evening," said the lawyer with an expression of distaste. "I'd sit on this side of the fireplace and he on that. 'Mannering,' I'd think to myself, 'I wonder how you'll end up. Drugs? Sexual perversion? Or murder?' Well, maybe we'll soon know the answer. Until we do, I suppose you, as next of kin, had better take charge here."

Saying this, the lawyer turned, about to go, and Mr. Mannering saw a malicious smile overspread the young man's face. The uneasiness which had overcome him at first sight of his nephew was intensified to fear and trembling at the sight of this smile.

When he had shown the lawyer out, the nephew returned to the study and looked round him with lively and sinister satisfaction. Then he cut a caper on the hearthrug. Mr. Mannering thought he had never seen anything so diabolical as this solitary expression of the glee of a venomous nature at the prospect of unchecked sway, here whence he had been outcast. How vulgar petty triumph appeared, beheld thus; how disgusting petty spite; how appalling revengefulness and hardness of heart! He remembered suddenly that his nephew had been notable, in his repulsive childhood, for his cruelty to flies, tearing their wings off, and for his barbarity toward cats. A sort of dew might have been noticed upon the good man's forehead. It seemed to him that his nephew had only to glance that way, and all would be discovered, although he might have remembered that it was impossible to see from the lighted room into the darkness of the hothouse.

On the mantelpiece stood a large unframed photograph of Mr. Mannering. His nephew soon caught sight of this, and strode across to confront it with a triumphant and insolent sneer. "What? You old Pharisee!" said he. "Taken her off for a trip to Brighton, have you? My god! How I hope you'll never come back! How I hope you've fallen over the cliffs, or got swept off by the tide or something! Anyway—I'll make hay while the sun shines. Ugh! you old skinflint, you!" And he reached forward his hand, and bestowed a contemptuous fillip upon the nose in the photograph. Then the usurping rascal left the room, leaving all the lights on, presumably preferring the dining room with it cellarette to the scholarly austerities of the study.

All night long the glare of electric light from the study fell full upon Mr. Mannering and his Cousin Jane, like the glare of a cheap and artificial sun. You who have seen at midnight in the park a few insomniac asters standing stiff and startled under an arc light, all their weak color bleached out of them by the drenching chemical radiance, neither asleep nor awake, but held fast in a tense, a neurasthenic trance, you can form an idea of how the night passed with this unhappy pair.

And, toward morning, an incident occurred, trivial in itself, no doubt, but sufficient then and there to add the last drop to poor Cousin Jane's discomfiture and to her relative's embarrassment and remorse. Along the edge of the great earthbox in which the orchid was planted, ran a small black mouse. It had wicked red eyes, a naked, evil snout, and huge, repellent ears, queer as a bat's. This creature ran straight over the lower leaves of Cousin Jane's part of the plant. It was simply appalling. The stringy main stem writhed like a hair on a coal-fire, the leaves contracted in an agonized spasm, like seared mimosa; the terrified lady nearly uprooted herself in her convulsive horror. I think she would actually have done so, had not the mouse hurried on past her.

But it had not gone more than a foot or so when it looked up and saw, bending over it, and seeming positively to bristle with life, that flower which had once been called Tib. There was a breathless pause. The mouse was obviously paralyzed with terror, the cat could only look and long. Suddenly the more human watchers saw a sly frond of foliage curve softly outward and close in behind the hypnotized creature. Cousin Jane, who had been thinking exultantly, "Well, now it'll go away and never, never, never come back," suddenly became aware of hideous possibilities. Summoning all her energy, she achieved a spasmodic flutter, enough to break the trance that held the mouse, so that, like a clockwork toy, it swung round and fled. But already the fell arm of the orchid had cut off its retreat. The mouse leaped straight at it. Like a flash, five tendrils at the end caught the fugitive and held it fast, and soon its body dwindled and was gone. Now, the heart of Cousin Jane was troubled with horrid fears, and, slowly and painfully, she turned her weary face first to one side, then to the other, in a fever of anxiety as to where the new bud would appear. A sort of sucker, green and sappy, which twisted lightly about her main stem, and reared a blunt head, much like a tip of asparagus, close to her own, suddenly began to swell in the most suspicious manner. She squinted at it, fascinated and appalled. Could it be her imagination? It was not.

Next evening, the door opened again, and again the nephew entered the study. This time he was alone, and it was evident that he had come straight from table. He carried in his hand a decanter of whiskey capped by an inverted glass. Under his arm was a siphon. His face was distinctly flushed, and such a smile as is often seen in saloon bars played about his lips. He put down his burdens and, turning to Mr. Mannering's cigar cabinet, produced a bunch of keys, which he proceeded to try upon the lock, muttering vindictively at each abortive attempt, until it opened, when he helped himself from the best of its contents. Annoying as it was to witness this insolent appropriation of his property, and mortifying to see the contempt with which the cigar was smoked, the good gentleman found deeper cause for uneasiness in the thought that, with the possession of the keys, his abominable nephew had access to every private corner that was his.

At present, however, the usurper seemed indisposed to carry on investigations; he splashed a great deal of whiskey into the tumbler and relaxed into an attitude of extravagant comfort. But after a while the young man began to tire of his own company. He had not yet had time to gather any of his pothouse companions into his uncle's home, and repeated recourse to the whiskey bottle only increased his longing for something to relieve the monotony. His eye fell upon the door of the orchid-house. Sooner or later it was bound to have happened. Does this thought greatly console the condemned man when the fatal knock sounds upon the door of his cell? No. Nor were the hearts of the trembling pair in the hothouse at all comforted by the reflection.

As the nephew fumbled with the handle of the glass door, Cousin Jane slowly raised two fronds of leaves that grew on each side, high up on her stem, and sank her troubled head behind them. Mr. Mannering observed, in a sudden rapture of hope, that by this device she was fairly well concealed from any casual glance. Hastily he strove to follow her example. Unfortunately, he had not yet gained sufficient control of his—his *limbs?*—and all his tortured efforts could not raise them beyond an agonized horizontal. The door had opened, the nephew was feeling for the electric light switch just inside. It was a moment for one of the superlative achievements of panic. Mr. Mannering was well equipped for the occasion. Suddenly, at the cost of indescribable effort, he succeeded in raising the right frond, not straight upwards, it is true, but in a series of painful jerks along a curve outward and backward, and ascending by slow degrees till it attained the position of an arm held over the possessor's head from behind. Then, as the light flashed on, a spray of leaves at the very end of this frond spread out into a fan, rather like a very fleshy horse-chestnut leaf in structure, and covered the anxious face below. What a relief! And now the nephew advanced into the orchid-house, and now the hidden pair simultaneously remembered the fatal presence of the cat. Simultaneously, also, their very sap stood still in their veins. The nephew was walking along by the plant. The cat, a sagacious beast, "knew" with the infallible intuition of its kind that this was an idler, a parasite, a sensualist, gross and brutal, disrespectful to age, insolent to weakness, barbarous to cats. Therefore it remained very still, trusting to its low and somewhat retired position on the plant, and to protective mimicry and such things, and to the half-drunken condition of the nephew, to avoid his notice. But all in vain.

"What?" said the nephew. "What, a cat?" And he raised his hand to offer a blow at the harmless creature. Something in the dignified and unflinching demeanor of his victim must have penetrated into his besotted mind, for the blow never fell, and the bully, a coward at heart, as bullies invariably are, shifted his gaze from side to side to escape the steady, contemptuous stare of the courageous cat. Alas! His eye fell on something glimmering whitely behind the dark foliage. He brushed aside the intervening leaves that he might see what it was. It was Cousin Jane.

"Oh! Ah!" said the young man, in great confusion. *"You're* back. But what are you hiding there for?"

His sheepish stare became fixed, his mouth opened in bewilderment; then the true condition of things dawned upon his mind. Most of us would have at once instituted some attempt at communication, or at assistance of some kind, or at least have knelt down to thank our Creator that we had, by His grace, been spared such a fate, or perhaps have made haste from the orchid-house to ensure against accidents. But alcohol had so inflamed the young man's hardened nature that he felt neither fear, nor awe, nor gratitude. As he grasped the situation a devilish smile overspread his face.

"Ha! Ha! Ha!" said he. "But where's the old man?"

He peered about the plant, looking eagerly for his uncle. In a moment he had located him and, raising the inadequate visor of leaves, discovered beneath it the face of our hero, troubled with a hundred bitter emotions.

"Hullo, Narcissus!" said the nephew.

A long silence ensued. The spiteful wretch was so pleased that he could not say a word. He rubbed his hands together, and licked his lips, and stared and stared as a child might at a new toy.

"Well, you're properly up a tree," he said. "Yes, the tables are turned now all right, aren't they? Do you remember the last time we met?"

A flicker of emotion passed over the face of the suffering blossom, betraying consciousness.

"Yes, you can hear what I say," added the tormentor. "Feel, too, I expect. What about that?"

As he spoke, he stretched out his hand and, seizing a delicate frill of fine, silvery filaments that grew as whiskers grow around the lower half of the flower, he administered a sharp tug. Without pausing to note, even in the interests of science, the subtler shades of his uncle's reaction, content with the general effect of that devastating wince, the wretch chuckled with satisfaction and, taking a long pull from the reeking butt of the stolen cigar, puffed the vile fumes straight into his victim's center. The brute!

"How do you like that, John the Baptist?" he asked with a leer. "Good for the blight, you know. Just what you want!"

Something rustled upon his coat sleeve. Looking down, he saw a long stalk, well adorned with the fatal tendrils, groping its way over the arid and unsatisfactory surface. In a moment, it had reached his wrist; he felt it fasten, but knocked it off as one would a leech, before it had time to establish its hold.

"Ugh!" said he. "So that's how it happens, is it? I think I'll keep outside till I get the hang of things a bit. I don't want to be made an Aunt Sally of. Though I shouldn't think they could get you with your clothes on." Struck by a sudden thought, he looked from his uncle to Cousin Jane, and from Cousin Jane back to his uncle again. He scanned the floor, and saw a single crumpled bathrobe lying in the shadow.

"Why!" he said. *"Well!*—Haw! Haw! Haw!" And, with an odious backward leer, he made his way out of the orchid-house.

Mr. Mannering felt that his suffering was capable of no increase. Yet he dreaded the morrow. His fevered imagination patterned the long night with waking nightmares, utterly fantastic visions of humiliation and torture. Torture! It was absurd, of course, for him to fear cold-blooded atrocities on the part of his nephew, but how he dreaded some outrageous whim that might tickle the youth's sense of humor, and lead him to *any* wanton freak, especially if he were drunk at the time. He thought of slugs and snails, espaliers and topiary. If only the monster would rest content with insulting jests, with wasting his substance, ravaging his cherished possessions before his eyes, with occasional pulling at the whiskers, even! Then it might be possible to turn gradually from all that still remained in him of man, to subdue the passions, no longer to admire or desire, to go native, as it were, relapsing into the Nirvana of a vegetable dream. But in the morning he found this was not so easy.

In came the nephew and, pausing only to utter the most perfunctory of jeers at his relatives in the glass house, he sat at the desk and unlocked the top drawer. He was evidently in search of money; his eagerness betrayed it. No doubt he had run through all he had filched from his uncle's pockets, and had not yet worked out a scheme for getting direct control of his bank account. However, the drawer held enough to cause the scoundrel to rub his hands with satisfaction, and, summoning the housekeeper, to bellow into her ear a reckless order upon the wine and spirit merchant.

"Get along with you!" he shouted, when he had at last made her understand. "I shall have to get someone a bit more on the spot to wait on me; I can tell you that. Yes," he added to himself as the poor old woman hobbled away, deeply hurt by his bullying manner, "yes, a nice little parlor-maid."

He hunted in the telephone book for the number of the local registry office. That afternoon, he interviewed a succession of maidservants in his uncle's study. Those that happened to be plain, or too obviously respectable, he treated curtly and coldly; they soon made way for others. It was only when a girl was attractive (according to the young man's depraved tastes, that is) and also bore herself in a fast or brazen manner, that the interview was at all prolonged. In these cases, the nephew would conclude in a fashion that left no doubt in the minds of any of his auditors as to his real intentions. Once, for example, leaning forward, he took the girl by the chin, saying with an odious smirk, "There's no one else but me, and so you'd be treated just like one of the family, d'you see, my dear?" To another, he would say, slipping his arm round her waist, "Do you think we shall get on well together?"

After this conduct had sent two or three in confusion from the room, there entered a young person of the most regrettable description; one whose character, betrayed as it was in her meretricious finery, her crude cosmetics, and her tinted hair, showed yet more clearly in florid gesture and too facile smile. The nephew lost no time in coming to an arrangement with this creature. Indeed, her true nature was so obvious that the depraved young man only went through the farce of an ordinary interview as a sauce to his anticipations, enjoying the contrast between conventional dialogue and unbridled glances. She was to come next day. Mr. Mannering feared more for his unhappy cousin than for himself. "What scenes may she not have to witness," he thought, "that yellow cheek of hers to incarnadine?" If only he could have said a few words!

But, that evening, when the nephew came to take his ease in the study, it was obvious that he was far more under the influence of liquor than he had been before. His face, flushed patchily by the action of the spirits, wore a sullen sneer; an ominous light burned in that bleared eye; he muttered savagely under his breath. Clearly, this fiend in human shape was what is known as "fighting drunk"; clearly, some trifle had set his vile temper in a blaze.

It is interesting to note, even at this stage, a sudden change in Mr. Mannering's reactions. They now seemed entirely egotistical, and were to be elicited only by stimuli directly associated with physical matters. The nephew kicked a hole in a screen in his drunken fury, he flung a burning cigar-end down on the carpet, he scratched matches on the polished table. His uncle witnessed this with the calm of one whose sense of property and of dignity has become numbed and paralyzed; he felt neither fury nor mortification. Had he, by one of those sudden strides by which all such development takes place, approached much nearer to his goal, complete vegetation? His concern for the threatened modesty of Cousin Jane, which had moved him so strongly only a few hours earlier, must have been the last dying flicker of exhausted altruism; that most human characteristic now had faded from him. The change, however, in its present stage, was not an unmixed blessing. Narrowing in from the wider and more expressly human regions of his being, his consciousness now left outside its focus not only pride and altruism, which had been responsible for much of his woe, but fortitude and detachment also, which, with quotations from the Greek, had been his support before the whole battery of his distresses. Moreover, within its constricted circle, his ego was not reduced, but concentrated; his serene, flower-like indifference toward the ill-usage of his furniture was balanced by the absorbed, flower-like single-mindedness of his terror at the thought of similar ill-usage directed toward himself.

Inside the study, the nephew still fumed and swore. On the

mantelpiece stood an envelope, addressed in Mr. Mannering's handwriting to Cousin Jane. In it was the letter he had written from town, describing his nephew's disgraceful conduct. The young man's eye fell upon this and, unscrupulous, impelled by idle curiosity, he took it up and drew out the letter. As he read, his face grew a hundred times blacker than before.

"What," he muttered, " 'a mere racecourse cad . . . a worthless vulgarian . . . a scoundrel of the sneaking sort' . . . and what's this? '. . . cut him off absolutely. . . .' What?" said he, with a horrifying oath. "*Would* you cut me off absolutely? Two can play at that game, you old devil!"

And he snatched up a large pair of scissors that lay on the desk, and burst into the hothouse—

Among fish, the dory, they say, screams when it is seized upon by man; among insects, the caterpillar of the death's-head moth is capable of a still, small shriek of terror; in the vegetable world, only the mandrake could voice its agony—till now.

ROMANCE LINGERS,
ADVENTURE LIVES

There is a great deal of devilry in a bright and windy midnight in the month of March. A little naked moon rides high over Fairlawn Avenue in the heart of the Sweetholme building development. The new houses are chalk-masked by its light, except for their darkened windows, which glare broodingly, like deep-set eyes, or the sockets of eyes. There are some young almond trees, which ordinarily look as if drawn by a childish hand. Now, as the wind sets their weak branches gibbering, they seem like shamanistic scratches on the white bone of the brittle bright night.

The wind causes a man to tuck his chin into his coat collar, to become a mere rag, curved against the wind. His bowler-hatted moon-shadow, apparently cut from a sheet of tin, scythes its way implacably through the asphalt, and seems the better man of the two, probably the real man, the genuine Mr. Watkins. Around the bend, just out of sight, comes another figure, bowler-hatted also, scythe-curved also, also chopping its way through the icy air. It might be the shadow of the shadow. It might be Death. It is, however, only Mr. Gosport.

The carriage from which he alighted out of the midnight train was the farthest from the station barrier. Also, his shoelace came undone. There is an explanation for everything, sometimes two explanations. These two explain why Mr. Gosport was a hundred yards or so behind Mr. Watkins.

Mr. Watkins, with his little grin slipped in like a scarfpin behind his upturned lapels, observed with a stare of desolate and hopeless superiority the monotony of the houses on Fairlawn Avenue. This was the vilest ingratitude, for the uniformity was due to the fact that each was the best possible house at the figure. Watkins, however, having drunk and sung away the Saturday evening in exclusively male company, was full of blood and villainy, intolerant of caution and incapable of gratitude. He decided that on Monday he would rob the bank at which he was employed, and fly to South America, where he would set up a seraglio.

How different were the thoughts of Mr. Gosport, as, out of sight, around the bend, he sheared his way into the wind and also regarded the monotony of Fairlawn Avenue! The good Gosport fully realized that each house was the best possible at the price; he knew that each chalky bump was a vertebra in the backbone of the country; he had read that the life of the little man was as full of romance and high adventure as that of any buccaneer of old; columnists had told him that the Fairlawn Avenues of the world are its very jewels, its necklaces of simple joys and sorrows, its rosaries in which each well-matched home is a pearl. The only trouble was, he had no great fondness for jewelry, and wished that he was dead. "I am unfit to appreciate the best of all possible lives in the best of all possible building developments," said he. "Tomorrow I will put my affairs in order, and be specially nice to Milly. On Monday I will go far away, to where there are trees larger than these little almond trees, and I will hang myself upon the branch of one of them."

Watkins, away ahead, roller-coastered in imagination over the curves of his future seraglio. He was brought to a halt by the appearance of a dim light behind a hall door. "Here we are," said he. He went up the little path and opened the door, and was at once received into the warmth of domesticity and greeted by the beauty of a three-piece hallway set of a pattern very popular on Fairlawn Avenue.

In a moment, the vigorous Watkins had hung hat and coat upon the peg, switched out the hall light, and was creeping up the stairs to bed.

Still out in the cold, still shearing with sensitive nose the arctic currents of the wind, Mr. Gosport passed the now darkened house. Four doors farther up, his watering eyes perceived a dim light behind a hall-door pane. "Here I am!" said he, with a sigh.

Upstairs in the first house, treading soft so as not to wake his sleeping wife, Watkins flung off his clothing, expanded his chest, scratched his rump, donned his pajamas, and slipped into the bed. His wife acknowledged his entry with a muted whinny.

Here were two human caterpillars, immobile in a cotton cocoon, awaiting the pupescence of sleep, the wings of dream.

There is, however, a great deal of devilry at midnight on a Saturday. What was the influence that drew the lady up from sleep like Sheba's queen from glowing Africa, and reclaimed the gentleman like Solomon from the contemplation of his seraglio? Was it that which had been moribund three years, or was it something totally different? It felt like something totally different.

Something very much the same—that is to say, something totally different—was happening at the very same time to Mr. Gosport.

Both couples slept late on Sunday morning, and when they woke the ladies did what they had not done since honeymoon days. That is to say, they rose smiling in the darkness of the curtained rooms, and hastened downstairs to prepare a morning cup of coffee.

Watkins, waking to full consciousness, heard the clink of the crockery below. He smiled, stretched, sniffed, expanded his chest, and with a coy smile abandoned himself to a warm flood of happiness. This, like a Gulf Stream, bore his thoughts away from South America and set the almonds all ablossoming on Fairlawn Avenue.

Watkins descended the stairs, and entered the little kitchen. There was the steaming coffee; there was a beloved figure in a fresh and flowery wrapper, bending over the gas stove. He bestowed a jovial but appreciative pinch, and took up the newspaper.

"How manly!" thought she.

At the same moment Mr. Gosport was descending the stairs, and in a similar mood. To him also was accorded the scent of new-made coffee, and the sight of a sweet figure in flowered wrapper bending over the stove. He bestowed a lingering and grateful kiss just where the hair twirls in little tendrils at the back of the neck, and took up the newspaper.

"How refined!" thought she.

"Hey, what's this?" said Mr. Watkins, when he had sipped his coffee, and skimmed smilingly over an account of a fugitive bank clerk being arrested at Southampton. "Hey, what's this? Where is the true detective story feature in this Sunday's *Telegram?*"

"That is not the *Telegram,*" said the lady, turning in surprise from the stove. "And you," said she on a rising note, "and you are not my husband."

With that she fell to the floor, in a faint of the third intensity. "I got into the wrong house last night," murmured Watkins. "I had better get off home."

He quickly assembled his clothes and left the house. On his way along the Avenue, he passed Mr. Gosport, with whom he was unacquainted. Each was too busy concocting an excuse for staying in town overnight, to take any notice of the other.

Mr. Watkins found Mrs. Watkins, and Mr. Gosport found Mrs. Gosport, highly agitated at the unaccountable absence of their husbands, and too relieved at their return to scrutinize very closely the likelihood of the excuses they made.

They each had a nice little cut of beef for their Sunday lunch, and after lunch they took a nap, while their wives looked out of the window. Their dreams were not unpleasant, and, when they woke, Fairlawn Avenue no longer seemed so monotonous as to justify resort to crime or suicide. How long this cheerful mood would have lasted without reinforcement it is impossible to say. Fortunately, Mrs. Gosport shortly afterwards made the acquaintance of Mrs. Watkins while seeking a strayed kitten, and the two families became the greatest of friends, and spent most of their evenings, their weekends, and their summer holidays together.

This happy relationship altogether banished monotony from Fairlawn Avenue, and it would have persisted to this day, had not a slight coolness arisen last spring owing to Mr. Gosport refusing Mr. Watkins the loan of his lawn mower.

BIRD OF PREY

The house they call the Engineer's House is now deserted. The new man from Baton Rouge gave it up after living less than a month in it, and built himself a two-room shack with his own money, on the very farthest corner of the company's land.

The roof of the Engineer's House has caved in, and most of the windows are broken. Oddly enough, no birds nest in the shelter of the eaves, or take advantage of the forsaken rooms. An empty house is normally fine harborage for rats and mice and bats, but there is no squeak or rustle or scamper to disturb the quiet of this one. Only creatures utterly foreign, utterly remote from the most distant cousinhood to man, only the termite, the tarantula, and the scorpion indifferently make it their home.

All in a few years Edna Spalding's garden has been wiped out, as if it had never existed. The porch where she and Jack sat so happily in the evenings is rotten under its load of wind-blown twigs and sand. A young tree has already burst up the boards outside the living room window, so that they fan out like the stiff fingers of someone who is afraid. In this corner there still stands a strongly made parrot's perch, the wood of which has been left untouched even by the termite and the boring beetle.

The Spaldings had brought a parrot with them when first they came. It was a sort of extra wedding present, given them at the last moment by Edna's mother. It was something from home for Edna to take into the wilds.

The parrot was already old, and he was called Tom, and, like other parrots, he sat on his perch, and whistled and laughed and uttered his few remarks, which were often very appropriate. Edna and Jack were both very fond of him, and they were overwhelmingly fond of each other. They liked their house, and the country, and Jack's colleagues, and everything in life seemed to be delightful.

One night they had just fallen asleep when they were awakened by a tremendous squawking and fluttering outside on the porch. "Oh, Jack!" cried Edna. "Get up! Hurry! Run! It's one of those cats from the men's camp has got hold of poor Tom!"

Jack sprang out of bed, but caught his foot in the sheet, and landed on his elbow on the floor. Between rubbing his elbow and disentangling his foot, he wasted a good many seconds before he was up again. Then he dashed through the living room and out upon the porch.

All this time, which seemed an age, the squawking and fluttering increased, but as he flung open the door it ceased as suddenly as it had begun. The whole porch was bathed in the brightest moonlight, and at the farther end the perch was clearly visible, and on the floor beneath it was poor old Tom parrot, gasping amid a litter of his own feathers, and crying, "Oh! Oh! Oh!"

At any rate, he was alive. Jack looked right and left for traces of his assailant, and at once noticed the long, heavy trailers of the trumpet vine were swinging violently, although there was not a breath of wind. He went to the rail and looked out and around, but there was no sign of a cat. Of course, it was not likely there would be. Jack was more interested in the fact that the swaying vines were spread over a length of several feet, which seemed a very great deal of disturbance for a fleeing cat to make. Finally, he looked up, and he thought he saw a bird—a big bird, an enormous bird—flying away. He just caught a glimpse of it as it crossed the brightness of the moon.

He turned back and picked up old Tom. The poor parrot's chain was broken, and his heart was pounding away like mad, and still, like a creature hurt and shocked beyond all endurance, he cried, "Oh! Oh! Oh!"

This was all the more odd, for it was seldom the old fellow came out with a new phrase, and Jack would have laughed heartily, except it sounded too pathetic. So he carefully examined the poor bird, and, finding no injury beyond the loss of a handful of feathers from his neck, he replaced him on the perch, and turned to reassure Edna, who now appeared in the doorway.

"Is he dead?" cried she.

"No," said Jack. "He's had a bit of shock, though. Something got hold of him."

"I'll bring him a piece of sugar," said Edna. "That's what he loves. That'll make him feel better."

She soon brought the sugar, which Tom took in his claw, but though usually he would nibble it up with the greatest avidity, this time he turned his lackluster eye only once upon it, and gave a short, bitter, despairing sort of laugh, and let it fall to the ground.

"Let him rest," said Jack. "He has had a bad tousling."

"It was a cat," said Edna. "It was one of those beastly cats the men have at the camp."

"Maybe," said Jack. "On the other hand—I don't know. I thought I saw an enormous bird flying away."

"It couldn't be an eagle," said Edna. "There are none ever seen here."

"I know," said Jack. "Besides, they don't fly at night. Nor do the buzzards. It might have been an owl, I suppose. But—"

"But what?" said Edna.

"But it looked very much larger than an owl," said Jack.

"It was your fancy," said Edna. "It was one of those beastly cats that did it."

This point was discussed very frequently during the next few days. Everybody was consulted, and everybody had an opinion. Jack might have been a little doubtful at first, for he had caught only the briefest glimpse as the creature crossed the moon, but opposition made him more certain, and the discussions sometimes got rather heated.

"Charlie says it was all your imagination," said Edna. "He says no owl would ever attack a parrot."

"How the devil does *he* know?" said Jack. "Besides, I said it was bigger than an owl."

"He says that shows you imagine things," said Edna.

"Perhaps he would like me to think I do," said Jack. "Perhaps you both would."

"Oh, Jack!" cried Edna. She was deeply hurt, and not without reason, for it showed that Jack was still thinking of a ridiculous mistake he had made, a real mistake, of the sort that young husbands sometimes do make, when they come suddenly into a room and people are startled without any real reason for it. Charlie was young and free and easy and good-looking, and he would put his hand on your shoulder without even thinking about it, and nobody minded.

"I should not have said that," said Jack.

"No, indeed you shouldn't," said Edna, and she was right.

The parrot said nothing at all. All these days, he had been moping and ailing, and seemed to have forgotten even how to ask for sugar. He only groaned and moaned to himself, ruffled up his feathers, and every now and then shook his head in the most rueful, miserable way you can possibly imagine.

One day, however, when Jack came home from work, Edna put

her finger to her lips and beckoned him to the window. "Watch Tom," she whispered.

Jack peered out. There was the old bird, lugubriously climbing down from his perch and picking some dead stalks from the vine, which he carried up till he gained a corner where the balustrade ran into the wall, and added his gatherings to others that were already there. He trod round and round, twisted his stalks in and out, and, always with the same doleful expression, paid great attention to the nice disposition of a feather or two, a piece of wool, a fragment of cellophane. There was no doubt about it.

"There's no doubt about it," said Jack.

"He's making a nest!" cried Edna.

"He!" cried Jack. *"He!* I like that. The old impostor! The old male impersonator! She's going to lay an egg. Thomasina—that's her name from now on."

Thomasina it was. Two or three days later the matter was settled beyond the shadow of a doubt. There, one morning, in the ramshackle nest, was an egg.

"I thought she was sick because of that shaking she got," said Jack. "She was broody, that's all."

"It's a monstrous egg," said Edna. "Poor birdie!"

"What do you expect, after God knows how many years?" said Jack, laughing. "Some birds lay eggs nearly as big as themselves—the kiwi or something. Still, I must admit it's a whopper."

"She doesn't look well," said Edna.

Indeed, the old parrot looked almost as sick as a parrot can be, which is several times sicker than any other living creature. Her eyes closed up, her head sank, and if a finger was put out to scratch her she turned her beak miserably away. However, she sat conscientiously on the prodigious egg she had laid, though every day she seemed a little feebler than before.

"Perhaps we ought to take the egg away," said Jack. "We could get it blown, and keep it as a memento."

"No," said Edna. "Let her have it. It's all she's had in all these years."

Here Edna made a mistake, and she realized it a few mornings later. "Jack," she called. "Do come. It's Tom—Thomasina, I mean. I'm afraid she's going to die."

"We ought to have taken the egg away," said Jack, coming out with his mouth full of breakfast. "She's exhausted herself. It's no good, anyway. It's bound to be sterile."

"Look at her!" cried Edna.

"She's done for," said Jack, and at that moment the poor old bird keeled over and gasped her last.

"The egg killed her," said Jack, picking it up. "I said it would. Do you want to keep it? Oh, good lord!" He put the egg down very quickly. "It's alive," he said.

"What?" said Edna. "What do you mean?"

"It gave me a turn," said Jack. "It's most extraordinary. It's against nature. There's a chick inside that egg, tapping."

"Let it out," said Edna. "Break the shell."

"I was right," said Jack. "It *was* a bird I saw. It must have been a stray parrot. Only it looked so big."

"I'm going to break the shell with a spoon," said Edna, running to fetch one.

"It'll be a lucky bird," said Jack when she returned. "Born with a silver spoon in its beak, so to speak. Be careful."

"I will," said Edna. "Oh, I do hope it lives!"

With that, she gingerly cracked the shell, the tapping increased, and soon they saw a well-developed beak tearing its way through. In another moment, the chick was born.

"Golly!" cried Jack. "What a monster!"

"It's because it's young," said Edna. "It'll grow lovely. Like its mother."

"Maybe," said Jack. "I must be off. Put it in the nest. Feed it pap. Keep it warm. Don't monkey with it too much. Good-bye, my love."

That morning Jack telephoned home two or three times to find out how the chick was, and if it ate. He rushed home at lunchtime. In the evening everyone came round to peep at the nestling and offer advice.

Charlie was there. "It ought to be fed every hour at least," said he. "That's how it is in nature."

"He's right," said Jack. "For the first month, at least, that's how it should be."

"It looks as if I'm going to be tied down a bit," said Edna ruefully.

"I'll look in when I pass and relieve your solitude," said Charlie.

"I'll manage to rush home now and then in the afternoons," said Jack, a little too thoughtfully.

Certainly, the hourly feeding seemed to agree with the chick, which grew at an almost alarming speed. It became covered with down, feathers sprouted; in a few months it was fully grown, and not in the least like its mother. For one thing, it was coal-black.

"It must be a hybrid," said Jack. "There *is* a black parrot; I've seen them in zoos. They didn't look much like this, though. I've half a mind to send a photograph of him somewhere."

"He looks so wicked," said Edna.

"He looks cunning," said Jack. "That bird knows everything, believe me. I bet he'll talk soon."

"It gave a sort of laugh," said Edna. "I forgot to tell you."

"When?" cried Jack. "A laugh?"

"Sort of," said Edna. "But it was horrible. It made Charlie nearly jump out of his skin."

"Charlie?" cried Jack. "You didn't say he'd been here."

"Well, you know how often he drops in," said Edna.

"Do I?" said Jack. "I hope I do. God! What was that?"

"That's what I meant," said Edna. "A sort of laugh."

"What a horrible sound!" said Jack.

"Listen, Jack," said Edna. "I wish you wouldn't be silly about Charlie. You are, you know."

Jack looked at her. "I know I am," said he. "I know it when I look at you. And then I think I never will be again. But somehow it's got stuck in my mind, and the least little thing brings it on. Maybe I'm just a bit crazy, on that one subject."

"Well, he'll be transferred soon," said Edna. "And that'll be the end of it."

"Where did you hear that?" said Jack.

"He told me this afternoon," said Edna. "He was on his way back from getting the mail when he dropped in. That's why he told me first. Otherwise he'd have told you first. Only he hasn't seen you yet. Do you see?"

"Yes, I see," said Jack. "I wish I could be psychoanalyzed or something."

Soon Charlie made his farewells, and departed for his job on the company's other project. Edna was secretly glad to see him go. She wanted no problems, however groundless, to exist between herself and Jack. A few days later she felt sure that all the problems were solved forever.

"Jack," said she when he came home in the evening.

"Yes," said he.

"Something new," said she. "Don't play with that bird. Listen to me."

"Call him Polly," said Jack. They had named it Polly to be on the safe side. "You don't want to call him 'that bird.' The missus doesn't love you, Poll."

"Do you know, I don't!" said Edna, with quite startling vehemence. "I don't like him at all, Jack. Let's give him away."

"What? For heaven's sake!" cried Jack. "This rare, black, specially hatched Poll? This parrot of romantic origin? The cleverest Poll that ever—"

"That's it," said Edna. "He's too darned clever. Jack, I hate him. He's horrible."

"What? Has he said something you don't like?" said Jack, laughing. "I bet he will, when he talks. But what's the news, anyway?"

"Come inside," said Edna. "I'm not going to tell you with that creature listening." She led the way into the bedroom. "The news is," said she, "that I've got to be humored. And if I don't like anything, it's got to be given away. It's not going to be born with a beak because its mother was frightened by a hateful monstrosity of a parrot."

"What?" said Jack.

"That's what," said Edna, smiling and nodding.

"A brat?" cried Jack in delight. "A boy! Or a girl! It's bound to be one or the other. Listen, I was afraid to tell you how much I wanted one, Edna. Oh, boy! This is going to make everything very, very fine. Lie down. You're delicate. Put your feet up. I'm going to fix dinner. This is practice. Stay still. Oh, boy! Oh, boy! Or girl, as the case may be!"

He went out through the living room on his way to the kitchen. As he passed the window, he caught sight of the parrot on the dark porch outside, and he put his head through to speak to it.

"Have you heard the news?" said he. "Behold a father! You're going to be cut right out, my bird. You're going to be given away. Yes, sir, it's a baby."

The parrot gave a long low whistle. "You don't say so?" said he in a husky voice, a voice of apprehension, a quite astonishing imitation of Charlie's voice. "What about Jack?"

"What's that?" said Jack, startled.

"He'll think it's his," whispered the parrot in Edna's voice. "He's fool enough for anything. Phew-w-w! You don't say so? What about Jack? He'll think it's his, he's fool enough for anything."

Jack went out into the kitchen, and sat down with his head in his hands for several minutes.

"Hurry up!" cried Edna from the bedroom. "Hurry up—*Father!*"

"I'm coming," said Jack.

He went to his desk, and took out the revolver. Then he went into the bedroom.

At the sound of the cry and the shot, the parrot laughed. Then, lifting its claw, it took the chain in its beak, and bit through it as if it were paper.

Jack came out, holding the gun, his hand over his eyes. "Fool enough for anything!" said the parrot, and laughed.

Jack turned the gun on himself. As he did so, in the infinitesimal interval between the beginning and the end of the movement of his finger on the trigger, he saw the bird grow, spread its dark wings, and its eyes flamed, and it changed, and it launched itself toward him.

The gun went off. Jack dropped to the floor. The parrot, or whatever it was, sailing down, seized what came out of his ruined mouth, and wheeled back through the window, and was soon far away, visible for a moment only as it swept on broader wings past the new-risen moon.

Variation on a Theme

A young man, with a bowler hat, cane, flaxen moustache, and blue suit, was looking at a gorilla in the zoo. All about him were cages floored with squares of desert. On these yellow flats, like precise false statements of equatorial latitudes, lay the shadows of bars. There were nutshells, banana skins, fading lettuce; there were the cries of birds who believed themselves mewed up because they were mad; obeisances of giraffes, the yawns of lions. On an imitation of moon crags, mountain goats bore about ignobly eyes that were pieces of moon. The elephants, gray in a humidity of grass and dung, shifted from one foot to another. Jurassic days, it seemed, would quite definitely never be here again. Mice, moving with the speed of a nervous twitch, were bold in the freedom of a catastrophe of values.

Perceiving that they were alone, the gorilla addressed the young man in an imitation of the American accent, which he affected for reasons of his own. "Pal, you look a decent sort of guy. Get me a suit like yours, only larger, a derby hat, and a cane. I guess I can do without the moustache. I want to get out of here. I got ambitions."

The young man was greatly taken aback to hear a gorilla speak. However, common sense reminded him that he was in a city in which many creatures enjoyed that faculty, whom one would hardly credit, at first sight, or at any hearing, with sufficient intelligence to have attained it. He therefore recovered from his wonder, but, having a nice sense of distinctions, he replied to the gorilla, "I do not see that I can do that. The place for a gorilla is either a cage or the Congo. In the society of men, you would be like a fish out of water, a bull in a china shop, or a round peg in a square hole. You would be a cause of embarrassment, and would therefore yourself be embarrassed. You would be treated as an alien, disdained on account of your complexion, and slighted because of your facial angle."

The gorilla was very much mortified by this reply, for he was extremely vain. "Here," he said, "you don't want to say that sort of thing. I'm a writer. Write you anything you like. I've written a novel."

"That alters the situation entirely!" cried the young man with enthusiasm. "I am a novelist myself, and am always ready to lend a hand to a struggling fellow author. Tell me one thing only, and my services are yours. Have you genius?"

"Yes," said the gorilla, "I certainly have."

"In that case," said the young man, "I shall bring your suit, hat, cane, shoes, and body-linen at this hour tomorrow. I will also bring you a file, and you will find me awaiting you under the large chestnut tree by the West Gate, at the hour of dusk."

The gorilla had not expected the file. As a matter of fact, he had asked for the outfit, not for purposes of escape, but in order to cut a figure before the public. He was rather like one of those prisoners who wrote from old Spain, and who were more interested in what they got in than in how they got out. However, he hated to waste anything, so, having received the file, he put it to such use as enabled him to join his benefactor under the dark and summer tree.

The young man, intoxicated by his own good action, shook the gorilla warmly by the hand. "My dear fellow," said he, "I cannot say how glad I am to see you out here among us. I am sure you have written a great novel in there; all the same, bars are very dangerous to literary men in the long run. You will find my little house altogether more propitious to your genius. Don't think that we are too desperately dull, however; everyone drops in on Sundays, and during the week we have a little dinner or two, at which you will meet the sort of people you should know. By the way, I hope you have not forgotten your manuscript."

"Fella came snooping in just as I was making my getaway," said the gorilla. "So I had to dump it. See?" This was the most villainous lie in the world, for the unscrupulous ape had never written so much as a word.

"What a terrible pity!" cried the young man in dismay. "I suppose you feel you will have to return to it."

"Not me," said the gorilla, who had been watching some singularly handsome limousines pass the spot where they were standing, and had noticed the faultless complexions and attractive toilettes of the ladies whom these limousines were conveying from one party to another. "No," said he. "Never mind. I got the whole thing in my head. You put me up; I'll write it out all over again. So, don't worry."

"Upon my word, I admire your spirit!" cried his deliverer enthusiastically. "There is something uncommercial about that which appeals to me more than I can say. I am sure you are right; the work will be even more masterly for being written over again. A thousand little felicities, necessarily brushed aside in the first headlong torrent of creativeness, will now assert their claims. Your characters will appear, so to speak, more in the round than formerly. You will forget some little details, though of course you will invent others even more telling; very well, those that you forget will be the *real* shadows, which will impart this superior roundness to your characters. Oh, there is nothing like literature! You shall have a little study on the second floor—quiet, austere, but not uncomfortable— where you shall reconstruct your great work undisturbed. It will undoubtedly be the choice of the Book Society, and I really don't see why we should not hope for the Hawthornden as well."

By this time they were strolling along under the dozing trees, each of which was full-gorged with a large block of the day's heat, still undigested, and breathed spicily upon them as they passed below.

"We live quite near here," said the enthusiast. "My wife will be delighted to make your acquaintance. You two are going to be great friends. Here is the house. It is small, but luckily it is of just the right period, and, as you see, we have the finest wisteria in London." Saying this, he pushed open a little wooden gate, one of some half-dozen in a quiet cul-de-sac, which still preserved its Queen Anne serenity and charm. The gorilla, looking discontentedly at certain blocks of smart modern flats that towered up on either hand, said never a word.

The front garden was very small. It had flagstones, irises, and an amusing urn, overflowing with the smoldering red of geraniums, which burned in the velvet dark like the cigarette ends of the lesser gods.

"We have a larger patch behind," said the young man, "where there is a grass plot, nicotianas, and deck chairs in the shade of a fig tree. Come in, my dear fellow, come in! Joanna, where are you? Here is our new friend."

"I hope," said the gorilla in a low voice, "you ain't given her the lowdown on *you know what.*"

"No, no," whispered his host. "I have kept our little secret. A gentleman from Africa, I said—who has genius."

There was no time for more. Mrs. Grantly was descending the stairs. She was tall, with pale hair caught up in an unstudied knot behind, and a full-skirted gown which was artistic, but not unfashionable.

"This is Ernest Simpson," said her husband. "My dear, Mr. Simpson has written a book which is going to create more than a passing stir. Unfortunately, he has lost the manuscript, but—what do you think?—he has consented to stay with us while he rewrites it. He has it all in his head."

"How perfectly delightful!" cried Mrs. Grantly. "We live terribly simply here, I'm afraid, but at least you will be quiet. Will you wash your hands? There is a little supper waiting for us in the dining room."

The gorilla, not accustomed to being treated with so much consideration, took refuge in an almost sullen silence. During the meal, he spoke mostly in monosyllables, and devoured a prodigious number of bananas, and his hostess, with teeth and eyes respectively.

The young couple were as delighted by their visitor as children with a new toy. "He is unquestionably dynamic, original, and full of that true simplicity which is perhaps the clearest hallmark of genius," said the young man when they were in bed together. "Did you notice him with the bananas?"

Mrs. Grantly folded her husband in her arms, which were delightfully long and round. "It will be wonderful," she said. "How I look forward to the day when both your books are published! He must meet the Booles and the Terrys. What discussions you will have! How delightful life is to those who care for art!" They gave each other a score of kisses, talked of the days when first they had met, and fell happily asleep.

In the morning there was a fine breakfast, with fruit juice, cereals, bacon and mushrooms, and the morning papers. The gorilla was shown his little study; he tried the chairs and the sofa, and looked at himself in the glass.

"Do you think you will be happy here?" asked Mr. Grantly very anxiously. "Is the room conducive to the right mood, do you think? There are cigarettes in that box; there's a lavatory across the landing. If you'd care to try a pipe, I have a tobacco jar I'll send up here. What about the desk? Is there everything on it that you'll require?"

"I shall manage. I shall manage," said the gorilla, still looking at himself in the glass.

"If there's anything you want, don't hesitate to ring that bell," said his host. "I've told the maids that you are now one of the family. I'm in the front room on the floor below if you want me. Well, I suppose you are burning to get to work. Till lunchtime, then!" And, with that, he took his leave of the gorilla, who continued to stare at himself in the glass.

When he was tired of this, which was not for some time, he ate a few of the cigarettes, opened all the drawers, had a look up the chimney, estimated the value of the furniture, exposed his teeth very abominably, scratched, and finally flung himself on the sofa and began to make his plans.

He was of that nature which sets down every disinterested civility as a sign of weakness. Moreover, he regarded his host as a bum novelist as well as a milksop, for he had not heard a single word about percentages since he entered the house. "A washout! A highbrow!" he said. "A guy like that giving the handout to a guy like me, eh? We'll soon alter that. The question is, how?"

This gorilla wanted suits of a very light gray, pearl tiepins, a noticeable automobile, blondes, and the society of "the boys." Nevertheless, his vanity itself was greedy, and snatched at every crumb; he was unable to resist the young man's enthusiasm for his nonexistent novel, and, instead of seeking his fortune as a heavyweight pug, he convinced himself in good earnest that he was a writer, unjustly hindered by the patronage and fussing of a bloodsucking, so-called intellectual. He turned the pages of half the books in the bookcase to see the sort of thing he should do, but found it rather hard to make a start. "This goddam place stifles me," he said.

"What's your plot like?" said he to the young man, one day soon afterwards, when they were sitting in the shade of the fig tree.

Grantly was good enough to recite the whole of his plot. "It sounds very trifling," he said, "but of course a lot depends on the style."

"Style? Style, the Hell!" observed the gorilla with a toothy sneer.

"I thought you'd say that!" cried his entertainer. "No doubt you have all the vitality that I so consciously lack. I imagine your work as being very close to the mainsprings of life—the sultry passions, the crude lusts, the vital urges, the stark, the raw, the dynamic, the essentially fecund and primitive."

"That's it," said the gorilla.

"The sentence," continued the rhapsodist, "short to the point of curtness, attuned by a self-concealing art to the grunts, groans, and screams of women with great primeval paps, and men—"

"Sure," said the gorilla.

"They knock each other down," went on his admirer. "As they taste the salt blood flowing over their lips, or see the female form suddenly grow tender under the influence of innumerable uppercuts, right hooks, straight lefts, they become aware of another emotion—"

"Yes!" cried the gorilla with enthusiasm.

"And with a cry that is half a sob—"

"Attaboy!" cried the gorilla.

"They leap, clutch, grapple, and in an ecstasy that is half sheer bursting, burning, grinding, soul-shattering pain—"

The gorilla, unable to contain himself any longer, bit through the best branch of Mr. Grantly's fig tree. "You said it! That's my book, sir!" said he, with a mouthful of splinters.

I hate to have to record it: this gorilla then rushed into the house and seized his hostess in a grip of iron. "I'm in a creative mood," he muttered thickly.

Mrs. Grantly was not altogether free from hero-worship. She had taken her husband's word for it that the gorilla was a genius of the fiercest description. She admired both his complexion and his eyes, and she, too, observed that his grip was of iron.

At the same time, she was a young woman of exquisite refinement. "I can't help thinking of Dennis," said she. "I should hate to hurt him."

"Yeah?" cried the ill-bred anthropoid. "That poor fish? That ham writer? That bum artist? Don't you worry about him. I'll beat him up, baby! I'll—"

Mrs. Grantly interrupted him with some dignity. She was one of those truly noble women who would never dream of betraying their husbands, except at the bidding of a genuine passion, and with expressions of the most tender esteem.

"Let me go, Ernest," she said, with such an air as compelled the vain ape to obey her. This ape, like all vulgarians, was very sensitive to any hint that he appeared low. "You do not raise yourself in my opinion by disparaging Dennis," she continued. "It merely shows you are lacking in judgment, not only of men but of women."

"Aw, cut it out, Joanna," begged the humiliated gorilla. "See here: I only forgot myself. You know what we geniuses are!"

"If you were not a genius," said Joanna, "I should have you turned out of the house. As it is—you shall have another chance."

The gorilla had not the spirit to interpret these last words as liberally as some of us might. Perhaps it was because he had lived so long behind bars, but they fell upon his ear as upon that of some brutalized coward snuffling in the dock. The timid husky saw no invitation in Mrs. Grantly's smile, and he was panic-stricken at the thought of losing his snug quarters.

"Say, you won't split on me, sister?" he muttered.

"No, no," said Mrs. Grantly. "One takes the commonsense view of these trifles. But you must behave more nicely in future."

"Sure," said he, much relieved. "I'll start in working right now."

He went straightaway up to his room, looked at himself in the glass, and thus, oddly enough, recovered his damaged self-esteem. "I'll show them," said he. "What did that poor worm say? 'Leap—clutch—grapple. . . .' Oh, boy! Oh, boy! This book's goin' to sell like hot cakes."

He scribbled away like the very devil. His handwriting was atrocious, but what of that? His style was not the best in the world, but he was writing about life in the raw. A succession of iron grips, such as the one he had been forced to loosen, of violent consummations, interruptions, beatings-up, flowed from his pen, interspersed with some bitter attacks on effete civilization and many eulogies of the primitive.

"This'll make 'em sit up," said he. "This'll go big."

When he went down to supper, he noticed some little chilliness in Mrs. Grantly's demeanor. This was no doubt due to his cowardly behavior in the afternoon. He trusted no one, and now became damnably afraid she would report his conduct to her husband; consequently, he was the more eager to get his book done, so that he should be independent and in a position to revenge himself. He went upstairs immediately after the meal, and toiled away till past midnight, pouring it out like one who confesses to a Sunday newspaper.

Before many days had passed in this fashion, he was drawing near the end of his work, when the Grantlys announced to him, with all the appearance of repressed excitement, that the best-selling of all novelists was coming to dine with them. The gorilla looked forward to the evening with equal eagerness; he urgently desired to pick up a tip or two.

The great man arrived; his limousine was sufficiently resplendent. The big ape eyed him with the very greatest respect all through the meal. Afterwards they sat about and took coffee, just as ordinary people do. "I hear," said the Best-Seller to Grantly, "that you are just finishing a novel."

"Oh, a poor thing!" said the good-natured fellow. "Simpson, here, is the man who's going to set the Thames on fire; I fear my stuff is altogether too niggling. It is a sort of social satire. I touch a little on the Church, War, Peace, Fascism, Communism—one or two things of that sort, but hardly in a full-blooded fashion. I wish I could write something more primitive—fecund women, the urge of lust, blood hatred, all that, you know."

"Good heavens, my dear Grantly!" cried the great man. "This comes of living so far out of the world. You really must move to some place more central. Public taste is on the change. I can assure you that before your book can be printed, Mr. P——" (he mentioned the critic who makes or breaks) "will no longer be engaged, but married, and to a young woman of Junoesque proportions. What chance do you think the urge of lust will have with poor P—, after a month of his marriage to this magnificently proportioned young woman? No, no, my boy, stick to social satire. Put a little in about feminism, if you can find room for it. Guy the cult of the he-man, and its effect on deluded women, and you're safe for a record review. You'll be made."

"I've got something of that sort in it," said Grantly with much gratification, for authors are like beds—even the most artistic requires to be made.

"Who's doing the book for you?" continued his benevolent mentor. "You must let me give you a letter to my publisher. Nothing is more disheartening than hawking a book round the market and having it returned unread. But my Barrabas is good enough to set some weight on my judgment; in fact, I think I may say, without boasting, you can look on the matter as settled."

"Say, you might give me a letter, too!" cried the gorilla, who had been listening in consternation to the great man's discourse.

"I should be delighted, Mr. Simpson," returned that worthy with great suavity. "But you know what these publishers are. Pigheaded isn't the word for them. Well, Grantly, I must be getting along. A delightful evening! Mrs. Grantly," said he, slapping his host on the shoulder, "this is the man who is going to make us old fossils sit up. Take care of him. Give him some more of that delicious zabaglione. Good night! Good night!"

The gorilla was tremendously impressed by the great man's manner, his confidence, his pronouncements, his spectacles, his limousine, and, above all, by the snub he had given him, for such creatures are always impressed by that sort of thing. "That guy knows the works," he murmured in dismay. "Say, I been barking up the wrong tree! I oughta gone in for *style*."

The Grantlys returned from the hall, where they had accompanied their visitor, and it was obvious from their faces that they, too, placed great reliance on what they had heard. I am not sure that Mr. Grantly did not rub his hands.

"Upon my word!" he said. "It certainly sounds likely enough. Have you seen poor P—'s fiancée? His views will certainly change. Ha! Ha! Supposing, my dear, I became a best seller?"

"It's terribly exciting!" cried Joanna. "Will it change your idea of going on a cruise when first the book comes out?"

"No, no," said he. "I think an author should detach himself from that side, however gratifyingly it may develop. I want to know nothing of the book from the moment it appears until it is forgotten."

"What? You going to spend a coupla days at Brighton?" struck in the gorilla bitterly.

"Ha! Ha! What a satirist you would make!" cried Grantly with the greatest good nature. "No. We thought of going for a trip round the world. I agree a shorter absence would outlast whatever stir the book may make; however, we want to see the sights."

The gorilla wrote never a word that night. He was overcome with mortification. He could not bear to think of the Grantlys sailing around the world, while the book he had despised piled up enormous royalties at home. Still less could he bear the thought of staying behind, left without a patron, and with his own book piling up no royalties at all. He saw a species of insult in his host's "striking gold," as he termed it, and then turning his back on it in this fashion.

"That guy don't *deserve* the boodle!" he cried in anguish of spirit. In fact, he uttered this sentiment so very often during the night that, in the end, an idea was born of its mere repetition.

During the next few days, he hastily and carelessly finished his own masterpiece, to have it ready against the *coup* he planned. In a word, this vile ape had resolved to change the manuscripts. He had alternative title pages, on which the names of the authors were transposed, typed in readiness. When, at last, the good Grantly announced the same; the two parcels were done up on the same evening, and the plotter was insistent in his offers to take them to the post.

Grantly was the more willing to permit this, as he and his wife were already busy with preparations for their departure. Shortly afterwards, they took their farewell of the gorilla, and, pressing into his hand a tidy sum to meet his immediate necessities, they wished his book every success, and advised that his next should be a satire.

The cunning ape bade them enjoy themselves, and took up his quarters in Bloomsbury, where he shortly had the pleasure of receiving a letter from the publishers to say that they were accepting the satirical novel which he had sent them.

He now gave himself airs as a writer, and got all the publicity he could. On one occasion, however, he was at a party, where he beheld a woman of Junoesque proportions in the company of a bilious weakling. The party was a wild one, and he had no scruples about seizing her in a grip of iron, regardless of the fury of her companion. This incident made little impression on his memory, for he attended a great many Bloomsbury parties.

All the same, nothing is entirely unimportant. It so happened that the bilious weakling was no other than P—, the greatest of critics, and the Junoesque lady was his promised spouse. The critic reviewed her behavior very bitterly, the engagement was broken off, and you may be sure he noted the name of the author of his misfortunes.

Very well, the two books came out: Grantly's, which the gorilla had stolen, and the gorilla's own raw outpourings, which now appeared under the name of Dennis Grantly. By a coincidence they appeared on the same day. The gorilla opened the most influential of the Sunday newspapers, and saw the stimulating headline, "Book of the Century."

"That's me!" said he, smacking his lips, and, fixing a hungry gaze on the letterpress, he discovered to his horror that it actually was. The critic, still a celibate, and by now an embittered one also, had selected the anthropoid's original tough stuff as being "raw, revealing, sometimes dangerously frank, at all times a masterpiece of insight and passion." Farther down, in fact at the very bottom of the column, the stolen satire was dismissed in two words only— "unreadably dull."

As if this misfortune was not sufficient, the next day, when the poor gorilla was leaving his lodgings, a young man in a black shirt tapped him on the shoulder and asked him if he was Mr. Simpson. The gorilla replying in the affirmative, the black shirt introduced him to a dozen or so friends of his, similarly attired and armed with blackjacks and knuckle-dusters. It appeared that these young gentlemen disapproved of certain references Grantly had made to their association, and had decided to give the wretched Simpson a beating-up by way of acknowledgment.

The gorilla fought like a demon, but was overpowered by numbers. In the end he was battered insensible and left lying in the mews where the ceremony had taken place. It was not until the next morning that he was able to drag himself home. When he arrived there, he found a bevy of lawyers' clerks and policemen inquiring for him. It appeared that Dennis, for all his delicacy and restraint, had been guilty of blasphemy, ordinary libel, criminal libel, sedition, and other things, in his references to the State, the Church, and so forth. "Who would have thought," the gorilla moaned bitterly, "there was all that in a little bit of style?"

During the various trials, he sat in a sullen silence, caring only to look at the newspapers, which contained advertisements of the book he had substituted for Grantly's. When the sales passed a hundred thousand, he became violent, and insulted the judge. When they reached double that figure, he made a despairing attempt at confession, but this was put down as a clumsy simulation of insanity. In the end his sentences amounted to a book in themselves, and were issued in serial form. He was carted off, and put behind the bars.

"All this," said he, "comes of wanting a suit of clothes for the public to see me in. I've got the clothes, but I don't like them, and the public aren't allowed in, anyway." This gave him a positive hatred of literature, and one who hates literature, and is, moreover, in prison for an interminable period of years, is in a truly miserable condition.

As for Dennis Grantly: by the time he returned he was so much the fashionable author that he never found a moment in which to open a book again, and thus he remained happily ignorant of the fraud. His wife, when she reflected on the fame and riches won by her husband, and remembered that afternoon when she had been almost too favorably impressed by the iron grip of the primitive, frequently went up to him and gave him an uninvited hug and kiss, and these hugs and kisses afforded him a very delicious gratification.

NIGHT! YOUTH! PARIS!
AND THE MOON!

Annoyed with the world, I took a large studio in Hampstead. Here, I resolved to live in utter aloofness, until the world should approach me on its knees, whining its apologies.

The studio was large and high; so was the rent. Fortunately, my suit was strongly made, and I had a tireless appetite for herrings. I lived here happily and frugally, pleased with the vast and shadowy room, and with the absurd little musicians' gallery on which I set my phonograph a-playing. I approved also of the little kitchen, sad with evergreens, that led to the street beyond. I saw no one. My mood was that of a small bomb, but one which had no immediate intention of going off.

Although I had no immediate intention of going off, I was unable to resist buying a large trunk, which I saw standing outside a junk shop. I was attracted by its old-fashioned appearance, for I myself hoped to become old-fashioned; by its size, because I am rather small; by its curved lid, for I was always fond of curves; and, most of all, by a remark on the part of the dealer, who stood picking his nose in the disillusioned doorway of his shop. "A thing like that," said he, "is always useful."

I paid four pounds, and had the large black incubus taken to my studio on a handbarrow. There I stood it on the little gallery, which, for no reason, ran along the farther end.

This transaction having left me without money, I felt it necessary to sublet my studio. This was a wrench. I telephoned the agents; soon they arranged to bring a client of theirs, one Stewart Musgrave, to inspect my harmless refuge. I agreed, with some reserve. "I propose to absent myself during this inspection. You will find the key in the door. Later you can inform me if my studio is taken."

Later they informed me that my studio was taken. "I will leave," I said, "at four o'clock on Friday. The interloper can come at four-thirty. He will find the key in the door."

Just before four on Friday, I found myself confronted with a problem. On letting one's studio, one locks one's clothes in a press reserved for the purpose. This I did, but was then nude. One has to pack one's trunk. I had a trunk but nothing to put in it. I had bidden the world farewell. Here was my studio—sublet. There was the world. For practical purposes, there is very little else anywhere.

The hour struck. I cut the Gordian knot, crossed the Rubicon, burned my boats, opened my trunk, and climbed inside. At four-thirty, the interloper arrived. With bated breath I looked out through my little air-and-peephole. This was a surprise. I had bar-gained for a young man of no personal attractions. Stewart Musgrave was a young woman of many.

She had a good look around, pulled out every drawer, peeped into every corner. She bounced herself on the big divan-bed. She even came up onto the little useless gallery, leaned over, recited a line or two of Juliet, and then she approached my modest retreat. "I won't open you," she said. "There might be a body in you." I thought this showed a fine instinct. Her complexion was divine.

There is a great deal of interest in watching a handsome young woman who imagines herself to be alone in a large studio. One never knows what she will do next. Often, when lying there alone, I had not known what I would do next. But then I was alone. She, too, thought she was alone, but I knew better. This gave me a sense of mastery, of power.

On the other hand, I soon loved her to distraction. The Hell of it was, I had a shrewd suspicion she did not love me. How could she?

At night, while she slept in an appealing attitude, I crept downstairs, and into the kitchen, where I cleaned up the crockery, her shoes, and some chicken I found in the icebox. "There is," she said to a friend, "a pixie in this studio." "Leave out some milk," said her friend.

Everything went swimmingly. Nothing could have been more delicate than the unspoken love that grew up between the disillusioned world-weary poet and the beautiful young girl-artist, so fresh, so natural, and so utterly devoid of self-consciousness.

On one occasion, I must admit, I tripped over the corner of a rug. "Who is there?" she cried, waking suddenly from a dream of having her etchings lovingly appraised by a connoisseur.

"A mouse," I telepathed squeakingly, standing very still. She sank into sleep again.

She was more rudely put to sleep some days later. She came in, after being absent most of the evening, accompanied by a man to whom I took an immediate dislike. My instinct never fails me; he had not been in the studio half an hour before he gave her occasion to say, "Pray, don't!"

"Yes," said he.

"No," said she.

"I must," said he.

"You mustn't," said she.

"I will," said he.

"You won't," said she.

A vestige of refined feeling would have assured him that there was no possibility of happiness between people so at variance on every point. There should be at least some zone of enthusiastic agreement between every couple; for example, the milk. But, whatever his feelings were, they were not refined.

"Why did you bring me here?" said he with a sneer.

"To see my etchings," she replied, biting her lip.

"Well, then—"

"I thought you were a customer."

"I am. A tough customer." With that he struck her on the temple. She fell, mute, inanimate, crumpled.

"Damn it!" said he. "I've killed her. I've done her in. I shall swing. Unless—I escape."

I was forced to admire the cold logic of it. It was, momentarily, the poet's unreasoning prostration before the man of action, the worldling.

Quickly he undressed her. "Gosh!" he said. "What a pity I hit so hard!" He flung her over his shoulder, retaining her legs in his grasp. He bore her up the stairs, onto the shadowy balcony. He opened the trunk and thrust her inside. "Here is a fine thing!" I thought. "Here she is, in her condition, alone with me, in my condition. If she knew she was dead, she'd be glad." The thought was bitter.

With the dawn, he went for a taxi. The driver came in with him; together they bore the trunk to the vehicle waiting outside.

"Strewth, it's heavy!" said the driver. "What yer got in it?"

"Books," said the murderer, with the utmost calm.

If I had thought of saying, *"Paradise Lost,* in two volumes," I should have said it, then and there, and this story would have come to an end. As it was, we were hoisted onto the cab, which drove off in the direction of Victoria.

A jet of cool night air flowed through the airhole. She, whom I had mourned as dead, inhaled it, and breathed a sigh. Soon she was fully conscious.

"Who are you?" she asked in alarm.

"My name," I said tactfully, "is Emily."

She said, "You are kidding me."

I said, "What is your name?"

She said, "Stewart."

I could not resist the reply, "Then I am Flora MacDonald."

Thus, by easy stages, I approached the ticklish question of my hitherto hopeless love.

She said, "I would rather die."

I said, "In a sense you have died already. Besides, I am your pixie. Or it may be only a dream, and you could hardly blame yourself for that. Anyway, I expect he will take us to Paris."

"It is true," she said, "that I have always dreamed of a honey-moon in Paris."

"The Paris moon!" I said. "The bookstalls on the *quais*. The little restaurants on the Left Bank!"

"The *Cirque Medrano!*" she cried.

"*L'Opéra!*"

"*Le Louvre! Le Petit Palais!*"

"*Le Boeuf sur le Toit!*"

"Darling," she cried, "if it were not so dark, I would show you my etchings, if I had them with me."

We were in absolute raptures; we heard the ticket being taken for Paris. We were registered; it was next door to being married, and we laughed at the rolling of the vessel. Soon, however, we were carried up an endless flight of stairs.

"*Mon Dieu, mais que c'est lourd!*" gasped the hotel porter. "*Qu'est-ce qu'il y a dans cette malle?*"

"*Des livres,*" said the murderer, with the utmost sang-froid.

"*Paradis Retrouvé, édition complète,*" I whispered, and was rewarded with a kiss.

Alone, as he thought, with his lifeless victim, the murderer sneered. "H'ya keeping?" said he coarsely, as he approached the trunk.

He lifted the lid a little, and thrust his head within. A rim ran round inside: while yet he blinked, we seized it, and brought the lid down with a crash.

"*La guillotine?*" I said cuttingly.

"*La Defarge!*" observed my adored one, knitting her brows.

"*Vive la France!*"

We stepped out; we put him inside. I retained his clothes. With a sheet from the bed, the bell rope, and a strip of carpet from before the washstand, she made a fetching Arab lass. Together we slipped out into the street.

Night! Youth! Paris! And the moon!

THE STEEL CAT

The Hotel Bixbee is as commercial a hotel as any in Chicago. The brass rail surmounts the banisters; the cuspidor gleams dimly in the shade of the potted palm. The air in the corridors is very still, and appears to have been deodorized a few days ago. The rates are moderate.

Walter Davies' cab drew up outside the Bixbee. He was a man with a good deal of gray in his hair, and with a certain careworn brightness on his face, such as is often to be seen on the faces of rural preachers, if they are poor enough and hopeful enough. Davies, however, was not a preacher.

The porter seized his suitcase, and would have taken the black box he held on his knees, but Davies nervously put out his hand. "No," he said. "Leave this one to me."

He entered the hotel carrying the box as if it were a baby. It was an oblong box, nearly two feet long, and perhaps a foot wide and a foot in depth. It was covered with a high-grade near-leather. It had a handle on the top side, but Davies preferred to cradle it in his arms rather than swing it by this handle.

As soon as he had checked in and was shown to his room, he set the box on the bureau and made straight for the telephone. He called Room Service. "This is Room 517," said he. "What sort of cheese have you?"

"Well, we got Camembert, Swiss, Tillamook . . ."

"Now, the Tillamook," said Davies. "Is that good and red-looking?"

"Guess so," said the man at the other end. "It's like it usually is."

"All right, send me up a portion."

"What bread with it? Roll? White? Rye?"

"No bread. Just the cheese by itself."

"O.K. It'll be right up."

In a minute or two a bellhop entered, carrying a platter with the wedge of cheese on it. He was a colored man of about the same age as Davies, and had a remarkably round face and a bullet head. "Is that right, sir? You wanted just a piece of cheese?"

"That's right," said Davies, who was undoing the clasps of his black box. "Put it right there on the table."

The bellhop, waiting for him to sign the check, watched Davies fold down the front side of the box, which carried part of the top with it. Thus opened, it displayed an interior lined with black velvet, against which gleamed an odd-looking skeletal arrangement in chromium-plated metal. "Now look at that!" said the bellhop, much intrigued. "Wouldn't be surprised if that ain't an *invention* you've got there."

"Interesting, eh?" said Davies. "Catches the eye?"

"Sure does," said the bellhop. "There ain't nothing much more interesting than an invention." He peered reverently at the odd-looking apparatus in the box. "Now, what sort of invention would you say that might be?"

"That," said Davies proudly, "is the Steel Cat."

"Steel Cat?" cried the bellhop. "No kidding?"

He shook his head, a plain man baffled by the wonders of science. "So that's the Steel Cat! Well now, what do you know?"

"Good name, you think?" asked Davies.

"Boy, that's a *title!*" replied the bellhop. "Mister, how come I ain't never heard of this here Steel Cat?"

"That's the only one in the world," said Davies. "So far."

"I come from Ohio," said the bellhop. "And I got folks in Ohio. And they're going to hear from me how I got to see this one and only Steel Cat."

"Glad you like it," said Davies. "Wait a minute. Fond of animals? I'll show you something."

As he spoke, he opened a small compartment that was built into one end of the box. Inside was a round nest of toilet tissues. Davies put his finger against this nest. "Come on, Georgie," he said. "Peep! Peep! Come on, Georgie!"

A small, ordinary mouse, fat as a butterball, thrust his quick head out of the nest, turned his berry-black eyes in all directions, and ran along Davies' finger, and up his sleeve to his collar, where he craned up to touch his nose to the lobe of Davies' ear.

"Well, sir!" cried the bellhop in delight. "If that ain't a proper tame, friendly mouse you got there!"

"He knows me," said Davies. "In fact, this mouse knows pretty near everything."

"I betcha!" said the bellhop with conviction.

"He's what you might call a demonstration mouse," said Davies.

"He shows off the Steel Cat. See the idea? You hang the bait on this hook. Mr. Mouse marches up this strip in the middle. He reaches for the bait. His weight tips the beam, and he drops into this jar. Of course, I fill it with water."

"And that's his name—Georgie?" asked the bellhop, his eyes still on the mouse.

"That's what I call him," said Davies.

"You know what?" said the bellhop thoughtfully. "If I had that mouse, mister, I reckon I'd call him Simpson."

"D'you know how I came to meet up with this mouse?" said Davies. "I was in Poughkeepsie—that's where I come from—and one night last winter I ran my bath, and somehow I sat on, reading the paper, and forgot all about it. And I felt something sort of urging me to go into the bathroom. So I went in, and there was the bath I'd forgotten all about. And there was Master Georgie in it, just going down for the third time."

"Hey! Hey!" cried the bellhop in urgent distress. "No third time for President Simpson!"

"Oh, no!" said Davies. "Lifeguard to the rescue! I picked him out, dried him, and I put him in a box."

"Can you beat that?" cried the bellhop. "Say, would it be all right for me to give him just a little bit of the cheese?"

"That's just demonstration cheese," said Davies. "Mice aren't so fond of cheese as most people think. He has his proper meal after the show. A balanced diet. Well, as I was saying, in a couple of days he was just as friendly as could be."

"Sure thing," said the bellhop. "*He* knows who saved him."

"You know, a thing like that," said Davies, "it starts a fellow thinking. And what I thought of—I thought of the Steel Cat."

"You thought of that cat from seeing that mouse in that bath?" cried the bellhop, overwhelmed by the processes of the scientific mind.

"I did," said Davies. "I owe it all to Georgie. Drew it up on paper. Borrowed some money. Got a blueprint made; then this model here. And now we're going around together, demonstrating. Cleveland, Akron, Toledo—everywhere. Now here."

"Just about sweeping the country," said the bellhop. "That's a real good-luck mouse, that is. He certainly ought to be called Simpson."

"Well, I'll tell you," said Davies. "It needs one really big concern to give the others a lead. Otherwise, they hang back. That's why we're in Chicago. Do you know who's coming here this afternoon? Mr. Hartpick of Lee and Waldron. They don't only manufacture; they own the outlets. Six hundred and fifty stores, all over the country! No middleman, if you see what I mean. If they push it, oh, boy!"

"Oh, boy!" echoed the bellhop with enthusiasm.

"He'll be here pretty soon," said Davies. "Three o'clock. By appointment. And Georgie'll show him the works."

"He don't never balk?" inquired the bellhop. "He ain't afraid of being drownded?"

"Not Georgie," said Davies. "He trusts me."

"Ah, that's it!" said the bellhop. "He trusts you."

"Of course, I make the water lukewarm for him," said Davies. "All the same, it takes some character in a mouse to take the dip every time like that. Never mind—if he puts this deal over, we get him a little collar made."

"Mister," cried the bellhop, "I want to see that mouse in that collar. You ought to get his photo taken. You could give it to anybody. They could send it back home to their families. Yes, sir, their folks 'ud sure be tickled to death to see a photo of that mouse in that collar."

"Maybe I will," said Davies, smiling.

"You do that thing, mister," said the bellhop. "Well, I got to be getting. Good-bye, Georgie!" He went out, but at once reopened the door. "All the same," he said, "if I had that mouse, I sure would call him Simpson."

Davies, left alone, set out his apparatus to advantage, washed, even shaved, and powdered his face with talcum. When he had nothing more to do, he took out his billfold, and laid six dollar bills one by one on the top of the bureau, counting them out as if he had hoped to find there were seven. He added thirty-five cents from one pocket, and a nickel from another. "We've got to put it over this time," said he to the mouse, who was watching him brightly from the top of the box. "Never get downhearted, Georgie! That gang of shortsighted, narrow-minded, small-town buyers, they just don't mean a thing. This fellow's the guy that counts. And he's our last chance. So do your stuff well, pal, and we'll be on top of the world yet."

Suddenly the telephone rang. Davies snatched it up. "Mr. Hartpick to see you," said the desk-clerk.

"Send Mr. Hartpick up right away," said Davies.

He stowed away the money, put Georgie back in his nest, and dried his moist palms on his handkerchief. He remembered, just as the tap came on the door, to banish the anxious expression from his face and put on a genial smile.

Mr. Hartpick was a square and heavy man, with fingers twice as thick as ordinary fingers, and the lower joints of them were covered with wiry, reddish hair.

"Mr. Hartpick," said Davies. "I certainly appreciate your coming up here like this."

"Long as I'm not wasting my time," returned Mr. Hartpick. "Let's see the goods. I got a rough idea from your letter."

Davies had set the box on the table. Now, getting behind it, he attempted a persuasive, hearty, salesman-like tone. "Mr. Hartpick, you know the old adage about the better mousetrap. You've been good enough to beat a path to my door, and . . ."

"Show me an idea, and I'll beat a path to it," said Hartpick. "However nutty it sounds."

". . . and here," said Davies, "is the Steel Cat." With that, he flung open the box.

"Selling name!" said Hartpick. "Might be able to use the name, anyway."

"Mr. Hartpick, the idea is this," said Davies, beginning to count off his points on his fingers. "More mice caught. More humanely. No mutilation of mice as with inferior traps. No mess. No springs to catch the fingers. Some women are just scared to death of those springs. No family disagreements, Mr. Hartpick. That's an important angle. I've gone into that angle psychologically."

His visitor paused in the rooting-out of a back tooth, and stared at Davies. "Eh?" said he.

"Psychologically," said Davies. "The feminine angle, the masculine angle. Now, the wife doesn't generally like to see a cat playing with a mouse."

"She can poison 'em," said Hartpick.

"That's what *she* says," said Davies. "That's the woman angle. Poisoners throughout the ages. Lucrezia Borgia—lots of 'em. But a good many husbands are allergic to having their wives playing around with poison. I think a nationwide poll would show most husbands prefer a cat. Remember, it was Nero—a man—fed the Christians to the lions. So, that starts an argument. Besides, you've got to put a cat out, get it fed when on vacation."

"Any mice *we* catch, the missus flushes 'em down the toilet," said Mr. Hartpick with a shrug.

"Feminine angle again," said Davies. "Cleopatra fed her slaves to the crocodiles. Only, many women haven't the levelheadedness of Mrs. Hartpick to take a mouse out of a trap and get rid of it that way."

"Oh, I dunno," said Mr. Hartpick in tones of complete boredom.

"In one way, this is the same sort of thing," said Davies, beginning to talk very fast. "Only more scientific and labor-saving. See— I fill the glass jar here with water, lukewarm water. It's glass in this demonstration model. In the selling product it'd be tin, to keep the cost down to what I said in my letter. The frame needn't be chromium, either. Well, having filled it, I place it right here in position. Kindly observe the simplicity. I take a morsel of ordinary cheese, and I bait the hook. Many scientific thinkers consider a piece of bread rubbed in bacon fat equally or more effective. Now, look! Please look, Mr. Hartpick! I'll show you what the mouse does. Come on, Georgie!"

"Live mouse, eh?" observed Hartpick, with a flicker of interest.

"*Mus domesticus,* the domestic mouse," said Davies. "Found in every home. Now, watch him! He's found the way in! See him go along that strip in the middle! Right to the bait—see? His weight tilts the . . ."

"He's in!" cried Hartpick, his interest entirely regained.

"And the trap," said Davies triumphantly, "has automatically set itself for another mouse. In the morning you just remove the dead ones."

"Not bad!" said Hartpick. "Gosh—he's trying to swim! My friend, I think you may have something there."

"You know the old adage, Mr. Hartpick," said Davies, smiling. "It's the better mousetrap!"

"Like Hell it is!" said Hartpick. "Pure nut, that's what it is. But what I always say—there's a nut market for nut inventions. Play up the humane angle . . . get the old dames het up . . ."

"Gee, that's great!" said Davies. "I was beginning to . . . Well, never mind! Excuse me! I'll just get him out."

"Wait a minute," said Hartpick, putting his heavy hand on Davies' wrist.

"I think he's getting a bit tired," said Davies.

"Now look," said Hartpick, still watching the mouse. "We've got our standard contract for notions of this sort. Standard rate of royalties. Ask your attorney if you like; he'll tell you the same thing."

"Oh, that'll be all right, I'm sure," said Davies. "Just let me . . ."

"Hold on! Hold on!" said Hartpick. "We're talking business, ain't we?"

"Why, sure," said Davies uneasily. "But he's getting tired. You see, he's a demonstration mouse."

Mr. Hartpick's hand seemed to grow heavier. "And what's this?" he demanded. "A demonstration—or what?"

"A demonstration? Yes," said Davies.

"Or are you trying to put something over on me?" said Hartpick. "How do I know he won't climb out? I was *going* to suggest you step around to the office in the morning, and we sign. If you're interested, that is."

"Of course, I'm interested," said Davies, actually trembling. "But . . ."

"Well, if you're interested," said Hartpick, "let him alone."

"But, my God, he's drowning!" cried Davies, tugging to free his wrist. Mr. Hartpick turned his massive face toward Davies for a moment, and Davies stopped tugging.

"The show," said Hartpick, "goes on. There you are! Look! Look! He's going!" His hand fell from Davies' arm. "Going! Going! Gone! Poor little bastard! Okay, Mr. Davies, let's say ten-thirty o'clock then, in the morning."

With that, he strode out. Davies stood stock-still for a little, and then moved toward the Steel Cat. He put out his hand to take up the jar, but turned abruptly away and walked up and down the room. He had been doing this for some time when there came another tap on the door. Davies must have said, "Come in," though he wasn't aware of doing so. At all events, the bellhop entered, carrying a covered platter on a tray. "Excuse me," said he, smiling all over his face. "It's on the house, sir. Buttered corncob for Brother George Simpson!"

SLEEPING BEAUTY

Edward Laxton had everything in the world that he wanted except a sweetheart, fiancée, or wife.

He had a very civilized little Regency house, whose ivory façade was reflected in a few acres of ornamental water. There was a small park, as green as moss, and well embowered with sober trees. Outside this, his land ran over some of the shaggiest hills in the south of England. The plowed fields were on the small side, and lay locked in profound woods. A farmhouse and a cottage or two sent their blue smoke curling into the evening sky.

With all this, his income was very small, but he was blessed with good taste, and was therefore satisfied with simple fare. His dinner was a partridge roasted plain, a bottle of Hermitage, an apple pie, and a crumb of Stilton cheese. His picture was a tiny little Constable left to him by his great-uncle. His gun was his father's old Holland and Holland, which fitted him to a hair. His dogs were curly-coated retrievers, one liver colored and one black. Such dogs are now considered very old-fashioned, and so, by those who knew him, was their master. He was now over thirty, and had begun to tell his tailor to make him exactly the same suits as last year, and, when his friends went abroad, it did not occur to him to find out others.

He turned more and more to the placid beauty of his house, and to the rich, harsh beauty of the upland farms. A man should beware of surrendering too much of himself to this sort of thing, for the beauty of a place can be as possessive as other beauties. Believe it or not, when Edward met a girl who attracted him, a certain hill would thrust its big shoulder, furred with oak woods, between them, for all the world like a jealous dog. It would at once be obvious that the girl was weak in the ankles, and wore too much makeup. The bare, prim front of a certain stockman's cottage, like the disapproving face of an old servant, could make a merry girl seem altogether too smart, and there was a certain faded little nursery room, the memory of which could make any young woman of these days look like something out of the cinema.

Thus Edward was under the necessity of sitting alone after din-

433

ner and telling himself, firmly, that he was the most fortunate man in the world. Into this felicity came a letter: it was from his oldest friend, inviting him to spend a season on his ranch in New Mexico. Edward reflected that he had never had the pleasure of seeing his own place after a long and homesick absence. He telegraphed, packed, and set forth.

He arrived in New Mexico, and admired immensely the beautiful immensities of that state. Nevertheless, he soon began to long excruciatingly to see a certain turn in a certain lane at home—a very ordinary corner, of which he had never taken any particular notice when he was there. He said good-bye to his host, and started for New York, but, wishing to see something of the country before leaving it, he bought an old car and set out by road.

His way lay along the northern edge of the area known as The Dust Bowl, a landscape from which, after a few hours of driving, the eye seems to recoil in blank disbelief. This is a very dangerous tendency, especially in one who is dreaming of a far-distant lane. Edward followed a gentle curve which happened to be some four thousand miles away, and found himself halted in a back alley, with a severe pain in his ribs, a watermelon by his side, and an impression of having driven through a small country store. "Now I am in trouble," thought Edward. He was soon to learn that he was also in Heeber's Bluff, Arkansas, and, what with settling up for the damage and getting his car repaired, he was likely to be there some days.

Heeber's Bluff is the dreariest town that ever sweltered on the devastated prairie. Sickly trees, tipsy posts, and rusty wire effectively dissipate the grandeur of the endless plain. The soil has all been blown away in the droughts; the fields are nothing but a hideous clay, with here and there the skeleton of a horse or a cow. A sunken creek, full of tin cans, oozes round a few hundred shacks whose proportions are as mean as the materials of which they are built. The storekeepers have the faces of alligators; all the other people have the faces and voices of frogs.

Edward deposited his bags in Mergler's Hotel, which stands opposite the funeral parlor. After a minute or two, he stepped outside and checked up on the signs. He went into the hotel dining room and was confronted with a corned-beef hash more terrible than the town itself, because, after all, he did not have to eat the town. Emboldened by this consideration, he went out to stroll along the main street.

When he had strolled a few yards, he had a strong apprehension that he was losing his mind, so he returned to Mergler's Hotel. Here he soon found himself biting the ends of his fingers, and shaken by a strong impulse to rush out again. He was restrained by a quaking and a dread which seized upon him as he stepped into the doorway. "Here is a place," said he to himself, "in which one suffers simultaneously from claustrophobia and agoraphobia. Now I see the purpose of the porch, and understand the motion of the rocking chair!"

He hastened to plant himself in one of these agreeable devices, and oscillated every few seconds between the horrors of the hotel and the terrors of the street. On the third day, at about eleven in the morning, this therapy failed of its effect, and something within him broke. "I must get out of this," said he. "And quickly!"

His money had arrived. His fine was paid, and his ribs were taped. He still had to settle with the owner of the store, but what had seemed disproportionate as damages appeared dirt-cheap when regarded as ransom. He paid it, and was free to go. He went to collect his car from the garage where it was being repaired, and there he met with a little disappointment. He returned to the hotel, packed his bag, and called for his bill. "At what time does the next train leave this town?" he asked.

"Eight o'clock," said the hotelkeeper calmly.

Edward looked at his watch, which now expressed the hour of noon. He looked at the hotelkeeper, and then he looked across the street at the funeral parlor. "Eight hours!" said he in the low, broken voice of despair. "What am I to do?"

"If you want to fill in the time," said the hotelkeeper, "you can always have a look at the carnival. It opens up at one."

On the very stroke of one, Edward was at the turnstile, and the first blast of music engulfed him as he passed through.

"I must restrain myself," he thought, "from dashing too madly at the sideshows. I will see the calf at half past one, the fat lady at two, and the pigtailed boy at half past, and the circus itself at three. At four-thirty, I will indulge myself in the glamor of the fan dance, the memory of which will color the giant rat at five-thirty, and at half past six I will see the sleeping beauty, whatever she may be, and that will leave me half an hour to pick up my bags, and a happy hour on the place where the platform would be if there was one. I hope the train will not be late."

At the appointed hours, Edward gravely inspected the heads of the two-headed calf, the legs of the fat lady, and the bottom of the pigtailed boy. He was glad of the fans when it came to the fan dance. He looked at the giant rat, and the giant rat looked at Edward. "I," said Edward, "am leaving on the eight o'clock train." The giant rat bowed its head and turned away.

The tent that housed the sleeping beauty was just filling up as Edward approached. "Come on!" cried the barker. "Curtain just going up on the glamorous face and form of the girl who can't wake up. In her night attire. Asleep five years. In bed! In bed! In bed!"

Edward paid his twenty-five cents and entered the crowded tent. An evil-looking rascal, dressed in a white surgical coat, and with a stethoscope hung round his neck, was at that moment signaling for the curtain to be drawn aside.

A low dais was exposed, and on it a hospital bed, at the head of which stood a sinister trollop tricked out in the uniform of a nurse.

"Here we have," said the pseudo-doctor, "the miracle that has baffled the scientists of the entire world." He continued his rigmarole. Edward gazed at the face on the pillow. It was, beyond any question at all, the most exquisite face he had ever seen in his life.

"Well, folks," said the impresario, "I just want you to know, for the sake of the reputation of the scientific profession, that there has been absolutely no deception in the announcement made to you that this young lady is A, asleep, and B, beautiful. Lest you should be speculating on whether her recumbent posture, maintained night and day for five years, has been the cause of shrinkage or wasting of the limbs, hips, or bust—Nurse, be so good as to turn back that sheet."

The nurse, grinning like a bulldog, pulled back the grubby cotton and revealed the whole form of this wonderful creature, clad in a diaphanous nightgown, and lying in the most graceful, fawn-like posture you can possibly imagine.

"If," thought Edward, "all my woods and fields, instead of bursting into bluebells and cowslips and wild roses and honeysuckle, had hoarded their essences through the centuries to produce one single flower, this would be the flower." He paused to allow the *genius loci,* which had been so arbitrary on other occasions, to voice any objections it might have. None was forthcoming.

"My friends," the abominable showman was saying, "world science having got nowhere in waking this beautiful young lady from her trance which has lasted five years, I want to remind you of a little story you maybe heard around that dear old Mamma's knee, about how the sleeping beauty woke right up saying, 'Yummy,' when Prince Charming happened along with his kiss."

"There's no doubt," thought Edward, "that if all the good-night kisses and candlelight visions and dreams and desires that have gleamed and faded in that faded little nursery ever since the day it was built were fused into one angelic presence, this is she."

"Top medical attention costing plenty, as you very well know," continued the showman, "we are prepared, for the fee of one quarter deposited in the bowl on the bedside table, to allow any gentleman in the audience to step up and take his try at being Prince Charming. Take your places in line, boys, and avoid the crush."

Shaking his head, Edward pushed his way out of the tent and returned to Mergler's Hotel, where he sat in his bedroom devoured by rage and shame. "Why should I be ashamed? Because I didn't try to make a fight of it? No," said he, "that would be ridiculous. All the same, there's something . . . something disgusting. It isn't— it can't be—that I want to kiss her myself! That would be vile, base, despicable! Then why, in the name of all that's shy, wild, lovely, and innocent, am I walking back to this unspeakable spectacle?

"I'll turn back in a moment. This time, I'll take my bags to the station, and sit on them, and wait for that train. In an hour, I'll be on my way home.

"But what *is* my home?" he cried almost aloud. "What was it made for, but to be a shell, a dwelling place for this creature and no other? Or the image of her, the dream of her, the memory of her, that I could take home on my lips and live with forever, if I kissed her just once. And that, by God, is what I will do!"

At this moment, he had arrived at the booth, just as a lip-licking audience was issuing forth. "Very good," said Edward. "The curtain will be lowered while the tent fills up again. I'll arrange to have a moment alone with her."

He found the back entrance, and squeezed through a narrow flap in the canvas. The doctor and the nurse were taking a little refreshment between shows.

"Other way in, buddy," said the doctor. "Unless you're the press, that is."

"Listen," said Edward, "I want to spend a few minutes alone with this girl."

"Yeah?" said the doctor, observing Edward's flushed face and breathless speech.

"I can pay you," said Edward.

"Stool pigeon—vice squad," observed the nurse in a level tone.

"Listen, buddy," said the doctor, "you don't want to muscle in here with a low-down immoral proposition like that."

"I'm an Englishman!" cried Edward. "How can I be a member of the vice squad or anything else?"

The nurse examined Edward with prolonged and expert attention. "O.K.," she said at last.

"O.K., nothing," said the doctor.

"O.K., a hundred bucks," said the nurse.

"A hundred bucks?" said the doctor. "Listen, son, we all been young once. You want a private interview—maybe you *are* the press—with this interesting young lady. Well, could be. A hundred bucks, cash on the barrelhead, for—what do you say, Nurse?"

The nurse examined Edward again. "Ten minutes," said she.

"Ten minutes," continued the doctor to Edward. "After twelve o'clock tonight, when we close down."

"No. Now," said Edward. "I've got to catch a train."

"Yeah?" said the doctor. "And have some guy sticking his long nose in to see why we don't begin on time. No, *sir!* There's ethics in this profession—*the show goes on. Scram!* Twelve o'clock. Open up, Dave!"

Edward filled in part of the time by watching the thickening crowds file into the booth. At nightfall, he went away and sat down by the stinking creek, holding his head in his hands and waiting for the endless hours to drag by. The sunken water oozed past, darkly. The night over the great flat of lifeless clay was heavy with a stale and sterile heat, the lights of the fair glared in the distance, and the dark water crept on.

At last, the blaze of lights was extinguished. A few were left; even these began to wink out one by one, like sparks on a piece of smoldering paper. Edward got up like a somnambulist and made his way back to the fair.

The doctor and the nurse were eating silently and voraciously when he entered. The single harsh light in the tent, falling on their ill-colored faces and their fake uniforms, gave them the appearance of waxworks, or corpses come to life, while the girl lying in the bed, with the flush of health on her cheeks and her hair in a lovely disorder, looked like a creature of the fresh wind, caught in this hideous stagnation by some enchantment, waiting for a deliverer.

"Here is the money," said Edward. "Where can I be alone with her?"

"Push the bed through the curtain," said the doctor. "We'll turn the radio on."

Edward was alone with the beauty for which he, and his whole life, and his house, and his land, were made. He moistened his handkerchief and wiped away the blurred lipstick from her mouth.

He tried to clear his mind, to make it as black as a negative film, so that he could photograph upon it each infinitely fine curve of cheek and lip, the sweep of the dreaming lashes and the tendrils of the enchanted hair.

Suddenly, to his horror, he found his eyes were dimming with tears. He had made his mind a blank in order to photograph a goddess, and now his whole being was flooded with pity for a girl. He leaned forward and kissed her on the lips.

It is the fate of those who kiss sleeping beauties to be awakened themselves; Edward jerked aside the curtain and went through.

"On time," said the doctor approvingly.

"How much," said Edward, "will you take for that girl?"

"Hear that?" said the doctor to the nurse. "He wants to buy the act."

"Sell," said the nurse.

"Never did like her, did you?" said the doctor.

"Twelve grand," said the nurse.

"Twelve thousand dollars?" said Edward.

"She said it," said the doctor.

This was not a matter for haggling over. Edward cabled his lawyer to raise the money. It arrived two or three days later, and that same evening Edward and his wonderful charge set off for Chicago. There he took a hotel room for her to rest in between trains. He wrote some letters, and went downstairs to mail them. He noticed a man and a woman standing by the desk. He thought they looked extremely unsavory.

"This is the gentleman," said the receptionist.

"Mr. Laxton?" said the man.

"My daughter!" cried the woman in a heartrending tone. "Where's my little girl? My baby!"

"What does this mean?" cried Edward, moving with them to a deserted sidehall.

"Kidnapping, white slave trade, and violation of the Mann Act," said the man.

"Sold like a chattel!" cried the woman. "Like a white slave!"

"What is the Mann Act?" asked Edward.

"You move a dame, any dame but your wife or daughter, outa one state into another," said the man, "and that's the Mann Act. Two years."

"Prove she's your daughter," said Edward.

"Listen, wise guy," said the man, "if half a dozen of the home-town folks aren't enough for you, they'll be enough for the district attorney. Do you see that guy standing by the desk in there? He's the hotel dick. Boy, I've only got to whistle."

"You want money," said Edward, at last.

"I want my Rosie," said the woman.

"We drew twenty per for Rosie," said the man. "Yeah, she kept her folks."

Edward argued with them for a time. Their demand was for twenty thousand dollars. He cabled once more to England, and, soon afterwards, paid over the money, and received in exchange a document surrendering all parental rights and appointing him the true and legal guardian of the sleeping girl.

Edward was stunned. He moved on to New York in a sort of dream. The phrases of that appalling interview repeated themselves constantly in his mind. It was with a horrible shock that he realized the same phrases, or others very like them, were being launched at him from outside. A seedy but very businesslike-looking clergyman had buttonholed him in the foyer of his hotel.

He was talking about young American womanhood, purity, two humble members of his flock, the moral standards of the State of Kentucky, and a girl called Susie May. Behind him stood two figures, which, speechless themselves, were calculated to take away the power of speech from any man.

"It is true, then," said Edward, "about hillbillies?"

"That name, sir," said the clergyman, "is not appreciated in the pure air mountain country of ———."

"And so her real name is Susie May?" said Edward. "And I have her upstairs: Then the other parents were crooks. I knew it! And these want their daughter back. How did they hear of it?"

"Your immoral act, sir," said the clergyman, "has had nationwide press publicity for the last three days."

"My friends always told me I should read the papers," said Edward. "So these people want to take the girl back to some filthy cabin . . ."

"Humble," said the clergyman, "but pure."

". . . and no doubt sell her to the next rascally showman that passes." He spoke at length of the purity of his intentions and of the excellent care he proposed to take of Susie May.

"Mr. Laxton," said the clergyman, "have you ever thought what a mother's heart really means?"

"Last time," said Edward, "it meant twenty thousand dollars."

One should never be witty, even when in the depths of despair. The words *twenty thousand* were rumblingly echoed, as from a mountain cavern, from the deep mouth of the male parent, whose aged eye took on the red glow of rustic cupidity.

From that moment, the conversation was mere persiflage. Edward asked leave to walk up and down by himself for a little time, in order to think and breathe more freely.

"This will take the last penny of my capital," he thought. "I shall have nothing to live on. Susie will need the most expensive doctors. Ah, well, I can be happy with her, if I sell the estate and retain only the keeper's cottage. We shall then have four or five hundred a year, as many stars as before, and the deep woods all round us. I'll do it."

He did not do quite that, for he found that hasty sales do not usually result in prices proportionate to the beauty and the value of estates. There were also some legal fees to be paid, one or two little presents to be made in the interests of haste, and some heavy hotel and traveling expenses.

When all was done, Edward found his fortune had dwindled to a very little more than two hundred a year, but he had the cottage, with Orion towering above it, and the mighty woods all round. He would walk up and down outside, and watch the treacly yellow candlelight shine through the tiny pane, and exult in knowing that all the beauty of the world was casketed there. At such moments, he was the happiest of men.

There was only one fly in his ointment. The man who had bought the estate turned out to be something less than *simpatico*. He seemed, somehow, hardly right for the place. Edward was, no doubt, a little prejudiced, but it seemed to him that this man had the loudest, most hectoring and boastful voice ever heard, that his clothes were too new, his manicure too conspicuous, his signet ring too massive and too bright. His features, also, lacked delicacy. But if, as Edward maintained, he had the appearance of a hog, he made it very obvious that he was an extremely wealthy one. He had some bloodchilling intentions for what he called "little improvements" on the estate.

Compared with the fate of his beloved land, Edward's other troubles were of no great importance. In spite of his legal guardianship of his lovely charge, one of the local papers condemned him as a libertine, while the other treated the matter with revolting levity. His richer relations disclaimed further acquaintance with him; his poorer ones called to expostulate. A lady of strong moral principle struck him several times with an umbrella in the High Street at Shepton Mallet.

While all this was going on, he had by diligent inquiry found out an endocrinologist of acknowledged genius. The great man proved to be an enthusiast, and was always throwing up important engagements in London to rush down and take another look at Susie May. Edward trembled to think of what the bill would be.

At last a day arrived when the doctor came down the narrow little stairway, and, brushing a cobweb from his sleeve, regarded Edward with a complacent smile. "I have some good news for you," said he. "Yesterday, I heard from Vienna, from Wertheimer."

"Good news, you say?" said Edward, his heart beginning to beat very fast. "Do you mean you can wake her?"

"Not only wake her," rejoined the specialist, "but keep her awake. Here's the preparation, made up by Wertheimer's people in accordance with the reports I've been sending in. Very ordinary-looking capsules, as you see; nevertheless, they mark an epoch. Do you see the label? *To be administered at 9 A.M. and 6 P.M.* Not *about* nine, or *around* six. Is that quite comprehensible to you?" demanded the doctor.

"I understand you," said Edward. "These have to be given at exactly the right time."

"Or she will very quickly fall asleep again," continued the doctor sternly.

"Now, tell me when she will wake," demanded Edward.

"It may be twenty-four hours, or it may be forty-eight," replied the doctor. "Or it may be even longer."

He added a good many little instructions, repeated his admonition as to punctual dosage some half a dozen times or so, brushed another cobweb from his sleeve, and departed.

Edward passed the next two days in a state of exaltation, qualified by certain misgivings. Most of all he feared she might be frightened at waking and finding herself in a strange place, alone with a strange man. He thought of asking the village girl, who attended to her by day, to stay overnight and sit by her, but he could not give up the right to be with her when she woke.

On the second night and the third he sat by her bedside, dizzy and red-eyed from lack of sleep, but watching every moment for the faintest flicker of her lowered eyelids. The third night wore on; the candle guttered and went out. The window was already pale with the coming dawn. Soon the first rays of the sun struck through the little window and fell aslant on the bed. The sleeper stirred, sighed, and opened her eyes. They were certainly the most beautiful eyes in the world. They dwelt upon Edward.

"Hey!" said Susie May uncertainly.

"How do you do?" said Edward. "At least . . . I mean to say . . . I expect you wonder where you are."

"Where I am, and how I goddam well got here," said his lovely guest, sitting up on the bed. She rubbed her brow, obviously trying hard to remember. "I must have passed right out," she said. And then, pointing at him accusingly: "And you look like a son of a bitch who'd take advantage of me."

"I assure you," said Edward faintly, "you are utterly mistaken."

"You better hope I am," responded the young lady. " 'Cause, boy, if you have, you're going to pay through the nose for it."

"I think you'd better let me tell you exactly what has happened," said Edward.

He proceeded to do so.

"You mean to say," said Susie May, when he had finished. "You mean to say you took me out of show business and brought me to this dump?"

"But, my dear girl, you were asleep, you were sick. . . ," expostulated Edward.

"Aw, phooey!" said she, "I'd have woke up. I betcha I'd have woke up the minute that show hit Hollywood. And, now, what am I going to do?"

"I can answer that question very easily," said Edward. "You will eat the food that's set before you, or you'll go hungry. You'll spend a few days learning to walk again, or you'll waste the rest of your life sitting on your backside. As soon as you can look after yourself, we'll talk about what you shall do. By that time, you'll know this place, and you'll know me, a great deal better than you do at present."

These words were uttered with a forcefulness that surprised both of them. Susie, somewhat daunted, and perhaps fatigued by the liveliness of her first waking impressions, said nothing in reply, but soon dropped her delicate eyelids and fell into a light doze.

Watching her, Edward found all his tender feelings, so rudely scattered, come fluttering home again. "I have just seen," thought he, "the scars of an appalling childhood. Somewhere, far, far below the pathetic surface, there must be a mind to match that lovely face. *That* is the real sleeper, and it's going to be devilish hard to awaken her."

In the days that followed, he buckled to his task, and enfolded her in a warm and cheerful affection. He offered her, as one lays one toy after another to the hand of a sullen child, a smile, a flower, a word of endearment, or an American cigarette procured especially from London. He invited her to note the flavor of the speckled trout he caught for her, the fragrance of the September honeycomb, and the luster of the beaded raindrops on the windowpane as they sparkled under the returning sun with a brightness exceeding that of diamonds.

Had any cynical person told him he was wasting his time, Edward would have replied with terrifying logic. "Look at that face!" he would have said. "It seems suitable to this place, does it not? It should, for it was made here. That, my dear sir, is a face straight out of eighteenth-century England, and it has been preserved unchanged (as if in a sleep two or three hundred years long) in the Cumberland Mountains of Kentucky. Depend upon it, her sleeping soul is of the same order of beauty, and will awaken, if it wakes at all, in response to surroundings like these, from which it originally sprung. Wait till I take her into the woods!"

The days went by, and her strength returned rapidly, and she was able to walk around the little garden patch, where the straggled flowers of late summer leaned out to catch her eye, but without success. At last, Edward was able to take her by the arm, and lead her out into the great woods which had once been his own.

He took her down a mile-long ride, over rabbit-nibbled turf as smooth as green velvet. Immense beeches walled it on either side; behind them the slimmer trunks stood hushed in a silvery dimness, regardful of the dryad. Farther down, towards where his old house stood, the beeches gave place to mighty oaks, bronzed, lichened, antlered, Virgilian. He had her peep into glades aflame with willow herb, and others rusty with the turning bracken. The rabbits scuttled off in all directions; the hare limped away with many a backward glance; the coppery pheasant rose, clattering like a dragon, its long tail rippling dragon-like behind it. The great woodpecker, laughing heartily over something or other, swooped on from tree to tree before them all the way home.

All this time, Edward had said scarcely a word, and had hardly dared to look into her face to see what she was feeling. Now, on the threshold of the cottage, he took her hands in his, and, gazing deep into her eyes, he asked her: "Well? How did you like it?"

She replied: "Lousy."

Edward's chagrin was so sudden and so fierce that, for a moment, he was bereft of his senses. Recovering them, he saw Susie cowering away in the very likeness of a spitting cat, and he realized his right hand was raised menacingly in the air. He lowered it. "Don't be afraid," he said breathlessly. "I am incapable of striking a woman."

Susie must have believed him, for she did not hesitate to offer some very unflattering reasons for this incapacity. Oddly enough, he himself was not so convinced, and his conscience so bit and tore at him that he scarcely heard what she was saying. He waited till six, gave her her capsule, and then strode out of the cottage and off over the dark and windy hills like a man pursued. After several miles at a very high speed, the turmoil within him abated a little, and he came to his conclusion. "I was enraged because she would not accept my standards—the standards of a man who is capable (for I lied when I said I wasn't) of striking a helpless girl. There is only one thing to do."

It is a sad reflection on life that, when there is only one thing to do, it is always extremely unpleasant. Next day, Edward arranged for the little daily maid to stay with Susie overnight, while he himself went up to town to see his lawyer.

"How much would I get if I sold everything I have?" asked Edward, in a somewhat grating voice.

"Including the little place you are living in?"

"The whole damned shoot."

The lawyer consulted his files, scribbled on a pad, deprecated the state of the market, and finally told Edward he might expect between four and five thousand pounds.

"Then sell," said Edward, and, brushing aside all expostulation, he repaired to a hotel, and next day took the train back home.

Just as he approached the cottage, he saw his Susie coming towards him along the path that led from the woods. Her cheeks were flushed, her eyes were bright, her hair was a little disordered.

"What is this?" said he, as they met. "Don't tell me you have been in the woods!"

"I don't know where else there is to go," she replied.

"Come inside," said Edward, "and I will tell you of somewhere else. How would you like us to go to Hollywood, California?"

"Are you kidding?" she asked in astonishment. "I thought you was broke."

"I am selling what I have left," said Edward. "It will not bring enough to live there very long, or on a very grand scale, but since that is what you want it seems to me you should have it."

Susie was silent for a little. "Aw, shucks!" she said at last. "Not if it's your last cent."

Edward, astounded at her magnanimity, tried to explain the reasons for his change of heart. However, she cut him short. "Forget it," she said. "I'd just as soon stick around here. For a while, anyway."

Edward heard this with the emotions of a man reprieved, if not from the gallows, at least from transportation. "What has happened?" cried he. "Is it possible we have both changed, only in opposite directions? Ah, I know! You have been in the woods. Something there has touched you."

"You'd better shut your big trap," said she almost angrily. "You don't know what the Hell you're talking about."

"I know," said he, "that these feelings can be very delicate and private ones; vague gropings that one prefers not to discuss. For example, I think you would not have felt what you felt today had I been there. My presence on Monday was a mistake, much as I hoped to share these sensations with you. In future, you shall go alone."

So, thereafter, she went every afternoon alone into the woods, and Edward remained at home, and everyday she came back smiling more sweetly than before.

"The woods are working for me," thought Edward, and his imagination followed her like a dog. He seemed to see her in the dappled sun and shade under the great trees, or paddling in the brook, or fanning herself with a fern frond, or staining her mouth with blackberries. Finally he felt he could live no longer without seeing these pretty things with his own eyes, so one afternoon he slyly followed her among the trees.

He kept a good way behind her, thinking to come up quietly when she stopped to rest, but instead of stopping she went on faster and faster, and at last broke into a run, and for a while he lost her altogether. He pressed on to where he heard a jay scolding in the distance, and when he got there he looked all around, but saw no sign of her. Suddenly, he heard her laugh. "She must have seen me all the time!" he thought.

Her laugh had a low, sweet, inviting quality that made his heart beat fast. It came from a little dell near by, where the ground fell away at the wood's edge. Edward stepped softly to the upper edge of this dell, half-expecting, yet not daring to expect, that he'd see her there looking up at him, and with her arms spread wide. He parted the twigs and looked down. She was there, indeed, and her arms were spread wide, but it was the better to embrace Edward's corpulent and detested neighbor.

Edward walked quietly away, and returned to the cottage. There he awaited Susie, who came back very late, and smiling more sweetly than ever.

"You may take that smile off your face," said Edward. "You dirty, double-crossing little harlot. . . ."

She at once obliged him in the matter of the smile. "Why, you low-down, snooping bastard," she began, and the conversation continued with the utmost vivacity. Edward so far forgot himself as to utter a threat or two, which she treated with the most galling derision, as if secure in the protection of her paramour.

"He's got a big film company up in London," she said, "and he's promised to put me in a picture."

"You forget," said Edward, "that I happen to hold your contract."

"You mean to say you'd stop me?"

"Why not?"

"Because I'm going to the cops right now," said Susie. "And do you know what I'm going to tell 'em? About when I was asleep?" She was about to supply the information when she was interrupted by an enormous yawn.

Edward glanced at his watch, and saw that the hour of six had long ago slipped by unnoticed.

"Well?" said he. "What?"

"Enough to . . . put you in jail for . . ." she muttered, in a voice like a slowing phonograph record, and she yawned again. Her head dropped down and down till her cheek rested on the table.

"Pleasant dreams!" said Edward, and, taking the little box of capsules from the mantelpiece, he pitched it into the fire. Susie observed this operation with a glazing eye. A little flame of fury flickered up in it to match the leaping flame on the hearth. It died, and the eye closed. She looked ravishing.

Edward put her to bed, and came downstairs and wrote a letter to a firm that advertised motor caravans and trailers. Next summer, he was at Blackpool, in a spotless white coat, addressing the multitude from under a sign that read:

THE SLEEPING BEAUTY
Dr. von Strangelberg presents
the Wonder of Modern Science.
Adults only.

THE SLEEPING BEAUTY
Admission sixpence.

They say he is rapidly recovering his fortune.

INTERPRETATION OF A DREAM

A young man entered the office of a well-known psychiatrist, whom he addressed as follows: "Doctor, save me!"

"By all means," responded the mind specialist suavely. "After all, that is what I am here for."

"But you can't," cried the young man distractedly. "You can't! You can't! Nothing can save me!"

"At all events," said the psychiatrist soothingly, "it will do no harm to talk it over."

With that, he waved his hands a little, smiled with a rather soapy and ingratiating expression, and before he knew it the young man was seated in a deep armchair, with his face to the light, pouring out his story.

"My name," said he, "is Charles Rotifer. I am employed in the office of an accountant, who occupies the top story of this skyscraper. I am twenty-eight years of age, single, engaged to be married. My fiancée is the best and dearest girl in the world, beautiful as an angel, and with lovely golden hair. I mention this because it is relevant to my story."

"It is, indeed," said the psychiatrist. "Gold is a symbol of money. Have you a retentive attitude toward money? For example, you say you are employed in an office. Have you saved anything considerable out of your salary?"

"Yes, I have," said the young man. "I've saved quite a bit."

"Please continue, Mr. Rotifer," said the psychiatrist, benevolently. "You were speaking of your fiancée. Later on, I shall have to ask you one or two rather intimate questions on that subject."

"And I will answer them," returned the young man. "There is nothing in our relationship that needs to be concealed—at all events, from a psychologist. All is complete harmony between us, and there is nothing about her that I could wish altered, except, perhaps, her little habit of gesturing rather too freely as she speaks."

"I will make a note of that," said the other, scribbling on his pad.

"It is not of the least importance," said the young man. "I hardly know why I mentioned it, except to indicate how perfect she is. But, Doctor, thirty-eight nights ago I dreamed a dream."

"Thirty-eight, indeed!" observed the mind doctor, jotting down the figure. "Tell me frankly, when you were an infant, did you by any chance have a nurse, a teacher, or a female relative, on whom perhaps you might have had a little fixation, who happened to be thirty-eight years of age?"

"No, Doctor," said the young man, "but there are thirty-nine floors to this skyscraper."

The psychiatrist gave him a penetrating glance. "And does the form and height of this building suggest anything to you?"

"All I know," said the young man obstinately, "is that I dreamed I was outside the window of our office at the top, in the air, falling."

"Falling!" said the psychiatrist, raising his eyebrows. "And what were your sensations at that moment?"

"I was calm," replied the young man. "I imagine I was falling at the normal rate, but my mind seemed to work very fast. I had leisure to reflect, to look around me. The view was superb. In a moment, I had reached the ornamental stonework which separates our windows from those immediately below. Then I woke up."

"And that simple, harmless, perfectly ordinary little dream has been preying on your mind?" asked the psychiatrist in a jocular tone. "Well, my dear sir . . ."

"Wait a moment," said his visitor. "On the following night, I dreamed the same dream, or, rather, a continuation of it. There I was, spread-eagled in midair—like this—passing the ornamental stonework, looking into the window of the floor below, which is also occupied by our firm. I saw my friend, Don Straker, of our tax department, bending over his desk. He looked up. He saw me. His face took on an expression of the utmost astonishment. He made a movement as if to rise from his seat, no doubt to rush to the window. But compared with mine, his movements were indescribably slow. I remember thinking, 'He will be too late.' Then I dropped below his window, and down to the dividing line between that floor and the next. As I did so, I woke."

"Well," said the brain doctor. "What have we here? The dream of one night is resumed on the night following. That is a very ordinary occurrence."

"Possibly," said the young man. "However, on the next night, there I was, having just passed the dividing line between that floor and the floor below it. I had slipped into a recumbent posture, with one leg slightly raised, like this."

"Yes, yes," said the psychiatrist, "I see. It is not necessary to demonstrate. You nearly knocked over my ashtray."

"I'm sorry," said the young man. "I'm afraid I have picked up the habit from Maisie. Maisie is my fiancée. When she wants to say how she did a thing, she just shows you. She acts it out. It was the night she told me how she slipped and fell on the icy pavement on Seventy-second Street that we became engaged. Well, as I say, there I was, falling past another floor, looking about me in all directions. The hills of New Jersey looked magnificent. A high-flying pigeon coasted in my direction, and regarded me with a round eye, devoid of any expression whatsoever. Then he banked and sheered off. I could see the people in the street below, or rather their hats, jammed as closely as black pebbles on a beach. Even as I looked, one or two of these black pebbles suddenly turned white. I realized I was attracting attention."

"Tell me this," said the psychiatrist. "You seem to have had a good deal of time for thought. Did you recollect why you were falling? Had you thrown yourself out on purpose, or had you slipped by seeming accident, or what?"

"Doctor, I really don't know," said the young man. "Not unless my last dream, which I had last night, sheds any light on the matter. Most of the time I was just looking around, falling faster all the time, of course, but thinking faster to make up for it. Naturally, I tried to think of subjects of importance, seeing it was my last opportunity. Between the seventeenth and the sixteenth floors, for example, I thought a lot about democracy and the world crisis. It seemed to me that where most people are making a big mistake is . . ."

"Perhaps, for the moment, we had better keep to the experience itself," said the brain doctor.

"Well," said the young man, "at the fifteenth floor I looked in at the window, and, really, I never believed such things happened! Not in offices, anyway. And, Doctor, next day I paid a visit to the fifteenth floor here, just out of curiosity. And those offices are occupied by a theatrical agent. Doctor, don't you think that confirms my dream?"

"Calm yourself," said the psychiatrist. "The names of all the firms in this building are listed on the wall directory on the main floor. You no doubt retained an unconscious memory which you adroitly fitted into your dream."

"Well, after that," said the young man, "I began to look down a good deal more. I'd take just a quick glance into each window as I passed, but mostly I was looking downwards. By this time there were big patches of white among the dark, pebble-like hats below. In fact, pretty soon they were clearly distinguishable as hats and faces. I saw two taxicabs swerve toward one another and collide. A woman's scream drifted up out of the confused murmur below. I felt I agreed with her. I was in a reclining posture, and already I felt an anticipatory pain in the parts that would touch the ground first. So I turned face downwards—like this—but that was horrible. So I put my feet down, but then they hurt. I tried to fall head first, to end it sooner, but that didn't satisfy me either. I kept on twisting and turning—like this."

"Please relax," said the psychiatrist. "There is no need to demonstrate."

"I'm sorry," said the young man. "I picked up the habit from Maisie."

"Sit down," said the psychiatrist, "and continue."

"Last night," said the young man despairingly, "was the thirty-eighth night."

"Then," said the psychiatrist, "you must have got down to this level, for this office is on the mezzanine floor."

"I was," cried the young man. "And I was outside this very window, descending at terrific speed. I looked in. Doctor, I saw you! As clearly as I see you now!"

"Mr. Rotifer," replied the psychiatrist with a modest smile, "I very frequently figure in my patients' dreams."

"But I wasn't your patient then," said the young man. "I didn't even know you existed. I didn't know till this morning, when I came to see who occupied this office. Oh, Doctor, I was so relieved to find you were not a theatrical agent!"

"And why were you relieved?" asked the specialist blandly.

"Because you were not alone. In my dream, I mean. A young woman was with you. A young woman with beautiful golden hair. And she was sitting on your knee, Doctor, and her arms were around your neck. I felt certain it was another theatrical agency. And then I thought, 'That is very beautiful golden hair. It is like my Maisie's hair.' At that moment you both looked toward the window. It was she! Maisie! My own Maisie!"

The psychiatrist laughed very heartily, "My dear sir," said he, "you may set your mind entirely at rest."

"All the same," said the young man, "this morning, in the office, I have been prey to an unbearable curiosity, an almost irresistible urge to jump, just to see what I should see."

"You would have had the mortification," said the psychiatrist, "of seeing that there were no grounds whatever for your rash act. Your fiancée is not a patient of mine; therefore, she could not have had one of those harmless little transferences, as we call them, which have been known to lead to ardent behavior on the part of the subject. Besides, our profession has its ethics, and nothing ever happens in the office. No, my dear sir, what you have described to me is a relatively simple condition, a recurrent dream, a little neurotic compulsion—nothing that cannot be cured in time. If you can visit me three or four times a week, I am confident that a very few years will show a decided improvement."

"But, Doctor," cried the young man in despair, "I am due to hit the ground at any moment!"

"But only in a dream," said the psychiatrist reassuringly. "Be sure to remember it clearly, and note particularly if you bounce. Meanwhile, return to your office, carry on with your work, and worry as little as possible about it."

"I will try to do so," said the young man. "But, really, you are astonishingly like yourself as I saw you in my dream, even to that little pearl tiepin."

"That," said the psychiatrist, as he bowed him smilingly out, "was a gift from a very well-known lady, who was always falling in her dreams." So saying, he closed the door behind his visitor, who departed shaking his head in obstinate melancholy. The psychiatrist then seated himself at his desk and placed the tips of his fingers together, as psychiatrists always do while they are pondering on how much a new patient may be good for.

His meditation was interrupted by his secretary, who thrust her head in at the door. "Miss Mimling to see you," she said. "Her appointment is at two-thirty."

"Show her in," said the psychiatrist, and rose to greet the new entrant, who proved to be a young woman with the appearance of a rather wild mouse upon whose head someone has let fall a liberal splash of peroxide. She was in a very agitated state. "Oh, Doctor," she said, "I just *had* to telephone you, for when I saw your name in the book, of course I knew it was you. I saw your name on the door. In my dream, Doctor. In my dream."

"Let us talk it over very quietly," said the healer of souls, trying to maneuver her into the deep armchair. She was fidgety, however, and perched herself upon the corner of his desk. "I don't know if you think there is anything *in* dreams," she said. "But this was such an extraordinary one.

"I dreamed I came up to your door, and there was your name on it, just as it is out there. That's how it was I came to look you up in the telephone book, and there it was again. So I felt I just had to come and see you.

"Well, I dreamed I came into your office, and I was sitting here on the desk, just like this, talking to you, and all of a sudden—of course I know it was only a dream—I felt a feeling . . . well, really, I hardly know how to tell you. It seemed to me as if you were my father, my big brother, and a boy I once knew called Herman Myers, all rolled into one. I don't know how I could feel like that, even in a dream, for I am engaged to a young man I love with all my conscious mind, and I thought with my unconscious, too. Oh, it's awful of me!"

"My dear young lady," purred the psychiatrist, "this is nothing more or less than the phenomenon of transference. It is something which can happen to anybody, and usually it does."

"Yes," said she, "but it made me transfer myself to your knee, like this, and put my arms around your neck, like this."

"Now! now!" murmured the psychiatrist gently, "I'm afraid you are acting out a neurotic impulse."

"I always act things out," she said. "They say it makes me the life and soul of a party. But, Doctor, then I happened to look out of the window, like this, and . . . Wow! There he is! There he was! It was Charlie! Oh, what a terrible look he gave us as he went by!"

Mary

There was in those days—I hope it is there still—a village called Ufferleigh, lying all among the hills and downs of North Hampshire. In every cottage garden there was a giant apple tree, and when these trees were hung red with fruit, and the newly lifted potatoes lay gleaming between bean-row and cabbage-patch, a young man walked into the village who had never been there before.

He stopped in the lane just under Mrs. Hedges' gate, and looked up into her garden. Rosie, who was picking the beans, heard his tentative cough, and turned and leaned over the hedge to hear what he wanted. "I was wondering," said he, "if there was anybody in the village who had a lodging to let."

He looked at Rosie, whose cheeks were redder than the apples, and whose hair was the softest yellow imaginable. "I was wondering," said he in amendment, "if *you* had."

Rosie looked back at him. He wore a blue jersey such as seafaring men wear, but he seemed hardly like a seafaring man. His face was brown and plain and pleasant, and his hair was black. He was shabby and he was shy, but there was something about him that made it very certain he was not just a tramp. "I'll ask," said Rosie.

With that she ran for her mother, and Mrs. Hedges came out to interview the young man. "I've got to be near Andover for a week," said he, "but somehow I didn't fancy staying right in the town."

"There's a bed," said Mrs. Hedges. "If you don't mind having your meals with us—"

"Why, surely, ma'am," said he. "There's nothing I'd like better."

Everything was speedily arranged; Rosie picked another handful of beans; and in an hour he was seated with them at supper. He told them his name was Fred Baker, but, apart from that, he was so polite that he could hardly speak, and, in the end, Mrs. Hedges had to ask him outright what his business was. "Why, ma'am," said he, looking her straight in the face, "I've done one thing and another since I was so high, but I heard an old proverb once, how to get on in the world. 'Feed 'em or amuse 'em,' it said. So that's what I do, ma'am. I travel with a pig."

Mrs. Hedges said she had never heard of such a thing.

"You surprise me," said he. "Why, there are some in London, they tell me, making fortunes on the halls. Spell, count, add up, answer questions, anything. But let them wait," said he, smiling, "till they see Mary."

"Is that the name of your pig?" asked Rosie.

"Well," said Fred, shyly, "it's what I call her just between ourselves. To her public, she's Zola. Sort of Frenchified, I thought. Spicy, if you'll excuse the mention of it. But in the caravan I call her Mary."

"You live in a caravan?" cried Rosie, delighted by the doll's-house idea.

"We do," said he. "She has her bunk, and I have mine."

"I don't think I should like that," said Mrs. Hedges. "Not a pig. No."

"She's as clean," said he, "as a newborn babe. And as for company, well, you'd say she's human. All the same, it's a bit of wandering life for her—up hill and down dale, as the saying goes. Between you and me, I shan't be satisfied till I get her into one of these big London theaters. You can see us in the West End!"

"I should like the caravan best," said Rosie, who seemed to have a great deal to say for herself all of a sudden.

"It's pretty," said Fred. "Curtains, you know. Pot of flowers. Little stove. Somehow I'm used to it. Can't hardly think of myself staying at one of them big hotels. Still, Mary's got her career to think of. I can't stand in the way of her talent, so that's that."

"Is she big?" asked Rosie.

"It's not her size," said he. "No more than Shirley Temple. It's her brains and personality. Clever as a wagonload of monkeys! You'd like her. She'd like you, I reckon. Yes, I reckon she would. Sometimes, I'm afraid I'm a bit slow by way of company for her, never having had much to do with the ladies."

"Don't tell me," said Mrs. Hedges archly, as convention required.

" 'Tis so, ma'am," said he. "Always on the move, you see, ever since I was a nipper. Baskets and brooms, pots and pans, then some acrobat stuff, then Mary. Never two days in the same place. It don't give you the time to get acquainted."

"You're going to be here a whole week, though," said Rosie artlessly. But at once her red cheeks blushed a hundred times redder than before, for Mrs. Hedges gave her a sharp look, which made her see that her words might have been taken the wrong way.

Fred, however, had noticed nothing. "Yes," said he, "I shall be here a week. And why? Mary ran a nail in her foot in the market-place, Andover. Finished her act—and collapsed. Now she's at the vet's, poor creature."

"Oh, poor thing!" cried Rosie.

"I was half-afraid," said he, "it was going wrong on her. But it seems she'll pull round all right, and I took opportunity to have the van repaired a bit, and soon we'll be on the road again. I shall go in and see her tomorrow. Maybe I can find some blackberries, to take her by way of a relish, so to speak."

"Gorsley Bottom," said Rosie. "That's the place where they grow big and juicy."

"Ah! If I knew where it was—" said Fred tentatively.

"Perhaps, in the morning, if she's got time, she'll show you," said Mrs. Hedges, who began to feel very kindly disposed toward the young man.

In the morning, surely enough, Rosie did have time, and she showed Fred the place, and helped him pick the berries. Returning from Andover, later in the day, Fred reported that Mary had tucked into them a fair treat, and he had little doubt that, if she could have spoken, she would have sent her special thanks. Nothing is more affecting than the gratitude of a dumb animal, and Rosie was impelled to go every morning with Fred to pick a few more berries for the invalid pig.

On these excursions, Fred told her a great deal more about Mary, a bit about the caravan, and a little about himself. She saw that he was very bold and knowing in some ways, but incredibly simple and shy in others. This, she felt, showed he had a good heart.

The end of the week seemed to come very soon, and all at once they were coming back from Gorsley Bottom for the last time. Fred said he would never forget Ufferleigh, nor the nice time he had there.

"You ought to send us a postcard when you're on your travels," said Rosie.

"Yes," he said. "That's an idea. I will."

"Yes, do," said Rosie.

"Yes," said he again. "I will. Do you know, I was altogether downhearted at going away, but now I'm half wishing I was on the road again already. So I could be sending that card right away," said he.

"At that rate," said Rosie, looking the other way, "you might as well make it a letter."

"Ah!" said he. "And do you know what I should feel like putting at the bottom of that letter? If you was my young lady, that is. Which, of course, you're not. Me never having had one."

"What?" said Rosie.

"A young lady," said he.

"But what would you put?" said she.

"Ah!" said he. "What I'd put. Do you know what I'd put? If— *if*, mind you—if you was my young lady?"

"No," said she, "what?"

"I don't hardly like to tell you," said he.

"Go on," she said. "You don't want to be afraid."

"All right," said he. "Only mind you, it's *if*." And with his stick he traced three crosses in the dust.

"If I was anybody's young lady," said Rosie, "I shouldn't see anything wrong in that. After all, you've got to move with the times."

Neither of them said another word, for two of the best reasons in the world. First, they were unable to; second, it was not necessary. They walked on with their faces as red as fire, in an agony of happiness.

Fred had a word with Mrs. Hedges, who had taken a fancy to him from the start. Not that she had not always looked down upon caravan people, and could have been knocked over with a feather, had anyone suggested, at any earlier date, that she would allow a daughter of hers to marry into such a company. But right was right; this Fred Baker was different, as anyone with half an eye could see. He had kept himself to himself, almost to a fault; his conversation showed that he was as innocent as a newborn babe. Moreover, several knowledgeable people in the village had agreed that his ambitions for Mary, his pig, were in no way unjustified. Everyone had heard of such talented creatures, reclining on snow-white sheets in the best hotels of the metropolis, drinking champagne like milk, and earning for their fortunate owners ten pounds, or even twenty pounds, a week.

So Mrs. Hedges smilingly gave her consent, and Rosie became Fred's real, genuine, proper young lady. He was to save all he could during the winter, and she to stitch and sing. In the spring, he would come back and they were to get married.

"At Easter," said he.

"No," said Mrs. Hedges, counting on her fingers. "In May. Then tongues can't wag, caravan or no caravan."

Fred had not the faintest idea what she was driving at, for he had lived so much alone that no one had told him certain things that every young man should know. However, he well realized that this was an unusually short engagement for Ufferleigh, and represented a great concession to the speed and dash of the entertainment industry, so he respectfully agreed, and set off on his travels.

My Darling Rosie,

Well here we are in Painswick having had a good night Saturday at Evesham. Mary cleverer than ever that goes without saying now spells four new words thirty-six in all and when I say now Mary how do you like Painswick or Evesham or wherever it is she picks F I N E it goes down very well. She is in the best of health and I hope you are the same. Seems to understand every word I say more like a human being every day. Well I suppose I must be getting our bit of supper ready she always sets up her cry for that specially when I am writing to you.

With true love
Fred XXX

In May the apple trees were all in bloom, so it was an apple-blossom wedding, which in those parts is held to be an assurance of flowery days. Afterwards they took the bus to the market town, to pick up the caravan, which stood in a stableyard. On the way, Fred asked Rosie to wait a moment, and dived into a confectioner's shop. He came out with a huge box of chocolates. Rosie smiled all over her face with joy. "For me?" she said.

"Yes," said he. "To give to her as soon as she claps eyes on you. They're her weakness. I want you two to be real pals."

"All right," said Rosie, who was the best-hearted girl in the world.

The next moment, they turned into the yard: there was the caravan. "Oh, it's lovely!" cried Rosie.

"Now, you'll see her," said Fred.

At the sound of his voice, a falsetto squeal rose from within.

"Here we are, old lady," said Fred, opening the door. "Here's a friend of mine come to help look after you. Look, she's brought you something you'll fancy."

Rosie saw a smallish pig, flesh-colored, neat, and with a smart collar. It had a small and rather calculating eye. Rosie offered the chocolates; they were accepted without any very effusive acknowledgment.

Fred put the old horse in, and soon they were off, jogging up the long hills to the west. Rosie sat beside Fred on the driving seat; Mary took her afternoon nap. Soon, the sky began to redden where the road divided the woods on the far hilltop. Fred turned into a green lane, and they made their camp.

He lit the stove, and Rosie put on the potatoes. They took a lot of peeling, for it seemed that Mary ate with gusto. Rosie put a gigantic rice pudding into the oven, and soon had the rest of the meal prepared.

Fred set the table. He laid three places.

"I say," said Rosie.

"What?" said Fred.

"Does she eat along with us?" said Rosie. "A pig?"

Fred turned quite pale. He beckoned her outside the caravan. "Don't say a thing like that," said he. "She won't never take to you if you say a thing like that. Didn't you see her give you a look?"

"Yes, I did," said Rosie. "All the same—Well, never mind, Fred. I don't care, really. I just thought I did."

"You wait," said Fred. "You're thinking of ordinary pigs. Mary's different."

Certainly, Mary seemed a comparatively tidy eater. All the same, she gave Rosie one or two very odd glances from under her silky, straw-colored lashes. She seemed to hock her rice pudding about a bit with the end of her nose.

"What's up, old girl?" said Fred. "Didn't she put enough sugar in the pudden? Never mind—can't get everything right first time."

Mary, with a rather cross hiccup, settled herself on her bunk. "Let's go out," said Rosie, "and have a look at the moon."

"I suppose we might," said Fred. "Shan't be long, Mary. Just going about as far as that gate down the lane." Mary grunted morosely and turned her face to the wall.

Rosie and Fred went out and leaned over the gate. The moon, at least, was all that it should be.

"Seems funny, being married and all," said Rosie softly.

"Seems all right to me," said Fred.

"Remember them crosses you drew in the dirt in the road that day?" said Rosie.

"That I do," said Fred.

"And all them you put in the letters?" said Rosie.

"All of 'em," said Fred. "I remember every one."

"Kisses, that's what they're supposed to stand for," said Rosie.

"So they say," said Fred.

"You haven't given me one, not since we were married," said Rosie. "Don't you like it?"

"That I do," said Fred. "Only, I don't know—"

"What?" said Rosie.

"It makes me feel all queer," said Fred, "when I kiss you. As if I wanted—"

"What?" said Rosie.

"I dunno," said Fred. "I don't know if it's I want to eat you all up, or what."

"Try and find out, they say," said Rosie.

A delicious moment followed. In the very middle of it, a piercing squeal rose from the caravan. Fred jumped as if he were shot.

"Oh, dear!" he cried. "She's wondering what's up. Here I come, old girl! Here I come! It's her bedtime, you see. Here I come to tuck you in!"

Mary, with an air of some petulance, permitted this process. Rosie stood by. "I suppose we'd better make it lights out," said Fred. "She likes a lot of sleep, you see, being a brain worker."

"Where do *we* sleep?" said Rosie.

"I made the bunk all nice for you this morning," said Fred. "Me, I'm going to doss below. A sack full of straw, I've got."

"But—" said Rosie. "But—"

"But what?" said he.

"Nothing," said she. "Nothing."

They turned in. Rosie lay for an hour or two, thinking what thoughts I don't know. Perhaps she thought how charming it was that Fred should have lived so simple and shy and secluded all these years, and yet be so knowing about so many things, and yet be so innocent, and never have been mixed up in bad company. . . . It is impossible to say what she thought.

In the end, she dozed off, only to be wakened by a sound like the bagpipes of the devil himself. She sat up, terrified. It was Mary.

"What's up? What's up?" Fred's voice came like the ghost's in *Hamlet* from under the floor. "Give her some milk," he said.

Rosie poured out a bowl of milk. Mary ceased her fiendish racket while she drank, but, the moment Rosie had blown out the light, and got into bed again, she began a hundred times worse than before.

There were rumblings under the caravan. Fred appeared in the doorway, half dressed and with a straw in his hair.

"She *will* have me," he said, in great distress.

"Can't you—Can't you lie down here?" said Rosie.

"What? And you sleep below?" said Fred, astounded.

"Yes," said Rosie, after a rather long pause. "And me sleep below."

Fred was overwhelmed with gratitude and remorse. Rosie couldn't help feeling sorry for him. She even managed to give him a smile before she went to get what rest she could on the sack of straw.

In the morning, she woke feeling rather dejected. There was a mighty breakfast to be prepared for Mary; afterwards Fred drew her aside.

"Look here," he said. "This won't do. I can't have you sleeping on the ground, worse than a gippo. I'll tell you what I'm going to do. I'm going to get up my acrobat stuff again. I used to make a lot that way, and I like it fine. Handsprings, double somersaults, bit of conjuring—it went down well. Only I didn't have time to keep in practice with Mary to look after. But if you'd do the looking after her, we'd make it a double turn, and soon we'd have a good bit of cash. And then. . . ."

"Yes?" said Rosie.

"Then," said Fred, "I could buy you a trailer."

"All right," said Rosie, and turned away. Suddenly she turned back with her face flaming. "You may know a lot about pigs," she said bitterly. "And about somersaults, and conjuring, and baskets, and brooms and I don't know what-all. But there's *one* thing you *don't* know." And with that she went off and cried behind a hedge.

After a while she got the upper hand of it, and came back to the caravan. Fred showed her how to give Mary her morning bath; then the depilatory—which was very hard on the hands; then the rubbing with Cleopatra Face Cream, and not on her face merely; then the powdering; then the manicuring and polishing of her trotters.

Rosie, resolved to make the best of it, conquered her repugnance, and soon mastered these handmaidenly duties. She was relieved, at first, that the spoiled pig accepted her ministrations without protest. Then she noticed the gloating look in its eye.

However, there was no time to brood about that. No sooner was the toilet finished than it was time to prepare the enormous lunch. After lunch Mary had her little walk, except on Saturdays when

there was an afternoon show, and after the walk she took her rest.
Fred explained that during this period she liked to be talked to, and
to have her back scratched a bit. Mary had quite clearly decided that
in the future she was going to have it scratched a lot. Then she had
her massage. Then tea, then another little walk, or the evening show,
according to where they were, and then it was time to prepare dinner. At the end of the day, Rosie was thankful to curl up on her
poor sack of straw.

When she thought of the bunk above, and Fred, and his simplicity, her heart was fit to break. The only thing was, she loved
him dearly, and she felt that if they could soon snatch an hour alone
together, they might kiss a little more, and a ray of light might dispel
the darkness of excessive innocence.

Each new day, she watched for that hour, but it didn't come.
Mary saw to that. Once or twice, Rosie suggested a little stroll, but,
at once, the hateful pig grumbled some demand or other that kept
her hard at work till it was too late. Fred, on his side, was busy
enough with his practicing. He meant it so well, and worked so
hard—but what did it lead to? A trailer!

As the days went by, she found herself more and more the slave
of this arrogant grunter. Her back ached, her hands got chapped and
red, she never had a moment to make herself look nice, and never
a moment alone with her beloved. Her dress was spotted and
spoiled, her smile was gone, her temper was going. Her pretty hair
fell in elf locks and tangles, and she had neither time nor heart to
comb it.

She tried to come to an explanation with Fred, but it was nothing
but cross-purposes and then cross words. He tried in a score of little
ways to show that he loved her, but these seemed to her a mere
mockery, and she gave him short answers. Then he stopped, and she
thought he loved her no longer. Even worse, she felt she no longer
loved him.

So the whole summer went by, and things got worse and worse,
and you would have taken her for a Gypsy, indeed.

The blackberries were ripe again; she found a whole brake of
them. When she tasted one, all sorts of memories flooded into her
heart. She went and found Fred. "Fred," she said, "the blackberries
are ripe again. I've brought you one or two." She held out some in
her grubby hand. Fred took them and tasted them; she watched to
see what the result would be.

"Yes," said he, "they're ripe. They won't gripe her. Take her and pick her some this afternoon."

Rosie turned away without a word, and, in the afternoon, she took Mary across the stubbles to where the ripe berries grew. Mary, when she saw them, dispensed for once with dainty service, and began to help herself very liberally. Rosie, finding she had nothing more urgent to attend to, sat down on a bank and sobbed bitterly.

In the middle of it all, she heard a voice asking what was the matter. She looked up, and there was a fat, shrewd, jolly-looking farmer. "What is it, my girl?" said he. "Are you hungry?"

"No," said she, "I'm fed up."

"What with?" said he.

"A pig!" said she, with a gulp.

"You've got no call to bawl and cry," said he. "There's nothing like a bit of pork. I'd have the indigestion for that, any day."

"It's not pork," she said. "It's a pig. A live pig."

"Have you lost it?" said he.

"I wish I had," said she. "I'm that miserable I don't know what to do."

"Tell me your troubles," said he. "There's no harm in a bit of sympathy."

So Rosie told him about Fred, and about Mary, and what hopes she'd had and what they'd all come to, and how she was the slave of this insolent, spoiled, jealous pig, and, in fact, she told him everything except one little matter which she could hardly bring herself to repeat, even to the most sympathetic of fat farmers.

The farmer, pushing his hat over his eyes, scratched his head very thoughtfully. "Really," said he. "I can't hardly believe it."

"It's true," said Rosie, "every word."

"I mean," said the farmer. "A young man—a young gal—the young gal sleeping down on a sack of straw—a pretty young gal like you. Properly married and all. Not to put too fine a point on it, young missus, aren't the bunks wide enough, or what?"

"He doesn't know," sobbed Rosie. "He just doesn't know no more'n a baby. And she won't let us ever be alone a minute. So he never gets a chance to find out."

The farmer scratched his head more furiously than ever. Looking at her tear-stained face, he found it hard to doubt her. On the other hand, it seemed impossible that a pig should know so much and a young man should know so little. But, at that moment, Mary came trotting through the bushes, with an egotistical look on her face, which was well besmeared with the juice of the ripe berries.

"Is this your pig?" said the farmer.

"Well," said Rosie, "I'm just taking her for a walk."

The shrewd farmer was quick to notice the look that Rosie got from the haughty grunter when it heard the expression "your pig." This, and Rosie's hurried, nervous disclaimer, convinced the worthy man that the story he had heard was well-founded.

"You're taking her for a walk?" said he musingly. "Well! Well! Well! I'll tell you what. If you'd ha' been here this time tomorrow you'd have met *me* taking a walk, with a number of very dear young friends of mine, all very much like her. She might have come along. Two young sows, beautiful creatures, though maybe not so beautiful as that one. Three young boars, in the prime of their health and handsomeness. Though I say it as shouldn't, him that's unattached— he's a prince. Oh, what a beautiful young boar that young boar really is!"

"You don't say?" said Rosie.

"For looks and pedigree both," said the farmer, "he's a prince. The fact is, it's their birthday, and I'm taking 'em over to the village for a little bit of a celebration. I suppose this young lady has some other engagement tomorrow."

"She has to have her sleep just about this time," said Rosie, ignoring Mary's angry grunt.

"Pity!" said the farmer. "She'd have just made up the party. Such fun they'll have! Such refreshments! Sweet apples, cakes, biscuits, a whole bucket full of ice cream. Everything most refined, of course, but plenty. You know what I mean—plenty. And that young boar —you know what I mean. If she *should* be walking by—"

"I'm afraid not," said Rosie.

"Pity!" said the farmer. "Ah, well, I must be moving along."

With that, he bade them good afternoon, raising his hat very politely to Mary, who looked after him for a long time, and then walked sulkily home, gobbling to herself all the way.

The next afternoon Mary seemed eager to stretch out on her bunk, and, for once, instead of requiring the usual number of little attentions from Rosie, she closed her eyes in sleep. Rosie took the opportunity to pick up a pail and go off to buy the evening ration of fresh milk. When she got back, Fred was still at his practice by the wayside, and Rosie went round to the back of the caravan, and the door was swinging open, and the bunk was empty.

She called Fred. They sought high and low. They went along the roads, fearing she might have been knocked over by a motorcar. They went calling through the woods, hoping she had fallen asleep under a tree. They looked in ponds and ditches, behind haystacks, under bridges, everywhere. Rosie thought of the farmer's joking talk, but she hardly liked to say anything about it to Fred.

They called and called all night, scarcely stopping to rest. They sought all the next day. It grew dark, and Fred gave up hope. They plodded silently back to the caravan.

He sat on a bunk, with his head in his hand.

"I shall never see her again," he said. "Been pinched, that's what she's been.

"When I think," he said, "of all the hopes I had for that pig—

"When I think," he said, "of all you've done for her! And what it's meant to you—

"I know she had some faults in her nature," he said. "But that was artistic. Temperament, it was. When you got a talent like that—

"And now she's gone!" he said. With that, he burst into tears.

"Oh, Fred!" cried Rosie. "Don't!"

Suddenly, she found she loved him just as much as ever, more than ever. She sat down beside him and put her arms around his neck. "Darling Fred, don't cry!" she said again.

"It's been rough on you, I know," said Fred. "I didn't ever mean it to be."

"There! There!" said Rosie. She gave him a kiss. Then she gave him another. It was a long time since they had been as close as this. There was nothing but the two of them and the caravan; the tiny lamp, and darkness all round; their kisses, and grief all round. "Don't let go," said Fred. "It makes it better."

"I'm not letting go," she said.

"Rosie," said Fred. "I feel—Do you know how I feel?"

"I know," she said. "Don't talk."

"Rosie," said Fred, but this was sometime later. "Who'd have thought it?"

"Ah! Who would, indeed?" said Rosie.

"Why didn't you tell me?" said Fred.

"How could I tell you?" said she.

"You know," said he. "We might never have found out—never! —if she hadn't been pinched."

"Don't talk about her," said Rosie.

"I can't help it," said Fred. "Wicked or not, I can't help it—I'm glad she's gone. It's worth it. I'll make enough on the acrobat stuff. I'll make brooms as well. Pots and pans, too."

"Yes," said Rosie. "But look! It's morning already. I reckon you're tired, Fred—running up hill and down dale all day yesterday. You lie abed now, and I'll go down to the village and get you something good for breakfast."

"All right," said Fred. "And tomorrow I'll get yours."

So Rosie went down to the village, and bought the milk and the bread and so forth. As she passed the butcher's shop she saw some new-made pork sausages of a singularly fresh, plump, and appetizing apearance. So she bought some, and very good they smelled while they were cooking.

"That's another thing we couldn't have while she was here," said Fred, as he finished his plateful. "Never no pork sausages, on account of her feelings. I never thought to see the day I'd be glad she was pinched. I only hope she's gone to someone who appreciates her."

"I'm sure she has," said Rosie. "Have some more."

"I will," said he. "I don't know if it's the novelty, or the way you cooked 'em, or what. I never ate a better sausage in my life. If we'd gone up to London with her, best hotels and all, I doubt if ever we'd have had as sweet a sausage as these here."

Hell hath no fury

As soon as Einstein declared that space was finite, the price of building sites, both in Heaven and Hell, soared outrageously. A number of petty fiends, who had been living in snug squalor in the remoter infernal provinces, found themselves evicted from their sorry shacks, and had not the wherewithal to buy fresh plots at the new prices. There was nothing for it but to emigrate. They scattered themselves over the various habitable planets of our universe; one of them arrived in London at about the hour of midnight in the October of last year.

Some angels in like case took similar measures, and, by a coincidence, one of them descended at the same hour into the same northern suburb.

Beings of this order, when they take on the appearance of humans, have the privilege of assuming whichever sex they chose. Things being as they are, and both angels and devils knowing very well what's what, both of them decided to become young women of about the age of twenty-one. The fiend, as soon as he touched earth, was no other than Bella Kimberly, a brunette, and the angel became the equally beautiful Eva Anderson, a blonde.

By the essential limitation of their natures, it is impossible for an angel to recognize fiendishness on beholding it, and equally so for a fiend even to conceive the existence of angelic virtue. As a matter of fact, at such a meeting as now took place in Lowndes Crescent, St. John's Wood, the angel is innocently attracted by what seems to her the superior strength and intensity of the fiendish nature, while the devil experiences that exquisite interest aroused in some by the purity and coolness of a first-class martini.

The two girls accosted one another, and each asked if the other knew of a suitable lodging house in the neighborhood. The similarity of their need caused them first to laugh heartily, and then to agree to become roommates and companions of fortune. Bella suggested that it was perhaps too late to make respectable application for a lodging, therefore they spent the night strolling on Hampstead Heath, talking of how they would earn their livings, and of what fun they would have together, and of love, and then of breakfast, which is not an unnatural sequel.

They had some poached eggs in the little Express Dairy in Heath Street, and afterwards found a pleasant room on the third floor of a large house in Upper Park Road. Then they went out in search of employment. Bella was soon taken on as a dancing instructress, and Eva, with a little more difficulty, secured a situation as harpist in a ladies' orchestra.

Once they were settled thus, they began to enjoy themselves as girls do, chattering and giggling at all hours. It is true that some of the things Bella said made Eva blush from the crown of her head to the soles of her feet, but she already loved her dark friend, and found her daring humor quite irresistible. They made amicable division of the chest of drawers, and shared the same bed, which no one thought was extraordinary, nor would have if they had known them in their true characters, for nothing is more common than to find a fiend and an angel between the same pair of sheets, and, if it were otherwise, life would be hellishly dull for some of us.

Now there was living in this lodging house a young man scarcely older than Bella and Eva, who was studying to become an architect, and who had never known love, nor been put off for long by any imitation. His name was Harry Pettigrew, and his hair was a very medium color, neither too dark nor too fair.

His means were limited, and his room was on the topmost floor, but not so far above that inhabited by the two girls but he could hear their delicious giggling at that still hour when he should have been at his latest studies. He longed to go down and tap at their door and ask them what the joke was, but he was too shy.

However, when three such young people are in the same house, it is not long before they become acquainted. On one occasion, Bella forgot to lock the bathroom door, and the reason for this must have been that in Hell there are no baths, and hence no bathrooms, and consequently no bathroom doors.

It was a Sunday. The young man himself was descending in a dressing gown to take his morning dip. There was a delicious little *contretemps,* in which, fortunately, he saw no more than any decent young man would wish to see. All the same, he retreated in great confusion, for he had no notion of the wishes of decent young women. His confusion was so extreme that he counted neither stairs nor landings in ascending, and, flinging open a door which he took to be his own, he discovered Eva in the third position of Müller's exercise for the abdominal muscles, and in nothing else at all.

Now angels, as every man knows, are, by virtue of their very innocence, or the simplicity of the celestial costume, sometimes far less conventionally modest than the squeakers of the darker sister-hood. Eva hastily, but without panic, threw a wrap about her shoulders: "You look quite upset," she said. "There is no reason to be upset. Did you want anything?"

"No . . . ," he said, ". . . I *did* not. In fact, I came in by mistake. It is nice of you not to scream or be angry with me."

They exchanged one or two more little civilities. In the end, Harry was emboldened to suggest a walk on the Heath. Before Eva could reply, Bella entered, and, not seeing him there, she burst out, with a giggle, "Whatever do you think happened to *me?*" Then, catching sight of him, she subsided into a confusion doubly arch.

This took off a little from the exquisite naturalness of the other encounter, a service for which Harry was not as grateful as he might have been, had he known to what a quarter, and from what a quarter, his fancy was being inclined. The truth is that, where a fiend and an angel, both in female form, are seen by the same young man, in precisely the same illuminating circumstances, he will, fifty or fifty-five times out of a hundred, choose the angel, if he is a nice young man, and if he has time enough.

Therefore, when they were all three on Hampstead Heath that afternoon, Harry addressed Bella with very pleasant words, but with words only, while to Eva he accorded certain looks as well.

Bella was not very slow at putting two and two together. She had been looking forward to a long period of mortal sin with this attractive young man, and to flying off with his soul afterwards. The soul of an architect, especially if he is of strong Palladian tendencies, is well worth a handsome villa, standing in two or three acres of well-laid-out grounds, in the most desirable residential quarter of Hell. You can imagine this homeless fiend's mortification, against which could have been measured the fury of the woman scorned, since they were here resident in the same anatomy.

She saw every day that Harry was growing fonder of her blonde companion, and conceived the idea of adding a fourth to their party, in the shape of a young man nearly as swarthy as herself whom she had met at the dancing-hall and with whom she was already quite sufficiently familiar.

She represented to him that Eva was likely to inherit a large sum of money. This, and her blonde locks and guileless air, were quite enough for the dance-hall Valentino, and all he asked was opportunity to come at her.

"It's no good just trying to do the sheik," said Bella, "for she's already crazy about Harry Pettigrew, who should be my boyfriend by rights. What you want is to give him the idea you and she are like that. That'll make him sheer off quick enough, if I know his lordship." It will be observed that Bella's speech was vulgar in the extreme; this is a very usual deficiency of fiends.

Her dancing partner, whom she had made well-acquainted with the stings of jealousy, soon found means to introduce them to Harry. For example, on one Sunday when they were all walking in the sylvan shades of Kenwood, he had Bella fall behind with Harry on some pretext or other, and when he and Eva had gone ahead a turn or two of the winding pathway, he put his arm behind her, without touching her in the least (or he would have had a severe rebuke), but so that it should appear to Harry, when he rounded the bend, that his hastily withdrawn arm had been about her consenting waist.

Not only this, but he once or twice made a sudden movement, and appeared flustered, when Harry entered a room in which he and Eva had been left alone by his accomplice. He was not above making, when he heard his rival's step outside the door, a little kissing sound with his perjured lips. On one occasion, when Bella was away for the weekend, he went so far as to throw a sock in at Eva's window.

Here he overreached himself. Harry, returning with Eva from a walk, was so overcome by the sight of this sock that he could no longer suffer in silence, but, first of all asking (as it were carelessly) whose sock that could be, he soon burst out with all the accumulated suspicions of the past few weeks, and had the infinite pleasure of hearing them denied frankly, emphatically, unmistakably, and, above all, angelically.

A pretty little scene ensued, in which they discovered that their love partook of the nature of perfection. In fact, the only attribute that was wanting was completeness, which is recognized as being as essential to perfection by many of the ancient philosophers, several of the Fathers of the Church, and by all young lovers. It is the nature of men to strive after perfection, and of angels to attain it. Our young pair were true to type, and, after a little amicable discussion, it was agreed that they should endeavor to realize perfection in Eva's room that very night, when all the house was asleep. If perfection itself is insufficient for the censorious, such are reminded that in Heaven there is no marrying or giving in marriage, and among architectural students very little.

Now, it so happened that Bella had returned that very afternoon, and had gone into conference with her accomplice to devise some bold stroke by which they might each achieve their impatient ends. At last, they agreed on the boldest of all. Bella that very night was to visit Harry in his bedroom, and the swarthy dancing-man was to play the Tarquin in Eva's.

That night, at about the middle hour, they repaired to Hampstead. It was as black as pitch, no moon, a mist over the stars; no lights in the other lodgers' rooms, for they were all asleep; no light in Harry's, because he was not there; no light in Eva's, because he was.

Bella, not knowing this, goes up to the top, finds him absent, and gets into his bed by way of a little surprise for him when he returns.

The dancing-man, making his entry a little later, gropes his way up the stairs, and, stopping at Eva's door, hears a murmuring within, which is, in fact, our young pair expressing to one another their great admiration of the perfection of perfection. He concludes he is a flight too low, goes higher, opens the door of Harry's room, and, all in the dark, seizes upon the waiting Bella, who, in high delight at his enthusiasm, lets down a losing battle in a very convincing way.

Several hours passed, in which the good enjoyed that happiness which is the reward of virtue, and the wicked that illusion of it that is the consolation of vice.

In the first gray of dawn, our good Harry made a very pretty speech of thanks to his charmer, in which he told her that she was an angel and had transported him to Heaven itself.

Bella and her companion, on the other hand, damned one another with more heat than grace. They were sufficiently realistic, however, to agree that a good illusion is better than nothing at all, and they resolved to perpetuate their error by seeking it in an eternity of darknesses, but, at this, I believe, they were not particularly successful.

IN THE CARDS

The Vascal System is the most reliable, the most up-to-date, and the most scientific method of foretelling the future by cards. It is true the operator cannot tell his own fortune, but that drawback seems to be common to all methods, and in every other way the successes of the Vascal System have been prodigious.

A wife, who studied Vascal in her spare time, laid out the cards for her husband on the breakfast table. She revealed to him that he would be involved in an unfortunate collision, and suffer a severe shock at the very least, if by any chance he drove his car home between three and five that afternoon. He now regularly desires his wife to lay out the cards for him, and never drives home before the hours she announces as propitious, with the result that he is almost the only person in the whole neighborhood who has not been considerably shocked during the period in question.

A young girl, holder of a Grade-A Vascal Diploma, was able to warn her still younger sister that she might that evening expect to lose something she had possessed all her life, through the agency of a tall, dark man, but though this would cause her some little distress at the outset, it would in the end lead to lasting happiness and satisfaction. Sure enough, the young sister left for a blind date that evening in such haste that she forgot to lock the door behind her. A tall, dark sneak thief, entering, took away her baby seed-pearl necklace, which was a tatty little number anyway, and she was successful in gypping the insurance people for at least three times its value, and bought that very same rhinestone clip which first attracted the attention of Mr. Jerry Horrabin, now her fiancé.

Mr. Brewster, when only halfway through the Vascal Course, laid out the cards for his wife, and told her she would be wrong to insist on going to the theater that evening, because the show would stink. She did insist, and it did stink.

Convinced by these, and by scores of other unsolicited testimonials, Myra Wilkins decided she could hardly do better than enroll as a student. Her idea was a big one—she meant to play her cards properly. She considered that, sooner or later, among the numerous young men who would flock to consult her, she would strike one for whom she could foresee an enormous fortune arriving in the near future from some unsuspected source. She had no intention of unsettling this happy young man by telling him what the future held, but thought rather she might warn him against any Queens of Hearts or Diamonds with whom he might be involved, and guide him gently toward a marriage with a high-grade Spade, for Myra was a brunette.

She graduated with the highest honors, and set up in a shadowy little nook in the West Forties, above the establishment of a dancing instructress with whom she was acquainted. She figured that young men who took dancing lessons often had a great yearning to know what the future held for them, and she hoped these would form the nucleus of a clientele.

Myra had very little capital, and this was exhausted in furnishing her nook with bead curtains, witch balls, images of Buddha, and similar junk, to create a convincing atmosphere for her visitors. She set her fee very low, in order to get the widest possible range of clients, and thus increase her chances of finding a future millionaire among them.

She shuffled and spread her greasy pack of cards, foretelling for innumerable insignificant young men the details of futures that were little better than pasts, which of course they would become one of these days. As far as the imminent fortune was concerned, the whole business was like a game of solitaire that never came out. The average future wealth of her clients was somewhere about the Two of Diamonds, and work and worry loomed up like a straight flush in clubs or spades.

The months stretched on into years, and the dust lay thick upon the witch ball and the Buddha. Myra had nothing but her dreams of wealth, and these, like an old knife, were sharpened to a razor keenness. At last, late one afternoon, when the shadows were at their deepest, the stairway groaned beneath a heavy tread, and a hulking figure tried to get four ways at once through the bead curtain that screened her alcove.

The new customer was an ugly one, and a more prosperous fortune-teller would probably have sent him straight back to the zoo. Myra, however, could not afford to pass up a dollar, so she wearily laid out her pack. The Two of Clubs frisked around fairly actively in the near foreground, in a context which gave it the significance of a cop's nightstick. She saw that her client was in some danger of visiting a large building, full of men in strange clothes, but vaguer influences seemed to indicate a postponement of this necessity.

Suddenly she had to repress a cry that rose unbidden to her lips. It was as if his future, dark as a cannibal king, had smiled, and revealed a golden tooth. Vascal declared unequivocally that a handsome fortune was coming to this young man on the death of someone very near to him.

"Have you any relations?" she asked. "Any near relations, I mean, who are well off?"

"No," said he. "Not unless Uncle Joe soaked anything away before they got him."

"That must be it," she thought. "Well," she said aloud, "it doesn't matter much. There's no sign of any uncle leaving you anything. This card means money troubles. This means you're double-crossed by a blonde. Looks like you're beaten up, too. I don't know what these two men in uniform are doing."

She continued prattling and laying out the cards, her mind working meanwhile like a three-ring circus. One ring was taken up with the story she was telling to her visitor, the second in reading the real future as it unfolded itself, and the third in wondering what she was going to do about it.

She stole another glance at her unattractive client. The fortune, as far as she could judge, appeared to be rather more than a million. Her visitor, on the other hand, seemed a good deal less than human. Myra had not expected romance, but there are things which make a nice girl hesitate, and he was one of them.

While she pondered, she was still automatically laying out the cards. Suddenly, her eyes brightened. She looked again. It was true. All her troubles were ended. The cards indicated, beyond the shadow of a doubt, that her client would die of a sudden, violent shock within a few months of inheriting the money. This made quite an eligible bachelor of him.

Myra at once began her maneuvers. "You seem," said she, "to be at the parting of the ways. One road leads to misery, poverty, sickness, despair, prison . . ."

"I'll take the other," said the young man.

"You show great powers of judgment," said Myra. "But, I can tell you, it is not as easy as all that. The other road, which leads to riches and happiness, can be traveled only hand-in-hand with a good woman. Do you know a good woman?"

"Oh, phooey!" said her client in dismay.

"What a pity!" said Myra. "Because, if you did, and if she was dark, and not bad-looking, and wore a number-five shoe, all you'd have to do would be to marry her, and you'd be rich for life. Very rich. Look—here it is. Money, money, money—coming to you from someone very near to you. If you marry the right girl, that is. Look —this card means you at the Waldorf. Look—this is you at Palm Beach. Here you are at Saratoga. Gosh! You've backed a big winner!"

"Say, lady," said her client. "What size shoe do *you* wear?"

"Well," said Myra with a smile, "I *can* squeeze into a four. But, usually . . ."

"Look, baby," said he, taking her hand. "It's you and me. Like that. See?" With that, he extended his other hand with two fingers crossed, as an emblem of connubial bliss.

Myra controlled a shudder. "When he's dead," thought she, "I'll have a million, and get me one of these young filmstars, in order to forget!"

Soon afterwards they were married, and took a small shack in an unprepossessing part of Long Island. Lew appeared to have strong reasons for living in inconspicuous retirement. Myra commuted, and drudged harder than ever with her greasy pack of cards in order to keep them both until death did them part, leaving her a rich widow.

As time went on, and the fortune still failed to materialize, she was bitterly reproached by her hulking husband, whose stunted mind was as impatient as a child's, and who began to fear he had been married under false pretenses. He was also a little sadistic.

"Maybe you ain't the right dame after all," said he, pinching her black and blue. "Maybe you don't wear a five. Maybe you wear a six. Gimme a divorce and let me marry another dark dame. The money don't come along, and you're black and blue anyway. I don't like a black and blue dame. Come on, gimme a divorce."

"I won't," said she. "I believe marriages are made in Heaven."

This would lead to an argument, for he claimed to have evidence to the contrary. In the end, his brutish wits would be baffled; he would fling her to the ground with a curse, and go into the backyard, where he would dig an enormously deep hole, into which he would gaze for a long time, and then fill it in again.

This continued for some months, and Myra herself began to wonder if the Vascal System could possibly have let her down. "Supposing he doesn't come into the money. Here I am—Mrs. King Kong, and working for it! Maybe I'd better get that divorce after all."

These defeatist notions came to a head one gloomy, winter evening as she trudged home from the ferry. Crossing the dark yard of the shack, she stumbled into another of the enormous holes dug by her simpleminded husband. "That settles it," thought she.

When she entered the squalid kitchen, Lew greeted her with an unusual smile. "Hello, sweetie," said he. "How's my darling little wifie tonight?"

"Cut the sweetie stuff out," said she tersely. "And the wifie stuff, too. I don't know what's bit you, you big gorilla, but my mind's made up. You can have that divorce, after all."

"Don't talk like that, honey," said he. "I was only joking. I wouldn't divorce you, not for all the world."

"No, but I'll divorce you," said she. "And quick."

"You gotta have grounds for that," observed her husband, with a frown.

"I've got 'em," said she. "When I show that judge where I'm black and blue, I'll get my divorce pronto. I'm sitting pretty."

"Listen," said he. "Have a look at this letter that came for you. Maybe you'll change your mind."

"Why did you open my letter?" said Myra.

"To see what was inside," said he with the utmost candor. "Go on, read it."

"Uncle Ezra," cried Myra, staring at the letter. "Left a million and a half dollars! All to me! Gee, the old geezer must have made good! But, say, the cards must have slipped up, then. It was supposed to come to you."

"Never mind," said Lew, stroking the back of her neck. "Man and wife are one, ain't they?"

"Not for long," cried Myra in triumph. "I'm rich! I'm free! Or, I will be."

"And what shall *I* do?" asked her husband.

"Go climb a tree," said Myra. "You ought to be good at it."

"I thought you might say that," said he, clasping her firmly around the throat. "Gypped me a dollar for that fortune, too, didn't you? Well, if you won't do right by me, the cards must. Death of someone very near to me—that's what they said, didn't they? So they was right after all!"

Myra had no breath left to thank him on behalf of the Vascal System, or to warn him of the sudden, violent shock that awaited him.

SPRING FEVER

There was a young sculptor named Eustace whose work was altogether too lifelike for the modern taste. Consequently he was often under the necessity of dropping in upon his friends at about seven in the evening, in the hungry hope of being pressed to stay for dinner. "I carve the stone," said he to himself, "and chisel my meals. When I am rich, it will be much the same thing, only the other way round."

He would eagerly snuff up the odors of sputtering roasts and nourishing stews that crept in from the kitchen, and, excited by the savor, he would exult in his incorruptible ideals and furiously inveigh against the abstractionists. But nature and art were combined against the unfortunate Eustace, for the stimulating vapors worked powerfully upon his salivary glands, and the moderns he most hissingly denounced were Brancusi, Lipchitz, and Brzeska.

It was usually the wives who, thus clumsily reminded of Niagara, demanded that Eustace be got rid of without delay. Numerous devices were employed to this end; one of the most humane was to give him a ticket for some show or other and bid him hurry off and get there before it started.

Thus it came about one evening that Eustace, defeated of a seven-rib roast, found himself unexpectedly watching Charlie McCarthy, whom he regarded with the humorless and critical eye of a hungry sculptor. "I don't know what all the applause is for," said he to the man beside him. "Those jokes are not his own; it's obviously all done by ventriloquism. And, considered as a work of art—well, I happen to be a sculptor myself, and I can assure you he's an all-time low."

"All the same," returned the stranger, "he earns I don't know how many hundred thousand bucks a year for his owner."

"By god!" cried Eustace, standing up and brandishing his fists. "What sort of civilization is this, anyway? Here's a coarse, crude, comic-looking dummy, not fit even to be called a piece of sculpture, and earns this fellow doesn't know how many hundred thousand a year, while the most lifelike work of the century is . . ." At this point, the ushers took him by the seat of the pants and slung him out of the auditorium.

Eustace picked himself up, and shuffled off in the direction of Brooklyn, where the old garage was situated that was at once his abode and his studio. In the near neighborhood of this place there was a dingy little bookshop, with a tray of secondhand books in the entrance. One of these bore the conspicuous title, Practical Ventriloquism. Eustace's eye fell upon this title, and he stopped and picked up the book and looked at it with a sneer. "Art and the Ideal," said he, "have brought me to this pass. If that fellow's figures were correct, Ventriloquism and the Practical may get me out of it." He glanced into the interior of the shop and saw that no one was looking at him. He at once slipped the book under his jacket, and made his way off. "I am now a thief," said he to himself. "How does it feel to be a thief, Eustace?" And he answered, "It feels fine."

Arrived home, he studied the book with great concentration. "This is perfectly simple," said he. "You just take your voice and bounce it, as if it were a ball, immobilizing the jaws as you do so. I used to bounce a ball as a youngster, and my jaws have had good practice at resting immobile. Here, too, is a little picture of the larynx, with A, B, C, D—everything. I can learn to ventriloquize as well as anyone, and with a dummy that is a real work of art I shall soon be making a fortune."

He at once dragged out all his long accumulated works to find one suitable to set up as a rival to Charlie McCarthy. But, though he had renounced his ideals, something of the old artist still survived within him. "They are all marvelous," he said, "but I can do better. I will model so lifelike a dummy that the audience will swear he's a stooge, and I shall have to invite them to step up on the platform and stick pins in him."

He looked about for material from which to carve this masterpiece, but he had been so long on the rocks that he had no longer a piece of stone to work upon. "Never mind," said he, "I will model him in clay, which has the advantage of being lighter and less chilly, and will yield a little to the points of the pins. This will provide an agreeable sensation for those who step up to make the test, for such people are bound to be sadistically inclined."

Next morning he went out into the yard behind his studio, and toiled with pick and shovel until he had uncovered a bed of red clay, of a quality very noticeably superior to that which is sold in the art stores. From this he fashioned a male figure of singularly attractive appearance, with crimpy hair and a Greco-Roman profile. He thought the face wore a slightly supercilious expression, and this he strove to modify, but in spite of his skill his efforts were unavailing. "After all," he said, "he is a work of genius, and as such he is entitled to a slightly supercilious expression."

In order to impart a sufficient flexibility to his creation, he jointed the limbs and neck with pieces of old bedsprings, such as are indigenous to the soil of the back yards of Brooklyn. This experiment was so successful that he broke up two or three battered alarm clocks he found, which his neighbors had thrown at the cats, and fixed up the fingers, the toes, and the eyelids. He scrabbled about in the debris, and found other springs of all shapes and sizes, which he employed to the utmost advantage, not even neglecting those details that were least likely to be seen by the audience. In the end, the figure had good reason to look supercilious.

Next, he heated his old rusty furnace to the point of incandescence, and baked the clay to a light, porous, and permanent texture. He had given it a low glaze, and tinted it in the most agreeable colors. Finally he borrowed a little money and got his best suit out of hock, and found to his delight that it fitted the figure to perfection, which had not been the case when he himself had worn it. Our friend admired the effect for an hour or two; then he took up the telephone and called Sadie. "Sadie," said he, "I want you to come around at once. I've a grand surprise for you."

"I don't think I ought to come around unless we're able to get married," said she. "It doesn't do a girl any good to be seen going to a sculptor's studio."

"Don't worry," said he. "The years of waiting are over. We can afford to flout the conventions, for I shall soon be earning I don't know how many hundred thousand a year."

"In that case," she said, "I'll be around immediately."

Pretty soon she was tapping at the door, and Eustace hastened to let her in. "I can hardly believe it," said she. "Oh, Eustace, it has seemed so long!"

"Never mind," said he. "It's all over now. Let me introduce you to the author of our good fortune. This is Mr. Bertie McGregor."

"Oh, how do you do?" said she with a blush and a smile. "If what Eustace says is true, you are my favorite author from now on. Yes, I think you're wonderful."

"Wonderful is the word," said Eustace. "However, you need not go on buttering him up, for he is only a dummy, and the praise is due to me."

"A dummy?" she cried. "And I have been talking to him all the time! How handsome he is for a dummy! But, Eustace, when I spoke to him first, it seemed to me he smiled and nodded."

"He is handsome," said Eustace, "because I took pains to make him so. As for smiling and nodding, that is not unlikely, for I have fixed him up with springs. He is perfect in every particular."

"Is that really so?" said she.

"Yes," said he, "in every particular. I will explain it all to you when we are married. But tell me frankly—you don't think his expression is a little too supercilious?"

"Oh, no," said she. "I think he just looks sort of cute and

masculine; sort of . . . I'll explain it to you when we are married. But, Eustace, if he is really a dummy, how can he be the author of our good fortune? That sounds a bit like fiction to me."

"I assure you," he replied, smiling, "it is straightforward biography." With that, he told her of his great plan. "And here," said he in conclusion, "is a bill I'm designing, announcing us to the public. I thought we might use your savings, and start in by hiring a hall. I think the lettering is pretty effective. See where I invite the audience to stick pins in him at the end of the performance, to assure themselves that he is not really alive, in spite of his lifelike appearance and rapier wit."

"Shall we really have you don't know how many hundred thousand a year?" said she. "You know how long it has taken me to save up that little nest egg."

Eustace pointed proudly to his creation. "Which is the more life-like?" he demanded.

"In some ways he is, and in some ways you are," responded Sadie.

"Come, come!" said Eustace, "I meant he or Charlie McCarthy."

"Oh, he is," replied Sadie. "There's no doubt at all about that."

"Then there's no doubt about the money," said Eustace. "And as for your own pitiful little hoard, we'll get it all back the very first evening." With that, he took her in his arms, as masterfully as his somewhat debilitated condition allowed. Suddenly Sadie squealed and thrust him from her. "Eustace," said she, "I wish you would not pinch me like that, even if we *are* going to be rich. After all, we are not yet married."

"Pinch you?" said he. "I wouldn't dream of doing such a thing."

"I didn't say don't dream of it," said she captiously. "You're in love. You're young. You're an artist. There's nothing wrong in dreaming."

"I am glad you think so," said he, "for you must have dreamed you were pinched."

"No. *I* wouldn't dream it," said she, "because I'm a healthy, normal girl, and therefore dream differently. But if you are healthy and normal, as I thought you were, *you* might very well dream of it, because you are a man. But are you? Or are you a mouse?"

"I am a man, Sadie," said he. "But hitherto I've been an artist also, and that sort of thing has been absorbed in the creative impulse. Now, I am altogether practical, and I expect I shall dream like a demon. Don't let us quarrel, my dear. After all, what's a pinch, be it real or imaginary? Perhaps I did it unconsciously—who can tell? Let us go to the bank and draw out your money, and then we will hire the hall."

This was done, and Bertie and Eustace were billed all over the neighborhood in large lettering. The fateful night arrived, and Sadie had a seat in the front row, and nearly twisted her head off looking back to count the audience, for, the truth is, she was extremely anxious about her nest egg.

Her fears were quickly laid to rest, for the hall filled up very pleasantly, and soon the curtain was raised, and there was Eustace bowing and smiling like a Svengali. Bertie also graciously responded to the applause. "What wonderful springs Eustace must have fixed in him!" thought Sadie. "I should think there is hardly anything he couldn't do. Certainly he is very much handsomer than Charlie McCarthy."

Now the show began, and, to Sadie's dismay, a slight hitch soon became apparent. Eustace took the figure on his knee, and addressed some old and corny gags to it, which he had found in the back pages of the book on ventriloquism. It at once became apparent that he had not studied the front pages sufficiently, for his voice had no more bounce in it than a lump of lead. Moreover, the springs in the figure's jaws obstinately refused to work, and all became aware that Eustace was a lousy ventriloquist.

The audience began to hoot and jeer. Eustace, who had no idea of what was wrong, took this to be a sign that they found the performance altogether too good to be true, so he advanced smiling to the footlights and invited them to come up straightaway and stick pins in the dummy.

There are always some who find an invitation of this sort irresistible. These filed upon the platform, and were handed outsize pins with souvenir heads on them, but, as soon as the first of these was applied to Master Bertie, an agonized "Ouch!" reechoed through the hall and convinced everyone that he was not even a genuine dummy.

This completed the disgust of the audience, who felt they had been taken for two rides, in opposite directions. A riot immediately started; the police burst in, and all the money had to be refunded. Eustace, who had come in a cab, had to stagger home on foot, overwhelmed by Bertie's considerable weight and by Sadie's upbraidings, which were no less hard to bear.

Arrived home, he deposited the figure on the divan, and stood like a man utterly beaten, hanging his head. Sadie continued to reproach him, for she felt the loss of her money very keenly, and no longer believed in the I don't know how many hundred thousand a year. "You did it on purpose," said she. "You ruined everything on purpose."

"No, my dear," said he. "I did not do that. My ventriloquism was not very effective, I admit."

"Don't be so brazen," said she. "Don't be so barefaced. That final 'Ouch' was the work of a master. You paraded your powers just where they were most destructive."

"No. No," said he. "I didn't let out that 'Ouch.' I was as much surprised as anyone."

"If you didn't do it, who did?" said she.

"How can I tell?" said he. "Unless, possibly, it was Charlie McCarthy's impresario, who may have attended the show in a false beard, eager to ruin so promising a rival."

"Stuff and nonsense!" said she. "You did it yourself, and you know it."

"It may be possible," said he. "After all, the pin was stuck into the child of my genius, and I have a sensitive nature, though I am now a practical ventriloquist. But, if so, Sadie, I assure you it was unconscious."

"About as unconscious as that pinch you gave me," said Sadie with a sneer.

"I swear to you that was an unconscious pinch," said Eustace.

"Oh, no, it wasn't," said Bertie, who had been regarding this regrettable scene with his supercilious smile. "Sadie is right, as usual. It was *I* who gave her the pinch. What's more, I was perfectly conscious of doing so, and the memory lingers yet."

"But we are not married," squealed Sadie. "We are not even engaged. What can we do?" She tittered, placed her hand on her mouth, and regarded the dummy with big, reproachful eyes.

"What are you?" cried Eustace, utterly flabbergasted. "Speak! Speak!"

"I speak when I want to, and I keep quiet when I want to," replied the image.

"Are you some damned soul," cried Eustace, "let out on parole from Hell, who nipped into my furnace to get a brief warm-up, and found my masterpiece there?"

The figure smiled superciliously.

"Is it possible," cried Eustace, "that the clay in my backyard is the original clay from which Adam was made? But that would imply that Brooklyn is on the site of the Garden of Eden."

The figure laughed outright.

"Or have I succeeded," said Eustace, "where all the scientists have failed, and changed dead clay into organic colloidal matter, charged with pep and energy? That must be it. In that case, I'm the Hell of a sculptor!"

"Have it your own way," said the figure. "In any case, you're a lousy ventriloquist, and it's ventriloquism that rakes in the I don't know how many hundred thousand a year."

"There is something in that," said Eustace. "But since you can speak so well, surely we can give terrific performances."

"Not with me as the stooge," said Bertie. "I have the looks and I have the personality. I'm not sitting on your knee anymore. You can sit on mine if you like, and I'll run the show and draw the money."

"Me sit on your knee?" cried Eustace. "No!"

"Oh, it's not so bad," said the other. "Come on, why don't you try it? You don't want to? Well, perhaps the little lady will try."

"Yes, I will," said Sadie. "I don't think I don't know how many hundred thousand a year is to be sneezed at." With that, she seated herself on the image's knee.

"How d'you like it, honey?" asked the image.

"I think we ought to be engaged," said she. "In fact, I think we ought to be married."

"Don't worry about that," said the image, chucking her under the chin. "On the stage, it's different. We troupers are practical."

"Then take your practicality out of my studio," said Eustace. "I'm going back to ideals. No more ventriloquism, no more clay, no more springs! I'm going to make tombstones, and, by gosh, I'll make 'em heavy!"

"Just as you please," said the image. "Sadie and I will get on very well as a couple."

"She will not like the pins," said Eustace.

"I shall allow no pins," said the image with a reassuring glance at Sadie. "Just a little matter of this sort." As he spoke, he gave her another pinch, similar to the first he had given her, only this time her squeal was in a deeper, fuller tone.

"Your squeal is very deep and full," said Eustace to her, as he icily opened the door for their exit. "You had better remember that some of the springs I used were abominably old and rusty."

With that, he shut the door after them, and, contrary to his expressed intention, he approached a chunk of clay that stood handy, and began to model it into a very fetching Eve-like figure. Halfway through, however, he changed his mind yet again, and turned out a cute little Sealyham.

YOUTH FROM VIENNA

Young men with open faces, red cheeks, and brown hair all behave in the same way, and nothing in the world could be more reasonable. They fall in and out of jobs and love with the utmost readiness and enthusiasm. If oil and Lucille let them down, they pretty soon console themselves with steel and Estelle.

Other young men seem born for one passion only, or maybe two: one job and one woman. If both passions are there, they run together like railway lines; they are strong as steel, and as devoid of romantic coloring. They are meant to go on forever, and, if one or the other fails, the results are apt to be serious. Young men of this sort are sometimes very tall, lean to emaciation, with skull-like faces, deep-set and rather burning eyes, and mouths either terribly sensitive or terribly cruel, it is hard to say which. If they are poor they look like nothing on earth; if they are rich they look like Lincoln in the rail-splitting period.

Such young men frequently devote themselves to science, sometimes to medicine. The research side appeals to them. If they are brilliant enough, and have money enough, they study under the world's greatest authorities. If they are interested in certain functions of the glands, this takes them to Lilly's or the Ford Foundation, but, in the old days, in the days of our youth, it took them to Vienna.

Before going to Vienna, Humphrey Baxter went to dine with a married couple of his acquaintance. These, not having a word to say about glands, had provided themselves and him with tickets for the theater. The play turned out to be a light romantic comedy which was only indirectly concerned with the glands. Humphrey sat regarding it with forbearance until, at a well-chosen moment early in the first act, Caroline Coates walked onto the stage. Humphrey leaned forward in his seat. The movement passed unnoticed because everyone else in the theater also leaned forward.

It may well be asked why this considerable expenditure of human energy was exerted on account of a girl who escaped being the worst actress in the world only by being so very obviously not an actress at all. The fact is, Caroline Coates was a goddess. I think it was Alexander Woollcott who wrote: "To inquire as to her capacity as a mummer would be like asking, of a real actress, what is her prowess in trapeze work. Talent in this young woman would be a mere dilution, like soda in a highball; the less of it the better. When the divine Aphrodite walks on the stage, we do not wish her to perform like the divine Sarah."

Caroline had been put into a play by some fantastic mistake in the very year she left Bennington. It was at once apparent that she was one of those girls—there is only one in each generation—whose fortune it is to stand for something greater than talent and greater than beauty, and hence to be universally adored. The essential quality in Caroline was her youth. It aroused in the beholder the keenest, liveliest, and most exquisite sensation of pure joy, which is the rarest and finest of all sensations. And, into the bargain, as I happen to know from private sources, this Caroline was a good-natured, well-bred, truthful, simple, kind, merry, and unaffected girl, and she smelled like a florist's shop, which is not always the case with goddesses.

Humphrey observed this phenomenon with a concentration he had hitherto reserved for sections of the obscurer glands mounted on microscope slides. As they left the theater, he turned to his host and hostess. "Do you by any chance happen to know that girl?" He saw the question surprised them, so he continued without waiting for an answer. "Or do you know anyone who knows her?"

"No, Humphrey. She lives in the great world. She's altogether beyond our class. She lives with people with the names of buildings and breakfast foods. And when she's not on the stage she's on yachts and polo fields and such like, and we wouldn't know even this if we didn't read the Sunday papers."

Humphrey was in no way dismayed by this answer. He knew very well it needs only two or three introductions to bridge the gap between oneself and anyone anywhere in the world. He therefore asked everyone he knew, stating his purpose very clearly, and before

many weeks had passed he found himself on a certain terrace, looking over Long Island Sound, being curiously regarded by the name-
sakes of buildings and breakfast foods, and talking to Caroline
Coates. He found her amazingly ignorant of the immense importance
of recent researches into the functions of the ductless glands, and
it was a keen pleasure to him to tell her of the great strides in human
health and happiness and longevity that were promised by the new
knowledge. You may imagine the effect of this gaunt, gauche, hollow-
cheeked young man, in altogether the wrong sort of jacket, sitting
among that well-groomed crowd, lecturing a popular idol of twenty-
three on the effects of certain unsavory juices upon horrible insane
little girls who wallowed in their own dung. Of course, she fell
wildly, madly, head-over-heels in love with him, and before the
month was out it was announced they were engaged to be married.

Certain buildings rocked a little; certain breakfast foods popped
and crackled even more snappishly than usual. But in the main
people felt that it showed what a fine girl Caroline was, and yet it
was in no way a threat, because it couldn't possibly last. For example, what would happen when Humphrey went to Vienna, to work
under the celebrated Vingleberg?

"I shall be there," said Humphrey, "for three years straight. And,
if I get out of that lab for forty-eight consecutive hours any time
in those three years, it'll be because the place has burned down.
I can't get back here to see you."

"Maybe I'll come over between shows."

"I wish you'd change your mind."

"Darling, I'd like to get married now, just as much as you would.
But I simply *cannot* walk out on a new show and leave everyone
flat. Besides . . ."

"You want just one more."

"Yes, I do. Maybe I could come when it's over."

"They say the damned thing'll run for years."

"It may fold up in six months. Humphrey, I know you think I'm
just greedy to have a fuss made over me . . ."

"I've never suggested such a thing."

"But you think so. And if you didn't you'd be crazy. Because
I am, just a bit. But if ever I feel it getting a *real* hold on me . . ."

"And what do you think a real hold feels like? Like this?"

This terminated the conversation just as they were on an important
point, which was rather a pity. Humphrey's boat sailed; Caroline's
play opened; she was more idolized than ever, and everyone expected

her to fall in love with someone else. But the first year passed, and the second year passed, and the third year wore on, and Caroline was still faithful. There were two excellent reasons for this. She was so extremely fond of Humphrey, and she was so extremely fond of herself.

When the three years were over, Humphrey Baxter was on the boat, and the boat was docking. For some weeks he had had a picture in his mind of how Caroline would look when she greeted him, and this picture was so much with him that when he was reading the right-hand page of his book, it hovered like an illustration on the left. Because this was the 1920s, he had costumed her in silver fox and violets. He looked down on the landing stage, and saw plenty of fur and flowers, but he saw no sign of Caroline.

He went down the gangway and through the barrier. Two people came up and grasped his either hand. They were Dick and Stella Archer, the very people who had introduced him to Caroline in the first place and thus established squatter's rights in the relationship. They held his hands and looked at him, and uttered the pleasantest and friendliest of greetings. Humphrey looked this way and that. "Where's Caroline?" said he.

The greetings were gone like a burst bubble. Three altogether grayer people stood, in an east wind, in the giant cheerlessness of the landing shed.

"Carrie couldn't come," said Stella.

There was no doubt at all that Humphrey's mouth was sensitive, extremely sensitive. "Is she ill?" he asked.

"Well . . .," said Dick.

"She's not ill," said Stella. "But she couldn't come. Humphrey, get your things through, and we'll go to lunch at the Revestel, and we'll tell you about it."

"Very well," said Humphrey.

They went to the Revestel, where they had eaten so often in the old days. They ordered lunch. "I think it's about time you told me what it is," said Humphrey.

"Humphrey," said Stella, "you've got to understand."

It was perhaps, after all, rather difficult to decide whether Humphrey's mouth was very sensitive or a little cruel. "Go on," he said.

"We're old friends," said Dick. "We've known you and Carrie the hell of a long time, you know." Humphrey looked at Stella.

"Carrie's fallen in love," said Stella.

Humphrey closed his eyes. He might have been asleep, or dead. These skull-faced men can look astonishingly dead at times.

However, after a few long seconds, he opened them again. Dick was saying something.

"When?" asked Humphrey of Stella.

"Last month, Humphrey. And almost at once it was too late to write."

"With whom?"

"He's quite a decent sort," said Dick. "In fact, it's Brodie."

"Alan Brodie the tennis champion," said Stella.

"National Singles eight times," said Dick. "The last six years in succession."

"Alan Brodie toured Europe the first year I was there," said Humphrey. "He came to Vienna. There was some sort of fuss at his hotel. A mob of women scuffling. It doesn't often happen over there."

"He's a popular idol," said Stella.

"Do you mean like Carrie?"

"He's a beautiful creature, Humphrey. He gives people the same sort of thrill that Carrie does. And the two of them together . . . !"

"She must have changed a great deal."

"Not really, Humphrey. I think she's realized what she's meant for."

"She's not meant for that sort of thing at all," said Humphrey, not loudly or emphatically, but with complete finality.

"Humphrey, you'll just have to wait till you see them together."

"I can wait," said Humphrey.

In New York it is seldom necessary to wait very long. Humphrey had a book to publish, and therefore a publisher, and therefore an invitation to lunch, and at a certain restaurant frequented by the people who are known to each other and to the gossip columnists. A woman for whose glands he would have paid a small fortune was sitting at the next table. Suddenly she uttered a sort of squeal. Then Humphrey, with a sensation that made of him a lifelong opponent of electrocution, heard her utter the following words: "Oh, look! The lovers!"

Humphrey had no reason to turn his head. He saw other people looking in the direction of the door. He had time enough to observe, on faces horribly besmeared with success, a look of simple pleasure such as made even those faces seem quite attractive. Humphrey not only observed this, but reflected on it. "It must be a good thing," he thought, "that can so transfigure faces like these."

All this time the faces in question were turning, like searchlights converging on an unseen objective, as they followed Caroline and her Alan Brodie. Suddenly Humphrey found himself caught, as it were, in the full blaze, which meant she was close behind him. He turned, and they met.

Everything was very pleasant, good-humored, and gay. Caroline and Brodie sat down with Humphrey and his publisher; other people came to greet them and were induced to sit down also. Everyone talked a great deal except Humphrey, who was not expected to talk a great deal.

The truth is, Humphrey had a decision to make. He was prepared to believe this new impression of his, that Caroline's approaching marriage was a good thing. He wanted to believe it, as far, at least, as a man nearly insane with jealousy could be expected to. Indeed, as far as is consistent with that very human weakness, and with knowing deep down that the whole business was nothing but an imbecile, narcissistic delusion, it may be said he *did* believe it was a good thing, and that his impulse to kick it to pieces and drag Caroline out of it was barbarous, atavistic, and on no account to be indulged in.

Caroline helped him in this noble endeavor. Her every word and every look was exactly right for the occasion. She made no bones about asking the publisher to move so that she could sit next to Humphrey. She spoke to him with the utmost tenderness and concern. Her look appealed to him to understand. Her smile, and the glow about her, proclaimed that, even if he didn't understand, there are values and glories in life which must be held paramount. And when she looked at her lover it was perfectly plain what those glories were. "So be it!" thought Humphrey. "It's a good thing." And he joined with the rest of the circle in watching the happy pair, and the light that was reflected on the faces of the others was reflected on his own, though, no doubt, in a broken sort of way.

There then ensued a *divertissement* such as often happens in restaurants frequented by celebrities. Sallow young men arrived with cameras and flashbulbs. Caroline and Alan were required to get together and to take first this pose and then that. The process was more elaborate than the usual snapping of pictures in a restaurant, partly because an important magazine was involved, partly because there was a great deal of byplay with the manager and with people at other tables. It was the sort of thing that would be an awful pain in the neck unless you like that sort of thing, in which case, of course, it could be very gratifying.

Caroline was flushed, smiling, and immensely gratified when she sat down again beside Humphrey. It is in such states of happy excitement that words pop out that are utterly different from what one really means, words that anyone but a cold-blooded scientist would have the decency to ignore. "Well?" said Caroline. "What do you think of us?" She stopped herself suddenly, and looked at Humphrey in blushing embarrassment, for such words are not fit to be heard by a psychoanalyst, much less by a forsaken lover.

"I think," said Humphrey, "you're both charming, and I hope we'll be friends. Why not bring your young man around to see me?"

"We go off on Friday, you know," said Caroline, still confused. "There's not a chance in the world before then."

"But you will when you get back?"

"Of course. We'd love to. But it won't be for two months, at least."

"I can wait," said Humphrey.

About a week before Alan and Caroline were due back from their honeymoon, Humphrey, who had been thinking a great deal while he waited, called up a man named Morgan. This was Albert Morgan, whose vocation it is to take the ambiguous and uncertain mutterings of scientists and transform them into clear, downright, and extremely thrilling articles for the weekly magazines. "Morgan," said Humphrey, "it's now three months since you last pestered me to give you some private information about Vingleberg's experiments."

Morgan explained why he had abandoned the attempt to get Humphrey to talk.

"If you think clams do that sort of thing," said Humphrey, "I can understand why your articles are so extremely inaccurate. But, anyway, I'm not a clam, and to prove it I'm calling you to say I've just had a letter from Vingleberg. It concerns some tests we started just before I left. Now, listen; I shall tell you nothing that's in the least confidential, because I know damned well I'll see it in all the headlines tomorrow morning. But if you want to hear about twenty very carefully chosen words . . ."

"Hold it!" said Morgan. "I'll be right over."

It was really remarkable what Morgan could do with twenty

carefully chosen words. Or, possibly, Humphrey, being a guileless scientist, had been cozened into uttering twenty-five or even thirty. At all events, the news broke, not in the headlines, it's true, but in very impressive articles on important pages, to the effect that stocky, balding, Viennese endocrinologist Vingleberg and Johns Hopkins' Humphrey Baxter had succeeded in isolating V.B. 282. And V.B. 282, it appeared, was neither more nor less than the glandular secretion that controls the aging of the tissues. And, since we all have tissues, all aging, the promise in these paragraphs was seized on with avidity by all who read.

Meanwhile Caroline and Alan returned, and soon came round to Humphrey's apartment for a drink. He received them with the utmost cordiality, and asked them a thousand questions about themselves, all of which they answered fully and frankly, like people who had nothing to conceal. They were so anxious to give him all the information that might be of interest to him that neither of them observed his reactions very closely. Had they done so, they might have noticed that at certain answers, particularly from Caroline, his cruel and sensitive mouth tightened itself with that painful satisfaction with which a pathologist might regard the slide which tells him that his difficult diagnosis was right in every particular, and his best friend needs immediate surgery.

I do not wish to convey that the conversation of the newly married pair was entirely egotistical. Before a single hour had passed, Caroline herself broached a new subject. "Humphrey, dear," she said, "we hear you've become famous. Is it true?"

"It's true if you've heard it," he replied. "That's what fame is."

"But is it true about eternal youth and all that?"

"My dear girl," said he, "I think you've got all the scientists beaten as far as eternal youth is concerned. You looked eighteen when I met you, and you were twenty-three. Now you're twenty-six. . . ."

"Twenty-seven last week, Humphrey."

"And you still look eighteen."

"But I shan't always."

"I can't say I've noticed myself slowing up any," said Brodie. "But some of these youngsters from the West Coast . . ." He shook his head with that air of melancholy always induced in tennis players by a mention of the West Coast.

Humphrey ignored this interjection. His eyes were fixed on Caroline. "Of course, you won't be young always," said he. "I imagine you'd hardly want to. Those people you see around, who never seem to mature, they belong to a particular frigid, inhibited, narcissistic type. They're in love with themselves; they can't love anyone else; therefore, they don't really live; therefore, they don't get any older."

"Yes, yes. But this stuff you've discovered . . . ?"

"Oh!" said Humphrey. And smiling, he shook his head.

"It's not true, then?" cried Caroline. Her disappointment would have moved a heart of stone.

"I told you it was all a lot of hooey," said Brodie.

"These journalists always omit to mention the snags," said Humphrey.

"And they wrote as if you'd really truly discovered it," lamented Caroline.

"It's completely untrue," said Humphrey. "It was Vingleberg, almost entirely."

"You mean it *has* been found," said Caroline, her face lighting up again.

"I didn't say so, to the newspaper men," said Humphrey. "However, they chose to take it that way." His tone suddenly became very cold and hard. "Now, I want both of you to understand this. This is something no one in the world must know about."

"Oh, yes! Yes!"

"Do you understand that, Brodie?"

"You can rely on me."

"Very well," said Humphrey. He sat very still for a moment, as if conquering some final reluctance. Then he rose abruptly and went out of the room.

Caroline and Alan didn't even glance at each other. They sat there looking at the door through which Humphrey had disappeared, expecting him to return with a crucible or an alembic at the very least. Instead, he came back almost immediately, dangling a piece of very ordinary string.

He smiled at his guests. He gave the string a jerk or two, and in through the door, leaping, frisking, clapping its paws in hot pursuit, came a kitten. Humphrey enticed it right over to where Caroline was sitting, made it jump once or twice. Then he picked it up and handed it to her.

"It's sweet," said Caroline. "But . . ."

"It had a birthday last week," said Humphrey. "Five years old."

Caroline dropped the kitten as if it were hot. "I hope people will be able to overcome that sort of instinctive prejudice," said Humphrey, picking it up again and handing it back to her. "Before very long, the world will have to get used to this sort of thing."

"But, Humphrey," said Caroline, quite agitated, "it's a dwarf or a midget or something."

"I assure you," said Humphrey, "that kitten is as normal as any kitten you've ever seen in your life."

"But what will happen to it? Will it go on forever?" And, as Humphrey shook his head: "Will it go off bang, or crumble into dust, or something?"

"Almost surely heart failure," said Humphrey. "But only after forty years of glorious youth. That's two hundred for a human being. But remember this, both of you . . ." He paused impressively.

"Yes? Yes?"

"I went to Vienna," said Humphrey very slowly and clearly, "exactly three years and four months ago. This kitten is five years old. So, you see, it's Vingleberg's discovery."

"Oh, yes. Yes, of course. But they said in the papers it was human beings," said Caroline.

"I was helping Vingleberg adapt it to human beings."

"And you succeeded?"

"Remember you have promised not to mention this to a living soul. Yes, we succeeded. To a limited extent, that is."

Alan spoke in a voice at once impatient and businesslike.

"Mr. Baxter, you said before very long the world . . ."

"Humphrey," said Humphrey with a friendly smile.

"Yes—Humphrey. But . . . but *when?*"

"It's a question of finding a new source for the extract," said Humphrey. "Or possibly making it synthetically, though I doubt we'll ever do that. I should say thirty years. With luck—twenty."

"Ah!" said Caroline. "I thought you meant now."

"To get this stuff," cried Humphrey, "we have to perform an extremely delicate operation which, unfortunately, is fatal to the animal we get it from. So, it's terribly difficult."

"What animal?" asked Alan.

"It's quite a common one," said Humphrey. "Man."

"Oh!"

"I think we've discovered another source, but it'll take years to test, and more years to manufacture an adequate supply. That's the point. That's why I swore you to secrecy. All merry Hell would break loose on this planet if people knew there was just *some* in existence, being kept for the privileged few."

"There *is* some, then?" said Caroline.

"The extract has been made," said Humphrey, "in very odd circumstances, about which I'll tell you exactly nothing—it has been made three times."

"Three!" exclaimed Alan, as if impressed by the coincidence, because there were three people right there in the room.

"I took one," said Humphrey with a smile.

"And the others?" cried Caroline.

"Fortunately, one dose is enough," continued Humphrey. "I don't want to bore you with technicalities, but this is extremely interesting. This secretion actually changes the functions of two distinct glands, neither of them the gland from which we originally extracted it. Now . . ."

"But, Humphrey dear, what happened to the other two doses?"

"Vingleberg took one of them. He's sixty-eight and as ugly as a monkey. He'll stay sixty-eight, and stay ugly, for the next two hundred years."

"For god's sake!" said Alan bitterly.

"And the third?" asked Caroline.

"Caroline, my dear," said Humphrey, "I brought that back with me. I needn't tell you why." As he spoke, he unlocked a little drawer in his desk. "Here it is," he said, holding an ordinary phial full of a colorless liquid. "Life, youth, love, for nearly two hundred years! Probably more, because in that time we'll have found out all sorts of things. I nearly poured this away, the day I landed."

"Oh, Humphrey, I . . . What can I say?"

"I don't feel that way any longer," said Humphrey. "In fact, I didn't from the very first moment I met you both. So, I'd like you to have this, if you'd care for it. Call it a sort of belated wedding present. Here you are. To both of you."

He held out the phial and, finding two hands extended to receive it, he brought them together. "But you do solemnly swear never to say a word?" he asked.

"I do," said Caroline.

"I do," said Alan.

"It sounds quite like the wedding service," said Humphrey with a smile. He laid the phial in their joined hands. "But, of course, it isn't. Well, there it is, for both of you."

"We shall take half each," said Caroline.

"A hundred years apiece!" said Alan.

"Here! Wait a minute! Hold on!" said Humphrey. "I'm afraid I've misled you. I suppose one works on a subject for years, and gets so close to it, one forgets other people don't know the first thing. There was an interesting example of that . . ."

"*Why* can't we take half each?" said Caroline rather loudly.

"Because, my dear, glands don't understand arithmetic. A half-changed gland won't give you half two hundred years of youth and beauty. Oh, no! Caroline, I remember the very first time I met you I told you what people were like when certain glands were deranged."

"You mean those awful idiots?"

"Exactly. This is one dose here, and one dose only. It can be drunk in one gulp; it's got a little flavor, but hardly unpleasant. It's simple, but it's dangerous if you fool with it—like dynamite. Keep it as a curiosity. It's no use; it isn't pretty; it's a wedding present. At least, it's unique."

"Well, thank you, Humphrey. Thank you very, very much."

Thereupon Caroline and Alan went home, where they set this interesting little bottle on the mantelpiece. They then took a long look at it, and a long look at each other. Had it been possible, they might have taken a long look in that enormous mirror, the public eye, before which—almost *in* which—their lives were lived, and in which they were the perfect lovers.

"You must take it right away," said Alan. "I'll get you a glass of water to drink afterwards."

"I shall do no such thing. Alan, I want you to drink it."

"Darling, come here and look in the glass. Do you see? I'm being perfectly selfish. I want you to be like that forever."

"I can see you, too, Alan. And that's how you've got to be."

Some compliments were exchanged. They were sincere and enthusiastic, and became more so. In the end, the little bottle was entirely forgotten. But the next morning it was still there.

Alan and Caroline were as determined as ever, each that the other should drink the precious potion. It is impossible to say exactly what it was in their protestations that suggested that each of them may have thought a little about it during the night.

"We can't spend the rest of our lives doing a sort of 'After you, Alphonse,' " said Caroline. "I swear to you—I cross my heart and hope to die—I *want* you to take it. Now, please do."

"Get this straight once and for all," said Alan. "You're going to take it, and I'm not. I'm going to be like that fellow what's-his-name who fell in love with—you know—the goddess."

"But darling, think of your overhead smash!"

"What's wrong with it? Are you trying to tell me it's not holding up?"

"Of course not. It's wonderful how it holds up. Everyone says so."

"Holding up! Wonderful! Is that what they say? Of course, that's the kiss of death."

"But you'll be up against that awful boy from California in August, you know."

"I can take care of that pip-squeak without any monkey gland," said Alan. "I must say, I'm rather surprised you think I can't."

"I don't think you can't," said Caroline. "But . . ."

"Oh, there's a 'but' to it!"

"But you *are* six years older than I am."

"Oh, listen! A man's got ten years at least on a woman."

"Not every woman. It's true some women like going around with men old enough to be their fathers." She studied him thoughtfully. "I think you'll look awfully distinguished with gray hair."

Alan looked unhappily into the mirror. Then he looked at Caroline. "I can't imagine *you* with gray hair. So, you see, if I *did* drink it, just to please you . . ."

"I wish you would," cried Caroline, whose basic goodness and kindness are a matter of record. "Alan, I *won't* see you get old, and ugly, and ill . . . and die. I'd rather it was me. Truly, I would. Rather than have you die and be left without you."

"And that goes for me," said Alan, with just as much emphasis, but yet in a way that caused her to look at him searchingly.

"But you'd love me?" she asked, "even if I did get old? Wouldn't you?" Then, giving him no time at all: "Or would you?"

"Carrie, you know I would."

"No, you wouldn't. But I would you."

"If that's what you think," said Alan, "you'd better take it yourself. It's obvious. Go on—take it. And let *me* get old."

"I wish Humphrey had never given us the wretched stuff!" cried Caroline. "Let's pour it down the sink. Come on! Right now!"

"Are you crazy?" cried Alan, snatching the phial from her hand. "The only bottle in the whole world! From what Baxter said, a man died for the sake of what's in that bottle."

"And he'd be awfully hurt if we threw it away," murmured Caroline.

"To Hell with *him*," said Alan. "But, after all, it's a wedding present."

So they left it right there on the mantelpiece, which is a good place for a wedding present, and their wonderful life went on.

The only trouble was, they were both becoming age-conscious to a degree which gradually amounted to an obsession. Caroline became extremely exacting at the beauty parlor. It was pathetic to see Alan hovering in front of the mirror, trying to decide if that was only a sunbleached hair on his temple, or a gray one. Caroline watched him, and in the mirror he saw her watching him. They looked at themselves, and they looked at each other, and whoever looks in that way can always find something. I shall not describe the afternoon when Alan's birthday cake was brought in with the wrong number of candles on it.

However, they both tried desperately to be brave about it, and Caroline might have succeeded.

"It won't be so bad," she said. "After all, we can grow old together."

"A nice old couple!" said Alan. "Silver hair, plastic dentures . . . !"

"Even so, if we still love each other," maintained Caroline.

"Sure! On a porch! With roses!"

It was that very night, in the middle of the night, Alan was suddenly awakened. Caroline had turned the light on, and was bending over him, looking at him.

"What is it? What's the matter? What are you looking at me for?"

"Oh, I was just looking at you."

Most men, if they woke up in the middle of the night and found Caroline bending over them, would think they must have died and gone to Heaven, but Alan took it very peevishly. He seemed to think that she was examining him for enlarged pores, deepening wrinkles, sagging tissues, blurring lines, and other signs of incipient decay, and she found it hard to make a convincing denial, because she had been doing exactly that.

"I've a good mind to take that stuff and swallow it down right now," said Alan in a rage.

"Yes, it's just the sort of thing you *would* do," retorted Caroline.

It will be seen that a situation had developed in which almost anything that either of them did would be certain to offend the other.

Things went on like this until the last day of the tournament at Forest Hills. It was on this day that Alan encountered the boy-wonder from California. He saw, as he had seen before, that the stripling had a game very noticeably lacking in finesse. He had tremendous force and a great deal of speed, but no finesse at all. His reflexes were uncanny; it was impossible to fool him by a change of pace. But reflexes are one thing; finesse is quite another. "Why the Hell do I keep thinking about finesse?" said Alan to himself before the first set was over. When the last set was done, the answer was there as big as the scoreboard. The stringy boy from California put his hand on Alan's shoulder as they walked off the court together. To a man who has been played to a standstill, the hand of the victor is a heavy load to carry.

Nevertheless, Alan took his defeat very well. All through the evening, he firmly discounted the alibis that his friends invented for him. "The son of a bitch just plain battered me off the court," said he with a rueful grin. Even when Caroline explained to everyone how tense and nervous he'd been lately, he showed no slightest sign of the rage and desolation which howled within him.

That night, in spite of his aching weariness, he lay awake long after Caroline was sound asleep. At last he got up and crept with infinite caution into the living room. He took up the little phial, unscrewed the top, and drained the contents at a single gulp. He went to the little faucet behind the bar and refilled the phial with water. He was about to replace the cap when a thought struck him, and he looked about among the bottles until he settled on some bitters. He added several drops to the water in the phial, to give it a flavor, and then put it back on the mantelpiece. Over the mantelpiece. Over the mantelpiece was a mirror; Alan took a long look in this mirror, and he smiled.

Now, it happened that at this time Caroline was playing the part of a girl who was encumbered with an amiable fool of a younger sister. The girl who played this sister walked out in a fit of temper, and a new girl had to be found in a hurry. One of the producers, without even the excuse of a villainous motive, but out of sheer, sottish good nature, nominated the niece of a friend of his. The girl had to be sent for and looked at, and, at once, everyone saw that she was the crazy kid sister in person, for she was nothing more or less than a long-limbed, wide-mouthed, dazzle-eyed version of Caroline in slang, so to speak, with a grin instead of a smile, and a stumble instead of Caroline's wonderful walk; and, instead of that look of spring morning joy that beamed from Caroline's face, the newcomer had an expression of slaphappy bewilderment, as if the world was playing a succession of highly diverting tricks on her.

Everyone thought she was charming, and everyone approved the choice, Caroline included. The first time she went on, Caroline stood in the wings to see how she took to it. She could see just by looking at her back that the girl lit up as she stepped into view of the audience. It hardly amounted to a premonition, but she stepped forward and watched attentively as the girl blundered through the agreeable little routine that the part called for. It was a scene that always drew a pleasant round of applause. This time, as the girl came off the stage: "My god!" thought Caroline, "that's *my* applause."

She was perfectly right. The sound that was mounting out front was of a timbre discernibly more feverish, and with more of the humming undertone of the human voice in it, than the applause that rewards a good piece of acting. This was the sound made by an audience that has fallen in love. Caroline knew it well. She had heard it every night for a good many years, and she heard it that same night when, a few minutes later, she made her own entrances. But, rightly or wrongly, it now seemed to her that a certain amount was missing, and, to Caroline's ear, that amount was exactly equal to what had been bestowed on the gangling youngster.

In the passage outside her dressing room, a small group was listening with new respect to the producer who had found the girl. "What do you think of her, Carrie?" he asked amiably as Caroline approached.

"I think she's a darling," replied Caroline.

"Carrie," said he, "she's the biggest discovery since you walked on that night in Newport."

Caroline smiled and entered her dressing room. Through the half-open door she heard someone say, "But do you think she'll make an actress?"

"Let me tell you, my boy," returned the fortunate discoverer. "I was out front all through the second act. Now, when you're talking to that kid the way I'm talking to you, what is she? Just a kid. But, my boy, when she walks on the stage—she's YOUTH. The crazy, lovely, dizzy, unlucky, stumblebum youth of this day and age, my boy! And she tears your goddam heart out. So, I don't give a hoot in hell if she ever learns to act. In fact, I hope to god she never will. I've put on as many good shows as anyone else over the last fifteen years, and I remember what Wolcott Gibbs said about some dame quite a time ago. 'When youth and beauty walks on the stage,' he said, 'to Hell with Sarah Bernhardt!' "

Caroline closed her door.

That night, she couldn't get home fast enough. She felt she needed Alan. She felt like a wounded animal that instinctively seeks some bitter herb, the one thing that will cure it. She knew, as it were, the flavor of what she needed from him: harsh, astringent, healing to the bruised ego; the acrid emanation of . . .which of his qualities? "Anyway, it's there," she thought in the elevator. "It's there in his ugly smile; in the way he. . . ." Here she stopped short. "Alan's smile? Ugly? I'm certainly good and mixed up. Never mind! At least I'm home."

She went in, and the place was empty. The emptiness of one's own home at midnight, when one has fled there for comfort, is an abomination and an injury, and Caroline took it as such, though it was the most ordinary thing in the world for Alan to go out while she was at the theater, and to get home after she did. Recently, he had done so almost every night, and she hadn't given it a thought. But tonight she was injured and angry.

She walked from one room to another, looked at the largest photograph of Alan, and felt dissatisfied with his smile. "It's not mature," she said. She looked in the glass and tried, with considerable difficulty, a smile of her own. This she found even more unsatisfactory, but for the opposite reason. "I may as well face it," said this valetudinarian of twenty-seven, "I'm old." She stood there watching her reflection as she drew down the corners of her mouth, and in the stillness and silence of the apartment she could feel and almost hear the remorseless erosion of time. Moment after moment, particles of skin wore away; hair follicles broke, splintered, and decayed like the roots of dead trees. All those little tubes and miles of thread-like channels in the inner organs were silting up like doomed rivers. And the glands, the all-important glands, were choking, clogging, abrading, falling apart. And she felt her marriage was falling apart, and Alan would be gone, and life would be gone.

Her eyes were already on the little phial. She took it up, she unscrewed the top, and she drank the contents. She was very calm and controlled as she went to the bathroom and refilled the phial with water, and added a little quinine to give it the bitter taste. She put the phial back in its place, eyed her reflection again as she did so, and called herself by a name so extremely coarse and offensive that it is almost unbelievable that so charming a girl as Caroline could have uttered the word.

When Alan returned that night, she did not ask him where he had been, but overwhelmed him with tenderness, feeling, of course, as if she had unspeakably betrayed him, and was going to desert him, and go away into an endless springtime where he could never follow her.

This mood continued over the weeks that followed, and should, one would say, have been matched by an equal remorseful tenderness in Alan, but things are not always as they should be. The fact is, the only inconvenience he suffered from his little secret concerning the phial was the thought of being married to an aging woman, which makes a man feel like a gigolo.

So time, which was the cause of all this trouble, went on, and Caroline and Alan, each secure in imperishable youth, each saw in the other, as through a magnifying glass, more and more of the hastening signs of decay. Alan began to feel very much ill-used. He felt that Caroline, at the very least, should have provided herself with a younger sister. One night, he dropped into the theater and discovered that, in a manner of speaking, she had done so.

Soon after this, Alan began to win his matches again, and by the same comfortable margin as before. The experts all noted that he had entirely regained his old fire and aggressiveness, and they confidently expected him to win back the championship the following year.

All this time, Humphrey, being trained to await patiently the outcome of his experiments, waited patiently. It may be asked how he knew that both of them would take the potion. The answer is, he was completely indifferent as to whether both of them took it, or one of them, or neither. It was his opinion that a good marriage would survive the phial, and a bad one would be wrecked by it, whichever way it happened.

Very late one evening, his doorbell rang three or four times in rapid succession. He raised his eyebrows and hurried to open it. There stood Caroline. Her hat, hair, dress, and all the rest of it looked just as usual; yet she gave the impression of having run all the way. Humphrey gave her his ugly smile, and saying never a word, he led her through into the living room, where she sat down, got up, walked about a little, and at last turned to him. "I've left Alan," she said.

"These things happen," said Humphrey.

"It's your fault," she said. "Not really yours, perhaps, but it was that horrible stuff you gave us. Humphrey, I'm the lowest, the most despicable rat; I'm such a hypocrite and traitor as you can't ever imagine."

"I very much doubt it," said Humphrey. "I suppose this means you drank the stuff."

"Yes, behind his back."

"And what did he say when you told him?"

"I haven't told him, Humphrey. I wouldn't dare. No. I filled the thing up with water and put some quinine in it, and . . ."

"Tell me why you put quinine in it."

"To give it that bitter taste."

"I see. Go on."

"Oh, I felt so horrible afterwards. I can't tell you how awful I felt. I tried, I tried so hard to love him more than ever to make up for it. But you can't make up for a thing like that. Besides . . ."

"Yes?"

"Oh, it just ruined everything, in all sorts of ways. I suppose I've been watching him—you can't help watching a person who's aging in front of your eyes. And when you watch anyone like that you see all sorts of things wrong with them. And I know he's felt it because he . . . well, he hasn't been very nice lately. But it's my fault, because I don't love him anymore. Maybe I never did." With that, she began to weep, which showed a very proper feeling.

"Don't tell me," said Humphrey, "that you don't want to be young forever."

"Not if I can't ever love anyone again."

"There's always yourself, you know."

"It's cruel of you to say that. It's cruel even if it's true."

"It's lonely being like this," said Humphrey. "But that's the price we pay for our little immortality. You, and me, and, of course, old Vingleberg. We're animals of a new species. There's us"—his hand swept a little circle around them—"and the rest of the world." They sat for quite a long time in silence, alone together in this imaginary circle. The sensation was not at all unpleasant. "Of course," added Humphrey, "I used to think we were like that for quite a different reason."

"If it could . . . Oh, but I'm so worthless! I let you down. Now I've let him down."

"The first was a mistake. It can be put right."

"But not the second. That we can't live with."

"Yes, I think so. You say the stuff tasted bitter? There's no mistake about *that*, I suppose?"

"No, oh, no, it was very bitter."

"You see, that has far-reaching implications. *I* used nothing but ordinary salt in the water."

Possession of
Angela Bradshaw

There was a young woman, the daughter of a retired colonel, resident in one of London's most select suburbs, and engaged to be married to Mr. Angus Fairfax, a solicitor who made more money every year. The name of this young woman was Angela Bradshaw; she wore a green sweater and had an Aberdeen terrier, and when open-toed shoes were in fashion, she wore open-toed shoes. Angus Fairfax was as ordinary as herself, and pleasant and ordinary were all the circumstances of their days.

Nevertheless, one day in September this young woman developed symptoms of a most distressing malady. She put a match to the curtains of the drawing room, and kicked, bit, and swore like a trooper when restrained.

Everyone thought she had lost her reason, and no one was more distressed than her fiancé. A celebrated alienist was called in; he found her in a collected frame of mind. He made a number of little tests, such as are usual in these examinations, and could find none of the usual symptoms of dementia.

When he had done, however, she burst into a peal of coarse laughter, and, calling him a damned old fool, she reminded him of one or two points he had overlooked. Now, these points were extremely abstruse ones, and most unlikely to be known to a young girl who had never studied psychoanalysis, or life, or anything of that sort.

The alienist was greatly shocked and surprised, but he was forced to admit that, while such knowledge was most abnormal, and while the term she had applied to him was indicative of ignorance and bad taste, he did not feel that she could be certified on these grounds alone.

"But cannot she be certified for setting fire to my curtains?" asked her mother.

"Not unless I find symptoms of insanity," said the specialist. "You can, of course, charge her with arson."

"What? And have her go to prison?" cried her mother. "Think of the disgrace!"

"I could undertake her defense, free of charge, and doubtless get her off with a caution," said Mr. Fairfax.

"There would still be the newspapers," said the colonel, shaking his head. "At the same time, it seems extraordinary that nothing can be done about it." Saying this, he gave the eminent alienist his check and a look. The alienist shrugged his shoulders and departed.

Angela immediately put her feet on the table (her legs were extremely well turned) and recited a string of doggeral verses, celebrating the occasion in great detail, and casting scorn on her parents and her fiancé. These verses were very scurrilous, or I would reproduce them here.

During the next few days, she played some other tricks, all of them troublesome and undignified; above all, she rhymed away like the principal boy in a pantomime. A whole string of doctors was called in. They all said her misbehavior was not due to insanity.

Her parents then tried a few quacks, who, powerless to certify, were also impotent to cure. In the end, they went to a seedy Madame who claimed to see into the soul. "The whole thing is perfectly clear," said this unprepossessing old woman. "Your daughter is possessed of a devil. Two guineas."

They asked her to exorcise the intrusive fiend, but that was ten, so they said they would think the matter over, and took Angela home in a taxi.

On the way, she said to them with a smile, "If you had had the decency to ask me, I could have told you that was the trouble, all along."

When they had finished berating her for allowing them to go to so much expense unnecessarily, they asked her how she knew.

"In the simplest way," she said. "I see him very frequently."

"When?" cried the colonel.

"Where?" cried her mother.

"What is he like?" cried her fiancé.

"He is young and not at all bad-looking," replied Angela, "and he talks most amusingly. He generally appears to me when I am alone. I am seldom alone but in my bedroom, and it is there that I see him, between eleven at night and seven in the morning."

"What does he say?" cried her father, grasping his Malacca.

"Is he black?" cried her mother.

"What does he—? How do you know it is not a she-devil?" cried her fiancé.

"But how does he appear?" asked her mother.

"Frequently I find him beside me when I have got into bed," said Angela, with the greatest composure in the world.

"I have always asked you to let me order a wider bed for that room," observed her mother to the colonel.

"This fiend must be exorcised at once," said Angus Fairfax, "for there is no bed wide enough to sleep three, once we are married."

"I'm not sure that he wants to be exorcised," said Angela. "In any case, I must ask him first."

"Colonel Bradshaw," said Angus Fairfax, "I hope you realize my position. In the face of these revelations, *and of all that lies behind them,* I cannot but withdraw from the engagement."

"A good riddance, *I* say," observed the fiend, now speaking for the first time.

"Be quiet, dear," said Angela.

Mr. Fairfax rapped on the glass, stopped the taxi, and got out.

"In the face of what we have just heard," said he, "no action for breach of promise can possibly lie."

"It is not the custom of the Bradshaws to bring actions for breach of promise," said the Colonel. "No more shall we sue you for your share of the taxi-fare."

The fiend, while Mr. Fairfax hastily fumbled for his money, recited a valedictory quatrain, rhyming most obscenely upon his name.

To resume our tale: they got home. The colonel immediately telephoned for the old Madame to come, regardless of cost.

"I'll have this fiend out before eleven tonight, anyway, Miss," said he to his daughter, who laughed.

The old Madame turned up, bearing a great box of powders,

herbs, bones, symbols, and heaven knows what else. She had the drawing room darkened, and the wireless disconnected from its aerial, just in case, and, as an afterthought, had the colonel go out with a sardine to tempt a cat in from the street. "They often like to go into a cat," she said. "I don't know why."

Then, Angela being seated in the middle of the room, and the ornamental paper being taken out of the fireplace, because fiends very frequently like to make an exit by way of the chimney, the old woman lit a joss stick or two and began to mumble away for dear life.

When she had said all that was required, she set fire to a saucerful of Bengal Light. "Come forth, Asmodeus!" she cried.

"Wrong," said the fiend, with a chuckle.

"Bother!" cried the old woman in dismay, for the flare had shown the cat eating one of the bones she had brought. "That was a bone of St. Eulalia, which was worse than Keating's Powder to devils, and cost me twenty guineas," she said. "No devil will go into that cat now, and the bone must go into the bill, and the colonel must go into the street to fetch a fresh cat."

When everything was resettled, she began again, and, lighting a new saucerful, "Come forth, Beelzebub!" she demanded.

"Wrong again," said the fiend, with a louder chuckle than before.

"They'll never guess, darling," said Angela.

The old beldam went on, at a prodigious expense of the Bengal Light, which was of a special kind. She called on Belial, Belphegor, Mahound, Radamanth, Minos, all the fiends ever heard of, and all she brought forth were taunts and laughter.

"Then who the devil are you?" cried the colonel at last.

"William Wakefield Wall," replied the fiend.

"You might have asked that at the beginning," said Angela quietly.

"And who, if you please, is William Wakefield Wall?" inquired her mother, with dignity. "At least, dear, he is not one of those foreign fiends," she added to the colonel.

"He is some charlatan," said the old woman. "I have never heard of him."

"Very few Philistines have," rejoined the fiend, with great equanimity. "However, if there is, by any odd chance, anyone in this suburb who is familiar with the latest developments of modern poetry, I advise you to make your inquiries there."

"Do you mean to say you're a poet?" cried the colonel.

"I am not a Poona jingler," replied the other, "if that is what you mean by the term. Nor do I describe in saccharine doggerel such scenes as are often reproduced on colored calendars. If, however, by the word 'poetry' you imply a certain precision, intensity, and clarity of—"

"He *is* a poet, Father," said Angela, "and a very good one. He had a poem in a magazine printed in Paris. Didn't you, Will?"

"If the rascal is a poet," cried the colonel, "bring in a bottle of whiskey. That'll get him out, if I know the breed."

"A typical army idea!" replied the poet. "Perhaps the only one. No, colonel, you need not bring whiskey here, unless you need some yourself, and you may send away that old woman, at whom I do nothing but laugh. I shall come out on my own terms, or not at all."

"And your terms are—?" said the colonel.

"Permission to marry your daughter," said the poet. "And the settlement upon her of a sum commensurate with the honor which my profession will bestow upon the family."

"And if I refuse?" cried the outraged father.

"I am very comfortable where I am," replied William Wall. "Angela can eat enough for two, and we are both as happy as anything. Aren't we, Angela?"

"Yes, dear," said Angela. "Oh, *don't!*"

"We shall continue to have our bit of fun, of course," added the poet.

"My dear," said the colonel to his wife, "I think we had better sleep on this."

"I think it must be settled before eleven, my dear," said Mrs. Bradshaw.

They could see no way out of it, so they had to come to an agreement. The poet at once emerged, and proved to be quite a presentable young man, though a little free in his mode of speech, and he was able to satisfy them that he came of an estimable family.

He explained that he had first seen Angela in the foyer of a theater, during the *entr'acte,* and, gazing into her eyes (for he was much attracted), he had been amazed and delighted to find himself enter into possession of her. He was forced to reply in the affirmative to a certain question of Mrs. Bradshaw's, but, after all, young people have their own standards in these days. They were married at once, and, as he soon took to writing novels, the financial side worked out very satisfactorily, and they spent all their winters on the Riviera.

THE CHASER

Alan Austen, as nervous as a kitten, went up certain dark and creaky stairs in the neighborhood of Pell Street, and peered about for a long time on the dim landing before he found the name he wanted written obscurely on one of the doors.

He pushed open this door, as he had been told to do, and found himself in a tiny room, which contained no furniture but a plain kitchen table, a rocking chair, and an ordinary chair. On one of the dirty buff-colored walls were a couple of shelves, containing in all perhaps a dozen bottles and jars.

An old man sat in the rocking chair, reading a newspaper. Alan, without a word, handed him the card he had been given. "Sit down, Mr. Austen," said the old man very politely. "I am glad to make your acquaintance."

"Is it true," asked Alan, "that you have a certain mixture that has—er—quite extraordinary effects?"

"My dear sir," replied the old man, "my stock in trade is not very large—I don't deal in laxatives and teething mixtures—but, such as it is, it is varied. I think nothing I sell has effects which could be precisely described as ordinary."

"Well, the fact is—" began Alan.

"Here, for example," interrupted the old man, reaching for a bottle from the shelf. "Here is a liquid as colorless as water, almost tasteless, quite imperceptible in coffee, milk, wine, or any other beverage. It is also quite imperceptible to any known method of autopsy."

"Do you mean it is a poison?" cried Alan, very much horrified.

"Call it cleaning fluid if you like," said the old man indifferently. "Lives need cleaning. Call it a spot-remover. 'Out, damned spot!' Eh? 'Out, brief candle!' "

"I want nothing of that sort," said Alan.

"Probably it is just as well," said the old man. "Do you know the price of this? For one teaspoonful, which is sufficient, I ask five thousand dollars. Never less. Not a penny less."

"I hope all your mixtures are not as expensive," said Alan apprehensively.

"Oh, dear, no," said the old man. "It would be no good charging that sort of price for a love-potion, for example. Young people who need a love-potion very seldom have five thousand dollars. If they had they would not need a love-potion."

"I'm glad to hear you say so," said Alan.

"I look at it like this," said the old man. "Please a customer with one article, and he will come back when he needs another. Even if it *is* more costly. He will save up for it, if necessary."

"So," said Alan, "you really do sell love-potions?"

"If I did not sell love-potions," said the old man, reaching for another bottle, "I should not have mentioned the other matter to you. It is only when one is in a position to oblige that one can afford to be so confidential."

"And these potions," said Alan. "They are not just—just—er—"

"Oh, no," said the old man. "Their effects are permanent, and extend far beyond the mere carnal impulse. But they include it. Oh, yes, they include it. Bountifully. Insistently. Everlastingly."

"Dear me!" said Alan, attempting a look of scientific detachment. "How very interesting!"

"But consider the spiritual side," said the old man.

"I do, indeed," said Alan.

"For indifference," said the old man, "they substitute devotion. For scorn, adoration. Give one tiny measure of this to the young lady—its flavor is imperceptible in orange juice, soup, or cocktails—and however gay and giddy she is, she will change altogether. She'll want nothing but solitude, and you."

"I can hardly believe it," said Alan. "She is so fond of parties."

"She will not like them anymore," said the old man. "She'll be afraid of the pretty girls you may meet."

"She'll actually be jealous?" cried Alan in a rapture. "Of me?"

"Yes, she will want to be everything to you."

"She is, already. Only she doesn't care about it."

"She will, when she has taken this. She will care intensely. You'll be her sole interest in life."

"Wonderful!" cried Alan.

"She'll want to know all you do," said the old man. "All that has happened to you during the day. Every word of it. She'll want to know what you are thinking about, why you smile suddenly, why you are looking sad."

"That is love!" cried Alan.

"Yes," said the old man. "How carefully she'll look after you!

She'll never allow you to be tired, to sit in a draft, to neglect your food. If you are an hour late, she'll be terrified. She'll think you are killed, or that some siren has caught you."

"I can hardly imagine Diana like that!" cried Alan, overwhelmed with joy.

"You will not have to use your imagination," said the old man. "And, by the way, since there are always sirens, if by any chance you *should,* later on, slip a little, you need not worry. She will forgive you, in the end. She'll be terribly hurt, of course, but she'll forgive you—in the end."

"That will not happen," said Alan fervently.

"Of course not," said the old man. "But, if it does, you need not worry. She'll never divorce you. Oh, no! And, of course, she herself will never give you the least, the very least, grounds for—not divorce, of course—but even uneasiness."

"And how much," said Alan, "how much is this wonderful mixture?"

"It is not so dear," said the old man, "as the spot-remover, as I think we agreed to call it. No. That is five thousand dollars; never a penny less. One has to be older than you are to indulge in that sort of thing. One has to save up for it."

"But the love-potion?" said Alan.

"Oh, that," said the old man, opening the drawer in the kitchen table and taking out a tiny, rather dirty-looking phial. "That is just a dollar."

"I can't tell you how grateful I am," said Alan, watching him fill it.

"I like to oblige," said the old man. "Then customers come back, later in life, when they are rather better-off, and want more expensive things. Here you are. You will find it very effective."

"Thank you again," said Alan. "Good-bye."

"*Au revoir,*" said the old man.

MADEMOISELLE KIKI

La Caillot, on the rocky coast near Marseilles, has the smallest harbor in the South of France. Its horseshoe basin shelters a score of fishing boats, and the owners of these boats spend their evenings in the Café Roustand.

Beside the café there is a little angular space with a street lamp and a wind-bitten tree. In front lies the roadway, and beyond it the lapping waters of the harbor. Inside, there are six or eight tables, and the usual small zinc bar near the door. Near one end of this bar stands a rack of postcards, showing views of La Caillot. These are mostly in a rather faded sepia, and have been there for some time. One of them includes the figure of the present proprietor, at a rather earlier age, standing with a hoop in his hand and a vacant expression on his face. Beyond the rack comes the last foot or so of the counter, and it is here that Kiki sleeps the whole day through. Kiki is a cat in her middle years, but looking rather older owing to the ravages of a passionate temperament.

Had the cat world its Kinsey, he could tell us some remarkable things. For example, there are certain spells in the life of the female of that species when she becomes more than ordinarily interested in the conversation of the opposite sex. These spells are very variable both in their frequency and their duration. Sometimes they occur twice in the year, sometimes thrice, and, in the ardent South, instances have been known of the manifestation recurring as often as four or five times. Kiki, though no prude, would have disdained such intemperance. In her case, the condition prevailed only once in every year. It must be admitted, however, that it lasted, except in leap years, for three hundred and sixty-five days.

Now Kiki, though unusually large and powerful, could not be called a beautiful cat. Her angular frame seemed to have been draped in a ragged, patchy, and discolored fur gleaned from some rubbish heap, and her sides were so knobbly and uneven as to suggest that this fur was stuffed with old bedsprings from the same source. In the amorous discourse of cats, a vitally important part is played by the vocal preliminaries. In this respect, Kiki suffered a disadvantage greater even than that of her appearance. No such dismal, dolorous, and uninviting croak has ever been heard as that which issued from Kiki. It effectively chilled the hot blood of the male cats of La Caillot, a feat otherwise accomplished only by death or the mistral.

Nevertheless, this grim, gaunt, hideous scarecrow of a female lived the life of Riley, and enjoyed the highest consideration both of the human kind and of her own. In La Caillot, the ordinary run of cats are nothing but anonymous scavengers, but no fisherman left Roustand's at closing time without a very civil *bon soir* to Mademoiselle Kiki. Still more to the point, every evening one or another of them would stop at his boat on his way to the café, and bring up, in a strip of net or an old can, a mess of such sorts of fish as were too bony or flavorless to be marketable. As often as not, some rich sardines or delicate *merlans,* which had been a little trodden upon in the bottom of the boat, were included in the offering.

Such distinction, in a community so utterly neglectful of its cats, needs a little accounting for. The fact is that when an exceptionally fierce and icy mistral was on its way, and all the local cats kept huddled in whatever shelter they could find, regardless of their hunger and all other earthly appetites, Kiki, foreseeing a lonely midnight, would lift her bristly chin and utter cries of disappointment and fury such as would set the flesh crawling on a man's bones in precisely the same way as did the bitter wind itself. When the record mistral of 1951 was on its way down the valley of the Rhône, and even before it began to flatten the wastes of reeds on the Camargue, Kiki had raised a banshee wail that was long remembered. It was remembered also that early next morning two of the open boats were blown out to sea and never returned. Much the same thing happened in the big blow in 1953, and Kiki was credited with supernatural powers. When she uttered her most piercing cries, the fishermen took warning, stayed at home, listened to the fury of the wind, and agreed that Kiki deserved all the fish she could eat.

They brought her, in fact, rather more than she could eat, but not more than she had a use for. Late in the evening, when the last customer had departed, Roustand would set the chairs on the tables, turn down all the lights but one, and bring from the kitchen a wide platter heaped with the daily tribute of fish. This he would carry outside, and set it down in the little angular space under the tree. Kiki, you may be sure, was close beside him, and had her nose to the platter the moment it clinked upon the ground.

The honest Roustand then reentered his café, secured the door, extinguished the remaining light, and betook himself to bed.

With the extinction of this last light, there remained only the weak and rather ghastly radiance of the streetlamp, and the round, flat, and greenishly shining eyes of some half a dozen tomcats, seated on the low wall, or under the bench, or between the cases of empty bottles or at various other points of vantage. There are grades even among the downtrodden cat population of La Caillot, and these represented the lowest grade. These toms were hams.

Not one of the hungry wretches dared to creep over to take a share in the magnificent banquet on which Kiki proceeded to regale herself in full view of them all. Being more powerful than any of them because she was better fed, the Amazon uninterruptedly continued to feed better. Her audience observed with breathless interest the way she took each fish by the snout and crunched it between her side-teeth until she got down to the tail. The more philosophic among them might have noted that riches are not always a guarantee of beauty; the knobbliness of the harridan's sides was not smoothed out by the rich lining of fish. In fact, the existing lumps and bumps seemed to project more hideously than before. There is, however, no evidence that this observation was ever actually made.

By the time Kiki had finished her meal, the sizable platter was somewhere about half empty. At this moment, a suppressed exclamation of impatience might have been heard from one or more of the famishing watchers. Kiki paid no heed to this unmannerliness, but embarked on a leisurely toilette, for all the world like some elderly charmer who lingers at her dressing table in full confidence that her riches will keep her gigolo kicking his heels below.

When at last she considered herself ready, she moved a pace or two away from the platter, and, sadly out of tune, she hummed a few bars of the feline equivalent of *"Parlez moi d'amour."* Her calculating admirers, creeping stealthily forward, their bellies low to the ground, soon ringed her about, turning their round and unwinking gaze upon her hideousness, and uttering amorous cries which were so insincere, so contrary to every normal instinct, and brought forth with such desperate, competitive effort, that they sounded like the desolate howls of the lost souls in Hell itself. It was largely because of this hideous racket that the cats of La Caillot were held to be more raucous than those of other places, and were accordingly more execrated and less fed, which in turn laid them under all the greater compulsion to vie with each other in the nightly concert. It will be seen that Kiki's circle of admirers was in every sense a vicious circle.

Kiki alone enjoyed the music, and listened with the air of a connoisseur. In the end, the voice of one or another having attracted her by some resonant suggestion of virility, she advanced her nose to within an inch of that of the chosen swain, and breathed upon him a fragrant reminiscence of her recent meal, rich with the promise of the second course yet to come. She then gratified him with a single harsh croak of approval, on which the rest of the infernal choir at once fell silent, for they realized the game was up.

Everything being well understood by everyone concerned, the business of the evening was then transacted with no concessions to false modesty or sentimental preliminaries. At this juncture a peculiar phenomenon was to be observed, such as makes it all the more regrettable that Dr. Kinsey never turned his attention to the behavior of cats. Naturally, Kiki was entirely preoccupied; so was the drudging mercenary whom she had chosen as her cavalier of the evening. The platter, still well garnished with the remaining fish, thus lay unguarded, yet not one of the rejected suitors, ravenous as they were, stole over to enjoy a free meal. This was in no way due to any nice scruples of honesty, but entirely to the obsessive *voyeurism* of their species, examples of which may be witnessed by whoever walks after midnight through the back streets and vacant lots of any great city. The round eyes of the rejected were fixed unwinkingly on the spectacle of the unhallowed mating, and the circle, also a vicious one, remained unbroken. Now and then, a low moan would issue from under the skeleton ribs of one or another of the watchers, for there are few of us so besotted with our vice or folly as not to be dimly aware of the price we are paying for indulging in it, but these cats were spellbound, fascinated, and hypnotized, and they remained riveted to the spot.

After a certain interval Kiki would sit up, stroke her whiskers, glance around her, and stroll back to the neglected platter. Her lover was permitted to accompany her; he did so with no very noticeable signs of shame or embarrassment. The others, their virtue and their appetites undiminished, wandered disconsolately off on a round of the garbage cans of La Caillot, which are by no means notable for the richness and profusion of their contents.

Thus it was that the unlovely Kiki lived as pleasantly as the sleekest little tabby that ever lapped milk. The only exception was on those nights when the presage of the icy mistral kept the hungriest toms crouching in their lairs, and it was on those nights she set up that dolorous and discontented cry which gave warning to the fishermen, who therefore repaid her out of their catch, and thus enabled this faded Cleopatra to feed her Caesars and her Antonys. Here is yet another vicious circle: perhaps there are more of them in the world than is generally realized.

This state of affairs had continued for some years, when a lady of a very vivid complexion sold a large house she owned in Marseilles and bought a small one at La Caillot, which happened to be her birthplace. There she proposed to end her days in retirement and respectable ease. She brought with her her own cat, who was called Papillon. He was a neat, trim, cheerful, and well-cared-for animal, as clean as a new pin, nicely marked, and with a coat like satin, and he proudly carried the adornment of a fine red collar, made of patent leather.

No one is absolutely perfect; this Papillon had suffered a certain little deprivation—a mere trifle, nothing to make a fuss about; on balance it may have added very considerably to his general comfort and well-being, but it was something quite unknown in this primitive village, where the cat is hardly regarded as a domestic animal, and therefore never domesticated.

Very well, on the first night he was set at liberty, Master Papillon came mincing down to the port, for all the world like a male milliner on holiday, the living principle of plumpness and the incarnation of urbanity and self-esteem. He arrived outside the café at the very moment when Roustand was setting down the big platter of fish, and he estimated that there would be plenty to spare for such a visitor as himself, who had a thousand interesting little stories to recount, of curious things he had happened to witness in Marseilles. So he uttered a birdlike chirrup of satisfaction, lifted his tail, and came tripping across to join in the banquet.

Kiki, though momentarily stupefied by his impudence, soon saluted him with a stinging blow in the face, such as he had never dreamed of in all his life before. He began to gibber and back away, but he was wrong even in this. He should have made a full and helter-skelter retreat, for Kiki, feeling he didn't retire with sufficient respectful speed, fell upon him like a thunderbolt and drubbed him with two fistfuls of fishhooks until he fled scampering up to the house of his protectress, leaving half his handsome coat puffing about the quay.

All the same, he had sniffed at the fish, and its fragrance haunted him. It was not long before he ventured out again. The regular circle, had they had the attention to spare, might have noticed his wistful face peeping from behind the tree. He soon understood very well what was going on, having seen something rather similar in Marseilles, and the next night he edged up and took his place among the suitors. These regarded him with more of astonishment than hostility. This was less due to his citified air, his general sleekness, and his shining collar, than to something at once subtler and more profound, which completely baffled and nonplussed these rugged mercenaries. An intruder of their own kind would quickly have been sent packing, but they felt that Papillon was somehow different. It was something on which they could not put a finger, partly, of course, because they hadn't a finger among them, and partly because there was nothing for them to put it on even if they had had one. Papillon, therefore, was suffered to remain.

Kiki, finding him among the others, saw him with a new eye. She was vastly impressed by his collar, which perhaps put certain social ideas into her head, to which even the drabbest of her sex are not altogether immune. She also noticed how extremely well-fed and plump he was, and she was not the first to be misled by appearances. Like his rivals, she was vaguely aware of something different about him, but he came from Marseilles, and, "What the Hell!" thought Kiki. "Who knows?"

Accordingly, she approached her nose to that of Papillon, and uttered her hoarse croak of approval. The vain cockney, with a flirtatious smirk, piped a wooing note or two, and proceeded to imitate, to the best of his ability, the conduct that was rewarded by the fish.

The fascinated onlookers shifted their round eyes, exchanged glances, and edged nearer, as if in need of spectacles. Kiki was patient for a while, for she believed she was being introduced to sophisticated ways, but after one or two rather broad hints had been disregarded she became completely disillusioned. She faced around, and with one sweep of her paw she sent the hapless eunuch rolling in the gutter. In less time than it takes to tell, she had chosen his successor, and all proceeded as it had done so often before.

Papillon picked himself up, trembling with mortification. He removed certain unsavory matter from one of his ears, and looked about him, and saw what was going on. His eye fell upon the neglected platter of fish. Now, Papillon, if not altogether a tom, was for that very reason not a Peeping Tom. He was under no such obsessive compulsion as the others were, and nothing that he saw seemed to him of the least interest compared with the platter of fish.

He crept towards the feast, at first in hope of snatching a single sardine and bounding away with it, but he quickly realized the tremendous advantage he possessed over the roughnecks he had almost been tempted to envy. He saw them shoot brief and agonized glances in his direction, he heard some low growling sounds, and noticed a convulsive start or two, but nothing could break the spell that bound them, and they remained riveted to the spot. Papillon, reflecting that it takes all sorts to make a world, devoured the last morsel at his leisure, licked the platter clean, and strolled away up the hill beyond any possibility of pursuit.

Shortly afterwards, the interested circle broke up, and Kiki, followed by her expectant paramour, came over towards the platter. They looked with a blankness absolutely beyond description at the equally blank and empty surface of the dish, upon which not so much as a single scale remained.

What followed was altogether without precedent. The bilked gigolo, using a vile expression, struck Kiki a savage blow on the ear. The unhappy debtor, conscious of the moral weakness of her position, had not the spirit to resent it, but cowered down with her ears close to her head. The enraged tom then withdrew to join his less successful rivals at the garbage cans.

The next evening, instead of six admirers, Kiki had only five. The defrauded hireling of the previous night had decided not to show up, either because of his very natural resentment, or because he thought it better to get first go at the garbage than to risk further labors of love that might be equally unrequited.

His judgment was justified. As soon as all was in train, Master Papillon sauntered easily upon the scene. He met with insouciance the hopeless glare of the immobilized Kiki, and he listened to the moans of the hypnotized circle as a diner-out listens to the agreeable strains which a wandering violinist draws from the agonized catgut.

At the same time, he was busily at work on the platter, and again he devoured the fish to the very last crumb.

The next night, the number of Kiki's suitors was reduced to four, and the night after that to only three, and by the end of the week there was not even one.

Kiki spent the next few days in a condition of shock and depression that was truly pitiable to witness. She sat with her eyes closed and her mouth half open, moving only when now and then she raked her paw from behind her ears to the tip of her nose, as if trying to comb an idea out of her bewildered head. And in the end she succeeded in doing so. She got up, stretched herself, and sailed out in the early afternoon, and went up the little hill in search of Papillon.

Papillon, observing her through the window of his well-warmed house, showed no very strong desire to take a walk in the January air. However, the hour arrived when his mistress urged upon him the necessity of a little constitutional, and he came trembling out into the presence of the cat he had wronged. You may imagine his relief when he found himself greeted with the utmost cordiality and offered all the advantages of a warm, though platonic, friendship. His distrust was finally melted by an invitation to a complimentary place at the fish platter; he accepted with alacrity and joined her there that very midnight.

It is true that, when she saw him snugly devouring his portion, his hostess was unable to repress a low rumbling in her throat, but this she may have explained as being due to the presence of a bone there. Alas, it was the very bone she had to pick with poor Papillon!

For some time these two were inseparable, and the whole town wondered at their friendship, and none more than the disappointed mercenaries, who, skulking around, were affronted by the sight of Kiki and her confidant taking their meals together. At other hours the oddly assorted pair were to be seen visiting various corners of the port, or sitting, their noses almost touching, for hours at a stretch, engaged in the endless quiet conversation of their kind. Unquestionably, Kiki was hearing the most extraordinary stories about Marseilles, and Papillon was being fully instructed in the amenities of La Caillot.

There came a day when two incredibly elongated clouds stretched themselves across the sky, and a chill came into the sunlight which made the flesh creep and crawl upon the bones. It was obvious that a mistral was on its way; the only question was, how long and how fiercely it might blow. Kiki sniffed the foreboding air and led Papillon out upon the jetty, where they spent another hour or so in the shelter of the seawall. It was then that Kiki, deprecating her own hospitable platter, spoke fervently of her youthful voyages as a stowaway, and the flavor of the fresh-caught sardine eaten while it was still leaping and quivering in the bottom of the boat.

Papillon, whose pleasures were confined to those of the table, was all the more an epicure on that account. He wiped a spot of eager saliva from his lip, and hastened to take a sniff at the boats that offered such divine opportunities. Kiki gave a three-star recommendation to a crazy old hulk called *Les Frères Gobinet,* the least seaworthy boat in all the port, and the infatuated greenhorn leapt aboard and concealed himself.

Kiki then returned to the Café Roustand, where the fishermen were gathered, debating whether to put to sea or not in face of the oncoming mistral. "Don't worry," said one of them as he caught sight of her. "Look at Mademoiselle Kiki. She is calm; she is tranquil; she is completely at her ease. You may take it from me, the blow will die down before midnight."

"I'm not so sure," said another. "It looks like being a regular hurricane."

"If that was the case," said a third, "Kiki would be howling worse than the wind itself. She knows her stuff. She never fails. I've gone by Kiki for seven years now. She is better than a barometer; she is better than the radio, and I, for one, am not going to miss the catch."

The discussion continued for some time, but Kiki's placid demeanor ultimately convinced even the most skeptical, and soon after midnight they one and all repaired to their boats.

Before dawn the worst mistral in living memory swept over the Bouches-du-Rhône. The fishing fleet was blown far out to sea, and when at last it limped back to port it reported the loss of *Les Frères Gobinet* with all hands.

Kiki was justly blamed. "The dirty old bitch has deceived us," said the fishermen. "She knows no more about the weather than that post. She ought to be slung in the port."

In spite of these hard words they still brought up the nightly mess of fish, because they had always done so. Kiki, as she had always done, ate but half the platterful, and it became known among the underprivileged of the cat world that a share of the remainder might be enjoyed by the industrious and deserving. The veterans of the informal little club resumed their midnight congregation, and Kiki raised her voice in complaint only when the approach of the bitter wind threatened an interruption of proceedings. This restored her reputation as a weather prophet, thus assuring a continuance of the offerings, and the vicious circle was intact again.

Son OF KIKI

Up in the white hills behind La Caillot is the smallest cement factory in the world, more like a coffee grinder than a cement factory. Every few months it accumulates a shipload of its product, and then the *Étoile de la Méditerranée* drops in to carry the load off to Algiers. So it happened that, one night in the spring, when the tiny port seemed gutted by moonlight as if by fire (the houses were so ashen-white and their windows stared out so blank and deathly), the old steamer came hooting in and made her mooring.

At one moment she had been a mere black patch wallowing in the glittering water outside. She slipped through the narrow neck of the harbor, and at once became a veritable tower of a ship, filling the whole port, dwarfing the little horseshoe of houses, with lights here and there upon her, and faces bending over the lights, like a city filled with men. Her outrageous funnel rose above the rooftops. Without the slightest necessity, she emitted three devastating bellows from her siren; then her lights went out one by one, and she settled to await the morning.

The good people of La Caillot turned in their beds, for it was about one o'clock, and soon fell asleep again. Then there was nothing but the drenching moonlight, the white-faced houses, and the new vast bulk in the harbor.

Nothing, that is, in the way of human activity. On the terrace of the Café Roustand, the aged and hideous Kiki was demolishing the first half of her huge platter of fish, while, at a discreet distance, her circle of mercenary admirers crouched and watched her unwinkingly. They were waiting till she should have finished the first stage of her repast, when she would stroll over and select her hireling for the evening, who, when he had paid his tribute to her loathsome charms, would be privileged to join her in the second half of the banquet. It was thus that this abominable Kiki had corrupted the ravenous and unprincipled toms of La Caillot.

This night, however, the mercenary rites were strangely interrupted. A single plank had been pushed out to the quay from the side of the *Étoile de la Méditerranée.* Down this plank there advanced, with a somewhat rolling gait, a creature whom only a pedantic zoologist would unreservedly have called a cat. The face of this monster was so arrogantly round that all other round things —full moons, dinner plates, mill wheels—would have seemed angular and caved-in by comparison. His whiskers had the formidable appearance of quills. His chest had the contours of a barrel, though his ribs had been stove in more times than he could remember. His forelegs were stumpy, but ended in huge and ridgy feet, garnished with claws like reaping hooks. His loins tapered away behind this appalling façade, but they tapered as do the loins of a lion. A stumpy, half-length tail, carried erect like a cockade, exposed the powerful motors which drove this boar-cat on his destructive career.

His fur was matted with tar, grease, and the blood of recent wounds. In most areas it stood up in prickles, but, in some places, the tricks of fate had torn it completely away, leaving nothing but a hide as dark and tough as leather. This atrocity of a cat must have joined the ship at some festering port in North Africa, where in times of old jinns and demons consorted hideously with the feline kind in the insomniac watches of the desert.

He no sooner felt solid ground beneath his feet than he uttered a barbarous grunt, and trotted rapidly in the direction of the Café Roustand, as if he had scented the banquet from afar.

He arrived at the moment when Kiki was engaged in her luxurious and tantalizing toilette, while the waiting mercenaries importuned her with cries in which the motif of lure and longing availed little to hide a counterpoint of rage and despair.

The visitor took in the scene as he advanced. He had no need to pause, as ordinary cats do, to make sure of his ground. He came briskly up, scattered the mercenaries like chaff, thrust the outraged Kiki to one side, and wolfed the generous half-plateful of sardines —at once food and the guerdon of love—in less time than it takes to tell.

Then an amazing thing happened, a thing that Kiki was never to forget. This swaggering and ogreish boar-cat was licking his upper lip with a tongue like a two-inch file, when his eye fell upon Kiki, crouching and snarling in a corner of the terrace. Without so much as a by-your-leave, the monster leaped in her direction, sunk his teeth behind her ears, and gratified her with a demonstration of the legendary proficiency of seafaring men. This done, he bestowed no further notice on her, but gave himself a shake and a scratch, and ambled superciliously up the street, where he saluted the door of the *Mairie* itself in the offensive and almost ineradicable manner of his kind, only twenty times more pungently. He then rolled back to his ship, ascended the gangplank, and was seen no more.

Kiki, left altogether in a daze, lifted her eyes to heaven. She could not find it in her heart to be offended at the somewhat offhand manner of the stranger, there was so much about him that appealed to her. Above all, he had eaten the fish first. "This, then, must be love," thought Kiki, a new spring burgeoning in her desiccated heart.

From that hour, she was a changed cat. The mercenaries were no longer entertained, but sent spitting off with additional fleas in their ears. Nor was the superfluous fish wasted. Kiki ate the lot. One miracle had succeeded upon another: She had now more than one life to maintain; she was conscious of bearing a pledge of her sailor's affection.

Such tender secrets cannot be everlastingly concealed. Soon, the whole town was agog with news of Kiki's condition. Everybody stared as she went by, carrying a vast and knobbly abdomen slung like a hammock full of rocks beneath her ridgy spine. People counted on their fingers, engaged in arguments and even quarrels concerning her age. She, meanwhile, dragged herself blissfully from one patch of sunlight to another, and distended daily, until everyone swore that nature could endure no more.

When her time came, Kiki removed herself to a nook in a deserted house, a little way along the quay. Roustand still put her fish out every night, and there she was, lurking like a shadow to pounce upon it, and devour the lot, as soon as he had closed the door behind him. Otherwise, the town knew her no more.

After a certain number of weeks, a cry was raised. Heads were turned all along the quay; the fishermen looked up from their nets, the shopkeepers hastened to their doors. Kiki was bringing home her litter.

But, what was this? Where were the rest? Was there only one? And what a one! My God, regard that kitten!

Behind Kiki, walking with something of a rolling gait, and regarding the world through a pair of eyes comparable to nothing but glass gooseberries, strutted a stump-tailed catling, at whom it was impossible to glance without bursting into a roar of uneasy laughter. This minuscule, which bristled at every shadow, shared the peculiar hideousness of his mother and the outrageous toughness of his distant dad.

Kiki, taking all the commotion as applause, stalked proudly on, and entered the café of the honest Roustand, who dropped a dish of *pieds et pacquets* which he was setting out for his own delectation in a corner.

"There is no doubt about it," said the sexton. "He has all the look of a veritable infidel, and should be called Voltaire."

The juvenile Voltaire, as if responding to his name, crossed the table where he had been set for exhibition, and lapped up the dregs of beer in the sexton's saucer.

From that moment, he was well-established in the café, spurned his mother's withered dug, and took all the beer that was offered to him. He would now and then cool his tongue in a saucer of milk, but relished it only if a liberal dose of rum or cognac was added. In the solid line, he was prepared to fortify himself with whatever came his way, but liked nothing so well as a pickled herring or a slice of salami. His personal habits were unclean.

Kiki, delighted by every attention he received, lavished upon him a besotted affection, to the infinite chagrin of her old-time playmates, who had been waiting hungrily for her return to the rites of earlier days. These, though they showed up hopefully every night, trusting that when he reached the gangling age there would be the usual rift between mother and son, were disappointed. Every night they were driven far from the platter of sardines, and were mortified to see the hated Voltaire bloat his elastic belly on the best of the dish.

He grew alarmingly, and grew uglier as he grew older. At an early age, he was as big as his doting mamma, and assisted her in driving off her admirers. The old cat never took her eyes from his unlovely form, and would have continued to wash his face for him, but this he would no longer permit, owing to an infirmity of her breath.

Unfortunately there came a day when Kiki, returning from the pursuit of her late mercenaries, approached the platter of sardines, and was about to close her lips on the snout of one of the juiciest, received a cruel buffet, looked up, and there was her beloved son Voltaire, advancing upon her with the fury of a tiger.

She uttered a desolate howl, which was cut short by a second blow, a hundred times harder than the last. Next moment, he was upon her, she was rolled over and over, and ended up crouching and shivering in the gutter.

She heard a soft chirrup of invitation, uttered in the well-known and rather cracked voice of her son, and looked hopefully up, telling herself that perhaps it was all a joke, just one of his boyish pranks. Her old heart broke when she saw, creeping out from the shadows, a little, insignificant, doll-faced chit of a ginger she-cat who hurried to the plate and speedily ate her share of it.

When the pair of them had dispatched every morsel, while Kiki watched and starved, they advanced their noses each to within an inch of the other, and the port reechoed with their amorous serenade. Kiki, watching the scene that followed, was more than once reminded of the seafaring stranger who had fathered this bitterness upon her.

Now the unfortunate Kiki entered upon the most woeful period of all her long and checkered life. She tasted the super-serpent sharpness of the tooth of filial ingratitude. She was forced to witness, night after night, scenes which filled her heart with memories that burned but did not bless, and, above all, she was starving. Her morale was so low that her old gigolos, whom she had ruled with claws of iron, now drove her squalling from the garbage cans.

Her face miraculously became more drawn than it was already, her ribs stood out piteously, her spine was like a comb, her tail was no better than a piece of string. Suicide is rare among cats, but Kiki was on the very verge of casting herself into the port.

It was while she was engaged in somber contemplation of this desperate act that the town was wakened again by the bellowing siren of the cement boat. At the first hoot, Kiki shuddered. At the second, she uttered a low moan. At the third, a wild gleam shone in her eyes, and she set off in the direction of the mooring place.

It was the same hour. The same plank was thrust out to the quay-side. After a short interval, the huge face of the seafaring boar-cat appeared; he surveyed the scene, and advanced upon the shore.

Kiki accosted him, but it must be admitted he paid her very little attention. However, he began to leg it for the Café Roustand, and this was all she wanted. She followed close at his flank, probably pouring her woes into his ears, but he neither mended nor moderated his pace. This boar-cat had a very tenacious memory, especially for sardines.

He therefore bowled confidently into the terrace as before, and there was his son Voltaire, in the very act of inviting his coy little ginger friend to join him in the evening meal. The little ginger looked up, and made one bound for the shelter of a tubbed privet, where she crouched to watch developments.

Voltaire, it must be admitted, blanched when he saw what was bearing down upon him. Nevertheless, he had never tasted a good drubbing in the whole of his short life, his mother had so valorously protected him in his kittenhood, and in recent months his share of his father's physique had rendered him safe and bold. He was bolder yet, on the present occasion, because the fishermen had liquored his milk unusually generously that evening, so the brash youth stood his ground and struck out right and left.

His seafaring parent, ignorant of their relationship, as he would have been indifferent to it had he known, was somewhat nettled at certain pinpricks he received in the tip of the nose, and obliged the unhappy Voltaire with a little demonstration of how these matters are carried off in Africa. Voltaire, alas, was in no shape to profit by this lesson, owing to the meeting of his opponent's teeth in a region just under the hinge of his jawbone, which effectually paid his reckoning.

Kiki watched this scene with the icy triumph of one revenged, a sensation which finally melted into a warm glow of admiration for the victor. She saw her ungrateful son laid lifeless on the terrace, and the conqueror turn nonchalantly to the platterful of sardines. Before he had eaten the last of them, she was again at his side, desiring nothing more than to relive one precious moment of the past. Alas, she was rudely brushed aside; the author of her joys and sorrows thrust past her as if she was not there, and, in another moment, with scarcely as much as a by-your-leave, he was paying his attentions to the little ginger.

Kiki, considerably mortified, was sufficiently exhausted by her emotions to regard this last development philosophically. "At least," she thought, "there will be no treacherous, ungrateful, overgrown hobbledehoy to insult and injure me as did that abominable Voltaire. Tomorrow, the boat will be gone; I shall enjoy my fish in peace, and, when I have eaten all I can, there will no doubt be those who will be glad to be a little civil for the sake of a share of the remainder."

She therefore possessed her soul in patience, and it seemed that her patience was to have its reward. The boat, with its disturbing supercargo, departed; the little ginger cat fled down side streets and alleys at the mere sight of Kiki. Kiki did not pursue—she was placid in the enjoyment of her sardines and her gigolos. Besides, she no longer burned with resentment at the sight of the ginger nonentity; she rather pitied and despised her.

It was therefore only natural that she should barely notice that her insignificant rival retired from public life exactly eight weeks after the departure of the cement boat. During the weeks that followed, she forgot her entirely, and was the more stupefied to encounter her one afternoon upon the quay, leading, with the air of one drunk with pride, six hideous but lusty kittens. These walked with something of a rolling gait, and regarded the world through eyes comparable only to glass gooseberries. Each was the spitting image of his half-brother Voltaire, and each stumpy half-length tail was carried like the standard of a new order, under which peace, sardines, and gigolos must soon be swept away.

A MATTER OF TASTE

Small and exclusive as it is, the Medusa is unquestionably the best-known of London clubs. It is there, on the first Friday of each month, a circle of intimates gathers, whose pleasure it is, after enjoying an admirably-cooked dinner accompanied by well-chosen wines, to retire to the smoking room and there to discuss the more interesting of the murders they have happened upon in the interval since last they met.

The circle is well-constituted for its purpose. Its regular members include a leading barrister, a well-known criminologist, a famous explorer, an eminent psychiatrist who makes a specialty of the homicidal impulse, and an amiable nonentity whose simple utterances are not always unworthy of attention. Others are now and then invited to join the group: a detective inspector from the Yard, a country parson, an Egyptologist (for asps), a distinguished *savant* (for general purposes), and, on occasional gala nights, a murderer in person, whose firsthand experience lends a salty touch of realism to the lively debate.

One evening not long ago, the circle was in full session. The servants had removed the coffee cups, placed every man's favorite beverage at his elbow, subdued the lights, and noiselessly withdrawn. "I wonder," said the nonentity amiably, "I wonder if there really is such a thing as 'the perfect murder.' What do you chaps think?"

This started the ball rolling with a vengeance. The explorer expatiated on the Polar Poignard, or ice dagger, which has the advantage of melting away and leaving no trace of a weapon. The psychiatrist, contemptuous of all material agents, described methods of inducing suicidal mania in unwanted spouse or obstructive uncle. A celebrated mycologist who was present gave a short, interesting talk on the toxic fungi, their use and abuse.

"All this, however, is purely theoretical," observed the amiable nonentity. "Can't we get down to cases?"

"You are right, Smithers," said a voice that had not been heard for some time in the little symposium. It was that of Sir Barnard Wigmore, consulting pathologist to Her Majesty's Home Office, who had been away for several months, taking the cure at a famous continental spa. "It is only to be expected, of course, that the perfect murder will be concealed from our sight in the very brightness of its own perfection. It so happens, however, that just before my recent indisposition I was called on by the Yard in connection with a case which was not only unique in my own limited experience, but which possibly has no parallel in the entire annals of crime. I wonder if you fellows would like to hear about it?"

Needless to say, a general murmur of assent greeted this modest inquiry.

"Very well," continued Sir Barnard, first taking a sip from the glass of effervescent liver salts that stood beside him. "Since we are all friends, and since no whisper of what passes here is ever allowed to reach the ears of a public already addicted to sensationalism, I shall not attempt to disguise the personalities involved. The case was that of Lady Jerningham, who died so suddenly last spring. Whether because of an indiscretion on the part of her doctor, or through the gossip of the servants, her symptoms became generally known, and were widely discussed. They included acute abdominal discomfort, nausea, dizziness, spots before the eyes, and, finally, convulsions, syncope, and coma. Death supervened in less than twelve hours.

"I need hardly remind you, gentlemen, that, while symptoms such as these are exhibited in various quite ordinary forms of violent gastric disturbance, and particularly in cases of food poisoning of an innocent nature, they are also typical of the effects of many types of irritant poisons criminally administered. In view of certain corollary circumstances which were a matter of common knowledge, rumor was rife in the clubs, and suspicion fastened upon Sir Jervase Jerningham, eleventh baronet of that name, and husband of the unfortunate lady in question. It is generally known that Lady Jerningham was several years older than her husband, and it was a matter of frequent debate as to whether her appearance or her personality was the more regrettable. Moreover, immediately before her seizure, Sir Jervase had presented her with an unusually large box of chocolates. This box, its contents about two-thirds consumed, was found in the deceased lady's boudoir, and preserved by the butler—to quote him, 'Just in case!'

"It is not uncommon for a husband to present a box of chocolates to his wife. I have done so myself; those of you who are married have doubtless also made such trifling gifts, and with motives as innocent as my own. But there is a very widespread opinion that in instances where the wife is so conspicuously lacking in feminine charm as to be unlikely to inspire any gallant generosity in her spouse, gifts of this sort may be suspect as indications of a guilt feeling, such as is experienced even by the most cynical in connection with an act of infidelity. I think our eminent psychiatrical friend will probably confirm the prevalence, if not the validity, of this opinion."

The eminent psychiatrist having nodded, Sir Barnard resumed his narrative. "Now, at that time, the name of Sir Jervase was linked by wagging tongues to that of the celebrated film star, Miss Gloria Mundy, whom, as you probably know, he has recently married. Miss Mundy is a young lady of outstanding attractions, and this was an outstandingly large box of chocolates, weighing, in fact, no less than fifteen pounds. It was very generally assumed that Sir Jervase had, so to speak, killed two birds with one stone, wiping out both guilt feeling and wife with the same expiatory offering. The daily press was alert to capitalize on the sensation, and in capitals exhorted Scotland Yard to 'GET A MOVE ON.'

"Our omniscient journalists were not aware that Scotland Yard had moved already. The Commissioner was fully cognizant of the marital situation of the Jerninghams, and I am revealing only the most open of secrets in telling you that his eye, gallant as befits an old soldier, had rested with particular attention on Miss Mundy. That same eye, keen as befits a chief of police, had observed with some distaste her sudden involvement with Sir Jervase. The Commissioner was out to get his man, and he immediately summoned me to the Yard. The box of chocolates, of which only a third remained, had been brought in and placed upon his desk.

" 'We have,' said he, 'corpse, chocolates, and motive. In fact, we have two motives. Look here, upon this picture' (showing me a photograph of Miss Mundy, a face capable of launching a thousand ships) 'and on this!' (showing me one of Lady Jerningham, who might with equal ease have sunk them). 'If you will oblige us,' said he, 'with the formality of a quick autopsy, I think we can at once proceed to an arrest.'

" 'An open-and-shut case, I imagine?'

" 'In the bag. We've not yet found out where he procured the chocolates. But that's a minor question.'

" 'And one very easily solved,' I observed. 'Here is the manufacturer's name on the box. This firm sells its products only in its own expensive shops, one of which is in Bond Street and the other, I believe, in Hanover Square.'

" 'The box presents no problem,' said he, with a slight touch of pique in his tone. 'It was sold in the Bond Street establishment, at four o'clock last Thursday afternoon, and to a person well-known to the manageress as Sir Jervase Jerningham himself. The chocolates are another matter. A representative of the firm has been here to inspect them, and declares that those at present in the box must have been made elsewhere and substituted for the originals. Our men are visiting every chocolate factory in England, and, if necessary, will proceed to the Continent.'

" 'An enjoyable trip, no doubt,' I replied, 'especially at the taxpayers' expense. However, I believe they are wasting their time. In my opinion, Sir Jervase was fully capable of making these chocolates himself, and I have very little doubt that he did so.'

" 'You scientists are brilliant fellows,' retorted the Commissioner, 'but practical matters are not always your strong point. Believe me, the making of chocolates of this standard—like, in its humbler way, the detection of crime—requires the touch of a professional.'

" 'Amateurs have been known to distinguish themselves in one field,' said I with a smile, 'and I happen to know that Sir Jervase was no ordinary amateur in the other. Many years ago I had some slight acquaintance with your suspect, and can possibly assist you with a clue. He was then in very different circumstances. He had not yet succeeded to the title, nor used it as a stepping-stone to his cynical and mercenary marriage to the unprepossessing relict of a Texas billionaire. He was extremely hard-up; I myself was struggling to gain a foothold in my profession; we were both members of a wide circle of similarly circumstanced young men.'

" 'And as to the chocolates?' interjected the Commissioner.

" 'I am approaching them, if a little circuitously. Jerningham, like a good many young fellows of his sort, prided himself on his discernment as a *gourmet,* and his skill as a cook. What is, unfortunately, far less common, in his case his pretensions were justified. He was gifted by nature with an extraordinarily sensitive palate; in fact, he possessed the equivalent of what music lovers term "absolute pitch." As some fortunate persons can distinguish every note that contributes to a musical chord, so could Jerningham infallibly detect, in *pilaf, cassoulet,* or *ragout,* not merely the major ingredients, but the very minims, so to speak, of herb or spice, and even the demi-semiquavers of the salt and pepper involved, as to the quality and freshness of which he was exceedingly hard to please. His taste in wine was no less perceptive; he could not only unhesitatingly give the name and year of any vintage he sampled, but, in cases where he had visited the vineyard and was acquainted with the staff, he could unerringly identify the peasant who had trodden out the grapes.'

" 'Interesting to a wine lover,' said the Commissioner. 'Personally, I prefer a good whiskey. May I ask to what point all this is leading us?'

" 'I thought I had mentioned, my dear Commissioner, that Jerningham, not content with his *réclame* as a critic, applied his talents equally successfully to the creative side. Poor as he was in those days, he could produce positive symphonies from a few cheap cuts of meat, embellished, of course, by the most exquisitely balanced flavoring agents. It was said that at his table one always ate too much, yet never enough, and newcomers were warned to leave room for the dessert. His confectionery was, if anything, more deliciously subtle than his other dishes, and to him the making of presentable chocolates would be the merest child's play. You may be sure he could easily disguise the flavor of whatever fatal ingredient he may have chosen to employ, and would, indeed, consider himself to be lacking in taste, as well as in discretion, if he neglected to do so. Naturally, he could disguise the flavor only if he made the chocolates himself. Moreover, if he stooped so low, artistically, as to introduce crude poisons into the centers of chocolates already manufactured, he would have no need to find substitutes for those originally in the box.'

" 'Well, whether he made them or not, he certainly gave them to her. The woman is dead; the man must hang; and, since he is such a connoisseur, we'll try to secure a worthy *chef* to prepare his last breakfast. Meanwhile, Sir Barnard, perhaps you will be good enough to determine, in your very different but equally precise manner, exactly what little extra fillip he has added to his latest recipe. And, since we are using musical similes today, the organs are awaiting you in the morgue.'

"His tone indicated that our interview was at an end. I withdrew. In less than twenty-four hours I was once more seated at his desk. He was in the best of good spirits, and permitted himself to rub his hands. 'Well, Sir Barnard, what's the good word? Arsenic? Cyanide? Prussic acid?'

" 'I have found no trace, Commissioner, of any of those.'

" 'No, indeed? Something a little *recherché,* perhaps? After all, the man is a *gourmet.* A product of the gorgeous East? A little present from up the Amazon?'

" 'Commissioner, you are getting no warmer.'

" 'Tiger whiskers, finely chopped?'

" 'No.'

" 'Then what?'

" 'I have found no trace of any poison whatever.'

" 'But the woman's dead.'

" 'Definitely.'

" 'And she ate the chocolates.'

" 'No doubt about that.'

" 'Aha! I have it! The chocolates were a blind. He did the deed with a *sauce Tartare,* a *Béarnaise,* some foreign kickshaw of that description.'

" 'There was no indication of poison of any sort, introduced by the chocolates or anything else, in the intestines of the late Lady Jerningham. I am accordingly returning them to the morgue.'

" 'No poison? You must have missed it.'

"I smiled.

" 'It's all very well to smile, Sir Barnard. We're none of us getting any younger. Maybe there are new poisons in these days. Atomic stuff, something of that sort. Pardon the bluntness of an old soldier, but I can't help thinking this may be a case for a younger man.'

"To restore his confidence, I infused a contemporary note into my reply. 'I assure you, Commissioner, when it comes to poisons, I am hep.'

" 'When it comes to murder, so am I. I maintain this woman was murdered. I don't want to impugn your judgment, Sir Barnard, but if you are so sure these chocolates are innocuous I should uncommonly like to see you eat one.'

"My reputation was at stake. I reached for the box. I took a chocolate. I looked it over. I took a nibble. I must admit, I savored the sweetmeat with great deliberation. Sir Jervase's accomplishments, both old and new, were such as to inspire respect. I encountered, as I expected, no bitterness, no burning of the tongue, no taste of almonds. On the other hand, there was unquestionably a novel flavor, almost impossible to describe—faint, elusive, provocative, alluring. The Commissioner, meanwhile, was watching me keenly.

" 'Feeling all right, Sir Barnard?'

" 'Extremely well, thank you.' And I casually helped myself to another chocolate.

" 'Is that so? Well, as an old army man, I never ask a fellow to do anything I'm not prepared to do myself.' With that, he took up one of the chocolates, eyed it for a moment, then nibbled, slowly at first, then with mounting interest and speed. He reached for another. So did I.

" 'Rum flavor,' said the Commissioner thoughtfully.

" 'I detect no taste of rum.'

" 'I meant, strange.'

" 'Oh, quite!'

"By now, we were on our fifth and sixth, respectively. Silence, broken only by faint sounds of mastication, fell upon the austere, official room, its tall windows overlooking the Thames. At length, our eyes met.

" 'I see it all now.'

" 'It's reasonably clear, Commissioner.'

" 'The wretched woman couldn't stop eating them.'

" 'Exactly. Would you mind pushing the box a little this way?'

" '*I* could stop if I wanted to.'

" 'Could you, Commissioner?'

" 'Well . . . I'll just have one more.'

" 'So will I.'

" 'But we're eating the evidence, man, we're eating the evidence!'

" 'If we *could* stop, it would be evidence of the possibility of stopping. That would hardly sit well with the jury.'

" 'So the fellow's going to get away with it!'

" 'I see little chance of a successful prosecution.'

" 'Hm!' And the Commissioner took two at once. I raised an eyebrow. He flushed. 'It makes us even.'

"Once more silence fell upon the austere, official room. It was some time before the Commissioner spoke again. 'I say, Sir Barnard, have you acute abdominal discomfort?'

" 'Decidedly. Nausea, too.'

" 'A touch of dizziness, I expect?'

" 'And spots before the eyes. I'm rather glad there are not too many of these chocolates left. It's probably as well that Lady Jerningham consumed ten pounds before she was overcome. I'm grateful to you, in a way, for sharing the burden with me. We shall probably escape convulsions, syncope, coma, and death. Really, this flavor is altogether *too* intriguing!'

"Little more was said. We finished the few remaining chocolates, sighed with mingled relief and regret, and hastened to our doctors, and later to our respective spas. Sir Jervase married Miss Mundy, and seems likely to live happily ever after."

Sir Barnard paused, sipped again at his liver salts, and looked brightly around. "Well, gentlemen, let me have your verdict. Do you consider this case deserves the title of 'the perfect murder'?"

There was rather a long interval of pipe-sucking and pondering.

"It's a murder all right," observed the nonentity amiably.

"I suppose it's a matter of taste," said the celebrated mycologist. "The chocolates fulfilled their function. But, frankly, I feel there is something more natural, more woodsy, to use an American expression, about a well-chosen fungus."

"Would it not have been rather nearer perfection," asked the eminent psychiatrist, "if Sir Jervase, instead of combining merely material ingredients, had achieved his compulsive effect by mental suggestion, hypnotic or otherwise? It would surely have lifted the whole affair to a higher plane."

"A successful murder, most emphatically," said the Arctic

explorer. "Nevertheless, the chocolates did, in part at least, remain in existence after their purpose was accomplished. Even granting that their discovery led inevitably to their elimination, a subtle touch I by no means underrate, this seems to me a fault of style. How much better to have employed, for example, a giant ice cream sundae, the residue of which would have melted away before suspicion was aroused, and in a manner reminiscent of the Polar Poignard, or ice dagger!"

A DOG'S A DOG

It was an hour or two after dinner on the day of the General's funeral. The drawing room was large but ill-lit and the fire smoked a little. Mrs. Bulteney was alone with Harry Despencer, a lawyer who had charge of the affairs of two or three of his cousins and second cousins, and who rode to hounds three days a week. He was down there in his legal capacity.

"I must say, Di, I wish you'd called in someone other than Harding."

"Harding's all right. He's the doctor here. He set my leg damned well when I came off Blazer."

"I know. But I wish you'd had someone else in."

"Why exactly do you wish that, Harry?"

"Well, the poor bloody old man! Everyone knows he's drunk as a fiddler's bitch any time after ten in the morning."

"And a sober doctor might have pulled him through? Is that what you think? Is that why you wish I'd called someone else in?"

"You know very well what I wish."

"I hope I do. Because it's going to come true. Isn't it?"

"It most certainly is."

"Then why think of anything else in the world?"

"One has to think sometimes of what people may say."

"We've thought of it. I'm sick of it. Now we don't need to anymore. Look, darling, everyone knows about septic pneumonia. The doctor doesn't count. The penicillin works—or it doesn't work."

"Harding gave him penicillin? I didn't know he'd even heard of it."

"He's drunk, but he's not such a fool. I filled the hypodermic myself. His hand was a bit shaky, so I did it for him. Four times!"

"It didn't do much good."

"No good at all, Harry. It might just as well have been tap water."

"Well, at least it gave him a sporting chance. I mean, it'd be a bit of a fly in the ointment if he'd died of any sort of neglect."

Mrs. Bulteney always had her servants knock before entering. The cook-housekeeper now knocked, and was told to come in.

"If you please, ma'am, is there anything else you require?"

"Nothing at all. I think you might all go to bed. Good night!"

"Please, ma'am, there's a poor dog out there at the back."

"A dog? What sort of a dog?"

"A cold one, ma'am, and a hungry one. Only we gave it a plate of scraps. Briggs thought if he might let it into one of the stalls, just for tonight. I mean, a night like this you don't hardly like to turn a dog out in."

"Proper wild goose weather!"

"That's what it is, sir, a night for the geese. Briggs said—you know his way of talking, sir—what with the wind and the sleet, he said, you'd think the old devil was standing astride the house, a-laying on to it with a cat o'nine tails."

"Parfit, I asked you what sort of a dog it was. Do you know one breed of dog from another? Or don't you?"

"Well, I must say, ma'am . . ." Mrs. Parfit was a woman of character, but she was exceeded in this respect by her mistress, who had the additional advantages of great size, great beauty, and great arrogance. "No special breed, ma'am. Just one of them middle-sized, black, shiny ones. A good deal of the Labrador in him, I'd be inclined to say, ma'am."

"Well, a dog's a dog, I suppose. No sort of dog's been turned away from this house on a night like this. But, I don't want mongrels hanging about the place with Christabel and Lady coming in heat any minute. Give him a bed, and get him off first thing in the morning. Make sure he goes. You understand me?"

"Yes, ma'am. Thank you, ma'am! Good night, ma'am! Good night, sir."

"Good night, Mrs. Parfit! I say, Di, I wonder if that's the dog that came to the funeral."

"And supposing it is?"

"It must have followed us home."

"Obviously, if it's the same one. Of course it's the same. What's the point?"

"No point. Idle remark. I'm just as glad it's got a bed for the night. Listen to the wind! I bet the horses are snugger than we are. I'll say this for old Gilbert—he let the house go to pot, but you've still got the best stables this side of Norwich. You could say worse things about a place."

"I'm glad you like the place, Harry. It's snug enough upstairs. Do you want some whiskey, or shall we go up?"

They went up. Despencer's bedroom was in the left corridor at the head of the stairs; Mrs. Bulteney's was in the big bay in the center. They both went into Mrs. Bulteney's room. As soon as they had closed the door, they fell into an embrace which was ravenous to the point of ferocity. There was that about this savage lovemaking, if the word can be applied to the congress of tigers, which indicated it was occurring by no means for the first time. It was less observable, but no less true, that this violence was natural, and a supreme fulfillment, to Diana Bulteney, and unnatural, an intoxication, though in a way all the more exciting for that, to Harry Despencer.

"Well, I suppose I'd better get back to my room."

"I don't think you really need to, Harry."

"I think I better had."

"Come back a moment! Just a moment. Must it really be six months?"

"Darling, you know just as well as I do. You can come up to town. Maybe we can go abroad for a month."

"I don't think I like this place anymore, Harry."

"Oh, that's just the funeral and the damned wind and everything. You love it really; you always have."

"No! I'd like to sell out, pack up, and go to Italy or somewhere tomorrow."

"You wouldn't get much hunting. Besides, what do you get for a place like this in these days? We've been into all that. We'll be all right here. Couldn't be better, as long as we take our time and don't put people's backs up. If I could get two or three more estates to handle, I could pay my shot."

"Who cares, you stuffy old lawyer, you?"

"I do, a bit. Not too much. But you've got a temper, you know. I mean, a fellow likes to stand on his own feet."

"Good night! Kiss me first! Oh, Harry, you don't know how different you are from him! Good night!"

Next day was clear, still and frozen, as often happens after the northeast gales in the coastal districts of Norwich. Hunting was out of the question so soon after the funeral, but Despencer felt it was all right to walk round the hedges with a gun. Mrs. Bulteney accompanied him. They ate their lunch under a big ash on the edge of a wood.

"There's that cursed dog sneaking after us! I gave word for Briggs to get rid of it first thing this morning. You heard me yourself. One of these days, I'm going to sack the whole damned gang of them. Don't throw food to it, Harry, the wretched thing gives me the creeps."

"What's wrong with it? Perfectly ordinary sort of a dog."

"You didn't hear it howl in the night."

"Not I, nor you neither. With that wind, you wouldn't have heard a pack of wolves howling. What you heard was the wind in some chimney or other."

"I seemed to hear it under the wind."

"Definitely not."

"Well, it kept me awake, anyway. I can tell you, I feel like absolute Hell today, and I don't want that damned creature looking at me. I don't like its eyes."

"Perhaps they remind you of somebody else's eyes?"

"There you are! You see it too! They're the same. I saw it yesterday as soon as he came up to us. I don't like it."

"There's a lot of black, beady eyes in the world, and that sort of dog usually has them. I wouldn't let it worry you."

"Well, it does, and if it comes crawling after us anymore, by God, I'll take that gun and shoot the bloody thing."

"Don't talk like that, Di! You know perfectly well you wouldn't. After all, a dog's a dog, you know."

"Yes, I suppose it is. Drive it off! Chuck a stone at it! Drive it away!"

"Here, you! Clear off! Go on! Get out, I say! There you are, darling! He won't come back in a hurry."

However, the dog, though timid, was seen about the house late that afternoon. After dinner Mrs. Bulteney questioned her housekeeper.

"Parfit, is that dog finally got rid of, or not?"

"Well, ma'am, it's been chased off with a broom three times."

"Has it stayed off? That's what I'm asking you."

"I haven't seen it since the last time, ma'am. We was as hard with it as we could bring ourselves to be."

"Well, if it shows up tomorrow, I want Briggs to get out the Austin and take it into Norwich. There's some sort of lost animals' home there. I want that *done,* do you hear?"

"If it'll let us lay hand on it, ma'am. It's got pretty shy of us now we've been after it with brooms. And, I must say, no wonder!"

"That's quite enough, Parfit. Go downstairs. I'll serve the coffee myself."

"Very well, madam. Good night, madam!"

"Brandy, Harry?"

"Thank you, yes, I think so. Easy though! My God, Di! Easy does it!"

"Oh, come on! It'll cheer us up."

"I don't know that I want any cheering up."

"Then why sit there looking like a wet week?"

"Was I? Sorry! I was just thinking."

"What do you mean? Thinking of what?"

"Look here, if we were going to throw everything overboard and to Hell with everybody, I wouldn't say a word. But we're going to get married after a decent interval: We're going to live here, and we want to stand well with the neighbors, and we don't want any stink. You know what backstairs gossip can be; we don't want any. You're altogether unreasonably worked-up about that dog. What's more to the point, you're showing it."

"Well, if I can't have a nasty, mongrel stray run off my own place, when I've got two champion bitches coming in heat any day, I'd like to know why, that's all."

"Di, you've been through a lot in the last few days. I can understand, but they can't. All the same, they've got eyes in their heads, and tongues, too. They can spot a likeness just as well as you can. As a matter of fact, they've spotted it already."

"How do you know?"

"I could hear them down in the yard when I was dressing."

"Your dressing room doesn't overlook the yard."

"All right then; when I was in the lavatory. Briggs and the boy were down there. I suppose they'd just been chasing it away. I heard Briggs say, 'Well, let's hope that's good-bye to the poor old General!' "

"I think that's the damnedest cheek I ever heard of in my life."

"Oh, I don't know. You saw it; I saw it; why shouldn't they see it? I mean, when that dog put his head on one side and looked at us when we were having lunch, I'd have sworn it was old Gilbert himself. But the point is, these people read nothing but the Sunday papers, and you can be quite sure they know it wasn't any sort of a marriage, and . . . are you listening?"

"Yes, I'm listening."

"Well, the dog turns up on the very day of the funeral and you seem afraid of it; you can just imagine the sort of nonsense they could make up. And that sort of thing's no better for being non-sense, let me tell you. In fact, it's all the harder to nail down."

"I see. I suppose you're right. It seems a bit strange to have to mind one's p's and q's in front of the servants, I must say. I didn't tell you, but, last night, the creature gave me a nightmare, and I couldn't sleep after it, and, somehow, I can't shake it off."

"A nightmare can weigh on you all the next day. Do you know, in the last few months I've had the same absolutely identical night-mare six times at least, probably more? I'm in one of those terrific great cars they're putting out now. Best-looking car you ever saw in your life. Cream-colored, open, buzzing along at a hundred miles an hour . . ."

"I wish you were with me, Harry."

"Oh, but, darling, I am, I assure you. Sorry! I didn't mean to interrupt."

"After you went last night, after I'd heard the damned thing howling, I dreamt I was down there in the churchyard. I think I'd followed it down there, trying to kill it. Yes, that's how it was. And it was there on the grave, and I had to go up close, and it fixed its damned, beady, black eyes on me, and, by God, Harry, it *was* Gilbert! I tell you, Harry, I . . ."

"Keep your voice down, darling, for heaven's sake! I know what it is. You've got what they call a guilt complex. Now, listen! Let me explain. I've read books on this Freudian stuff; a lot of it's awful rot, but all the same, there's something in it. They say when people wish other people were dead and all of a sudden they kick the bucket, the person—it's generally a kid, but it can be anybody—

he feels just as responsible as if actually he'd done 'em in. You see, it's all unconscious, so he can't be reasonable about it. So he gets the jimjams. Then the mind doctor gets to work, and tells him what's biting him, and he feels better."

"It's not like that."

"Of course it is. You've wished he'd die; I've wished he'd die. We've said as much to each other. It's only natural. If I'd had money enough, there could have been a divorce, but, as it was, we were stuck. Now we both feel the same; glad as the devil and yet a bit sick inside, and, of course, you feel it more than I do."

"You think I'm making it up about that bloody dog?"

"I think you're making the Hell of a lot of a perfectly ordinary little coincidence. You want a good night's sleep, that's what it is. Got any pills in the house?"

"Sleeping pills? Yes, I have. Harding gave me some when I broke my leg. I didn't take them, though; I don't go in for that sort of thing."

"Well, take one tonight. Get eight solid hours; no nightmares, no nonsense, and in the morning you'll laugh at the whole silly business."

"All right, Harry. Stay with me till I go to sleep, though, won't you?"

"Of course I will."

Perhaps Despencer should have taken a pill himself. At all events, he experienced a return of the recurrent nightmare he had spoken of. Once more, he was in that incredibly beautiful and powerful car, cream-colored, or flesh-colored, open; she was rushing along at a hundred miles an hour. Again, he realized his foot was not pressing the accelerator. She was going by herself, and faster and faster, and there was no such thing as a brake, and faster and faster, the wind rising to a menacing howl in his ears, and he tried to get out, but the seat held him. The seat gripped him, enfolding his loins in the close and fleshy grip of foam rubber that was somehow alive. And suddenly there was a loud crack, as if an axle had gone, and he was wide awake.

The crack was something new in the dream. Perhaps it wasn't in the dream at all. Perhaps it had come from outside. The thought moved him before it made itself known to him; he was already on his feet, on his way to the window. His pajamas were wet through and it was abominably cold.

Outside there was a breathtaking stillness and moonlight as

bright as ever he'd seen it. The rather ugly fir plantations were black blocks defining the circle, its center also black with a pyramid of conifers, in which the drive ended in front of the house. The ground had that glitter which foretells a thick hoarfrost in the morning. It was incredibly beautiful, but too disturbing to be altogether pleasant. There was a dark movement; then a flicker of light which could have been the moon on the barrels of a gun. Someone had passed from blackness to blackness across one of the rides that radiated between the encircling firs.

"If that fellow's after the birds, if that fellow fired a shot right under the very windows, all I can say is he's got the Hell of a nerve. Perhaps I'd better wake Briggs."

He put on slippers and a dressing gown and set off on this errand. In the corridor, looking towards the stairwell ahead of him, he could see there was an unusual amount of light there, as though the moonlight, though more attenuated and ghostly, was leaking into the house. After a few more steps, he saw the reason for this. Mrs. Bulteney's door was wide open and the light inside was nearly as bright as day. Looking in, he saw her bed was empty; the sheets, thrown back, had in every fold the likeness of sculptured marble. He was reminded of a tomb he'd seen in Italy or somewhere.

This changed his mind about waking Briggs. He went down into the big hall and found that the outer door, though closed, was not completely shut. He put out his hand to open it, but it moved of itself, like the car in his dream. He found himself face-to-face, very close, with Mrs. Bulteney. Her face was so streaked and cratered by the blue moonlight that he didn't recognize her at first. When he did, he realized she must have been deathly white underneath. She had a fur coat on over her pajamas and she was carrying a gun. She spoke quietly, but in such a way that he thought her next words might be very loud, indeed.

"I missed him!"

"Come in, for god's sake, and don't make a noise! Let me put that thing down. Come up to your room!"

"Thirty feet! Clear as daylight! And I missed him! I never missed like that before."

"Just as well you did! Are you absolutely mad, Di? If you shoot a man like that, it's murder."

Diana Bulteney began to laugh. Her laugh had undergone exactly the same sort of change as her face. Moonstruck! thought Despencer, who was by no means given to fanciful expressions. At the same time, he thought, "She weighs as much as I do; I can never carry her up."

He pulled at her coat and, to his surprise and relief, she yielded to the pull, not in the least responsively, but as if she had abandoned her body to any force that might act on it. Now, Mrs. Bulteney, more than anyone else in the world, had lived in and for her large and magnificent body, feeding it great lumps of raw sensation at its slightest demand. This drifting hulk, uncertainly and stumblingly following the rude pull on its fur exterior, seemed to have suffered the same lunar ruin as her face and her laugh. The laugh continued as they ascended the stairs, but fortunately seemed to have no sort of force or breath behind it. By the time they got into her room it had altogether ceased.

He seated her on the bed and went to close the door. Turning back, he found her with her head sagging forward and her eyes almost closed. He remembered the sleeping pill.

"Di, it's that pill you took. You're drunk on it. I say, you're sure you really did miss that fellow, aren't you?"

"I missed him. I might have known I would."

"You'd better lie down and sleep it off."

"He wouldn't have died if I'd given him both barrels point-blank."

"You're half frozen. You're out of your mind. Get into bed and I'll cover you up."

"You can't kill them and you can't chase them away."

"All right. Don't worry. Just go to sleep."

"I went to sleep. It wasn't any good. I woke up and he was out there, right under the window, howling for me."

"Do you mean the dog? Are you talking about the dog? Was it the dog you tried to shoot?"

"Damned silly thing to do! He's dead already. Know what he died of?"

"Do you mean Gilbert? Are you talking about Gilbert now? Here, wake up! Tell me!"

"Tap water, Harry. That's what I put in."

Her mouth moved as if she was going to laugh again, but, before she could do so, she was asleep, and she slept till the low winter sun fell on her face in the morning. Then she woke and rang the bell.

"Good morning, ma'am!"

"Good morning, Parfit. What time is it?"

"Just gone half-past-ten, ma'am. Mr. Despencer said you weren't to be disturbed. He left this for you, ma'am."

"Left it? What do you mean? Where's he gone?"

"Up to town, ma'am. He had to go all of a sudden, so he left the letter."

"Di, I've absolutely forgotten what was said last night. I do know, however, that no sort of life is possible for you and me. I have to get out if it kills me.

Regretfully,
H."

"The dog's gone too, ma'am. Gone for good this time, you'll be glad to hear. A little boy came from Church Farm where the new people have moved in. No higher than that, ma'am, and frightened out of his life coming here. I think he had the idea we'd stolen his precious dog. The postman told him he'd seen it hanging about. 'I want my Blackie,' he says, trembling all over. So, off he went with his Blackie on a piece of string, happy as a sandboy!"

"Parfit, I don't feel well today."

"Why, I'm sorry to hear that, ma'am, I'm sure. Would you wish me to send for the doctor?"

"Dr. Harding? No. On the dressing table there, or in the bathroom, there's a little bottle of reddish sort of pills. Give it to me, will you? Thank you! Parfit, unless I ring, I'm not to be disturbed on any account."

"Not even for a little luncheon, ma'am?"

"Not for lunch or dinner, either. I want to sleep. I may sleep right through. You may come in at this time tomorrow morning. Not before. Do you understand?"

"Well, yes, ma'am, if you say so. I hope it'll make you feel better, ma'am."

Man Overboard

Glenway Morgan Abbott had the sort of face that is associated with New England by those who like New England. It was so bony, so toothy even, so modest, so extremely serious, and so nearly flinchingly unflinching, that one hardly noticed that he was actually a very good-looking man.

He also had the yacht *Zenobia*, which was handsome enough to take one's breath away at the very first glance; it showed its seriousness only on closer inspection. Once in a very great while, I used to go on a long cruise with Glenway. I was his best, and his only intimate, friend.

Those who have seen the *Zenobia*, or its picture in books on sailing, may be impolite enough to wonder how I came to be so specially friendly with the owner of a three-masted schooner which is certainly among the dozen, perhaps among the half dozen, most famous of the great yachts of the world.

Such people should realize that, though I may lack wealth and grace and charm, I do so in a special and superior way. Moreover, in spite of the glorious *Zenobia* and the impressive associations of his name, Glenway's way of life was far from being sophisticated or luxurious. His income, though still very large, was only just large enough to pay for his yacht's upkeep and her numerous crew. When he wanted to get a piece of research done, he had to dip into his capital.

The fact is, Glenway had at one time been married, and to a filmstar, and in highly romantic circumstances. As if this wasn't enough, he had at once been divorced. The star in question was Thora Vyborg, whose beauty and personality are among the legends, or the myths, of our time. All this happened before I met him, but I had gathered, though not from Glenway, that the divorce had been distinguished by a settlement such as can result only from the cruelest heartbreak, the bitterest injury, and the most efficient lawyers on the one side and honest eyes and rather prominent front teeth on the other.

Therefore, if the word "yacht" suggests music, ladies, awnings, white-jacketed stewards, caviar, and champagne, the suggestion is altogether misleading. The only music was the wind in the rigging; there were no ladies; the solitary steward wore no jacket; and the crew wore no shirts, either. They were all natives of different parts of the Pacific with different complexions and different tongues. The language used on board was a sort of sub-Basic English, adequate for work, expressive in song, but not very suitable for conversation. Glenway might have had an American or a British captain or mate; however, he did not.

Anyway, every man on board knew his job. It was a pity that the cook's job was all too often only the opening of cans of frankfurters or baked beans. This was not so much due to New English frugality as to that gastronomical absentmindedness which is so often found linked with honesty, teeth, etc., and especially with devotion to a cause.

Glenway was devoted to a cause, and so was the *Zenobia*. All these great yachts are, of course, capable of ocean cruising; this one was used for it, and for nothing else at all. She was used and hard-used, and, though as clean as a pin, she was by no means as shiny. On the horizon, she looked like a cloud; at her mooring, like a swan to the poetically-minded, or, to the materialistic, like a floating palace. But, as soon as you stepped aboard, she had more the appearance of something sent out by an oceanographical institute. All manner of oddly-shaped nets and trawls and scoops were hung, or spread, or stowed around her deck. On either side of the fore-mast, there were two objects on pedestals, shoulder-high, and made of that ugly, gray, rust-resisting alloy which was used everywhere on this boat in place of brass or chromium. These objects were not ventilators. They had rotating tops; these tops were hooded or cowled, or whatever you'd call it; and closely shuttered against the salty spray. If you turned one of the tops towards you, and slid open the shutter, and looked inside, you would find yourself being looked back at, quietly, by the darkly gleaming eye of a movie camera.

Up in the bows, there was a bulky object lashed down under quickly removable canvas. This was a searchlight. Long chests, seat-high, almost as high as the low gunwale into which they were built, contained rockets and flares. Glenway was hoping to photograph something which he believed might be nocturnal in its habits. He thought that, otherwise, being a very large, noticeable creature, and being a reptile, and therefore breathing air, it would have been seen more often by daylight.

Glenway, in a word, was looking for the sea serpent. As he detested the sensational newspaper stories and the tiresome jokes associated with the term, he preferred to think of it as a "large marine saurian." For short, we called it, not inaptly, "It."

People all over the Pacific knew of Glenway's quest. They were, though tactful about it, rather too obviously so. Something about Glenway caused them to refrain from guffaws; but they put on leaky masks of politeness over their grins, or, if they took the matter seriously, they seriously sought to reclaim him from his folly. Either way, they made it all too clear that they thought him a crank and perhaps a zany because he believed in the existence of such a creature. For this reason, he avoided ports as far as possible, and, when taking in supplies or docked for overhaul, he avoided the society of his kind. Now, it so happens that, though I am of a skeptical nature in most matters, I am strongly inclined to suspend disbelief when it comes to a large marine saurian. Without at least the possibility of such a creature, it seems to me that the world would be a poor and a narrow place. Glenway perceived this at our very first meeting, and it was the reason for the beginning of our friendship. I was forced to tell him I thought the chances were a million-to-one against his ever seeing his quarry, and I thought he was crazy to waste his time and his lovely money on hunting for it. This didn't worry him in the least.

"I shall find it sooner or later," said he, when first we debated the question, "because I know where to look."

His theory was a simple one, and made sense up to a point. If you know how an animal is constructed, you can deduce a great deal as to how it lives, and especially as to what it lives on. When you know what it eats, and where that particular abounds, you have already a very good clue as to where to look for it.

Glenway had taken all the best authenticated reports, and he had had an outline drawn up from each of them. Almost all these reports, from whatever corner of the world they may come, describe more or less the same sort of creature, so he had no trouble in getting a composite picture made by an expert hand. This, of course, showed a reptile of the plesiosaur type, but very much larger than any of the fossil plesiosaurs, being only a few inches under eighty feet in length. But here there was a snag.

Glenway had every reason to know what each extra foot on the length of a yacht adds to its maintenance bills, and he knew that an eighty-foot plesiosaur is not a practical proposition. It was not hard to calculate what its weight would be, or the size of its bite, or how large a fish could pass down its narrow gullet. "It would spend more energy just picking up fish of that size one by one," said Glenway, "than it would gain by eating them. Also, schools of herrings, mackerel, haddock, and so forth are mostly found in coastal waters, and fishermen have been after them by day and by night ever since fishermen existed. An air-breathing creature has to show itself on the surface fairly often; if it followed fish of that sort it would be as familiar to us as the basking shark. And, finally, it would be extinct, because with those jaws it couldn't defend itself against killer whales, or threshers, if it hadn't been finished off by carcharodon, and the other big sharks of the Miocene."

"Glenway, if all this is correct, you've slain your own goddam Jabberwock."

"I was afraid I had," said he. "It depressed the Hell out of me. But one day it struck me that people who see something very surprising, and see it suddenly, briefly, in bad visibility and so forth, will naturally tend to exaggerate the most surprising aspect of whatever it is they see. Thus, an astonishingly long, snaky neck will look longer and snakier than it actually is, a small head smaller, and so forth. So, I had a couple of young chaps from Uncle Fred's Institute of Industrial Psychology do a series of tests. They found a deviation running up to about twenty-five percent. Then I told them what I wanted it for, and asked them to modify this outline accordingly. We got this." He handed me a second sheet. "We can take it this is what was actually seen."

"Why, this damned thing's only sixty feet long!" said I, rather discontentedly. "It seems to me you're correcting eyewitness reports on pure speculation."

"No, I'm not," said he. "I double-checked it. I hired a reptile man and an icthyologist, and I asked them to work out what the nearest thing to a sixty-foot plesiosaur would be like if it were to be a practical proposition in terms of food, energy, defense, and all that. They came up with two or three alternatives. The one that interested me was this." He pulled out at third outline. "If you put this on top of the psychologists' corrected version," said he, "you'll see they correspond in everything essential."

"All the same, if I'm going to believe in a large marine saurian, I'd rather have an eighty-footer."

"This one weighs more than an eighty-footer," said Glenway, "and he's probably ten times as powerful. Those jaws have a bite of over three feet. This fellow could swallow a big barracuda at a gulp. He might have to make two snaps at a porpoise. He'll follow schools of tuna, albacore, any sort of fish ranging from fifty to a hundred-and-fifty pounds. Not cod, of course."

"And why not cod?"

"Fishermen. He'd have been seen."

"Oh!"

"So, evidently, he doesn't follow cod."

"And, evidently, you can sweat a positive out of a couple of demolished negatives. Even so, it may make some sort of sense."

Glenway accepted this, which at least was better than he got from other people. He eagerly showed me innumerable charts he had drawn up, and had emended by his own observation. These showed the seasonal movements of deep-sea fish in the East Pacific, and, where these movements weren't known, he had what data there was on the smaller fish that the larger ones preyed on. He went on down through the food chains, and down to plankton drifts and current temperatures and so forth, and, with all these, modified by all sorts of other factors, he had marked out a great oval, with dates put in here and there, which tilted through those immense solitudes of ocean which stretch from the coast of Chile up to the Aleutians.

This was his beat, and two or three times I sailed it with him. There were almost no islands, almost no shipping lanes. I used to take a regular spell in the crow's nest; two hours in the morning and two more in the late afternoon. You can't sit day after day looking for something without an admission, deep in your mind, of the possibility of seeing it. Anyway, I was extremely fond of Glenway, and it would have given me great pleasure to have been the one who sighted his saurian for him somewhere far out on the flat green or the rolling blue. The very wish lent a sinewy twist to every waterlogged palm trunk that drifted across our bows, and every distant dolphin leap offered the arc of a black, wet, and leathery neck.

At the first sight of such things, my hand, more wishful even than my thoughts, would move towards the red button on the rail of the crow's nest. This, like another in the bow, and a third by the wheel, was connected with a loud buzzer in Glenway's cabin. However, the buzzer remained silent; the immense horizon, day after day, was empty.

Glenway was an excellent navigator. One morning, when I was aloft, he called up to ask if I could see anything ahead. I told him there was nothing, but I had no sooner raised my glasses again than I discerned a thickening, a long hump gathering itself in the infinitely faint pencil line that marked the juncture of sky and sea. "There's something. It's land! Land ahead!"

"That's Paumoy."

He had not bothered to mention that he was going to touch at Paumoy, the main island of an isolated group northeast of the Marquesas. I had heard of the place; there were eight or ten Americans there, and someone had said that, since the war, they almost never got their mail. Glenway's beat took him within fifty miles of the island, and he now told me he had agreed to touch there as he passed. Sensitive as he was to crude jokes about the sea serpent, he was still a New Englander, and he felt that people should have their mail.

The island, as we drew nearer, revealed itself as several miles of whaleback, covered with that hot froth of green which suggests coconut palms and boredom. I put down the light binoculars I was using and took up the telescope, which had a much greater range. I could see the harbor, the white bungalows spaced out around it, and I could even see the people quite clearly. Before long I saw a man catch sight of the yacht. He stared under his hand, and waved, and pointed; another man came out of a bungalow with a pair of glasses. I saw the two of them go off at a run to where a jeep was standing. The jeep crawled off around the harbor, stopped at another bungalow; someone got out, someone got in. The jeep moved on again, disappeared into a grove, came out on the other side, and went toiling up a little thread-like track until it went out of sight over the ridge.

By this time, other people on the shore level had turned out to look at us. They had plenty of time to do so, for the breeze fell off almost to nothing as we stood in towards the island. It was already late afternoon when the *Zenobia,* with every sail set, floated as softly as an enormous thistledown to her anchorage in the harbor of Paumoy.

"What a dreary-looking dump!" I said. "What do they do here? Copra?"

"That, and shell. One fellow dries a sort of sea slug and sells it to Chinese dealers all over the world. There was a Gauguin from San Francisco, but he didn't stay very long."

"You'd think they'd cut each other's throats out of sheer boredom."

"Well, they play poker every night of their lives, and I guess they've developed a technique of not getting on each other's nerves."

"They must need it." There seemed to be nothing on the island but coconut palms, which I don't like, and the blistering bungalows, all of which might have been prefabricated by the same mail-order house. What I had taken from a greater distance to be banks of varicolored flowers beside the bungalows were now recognizable as heaps of tin cans, some rusty, some with their labels still on. But I had no more time to look about me; we were on the quay, and being greeted by men in shorts and old-fashioned sun helmets, and the greeting was hearty.

"Now, listen to me," said Victor Brewer, "we've got two new guys here who've been in Java. We've had them working like dogs ever since we sighted you, fixing a *rijsttafel*. So you've got to stay to dinner. Or those guys are going to be hurt. Hell, you're not going to insult a couple of fellows who are slaving over a hot stove, fixing you a dinner!"

Glenway wanted nothing but to pick up the outgoing mailbag and be gone. On the other hand, he hated the idea of hurting anyone. He looked at me as if in the faint hope that I might step in and do it for him. It was at such moments, very rare with Glenway, that I felt Fitzgerald was right about the rich being different. This thought, and the thought of the *rijsttafel*, prevented me from obliging him. Instead, I pointed out there'd probably be no wind till nightfall, so we'd be losing hardly any time. Glenway at once surrendered, and we settled down to drinks and chat and to watching the sun go down.

Listening to the chat, I remembered Glenway's remark about the technique of not getting on each other's nerves. It seemed to me that this technique was being exercised, and especially for Glenway's benefit. At the end of almost every remark our hosts made, I felt myself dropping in the air pocket of a pulled punch; I experienced that disconcerting absence of impact which is the concomitant of velvet paws. It was clear they knew what Glenway was after, and they even referred to it, but with such collective tact that, if one of them seemed likely to dwell on it for more than a few seconds, he would be steamrollered out of the conversation, generally by Mr. Brewer. It was he who asked, very casually, when we had been sitting some time at dinner, if Glenway was sailing the same course as usual; if he was going to pass, give or take a hundred miles, the northern extremity of Japan.

Glenway having replied that he always followed the same course: "You know," said Vic Brewer, letting the words fall as casually as one lets fall the poker chips when the hands are high and the stakes are higher, "you know, you could do the Hell of a good turn to a guy. If you felt like it, that is."

"What sort of a turn?" asked Glenway. "And which guy?"

"You don't know him," said the man on Brewer's left. "He's a fellow called Geisecker. He's Charlie's brother-in-law's brother-in-law, if you can work that one out."

"He dropped in here to say hello," said the next man. "He came on the copra boat and he didn't know the mailboat doesn't call any more. So he's stuck."

"The point is, this poor guy is going to be in big trouble if he doesn't get to Tokyo in the next few weeks."

"When you get up in those latitudes you're certainly going to sight some boat or other bound for Japan."

"Any little tramp, or oiler, or fishing boat, or anything. He'll be tickled to death."

They spoke one after another all the way round the table, and, remembering that Glenway had said they played poker every night of their lives, I was irresistibly reminded of the process of doubling up.

"We hate to see him go," said Brewer, collecting the whole matter into his hands with the genial authority of the dealer. "He's wonderful company, Bob Geisecker. But it's almost life or death for him, poor fellow! Look, he'll pay for his passage—anything you like—if *that's* the obstacle."

"It ain't that," said Glenway. "But, I haven't seen him yet."

"He's over on the other side of the island," said Brewer. "He went off with Johnny Ray in the jeep less than half an hour before we sighted you."

"That's funny," said I, thinking of what I'd seen through the telescope.

"Damned funny," said Brewer, "if going off to give Johnny a hand makes him miss his chance of a passage." And, turning to Glenway, he added, "If you'd only seen old Bob, I know you'd have been glad to help him."

"I'll take him," said Glenway, "if he's back in time. But the wind's been failing us, and we're behind schedule, and . . ."

"Fair enough," said Brewer. "If he's back in time, you'll take him. If he isn't, that's his hard luck. More rice? More chicken? More shrimp? Boy, fill up that glass for Mr. Abbott."

The dinner went on and on, and not another word was said about Mr. Geisecker. At last, the heavy frondage above the table drew a deep breath and began to live and move. The wind was up, and Glenway said we could wait no longer. We all walked together down to the quay. Glenway and I were just stepping into the dinghy when someone pointed, and, looking back, as people were rightly warned not to do in the old stories, we saw, like a moonrise, the glow of headlights in the sky. The jeep was coming up the far side of the ridge. "That's Bob," said Brewer. "But don't wait. We'll get him packed up in no time, and bring him out in the launch before you can up-anchor."

Sure enough, just as we were ready to move out, the launch came alongside with Mr. Bob Geisecker and his bags. The latter had pieces of pajamas hanging out at their sides like the tongues of panting dogs. Geisecker himself seemed a little breathless. His face, as he came up the steps into the light hanging above, had something strange about it. At first, I thought it was just the flustered and confused expression of a man who had to pack and get off in such a hurry; then, I thought it was the fact that, after weeks and months under an equatorial sun, this considerable face still peeled and glowed as if fresh from a weekend at Atlantic City. Finally, still unsatisfied, I thought of that massive, opulently curved, wide-mouthed instrument which is included in every brass band, and which, when it is not playing at full blast, looks as if it ought to be, or at least is about to be. Mr. Geisecker greatly resembled this instrument, but he was very silent, and it was this that was strange.

There was a quick introduction, a brief welcome from Glenway, who was busy, an uncertain mumble of thanks from our guest, and a very hasty farewell from Brewer. Glenway had to give all his attention to taking the yacht out, and Geisecker stood neglected on deck, staring after the launch, his mouth open, looking something worse than lost. I took him down to his cabin, told him we break-fasted at seven, and asked him if there was anything he wanted before turning in. He seemed only vaguely aware that I was talking to him.

"Those guys," said he, speaking like a man in a state of shock, "I kept them in stitches. In stitches—all the time!"

"Good night," I said. "I'll see you in the morning."

Next morning Geisecker joined us at breakfast. He acknowledged our greeting soberly, sat down, and looked at his plate. Glenway apologized for having been so much occupied overnight and began to discuss where and when we might hope to encounter a boat headed for Tokyo or Yokohama. Geisecker lifted a face on which dawning enlightenment made me think of the rapid change from the blue-gray hush of the tropic night to the full glare and blare of tropic day; light, warmth, life, and laughter all came flooding in faster than one would think believable or even desirable.

"I knew it all the time!" said he exultantly. "Only I just didn't happen to think of it. I knew it was a gag. When those guys hustled me aboard this lugger I got the idea they were—you know—giving me the brush-off. They just about had me fooled. Now, I get it. Anything for a laugh! They swore to me last night you were heading for Lima, Peru."

"They told me very definitely," said Glenway, staring, "that it was of the greatest importance that you should get to Tokyo."

Geisecker slapped his plump and crimson thigh with startling effect. "Those guys," said he, "they'd ship a fellow to the moon on one of those goddam spaceships if they could get a laugh out of it. And that's what they've done to me! Tokyo's where I came from. Lima, Peru is where I was going to move on to. *That's* why they kept me all day over on the other side of the island. So I couldn't hear which way you were going."

"We're short of time," said Glenway, "but I'll put about and take you back to Paumoy if you want me to."

"Not on your life," said Geisecker. "It's a good gag and I'll be goddamned if I spoil it. All I'm doing is just going around the world saying hello to people, and, to tell you the truth, there's a little kimono lady back in Tokyo I won't mind saying hello to once again." With that, he obliged us with a few bars from *Madama Butterfly*.

"Glenway," said I, "it's just on eight. I think I'll be getting up aloft."

"Aloft?" cried Geisecker. "That sounds like the real saltwater stuff. I've never been on one of these windjammers before. You've got to give me the dope on marline spikes, splicing the main brace, and all the rest of the crap. I tell you, boys, I'm going to learn to be a sailor. Now, what's all this about going up aloft?"

"I'm just going up to the crow's nest for a couple of hours."

"What for? Looking for something?" Even as he asked the question, he turned, first on me and then on Glenway, a face which now resembled a Thespian as well as a porcine ham, it so overacted the simple feat of putting two and two together. Fixing his eyes on

Glenway, he slowly raised and extended an index finger of great substance. The lower joint of this finger was adorned with curving hairs, very strong and serviceable, and of a ruddy gold which glinted in the morning sun. The finger stopped about a foot short of Glenway's ribs, but its quality was so potent that it seemed to make itself felt there. In fact, I even felt it in my own.

"Abbott!" cried Geisecker triumphantly. "Now, that shows you how miffed I was last night when I thought those guys had given me the brush—it didn't ring any sort of a bell. Glenway Morgan Abbott! Christ, I've heard about you, pal. These birds told me all sorts of yarns. *You're* the guy who got married to Thora Vyborg! *You're* the guy who goes around looking for the sea serpent!"

At this point he became aware of Glenway's regard, which was, for one naked moment at least, quite deadly. Geisecker drew back a little. "But, maybe," said he, "maybe they were pulling my leg. I ought to have seen it right away. A fellow with your education wouldn't fall for that cheesy old bit of hokum."

By this time Glenway had recovered himself, which is to say that he was once more subject to his customary inhibitions and compulsions. These forbade him to be discourteous to a guest, and forced him to bear witness like a zealot in favor of his large marine saurian. "Perhaps," said he, after a painful swallow or two, "you haven't considered the evidence."

He went on to summarize the affidavits of numbers of worthy citizens, all describing what was obviously the same sort of creature, seen at widely dispersed times and places. He stressed especially the sworn evidence of naval officers and sea captains, and crowned the list with a reference to the reptile clearly seen by the bearded and impeccable gentlemen in charge of Queen Victoria's own yacht, the *Osborne*.

Geisecker, who had been listening with a widening smile, here heartily slapped Glenway on the back. "You know what it was *they* saw, brother? They saw the old girl herself, flopped overboard for a dip. What do you say, boys?" said he, addressing the question to me and to the man who was clearing the table. "That's about the size of it, believe you me! *Splash me, Albert!*"

He accompanied this last sentence with a flapping mimicry of regal and natatory gambols, which, considering he was neither on a throne nor in the water, seemed to me to show talent. Glenway, like the august personage represented, was not amused. There was such a contest between displeasure and hospitality visible on his face that it looked for a moment like a wrestling match seen on television, except, of course, that the pain was genuine.

This, and the thought that I had rather let him down over the dinner on Paumoy, moved me to an unwonted self-sacrifice. "Glenway," said I, "you take my spell in the crow's nest, and I'll take the wheel this morning."

Glenway, being one of nature's martyrs, refused this handsome offer, and elected to stay down in the arena. As I went aloft, I realized how those patricians must have felt, who, though inclined to Early Christian sympathies, were nevertheless pressured into taking a box in the Colosseum on a gala night in Nero's Rome.

Every now and then I heard a roar below me, and it was not merely that of a lion; it was that of Geisecker's laughter. Before long I saw Glenway come forward, and pretend to busy himself with the little nets that were used for taking up plankton and algae. In a very few minutes, Geisecker came after him, smiling, and spoke with jovial camaraderie to the two sailors who were spreading the nets. These men looked uneasily at Glenway before they laughed; it was sufficiently obvious that the jests were concerned with the sea serpent. Glenway then dropped his work and went aft, and below. Geisecker went bellowing along the deck and, getting no response, he went down after Glenway. There was a period of calm—deceptive calm, which is calmer than the other sort. Then, Glenway burst up out of the forward hatch and looked around him as if for refuge. But there is no refuge on a yacht, not even on a yacht like the *Zenobia*. I realized that he must have slipped through the pantry, into the galley, and thence into the men's quarters, leaving Geisecker ditched in the saloon. Geisecker was, of all men, the least likely to remain ditched more than three minutes. At the expiration of that time, I leaned far out and looked back, and saw his mighty, sweating torso emerge from the companionway.

There are certain big, fat men who, when they joke with you, seem almost to enfold you in a physical embrace. This caused me to wish we were farther from the equator, but it did not prevent me going down to try to run a little interference for Glenway.

I soon found that it was next door to impossible to draw Geisecker away from Glenway. There are certain people who, if they become dimly aware they are offensive to another, will fasten on that unfortunate with all the persistence of a cat which seeks out the one cat hater in a crowded room. They can't believe it; they think you really love them; they are tickled and fascinated and awesomely thrilled by the fantastic improbability of your dislike. They'll pluck at your attention and finger your very flesh for the unbelievable spectacle of your recoil, and they'll press yet closer for the marvel of your shudder, for all the world as if recoil and shudder were rapturous spasms induced by some novel form of lovemaking, to be evoked in wonder and in triumph again and again and again.

"Good old Glen!" said Geisecker, one afternoon when Glenway had jumped up with what I can only call a muttered exclamation, and sought refuge in his cabin. "I love that guy. I love the way he takes a bit of ribbing. You know—straight, deadpan—and yet you can tell that underneath he just loves it."

"Not on that subject," I said. "He detests it. And so do I. It's making him miserable. It's driving him just about crazy."

"Ah, don't give me that baloney!" said he with a good-humored flap of his hand. Geisecker was not in the least interested in what I said about my own reaction. Sensitive to nothing else on earth, he had, unconsciously, of course, better than a dog's nose for the exact nature of the feeling he inspired. This keen sense told him that I am of a type not offended by his sort of humor, and that my mounting anger was entirely on behalf of Glenway. To him, therefore, it was vicarious, secondhand, and as flavorless as a duenna's kiss. It gave him no sort of thrill, and he had no itch to increase it. I felt quite rejected.

I went down to see if I could be more effective with Glenway. I said, "If you had the least sense of humor, you'd enjoy this monster. After all, he's the sort of thing you're looking for. He belongs to a species thought to be extinct."

"I wish to god he was," said Glenway.

"He may not come from the Cretaceous, but he's at least a survival from the Jokebook Age. He's a human coelacanth. He's a specimen of Comic Picture Postcard Man. He's a living Babbitt. You ought to turn your cameras on him. Otherwise, people won't believe he exists."

It was like trying to skip and run over soft sand. Each new sentence got off to a worse start and sank deeper into Glenway's depression. At last I was altogether bogged down, and we sat there just looking at each other. Then, like the last trump, there arose an urgent, heart-stopping stridulation in the buzzer box on the wall over the bed. Glenway was out of his depression, out of his chair, into the doorway, and up the companion so quickly that one felt certain intervening movements must have been left out. I followed as fast as I could; after all, it was either the sea serpent or Geisecker, and in either case I thought I'd better be there.

It was Geisecker. He was standing by the wheel, hooting with laughter, pointing out over the ocean, shouting, "Thar she blows! Flukes on the starboard bow!"

Then the laughter doubled him up completely. I noticed that it can be true about people getting purple in the face. I noticed also that, even doubled up, Geisecker seemed bigger—there seemed to be more of him than at other times.

Sadder still, there seemed to be less of Glenway. He seemed to be shrunken and concentrated into a narrower and grayer column of tissue than was natural. I had time to think, "He'll be driven completely out of his mind if this continues," and then he turned and went down the companion out of sight.

I went over to Geisecker, wondering on the way what sort of words could possibly pierce his thick hide. "Jesus Christ!" said he. "I knew it was true. When those boys on Paumoy told me, I knew it was true, but I just felt I had to check up on it."

"What the Hell are you talking about?" I asked, cursing myself as I spoke for asking anything.

"About old Glen and Thora Vyborg," replied Geisecker, still gasping with mirth. "Don't you know about Glen and Thora Vyborg?"

I knew they had been married. I vaguely remembered something about a dramatic love-at-first-sight encounter in Honolulu. I had some sort of a picture in my mind of the more than famous filmstar —of her unfathomable personality, her unknowable beauty, and the fact that she talked to no one and traveled with no one and dined with no one except her Svengali, her current director, and her publicity man. I had a fairly clear idea of what these types were like, and I could imagine that Glenway—younger then, tall, angular, already dedicated, with the ocean behind him, winged with sail and haloed with sun and money—must have seemed to offer her a part in a rather better production.

I remembered, too, that the marriage had been extremely short-lived. Someone had said something about them sailing away with the sunset and returning with the dawn. No statement had been made by either party. There had been rumors, as there always are, but these were weak, uncertain; they had been drowned in a flood of better authenticated adulteries long before I ever knew Glenway. Now, it seemed that some of them had been washed ashore, horribly disfigured, swollen and salty, on the ultimate beaches of Paumoy. "You know what the boys there told me?" said Geisecker, watching me closely. "Seems they got married in no time flat and started out on this very same boat, on a big, front-page honeymoon. Believe it or not, the very first night out—round about eleven o'clock, if you get what I mean, pal—some fellow on deck sees something or other, maybe porpoises or kelp or any damn thing you like, and he gets the idea it's the old brontosaurus in person. So he presses the buzzer, and Glen comes rushing up on deck in ten seconds flat. Don't ask me any questions, pal; all I know is that first thing next morning the lugger was turned right around, and it's full steam ahead back to Honolulu, and Reno, and points in opposite directions."

I realized at once that this was true, and had a certain beauty. However, that was for my private contemplation and had nothing to do with Geisecker. He was regarding me with a sort of arrested gloat, his eye triumphant and his nose tilted up ready to join in the expected peal of laughter. "Geisecker," I said, and for the first time I heard, and he heard, a note of direct and personal hatred in my voice, "Geisecker, I'm not going to discuss the whys and wherefores, but from now on you're going to stay right away from Glenway. You can come on deck; you can have a chair on the port side there, between the masts. But if you step one inch . . ."

"Hold it!" said Geisecker. "Who's talking? The owner? Skipper? First mate? Or what the Hell else do you think you are? I'd like to hear what old Glen's got to say."

I am no good at all at a row. When my first damp squib of wrath has exploded, I am always overwhelmed by an immense weariness and blankness. At that moment I had neither the will nor the power to go on. But Geisecker obligingly came to my assistance. I could never decide whether he was a sadist, avid for the discomfort of his victim, or a masochist, indecently eager for the wound of being disliked. Whichever it was, he watched me with his little eyes, and he actually passed his tongue over his lips. "Anyway," said he, "I'm going down to ask him if there's any truth in that goddamn yarn or not."

The lip-licking was so crude and so banal that it transposed everything into a different key. There was a sailor of great good nature and phenomenal size, a man called Wiggam, a native of Hawaii, who was mending a net a little way along the deck. I called him and told him, in phrases which normally appear only in balloons in comic strips, to take his net and work on it outside Abbott's door, and, in the event of Geisecker approaching that door, to cut his belly open.

I gave these deplorable instructions in a rather cold, staccato tone, assumed in order to overcome a tendency to squeakiness, and I was reminded, even as I heard myself speak, of a small boy's imitation of a tommy gun. Had Geisecker laughed, or had the sailor looked surprised or reluctant, I should have been in a very ludicrous situation. However, it seems that sailors are simple folk; this one showed alacrity, his teeth, and a spring knife that seemed all the more purposeful for being of very moderate dimensions. He glanced at Geisecker, or rather at the belly in question, as if making certain precise and workmanlike calculations, and then he went and gathered up the long net and carried it below. Geisecker watched all this with growing seriousness.

"Look," said he, "maybe I got things wrong somehow, but. . . ."

"Listen, Fatso," said I, "if you get anything else wrong you're going to be put on a little Jap crab-fisher boat, see? And the name of that boat's going to be screwed up when we write it down in the log. 'Cause it'll be a Japanese name that means 'the boat that never returned.' Or never existed. Work that one out next time you feel like kidding."

I went down and found Glenway lying on his bed, not reading. I said, "I've fixed him. I can't believe it, but I have."

"How?" said Glenway, not believing it, either.

When I had told him, he said, "He won't say fixed, not by that sort of thing."

I said, "You think so because I've related it with a twinkle. When I spoke to Geisecker, my voice was cold and dead, like steel, and I let my eyelids droop a little. Like this."

"He certainly won't stay fixed," said Glenway.

"In that case, his belly will be cut open," said I. "Because to Hill Wiggam, who is sitting right out there in the passage, this is his moment of fulfillment. Or, it will be, if Geisecker tries to get past him. It's a case of a man suddenly finding his vocation."

"I don't want Wiggam getting into trouble," said Glenway.

"Nor," said I, "does Geisecker." With that, I went up and did my afternoon spell in the crow's nest, and later I had a drink with Geisecker, to whom I said as little as possible, not knowing what to say nor how to say it. I then dined with Glenway, in his cabin, and then had a smoke with Geisecker on the port deck, and, at about ten o'clock, I went to spend the last hour of the evening with Glenway, who was still extremely tense.

"What's the night like?" he asked.

I said, "It's the most wonderful night of the whole cruise. The moon's just on full, and someone's let it down on an invisible wire, and you can see the curve of the stars going up behind it. The wind's light, but there's a Hell of a big swell rolling in from somewhere. She's still got everything on but her balloon jib, and she's riding it like a steeplechaser. Why don't you go up and take the wheel for a bit?"

"Where's Geisecker?" asked Glenway.

"Amidships, on the port side, fenced in invisibly by threats," I said with some pride.

"I'll stay down here," said Glenway.

"Glenway," said I, "you're making altogether too much of this. The fact is, you've led a sheltered life; people like Geisecker have always treated you with far too much respect. It sets you apart, which I find rather offensive. It reminds me of what Fitzgerald said about the rich. He said you are different. Think of that! It's almost worse than being the same."

"You forget what Hemingway said," replied Glenway, who perhaps found little attraction in either alternative.

"The Hemingway rebuttal," said I, "proves only what it was intended to prove. That is, that Hemingway is a fine, upstanding, independent citizen, and probably with a magnificent growth of hair on his chest. All the same, Fitzgerald had a point. Just because your iniquitous old grandfather happened to build a few railways . . ."

"First of all," interrupted Glenway, "it was not my grandfather, but my great-grandfather. What's more . . ."

And, at that moment, just as I was exulting in having induced him to unclench his hands, and look out of his eyes, and stick his neck out, the buzzer sounded again. I had forgotten to have it disconnected.

What was quite pathetic was that Glenway couldn't control an instinctive movement towards leaping off the bed. He arched up like a tetanus victim, and then collapsed as flat as an empty sack. The buzzer went on. I had a panicky feeling that he might arch up again at any moment. I lost my head and picked up a stool that stood in front of the dressing table and pounded that rattlesnake box into silence.

The silence, once achieved, seemed deep and complete. This was an illusion; we soon noticed that there were all sorts of noises here and there in the large emptiness left by the death of the outrageous buzzer. We could hear the patter of running feet on deck, and voices, and especially Geisecker's voice, spouting large jets of urgent sound.

I opened the door and the words came rushing in. "Glen! Glen! Come up, for God's sake! Can't you hear me? Come on! Come up, quick!"

"My God!" I said. "Maybe they *are* cutting his belly open."

With that, I ran up. Geisecker was at the head of the companionway. He turned his head briefly to send another shout down the stairs; then he turned it back again to stare out over the sea. I barged into him. He blindly clutched at my arm and dragged me to the side of the boat, and pointed.

I saw something already disappearing into the great smooth side of one of the enormous waves. It was black, wet, shining, and very large. These words can be applied to a whale or a whale shark, and maybe to two or three other things. I can summon up with absolute precision the way Geisecker's face was turning as I came up the companionway; I can remember exactly how his shout went on a little after he had turned his head back to look over the sea again. But I haven't the same perfect mental photograph of what I saw disappearing into the wave. To the very best of my recollection, I saw the hinder half of an enormous back and, following on a curve, already half-lost in the black and moon-glitter, a monstrous tail.

The men who had run up were standing three or four paces away. I looked at them, and they nodded. As they did so, I heard Glenway's voice speaking to the men. "You saw it?" He had come up, after all, and had seen my look and their response as he came toward us. One of them said, "Yes, but he shout," pointing to Geisecker. "He shout, shout, shout, and it go under."

Glenway stepped toward Geisecker, thus turning his back on the men. They couldn't see his face, but I could see it, and so could Geisecker. I don't think Glenway even raised his hand. Geisecker stepped backwards, which brought him, at what I would have thought a very slight and harmless angle, against the low gunwhale. His big, fat, heavy torso went on and over; his feet went up, and he was gone. He was overboard.

I don't remember putting my hand on the life belt, but I can remember flinging it, skimming it almost parallel with the side of the boat, and feeling sure it hit the water within a very few feet of

Geisecker. Then the boat, whose six knots or so had been like nothing at all a moment earlier, seemed to be racing ahead faster than any boat had ever gone before.

Glenway shouted; the helmsman put the helm over and spilled the wind out of her sails. There was always a boat ready to be lowered at record speed. Two men were at the oars, Glenway took the tiller, and I stood in the bows looking for Geisecker, who could be no more than two or three hundred yards away.

The night was clear beyond all description. The enormous, smooth swells gleamed and flashed under the moon. The yacht, when we had drawn away from it, stood up like a snowy Alp on the water, and when, at the top of each swell, the men lifted their oars for a moment, it was a moment of unbelievable silence, as if some tremendous creature was holding its breath.

Then I saw Geisecker. We were lifted high on one of the great, glassy hills of sea, and he was beginning to slide down the slope of another. He had the life belt. I couldn't see his real features at that distance, but the white moonlight gave him such great, hollow, black eyes, and made such a crater of his open mouth, that I got the picture of a clown in comic distress. Then he went down, and we went down, and two or three ridges ten feet high humped themselves between us.

I said, "He's ahead of us; a couple of hundred feet. You'll see him from the top of the next one."

But we didn't. I began to wonder do a man and a life belt rise and fall faster or slower on a rolling sea than a fourteen-foot boat. Before I could work out the answer, we had gone up and down again and had arrived at a spot which certainly was extremely close to where I had seen him.

"You misjudged the distance," said Glenway, after perhaps half a puzzled minute.

"I must have. Anyway, he's got the life buoy. He'll be all right. Let's row around in a circle."

One of the men put out a bailing can as a marker. The giant swells were so smooth that, ballasted with a couple of inches of water, the can floated up and down without shipping another drop. We went round it on a hundred-foot radius and then at a hundred-and-fifty feet. Geisecker was not to be seen. And we could see, at one time or another, every square foot of water where he could possibly be.

"He's sunk!" said Glenway. "A cramp . . . A shark . . ."

"No shark would have taken the life belt down. It'd be floating right here. We'd see it."

The words were scarcely out of my mouth when we saw it. It breached up, right out of the water—it must have come up from god knows how many fathoms—and it fell back with a splash just a boat's-length ahead of us. Next moment, it was beside our bow and I reached out and lifted it aboard. I turned, holding it in my hands, and showed it to Glenway. It was easier than speaking, and not so silly. We both knew perfectly well that no known creature, except possibly a sperm whale, could have taken Geisecker and the life belt down to that sort of depth. And we knew that what I had seen, and what the men had seen, was not a sperm whale.

We rowed around in circles for a little longer, and then we pulled back to the yacht. When we were aboard again, I said to Glenway, "You didn't so much as touch him. You didn't even mean to touch him. You didn't even raise your hand."

"And some of the men were watching," said Glenway with the utmost calm. "They can testify to that."

If not the railway tycoon, his great-grandfather, it might certainly have been his grandfather, the banker, speaking. He saw my surprise, and smiled. "From the most scrupulous legal point of view," said he, "it was a pure accident. And we'll make a report accordingly. Of course, I killed the man."

"Now, wait a minute," said I.

"Excuse me," said he. We were near the wheel. He took it from the man who was steering, and said something to him, and the man ran forward calling to the rest of the crew who were still on deck. Next minute, the helm went up, the booms swung over, the sails bellied out on the other side, and the great boat was jibbed and sweeping round on to a new course.

"Where are we heading now?" said I to Glenway.

"Due east," said he. "To San Francisco."

"To make the report? Can't you . . .?"

"To put the boat up for sale."

I said, "Glenway, you're upset. You've got to see this business in proportion."

He said, "He was alive and enjoying himself, and now he's dead. I didn't like him—I detested him. But that's got nothing to do with it."

I said, "Don't be completely psychologically illiterate. It's got everything in the world to do with it. You hated his guts, a little too intensely, perhaps, but very understandably. You wished he was dead. In fact, you more or less said so. Now you've got guilt feelings. You're going to take the blame for it. Glenway, you're an obsessive type; you're a Puritan, a New Englander, an Early Christian. Be reasonable. Be moderate."

"Suppose you were driving a car," said Glenway, "and you knocked a man down and killed him?"

"I'd be very sorry, but I think I'd go on driving."

"If you were a speed demon, and it was because of that? Or a drunk? Or if there was reason to believe you were mentally unfit to handle a car?"

"Well . . ." I said.

But Glenway wasn't listening. He beckoned the man who had been steering, and turned the wheel over to him. He gave him the course and told him who was to relieve him in each watch. Then he turned away and walked forward. He walked like a passenger. He walked like a man walking on a street. He was walking away from his mania, and in the very hour of its justification.

I followed him, eager to bring him back to himself, but he walked away from me, too.

I said to him considerably later, "I've found out something very interesting, talking to the man. Shall I tell you?"

"Please do," said he.

I said, "I thought they rather liked Geisecker because he made them laugh. But they didn't. Not a bit. Are you listening?"

"Of course," said he as politely as a banker who has already decided not to make a loan.

I said, "They hated him almost as much as you did, and for the same reason—for making fun of It. They believed in It, all the time. They've all got different names for It, according to where they come from. Almost every man's got an uncle who's seen It, or a wife's grandfather, or someone. And it's quite clear It's the same sort of beast."

Glenway said, "I've decided I'm going to buy a farm or a ranch as far from the ocean as I can get. I'll breed cattle or hybridize corn or something."

I said, "You've been over seven years on this boat with these men, or most of them. Did you know they believed in It?"

"No," said he. "Or I might go in for soil biology. There's still a tremendous amount to be discovered in that field."

This made me feel very sick. I felt Glenway was indeed different

—different from me, different from himself. The beautiful *Zenobia* was to be sold, the crew disbanded, and the large marine saurian left to dwindle into a figure on an old map, distant and disregarded in its watery solitude. As for myself, all my friendship with Glenway had been aboard the boat—I was part of it; I was one of these things. I had been nothing but the accomplice of his obsession, and now he was, in a way I didn't like, cured. I felt that I, too, was up for sale, and we talked amiably and politely and quite meaninglessly all the way back to San Francisco, and there we said good-bye to each other and promised to write.

We didn't write in over three years. One can't write to the ghost of a banker, nor expect a letter from one. But, this summer, when I was in New York, I got home one night and found a letter awaiting me. The postmark was Gregory, South Dakota, which is about as far from either ocean as you can get.

He was there; he wondered if I knew those parts; he wondered if I was likely to be free; there were some interesting things to talk about. The lines were extremely few, but there was all the more space to read between them. I took up the telephone.

It was nearly midnight, but, of course, it was two hours earlier in South Dakota. All the same, Glenway was a very long time coming to the phone. "I hope I didn't get you out of bed," I told him.

"Heavens, no!" said he. "I was on the roof. We get wonderful nights here; as clear as Arizona."

I remembered that clear night in the Pacific, and the flash and glitter of the enormous, glassy waves, and the silence, and the boat rising and falling so high and so low, and the yacht like a hill of snow in the distance, and the little bailing can visible at over a hundred feet. I said, "I'd like to come out right away."

"I rather hoped you would," said Glenway, and began to tell me about planes and trains.

I asked him if there was anything he wanted from New York.

"There most certainly is," said he. "There's a man called Emil Schroeder; you'll find his address in the book; he's out in Brooklyn; he's the best lens grinder that ever got out of Germany, and he's got a package for me that I don't want sent through the mail because it's fragile."

"What is it?" I asked. "A microscope? Did you go in for soil biology after all?"

"Well, I did for a time," said Glenway. "But this is something different. It's lenses for a binocular telescope a fellow's designed for me. You see, a single eyepiece is no good for following anything that moves at all fast. But this binocular thing will be perfect. I can use it on the roof, or I can set it in a mounting I've had built into the plane."

"Glenway, do you mind telling me what the hell you're talking about?"

"Haven't you read the government report on unidentified flying objects? Hello! Are you there?"

"Yes, I'm here, Glenway. And you're there. You're there, sure enough!"

"Listen, if you haven't read that report, do please get hold of it first thing tomorrow, and read it on the way out here. I don't want to hear you talking like that unfortunate fellow fell overboard that night. Will you do that? Will you read it?"

"All right, Glenway, I will. I most certainly will."

THE TENDER AGE

How pleasant to have traveled the world as you have, Mr. Renvil! Six months here, a year there—always moving on! We parsons are tied to our parishes like watchdogs to their kennels, barking once a week, as best we can, to keep away the Eternal Prowler. Well, Mr. Dodd, I should not mind being tied to such a spot as this. I should like it very much; one gets weary of wandering. I am hoping to be able to stay here permanently; I hope it will turn out that way.

Go back to your chair, Patricia. Mr. Renvil did not come here to be bothered by little girls. He came here to have tea with your father and me. Oh, please, Mummy, let me sit with Mr. Renvil.

Pattikins, you heard your mother; sit in your place and show how well-behaved you can be. Oh, but please, Mr. Dodd, don't disturb your little daughter on my account.

Her mother likes her to obey; I am perhaps a little lax in that respect. Let me see—what were we saying? Oh, you really think of staying here for good? That will be very nice for us, I'm sure. It's a lonely part of the country. There are few people of our sort; very few farmers; very few cottagers, even. It will be very nice for me, Mr. Dodd, if I am able to stay. I have long wanted to make my home somewhere, but something has always come over me, call it a sudden urge if you like, and in a moment my plans are changed and I am off.

Moving on! Moving on! Well, you have certainly seen the world, no doubt about that! All sorts of places, all sorts of people! When you were in tropical parts, I suppose you saw savages—they have always interested me. Even cannibals perhaps? Savages, yes indeed. Savages one sees everywhere, and not only in the tropics. As to the cannibals and cannibalism, I can't pretend to be an authority on that sort of thing. But I have had enough of the tropics, and of foreign countries altogether. The English countryside is unbeatable. Your hills and woods here are the very best of it. A garden like this is my idea of Heaven. It is here I should like to stay.

Patty, I have told you once, you must not climb on Mr. Renvil. Mr. Renvil did not come here to be climbed and clambered upon. How do you know Mr. Renvil likes little girls? Not everyone likes them, especially when they are ill-behaved. Oh, but I do, Mrs. Dodd. I'm sure no one likes little girls better than I do. I think they are absolutely delicious, absolutely delightful.

I think, Mary, you are making too much fuss. Our guest has told us he has no objection. Let us do him the courtesy of taking his word for it. Patty has taken a great fancy to you, Mr. Renvil. She is not often so eager to sit on anyone's knee. It seems to me, George, you are putting Mr. Renvil quite on the spot, as they say. Do you expect him to come out with it to your face that he finds the child a nuisance? I'm sure he is too polite for that.

I might be, Mrs. Dodd, if it were necessary, but, in this case, it is not. I think little girls are delectable creatures, especially when they are six or seven. Now, Mr. Renvil, we are blunt people hereabouts. Brutally frank, as some might put it. And I couldn't help noticing last time you came to see us—or was it the first time, after you met my husband on the road? I think it must have been the first time; I don't think Patty was home last Tuesday. Well, whenever it was, she had already begun to clamber upon you, and it seemed to me you were anxious to be rid of her. When she came climbing and squeezing and nuzzling, I'm sure I saw you flinch away. I felt you were quite flustered and upset.

My dear, I really believe you are imagining things and perhaps embarrassing our visitor. If Mr. Renvil feels anything of that sort,

I'm sure he will be candid enough to say so, and Patty can go and play with her toys. Yes, dear, but some people hesitate to say they dislike children; it is so often said to be the sign of a bad heart.

I'm sure Mr. Renvil is above such a vulgar prejudice, and I hope he will give us credit for being above it ourselves. Novelists and the people who write for the cinema find it easy to identify the villain of the piece by giving him an aversion to children and animals. They have him kick a dog or slap a child, and this, in turn, strengthens the popular misconception. There was some sort of writer once staying in the village, Mr. Renvil, and he explained it all to us. It was most interesting. Children, dogs, and, I think, cats. Not so much cats, dear, because so many people have rather a horror of them. Lord Nelson did, for one, and all sorts of famous people. Dr. Johnson, though, loved his cat.

Dr. Johnson was a great friend of the Church, and now you tell me he was a cat lover. Perhaps I should be grateful on the first count, but I have never much liked the worthy Doctor, and I shall not change my opinion because of his fondness for cats. I hope you are not a great admirer, Mr. Renvil. I hope you don't think me guilty of lèse-majesté. Oh, no, Mr. Dodd, not in the least, I assure you. I myself could never feel very warmly about Dr. Johnson. A tremendous mind, no doubt, but he is not one of those great figures I could imagine myself meeting and liking if we were contemporaries. I was greatly put off when first I read of his eating habits. When I think of a man gorging and gulping like some ravenous cannibal, some ravenous animal, with his face bent over almost into his food, and the veins swelling out on his forehead, it makes me positively shudder, as if someone were walking over my grave. Excuse me, Mrs. Dodd, if my description is unpleasantly vivid. I am quoting almost exactly what I read.

Oh, I don't shudder so easily, Mr. Renvil. I am not one of your sensitive persons; I am thick-skinned. I am the practical, down-to-earth member of the family. But tell me frankly, and once and for all—are not sticky little fingers, and hugging and nuzzlings rather unpleasant to you? Because I really thought I saw you shudder, just as you describe, the first time Patty came climbing on your knee. Well, I am not a family man. I am unmarried, as you know. That may make me a little awkward. But, as it happens, I have the very greatest fondness for little girls. Little girls of six or seven—to me, at that age they are just at perfection. They are formed already, and still so fresh and tender, and they have such charming ways.

They have not yet reached the lanky stage or the scrawny stage. They positively melt in one's heart.

And little boys? Do you like little boys equally? We put Patty first, of course, but we have often wished she had a little brother. I like little boys, Mrs. Dodd, but they are so very tough in these days, with all the comic strips and the cowboy pictures. A little girl like this one on my knee—I don't think I could ask for more than just such a little girl.

Well, Patty, it seems that Mr. Renvil does not mind you too much. So I suppose you may stay where you are until he puts you down. I know Mr. Renvil likes me, Mummy. I knew it all the time. The very first day he came to tea he whispered in my ear. He whispered he could eat me up.

I think I know what misled you, Mrs. Dodd. I have some sort of little nervous twitch every now and then. I sometimes give a little start and shudder. Why, yes, I just noticed. I think no one would notice unless they were watching as I was—watching, I mean, to see if Patty was bothering you. I think highly-strung people, people of talent, often have a little nothing of that sort. Like Lord Nelson and his aversion to cats. Mr. Dodd has a cousin who is extremely gifted musically; it is thought he could have played at concerts had he really taken it up. He sometimes starts almost out of his chair.

Do you like pussycats, Mr. Renvil? Would you rather have a little girl or a pussycat? Oh, a little girl, Patricia. I don't like cats at all.

Would you rather have a little girl than a bunny rabbit? Why, yes, indeed. Rabbit is quite nice, but I would rather have a little girl.

There used to be lots of bunny rabbits, but they all died because of a wicked disease. I think there is one who lives in the big wood on the top of the hill, but Daddy won't take me there. Now, Patty, you are always whining and wheedling to go to the wood. Daddy has the parish to look after, and Daddy has his sermon to write, and he has told you there are no rabbits there.

Shall you keep the house you are living in at present if you decide to stay, Mr. Renvil? I hardly think so. I shall probably look around for something a little larger. One never knows, of course; one's plans may change at a moment's notice. But I do sincerely hope that nothing will prevent my settling here.

No more sudden urges, eh? Well, we shall be glad if you can avoid them. The wanderlust, I suppose you would call it? A hunger to be moving on, moving on. I suppose so, Mr. Dodd. It's a matter of fate, I suppose. I think you might describe it as a sort of hunger.

Mr. Renvil, if you had a little girl, would you take her to the wood? Yes, my dear, I very well might. I am not clever enough to write sermons, so I have more time than your father. It would be very nice to take a little girl to the wood.

Ah, the church clock, striking six! The sunset gun I think they call it in India or somewhere. We have finished tea long ago. Can I persuade you to take a glass of sherry, Mr. Renvil? An *apéritif,* as they say in France? No, thank you, Mrs. Dodd. I have no need of it. It is high time I was on my way. I am walking this evening, and if I am not home by seven I shall hear murmuring in the kitchen, quite loud, and very gloomy in tone. I am most grateful for your kindness, Mr. Dodd. Thank you both so much. And I will try, indeed I will, to control any sudden urge. Patricia, may I kiss you good-bye?

Mummy, can I walk up the road with Mr. Renvil? Can I walk with him as far as the wood? I could just peep inside and see a great big bunny rabbit. Now, Patty, Patty, Pattikins! I think Mr. Renvil has been more than nice to you already. It is time to stop asking things and bothering him.

It would be a pleasure to me, Mrs. Dodd. You have no idea what a pleasure it would be to me. But it must be at least half a mile to where the woods begin, and half a mile back again. I'm sure those plump little legs would not carry her more than half as far. And I could hardly see you walking back all alone, my dear. Oh yes, I could, Mr. Renvil. I go all by myself to the village, and that is farther than the wood. I walk there and back all by myself. Don't I, Daddy? Don't I, Mummy? Please, Mr. Renvil, ask Mummy to let me go with you to the wood!

Now, Patty, that is whining and wheedling and nuzzling up all in one. Mr. Renvil doesn't know what to do with little girls who cling. You are strangling him; you are taking his breath away. Mr. Renvil can hardly breathe. Mary, my dear, I think we are having altogether too much fuss over Patty this evening. The child can walk back by herself; Mr. Renvil has said she will be no trouble to him. It is daylight still; we have no bandits or wolves in this part of the world. She can be back in half an hour or so, in ample time for her supper. She will be off your hands when you are busy, just when she is most trouble to you.

Well, very well, if you really don't mind, Mr. Renvil. All I hope is that Patty is not too much for you. Don't let her give you one of your sudden urges, just as we are hoping you will settle here. Oh, as to that, Mrs. Dodd, it is a matter of fate, a matter of fate. No man can avoid his destiny.

Come, my little dear, we will walk together to the wood, and if there is time enough we will take a tiny peep inside it. Can we really, Mr. Renvil? We'll see a great big rabbit. Good-bye, Mummy! Good-bye, Daddy!

Good-bye, Patty! Good-bye, Pattikins! Good-bye, Mr. Renvil!

A NOTE ON THE TYPE

The text of this book was set in Garamond, a modern rendering of the type first cut in the sixteenth century by Claude Garamond (1510–1516). He was a pupil of Geoffroy Tory and is believed to have based his letters on the Venetian models, although he introduced a number of important differences, and it is to him we owe the type which we know as Old Style. He gave to his letters a certain elegance and a feeling of movement which won for their creator an immediate reputation and the patronage of the French King Francis I.

Composed by Cherry Hill Composition, Pennsauken, New Jersey. Printed, and bound by The Haddon Craftsmen, Inc., Scranton, Pennsylvania. Typography and binding design by Andrea Clark.